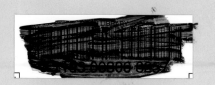

Learning to Read and Write in Colonial America

Studies in Print Culture and the History of the Book

Learning to Read and Write in Colonial America

E. JENNIFER MONAGHAN

University of Massachusetts Press
Amherst and Boston

in association with

American Antiquarian Society
Worcester, Massachusetts

LC 2004027600
ISBN 1-55849-486-3

Designed by Jack Harrison
Set in Adobe Garamond with Bickham Script display by Binghamton Valley Composition
Printed and bound by The Maple-Vail Book Manufacturing Group

Library of Congress Cataloging-in-Publication Data

Monaghan, E. Jennifer, 1933–
Learning to read and write in Colonial America / E. Jennifer Monaghan.
        p. cm. — (Studies in print culture and the history of the book)
Includes bibliographical references and index.
ISBN 1-55849-486-3 (cloth : alk. paper)
1. Literacy—United States—History—17th century.
2. Literacy—United States—History—18th century.
3. Books and reading—United States—History—17th century.
4. Books and reading—United States—History—18th century. I. Title. II. Series.
LC151.M65 2005
302.2'244'0973—dc22
                        2004027600

British Library Cataloguing in Publication data are available.

This publication was supported in part by the Waldo Lincoln Publication Fund
of the American Antiquarian Society.

For my husband, Charles Monaghan

Without you, not only would this book never have been completed,
it would not even have been begun.

CONTENTS

ILLUSTRATIONS

Figures

Graphs

ACKNOWLEDGMENTS

For assistance with this book, I am much indebted to the librarians at the libraries and historical societies that I visited for my research. My largest debt is to the American Antiquarian Society (AAS), particularly to John Hench and Nancy Burkett, to Georgia Barnhill, Joanne Chaison, Thomas Knoles, Caroline Sloat, and Marie Lamoureux. (Additional thanks to Therasa Tremblay, Laura Wasowicz, and Su Wolfe.) Every student of early America is deeply indebted to the present and past presidents of the AAS, Ellen Dunlap and Marcus McCorison, for their vision in making the society what it is—a haven for researchers. The depth of the society's holdings is extraordinary, the expertise and helpfulness of its librarians and staff legendary. I am honored to have this book published in association with the American Antiquarian Society.

Fellow researchers at the Goddard Daniels House, which the AAS maintains for visiting scholars (and which my husband, Charles, and I came to look on as our house in the country), were models of unselfish assistance. Very special thanks go to Konstantin Dierks, who unstintingly shared his ongoing research on letter writing in the last half of the eighteenth century.

I thank the librarians at other institutions, naming them in the order my research took me over the years from my home base in Brooklyn, New York. Foremost is the New York Public Library. Other valuable institutions in New York were the Brooklyn College Library of The City University of New York, the Brooklyn Public Library, the New-York Historical Society, the Pierpont Morgan Library, and Columbia University Library. Farther afield, the University of Rochester Library, the Beinecke Rare Book and Manuscript Library at Yale University, the Houghton Library of Harvard University, the Boston Public Library, the Massachusetts Historical Society, the John Carter Brown Library at Brown University, the Rhode Island Historical Society, and the Duke's County Historical Society of Martha's Vineyard all provided sources. As I traveled south from New York, my scholarly debts grew, to the librarians at the Historical Society of Pennsylvania, the Library Company of Philadelphia (with particular thanks to James Green), the Library of Congress, the Virginia Historical Society, the South Carolina Historical Society, the Southern Historical Collection at the University of North Carolina, and the Hargrett Rare Book and Manuscript Library of the University of Georgia. Our recent move to Charlottesville, Virginia, brought me within reach of the Alderman and other fine libraries of the University of Virginia.

For research undertaken abroad, I am grateful to librarians at the Osborne Collection at the Toronto Public Library, the Public Archives of Nova Scotia, the University of Edinburgh Library, the British Museum Library, the Cambridge University Library, the Pepys Library at Magdalene College, Cambridge, and particularly the librarians at Rhodes House Library, Oxford, which holds the papers of the Society for the Propagation of the Gospel.

Visiting this many institutions over so many years would not have been possible without travel grants from my own college, Brooklyn College of The City University of New York, and CUNY itself. I benefited from grants from The City University of New York, PSC-CUNY Research Award Program, no. 664048 (1984–1985), no. 666062 (1986–1987), and no. 665071 (1994–1995). Brooklyn College provided invaluable faculty research support over several semesters. Above all, I benefited from the luxury of an entire year free of all college responsibilities when the Ethyle R. Wolfe Institute for the Humanities awarded me one of their fellowships for a full academic year. I would like to pay tribute to the contributions of Robert Viscusi and the late President Robert Hess for the creation of this series of fellowships, and to President Christoph Kimmich for his continuing support.

Several scholars generously gave their time and insights, after reading various chapters: James Axtell, Benjamin Franklin IV, Lucille Schultz, Steven Spackman, Betty Wood, and my Brooklyn College colleague Anna Acosta. Thanks, too, to my friend Sandra Pierson Prior for medieval sources.

At a later stage, I learned much from the insightful comments and encouragement of Patricia Crain. I am especially grateful to Robert Gross, whose detailed review and timely bibliographical suggestions raised new questions, made me rethink the structure and thrust of the book, and even clarified some of my conclusions. A great debt remains to David Hall, who read every word of this book in its first version, and who then read it all again in its near final form. His knowledge, insights, suggestions, support, and kindness have sustained me over the twenty-year lifetime of this project.

David Rawson shared his invaluable expertise on colonial literacy by preparing the data for the graphs in the appendixes. Graphic designer Michaux Hood translated them into their present elegant form. Deborah Stuart Smith was most helpful in spotting errors and infelicities in the manuscript, and in suggesting solutions, on behalf of the University of Massachusetts Press. I thank all the folks at the press wholeheartedly for the care they have taken with this book, particularly Carol Betsch, managing editor. A special thank you to Paul Wright, senior editor, who had faith in this project even in its initial and most unpublishable form.

Several publishers have graciously given me their permission to adapt and reprint material from earlier articles of mine: the American Studies Association, "Literacy Instruction and Gender in Colonial New England," *American Quarterly* (1988); the History of Education Society, "'She loved to read in good Books': Literacy and the Indians of Martha's Vineyard, 1643–1725," *History of Education Quarterly* (1990); the International Reading Association, "Family Literacy in Early 18th-Century Boston: Cotton Mather and His Children," *Reading Research Quarterly* (1991); and "Readers Writing: The Curriculum of the Writing Schools of Eighteenth-Century Boston," *Visible Language* (1987). Additional thanks to ABC-CLIO for permission to use material from my chapter in *Girls and Literacy in America* (2003), edited by Jane Greer, and to Cambridge University Press for two graphs from *A History of the Book in America*, volume one.

I also wish to acknowledge here those who were not involved directly in this particular monograph but whose commitment to the importance of the history of literacy and literacy instruction has sustained me in a different way. As teachers of literacy to students in today's schools, colleges, and universities, and as members of the History of Reading Special Interest Group (SIG), founded in 1975, of the International Reading Association, we have worked together to convince our parent organization and its members that historical research is as meaningful for the present as it is for the past. Thanks are due, in order of their leadership as presidents of the SIG, to Janet Miller, June Gilstad, Miriam Balmuth, Richard Hodges, David Moore, the late Garr Cranney, Luther Clegg, Norman Stahl, Bernardo Gallegos, Peter Fisher, Arlene Barry (who mounted an exhibition of old reading textbooks at the 1999 International Reading Association convention and coauthored its catalogue with me), Richard Robinson, Joseph Zimmer, and Douglas Hartman (who has collaborated with me on several publications on the history of literacy).

Others who have supported this mission are my friends Bridget Cooke and Virginia Cantarella. Those who aided our quest in a different way are Philip Gough, James Hoffman, and the late Ralph Staiger. Yet others set me out on this long journey in the first place. I thank my friends Nina Bentley, Joan Sexton, Ellen Sporn, Wendy Hall Maloney, Madeline Lee, and Enid Pearsons. I am most grateful to my professors at Yeshiva University, Lawrence Kasdon and Susan Sardy, and to Moshe Anisfeld for his work on the acquisition of language, which opened new vistas for me, and for introducing me to Richard Venezky. To Dick, who became my mentor and friend and whose untimely death has left a void in the scholarship on the history of literacy, I remain forever indebted.

My last thanks go, as always, to my family. Our elder daughter, Leila, gave me the benefit of her perspective on the book as a linguistic anthropologist; our son, Anthony, warned me to back up my writing in the nick of time and reorganized my work space; our younger daughter, Claire, provided valuable comments and questions on several chapters. Thanks as well to our son-in-law, Kirk Tolchin, and our daughter-in-law, Dayna, née Shook. Thank you, my dears, for your comments on the work in progress and for your encouragement and patience with a project that took up so much of my time and attention. I have finished this book just as the first of our grandchildren begin their own journeys toward literacy. I hope all our grandchildren, Conor, Jane, Regan, and Liam Monaghan, and Quinn, Jake, and Aidan Monaghan Tolchin, will be the beneficiaries of my new influx of spare time.

My final bouquet of thanks is to my husband, Charles Monaghan, who has collaborated on this in ways that are invisible but crucial. He found sources for me, read and reread early and late drafts, gave me the benefit of his keen editing eye, stage-managed the project at key stages, and greatly enriched my understanding of American history by the capaciousness of his own. (And he even spared me from cooking.) His unflagging support of this effort bears witness to our treasured friendship and our love.

Learning to Read and Write in Colonial America

Introduction

The passion and heat generated in the United States over the past decades on the issue of reading methodology (all too often oversimplified as a phonics versus whole-language debate) show that we are still looking for the best way to teach children to read and write. At least we all agree on one thing: the importance of literacy acquisition. Virtually all other aspects of education in this letter-filled world hinge on our ability to master this skill, and education is almost universally acknowledged to be the pathway to job satisfaction and personal self-fulfillment. Moreover, illiteracy among disadvantaged groups, as Carl Kaestle warns, can threaten the survival of the American Republic. Just as our founders believed, we need a well-informed and thoughtful citizenry to make democracy work.[1]

Since literacy begins in childhood, children's literacy and literacy instruction are therefore of central concern to many. Certainly, it is of keen importance to parents and teachers; but it is also an object of study for distinct groups of scholars with overlapping interests: researchers into reading and writing, linguists, educational psychologists, sociologists, and anthropologists, among others. Scientific investigation into reading, in particular, has a long tradition in the United States, dating from the eye-movement measurements of readers conducted in the 1890s and early 1900s.

Although much attention has been paid to the literacy of the present, the same cannot be said for the literacy instruction of the past. Surprisingly little research has been undertaken by educational historians on how children in colonial America were taught to read and write. Lawrence Cremin, author of the three-volume *American Education*, pronounced the research on colonial reading instruction "scandalously thin." Even on Cremin's own broad canvas, a review of such instruction fills only a few pages. Virtually the only extended discussion of the topic is the twenty-five-page account in Nila Banton Smith's *American Reading Instruction*, written as a dissertation and first published in 1934; the colonial portion was not updated in later editions. Significantly, for a work written so long ago, Smith identified many key texts, but it is hardly surprising that she was not interested in areas that have become of importance to us today, such as gender and class, race and ethnicity. Even so, she is more informative than Mitford Mathews, whose 1966 study of teaching reading in America omits colonial literacy instruction entirely. Important studies of colonial writing instruction (penmanship) were undertaken by Ray Nash, but his work is not easily accessible today. The only exception to this general picture is the recent publication of *Literacy in America* by Edward Gordon and Elaine Gordon, whose use of personal evidence, such as diaries, has brought welcome coloration and context to the study of American literacy. Since, however, their ambitious work covers the story of literacy in America up to the present time, they inevitably cannot do full justice to the colonial period.[2]

This lack of attention to the details of instruction may be due to the wide acceptance of what is known as the Bailyn-Cremin thesis of education: the insistence first by Bernard Bailyn and then by Lawrence Cremin that there are many educating agencies (such as families, communities, and churches) in addition to schools. This position was itself a reaction to the work of earlier educational historians, who had focused on formal schooling to the exclusion of all else. An ironic consequence of this broader definition of education—one that I certainly accept— has been a decrease in attention to formal instruction, and nowhere is this more evident than in the details of literacy instruction.

If educational historians have had their reasons to slight the details of the transmission of literacy, so too has a group of social historians known as "literacy historians," whose major interest has been in quantifying how many people were literate, not in how they got to be that way. Literacy historians have studied the literacy of national groups as an offshoot of the new social history of the 1960s and 1970s. In those decades, the new social historians boldly asserted the importance of knowing about the lives of ordinary people and used quantitative methods as their tool. Studies of literacy, in which people were categorized as either literate, if they could sign their names, or illiterate, if they could not, became popular. Since about 1980, literacy historians have made great strides in investigating the number of people who were literate according to this criterion and in exploring relationships between literacy and such constructs as race, gender, social class, and locality (urban versus rural). They have shown a particular interest in how literacy rates have increased over the years and in debating the relationship between literacy and human progress.[3]

The net result has been an outpouring of works on the literacy and illiteracy of the past, covering places and times as distant from each other as ancient Egypt, classical Greece and Rome, medieval Europe, Scotland in the seventeenth and eighteenth centuries, Russia from the 1860s to the Russian Revolution, and the United States since 1880, among many, many others. Nor is this concern with literacy confined to the past: there are fierce arguments over the role to be played by literacy in the future, over its relationship to technology, indeed, over the future of literacy itself in an electronic age.[4]

In this enthusiasm for counting marks and signatures and for debating the relationship between concepts such as literacy and liberty, the literacy of ordinary people during the colonial period of America has not been ignored. In the study of literacy in colonial America the pioneer is indisputably Kenneth Lockridge, who as early as 1974 examined the literacy of New England, basing his account on signatures and marks affixed to some three thousand New England wills.[5] He has since been followed by many others, who have mined deeds, oaths, petitions, voter lists, and other documents for the information they can yield about how many people were signature literate and how many not. Their major finding has been that, for the literacy of white men, the colonial period is overall a dazzling success story. Despite a slump after the founding generation, by the time of the American Revolution the literacy of white men in New England had reached nearly universal levels, with that of the other colonies close behind. The signature literacy of white women, in contrast, lagged behind that of men throughout the entire colonial period even while it, too, gradually improved. A signature indicates at least a minimal amount of reading ability. (For details, see Appendix 1.)

Something that schoolteachers have known all along has belatedly been recognized, that there is no strict demarcation between literacy and illiteracy, as signature/mark counts imply, but numerous grades of variation between total illiteracy and the most accomplished literacy. This aside, what has also been lacking in most of these studies of colonial literacy is an attention to how people became literate (at various levels) in the first place. Those issues that are debated so hotly today— instructional purpose, instructional method, ideology, differential access to literacy instruction mediated by race, gender, ethnicity, and social class—have rarely been the central focus of the literacy historians. Schools, children, and teachers are often strikingly absent from their accounts. So are instructional texts, books written for or read by children, and the literacy activities of families, all of which we now know are important in fostering literacy acquisition. We miss the realities of both the classroom and the family educational experience.

This book aspires to fill that gap for the colonial period in America, and I have approached the topic from the dual perspective of a historian and practicing teacher of reading and writing. For the former, I have drawn on my training in the classical languages at Oxford University, which included the interpretive analysis of classical texts and an intensive study of the sources for Greek and Roman history in the original languages. For the latter, I have been aided by my doctoral studies in reading education at Yeshiva University. I have also learned much about the transmission of literacy from my colleagues at Brooklyn College of The City University of New York. In addition, I have learned a great deal from my students, whether they were inmates at Rikers Island prison in New York, children needing remedial help at a Brooklyn parochial school, or undergraduates at Brooklyn College, where I taught developmental reading, English as a second language (as it was then termed), and English composition.

The first purpose of this book, then, is to ask the questions omitted in many other studies of literacy during the colonial period of the present United States and discover what kind of literacy was taught, when, where, how, to whom, and why. I review the literacy instruction of individuals and groups, young and old, European and native American, enslaved and free, in family settings and in schools. I look at the motives for literacy instruction, the reasons for acquiring literacy, the texts used for literacy instruction, and the sequence of such instruction. I examine the intersections among literacy schooling, on the one hand, and community and family, on the other, and ask how literacy instruction was affected by the sex of the instructed and the instructors, by their social standing, by ethnicity and race, by commerce and socioeconomic progress. I also try to distinguish carefully between the two very different skills of reading and writing and discern the meanings of each skill to the newly instructed. In short, I look at the varied cultural contexts within which literacy was taught and acquired in colonial America. In an article published in 1988 I tackled some of these questions in an examination of literacy instruction and gender in colonial New England. The evidence, I argue there, shows that many people could read who could not write, and that therefore signing evidence underestimates the literacy of colonial Americans, particularly of women. Here I test this and other earlier conclusions against a broad array of new evidence.[6]

A second purpose of this book is to relate the improvement in signature literacy rates, which rose as if inexorably as the eighteenth century progressed, to the larger culture. What should be our explanatory model? Why did women's writing ability lag behind that of men? How does the increase in literacy rates relate to the development of the colonies in other aspects, such as commercial growth, increases in the publishing and importation of books, and the expansion of schooling? What were the continuities and what were the innovations in literacy instruction across regional and temporal boundaries? Does the increase in literacy parallel any kind of literacy innovation or cultural change within literacy instruction itself?

A third purpose of this book is to attempt to relate past literacy instruction to the present. Today we have become used to fierce arguments over reading methodology. Yet one of my earliest discoveries, interestingly, was that there was virtually no dispute in the colonial period over reading method: the alphabetic method ruled supreme, and few were the voices raised to object to it. Nonetheless, those few who did comment on it touched on a very contemporary argument: that the sharp focus of the alphabet method on individual letters and the relationship between letters and syllables encouraged children to ignore the meaning of what they read. "[C]hildren," the Congregational minister Jonathan Edwards wrote in 1751 as he discussed a possible boarding school for the Stockbridge Indians, "when they are taught to read, are so much accustomed to reading, without any kind of knowledge of the meaning of what they read, that they continue reading without understanding, even a long time after they are capable of understanding." He blamed this "word calling," as reading teachers term it today, on the children's "habit of making such and such sounds, on the sight of such and such letters, with a perfect inattentiveness to any meaning."[7]

Moreover, many other issues that have sparked disagreements over literacy instruction in America appear as themes throughout this study. One of these, the issue of whether literacy skills are "caught" or "taught"—that is, learned almost incidentally by an immersion in a rich print environment or deliberately imparted by direct instruction—has been at the heart of recent controversies. Other themes are the influence of motives on literacy instruction, the importance of families in literacy acquisition, the urgency felt by certain groups to reach children of different backgrounds, the role of schoolbooks, the tug-of-war between reading and writing, and above all, the mediating effects of race, class, gender, religion, and ethnicity on literacy instruction and acquisition.

I defer my discussions that address this third purpose until the afterword of this book. To address the book's second purpose, that of explaining the improvement in literacy rates, I have adapted the developmental theory offered by Jack Greene in *Pursuits of Happiness*, where he proposes a three-stage model of social development. Scholars used to regard the experience of Puritan New England as the model for the entire nation. Greene, however, convincingly argues that the experience of the Chesapeake was the norm and that of orthodox Puritan New England the exception, and that American colonies that once differed sharply became gradually more alike. This transformation occurred in three stages, experienced at somewhat different times by each colony.[8]

The first of Greene's stages is *social simplification*. Thanks to the rigors of settlement, the early social systems produced in colonies such as Virginia were greatly simplified versions of those in the mother country, setting a high value on individualism, autonomy, and personal acquisition. In contrast, up to about 1660, orthodox New England produced tightly controlled, orderly societies that, as a function of their deep commitment to Congregationalism, emphasized community. After the 1660s, however, even orthodox New England colonies were part of a common movement in the direction of the second stage, *social elaboration*. Colonies were increasingly settled and prosperous enough to create more elaborate social, political, economic, and cultural structures. (The substructures for transportation, for example, expanded greatly at this time, with an increased number of roads, bridges, and ferries.) Greene's third stage, *social replication*, relates to the rise of elite groups, a feature that had occurred in all the colonies by the 1750s. Members of the elite longed to share in all the elegance and sophistication of the British metropolis and strove to replicate the standard of living enjoyed by the British elite. All the colonies, Greene argues, between about 1660 and 1760 developed in a comparable manner, in a steady convergence of their cultures, laying the groundwork for colonies to regard themselves as a single united entity entitled to break with Great Britain in the American Revolution. Greene's concept of social replication needs to be enlarged in the light of Timothy Breen's *Marketplace of Revolution*, which sets American consumers and their ability to forgo British imports at the heart of the Revolution. Breen demonstrates that those of the middling sort as well as the elite aspired to gracious living and elegant British products, forming part of what Breen terms "a vast new consumer culture" in the second half of the eighteenth century.[9]

In addition to Greene's framework and Breen's insights, I have profited greatly from the relatively new "history of the book" scholarship. This interdisciplinary approach examines the connections that tie authors, printers, publishers, booksellers, reviewers, and so forth to readers. From the first, it has set literacy firmly as the foundation on which writing, printing, and reading are all based. In particular, I am much indebted to Hugh Amory and David Hall's jointly edited *The Colonial Book in the Atlantic World* (the first of the multi-volume *History of the Book in America*), in which I briefly present some of the themes of this book.[10] The remarkable work of Amory and Hall and of the other contributors to *The Colonial*

Book has been invaluable to my understanding of the larger world of books and adult literacy that surrounded the young.

Drawing on the history of the book scholarship as well as Greene's model of social progress and Breen's emphasis on a consumer culture, I propose a three-part developmental model of colonial literacy instruction and acquisition. While these parts, which provide the structure for this book, fall largely along chronological lines, the primary purpose of the division is to mark the points at which literacy instruction underwent significant transformations. Part I focuses on the religious underpinnings of literacy instruction, and of reading instruction in particular. The religious, specifically Christian, purposes of such instruction that run through all the chapters within this part dictated the content of reading instructional texts and the nature of missionary endeavors to the unconverted "heathen." This part spans the 1620s to roughly 1730. In certain contexts, however, particularly the Anglican ones of the final chapters, the characteristic features of this part last until the American Revolution.

Part II covers the years 1730 to 1750, a period when the spelling book emerged as a key instructional text in American reading instruction, inserting itself into the traditional instructional sequence—the hornbook, the primer, the Psalter (Book of Psalms), the New Testament, and the entire Bible—after the primer and before the Psalter. The "speller," as it was called informally, opened the door to secular texts and represented a shift in what the culture expected in its instructional texts for children.

Part III, covering 1750 to 1776, outlines an innovation and a convergence. The innovation, which would compete with the old view for decades to come, involved a rethinking of the child's supposedly innate sinfulness, and it was one of the factors that resulted in the creation of new books for children, designed to amuse them rather than convert them. The convergence was the literacy version of Greene's cultural convergence, as expanded by Breen's consumer culture. By 1750, most of the substructures that permitted better dissemination of books and stationery were in place and would continue to improve, such as swifter and more frequent transatlantic crossings, better roads, and a network of peddlers to carry books into rural areas. For eager American consumers of literacy-related objects, an increasingly wide choice was available from an influx of offerings into American ports as ships transported writing implements and books to each province while provincial presses reprinted imported books.

The central argument of this book is that literacy for children—broadly understood to embrace literacy offered in both family and school settings—underwent a transformation after about 1750, for which much of the groundwork was laid during the transitional decades of the 1730s and 1740s. The change was, in small part, a function of the new and competing view of the child and in large part the almost universal acceptance of the spelling book as the most important text for teaching reading.

As the colonial period opened, it seems that most adults shared the belief that children, like all humans, were the creatures of original sin: "In *Adam's* Fall / We

Sinned all," as the opening verse of the *New-England Primer* puts it. Furthermore, their memories were "weak and slipperie," as the English reformer Charles Hoole conceded in 1660, "like leaking vessels." The key to instruction was therefore "frequent repetitions."[11] But theories are open to challenge, and in the 1690s the work of the British philosopher John Locke offered a different view of children. Locke posited a concept of childhood in which the minds of children were to be regarded as blank slates, capable of receiving impressions, amenable to gentler treatment. He paved the way to an approach to teaching children and to the creation of reading materials that looked to children's amusement rather than to their salvation.

One of the consequences of this milder view of children was the publication of gilt-tipped "pretty books" by John Newbery of London, which, I suggest, were welcomed by the elite, who permitted their children to read them alongside the older, doctrinal works, apparently oblivious to their inconsistency of message. General acceptance, however, of this new kind of children's book would not be widespread until after the American Revolution, when Newbery books began to be reprinted in large numbers in the United States. Another aspect of the transformation of literacy can be found in the increasing secularism and commercialism of the eighteenth century after 1750, particularly in the commercial interests of those publishing the new "pretty books."

This study also highlights an instructional text—whose name, "*spelling* book," continues to mislead researchers—as the single most important innovation in American *reading* instruction. I claim that, beginning in the 1730s, its increasingly widespread use greatly facilitated the acquisition of reading, writing, and spelling. The main purpose of the spelling book was to teach reading through the alphabet method in a much more methodical way than had been offered through the traditional Christian texts of hornbooks, primers, and psalters (see Appendix 2). I argue that the speller fostered literacy acquisition by its thorough and carefully paced presentation of reading material. But it also introduced a tension that we have yet to resolve between an orderly presentation (one in which new words in a text are carefully restricted to those that conform to the elements or principles already taught) and a meaningful text (which may be compromised by the stilted language of the orderly presentation). The speller also opened up questions of professional preparedness, of how much teachers need to know about the alphabetic code in order to teach it.

Other themes weave through this book. One is that an instructional dichotomy existed in colonial times (and indeed later) between reading and writing. During the colonial period, the two literacy skills were taught at different times in the child's development, for different purposes, using different tools. The devotional motivations for reading instruction contrast strikingly with the perceived practicality of writing instruction, and they had important consequences for which sex learned which literacy skill. Another theme is that religion continued to suffuse and motivate most of the reading instructional activities covered by this study, even after the introduction of texts of a more lighthearted nature. A third is that formal schooling was of primary importance in the transmission of literacy. Other themes involve the continually mediating impact on literacy transmission of race, class, gender, and ethnicity.

In effect, this study presents colonial reading and writing in a new light. We should not be misled by the implicit colonial definition of writing as penmanship. Writing, it turns out, was not only the bedrock of all governing bodies (and in that respect an instrument of social control) but also the hallmark of the free. The definitions of the two literacy skills implied in so many colonial sources—of reading as a receptive and passive skill, of writing as the repetitious copying of the work of others—were in fact undermined and contradicted by actual practice. By the time of Thomas Paine, both reading and writing had emerged as potentially revolutionary practices, challenging every kind of religious and political orthodoxy. Children schooled by authoritarian means turned out to be the most anti-authoritarian of adults.

PART ONE

The Ordinary Road

PRELUDE TO PART ONE

Religious turmoil in England in the early seventeenth century drove thousands of dissenters across the Atlantic Ocean, seeking a better life in the region they would name New England. The first arrivals, who have come to be called "Pilgrims," had been so dismayed by the practices of their church, the Church of England, that they sought to separate from their mother church altogether. These "Separatists" reached the coast of New England in 1620 and founded the little colony of Plymouth.

In the 1630s and 1640s, other waves of English migrants reached Massachusetts Bay and founded the townships of Cambridge, Boston, and many others to form the Bay Colony of Massachusetts. These Congregationalists (dubbed "Puritans" by their detractors) had not separated from the Church of England but had tried to reform it from within; however, new repressive measures by the English authorities led them to create their own communities on this new continent. (The two colonies of Plymouth and Massachusetts Bay remained distinct until 1691, when Plymouth was absorbed by its sister colony.) Some of the migrants left Massachusetts to create the colony of Connecticut. Of these, a group of men who were disenchanted with what they perceived as spiritual laxness even in Connecticut, founded yet another little colony, New Haven. The latter would hold out against absorption into Connecticut until 1665.

Many brought literacy with them as they sought economic as well as spiritual betterment for themselves and their children. In common with all Christians, these Protestants shared the belief that children, like adults, were the creatures of original sin. Salvation could come only through conversion, and Protestants believed that reading the scriptures oneself was a vital path to that goal.

The concept of spheres is helpful in understanding the role played by different community members in the new townships of New England. Women belonged to the first and narrowest sphere, the domestic one. Excluded from any kind of direct participation in public life, with their property subsumed under their husband's, women were defined largely by their relationship to the men in their lives—as wife, mother, neighbor, mistress of servants—or, as Christians, by their relationship to a male deity.[1] The conventional wisdom was that they were as weak in mind as they were in body and, apparently, that their sphere excluded any engagement with the intellect. The opinion voiced by the

11

governor of the Massachusetts Bay colony John Winthrop was a standard one. In a journal entry in 1645, he discussed the plight of Ann Hopkins, who had accompanied her husband, Edward Hopkins, soon to become the governor of Connecticut, to New England. She had "fallen into a sad infirmity, the loss of her understanding and reason," Winthrop noted. He offered his insights on its cause: it had come upon her over the course of several years "by occasion of her giving herself wholly to reading and writing, and had written many books." Winthrop faulted his colleague for being too indulgent with her: "For if she had attended her household affairs, and such things as belong to women, and not gone out of her way and calling to meddle in such things as are proper for men, whose minds are stronger, etc.," she would, in Winthrop's opinion, have "kept her wits, and might have improved them usefully and honorably in the place God had set her." It was not female writing itself that Winthrop condemned—he could not express, he once told his own wife, Margaret Winthrop, how "welcome" her "sweet Lettres" were to him—but Anne Yale Hopkins's usurpation of male modes of writing.[2]

The second, wider sphere was inhabited by ordinary men. Some were able to read but not sign their name; others could read, write, and perhaps keep accounts. They could read the notes posted on the doors of the meeting-house informing townsfolk of straying cattle. They could write to family members left behind in England, sign documents, put their own hand to their wills, record economic transactions, and in general take full part in the life of their community. Many were deeply religious and members of their town's Congregational church.

The third and most exclusive sphere comprised the founding fathers of New England, who saw themselves as part of an international world of men of letters, committed to shared religious beliefs. They and comparable leaders across Europe had had a similar education. Back in England, the spiritual and political leaders of the colonies had been taught to read at petty schools before they attended so-called grammar schools, where they had learned Latin and Greek and perhaps a little Hebrew. They had attended Oxford or Cambridge (certain Cambridge colleges were famous—or notorious—as hotbeds of Puritanism) and could communicate, writing in Latin, with college graduates all over Europe. Their high level of literacy was taken for granted within the broad sphere of international leadership.

At the least accomplished end of the scale within the first two spheres, men and women read slowly and deliberately, fitting the profile of what David Hall calls "traditional literacy." In this realm reading was valued more than writing because it gave access to the scriptures, and memorizing was key for children to learn to read. The availability of books was very limited, though some books, the "steady sellers" of the printing business, had a comparatively large circulation and a long shelf life.[3] Books were treated with reverence and read again and again. "Reading" was equated with oral reading, an activity shared with others. In these contexts, reading offered no new insights but only reinforced previously held beliefs.[4]

At the most accomplished end of the scale, men and women read as we do today, copiously, intently, and presumably often silently. How they read depended on what they were reading. Cotton Mather, minister of the Congregational North Church of Boston from 1685 until his death in 1728, springs to mind as the most obvious example. As I show in a later chapter, he could skim texts or analyze them deeply with equal facility.

Although Mather and his highly literate colleagues could read silently, it is important to remember that oral communication was the norm among the early colonists, written the exception. From neighborly scoldings to ministers' sermons, literacy functioned within a broadly oral context.[5]

While John Winthrop, soon to be governor of Massachusetts Bay colony, was sailing toward New England in 1630, he preached a sermon to his fellow passengers, warning them that the settlement of New England was like a "Citty upon a Hill," a godly community of Christians that should be a shining example to the rest of the world. To achieve this goal, the founding fathers realized they would have to recreate their former educational institutions, like a "school upon a hill," as historian James Axtell has dubbed it.[6] Texts for reading and writing instruction would be foundational to the endeavor.

We can only guess at the books for reading instruction that the immigrants brought with them, but we do know the general contours of such instruction. The texts for teaching reading were virtually a course in Christianity. They composed what the English philosopher John Locke would call, in 1693, the "ordinary Road" of the reading instructional sequence: "the Horn-Book, Primer, Psalter, Testament, and Bible." The hornbook was a little paddle of wood with a single page tacked onto it that consisted of the alphabet, four lines of syllables, the invocation ("In the Name of the Father, and of the Son, and of the Holy Ghost") and the Lord's Prayer. The original meaning of a primer was a book of prayer. The instructional content of primers—the letters of the alphabet, the syllabary (ab eb ib ob ub, ba be bi bo bu), and a few tables of words—was brief in relation to the religious content. The Psalter was the Book of Psalms, printed as a separate book, and the "Testament" Locke refers to was the New Testament. The Bible was the climax of the reading sequence, capping this succession of ever more challenging Christian texts (see Chapter 3).[7]

All these books turned up in the colonies as imported items long before we know of any of them being reprinted in the colonies. Children would use the alphabet method as their means of reading them, spelling the letters of a word aloud, in syllables, in order to pronounce the word as a whole (see Appendix 2). In a culture in which so much interchange was conducted orally, this very oral approach fitted easily into the prevailing context. Of course, children also often learned texts by heart from listening to an adult reading them aloud repeatedly.

One text that lay outside this sequence of Christian texts, and that was missing from Locke's generalization about the "ordinary Road," was the spelling book. A spelling book was printed in about 1644 on British America's first press in Cambridge, Massachusetts.[8] We do not know its title, but it might have been a reprint of the *English Schoole-Maister* by Edmund Coote, first printed in London in 1596 and reprinted many times thereafter. (It was in two books, the first of which offered the syllabary and monosyllables and the second rules for reading and spelling.) This seems, however, too secular a choice for the Congregationalists, for it is very Elizabethan in tone. The final lesson on monosyllables, for instance, features a sentence that begins, "As I went through the cattl yard, I did chaunce to stumbl in a queach of brambls, so as I did scratch my heels and feet, and my gay girdl of gold and purpl." It would take almost a century before spelling books, as a useful genre, would become widespread in the colonies. Throughout the seventeenth century, the American colonies seem to have followed the "ordinary Road" of Christian texts almost exclusively.[9]

Immigrants who came to the colonies intending to teach writing and arithmetic must have brought with them a few printed "copybooks" or their own manuscript copybooks. The first printed copybooks in English, all of them designed for the professional who dedicated himself solely to the task of teaching penmanship, had arrived comparatively late on the scene. Although the earliest printed Italian copybook is dated 1514 and the first such Spanish text appeared in 1548, it was not until 1570 that a copybook was published in England—*A Book Containing Divers Sortes of Hands*. One of its authors was Jean De Beauchesne, a Huguenot who had escaped from Catholic oppression on the Continent and brought Continental writing styles with him. It was actually an English version of de Beauchesne's *Thresor d'escripture*, published at Lyons, France, two decades earlier. The work displays a range of scripts but features the secretary and italic "hands" (scripts) most prominently. These were the two standard scripts of the seventeenth century. The secretary hand was illustrated in a 1630 edition of Coote's speller, an indication of its preeminence among the English.[10]

On the European Continent, a great technical advance had already occurred by the time of the Puritan immigration: the invention of the copperplate printing process. The first copybook to use the new technique was an Italian work published in 1571. Writing masters could now entrust their work to engravers—or become engravers themselves—and be confident that every swirl and flourish they had made in ink would be faithfully reproduced in print. Throughout the seventeenth century, highly elaborate copybooks were produced all over Europe. In England, skilled penmen published a large number of texts, of which the first to be considered a fully English copybook is generally believed to be Martin Billingsley's *The Pens Excellencie* of 1618. Only a couple of colonial Americans before the American Revolution would gain enough expertise and risk enough money to produce such texts.[11]

Writing instruction was actually penmanship instruction, and it involved the frequent copying of models. William Kempe, an English schoolmaster whose *Education of Children in Learning* was printed in London in 1588, usefully provides some notion of how the master was to sequence his instruction. He should first teach the student how to hold the pen, then form the letters "in due proportion," and next join them together. Kempe suggests a gradual progression on the part of the scholar toward independence: "by practice, of drawing the Pen upon the figures of shadowed letters, then of writing without shadowed letters by imitating a Copie, lastly, of writing without a Copie."[12]

The secretary hand, popular in England, was a cursive gothic script that derived from medieval scripts. As early as the late sixteenth century it was being used in England and the Low Countries for business correspondence. (The printed version is the Black Letter font used in the first edition of Coote's *English Schoole-Maister*.) The second popular script, italic, was closely associated with the new learning that had spread from Italy in the Renaissance and was used by scholars and members of the Italian court. It was a simpler and clearer hand that is easily read by us today because our own script is descended from it. As Ray Nash has observed, in the sixteenth and early seventeenth centuries there was nothing unusual about an educated Englishman's being master of both of these very different scripts.[13]

In the American colonies, the secretary hand was used for correspondence and commerce alike. John Rolfe used it when he wrote to the governor of Virginia requesting his permission to marry Pocahontas, and most town clerks used it when they transcribed the first records of the New England colonies. Governor Winthrop kept his diary in that script from March 1630 on, although in correspondence he could switch between secretary and italic, Ray Nash informs us, even within the same sentence.[14]

In contrast, William Bradford, the second governor of the colony of Plymouth, wrote his history "Of Plimouth Plantation," in the italic script. His style of italic was influenced by that of Dutch writing masters, who were introducing a rounder version to their students. As was fitting for a work intended for the public, the italic Bradford used had most of its letters standing separately from one another, rather than joined in a true cursive. The result is a document of, to modern eyes, singular visual clarity, in marked contrast to Winthrop's hastily penned diary, which exhibits all the features of a work intended only for private consumption. As town records demonstrate, the secretary script was gradually supplanted by italic, in most cases by the end of the seventeenth century.[15]

No matter what script was used, writing was viewed by everyone, from governors to private individuals, as the single most essential element for authenticating an agreement. Like those who had signed the famous Mayflower Compact in 1620 on board the *Mayflower* as it sailed toward America, English Americans used quill pens and ink to give their assent to documents. Nonetheless, men and women did not need to know how to form the letters of their names in order to signal their agreement: their mark was as valid as their signature.

Once the early turbulent years were behind the immigrants, who were often obliged to teach their children to read and write themselves in the absence of formal schooling, imparting literacy to the young was turned over to schools. A note of caution is in order here on terminology. The ambiguity we experience today over the term "school," which is sometimes an abstraction and at other times a building, did not exist in the colonial period. A "school" to the colonists was equivalent to the schoolmaster or mistress who "kept" it, along with his or her students, in his or her own home or a rented room. No building was implied, and when one was built by a town, it was termed a "schoolhouse." Similar distinctions need to be made for other phrases. In the seventeenth century, a "grammar school" was always a Latin grammar school, never an elementary school, while "teaching English" meant teaching children to read, not teaching them to write. The implicit contrast of "teaching English" was with teaching children Latin.

Part I highlights two approaches to literacy instruction, both religiously based, along with two implicit definitions of the purposes and practices of literacy: the Congregational approach and the Anglican approach. First we look at the Congregationalists, who were unusual in their focus on legislating reading and writing instruction (Chapter 1), and the handful of men who attempted to convert the Massachusetts Indians to Congregationalism, an effort that inevitably brought literacy in its train (Chapter 2). Next we examine the overwhelmingly religious emphasis of the books selected for New England's children up to 1730 (Chapter 3) and at how two devout Boston families used literacy in the first quarter of the eighteenth century as they sought to come to terms with the early deaths of their young children (Chapter 4). Throughout these chapters, we track the orthodox view of original sin and the dire consequences believed to arise from dying young and unconverted. The "exceptionalism" of the orthodox New England colonies—Massachusetts Bay, Connecticut, and New Haven—set them apart, in their treatment of literacy, from their sister New England colonies such as Rhode Island, from any of the middle or southern colonies, and even from the Separatists in Plymouth colony.

The second section of Part I shifts from orthodoxy and Congregationalism to hierarchy and Anglicanism, the very denomination whose perceived excesses the Congregationalists had hoped to purify. The time frame is now the eighteenth century, and we look at the literacy instruction offered by the London-based Society for the Propagation of the Gospel, which attempted to export Anglicanism to poor children throughout the colonies (Chapter 5) and to the Mohawks, native Americans living in northern New York in the forests west of Albany (Chapter 6). According to the Anglican vision, teaching literacy meant providing training in obedience, deference, and a cheerful acceptance of one's lot in life, on the one hand, and in furthering the aims of British imperialism, on the other. Here the Bible is less of a final goal for reading instruction than is the Anglican Book of Common Prayer.

As we search for the earliest sources on the colonial adventure to illuminate the topic of literacy instruction, we turn to the township of New Haven, flagship of the small colony of New Haven, its buildings only recently constructed, its laws still being established. New Haven allows us to see men who peopled the second sphere of colony life (and a few women of the first sphere) as they struggled to transmit their literacy to their young.

THE CONGREGATIONALISTS AND
THE ORDINARY ROAD, 1620 TO 1730

1

Literacy and the Law in Orthodox New England

What pains the town clerks took. Week after week, in books brought specially over the seas, recorders in fledgling New England townships recorded court decisions, land transactions, town votes, earmarks, and the town's births, marriages, and deaths. Other men, or sometimes the same men, transcribed the laws enacted and the criminal trials conducted in each particular colony. For the conscientious, the keeping of the town and colony books was a heavy burden. In 1654, Francis Newman, faced with yet another annual reelection as the keeper of the New Haven town book, begged to be relieved of the position, because "by reason of much wrighting which he hath had in the place, for allmost seuen yeares past, he finds his eyesight much decayed." Pressed to continue, he served another three years.[1]

The earliest clues we have for deciphering reading and writing instruction often come from the town clerks, the men "chosen to keep the town book." Were it not for these literate men, we would know little about how colonies and townships tried to ensure that their young would become literate themselves in due course. The town and colony records these men kept form the basis of the chapter that follows. We begin with the town of New Haven, not so much because it was typical—although it did have many characteristics in common with other new townships—but because Francis Newman's records offer exceptionally rich detail on the town's initial struggles with literacy education in the town school.[2]

New Haven came into existence in 1639—three years after Harvard College opened in Cambridge, Massachusetts. This "new haven" for the orthodox was founded at the point where the Quinnipiac River meets Long Island Sound, two years after the bloody end of the Pequot War had made the southern New England coast available for English settlement. The two men most influential in the township's founding were John Davenport and Theophilus Eaton. During a period when he was converting from Anglicanism to Congregationalism, Davenport resigned as vicar of his London parish, in 1633, and left first England, then the United Netherlands, and finally Massachusetts Bay colony to found a plantation that would adhere to the true principles, as he saw them, of pure Christianity. He would be elected minister of New Haven township; Eaton, his boyhood friend, would serve as the governor of New Haven colony until his death in 1658.[3]

The plantation was soon transformed from a single township into the leading town of a small colony. The villages of Guilford and Milford joined New Haven township in 1643, and they and a couple of other towns constituted New Haven colony until it was absorbed into Connecticut in 1665. The general court of the colony acted as its legislative body, and records were kept of both colony and town rulings.[4]

Founding the Colony of New Haven

The settlement of New Haven on the southern shores of New England had begun, as it did elsewhere in New England, with the purchase of land from native Americans. In late November, 1638, Davenport and Eaton, together with some other Englishmen, had purchased a large tract of land from Momaugin, the Indian sachem of the Quinnipiac Indians. It cost the English a dozen overcoats, along with spoons, hatchets, knives, and scissors. Shaumpishuh, an Indian squaw and Momaugin's sister, had added her mark to the document. Two weeks later, Mantowese's bow and arrow and Sawseunck's depiction of an ax sealed a second sale of land.[5] The Indians, too, respected the authority of the written symbol. Now, on June 4, 1639,[6] all the free "planters" (the 70 founders of the township) in Quinnipiac, soon to be renamed New Haven, met together in a general meeting to set up a civil government and nominate those who would lay the foundation for gathering a church there. Robert Newman was "intreated to write in carracters and to read distinctly and audibly in the hearing of all the people whatt was propounded and accorded on," so that "itt might appeare thatt all consented to matters propounded according to words written by him." When, a little later, it came time to subscribe to the formally written covenant, New Haven had already increased in size. Now 111 men put their names to the covenant. Of this number, only 13 made marks; all the rest signed their names. As in other New England settlements, the founders enjoyed a high level of literacy.[7]

Like other New England townships, New Haven successfully established jurisdiction over clashes between Indians and Englishmen. Four months after the "fundamental agreement" of June 1639, the colony held its first murder trial. Nepaupuck, an Indian, was convicted—by his boast as much as his confession—of murdering an Englishman. He even said that he had "had his hands in other English blood." Declaring that he was not afraid of death, he laid his neck against the mantelpiece and told his listeners that he was prepared to die by having his head cut off, or in any other manner that the English should appoint, except by fire. Fire was his God, who was angry with him, he said, and he did not wish to fall into his hands. The court cited scripture to the effect that he who shed man's blood, "by man shall his blood be shed." Nepaupuck was executed the following day, and his head stuck on a pole in the marketplace.[8]

Within one year of the covenant of 1639, the little township of New Haven had begun to take shape along the lines of other settlements. It ordered the erection of a meeting house, restricted the felling of trees other than on a planter's own property, issued instructions on the obligatory possession of arms and ammunition, and offered a bounty for killing wolves and foxes. One servant was whipped for stealing and another one put in the stocks for drunkenness. Within three years, the authorities had ordered more whippings, of a culprit in a child molestation case and of Samuel Hoskins and Elizabeth Cleverley for their "filthy dalliance together." (A month later, the two were given permission to wed.)⁹

Again in common with most other settlements, the town and colony took measures for the education of their young. If we read carefully four decades of New Haven records—those kept between 1640 and 1680—the town's struggles with schooling and even some of its court cases yield a broader meaning. The New Haven laws express the colony's view of the roles that reading and writing were designed to play in the life of the new community and indicate the compromises that townsfolk were forced to make in response to the realities of colonial circumstances.

The town records also reveal details of instruction. They disclose that children were taught reading first, then writing, and finally (if at all) arithmetic, each skill presupposing the other, as in our conventional glossing of the three Rs as "reading, 'riting and 'rithmetic." (Learning arithmetic was heavily dependent on the writing of mathematical examples.)¹⁰ The records reinforce the close relationship between penmanship and arithmetic, together regarded as the tools of commerce. They expose the ready availability of elementary reading instructional texts (primers) in village stores, the sequence of the texts used, the methodology employed in reading instruction, and the objectives of writing instruction. They also hint at the difficulty of finding qualified schoolmasters for a Latin grammar school, as well as the uneven preparation in reading and writing and the unequal treatment of boys and girls.

Education in the Colony of New Haven

The first of New Haven's laws on education was passed in March 1642, ordering "that a free schoole shall be sett vp in this towne." John Davenport, the town's minister, was to form a committee with the town magistrates to determine what the schoolmaster's annual salary should be and where it would come from. (While a schoolhouse is not specified, one was indeed built, for in 1651 it already needed repairing.) In addition, private schooling was available from Mr. "Pearc," who announced in February 1646 that "if any will send their children to him, he will instruckt them in writing or arethmatick."¹¹

The records hint at two kinds of contemporary instruction. The first was provided by the "free" school. In England, most free schools were Latin grammar schools, which aimed to train boys for an education at the colleges of Oxford or Cambridge. The second kind of instruction was the one provided by Mr. Pearce, the private writing master. Instruction in penmanship was conventionally considered a separate discipline from reading instruction and was taught by someone, always a man, with specialized training. Pearce's offer to teach writing or arithmetic provides an early glimpse of the close relationship between the two skills. Arithmetic was the ally of writing instruction in the sense that both were commercially useful, and writing masters generally taught the keeping of accounts, or bookkeeping, along with penmanship.¹²

In 1645, the colony of New Haven ejected Thomas Fugill, the first keeper of the colony books, from his post, charging him with falsifying the records. His replacement was asked to recapitulate some of the colony's laws that had been passed earlier but improperly recorded. Among these was the colony's first school law: "For the better trayning vpp of youth in this towne, that through Gods blessinge they may be fitted for publique service hereafter, either in church or commonweale, it is ordered, that a free schoole be sett vpp." Accordingly, explained the summary, Ezekiel Cheever had taught for twenty pounds for the first two or three years, but this salary had not proved enough, and he had recently been receiving thirty pounds from the town treasury.[13]

Cheever was a graduate of Emmanuel College, Cambridge, and one of the seventy original founders of New Haven. (He had in fact opened a school in his own house and taken private pupils almost as soon as the township began.) New Haven's choice of him for the colony schoolmaster, and the salary he received, is evidence of the high level at which it and many other townships initially set their sights for town-funded schooling. The first masters to be salaried by the new towns at free schools were employed to teach Latin rather than reading and writing. Indeed, schools designated as free schools were given the appropriate financial support because townships felt obliged to support a school that functioned, at least theoretically, at such a high level.

Four years after this note in the records, Cheever fell out with the New Haven church and was ejected from it for his "overweening conceit of his own sufficiency." His departure from both church and town left New Haven without a town schoolmaster and in a quandary. In March 1651, the town discussed whether it would allow a salary to William Jeanes for teaching school at a much more elementary level than Cheever had: "much debate was aboute it, but nothing was ordered in it at present." One suggestion was that the town should offer Jeanes ten pounds a year, and (as this was a salary well below subsistence level) that he should supplement it with payments from his pupils' parents. This was the course chosen, but only a few months later, in October, Jeanes announced that he had been offered a better salary by the village of Wethersfield in the neighboring colony of Connecticut. The town then voted to allow him the same ten pounds a year for three years, perhaps in an attempt to provide job security. A few weeks later, however, Jeanes asked the town's permission to go to Wethersfield after all. He had heard that New Haven had invited another schoolmaster and he believed (correctly, as it turned out) that there would not be enough employment for both.[14]

New Haven's new schoolmaster was Thomas Hanford, who seems not to have been a Harvard graduate. Not until after his arrival in New Haven in November were his terms of employment finalized and the decision made to repair the schoolhouse. The town specified his responsibilities: he was to "perfect male children in the English, after they can reade in their Testament or Bible, & to learne them to wright, & so bring them on to Latin as they are capeable & desire to proceede therein." The wording "perfect male children in the English" is significant. Children were not to come to the town school for initial reading instruction; that was to have taken place elsewhere. In fact, they were supposed to have progressed beyond the primer and the Psalter to the two most advanced texts in the reading sequence: the New Testament or the whole Bible. Moreover, only the town's sons were entitled to town schooling.

Although the committee appointed to deal with Hanford had been empowered to offer him an annual salary of between thirty pounds and forty pounds, Hanford was in fact offered only twenty pounds, presumably because he was less well qualified than expected. He was, however, to enjoy certain privileges. The town was to pay for his food and lodging, his moving expenses, and a vacation in harvest time "once a yeare to goe see his friends." It was also to provide a portion of his salary in a form suitable for purchasing books. (Most of Hanford's salary was to be in produce, at a time when the majority of financial transactions were in that form rather than in scarce cash.) He would also have "the benefit of strangers" (that is, keep for himself the fees charged to children from outside the town). Hanford's last stipulation was that if he were to receive a call to the ministry elsewhere, he would be free to take it up.[15]

Hanford's high hopes for his school were soon disappointed. Only four months later, in March 1652, he was reported to be "somewhat discouraged, because he hath so many English scollers, which he must learne to spell, which was neuer the Townes mind." (Teaching children to spell syllables aloud was to teach them to read; so it is clear that, contrary to the town's intentions, the boys had not been taught to read before they came to school.) The town told Hanford that he could send home those children who could not read adequately and instructed their parents not to send them to school. Meanwhile, some seats were to be constructed for the schoolhouse, as well as a chest for the school's books. Only a few months later, in June 1652, Hanford was thoroughly disgusted with his job: "he finds his body vnable, and that it will not stand with his health to goe on in this worke of teaching scoole." He asked for the permission to leave that he had prudently written into his contract and accepted a call to the ministry in Norwalk, Connecticut.[16]

Theophilus Eaton, governor of New Haven colony, who seemed to feel personally responsible for the town's schooling, sent out letters to a couple of Harvard graduates. He informed the town in November that William Jeanes had notified him that he would be willing to return to New Haven to "teach boyes and girles to read and wright, if the Towne thought fitt." Some of the town thought that there "would bee neede of two scoolemasters; for if a Lattin scoole Master come, it is feared he will be discouraged if many English scollers come to him."[17] This distinction between "Latin" scholars, who would be taught to read and write Latin, and "English" scholars, who were still learning to read English, suffuses the colonial records. Moreover, the inclusion of girls as the potential recipients of elementary literacy instruction is both notable and rare.

John Bowers, who had graduated from Harvard four years earlier, arrived in June 1653. The town had a little difficulty in finding lodgings for him: "but now Thomas Kimberlys house is agreed vpon." He received the same salary as his predecessor and inherited the same problems. "A complainte was made," Francis Newman recorded the following May, "that the schoolmaster is so imployed in teaching children sent to him to Learne their Letters and to spell (which is contrary to order) that others for whom the scoole was cheifely intended (as Lattin scoollers) are neglected." Two of the "townsmen"—the standing committee of the town, called "selectmen" in most other townships—were dispatched to "send all such children home."[18]

Despite a salary increase to thirty-eight pounds that December, Bowers's troubles continued. Six years later, in April 1660, he complained that he had only eighteen students, and that their attendance was "so vnconstant that many times there are but 6 or 8; he desired to know the Townes minde, whether they would have a schoole or no schoole, for he could not satisfy himself to goe on thus." (As if to emphasize the town's generalized dissatisfaction with its young, the next entry in the town book was the registration of a complaint about the "Great disorders amongst children in the Meetinghouse in the time of divine worshipp.")[19]

Implicit in the grumbles of Hanford and Bowers is an acknowledgment of a universal reading methodology. Learning to read involved learning to identify the letters of the alphabet by name, spelling aloud syllables and words, and pronouncing the syllable or word as a unit (see Chapter 3). No wonder Hanford became discouraged when he was to teach so many of his young scholars "to spell," while Bowers was not only teaching spelling (the key to elementary reading) but was obliged to descend to the very beginning of the literacy curriculum and teach some of his boys the alphabet: they needed "to Learne their Letters."

Meanwhile, during the years that John Bowers was struggling with his underprepared students, New Haven colony had passed its first law that directly related to literacy. In July 1656, the townships that made up New Haven colony received the first copies of a book containing the statutes that had been passed up to that time, known as the "Code of 1656." (It had been printed in England.) To make sure that everyone knew what these laws enjoined, the colony ruled that each family should purchase a copy of the Code of 1656 for twelve pence.[20]

A section on children's education spoke reproachfully of parents and masters who neglected the education of children under their care. Those responsible were required, whether on their own initiative or by contributing to the support of a schoolmaster, to ensure that all children and apprentices should "attain at least so much, as to be able duly to read the scriptures, and other good and profitable printed Books in the English tongue, being their native Language, and in some competent measure, to understand the main grounds and principles of Christian Religion necessary to salvation." They were also to give appropriate answers to "plain and ordinary Questions" on these texts that might be posed them by the authorities. To ensure that these requirements were met, various court and town officials were ordered to keep a vigilant eye on their fellow townsmen. In short, all children were to learn to read (writing is not mentioned), and their comprehension of what they read would be tested.

The court put teeth into the law by providing a series of escalating penalties, beginning with a "warning" and proceeding through fines, doubled fines, and finally, as a last resort, the removal of the children from their parents or masters. The young illiterates would then be apprenticed to those "who shall better educate and govern them, both for publick conveniency, and for the particular good of the said children or Apprentices." The apprenticeship would last until the age of twenty-one for boys, and eighteen for girls—the standard age limits for apprenticeship at this time.[21]

Only a year later, in 1657, the colony rethought this legislation on reading instruction. Since, the court said, the town of New Haven had provided for a schoolmaster to be maintained at the town's expense, and that Milford had done the same, it now issued another law that made the support of a schoolmaster an obligation of every township; towns were to pay a third of his salary from the rates ("the good education of children being of publique concernment"), while the parents of his students were to pay the rest.[22] This offer was the kind that New Haven had made six years earlier to William Jeanes for elementary schooling: ten pounds to be paid from the town coffers and the rest to be made up by parents.

While the colony was emphasizing the need for schools to impart elementary literacy, pressure was growing within the colony for more advanced education. Many of the elders wanted to have a true "grammar" school, where boys would be taught not only Latin but Greek and even Hebrew and would therefore be prepared for admission to Harvard College. Francis Newman, who had served the colony so faithfully and for so long as its secretary, succeeded Theophilus Eaton as governor after Eaton died in 1658. Under Newman's leadership, the general court ordered that funds be set aside for the furtherance of such a school, which would function as a colony school, rather than just a town school. Despite its notable lack of success in attracting a constant student body at the township level when it was offering a more elementary level of education, New Haven colony formed a committee to explore the possibility.

A year later, John Davenport, minister of the town of New Haven since its foundation, put forward an even more ambitious plan. In an eloquent letter to the colony court, he urged its members to consider promoting a college and offered a portion of an estate that had been left by the late Edward Hopkins to further the cause. (Hopkins had served as governor, assistant governor, or deputy governor of Connecticut until 1656.) Davenport enjoined parents to keep their sons at school so that "at the least" they would be able to write, cast accounts competently, and make some entrance into the Latin tongue and urged the colony to find a schoolmaster to teach the Latin, Greek, and Hebrew that were the necessary preparation for college.[23]

The colony court (deeply sensible, it said, of the small progress that had been made in recent years in learning) responded in two ways. It provided a grant from the coffers of the town and the colony for the proposed Latin grammar school (to which it gave New Haven first refusal), and it added a rider to the education provisions in the Code of 1656. The code had demanded that all children, girls as well as boys, be taught to read; but this 1660 addition to the law now required that only one of the sexes be taught to write. "To the printed law, concerning the education of children, it is now added, that the sonnes of all the inhabitants within this jurisdiction, shall (vnder the same penalty) be learned to write a ledgible hand, so soone as they are capable of it."[24] This focus on legibility had implications: writing was being defined more in terms of its manner of presentation than on what was being presented: as product over process, as penmanship rather than composition. A "legible hand" was a phrase that would recur over and over again in this and the following century as the criterion for successful writing acquisition.

After becoming the earliest, by far, of all the colonies to make writing mandatory (for boys), New Haven continued its search for a master for its Latin grammar school. Jeremiah Peck, who had left Harvard in his junior year without a degree, was lured away from Guilford to become the new schoolmaster.[25] He was to teach Latin, Greek, and Hebrew. Clearly a young man brimming with self-confidence, he dispatched a lengthy letter to the court in May 1661, detailing fifteen propositions that he wished satisfied before he taught. They ranged far and wide and included the appointment of what he grandly called Rectores Scholae (a school committee); the selection of two men to screen students to make sure the scholars sent him were "fitted for his tuition" (perhaps town gossip about underprepared students had reached his ears in Guilford); free housing, a week's vacation and relief from paying any rates; and a salary of forty pounds from the colony along with another ten pounds from the town, to be paid semiannually. He also had a question: Did the court wish him to instruct his scholars in anything other than the ancient languages and oratory? To this, the court responded that "they expected he should teach them to write soe far as was necessary to his worke."[26] This answer reflected colonial compromises: whereas in England the boys would have gone off to learn penmanship from another master, at set hours, here Peck was expected to teach them to write himself. The incident reveals the gulf between the kind of writing deemed necessary for the Latin grammar school, on one hand, and the kind needed for commerce (offered by a master who linked penmanship and arithmetic instruction), on the other. Grammar school boys who learned Latin and Greek of course needed to be able to write, since they had to translate and to compose in the ancient languages, but in this context writing is strictly functional: the implication is that boys needed only to learn a simple script.

The fortunes of the colony grammar school need not detain us. Given the track record of earlier schools, the race was already lost well before young Peck left the starting blocks. By August 1662, only five or six boys from New Haven were attending the school—"it greived him," Davenport said, "to see how few schollars was there"—and in November the court reluctantly closed the school.[27]

The responsibility for education now reverted once again to the township of New Haven, and a note of realism creeps into the town records in December 1662. "Considering that there was but few boys that did learne Latting, it was thought best to haue a Schoole Master that may perfect schollars in English, to learne them to write, and arethmaticke, & to teach them the other tongues as they are capable." The salary of thirty pounds from the town treasury would be enough for this task.[28] Introductory reading instruction was still to be initiated outside the town school, but the town schoolmaster was to be responsible for continuing such instruction and for introducing the other two Rs.

After a short stint with a Harvard graduate, Recompense Osborn, the town was again without a school. In June 1663 a former ferryman named George Pardee was asked to take on the job of New Haven schoolmaster. He had John Davenport's confidence, and the town felt that there was "none soe fit at present as

George Pardee." Pardee was to "teach english" (teach introductory reading as opposed to "perfecting" it), as much Latin as he could, and writing. (Something was also said about teaching arithmetic, "as very necessary in these parts.") Pardee held out for full town funding, saying that he had a family to support. This demand produced some grumbling. Several men said that it was "scarce known in any place to haue a free schoole for teaching of English & writing." The town reached a compromise by allowing Pardee twenty pounds—more than the usual ten pounds but less than the thirty pounds a college graduate could command—for teaching reading and writing, with the usual proviso that the rest should be made up by the parents of the students. Pardee agreed to try the position for a year and was advised to be careful to instruct his pupils in "point of manners, there being a great fault in that respect as some exprest."[29]

The vicissitudes of the town school continued. In 1665 New Haven colony was absorbed into the colony of Connecticut. It was now subject to Connecticut's law (discussed below), which required towns of over a hundred families to support a grammar school. Two years later an instructor named Samuel Street did indeed conduct a grammar school in New Haven, but it was hard going, with only eight of its scholars in "Latting" the following year.[30] When he finally left in 1673, the town was without any school for an entire year, during which time nothing was done "to teach boys or youth in any kind of Learning." Once again, George Pardee stepped into the breach. (He had served as Davenport's attorney in the interim.) For a salary of eighteen pounds and the use of a house, barn, and home lot, his assignment was to "teach youth to read English and the accidence and any [Latin] Grammar ruels as farre as he could, and to write." (The "accidence" was the introduction to Latin grammar.) Pardee seems to have done an adequate job: "severall persons sayd they found some fruit of his labour in theyer chilldren & did desyer hee might goe on yet longer."[31]

This sort of schooling, however, fell far short of fulfilling Connecticut's legal requirement of a Latin grammar school for townships with over a hundred families, and in 1677 the orders of a displeased Connecticut General Court were read out at the July town meeting, that "this Towne must keep a Lattin schoole." There ensued a long and "louing [loving] debate" (Puritan code for a fierce argument), in which many voiced the opinion that the schoolmaster should "teach English allsoe and to write," because there were so few Latin scholars. The upshot was that the town made a decision that reflected how times had changed. The new schoolmaster was to teach a little of everything, expanding his offerings at both the top and the bottom level of difficulty. The school committee was to "prouide a sufficient schoolemaster, who shall not only teach the [Latin] Grammer & the [ancient] Languages, but allsoe to perfect the youth in reading English, they being entred in the primmer, & to teach to write a legible hand."[32]

This represents a classic and common solution to the problems caused by the hundred-family law: a compromise on various levels of instruction. Thomas Hanford had been hired in 1651 to teach a multipurpose school for boys only, providing advanced reading instruction, writing, and Latin for those who wanted it. After the collapse of the New Haven colony grammar school in 1662, the revised curriculum for the town school was very similar, except that arithmetic instruction was added to the schoolmaster's task. The compromise of 1677 was typical of other townships: in addition to teaching the ancient languages and Latin grammar, the schoolmaster was to provide writing instruction and even some elementary reading. Never part of the grammar school curriculum, arithmetic had apparently fallen by the wayside. Even more significant, admission standards had been dropped. Where once the ability to read the New Testament was an admission requirement, now the boys had to be entered only in their primers.[33]

The experience of New Haven, which was much like that of dozens of other townships across New England, reflects the remarkable efforts made by the founding members of the colony to recreate the educational circumstances under which they themselves had reached intellectual maturity. Their emphasis, once children of both sexes had supposedly mastered reading, was solely on the education of boys, who were to be groomed for Harvard College, which remained New England's only college throughout the seventeenth century. But the example of New Haven also reflects the tough realities of the colonizing experience and the growing conviction among men working their fields that an English education was far more practical than a classical one. New Haven also permits us to see the separate spheres to which the sexes were allocated.

Literacy in the Courts

The evidence on literacy provided by cases brought before the New Haven colony courts is as instructive as that provided by the town and colony records.[34] Court cases by definition show the aberrant, and the insights they provide on normalcy must be teased out of deviation. Inadvertently, New Haven court records shed light on the availability of the colonial equivalent of textbooks. Primers—which were preceded only by the hornbook in the traditional sequence of imparting reading—are mentioned very early. In December 1645, the colony court heard a case in which a man identified as Captain Turner was defending himself against Mistress Stolion, who kept a village store. Stolion alleged that the captain had backed down on a bargain they had struck, in which he had promised to give her two cows in exchange for six yards of her cloth. Turner responded by accusing Stolion of inflating prices, claiming that "she sold primmers at 9d [pence] apeece which cost but 4d here in New England."[35]

To those of us who are used to thinking of primers in terms of the famous *New-England Primer*, in its second impression in 1690, it comes as a surprise to learn that primers were readily available in New England in the 1640s.[36] (They were, of course, imported.) The cost of fourpence identified by Turner as the usual price of a primer was not a large sum. In the late 1630s the price of a quart of beer in Plymouth colony was regulated at twopence; and it cost fourpence to take a man and his horse across the river on a ferry. A fourpenny primer would have been only a third of the price of the law book embodying the New Haven Code of 1656, which everyone was supposed to buy. An inventory taken in 1647 of a store in

Roxbury, Massachusetts, valued the nineteen primers there at twopence, the same price as lace and the cheapest item in the store.[37]

Another instructive morsel, this time falling under the town's jurisdiction, is the tale of Captain How's daughter. In 1651, this girl was charged with a battery of misdeeds. She was alleged to have made oaths like "as she is a Christian" and "by the Holy name of God." In addition, she had supposedly shown a "stubborn miscarriage" toward her mother, and spoken in a profane way of the scriptures. Her mother insisted that her daughter had picked up some of these bad habits at Goodwife Wickam's, where she went to school. Two witnesses testified that young Miss How had made remarks about her mother such as, "a pockes of the devill what ayles this madd woman." Worse still, she had been seen to look in a Bible, turn over a leaf, and say that "it was not worth reading." The court found her guilty, fined her ten shillings for her oaths, and ordered a whipping "suitable to her yeeres" for everything else. It is not fanciful to suggest that Miss How had been asked to read the most advanced text in the "ordinary Road" to reading acquisition, the Bible—and that her disdain probably masked her inability to read it.[38]

A case some years later, in 1660, concerned the literacy and vocational training of an apprentice named Samuel Hichcock. The court wanted to know why John Tompson was holding Hichcock as a servant when there was no indenture. Tompson admitted that no indenture existed but said that Mr. Bowers (the schoolmaster) and his wife could testify to an agreement, made about three years earlier between Hichcock's father (then sick) and himself. According to Bowers's testimony, the agreement was that Hichcock should serve Tompson for seven years as an apprentice and be taught to read and write and the "practicall part" of navigation. The court withheld judgment for the moment on the legality of the agreement and asked Tompson whether the educational provisions of the agreement had been carried out. Tompson said that Hichcock "could read pretty well, & that he was now learning to write."[39] This case exemplifies the curricular sequence of acquiring reading skills to a considerable degree before being taught to write.

Another case, two years later, confirms the presence of adults who were literate in reading but not in writing. William Potter was accused of (and subsequently hanged for) the crime of bestiality. (His wife and son were his accusers.) In an effort to see whether he had any redeeming features, the court asked him if he had been educated. "He answered, well, and was taught to read."[40] Had he also been taught to write, he would surely have said so.

Patterns of Literacy in Seventeenth-Century New England

If pieced together, these snippets of information from New Haven's first few decades can provide us with portions of several patterns that were to emerge throughout New England during the seventeenth century.

For one, we encounter several of New England's forms of schooling, ranging from elementary schools, such as the town school that Jeanes kept briefly, where he taught reading and writing (the "English" school), to the "Latin" school, which in its most exalted form was a true "grammar" school, such as the one that New Haven colony initiated in 1661 when Jeremiah Peck was hired to teach Latin, Greek, and Hebrew, with no mention of any instruction in reading English. In theory, the boys who attended a Latin grammar school would already be fully literate in reading English, and the grammar schoolmaster would not have had to teach writing. In practice, however, successive New Haven boys disappointed their masters by their lack of preparation in reading, and any man who taught at the town school had to be ready to teach writing. In this way, the authorities combined the "petty school" they had known back in England—a school for teaching the "petties" or little ones—with the grammar school and even the writing school.

Another form of schooling in England was the "dame" or "reading" school, which was conducted by women in their own homes for small children of both sexes. Since dame schools were private and normally run by women who did not fall foul of the court system, they do not appear in the New Haven records, but they do surface in reminiscences. Joseph Green, born in Boston, Massachusetts, in 1675, used the term when recalling his introduction to education: "when I came to be big enough to go to school I went to the Dames School, where I was bad enough." Dame schools were often little more than the equivalent of nursery schools, but their ostensible purpose was always to teach reading.[41]

The lower boundaries of the age at which a child might attend a dame school emerge from an inquest: in Plymouth colony in 1664, Elizabeth Walker accidentally drowned when "being sent to scoole" at the age of two and a half.[42] The upper age boundary for schools taught by women is less clear. References to a "reading" school in the records may reflect the expansion of the quintessential dame school—where the texts used were only a hornbook and primer—into a school with a more advanced reading curriculum, where the children would reach the Psalter or even the entire Bible. At least in Boston, boys would then leave their reading mistresses to go to the town (Latin) grammar school; girls, however, might stay on at their private reading school. This latter kind of school, one that probably included girls of thirteen or fourteen (such as the rebellious Miss How), emerged in the New Haven records in the form of Goodwife Wickam's rather unsatisfactory school.

Except when a town insisted on, in effect, licensing them, as Boston did in the early eighteenth century, such private schools are rarely visible in seventeenth-century records. Nonetheless, it is important to remember that private schools, run in the home or lodging of the teacher, male or female, existed at all times and everywhere in the colonies.

Finally, the New Haven experience introduces us, if obliquely, to the division of literacy instruction by sex. Women introduced children to reading; men did the same for writing. The word *penmanship* is well chosen, for men were judged to be the sex ideally qualified to teach handwriting as part of boys' preparation for work. The corresponding utilitarian skill for girls was sewing.

New England Legislation on Reading

By the 1670s, all the New England colonies then in existence, except Rhode Island, had passed legislation like that in New Haven mandating that children be taught to read.

The Bay Colony of Massachusetts had had its first large migration of English settlers in 1630. Six years after that, its leaders founded Harvard College, and another six years later, in 1642, the colony led the way in legislating reading instruction. The Massachusetts law, surely the model for New Haven's Code of 1656, empowered the colony's selectmen, in effect, to monitor children's ability to read. The selectmen were to inquire into the vocation and employment of all children, "especially of their ability to read & understand the principles of religion & the capitall lawes of this country." If their inquiries proved unsatisfactory, the selectmen could impose fines on uncooperative parents and masters, and even, with the consent of a magistrate, remove from their parents or masters those children who were not being trained to a skill or taught to read, and apprentice them to someone else for such instruction. A Boston version of the law passed in 1672 reaffirmed that those responsible for children were not to permit "so much Barbarism in any of their families, as not to endeavour to teach, by themselves or others, their Children and Apprentices" enough learning "as may enable them perfectly to read the English tongue, and knowledge of the Capital Lawes." The fine was set at twenty shillings. The view of reading as a vehicle for social control emerges strongly from the wording of the law.[43]

Connecticut, where settlers had first migrated in large numbers in 1635, followed with similar legislation on children in 1650, reproaching parents and masters for being "indulgent" and "negligent." Like Massachusetts, Connecticut included in its law a reference to both teaching children a trade and teaching them how to read. Heads of families were not to permit so much "barbarisme" in their households as to fail to try to teach their children "by themselves or others . . . perfectly to read the English tongue." Children were also to know the capital laws. In addition, Connecticut required weekly catechizing of children.[44] (To catechize was to teach children to remember the answers to questions about Christian doctrine that could be found in dozens of different printed catechisms.) New Haven colony, as we have already seen, followed with its own reading law six years later. It was unique in making no reference whatsoever to mastering a trade, focusing only on teaching children to read.

New Plymouth colony had been founded earlier than any other colony in New England and enjoyed independent status until absorbed by Massachusetts in 1691; yet it published its legislation on reading in 1672—very late by New England standards. This late date allows us to see what the colony had learned from the experience of the others. Plymouth opted for the maximum coverage: its law required bringing children up in some trade or skill, catechizing them, and inculcating a knowledge of the laws. What Plymouth colony omitted, however, was significant. It differed from New Haven but resembled the other two colonies in that it nowhere mentioned the possibility of supporting a schoolmaster, simply saying that parents and masters of apprentices were to teach children to read "by themselves or others." New Hampshire cited ignorance, bad manners, and "Irreligion" as the motives for its own reading and apprenticeship law of 1712, which authorized a justice of the peace to examine "all Youth" aged ten years old to see whether they could read. Those unable to do so were to be apprenticed to "good Masters" who would teach them to read and write.[45]

The absence of any such legislation in Rhode Island is highly significant. The colonies of Massachusetts Bay, Connecticut, New Haven, and New Hampshire were considered "orthodox" in their religion: that is, they hewed to the tenets of Congregationalism with particular devotion. The Separatists who founded Plymouth were in a somewhat different category, and it is interesting to see how the founding fathers avoided legislation on literacy instruction for so long even while they gave lip service to it. Rhode Island, in contrast, was a home to Puritan exiles and founded on the principles of religious liberty. Jews settled in Newport as early as 1654, and Quakers soon followed. Laws that required the reading of Christian catechisms under these circumstances must have seemed inappropriate.

Adults living in the religiously orthodox colonies of New England, then, were responsible for teaching any child living under their roof to read and (except for New Haven) providing him or her with some vocational training. The notion of sending children into apprenticeship as the last legal resort for parents' or masters' failure to provide appropriate education needs to be interpreted in the colonial context. Learning a trade usually required that the apprentice live with the "master" in a status known generally as that of "servant." With or without formal indentures of apprenticeship, children of both sexes at virtually any age could be sent to live with someone other than their parents—often a relative—in a process known as "putting out." In formal apprenticeships, the master undertook to provide his servant's food, shelter, and clothing, and in addition often promised to introduce the child to a skill. Some indentures added a rider on educating the child.[46]

The English Poor Laws that had served as the precedent for all this New England legislation had also empowered the appropriate officials to remove from their parents or masters those children who were not being brought up in a trade and apprentice them elsewhere, lest they be a burden on the community as adults. There was, however, as Lawrence Cremin has noted, no precedent for the educational provisions written into the New England versions of the law.[47] Here, in a new land, the settlers took steps to legislate the reading acquisition of their young in a way that had no parallel in the country they had left. While lip service was paid in old England to the importance of teaching every child to read, no legislation provided any penalties for the parents who failed to do so. The legislation of reading instruction in the orthodox New England colonies, therefore, was an extraordinary departure from English custom that requires an explanation of the motivations that lay behind it. These motivations were complex, and the preambles to the laws suggest that they had a religious, social, political, and economic base.

The religious motive was paramount. The founding fathers of the New Plymouth, Massachusetts Bay, Connecticut, and New Haven colonies were men who had left communities that they felt were hostile to their faith. They longed for the chance to create a new system of spiritual and political governance that was purified of the excesses of Anglicanism. In their view, children needed to be able to read the Scriptures because personal access to the scriptures was a basic tenet of Protestantism.

The relationship, in the Puritan mind, between learning to read and piety was so intense that, as David Hall has argued, the two were virtually inseparable. As the articles of faith of 1549 had proclaimed, "Holy Scripture containeth all things necessary to salvation: so that whatsoever is not read therein" was neither to be believed nor thought necessary for salvation.[48] Like other devout Protestants everywhere, the Congregationalist founders of New England colonies believed deeply in the individual's right and duty to search out scriptural truth for himself or herself. Although reading the Bible by no means guaranteed conversion—that ineffable certainty that one had indeed been saved—it undeniably laid the groundwork for it. Belief in this relationship between reading the scriptures and understanding the tenets of Christianity inspired the New Haven law, and others like it, that decreed that children, as their capacity increased, should acquire enough learning to read the scriptures and understand Christian fundamentals "in some competent measure." (These last words were an acknowledgment of childish inadequacies.)[49] When Miss How said that the Bible was "not worth reading," she was committing blasphemy of a high order that violated the Bible's status as the wellspring of eternal truth. No wonder her punishment was severe.

The laws also draw a connection between reading and learning a "short" and "orthodoxe" catechism. Brevity was a nod to childish incapacity, orthodoxy an acknowledgment of the preeminence of Congregationalism. It was much easier to learn a catechism by heart if you could read it first. Conversely, knowing a text by heart promoted reading it. That is why the town book of Watertown, Massachusetts, characterizes the colony's reading law as the law for the "exercising reading to the advancing of Catachising."[50]

The social motive for mandating reading instruction, revealed in the wording of the New Haven version of the law, was the concern that children not taught to read were in danger of growing "barbarous, rude and stubborn, through ignorance." The 1648 amendment to the Massachusetts law and the 1650 Connecticut code both use the word "barbarisme." Civilization and education went hand in hand, in the Puritan view, and the fear that people who were making towns from "wildernesses" could themselves slip back into the wilderness is a recurring theme in Puritan thought.[51] In 1672, the selectmen of Dorchester, Massachusetts, "summoned in" Timothy Wales and his sons. Wales appeared before them without his sons and with offensive and contemptuous answers on his lips. When he finally brought the boys in, they were found very ignorant and unable to read. In Watertown, also in Massachusetts, two of the selectmen felt obliged to speak to William Knop early in 1671 about his daughter's education and also about her being "keept vnder restraint and Gouerment."[52] Implicit in these cases is the assumption that education served as an instrument of the state in keeping its citizens both civil and civilized.

A third motive was a refinement of these social considerations, and political in its thrust. Children needed to be able to read in order, as the Massachusetts law had put it, to "understand . . . the capital lawes of this country." For the communities to flourish in the wilderness, the rule of law must prevail, and all were required to know what the laws mandated by being able to read them. The laws of Massachusetts, Connecticut, and Plymouth all reflect this aspect, and that of New Haven did so by implication: the "good and profitable printed Books in the English tongue" certainly included the law books embodying the first printed laws, which every family was ordered to purchase.

The political aspect of knowing how to read appears within the framework of a person's familiarity with the law. A couple of New Haven examples illustrate how seriously communities took the fact that their laws were in print, readily available, and therefore to be obeyed. In June 1652, several years before the New Haven laws were published, Thomas Wickam (probably the husband of the school dame who was blamed for Miss How's delinquencies) was "complained of for not bringing the name & birth of his child to the Secretary in season; he said he is a stranger and knew not the order." The court accepted this as a reasonable excuse and did not fine him.[53]

In July 1656, however, the books of laws arrived in the colony from England, and every family was required to purchase one. Three years later, Francis Harvy, a Frenchman, was summoned before the town court on the charge that he had become engaged to Ann Small, a hired servant, without obtaining the permission of her parents or master. Like Wickam, Harvy said that "there was no such Law in the places where he hath beene, nor did he know that there was any such law here." Now, however, the court was not inclined to be lenient: "he was told that that excuses him not, & that he must (if he live heare) acquaint himself with the Lawes established & submitt to them." He received a steep forty-shilling fine.[54] It is clear that once the laws were in print, they were presumed to be accessible to all and the old principle of Roman jurisprudence applied: *ignorantia iuris neminem excusat* (ignorance of the law is no excuse). While others could read the laws aloud to a newcomer, the presumption was that the newcomer ought to be able to read them for himself or herself. This relationship between reading and the law is neatly encapsulated by a Watertown order of 1674: the town asked its selectmen to conduct a reading inspection, check that the children knew an orthodox catechism, and at the same time leave a free copy of the new colony laws at any house that lacked one.[55]

A fourth motive for requiring that children be taught to read was plainly economic. In both England and the colonies, it was widely accepted that male children had to learn a trade or skill and female children at least housewifery, and usually sewing. In most of the preambles to the colonial laws about reading, reading ability is linked to the skills necessary for economic survival. The economic aspect of the legislation emerges with especial clarity in the 1642 Massachusetts version, where a fuss was being made by the legislators over supplying children with hemp and flax; if children's only employment was to watch cattle, the selectmen were supposed to make sure that they were engaged in a constructive activity, such as knitting, as well.[56] The economic motivation had been at the heart of the English

Poor Laws, designed to protect communities from supporting unemployable indigents.

The economic necessity, however, of knowing how to read is by no means as clear-cut as the religious, social, or political ones. In fact, the vigor—or lassitude—with which all these laws were enforced illuminates how New England townships evaluated the importance of reading ability in relation to training in a trade or skill. All the laws stipulated that the selectmen of each jurisdiction were to keep an eye out for violators.

Some townships, in response to the reading legislation of their respective colonies, started off with a flurry of activity to survey their children's education. Cambridge, Massachusetts, seemed all energy and enthusiasm when, in November 1642, it first began to check on its children in compliance with the court order:

> John Bridg shall take care of all the families of that side the higheway his owne house stands on to my brother Winshepes . . . & Sergent Winshepe is to see to the families on the other side the common to Grissall . . . [and] George Cooke [is] to take care of all the ffamilies betwene that way & the highe way going ffrom the meeting house into the necke.

No report, however, is given of the results.[57]

Watertown, Massachusetts, in contrast, was unusual among New England townships in making consistent efforts to check up on whether all its children could read and knew their catechism. The town, situated on the banks of the Charles River, enjoyed both political and spiritual stability. Its minister, John Sherman—known from the beauty of his sermons as "the golden-mouthed preacher"—presided over Watertown's spiritual health from 1644 until his death in 1685. During and just after his long ministry, the town selectmen carried out ten inspections, between 1661 and 1686. On the first of these they discovered poverty as well as illiteracy: four families with eighteen children among them had failed to comply with the law on "excerising reading to the advancing of Catachising." Rather than instituting penalties, however, the selectmen offered the families some practical relief.[58]

In November 1670, a selectmen was assigned to visit the houses of another three families, those of John Fisk, George Lorance, and William Preist, to see whether their children had learned to read. A couple of weeks later, the "said John Georg and Willyam" were summoned to a meeting with the selectmen to be "admonished for not Learneing their Children to read the english toung"; they readily admitted that they were in the wrong and promised amendment. The next inspection of 1672 found no improvement in Fisk's children, and two years later Fisk was "warned in" again, both times being found "wholy negligent of Edducating his children as to Reding or cattecising." The town still took no punitive action.[59]

Yet Watertown did take action on the family of Edward Sanderson. Sanderson's family of six children had been the largest of those identified as illiterate back in 1661. In January 1671, the selectmen raised the possibility of apprenticing one of his children. Two months later the crisis came to a head. Complaints were being made by other townsfolk that the Sanderson family did not have enough for themselves or their children to live on. In consideration of the fact that "it would be the charge of the towne to prouide for the wholl fameley which will be hard to doe this year," the town decided that the best step would be to apprentice two of the children, "with the consent of their perants if it may be hade," otherwise with the help of the magistrate. In March, Sanderson's eight-year-old daughter was apprenticed to John Fleg, son of one of the selectmen, until the age of eighteen. Her education was covered by Fleg's undertaking to bring her up in all respects as an apprentice, as the law required. The Sandersons had apparently complied voluntarily, because there is no record that the town was forced to resort to the court and invoke the reading law.[60]

In a comparable incident in New Haven in 1652, "Old Bunill" had refused to allow his son to be apprenticed. The following year the villagers were still complaining about the Bunill children, whose mother was now ill. The town then decided to apprentice two of them "both for the good of the children (who are not educated as they should) & for the easing the Towne of charge."[61]

These examples strongly suggest that the law on reading, even when literacy was monitored, as it was by Watertown, was only invoked if it suited the town. All New England townships conscientiously looked after their own indigent, however quick they were to "warn out" the poor from anywhere else. In the 1670s, men like John Fisk and Edward Sanderson of Watertown were able to violate the law with impunity over a span of several years presumably because their families were not destitute and a potential expense for their towns. Only when Sanderson and his family, and others like them, threatened to become an economic burden to the town was the law invoked. All of this suggests that it was the economic aspects of the law rather than the educational ones that spurred towns to take action.

Even parents of apprentices apparently did not use the courts to insist that the literacy aspects of the reading law be honored. In a study of 267 young apprentices in the colony of Massachusetts between 1630 and 1698, of whom 235 were boys, Judith Walter found not a single example in the court records of an apprentice who took his master to court for failing to fulfill his literacy obligations, although she found several in which an apprentice's parent charged that his son's training in a trade had been neglected.[62]

There were steps that could be taken, however, by family members concerned about the education that their child or grandchild was receiving in someone else's household that fell short of legal proceedings. In Watertown, for example, William Knop had received a visit by the selectmen in January 1671 to inquire into his daughter's lack of education and unruly behavior. The girl turns up in the household of Thomas Smyth that October (probably sent to Smyth as a servant as a direct result of the earlier interview), when Smyth himself was summoned by the selectmen, as a result of a complaint presumably initiated by Knop. Smyth admitted that Knop's daughter had not been attended to in the matter of learning as well as she should have been. In the presence of her father, Smyth promised that he would be more careful in the future to make sure the girl would be taught to read.[63]

Seven years later, in an unrelated Watertown incident, Goodwife Ives complained to the selectmen that her son-in-law, Luis Allin, was "not taking ceare of his children which he had by hur daughtur: to giue them due Edducation & and bring them vp: in sum honnest imployment." Two of the selectmen were asked to look into her complaint so that they could "Reforme any such disordur."[64]

What, then, did the laws on reading achieve? It is safe to say that merely having a law requiring that all children be taught to read was not a guarantee that they were. As we have seen, the selectmen were inclined to invoke the penalties of the law only if it suited the economic needs of the town. If it was merely the educational interests of the child that were involved, it was unlikely that any action would be taken by the town other than a scolding. Nonetheless, the law was available to those who had an emotional stake in a child's welfare, and relatives could, and on occasion did, invoke the law to ensure that the child received reading instruction.

In another sense, however, the laws on reading have a broader meaning: they embodied the colonists' deeply held views on religion, society, and politics. To teach children to read, the legislation implied, was to give them access to the values held by the community. Reading offered a child a path toward salvation as an individual and led to a sense of social civility as a member of a group. In this, New England legislators had much in common with other governments, which have usually viewed the acquisition of reading by the nation's young as key to promulgating their values. Reading, in short, has been considered eminently serviceable in the cause of indoctrination.[65]

The New England legislators' further assumption that reading was a useful economic acquisition is more problematic. Men and women could and did survive in their New England townships without knowing how to read: they usually had access to those who did.

New England Legislation on Writing and Schools

In every colony, the reading laws preceded any legislation that related to writing instruction. When such instruction does appear in New England legislation, preambles to the laws mention none of the motivations that had inspired the reading laws—religious, social, political, or economic. Writing was not necessary for salvation. If writing were to be used in the cause of religion, it was for taking notes on sermons or creating the hortatory texts that would provide the faithful with edifying reading, those "other good and profitable printed Books" mentioned in the New Haven reading law. It was therefore much more useful for the producers than the consumers of devotional texts. Nor does any social aspect of writing appear in the legislative preambles. Writing did not have the social cachet it would acquire later. Similarly, its economic advantages are never mentioned. Instead, all the legislation on writing focused on its intellectual uses.

In 1642 Massachusetts had legislated the acquisition of reading skills without any discussion of schooling, laying on parents and masters the responsibility for teaching reading. In 1647, Massachusetts passed a law on writing that put the responsibility on towns by requiring them to hire a schoolmaster. (The instructor, not the literacy skill itself, was mandated by law.) The preamble to this famous schooling law, known as the "Old Deluder" law, declared that it was a "chiefe project of the ould deluder, Satan," to keep men from knowing the scriptures, formerly by keeping the scriptures in an unknown language and more recently by discouraging men from acquiring these languages. (The languages concerned were Hebrew for the Old Testament, Greek for the New, and Latin for the scholarly glosses.) In order, therefore, "that learning may not be buried in the grave of our fathers in the church & commonwealth," it was ordered that every township in the colony, once it had reached the number of fifty householders,

> shall then forthwith appoint one within their towne to teach all such children as shall resort to him to write & reade, whose wages shall be paid either by the parents or masters of such children, or by the inhabitants in general . . . ; & it is further ordered, that where any towne shall increase to the number of 100 families or householders, they shall set up a grammer schoole, the master thereof being able to instruct youth so farr as they may be fited for the university.[66]

The order in which the literacy skills are presented, "to write & reade," is most unusual. In its reversal of the actual order of instruction and of the common phrasing, it suggests that the schoolmaster in the fifty-family town was to be hired, above all, for his ability to teach writing, because introductory instruction in reading was supposed to have taken place already.

A careful analysis of the preamble tells us much about the working of the Congregational mind and about how the tool of writing was envisaged. At first glance, with its invocation of Satan, the law appears to be, like the one on reading five years earlier, mostly about religion. In fact, however, this new law is about the intellect.[67] Its major point is not that Satan is conspiring to keep men from a knowledge of the scriptures but that "learning" is in danger of being "buried" once the founding generation is gone. As one participant in the founding of New England put it, as soon as the settlers had secured the bare essentials of life, "we longed . . . to advance learning[,] . . . dreading to have an illiterate ministry to the Churches when our present ministers shall lie in the dust."[68] Ministers who were "illiterate" were not those who could not read or write, but those who did not know the ancient biblical languages.[69]

The 1647 schooling law, therefore, was laying the groundwork that would continue the Puritan intellectual tradition. It was creating the institutions that would enable a relatively small number of young men to attend schools where they would continue their reading instruction, learn to write, then advance to a Latin grammar school, and eventually go to Harvard College, founded, as we saw, in 1636, six years before Massachusetts passed any law on literacy education. Teaching writing, within this context, was to give young men a tool for the attainment of "learning" in a way that merely teaching reading could not.[70]

Just as they had done with the reading law, other New England colonies followed the lead of Massachusetts with regard to writing instruction, introducing schooling laws that were either copied or derived from the Bay Colony's law of 1647. Connecticut copied it in its entirety in 1650. In 1658 Plymouth colony recommended, distinctly halfheartedly, that its townships support schools: "they ought to take into theire serious consideration That some course may be taken that in euery Towne there may be a Schoolmaster sett vp to traine vp children to reading and writing." In 1660 New Haven, having three years earlier required every township in the colony to support a schoolmaster, actually stipulated writing as a minimum requirement for boys.[71] Once again, Rhode Island spurned any legislation relating to education. In every case, writing instruction was assumed to need the services of a schoolmaster.

When the "Ould Deluder" law of the Massachusetts Bay Colony created this two-tiered educational system, the educational structure was already in place.[72] Significantly, as Geraldine Murphy has demonstrated, the aims of seven of the nine Massachusetts towns that had opened schools before the passage of the schooling law of 1647 were identical to those of New Haven: they were trying to sponsor Latin grammar schools. The closer a town came to running a true grammar school, the more likely it was to fund the school and offer instruction free or partially free to its students, as was done in contemporary England.[73]

In this context, therefore, it is remarkable not so much that the "Ould Deluder" law of 1647 required grammar schools of one-hundred-family towns, but that it required fifty-family townships to employ a schoolmaster to teach writing and (advanced) reading. Presumably the law's two-tier system was based on a new awareness of the toll taken by colonial settlement—the discovery that, as in New Haven, the pupils entering the upper-tier school were ill prepared.

As we have seen with the reading laws, merely having a law on the books did not guarantee its compliance. Once again, therefore, it is necessary to ask what success the laws, this time on schooling, achieved. Murphy's overall conclusion in relation to Massachusetts is that its legislation did not succeed for another forty-five years, when a new law, in 1692, clarified the earlier one and found ways to enforce it.[74]

For decades the county courts, under whose aegis the school legislation fell, were much more interested in seeing that towns complied with the grammar school portion of the law than with the lower school one. In Massachusetts, for instance, while several one-hundred-family towns were taken to court for not having grammar schools, as late as 1668 not a single fifty-family town had been presented for lack of compliance, even though sixteen of twenty-six towns were out of compliance.[75]

The town schools of Massachusetts Bay, New Haven, and Connecticut had several features in common. First, the two-tiered system generally evolved into a single school: grammar schools transmuted into what Murphy calls "general" schools that offered a range of subjects, from writing to Latin. Second, the instructor chosen by the selectmen and voted on annually by the town was male. Although, as we shall see, townships after about 1670 would begin to employ women to teach elementary reading, these women would almost always be in addition to, not instead of, the master. Another element common to all the town schoolmasters was that they were expected to teach writing. It is rare indeed to find, in the records, instructions for a schoolmaster to teach just reading, like those given by the Dedham selectmen to the elderly and infirm Brother Joseph Ellice in 1664, "he being willing and we being hopefull he may doe some good in teaching some children to read English, for present and vntill one more able may be attayned." And even then it is clear that Ellice was hired as an adjunct to the main school of Dedham, the grammar school.[76]

The town schools had other features in common. Writing was valued more highly than reading, as the fees for each subject indicate. Indeed, it could cost as much as Latin instruction. When Watertown, Massachusetts, a hundred-family town, was presented to the court for not having a school, it responded by hiring Richard Norcross as its schoolmaster. He signed an agreement in 1652 that permitted any inhabitant to send his "sonnes or seruant for a weeke or two and to take them away agayne at his plesure." He was therefore required to keep "a strict accounte" of the number of weeks each boy was in school. Parents were to pay threepence a week for reading instruction, and fourpence for writing or Latin—a fee differential that was replicated elsewhere.[77]

The town schoolmasters also taught reading at some level. A crucial question is precisely what that level was. Like the grammar schools, the writing-reading schools were not intended, in theory, to provide initial reading instruction, because it was assumed that this skill would have been mastered at home or in a dame school. In practice, however, admissions standards for the town schools were progressively lowered until a knowledge of the alphabet was the only requirement. Newbury, Massachusetts, for instance, when it opened its lower-tier school, required the master of its new schoolhouse in 1652 "to teach all such inhabitants children, as shall be sent to him so soon as they know their letters and begin to read." Similarly, the same year, Salisbury, Massachusetts—which, like Newbury, was complying with the fifty-family law—contracted with its schoolmaster "to teach all their childeren (those only excepted that have nott the knowledge of the letters) in writing & reading & otherwise so farr as his abilities will reach unto." Elsewhere, townships had made it clear that boys should be able to "reade in their Testament or Bible" before admission, as New Haven had specified for its town school in 1651. But when New Haven opened its grammar school in 1684 with far loftier aims than those of the regular town school, its regulations required entering boys only to "have ben before taught to spell the letters well & begin to Read." Similarly, Farmington, Connecticut, a couple of years later, asked only that boys be through their hornbook.[78]

This new willingness to teach reading at a low level is borne out by the ages at which children could attend school: four years old for boys at the Dedham Latin school in 1652, five in Wethersfield, Connecticut, in 1661. Since children were not expected to be able to hold a quill pen much before the age of seven or perhaps six, the younger children could only have been there for beginning reading instruction.[79]

Similarly, towns seem to have taken seriously the injunction that the schoolmaster should teach all "the children that shall be sent to him." When Michael

Metcalf turned several boys away from his Dedham school in 1656 because they were over the age of fourteen (the top age limit at which parents of boys paid fees), some of the town's selectmen paid him a visit to remind him of the "covenant wherein it is expressed he should teach all that are sent to him to wright and read."[80] The implications of this "convenant" for the town instruction of girls would later prove crucial.

The last feature that town schools had in common was their clientele. One of the most crucial questions to be asked about New England education in the seventeenth century relates to the sex of the "scholars." Did the town schools admit girls? If so, to which kind of school?

One point is immediately clear: Latin grammar schools did not accept girls. Since the main motivation for the schooling laws of 1647 was to preserve the spiritual and intellectual standards of the colony—and the grammar schools were specifically designed to "instruct youth so farr as they may be fited for the university"—there was no reason to include girls in such schools, for they could play no role in the ministry. Nor could they attend Harvard or any other college (Yale would be chartered in 1701) or participate in the government. Dedham actually raised the issue: in 1652 the selectmen were asked to rule "whether the Town require that girls should be taught in this Schoole or not." The town answered decisively in the negative, and it continued to specify parents of "male children" as liable for the school tax to the end of the century. The same was true of Wethersfield, in Connecticut. When, in 1684, New Haven planned, yet again, to open a grammar school, the Hopkins Grammar School, it stipulated that "all Girles be excluded as Improper & inconsistent with such a Grammer Schoole."[81]

But what of the "general" schools that many towns opened as a compromise response to schooling laws that in theory required them to have both a writing-reading school and a grammar school? Here girls may have attended some early schools—but only for writing instruction. Richard Norcross was the Latinist hired to teach in Watertown, Massachusetts, to satisfy the new hundred-family requirement. In his initial contract of 1650, it was stipulated that "if any of the said towne, haue any maidens, that haue a desire to learne to write that the said Richard, should attend them for the Learning off them." These girls, if they came, would have been taught at a different time from the boys, but the wording of the law could also imply instruction at their homes.[82]

A much more important question, however, because it affected a much larger number of children, is whether girls were regularly admitted to the less ambitious town schools, those lower-tier writing-reading schools mandated in Massachusetts and Connecticut for townships of over fifty families. In 1656 Rowley, Massachusetts, opened such a school. It required the parents of all male children from the age of four to fourteen to pay for their schooling, and so clearly excluded girls.[83]

It is important to note here that the term *children* was implicitly defined as boys. Boston, for instance, had no town-supported schooling whatever for girls until 1789, yet its records routinely refer to "children."[84] Farmington, Connecticut, voted as late as 1686 to devote twenty pounds to a town school "for the instruction of all such children as shall be sent to it, to learn to read and write the English tongue." Yet a year later it had to issue a clarification: by "all such children as shall be sent is to be understood only male children that are through their horning book [hornbook]."[85] This sex-biased definition of "children" explains why Hampton, Massachusetts, when it opened a lower-tier school in 1649, felt obliged to be explicit when it ordered John Legate "to teach and instruct all the children of or belonging to our Towne, both mayle and femail (wch are capiable of learning) to write and read and cast accountes."[86] Imbedded in this inclusiveness is the implication that not all little girls were capable of instruction.

Everyone who has looked at education in the colonial period is beholden to Walter Small, who studied the records of almost two hundred New England schools. He found only seven town-supported schools that definitely admitted girls (including Hampton), and five that might have. Most of the schools known to accept girls did so at the end of the seventeenth century. Rehoboth, Massachusetts, engaged Robert Dickson in 1699 "To do his utmost endeavor to teach *both sexes* of boys and girls to read English and write and cast accounts"; a year earlier Deerfield, also in Massachusetts, had made heads of families of both boys and girls pay a poll tax to finance the school.[87]

While the comparative silence in the town records on the subject of the admission of girls to the lower-tier schools is by no means conclusive, other factors must be taken into consideration. First, it was widely believed in the seventeenth century that there was no compelling economic reason to require girls to learn to write. The social standing of elite girls permitted them to be taught to write privately, but since writing instruction was the first job of the town schoolmaster, fathers of lower social standing probably did not even contemplate it for their daughters. Bequests and wills in the early decades, if they mentioned any provision for children's education, routinely asked that sons should be taught both literacy skills but daughters only to read and sew. Apprenticeship indentures for those apprenticed voluntarily show a similar differentiation: boys were usually to be taught to read, write, and cipher, but girls were only to be taught reading and religion, occasionally sewing, and never writing. Seventeenth-century girls were being educated to be successful homemakers, not job holders.[88]

The colonists were part of a culture that consistently undervalued women's intellectual ability, and most men did not believe that women could or should engage in literacy at an advanced level, especially in composition. Anne Bradstreet, an immigrant to Massachusetts Bay and a devout Congregationalist whose poetry was first published in London in 1650, referred to the conflict between writing and sewing as mutually exclusive occupations for the hands: "I am obnoxious to each carping tongue / Who says my hand a needle better fits," she wrote. She was scorned, she said, for wronging "A Poets pen . . . / For such despite they cast on female wits."[89]

Moreover, the English model from which immigrants derived their ideas of schools precluded the admission of girls. Town-funded schools in England, whether they were petty schools or grammar schools, never included girls. The burden of proof is therefore on those who wish to argue that girls were included in the town schools, not the other way around, particularly since schooling was segregated by gender beyond the level of the dame school. In addition, the force of custom no doubt kept many "maidens" away from the town school even when the law did not. My conclusion, then, is that, up to perhaps the 1670s, girls, with a few rare exceptions such as that of Hampton, were not admitted to town schools of any kind. In general, the more ambitious a town's schooling was, the less likely it was that girls would be permitted to attend.

But restrictions against girls would eventually be relaxed. In particular, townships founded after 1670 would have a more inclusive definition of children. For instance, in 1678 the selectmen of Wallingford, Connecticut (founded eight years earlier), paid the schoolmaster ten pounds a year and asked for a subsidy of "three pence a weeke for all schollers males or females from six to sixteene years ould so long as they goe to schoole." Ten years later, the town was employing a woman in the summer school, and a man in the winter school. The juxtaposition of girls as students and women as teachers in town schools is not coincidental. Widespread change would only occur once the need was perceived for educated women—not as students but as teachers.[90]

Women as Reading Teachers

Women's aptitude for teaching reading, at home and in their own private dame schools (also called reading schools), had long been acknowledged. On the rare occasions when we know who taught a child to read at home, the mother is singled out. As texts for reading instruction in the seventeenth century were a sequence of Christian works (see Chapter 3), pious mothers were particularly motivated to teach their children to read. The Boston minister Increase Mather, born in 1639, only nine years after Dorchester, Massachusetts, was settled, reports that his mother, whom he describes as a "very Holy praying woman," taught him to read. (Significantly, his father taught him to write.)

The amount of reading dames offered must have varied according to the age of their pupils, while the length of time children continued with them depended on the children's sex: boys moved on to schoolmasters' schools while some girls, such as the rebellious Miss How, persisted with her dame. We know of schoolmistresses who taught a substantial amount of reading. John Barnard, born in 1681, recalled that when he was not yet six years old his schoolmistress made him "a sort of usher" and appointed him to teach children who were older as well as younger than he, "in which time I had read my Bible through thrice."[91]

Once townships acknowledged the need for town-supported reading instruction, they naturally turned to women for help. During the three last decades of the seventeenth century, towns began to hire women instructors to teach reading to children of both sexes. The change was probably born of necessity: parents and masters were being delinquent in fulfilling their legal responsibility to have their children taught to read, despite the 1672 revision to the old law that now imposed a twenty-shilling fine. Around 1700, Marblehead, Massachusetts, found 122 boys who could not read and could therefore not be admitted to the town school—and this at a time when minimal reading requirements required little more than a mastery of the alphabet.[92]

Walter Small found numerous references to town support of school dames in town records from the 1670s on.[93] Further town support of school dames would come in the first three decades of the following century and increase thereafter. Once towns funded school dames, we can be confident that little girls as well as little boys attended their schools for reading instruction. The girls' next step would be to attend the master's school for writing instruction, for the town schools evolved into summer schools taught by women and winter schools taught by men.

Just how firmly the orthodox colonies were committed to literacy education became apparent again in the eighteenth century, when the colony of New Hampshire (set off from Massachusetts in 1679) clarified its educational provisions. Its 1719 schooling law demanded that every town of fifty householders "be constantly provided of a School-Master to Teach Children and Youth to read and write," and pay his salary by a town rate.[94]

Despite the many failures to comply with the literacy laws passed by the orthodox New England colonies, the towns that complied offered their young something that was highly unusual: a town-sponsored school to impart literacy, at first to boys only but often, especially in newly founded towns in the last quarter of the century, to girls as well. Whether these schools were provided at no cost to the parents (as with a few grammar schools), at a subsidized cost, or even at full fees, this was still a remarkable instance of government-sponsored education.

No other region of colonial America replicated this educational provision. In Virginia, as elsewhere in the South, geography would have militated against a New England approach because its settlements were widely dispersed and thinly populated, reachable mostly by water. But the key difference was that the underlying motivations for literacy instruction that prevailed in much of New England were simply missing in a colony designed for commercial profit, not the pursuit of a model of Christian living. Virginia was outwardly a Christian settlement: it was one of only two colonies in which the Church of England was the established church. However, when Virginia passed a law in 1632 on instructing the young and ignorant, there was no mention of compulsory reading instruction, only of compulsory catechetical instruction—using the catechism in the Anglican prayer book—which the minister was to provide during the half hour before Sunday prayers. The Poor Laws passed by Virginia in 1646 resembled England's in permitting involuntary apprenticeship without any reference to reading instruction. In fact, during the entire colonial period, this Anglican colony closely resembled its mother country in passing no act on elementary education. The only law to mention children and be passed in successive legislative sessions was one that clarified the legal standing of children born to Negro women: they were to be bond or free, in accordance to the condition of their mothers.[95]

There is therefore a reason why the district schools, as they were later called, of New England became so famous. Overall, the Puritans established a model of education that had no precedent in the legislation of the mother country. Nothing in any English law set penalties for not teaching a child to read. No English statute required English townships of a certain size to have a schoolmaster to offer writing and advanced reading instruction. Nothing like this existed at the time in England, and, with the possible exception of Scotland, probably not anywhere else in the world.[96]

2

Literacy and the Indians of Massachusetts Bay

No trackless wilderness had confronted the first Europeans to reach the northeastern shores of the great American continent in the early sixteenth century. Instead, they had come upon a land already inhabited by hundreds of thousands of native Americans. Extending hundreds of miles inland from the eastern coast as far as the region around the Saint Lawrence (where Iroquoian-speakers lived), innumerable bands of Indians spoke various languages belonging to the Algonquian language family. In the east, many bands spoke languages belonging to the eastern branch of Algonquian, such as Narragansett, Nipmuck, Mohegan-Pequot, and Massachusett. Massachusett was spoken by Indians who lived in what came to be called the Massachusetts Bay colony. It was perhaps also spoken by the Pawtucketts, close by the Merrimac River to the north, and certainly by the Wampanoags (also known as the Pokanokets), who lived in southeastern Massachusetts, on Cape Cod, on the eastern shore of Narragansett Bay, and on off-shore islands such as Martha's Vineyard and Nantucket.[1]

The first successful New England settlement by the English was that of the "Pilgrims," who debarked from the *Mayflower* at what they named Plymouth in December 1620. A decade later, the first of several large waves of Puritan immigrants, led by John Winthrop, reached Boston Bay to found the Massachusetts Bay colony. These English settlers frequently discovered fields that had once been cultivated but were now reverting to the wild. Their cultivators, the local Massachusetts, had been ravaged by the lethal epidemics of 1616–19. Diseases such as smallpox, measles, and diphtheria, previously unknown in North America, had been introduced by contact with infected European traders. Lacking immunity, entire populations of native Americans had been consumed. Called simply "the plague" by Europeans who witnessed its terrible fruits—corpses of unburied Indians rotting on the ground—it reduced the native population of southern New England from perhaps as many as 126,000 or even 144,000 to a mere fraction of that total.[2]

A smallpox epidemic in 1633 further decimated the Indians of the Massachusetts coast. The "sad remnant" that was left was therefore vulnerable to new systems of belief that could offer an explanation for their shattered way of life. Many would prove to be receptive to a cultural change that would preserve their ethnic identity.[3]

In the spirit world of the Massachusetts, Hobbamock was a powerful force. (The Puritans paid him the compliment of regarding him as the Indian version of the devil.) Some Indians living as servants in Boston families were suddenly terrified by the appearance of this spirit, who materialized in various shapes but with a single message. As John Winthrop, governor of Massachusetts, reported it, Hobbamock was "persuading them to forsake the English, and not to come at the assemblies, nor to learn to read." Hobbamock was, in effect, warning the Indians against acculturation. He had correctly identified literacy and literacy transmission as an integral part of an alien culture. The ability to read would eventually expose literate Indians to English control and English bureaucracy through printed laws and written orders.[4]

The two cultures, native American and European, differed on many counts, but one of their most striking contrasts concerned a written language. Native Americans were certainly familiar with symbolic representation. Some kept records by notching sticks or using twigs to count with. Others used pictures to indicate their names: like other Indians selling land, Sawseunck had drawn an ax and Mantowese a bow and arrow as they signed the land deed with the founders of New Haven colony. But none of the Indians of North America had devised a written language.[5]

The magical aspects of writing were considerable for those who had never encountered them before. The oral culture in which native Americans lived ensured that the spoken word was regarded with great reverence. The Englishmen who attended Indian meetings were impressed by the deference accorded to speakers and the courtesy with which one Indian waited, with a respectful silence, until well after another had finished. Spoken words were as real as objects, and their power to cause good and ill was part of the intricate web of the native American belief system, in which there was no line drawn between the natural and the supernatural.[6]

When, on a mission to the Huron Indians in the 1620s, Gabriel Sagard sent a note back to the village to a fellow Recollect priest, asking for a replacement for his leaky canoe, the Indians who witnessed the arrival of the new canoe were impressed. "They said that that little paper had spoken to my brother . . . and all were filled with astonishment and admiration at this mystery." As James Axtell notes, writing enabled a man to read another man's mind at a distance, a gift much prized by native Americans. Moreover, the magical qualities of writing were enhanced by their so often occurring in a magical context—the white man's religion. (If things went poorly, of course, literacy could have the reverse effect and be considered as malevolent as the religion in which it was embedded.)[7] But the mystery of reading and writing did not last long. Indeed, Indians already had enough experience with symbolic communication, such as markings on trees, to perceive literacy as the same process in a different form. Amy Schutt, speaking of the Algonquians, points out, "the adoption of alphabetic writing did not require a complete transformation of thought patterns or adoption of an entirely new way of seeing the world."[8] The oral nature of literacy instruction and of literacy itself (where reading meant oral reading) also aided the adoption of literacy into a highly oral culture.

The English settlers' efforts to teach the Indians to read were almost invariably part of a missionary effort.[9] The notion that the English had a spiritual obligation to bring "salvation" to the "savages" was an important theme in immigration rhetoric in both Virginia and New England. The Massachusetts seal even portrayed an Indian with an appeal ballooning from his head, "Come over and help vs."[10] Most of the new settlers, however, early become so disenchanted with this idea, so hostile to Indians in general, and so preoccupied with their own concerns that only a handful—most notably John Eliot and the younger Thomas Mayhew—embraced the cause of preaching to the Indians. Englishmen actually living on American soil financed none of the efforts to convert native Americans and none of the schools that every proselytizer saw as essential to the conversion effort. Instead, all funds came from the home country.

Because efforts to impart literacy to native Americans were set within the larger context of religious proselytism, how scholars view such efforts has been colored by their judgment of mission activity in general. Scholarly opinions have changed markedly since the mid-1960s. In the older studies, missionary activity was usually exempted from criticism even when other aspects of Puritan aggression were not. Missions were viewed, in general, as benevolent attempts at "saving souls from savagery."[11] Bringing literacy to native Americans was considered part of the baggage of bringing them civilization—assumed to be an essential component of their conversion.[12] Beginning in the mid-1960s, however, scholars focused on "coercive" cultural change, in which the missionary was seen as a "cultural revolutionary" who imposed his ethnocentric world views on Indians able to respond to assaults on their culture only in "delimited" ways.[13] By implication, the introduction of literacy to the Indians was equally coercive and to be condemned in principle.

More recently, most scholars accepted the view that Indians were not merely passive in the face of "cultural imperialism" but active in a variety of ways in defense of their own culture.[14] This view suggests that to evaluate missions from the Indian point of view we must consider whether or not the Indians' acceptance of Christianity helped them to preserve their ethnic identity and even facilitated their survival as a people. From this perspective, the missions, by introducing native Americans to literacy, are said to have provided them with a "practical technique" that helped them adjust to a new world.[15] More recently still, however, the teaching of literacy to native Americans has come under a new attack. Those New England Indians who acquired literacy did so, according to Jill Lepore, at "great cost," placing themselves in a dangerous, if "powerful, position, caught between two worlds but fully accepted by neither." If, Lepore asks, "literacy can be wielded as a weapon of conquest and can effectively compromise a native culture, what then of that culture's history and who is left to tell it?"[16]

This chapter looks again at the introduction of literacy to native Americans, examining its impact on their culture and their reactions to it and asking whether the introduction of literacy to this population differed materially from its introduction to the immigrants from England. We look first at the literacy education that was an integral part of the mission of John Eliot in mainland Massachusetts, then at the Indian Library, the status of literacy among New England Indians in the early 1670s, and finally at the introduction of literacy to the Wampanoag Indians on the island of Martha's Vineyard.

John Eliot and the Massachusett Indians

The missionary efforts financed from England were reported in a series of small pamphlets published in London now known as the Eliot Tracts. Despite their clearly promotional aspects—they were designed to publicize the endeavor and raise money in England for the cause—they contain invaluable insights on the Indians' acquisition of literacy.[17]

John Eliot, after whom the tracts were named, was known even in his own time as the "Apostle to the Indians." A graduate of Cambridge University, where he attended Jesus College, he emigrated to America in 1631. He soon became the "teacher" of the church of Roxbury, Massachusetts, one of two ministers there. (The term "teacher" did not denote a schoolteacher, who was always called a schoolmaster, but a minister whose special function it was to teach the principles of Christianity to his flock.)[18] Eliot therefore had to fit his missionary activities around his other pastoral duties. He began his work with the Massachusetts in 1646.[19]

Eliot was not shy about promoting his cause, and in 1647 sympathizers in London published the first of the Eliot Tracts, titled *The Day-Breaking if not the Sun-Rising of the Gospell with the Indians in New England.*[20] This and subsequent pamphlets generated enough interest among English Puritans to lead to the organization of a society for the cause, which became a legal entity in 1649 under legislation passed by the English Parliament. (The year was tumultuous one for everyone but Puritans: it saw the beheading of Charles I and the naming of Oliver Cromwell as England's "Lord Protector.") The society was known at first as the "New England Corporation" and later as the "New England Company."[21]

This private, London-based society was able, through contributions from individuals in England, to provide extensive funding for the rest of the century to those "laboring in the Lord's vineyard." The corporation needed an administrative arm in New England, so the Commissioners of the United Colonies of New England (who, ironically, had joined together to coordinate the colonies' mutual defense against the Indians) were entrusted with the responsibility. The New England Commissioners, through a Boston agent, disbursed the funds remitted to them by the corporation and channeled requests to London for supplies. (By September 1655 they were forwarding John Eliot's urgent pleas for hornbooks and primers.)[22] While Eliot was laboring among the Massachusetts of the mainland, Thomas Mayhew was preaching to the Wampanoags of Martha's Vineyard, a small island— just over nineteen miles long—off the coast of southeastern Massachusetts.

The eight tracts published from 1647 to 1660 (another appeared as late as 1671) are in the form of a series of letters. Some were written by Eliot and Mayhew, others by supporters, such as Henry Whitfield, pastor of the church at Guilford in New Haven colony, who urged his readers to encourage Eliot and Mayhew "in this great work." With titles such as *The Clear Sunshine of the Gospel Breaking forth upon the Indians in New-England* and *Strength out of Weakness: or a Glorious Manifestation of the Further Progresse of the Gospel amongst the Indians in New England,* the tracts promoted the work as a continuing spiritual success story.[23]

These accounts disclose more than just the acquisition of literacy by native Americans. They allow us to share, however briefly, the experiences of those who were undergoing the stress of acculturation. The Indians' encounters with literacy were a crucial aspect of their confrontation with an alien way of life, and their rejection or adoption of literacy has much to tell us about the process of cultural transference and even the nature of literacy itself. The reactions of the Massachusett and Wampanoag Indians to learning to read and write are particularly telling because they were acquiring literacy in their own language. The creation of printed texts in the Massachusett tongue is therefore a key part of the story. These texts were among a small number of books translated into various dialects of Algonquian (mostly Massachusett) and printed in a series known today as the Indian Library.

After Eliot became interested in preaching to the Massachusett Indians, he began to learn the Massachusett language. (His skill as a linguist in analyzing a language so strikingly different from Indo-European languages has been belatedly acknowledged by many scholars.) Eliot had the assistance of a young Indian named Cockenoe-de-Long-Island who knew English. Cockenoe had been captured during the Pequot War and sold as a servant into the house of Richard Collacot, a prominent Dorchester man. (Cockenoe's name arose from the fact that he was not a Pequot but a native of Long Island.)[24]

Cockenoe was "ingenious, [and] can read," Eliot reported, "and I taught him to write, which he quickly learnt, though I know not what use he now maketh of it."[25] In this offhand way, Eliot disclosed his own creation of a written language for the Massachusett tongue. Cockenoe's clear pronunciation made him a good interpreter, and he helped Eliot translate the Ten Commandments, the Lord's Prayer, and several scriptural texts into Massachusett, even though his native tongue was not Massachusett. Eliot was also able to write several *Exhortations* and *Prayers* by his help." Cockenoe was on hand to assist Eliot as a translator when Eliot made his first missionary forays among the Massachusett Indians.[26]

Eliot's work among the Massachusetts, described in faithful detail in the Eliot Tracts, allows us to see the relationship between literacy and the Congregationalist interpretation of Christianity that Eliot represented. In October 1646, Eliot and three other Englishmen went to the wigwam of Waaubon to preach the Christian message, in the Massachusett tongue, to some survivors of the devastating smallpox epidemics of earlier times. This was not the first such meeting. Waaubon (or Waban) had earlier sent his son to the English to be educated, and the boy, dressed in English clothes, was standing beside his father as Eliot spoke. Turning occasionally to Cockenoe for help, Eliot preached for an hour and a quarter on the Ten Commandments. He explained their import, outlined in chilling terms the wrath of God that descends on those who break them, and "preached Jesus Christ" to the Indians as their only means of salvation from sin. Then he asked for questions.[27]

At a similar meeting among other Indians six weeks earlier, the questions had been along the lines of what causes thunder. Now, however, Waaubon's Indians seemed to reveal how well they had understood Eliot's preaching by asking, "How may wee come to know Jesus Christ?" Eliot told them "That if they were to read our Bible, the book of God, therein they should see most cleerely what Jesus Christ was." Since they could not do that, they should think about what they had heard out of God's book and pray that the Lord would make them know Jesus Christ. After a few more questions from the Indians, it was the turn of the English to ask some questions. The meeting between the two cultures ended with Eliot's handing out apples to the children and tobacco to the men.[28]

The first step in formal instruction was taken at another meeting in Waaubon's wigwam two weeks later. Eliot and his English companions taught the younger Indians the beginnings of a catechism—that exchange of questions and answers on doctrine that all Christian children had to memorize. Careful not to "clog their mindes or memories with too much at first," they began, still speaking in Massachusett, with only three questions. "Who made you and all the world?" The answer was "God." "Who doe you looke should save you and redeeme you from Sinne and hell?" "Jesus Christ." "How many commandments hath God given you to keepe?" "Ten." A few weeks later, several Indians made their own decalogue. Revealing some understanding of the "civility" being encouraged by Eliot, if not his religious message, the decalogue laid down rules on family relationships and the work habits of Indian males, and it included fines for women who left their breasts naked or allowed their hair to hang loose and for men "that weare long lockes."[29]

Whether or not the English were correct in asserting that the Indian men cut their hair of their own accord, it is clear that the Indians themselves had heard John Eliot's message, spoken or unspoken, that becoming a Christian meant becoming a Congregationalist in outward behavior as well as inward.[30] Long hair, to an Indian man, had unique value. More than anything else, it symbolized his identity. To the Puritans, however, long hair reeked of pride and independence.[31] John Eliot happened to be peculiarly opposed to it: long hair "was always very loathsome to him" (according to his biographer, the Boston minister Cotton Mather), whether in its natural form or as a wig.[32] The violation of their culture represented by cutting their hair was, nonetheless, a price that most of the Indians seemed ready to pay as their dues for conversion.

"Civilizing" the Indians was closely connected to converting them. As Eliot put it in the fall of 1649, "I find it absolutely necessary to carry on civility with Religion." Civilization implied education, and, thanks to a donation from an anonymous well-wisher, Eliot was able to pay five pounds each to a schoolmaster in Dorchester and a woman in Cambridge for teaching English to the children of nearby Indians. (The woman's pupils were said to have come along "very prettily" under her care.)[33] Eliot was also very much aware of the need for the Indians to receive schooling in their own language. "If the Lord bring us to live in a Towne and Society, we must have special care to have Schools for the instruction of the youth in reading, that they may be able to read the Scriptures at least." This necessitated finding the fees for "such Schoolmasters and Dames" as could be persuaded to teach them. He was therefore eager to translate some parts of the scriptures and print a primer in their language. This project would be very expensive, and Indian help for the work, he noted, would be essential.[34]

Eliot was already convinced that the Indians could be educated for conversion only if they adapted "cohabitation"—living in villages modeled on those of the English settlers, with a fort, a meetinghouse, and a school. In 1646 the General Court of the Massachusetts Bay colony had purchased land for the "Praying Indians" to settle in and named it Nonanetum or "Rejoicing."[35] ("Praying Indians" was the term given to Indian worshipers of Christ who had not yet attained church membership.) This was not the formal settlement Eliot had in mind, however, and it proved to be poorly situated because, ironically, it was too close to other habitation. The cattle of English settlers at nearby Watertown spoiled the Indians' corn, and their owners refused compensation because the Indians' lands were unfenced. In 1650, therefore, the general court granted the Indians a tract of land on the upper Charles River, to be named Natick.[36]

Natick straddled the river some sixteen miles southwest of Boston and eight miles from Dedham. It was the first of fourteen towns of Praying Indians that would be settled in the Massachusetts Bay colony. Eliot instituted a form of government that he believed to be based on scripture. With minimal English assistance, the Indians laid out three rows of streets (two on one side of the Charles, one on the other), constructed a bridge, built a fort, and within the fort erected a building that doubled as a meetinghouse on Sundays and a schoolhouse on weekdays. In the upper chamber, a small room was partitioned off for Eliot, who lodged there when he visited the village. In September 1651, the Indians at Natick entered into a formal covenant, devoting themselves to God.[37]

Eliot had voiced his aspirations for Indian schooling a year earlier. He wanted to have school exercises that would teach all the men to read and write, and, "if the Lord affords us fit instruments," all the women to read. (Literacy instruction differentiated by sex thus appears early in the account.) Because there were no books in the Massachusetts' own language, he realized that this plan involved teaching "them all to write, and read written hand [handwriting]"—a comment that took into account the difficulty of reading script rather than print. Referring to one of two potential Indian schoolmasters, Job Nesutan and Monequassun, Eliot said, in that same letter, "I have one already who can write, so that I can read his writing well, and he (with some paines and teaching) can read mine."[38]

By February 1651, the Natick school was in operation. With no books yet in print in the Massachusett tongue, all instruction was conducted by writing and by reading manuscript. "We have begun," Eliot wrote, and "though we cannot yet be constant in it, we have two men in some measure able to teach the youth with my guidance, and inspection." (By this time Monequassun had become the Natick schoolmaster and Job Nesutan was devoting most of his time to helping Eliot translate.) Eliot described the course of the school day. The schoolmaster prayed with his scholars and instructed them in their catechism. Eliot himself had composed the catechism and written it in the schoolmaster's book, "which he can read, and teach them." The schoolmaster also used the questions and answers of the catechism as the source for the copies he set the children when he was teaching them to write. "We aspire to no higher learning yet, but to spell, read, and write, that so they may be able to write for themselves such Scriptures as I have already, or hereafter may (by the blessing of God) translate for them." He had no hope,

Eliot added, of seeing the Bible translated, much less printed, in his own lifetime. His chief aim, therefore, was to "communicate as much of the Scriptures as I can by writing."[39]

By this time the Indian village was becoming the seventeenth-century equivalent of a tourist attraction. In October 1651, a month after the Natick covenant, John Endecott, the governor of Massachusetts, decided to visit Natick himself. He was accompanied by a group of twenty Englishmen on horseback, who came to hear Eliot give a sermon in Massachusett to the Indians. John Wilson, pastor of the Church of Christ at Boston, was one of the sightseeing party. A tour of the village impressed him. He admired the Indians' three "fair long streets," the English houses that some were building, and the English clothing that most Indians wore. He reported on the sturdiness of their fort and the strength of their footbridge, which had withstood a flood of ice earlier in the year when a similar bridge built by the English at Medfield had collapsed. He also commented favorably on the Indian schoolmaster (Monequassun), who was conducting a class in the school-house. "The Indian school master was there teaching the Children, who doth read and spell very well himselfe, and teacheth them to doe the like (besides writing)." This lesson must have been held for demonstration purposes, for when the service began in the fort, the schoolmaster led the singing, and "read out of his Book one of the Psalmes in meeter, line by line." All the Indians followed his lead, singing an English tune.[40]

A prerequisite for church membership for Congregationalists was their public "relation," a narrative of their conversion experiences. Eliot hoped that several of the Natick Indians would demonstrate, through their narratives, that they were well prepared for church membership. He therefore invited leading ministers and important laymen to come to listen to the Indians' narratives at Natick, in October 1652. One of those planning to speak was Monequassun.[41]

Unlike the sightseeing party of the year before, this venture was a public relations disaster from the start. None of the Englishmen whom Eliot had asked to come as interpreters, including Thomas Mayhew, turned up. "I was alone," Eliot said, "(as I have been wont to be in this work)." (He did, in fact, have one Indian interpreter on hand.) When the morning, spent on prayers and sermons, was almost over, the visiting elders expressed a wish to hear oral relations, although Eliot, in the absence of interpreters, would have preferred their questioning the converts.[42]

The program went on seemingly interminably. The fifteen Indians who were bidding for church membership had prepared their relations ahead of time, and Eliot had written them down and given them to important churchmen earlier for their comments. Eliot now read these prepared relations, one by one. After the lengthy readings, the initiates began to make their oral relations extemporaneously, while Eliot translated. Eliot dragged out the proceedings further by asking the converts to slow their speeches so that he could write them down, and by pausing occasionally to ask the one interpreter who was there—presumably Job Nesutan—to clarify some of the sentences for him. The gathered elders, few of whom could understand a word of Massachusett, grew more and more restless.[43]

When it was Monequassun's turn to speak, the day was far advanced. Had his listeners been able to comprehend, they would have witnessed a rare event. The vast majority of our sources are written by the English, and they inevitably report on Indians from a European perspective. Here, in contrast, as recorded by John Eliot, is a description from the Indian point of view of the emotional cost of acquiring literacy. Monequassun had not included any mention of learning to read in his formal relation transcribed in advance by Eliot, but now, as he spoke spontaneously, he returned to it time and again in front of the assembled crowd.

Monequassun's initial response to Christianity had been one of revulsion: "my heart did not like it, but hated it, yea and mocked at it." He even contemplated running away, "but I loved the place of my dwelling," and decided he would rather pray than run. Then he toyed with the idea of learning the Ten Commandments and parts of the catechism and even began to feel a spirit of repentance—"but I was quickly weary of repentance." After a period of pretending to be a believer, he despaired of being saved, for he knew that Christ saved only the truly penitent. Soon, however, he was able to recognize his sin of lust and ask pardon for it. "Afterwards when I did teach among the Indians," he went on, "I was much humbled because I could not read right, and that I sinned in it; for I saw that when I thought to do a good worke, I sinned in doing it, for I knew not what was right nor how to do it." For three nights he wondered what to do. At last, "God shewed me mercy. . . . And then I desired to learn to read Gods Word, and hearing that if we ask wisdom of God, he will give it, then I did much pray to God, that he would teach me to reade."[44]

After a year, Monequassun continued, his enthusiasm for reading waned. Indeed, he became convinced that he was sinning, "because I did not rightly desire to read Gods Word, and I thought my praying was sinful, and I feared, how should I, my wife, and child be cloathed, if I spend my time in learning to reade." This objection was overcome by a verse from the scriptures: "*Say not, what shall I eat, or drink . . . but first seek the Kingdom of Heaven, and these things shall be added to you.*"[45]

When the Indian church was being gathered at Natick, Monequassun had been reluctant to move there, because, he said, "my heart disliked that place." But then his family was struck with illness—first one of his children and then his wife died—and Monequassun blamed himself for not having followed Christ. He felt repentant, but yet another obstacle was his long hair: "I thought I loved not long hair, but I did and found it very hard to cut it off." Again scripture guided him: "*If thy right foot offend thee cut it off.*" He sacrificed his hair, he said, and prayed for forgiveness.[46]

By this time, even though Monequassun had not finished, his listeners were making it clear that they had had enough. Some of them left, while those who remained whispered to each other shamelessly. Eliot, keenly aware that Monequassun had lost his audience, "took him off"—an impresario removing an unsuccessful act. A little later, afraid that the sun would set in a place "so remote in the woods, the nights long and cold," with no suitable lodgings available for the English, Eliot brought the relations to a close, telling the audience that there was not time to finish the work. He pronounced himself more relieved than disappointed at the failure of his hopes: now his Indians would have longer to prepare themselves.[47]

None of those who listened to the translation of Monequassun's confession understood its import, not even John Eliot. The pain of making the transition from an oral to a literate culture has perhaps never been more lucidly stated. Monaquassun identified a very practical issue: acquiring literacy is time-consuming. He had agonized over how he would support his family if he spent his time on learning to read. This problem, at least, was resolved by becoming a salaried schoolmaster.

Nowhere in his relation did Monequassun mention learning to write. He had learned how to write, of course, because he was teaching his students to write. The explanation, then, of this omission is that he had correctly divined the purpose of reading acquisition. Eliot himself, in one of his earliest contacts with the Indians in Waaubon's wigwam, had raised the issue of reading the Bible as the key to understanding God's word. Monequassun had internalized the thrust of reading acquisition as thoroughly as any white New Englander. To learn to read, for him, was to embrace an alien culture and new religious beliefs. Writing, in contrast, did not involve cultural sacrifice.

It would be almost two more years before Eliot gathered his converts together again for another round of relations for the next attempt at church membership. This time, at the elders' insistence, it was held at Roxbury, and Thomas Mayhew was there to help interpret. Monequassun did not attend; he was mortally ill with tuberculosis.[48]

While Eliot was gathering Indians together into villages on mainland Massachusetts, Mayhew was doing much the same on Martha's Vineyard. Together with his father, Thomas Mayhew senior, the younger Thomas had become a joint patentee of Martha's Vineyard in 1641. He moved to the eastern tip of the island the following year with a handful of other Englishmen, becoming their minister almost by default. He began his missionary activities among the Wampanoags there in 1643, three years before John Eliot embarked on his own mission.[49]

Probably because of their relative isolation, the thousands of Wampanoags who lived on Noepe, as they called the Vineyard, had been spared—temporarily—the disastrous depopulation of the rest of the Indian population of Massachusetts. Although outbreaks of disease, such as those of 1643 and 1646, caused a population decline, for the entire seventeenth century the Wampanoags continued to outnumber the Europeans who migrated there.[50] They spoke Noepe, a dialect of the Algonquian language that differed only slightly from that spoken by the Massachusetts on the mainland.[51]

A Wampanoag named Hiacoomes took to visiting the homes of the English, and the younger Mayhew used to invite him to his house every Sunday evening to discuss Christianity.[52] Hiacoomes became Mayhew's first and most important convert. The reasons for Hiacoomes's conversion may relate to the low esteem in which he had previously been held by his fellow Wampanoags. His speech was slow and his features "not very promising."[53] "Esteemed by the *Indians* as a contemptible Person among themselves," as Mayhew's son Matthew put it later, Hiacoomes had "so great a measure of *Faith* and Confidence in this Power, that he is soon beyond the fear of concealing his contempt of *their gods*."[54] Hiacoomes had nothing to lose, as it were, by accepting a new way of life.

Late in 1643 a disease raked the Vineyard Indians; they blamed it on those who, like Hiacoomes, had deserted their traditional beliefs. But Hiacoomes held fast to his new faith and, according to the younger Mayhew, "continued his care about the things of God: and being desirous to read, the English gave him a Primer." With tutoring from the English, Hiacoomes became the first Indian on the Vineyard to acquire literacy—in English, for there were only English primers available. Seven years later, Hiacoomes was still carrying the primer about with him—a little book that symbolized his bridge across a cultural chasm.[55]

Hiacoomes's conversion brought him continuing derision. "*Here comes the English man*," the Wampanoags scoffed. But he was already teaching others about Christianity, and Wampanoags were amazed that a man who "had nothing to say in all their meetings formerly, is now become the Teacher of them all."[56] He began to bring others over to his new beliefs.

Although the younger Mayhew's aim was to persuade the Indians to convert to his faith, he did not see conversion as entailing the eradication of every vestige of their old customs and way of life. His rapid mastery of their tongue impressed the Indians, and he himself was early encouraged in his efforts by "the notable reason, judgement, and capacitie that God hath given unto many of them." His conversion efforts were materially aided by what he called "providences"—such as his apparent cure of a sick Indian and the fact that until 1650 no deaths occurred among any Wampanoags listening to his message. (Indeed, Mayhew's success at conversion has been attributed by scholars to his success in taking over the functions of the powwows—the Indians' traditional healers and soothsayers.)[57] The Indians drew their own conclusions about the relative strength of the powwows and the proselytizers and found the former wanting.

Mayhew had been living and proselytizing on the island for eight years when a contrary wind blew Henry Whitfield's ship into the harbor of the Vineyard in the fall of 1650, giving him the opportunity to observe Mayhew at his work. (Whitfield had been the pastor in Guilford, New Haven colony, since its founding and was returning to England.) For ten days he accompanied Mayhew on his lectures to the Indians in their own language and listened to his catechizing of the children, sometimes in English and sometimes in Massachusett. Whitfield was particularly keen to meet Hiacoomes. When they met, Whitfield quizzed him on his new faith with a battery of questions. Hiacoomes responded to each with "a very good satisfactory and Christian answer." He "seemed to me," Whitfield wrote, "to be a man of a prompt understanding, of a sober and moderate spirit."[58]

Whitfield was struck by Thomas Mayhew's poverty: "I saw but small and slender appearance of outward conveniences of life, in any comfortable way; the man himself was modest, and I could get but little from him." He learned from other Englishmen who had moved to the Vineyard that Mayhew, who had a wife and three small children, was indeed poor, often "forced to labour with his own hands," and was carrying on his mission to the Wampanoags with an income that was about half what he would have earned as an ordinary laborer.[59] Whitfield brought this news, together with a long letter that he had persuaded Mayhew to write, back to England after his ship finally sailed out of the Vineyard harbor. Their accounts of the Vineyard mission appeared in one of the Eliot Tracts.

In a later letter, dated October 1651, Mayhew was able to assert that 199 Indians had proclaimed themselves to be worshipers of God (or Praying Indians), and that Hiacoomes and another Wampanoag named Mumanquen were teaching Christian doctrine twice a day on Sundays, at two separate meetings. Each Saturday both men came to Mayhew to get information on the topics they planned to discuss. Mayhew hoped, he said, to set up a school that winter "to teach the Indians to read, viz. the children, and also any young men that are willing to learne."[60]

A bilingual English schoolmaster named Peter Folger (also spelled Foulger) was hired to teach the Wampanoags, and he opened his school early in 1652. He taught Indian youth both reading and writing and imparted religious instruction by catechizing them.[61] The obstacles in the way of literacy instruction were considerable, for it would be over a decade before any works were printed in the Massachusett tongue. The first essential text in religious instruction was a catechism, and Mayhew prepared a lengthy one, in manuscript, for the Indians.[62]

In October 1652, Thomas reported again on his progress. They were about to begin a town, he said, and some thirty Indian children were already at the school, opened early that year. They were "apt to learn," and more and more parents were sending in their children.[63] By now the corporation in England was financing much of the work, paying the salaries of Mayhew and John Eliot as well as of the Indians whom each employed as interpreters and schoolmasters. By 1656, Mayhew and Eliot were receiving fifty pounds each, Peter Folger thirty pounds, and the Indian schoolmasters and "interpreters," who included Monequassun and Hiacoomes, ten pounds each. As we saw earlier, ten pounds was a minimal salary, in the English-speaking context, for a schoolmaster expected to raise another twenty pounds from student fees.[64]

Moreover, the corporation was shipping over practical items, such as tools and linen, in aid of Eliot's efforts to introduce the Indians to English agricultural methods and modes of dress. From New England, the commissioners sent out a stream of requests to the corporation in London, most of them originating from Eliot, for items such as nails, axes and hoes, shoes and stockings, and blankets and haberdashery items. Notations on the cost of Bibles, books, paper, and inkhorns turn up in the commissioners' records. Even spectacles were on the list: English technology would make it easier for Indians to see print. Also among the items requested were hornbooks and primers.[65]

In 1656, Mayhew asked permission of the corporation, whose employee he now effectively was, to leave the Vineyard for a trip to England. He needed to clear up some problems with a legacy his wife had received. Because of his unique value to the Vineyard mission, the corporation was reluctant to let him go: "a worke of higher consideration would suffer much by his so long absence." They advised him to send someone else.[66] Perhaps his wife (who was his father's stepdaughter, Jane Paine) insisted on his going, for Mayhew himself, as we know, was singularly unworldly. In any event, the corporation relented, no doubt with an eye on the favorable publicity Mayhew's visit would generate for their fundraising efforts.

In November 1657 Mayhew embarked from Boston on the larger of two ships leaving for England. Daniel Gookin, newly appointed as the magistrate for the Indians of New England, changed at the last minute from that ship to the smaller one, after an altercation with the captain about his cabin. (It proved to be a decision that saved his life.) Accompanying Mayhew was a son of Miohqsoo, a Wampanoag from the Edgartown region of the Vineyard who had been converted by Hiacoomes.[67] Tradition has it that before Mayhew left the Vineyard, he gave a farewell service of worship and song to the Wampanoags at the point of their most distant assembly.[68]

Time passed and the ship became long overdue. The secretary of the corporation wrote to the New England Commissioners that he was greatly afraid that the ship had miscarried. The commissioners were stunned. The loss of Mayhew to the work, they responded, "is very great; and soe farr as for the present wee can see irreparable; . . . his father though ancient is healpfull." "The Lord," John Eliot said, "hath given us this amazing blow, to take away my brother Mayhew." Only Thomas's father could not accept the sad truth that the ship bearing his son had foundered in the Atlantic Ocean. As late as August of the following year, the elder Thomas Mayhew wrote, "I cannot yett give my sonne over." It was said that for many years after, the younger Mayhew was seldom named by the Wampanoags without tears.[69]

The loss of Thomas Mayhew proved, astonishingly, not to be irreparable. The reasons for what happened later are a matter of interpretation, but there is no quarrel about the facts: the conversion of the Vineyard Wampanoags continued without the younger Mayhew. It was furthered only by his father, the elder Mayhew, who as governor of the Vineyard had other concerns that took his attention, and, briefly—until he fell out with Mayhew—by the minister John Cotton, a son of the much better known Boston minister John Cotton. During the younger Cotton's ministry, the questions the Wampanoags asked him (as recorded in his diary) about verses in the Bible demonstrated their keen desire to understand Christian doctrine and Christian texts.[70]

Although Cotton's contribution was significant, his service to the Indians did not begin until 1666, nine years after Mayhew's death. The key, therefore, to the successful continuance of the Christian mission was undoubtedly Hiacoomes, who kept up the conversion effort aided by other converts. Able to speak English well by this time, he also studied, mostly on his own, to become a minister himself. Given the stringency of Congregational standards for a learned ministry, this was a challenging task. Nonetheless, in 1670, he and another Wampanoag named John Tackanash were ordained as, respectively, pastor and teacher of the Vineyard's second Indian church. (The first had been established in 1659, but without officers.) John Eliot, along with the younger John Cotton and Thomas Mayhew, was there to confer this extraordinary symbol of where the acquisition of literacy had led Hiacoomes.[71]

The New England Corporation, rechartered as the New England Company in 1662 after the restoration of the English monarchy, continued to pay indirectly, through disbursements by the New England Commissioners, for the salaries of schoolmasters and interpreters throughout the 1660s. In 1658 it supported two Indian schoolmasters on the Vineyard, eight between 1661 and 1664, and nine in 1667. (It stopped funding schoolmasters on the mainland for a year in 1663, but the New England Commissioners and John Eliot alike raised such a clamor that funding was renewed the following year.) In 1672, the commissioners' accounts no longer identified schoolmasters as such. They did, however, record the payment of sums totaling sixty pounds for ten Indian teachers and "rulers" (religious and secular leaders) in John Eliot's sphere of influence, fifteen pounds for three Indians guided by Richard Bourne of Sandwich (a layman involved in missionary work in the Plymouth region), and fifty-seven pounds for various Indian teachers and rulers on Martha's Vineyard and Nantucket.[72] Since schoolmasters were also teachers of doctrine ("teachers," in New England parlance), these salaries doubtless included payments for men who provided literacy instruction. (Native Americans were consistently paid a salary that was, at best, one-fifth of that paid to the English.)[73]

The corporation also funded an ambitious project—educating young Indians at Harvard College. It paid for the food, clothing, books, and schooling of "six hopfull Indians"—originally selected by Eliot and the Mayhews—who received a grammar school education from Elijah Corlet, a schoolmaster in Cambridge. Also included in the corporation's educational largesse was the late Thomas Mayhew's eldest son, Matthew, whom the corporation hoped would eventually take over his father's work. In addition, the corporation financed the construction, planned as early as 1653, of "the Indian College" at Harvard. This was a two-story building with enough room for twenty Indians to board in and, apparently, be tutored separately.[74]

Only four Indian students matriculated at Harvard before 1700. Two of them came from the Vineyard: Joel Hiacoomes, one of Hiacoomes's sons, and Caleb Cheeshahteaumauk, the son of a sachem of Homes Hole. They would both have been in the Harvard graduating class of 1665 had not disaster overtaken the ship Joel Hiacoomes was sailing on, as he was returning to Boston from a trip home shortly before the graduation ceremonies. His ship was found wrecked on the shores of Nantucket Island. It was presumed that he and the other passengers had survived but had then been murdered by hostile Indians for the goods on the vessel.[75]

Daniel Gookin, the magistrate for Indians, remembered young Hiacoomes well, for they had both lived in Cambridge. He was not only a "diligent student," Gookin recalled, "but an attentive hearer of God's word; diligently writing the sermons, and frequenting lectures; grave and sober in his conversation." Cheeshah-teaumauk did graduate from Harvard, the first and only Indian to do so in the colonial period. He was already suffering from tuberculosis, however, and died early in the following year. His Latin address to the corporation, which begins, "Honoratissimi benefactores" (Most honored benefactors), has been preserved.[76]

Even contemporaries came to appreciate how misguided it had been to rip the Indians out of their own culture. Gookin's verdict was, "In truth the design was prudent, noble, and good; but it proved ineffectual to the ends proposed." Several of the young Indians who had gone to school among the English grew "disheartened and left learning" shortly before they were to go to college. A few took up trades; others returned home. Several died of tuberculosis: Gookin and others attributed their deaths to "the great change upon their bodies, in respect of their diet, lodging, apparel, studies; so much different from what they were inured to among their own countrymen."[77]

The Indian Library

The New England Corporation, meanwhile, had embarked on a new venture, the creation of what was later known as the "Indian Library." To John Eliot's credit, he never wavered in his insistence that the mission must be carried on in the natives' own language. As a result, most of the texts in the Indian Library were printed in Indian tongues. Only a handful, such as Eliot's *Indian Grammar*, were in English, intended for an English audience.[78]

Prodded by Eliot, the New England Corporation began to subsidize the translation and publication of a series of texts, mostly composed in the Massachusett language. Eliot himself had devised its written system, using the Roman alphabet. In the fall of 1653, the commissioners authorized the Indian Library's first publication, a catechism translated by Eliot into Massachusett. It was published by Samuel Green, the manager of the press at Harvard College.

The next venture was a project that Eliot had once said he did not expect to see in his lifetime—the translation and publication of the entire Bible. Two Indians played a vital role in the translation and printing of these texts: Job Nesutan, who had been with Eliot in the early years in Natick, and a young Natick named Wowaus. Job Nesutan worked with Eliot as his translator not only of the Indian Bible but of subsequent publications.[79] Wowaus, born around 1640 and named James Printer by the English, assisted with the monumental task of typesetting and proofing the Bible, which would have been almost impossible without his help. Wowaus had been one of the young men taught to read and write at the corporation's expense, and in 1659 he was apprenticed to Samuel Green, possibly with the design of furthering the project of the Indian Library.[80]

Once Eliot and the commissioners had persuaded the corporation in London to publish the Bible in translation, the corporation took a more active role: in 1660 it dispatched one hundred reams of paper and a young printer, Marmaduke Johnson, to assist Samuel Green. In addition to the problem of typesetting a language that Johnson did not speak, the task had specific technical difficulties: Eliot had introduced accent marks. Moreover, because of its generous use of diphthongs, Massachusett required an exceptionally large number of vowels.[81]

Despite all these obstacles and the fact that, with the fall of Oliver Cromwell, the corporation ceased official existence in 1661, Eliot and Job Nesutan's translation of the New Testament was published in 1661 and was quickly followed by the issue of another fifteen hundred catechisms. When the missionary society was reconstituted as the New England Company the following year, the commissioners tactfully dedicated the Indian New Testament to the newly restored Charles II. By the fall of 1663, the entire Indian Bible had been published, the first Bible ever issued on an American press. Eliot's metrical version of the Psalms was issued at the same time. So was a single sheet, the only publication before the turn of the century to be printed in both Massachusett and English: a bilingual version of the *Christian Covenanting Confession*, presumably derived from the manuscript version that had been used in Natick.[82]

Eliot and Nesutan's translations of two devotional manuals soon followed: an adaptation of Richard Baxter's *Call to the Unconverted* (1664) and an abbreviated version of Lewis Bayly's popular *The Practice of Piety* (1665). Eliot's first reading instructional text, the *Indian Primer*, appeared in 1669 in an edition of two thousand copies, and an illustrated A B C (no longer extant) was printed two years later. In 1672 Eliot published *The Logic Primer*, intended to teach the Indians how to present their sermons and instructions logically and aimed at "teachers," those charged with teaching church doctrine.[83]

The Status of Literacy among the New England Indians

A year after the publication of the *Logic Primer*, the first of several attempts was made to take the pulse of the New England mission to the Indians. John Eliot was asked to report on the six Indian churches with which he was involved on the Massachusetts mainland. Did the Indians, he was asked, pray, read the scriptures, and catechize? They did, Eliot responded, according to their ability, "but sundry cannot read. [A]ll learne and rehearce catechise." What about schools? "We have schooles, many can read, some wright."[84]

The following year, in 1674, Daniel Gookin sent out a similar but lengthier questionnaire. Richard Bourne, pastor of the lone Indian church in Plymouth colony, counted 497 Indians living in twenty-two Indian villages on Cape Cod, of whom 35 were too far from his home for him to reach. Among the remaining 462, of whom 274 were adults, 142 (31 percent) could read Massachusett, 72 (17 percent) could write Indian, and 9 (2 percent) could read English. No Indians were reported to be able to write English. Bourne considered these figures on literacy an underestimate: "We have and do want books exceedingly to carry on the work. . . . I do not question but there is more than one hundred young ones, that are entered both in writing and reading, that are not put into this account."[85]

John Cotton the younger, who had once preached to the Martha's Vineyard Wampanoags and who had recently become pastor of the English church in Plymouth, reported back to Gookin on about 40 Indians at Kitteaumut, a settlement on Buzzard's Bay. About 10 of them, he said, could read the English books translated into Indian, and many more "are very desirous to learn to read the word," but there was a great need for Indian primers and Bibles. The elder Thomas

Mayhew, now over eighty years old, responded that there were at least 240 families on the Vineyard, 60 on Chappaquidick, and another 300 families on Nantucket. Almost all of them were Praying Indians. Mayhew's report on their literacy attainments is terse: "For schools, sometimes there are some; sometimes, not. But many can read and write Indian; very few, English . . . not above three or four; and those do it brokenly." He and his two grandsons Matthew and John could speak the language, he said, and John was now preaching to the Indians. In Nantucket, he added, Weekochisit, one of the four Indian teachers of Christian doctrine there, was also a schoolmaster. Weekochisit was anxious to learn to read and understand English, and Gookin had accordingly obtained an English Bible for him from the commissioners.[86]

Several conclusions may be drawn from these reports. All of the reports were seeking to cast the missionary effort in a good light, but even when we factor in this bias, it would appear that Christianity had made considerable headway in many Indian villages throughout Massachusetts. Progress in literacy was another matter. The rate of reading acquisition hovered at around 25 to 30 percent, writing at about half that level. It is also apparent that literacy instruction in the native language was not being adequately supported by publications. Despite the Indian Library project, books were in short supply. Even though two thousand copies of the *Indian Primer* had been printed in 1669, pastors were complaining only five years later of the shortage of this basic instructional text.

King Philip's War, 1675 to 1676

One man, according to Gookin, was a particular target of missionary hopes, the Indians' "greatest and chiefest sachem, named Philip," who was living in Mount Hope, now Bristol County in Rhode Island. "I have heard him speak very good words, arguing that his conscience is convicted." But he was held "under Satan's dominion," Gookin reported, by his "carnal lust."[87]

Philip or Metacomet—usually called "King" Philip by the English because of the authority he held—was the son of the late sachem Massasoit, who had been the acknowledged leader of the Wampanoags when the Pilgrims first reached Plymouth harbor in 1620. Philip seems to have been attracted by the colonists' literacy at the same time as he held firm against their beliefs. In the winter of 1663 he had sent to John Eliot "for books to learne to read, in order to praying unto God." Eliot twice sent his son John to preach to Philip and his people, and John Sassamon, a convert, was teaching Philip and his men to read. A copy is still extant of a 1662 deed initialed by Philip. (The literate impression is rather spoiled by the fact that the *P* is lying on its back.)[88] Philip's reaction to Christianity overall, however, is best summed up by a story recounted by Cotton Mather. Philip once took hold of a button on John Eliot's coat and said that "he cared for his Gospel, just as much as he cared for that Button."[89]

Philip may have been intrigued by literacy, but he was also coming to understand the drastic changes that the English had wrought, reflected in the increasing resentment of the mainland Wampanoag Indians. In 1675, a year after Gookin sent out his questionnaire, Philip appealed to all within and outside his domain to join him in his attempt to dislodge the English. The spark was struck that ignited the conflict called "King Philip's War." Most unconverted mainland Wampanoags joined the cause, though the Martha's Vineyard Wampanoags declined to become involved. For nearly two years, New England would be engulfed in warfare. It would be the costliest conflict in America, in terms of the loss of human life, until the Civil War. Its first victim, whose death helped spark the war, was John Sassamon: he was murdered by fellow Indians on his return from a trip to the governor of Plymouth colony, whom he had just warned that Philip was about to declare war.[90]

By this time there were seven "old praying towns" of Indians on mainland Massachusetts, of which Natick was the oldest. Of all the communities, English or Indian, that were ravaged by the conflict, few suffered more hardship than these seven. Such was the prejudice of the English against all Indians that Daniel Gookin's account of the sufferings of the Christian Indians during King Philip's war was never published in his lifetime.[91]

In July 1675 Gookin asked for a third of the Praying Indians' men to enlist. Fifty-two did so and acquitted themselves bravely. At a fight near Mount Hope, Job Nesutan, whose skill at translating had proved indispensable for the Indian Library, was slain. Despite this show of loyalty to the English by the Praying Indians, Gookin reports, the "animosity and rage of the common people [so] increased against them, that the very name of a praying Indian was spoken against." Because some Indians had been "perfidious . . . all the Indians are reckoned to be false and perfidious." Had they been allowed to remain in their villages, aided by English reinforcements, they would have been, in Gookin's words, "a living wall to guard the English frontiers." Instead, in October, the Natick Indians were removed to Deer Island, a small island off the Massachusetts coast. Two months later, with others sent there as well, there were five hundred Indians on the island, living on clams and shellfish. According to Gookin, "the Island was bleak and cold, their wigwams poor and mean, their clothes few and thin." Many sickened and died there.[92]

Other Indians, captured earlier, were sold into slavery. Only through Eliot's importunity were any redeemed. Others were killed in battle. When the English realized that Indian help was indispensable, some of the Indians on Deer Island were recruited as scouts. By the time the war ended in 1676, when Philip was finally hunted down and killed, the population of Christian Indians on the mainland had been dealt a nearly mortal blow.[93]

The possession of literacy in such a context seems almost irrelevant. Yet there are two striking wartime instances of the extraordinarily disparate uses to which each literacy skill could be put. Those Praying Indians who had not been transported to Deer Island melted into the woods. The Wamesit Indians were later asked what they had done there. Their teacher, Symon Betokom, said that they had kept three Sabbaths in the woods. On the first he had read and taught the people out of Psalm 35 ("Contend, O LORD, with those who contend with me"); on the second from Psalm 46 ("God is our refuge and strength, a very present help in trouble"); and on the last from Psalm 118 ("With the LORD on my side I do not fear"). The hostile Indians loyal to Philip used their literacy for a very different purpose. An English trooper found a paper written by one of them stuck in a cleft in a bridge post in Medfield: "Know by this paper," it read, "that the Indians that thou has provoked to wrath and anger, will war this twenty one years if you will."[94] The skill of reading, in short, was still being used in the service of the new faith of the Indian converts, who were deriving consolation from the Bible in a time of hardship. The skill of writing, in contrast, was the vehicle for the native Americans to express their angry self-determination and trumpet their independence.

Literacy among the Wampanoags of Martha's Vineyard

While the Massachusetts and Wampanoags on the Massachusetts mainland were suffering on each side of the conflict, the Wampanoags on the Vineyard survived the war unscathed. Philip was unable to attract them to his cause and they stayed out of the conflict altogether. Matthew Mayhew (who had not followed his father into the ministry, despite his education at the expense of the New England Corporation) told the following tale. Early in the course of King Philip's war, some of the English, in the grip of anti-Indian hysteria, demanded that the Vineyard Indians lay down their arms. An English officer was dispatched to Gay Head, the western tip of the island, to make this proposal to the leaders of the Gay Head Wampanoags. He returned with a very courteous message from the sachems, written in Noepe (the Massachusett dialect), to the effect that as they had already submitted long ago to the Crown of England, they would assist the English against their enemies by all the means in their power. This document—which Matthew said he would have inserted into his text had he not misplaced it—was "subscribed by Persons of greatest note among them." Matthew also disclosed that the Wampanoags, within their own court system, had records kept "by such who having learned *to Write* fairly, were appointed thereto."[95]

By these almost casual references, Matthew revealed the prevalence of literacy among the leading men of the Vineyard Indians at the end of the seventeenth century—he was writing in 1694—nearly four decades after his father sailed from the Vineyard, never to return. The spread of literacy in their own language among the Vineyard Wampanoags was initially linked, as we have seen, to the spread of Christianity. After the death of the younger Thomas Mayhew, the Wampanoags on Martha's Vineyard had become largely Christianized in a process that the ethnohistorian William Simmons has called the "most profound social conversion to occur anywhere in New England."[96] Thanks to the leadership of Hiacoomes, the Indians themselves had taken on the conversion effort, and Christianity had become the prevalent faith on the island.

The successful spread of Christianity was due, in part, to the character and style of the younger Thomas Mayhew. In striking contrast to Eliot, Thomas had never insisted on radical cultural change as the price of conversion. Consequently, as James Ronda has demonstrated, the Vineyard Indians were able to become Christians while still retaining their own culture. As Christian ministers, they took on the functions of the old Indian powwows and continued ancient Wampanoag ritual traditions of healing, thanksgiving, and charity. Laymen assumed the duties of ruling elders or deacons, laywomen those of catechists or counselors. The Vineyard Indians, in short, adopted only those forms of English culture that appealed to them: they acquired looms and plows—and literacy—while continuing to retain their long hair, live in wigwams, and preserve their Indian names.[97]

Most of our information about the literacy of the Vineyard Wampanoags comes from Experience Mayhew. He was the oldest son of John Mayhew, who was the youngest son of the younger Thomas Mayhew. Like his father, John Mayhew became a minister and preacher to the Wampanoags of the Vineyard and, again like his father, died relatively young; he died in 1689, when Experience was sixteen. Five years later Experience began to preach to the Indians himself.[98]

As time passed, Experience became as well-known as his grandfather, the younger Thomas Mayhew, for his labors on behalf of the missionary cause, and in 1720 he was asked to report on the "Condition" of the Vineyard Indians. (His account appeared in Cotton Mather's *India Christiana* a year later.) European microbes had caught up with the Vineyard Indians: Experience noted how much their numbers had been reduced by disease since the first English settlements of 1642, when they had numbered in the thousands. By 1720 only six small Indian villages remained on the island, containing some 155 families and totaling perhaps 800 persons.

"There has," Experience Mayhew wrote, "from time to time been much care taken that the several Villages might be provided with School Masters to teach the children to Read and Write; yet some of them have not been so constantly supplied as is to be desired." One problem, he said (voicing the obstacles to schooling endemic to farming families), was that the Indians would remove their children from school in spring, "alleging they want them for Tillage of the land; and so the Schools fail till the Fall." This, he said, "has much hindred their Progress in Learning: Nevertheless, I think the greatest Number can Read, either in the *English* or in the *Indian* Tongue; and some in both." But they understood "the *Indian* Tongue much better than that of the *English*."

Mayhew also reported on the texts available to the Indians in their own language. He said that the Vineyard Indians "complain much for want of *Indian* BIBLES, having now but very few among them. Nor are there any to be had; the last Edition [of 1685] being now gone." This disadvantage was somewhat offset, he said, by the care that the commissioners had taken to supply the Indians with "other useful Books in their own Language."[99]

Mayhew was referring to the later publications of the Indian Library. The New England Commissioners had continued to oversee the translation and publication of texts financed by the New England Company. The first edition of the Indian Bible was obliterated in King Philip's War, but John Eliot had contrived to get a second edition published in 1685; John Cotton helped him in its revision. ("I desire to see it done afore I dye," he had told the London office, and the printers in Cambridge, Massachusetts, were already peeling pages of Leviticus, the third book of the Old Testament, off the press before the authorities in London quite realized what Eliot was up to.) The New England Commissioners then printed a second edition of Bayly's *Practice of Piety* and, in 1688, of Baxter's *Call to the Unconverted*. With the assistance of Grindal Rawson, a pastor for the town of Mendon, Eliot translated his last work. Their joint translation of Thomas Shepard's *Sincere Convert* appeared in 1689. Eliot died a year later.[100]

After Eliot's death, the nature of the books translated and published for the Indians changed. The New England Commissioners now ordered the publication of several shorter works rather than undertaking any major projects, and the subtext of the commissioners was that the Indians should learn English. These less ambitious publications included translations of sermons by Increase Mather, minister of Boston's North Church, and publications by his son Cotton Mather, who assisted his father in the Boston pulpit. Two of the new imprints were for children—a catechism and a primer. In 1691 Grindal Rawson translated the well-known catechism by John Cotton (father of the Vineyard missionary), *Spiritual Milk for Boston Babes*, and he also worked on a new edition of the *Indian Primer*. Three thousand copies of the primer were printed in late 1699 or 1700. This primer, like the first, was in Massachusett only, but after the turn of the century, the new practice was to issue bilingual publications, with parallel columns of English and Massachusett.[101]

The possibility of a third edition of the Indian Bible was raised in 1705, and the New England Company actually sent over large quantities of high-quality Genoa paper and new fonts for it. But the project was sabotaged in no small part by the opposition of Cotton Mather, who thought that "the best thing we can do for our Indians is to Anglicise them," including anglicizing their language—which, he said, they could scarcely retain "without a Tincture of other Salvage Inclinations." By no means as hesitant about the publication of his own work as he was about a new edition of the Bible, Mather promoted the translation and publication of his *Family Religion Excited* in 1714 and, two years later, his *Monitor for Communicants*.[102]

As a result of the opposition to reprinting the complete Bible, the commissioners decided to publish just the Book of Psalms. The three-man committee appointed to further this project included Cotton Mather and Samuel Sewall, a Boston judge who continued to be a staunch supporter of the third edition of the Indian Bible. The committee asked Experience Mayhew to undertake a revision of Eliot's original translation of the Psalms, to be bound together with the Gospel According to John. He was to be assisted by Job Neesnummin, the Indian preacher in Natick, and James Printer. The translation, titled the *Massachuset Psalter*, bears the publication date of 1709, although it did not appear until the following year. It follows the new format of parallel columns in Indian and English.[103] Of all the translations in the Indian Library, this, written in the dialect of the Vineyard Wampanoags by a man who had learned it as a child, was surely the finest. The last title in the Indian Library was a text for children: a new version of the *Indian Primer* was issued in 1720, this time with a matching English translation.[104]

A useful overview of the status of the Indian Library is available from May 1724,

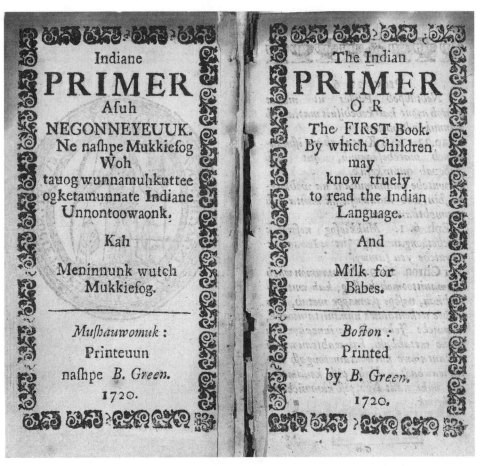

FIGURE 1. Title page of *The Indian Primer or The First Book* (Boston: B. Green, 1720). This page captures the dual purpose of the primer in teaching reading and Christianity. The third version of the Indian primer, this edition was the first one to be printed bilingually in Massachusett and English. (Courtesy, Rare Books Division, The New York Public Library, Astor, Lenox and Tilden Foundations)

when an inventory was made of the stock in hand in the possession of the New England Commissioners. It included 894 copies of the "New primmers" (that is, the 1720 edition), 408 *Confessions of Faith*, 45 *Practice of Piety* (the 1685 edition), 48 *Sincere Converts*, and 324 copies of the *Massachuset Psalter*.[105]

Indian Literacy as Revealed in Experience Mayhew's *Indian Converts*

Experience Mayhew's insights into Wampanoag literacy appear in his book, titled *Indian Converts: Or, Some Account of the Lives and Dying Speeches of a Considerable Number of the Christianized Indians of Martha's Vineyard, in New-England*. It was published in London in 1727.[106] By the time Mayhew began to collect material for the book in the early 1720s, three or even four generations of Christian Indians had lived and died on the Vineyard. All the subjects of Experience's biography had two features in common: piety and death. Because conversion was a state from which one might relapse, Mayhew, along with most other Puritan biographers, wrote only about the dead. Deathbed scenes had great significance in this context, because "Dying Speeches" offered the best indication of whether a person was dying under the conviction of salvation. (Deathbed conversions, however, were suspect, and Experience excluded them from his text, on principle.) It was more than a morbid interest, then, that led Experience to collect such speeches, although one can hear the regret in his voice when he occasionally mistimed his last visit. (John Eliot, in contrast, although he also made an attempt to record dying speeches, said, "It was an humbling to me that there be no more, [but] it was not in my heart to gather them.")[107]

No one could have been better qualified than Experience for such a work: he was completely bilingual in English and the Wampanoag dialect. Moreover, he had known many of the Indians whose lives he recounted. For instance, he had clear memories of Hiacoomes, who had died when Experience was seventeen and whom Experience had seen frequently as a child. He recalled the "Gravity of [Hiacoomes's] Countenance, Speech and Deportment: He seemed always to speak with much Thought and Deliberation, and I think very rarely smiled." Where Experience's first-hand knowledge was lacking, he had had recourse to other trust-worthy sources, such as accounts written by his father and grandfather and, once the Indians became aware of his work, memoirs they wrote specifically for his book. The net result, as James Ronda has put it, is that *Indian Converts* is a "kind of oral history assembled by an informed observer with a sharp eye for detail and a keen ear for arresting tales."[108]

Indian Converts presents a series of snapshots of native American literacy. These in turn are set within the larger framework of short biographies of 94 Christian Indians who lived and died on Martha's Vineyard. (Another 34 Indians are noted in brief supplements to the first three chapters.) The book is organized into four chapters, by dates of death. The first chapter recounts the lives of 22 Indian men who were pillars of the church in some way, working as pastors, ruling elders, or deacons. The second memorializes 20 Indian men of lesser rank who held no formal position in any church. Experience's third chapter is a rarity among colonial records: it is devoted to 30 Indian women. His last recounts the lives of 22 Indian children. Although Mayhew had known many of his adult subjects, he had not met most of the children, and the portrayals in this chapter lack the freshness of the others, often bordering on stereotype.[109]

Mayhew took pains to validate the accuracy of his accounts. As befitted one who regarded himself as a historian, he had sought the testimony of those hostile, as well as sympathetic, to the Wampanoags. "Nor can I think that I have repre-sented any, as if they lived better Lives than they really did." He had no hesitation, for instance, in chronicling alcoholism or marital violence. In fact, Puritan biog-raphers as a group were not motivated to tone down their accounts: sinfulness before conversion was no impediment to a Puritan narrative, because, they believed, all sins are forgiven in Christ.[110]

The accuracy of Mayhew's account is important to our assessment of his reliability when he discusses the Indians' literacy. His testimony on how well, or poorly, the Indians read and wrote should be viewed within the context of his general claims to veracity. While one senses that Mayhew was somehow eager for his subjects to be able to read well, his discussions nevertheless ring true.

Although literacy was not the main focus of Mayhew's account, he was genuinely interested in the Indians' educational attainments and usually devoted one paragraph in each of his biographies to the topic. Of a total of 128 children and adults in *Indian Converts*, including those in the chapter supplements, 60 are identified as being able to read. In contrast, Mayhew comments on the writing ability of only 7 of them.[111]

Experience entered a caveat about the reading ability of the converts. His caution stands as a rare example of a distinction being made, by a colonial American, between different levels of literacy attainment. "And tho considerable numbers of the *Indians* have learned to *read* and *write*, yet they have mostly done this but after the rate that poor Men among the *English* are wont to do." They did not, he said, have the same advantage as the English did of having books in their own language. Mayhew was, in effect, referring to what David Hall has called "traditional literacy," in which men and women read slowly and deliberately from a restricted set of religious texts.[112]

Mayhew is frank about the poor reading ability of some of his subjects. Akoochuk was a Gay Head Indian whose conversion to Christianity had enabled him to conquer his excessive drinking: "tho he was not a very good Reader, yet used Books, endeavouring to get Good out of them, and took Care to Learn his Children to read better than he could." Hepziah Assaquanhut read even more poorly: she "appeared willing to learn to read, but did not take her reading so easily as many do, and so did not learn to read so well as was to be desired." In contrast, Mayhew recalls skilled readers who loved to read. Jerusha Ompan, who had been taught to read by her parents, enjoyed reading so much that if she "could not get time in the Day, she would not ordinarily fail of reading in the Night," and made sure that she always had something by her that she could use for illumination.[113]

The most avid reader Mayhew found was surely Abel Wauwompuhque, a deacon of a church on the western end of the Vineyard. In 1690 a deadly fever swept the island. Wauwompuhque survived but lost his hearing, "a great Affliction to a man who was much delighted in Conversation." The written language helped him during services, since he had someone write down the main points of the sermon or at least direct him to the texts of scripture being discussed. If preachers used notes for their sermons, he borrowed them. He even learned to lip read. But reading books became his great consolation, "for having no Use of his Ears, he made the more Use of his Eyes." Before morning and evening prayers he used to read *The Practice of Piety*, one of the few books available in Massachusett. He also struggled to read books in English, and he would badger his companions with questions about them until he elicited some kind of signaled or written response.

His favorite book, once it was published, was the *Massachuset Psalter*, translated by Experience Mayhew with the aid of Job Neesnummin, a teacher in Natick. After its publication, it became Abel's constant companion: "this godly Man delighted much to read and meditate therein; he therefore carried it about with him wherever he went to work, and whenever he sat down to rest him, he would look into it."[114]

The Bible was the text most frequently read by Christian Indians of any age. At least one Indian preacher knew it almost by heart. Elisha Paaonut, who preached in the early 1700s, could turn to "almost any Text than one could mention to him, if a Word or two of it were but named." Because the Indian Bible was not reprinted again after its second edition in 1685, any Bibles available in the early eighteenth century must have been treasured heirlooms, passed down from one generation to next. The *Massachuset Psalter*, in print by 1710, was the only readily available text with biblical content. It has been said that it is now virtually impossible to find a copy of this particular psalter in good condition. Years of devoted usage have worn the book out. The only other texts whose titles are identified by Mayhew are Bayly's *The Practice of Piety* and William Perkins's *Six Principles of Religion*. (Since there is no independent evidence that this last work was an imprint of the Indian Library, Mayhew may be mistaken here.)[115]

The picture of literacy that emerges from *Indian Converts* is of Christian Indians who used their reading and writing skills in much the same ways as their Congregationalist English counterparts did on the mainland. Ministers used their reading professionally and within the family. John Tackanash had been ordained in 1670 along with Hiacoomes, whom Experience considered he exceeded in natural ability. A committed student, Tackanash "followed his Study and Reading closely," and, like other Indians, sought help from Englishmen in the neighborhood to obtain further information on what he was studying. Tackanash's use of literacy in his home was similar to that of any devout Puritan. Janawannit, who also became a minister, was remembered as "a very diligent Reader of the holy Scriptures, and very constant and serious in his Performance of other religious Duties." He used to read a chapter of the Bible to his family and sing a psalm each morning and evening. Tackanash and Janawannit were not exceptional: Mayhew characterizes the ministers and church leaders almost to a man as using their reading ability as part of their daily devotions.[116]

While Mayhew frequently mentions reading as an intrinsic part of the converts' devotional life, he comments on the writing of only seven converts—three ministers, three laymen, and one woman. But because reading was so much more central to the Christian experience than writing, and therefore of greater interest to Mayhew, this number is certainly an underestimate of those who could write. All ordained ministers, for instance, had to acquire writing. Mayhew himself implies as much when he says that Elisha Paaonut (who knew the scriptures, according to Mayhew, better than any Indian he had ever met) used "no Notes in preaching, nor did he seem to need any." This observation suggests that notes for a sermon— and so the ability to write—were the norm. Mayhew also mentions other Indians (all men) who could write but who were not the subject of biographies. He refers to their jotting down the "discourses" or dying words of family members.[117]

The only woman whom Mayhew indicates could write was Rachel Wompan-ummoo, who died in 1724 at the age of twenty-five. Her devout parents taught her as a child to read, and, as an adult, she worked in the homes of the English, including that of Experience Mayhew. He says of her: "Having been much among the *English*, and so got the Knowledge of their Language; she, after she was a Woman grown, learned to read *English*, and also to write a legible Hand, (having only learned to read Indian before.)"[118]

The appeal of literacy as part of the Christian message—or even the appeal of literacy on its own merit—was felt by those who had recently acquired it for themselves. Several leading Wampanoags sent their children to the English to be educated: Hiacoomes sent his son Samuel Coomes to the elder Thomas Mayhew. Miohqsoo's son was sent to live with the younger Thomas Mayhew and accompanied him on his fateful voyage to England, perishing with him at sea.[119]

To some Indians, the allure of literacy was so compelling that they acquired it without the benefit of formal schooling. Hiacoomes, of course, is the most striking example, but there were others who became literate as adults because they were converted as adults. Joash Panu, grandson of a Christian convert, decided as an adult to learn to read and write. Without the help of any school, he learned to read Indian well and mastered enough English to use an English Bible and even an English concordance. He was ordained in 1716 as the minister of an Indian church.[120]

Other Wampanoags never acquired literacy themselves but made sure that their children learned to read. David Paul, a member of the third generation of Christian Indians, died in 1718. He had never been to school and neither he nor his siblings knew how to read. He married the daughter of a Praying Indian and became a committed Christian when a child was born, after a long spell of childlessness, in answer, he believed, to his prayers. A man of considerable wealth, owner of a cart and plow, as well as oxen and horses, he was able to pay for a private education for his children. First he paid for their boarding expenses so they could attend a distant school and then he hired a young man, a candidate for the ministry, to teach his children to read and give them catechetical instruction.[121]

Once Christianity had become widely established and with it the culture of formal schooling, most Wampanoags who became literate did so as children. Mayhew indicates that fifteen of his adult subjects learned to read as children, either at home or school. Significantly, the parents of all but three of the fifteen are simultaneously identified as Christians, ranging from Praying Indians to church deacons. Of the remaining three, Sarah Peag was taught to read in a "good English Family" in Chilmark on the Vineyard, while Abigail Ammapoo's father was a "petty sachim" (minor chieftain). Her brother, Caleb Cheeshahteaumauk, was, as we have seen, a Harvard graduate, so it appears that a certain social cachet was associated with literacy education, and the more prominent Wampanoags insisted on it for their children.[122]

Those Vineyard Indians who became literate usually made sure that their children became literate as well. Ronda has documented the familial transmission of Christianity from one generation to the next; it was accompanied by the familial transmission of literacy. In fact, to judge by the number of children who disappointed their pious Christian parents by their wild behavior, literacy may sometimes have been the easier of the two to transmit. Samuel Coomes mortified his pious father, Hiacoomes, by his drinking and his relationship with a white woman, but he was fully literate in both Indian and English.[123]

It is possible to trace literacy acquisition through several generations of Christian Wampanoags. The Hannit family is one example. Japheth Hannit was born before the English arrived at the Vineyard. His parents were converted by the younger Thomas Mayhew a few years later, and they sent Japheth to Peter Folger's school, where he became literate in both Indian and English. Japheth married Sarah, daughter of Keestumin, and joined the church himself. He was made a captain over an Indian company and then a magistrate, and during King Philip's War he was employed by the English as a spy on his own people. Called to the ministry, he succeeded John Tackanash early in 1684 as the third pastor of the Vineyard's first Indian church. His wife, Sarah, was characterized by Mayhew as a poor, though eager, reader. (She had other virtues, according to Mayhew: the family's spacious wigwam, with its embroidered mats, was largely the product of her hands.) She could not, however, "read very well, yet she was not discourag'd from making the best use of Books she was capable of."[124] (Here Experience Mayhew's eagerness to put a good face on his subject's reading abilities has led him into an implausible conclusion, for how can such a poor reader make good use of books?)

Japheth and Sarah Hannit's children included his eldest son, Jeremiah, born in about 1671, who was sent to school, and his daughter Jedidah, who was taught to read but apparently not to write. Japheth also made himself responsible for continuing the education of a boy named Joseph Nahnosoo, who, after his father died, had been entrusted to Japheth. According to Mayhew, Joseph "was taught to read both in *English* and *Indian*, . . . and," he adds, "I doubt not but that he was taught to write also."[125]

A grandson, Japheth Skuhwhannan, represents the third generation of Hannit literacy. He was the son of Bethia, another of Japheth and Sarah's daughters. He came to live with his grandparents to fill the void left by the deaths of all of their sons. Japheth Hannit saw to it that his grandson continued his literacy education. By the time the younger Japheth died of tuberculosis in 1715, outliving his grandfather by just three years, he was not only fully literate in Indian but had also made considerable progress in learning to read English.[126]

Another family line, in which four generations separated the minister Wunnanauhkohun from his great-granddaughter, Bethia Sissetom, represents a somewhat different pattern of bequeathing Christianity and literacy. Wunnanauhkohun was an early convert who preached at what became Christian Town and died in about 1676. "I'm informed," Mayhew writes, "that he constantly read the Scriptures in his Family." A man whose only means of support was the work of his own hands, he nonetheless spent some time every day reading and meditating.[127]

Two generations later, the literacy chain had been broken. Wunnanauhkohun's Christianity had apparently not been passed down to his grandson, Oggin Sissetom, a drinker and a spender. The latter's wife, Hannah Sissetom, was the daughter of a convert, but her education had suffered. She had lived as a servant with a religious English family on the island, where she had been taught to read, Mayhew writes, "tho not very well." She read so poorly, in fact, that she was incapable of helping her daughter Bethia, born around 1702, with her elementary lessons. Although no school was nearby and Bethia's father, another potential resource, was "seldom at home," Bethia refused to be discouraged. She seized every opportunity she could to read a lesson to anyone who would listen to her. Some of her neighbors promised to help by hearing her lessons if she could come to their homes. She seldom could, as Mayhew points out, for "the Circumstances of the Family to which she belonged, were such that she could scarcely be spared long enough from it to go and read a Lesson or two in a Day"; nevertheless, "she would by her great Industry redeem time." Her motivation was so strong that she "learned to read better than many do who have a School to go to, and time to attend it."[128]

It may be significant that it was a daughter, rather than a son, who insisted on learning to read as part of her Christian beliefs. As James Ronda has demonstrated, Christianity held a special attraction for Indian women. It not only validated their traditional roles as housekeepers but also rewarded any unusual abilities they had by opening the way for them to become Christian women healers. In addition, it provided them with crucial emotional support in the face of the growing problem of alcoholism. Mayhew himself considered that the number of women "truly fearing God" exceeded the number of men. In this, the Wampanoag experience with Christianity mirrored its role in the broader English context on the New England mainland, where far more women than men were church members.[129]

Christian literacy, Mayhew's account implies, played an important role in mitigating family stress. Margaret Osooit of Gay Head, a third-generation Christian who learned to read well a child, lived with her alcoholic husband Zachariah for thirty-three years. Her children remembered with great affection her piety and her efforts to bring them up in her beliefs: "several of them have with Tears told me," Mayhew reports, "what Pains she used to take with them, as by teaching them their Catechisms, and also reading the Scriptures to them, and pressing them to the Duties mentioned in them." If she did not attend Sabbath services as much as some thought she should, it was because both she and her children were so "miserably clothed." She never felt sufficiently sanctified to become a church member and would turn to texts in the Bible that she felt supported this decision. "She mightily delighted," Mayhew recalls, "in *The Practice of Piety*, a Book which our *Indians* have in their own Language, and would scarce pass a Day without reading something in it."[130]

The evidence gathered by Mayhew on adult literacy spans a large number of years, from 1643, when Hiacoomes began learning to read, up to 1724, when the last adult subject died. In contrast, the twenty-two children he discusses form a more compact group, in terms of both their ages and the period in which they lived. All but five were born between 1682 and 1712. Of these, all but two of the children over six are identified as being able to read.

Once again, writing ability is associated with boys but not girls. A generalized expectation that boys would be taught to write can be inferred from Mayhew's comment about Japheth Hannit's ward, Joseph Nahnosoo: "He was taught to read both in *English* and in *Indian* . . . and I doubt not but that he was taught to write also." As in its English context, writing instruction is mentioned only in connection with schooling: Jeremiah Wesachippau and Eleazar Ohhumuh both attended school, where they learned to "write a legible Hand." None of the twelve girls, however, is identified as being able to write.[131]

The accounts discloses meager information on the age at which literacy instruction was begun, whether at home or school. Jesse Quannoohuh, who died a couple of months after his seventh birthday, had earlier been sent to school to learn to read. Instruction in the school setting for reading as well as writing emerges as the norm. In fact, schooling for boys seems to have been so widely accepted by the Indians that even nonbelievers sent their sons to school. Jeremiah Wesachippau, who was born in 1687 and died of a fever at the age of eighteen, was a child of such parents. His "vicious" parents had drowned at sea; they were alleged to have "drowned in Rum at the same time." Nonetheless, they had sent Jeremiah to a school where he had learned his catechism, been taught to read and write, and had heard Christian prayers—"for it is the custom of our *Indian* Schoolmasters to pray with their Scholars." Long after Mayhew's witness, Massachusett education in English as well as Indian continued to be, in essence, religious education.[132]

Whereas schooling seems fairly commonplace before the turn of the century, children born in the Vineyard after 1700 were several times confronted by failing schools or no school at all, because of a lack of schoolbooks and inadequate financial support for schoolmasters. Indeed, in some places such shortages happened earlier. When, in 1698, the pastors Grindal Rawson and Samuel Danforth conducted a survey for the New England Company of all the Indian plantations in the eastern part of Massachusetts, they noted that in Nantucket three schools had once existed that were no longer open, "for want of primers." The evidence bears out Mayhew's comments of 1720 that the Indian villages were not as "constantly" supplied with schoolmasters as was desirable.[133]

The themes for these Wampanoag Christian children, as they appear in Mayhew's account, are similar to those for other children raised as believing Christians. A child's "delight" in reading the scriptures "and other good Books" is noted in several instances. Like the adults, the children drew praise for thinking about what they read. An enthusiasm for reading is seen as an asset and contrasted with earlier poor, nonreading behavior.

Laban Panu was one of those children whose wildness had disappointed his pious father, Joash Panu. Laban had been "rude and disorderly" when nine years old and could barely be restrained from profaning the Sabbath by fooling around during the services. After his parents began to deal with him "more sharply," he became a believer and "applied himself with Diligence to the reading of his Books, which he had before too much neglected." Mayhew has high praise for Japheth Hannit's daughter Jedidah, who chose books over her friends: she "delighted much in reading her Book. Nor was she much inclined to go into such vain Company as many young People delight in."[134]

For both children and adults, according to Mayhew, books were treasured possessions, with their Christian messages offering consolation at life's close. For Bethia Sissetom, during the year and a half that she was suffering from tuberculosis and was rarely able to attend religious services, books became more precious than ever. When Abigail Kenump became too ill, at the age of sixteen, even to be carried to the meeting house, she consoled herself by reading. When even that became too much for her, she used to ask those of her friends "as she knew could read, to read some Portion of God's Word to her."[135]

The consolations of Christianity in the face of death were perhaps best expressed by Abel Wauwompuhque. When Mayhew visited him in his last sickness in the fall of 1722, Abel said that he believed that he was leaving all his troubles behind him. "And tho now I cannot hear, and can hardly see, but am every way weak and feeble; yet I shall shortly both see and hear, and walk, and leap in the Presence of the Lord."[136]

Writing and Native American Culture

The evidence Experience Mayhew provides on Vineyard literacy gives the impression that the most pervasive use of literacy among the Christian Wampanoags was in the service of their Christianity, and that reading was the skill that mattered most in such a context. But there is other evidence available that provides a different perspective on Indian literacy: the surviving writings in Massachusett. As Ives Goddard and Kathleen Bragdon observe, these documents suggest that writing supplemented, rather than supplanted, the native oral culture and, by the mid-eighteenth century, reduced dialect variation.[137] Some records reveal how difficult it was to understand what was read and therefore provide a useful counterpoint to Experience Mayhew's rather glowing portraits of literacy acquisition.

A major segment of the surviving records in Massachusett comprises legal documents: land deeds, petitions and wills, notes and arrest warrants. The transfers of lands are notable, as Goddard and Bragdon have pointed out, for reproducing written versions of earlier oral forms. Here writing supplemented earlier ways of carrying on business by providing a convenient way of reminding those concerned of a transaction often undertaken much earlier.[138]

A portion of the town records of Natick written by the town clerk Thomas Waban from 1700 to 1720 has been preserved. A letter to the commissioners has survived, sent by the Mashpee church in 1753 on behalf of the township, asking for financial support for their minister, Solomon Briant, who had incurred debt because "he was much troubled concerning the sickness and death of his late children, all eleven of whom have died." The letter adds, "regarding the English schoolmaster: we have no need for him yet, because we cannot understand him, only a few can." A notice of marriage bans posted in Gay Head in the fall of 1764 still exists, as does the record kept by the minister Zachary Hossueit of the thirty-six marriages he solemnized at the Gay Head Congregational Church from January 1750 to May 1771.[139]

Revealing insights on literacy come from the marginalia on Indian Bibles, scribbled by different writers (all, apparently, male) as the Bibles were handed down

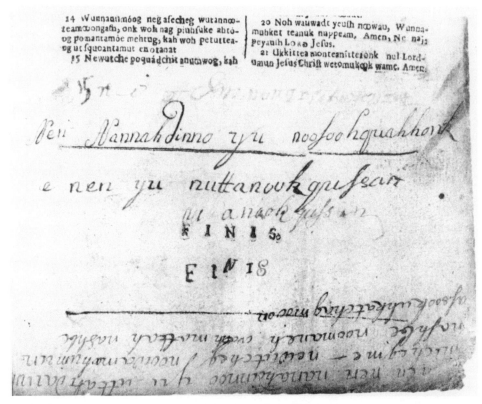

FIGURE 2. Marginalia written by Nannahdinno, a Massachusett or Wampanoag Indian, on the Book of Revelations in a 1685 Indian Bible. Under the final verses of the Book of Revelations, Nannahdinno notes his pleasure in owning this Bible: "I, Nannahdinno, this is my book . . . I, I Nannahdinnoo, own this forever. Because I bought it with my money." *Native Writings in Massachusett*, pt. 1, trans. Ives Goddard and Kathleen J. Bragdon (Philadelphia: American Philosophical Society, 1988), 396–97. (Courtesy, Congregational Society Library)

through the generations. Several writers used the relatively wide margins for practice with letter formation, from simple alphabets to elaborate capital letters. Others made little comments of all sorts, such as, "I Laben Hossuit own [?] this bible, June 11, 1747. Solomon Pinnion sold it to me. It cost four pounds"; and "This chapter I read / the first chapter of Nahum." "You, Thomas, remember: do not fornicate" appears in the margins of the Book of Daniel. Several men were concerned about their lack of understanding of the Bible, which must have become less and less comprehensible as time passed and linguistic changes occurred. A member of the Papenau family wrote despairing marginalia on the Book of Numbers that run:

I do [n]ot like very much to read
many writings, because I am too . . .

I am forever a pitiful person in
the world. I am not able clearly
to read this, this book.

A more hopeful annotation by the same man or another family member, written on the same chapter in the same Bible, runs:

I Joseph Papenau, this is my book.
I say this at this time July 22, 1712

This is your book, you Papenau.
Read it with c[oncentr]ation [?]. Your God will bless you.

This Bible came into the hands of the minister Zachary Hosueit.[140]

As these records suggest, a minority of Wampanoags continued to possess and use their literacy during the eighteenth century, despite the declining availability of texts. Signatures of men tabulated by David Silverman from these and other records reveal that between 1700 and 1749, roughly half of those signing documents could write their own name. (Predictably, fewer than one in five women could do so.) Male signature literacy dropped sharply in the 1760s and 1770s (although the data base is small), but was back to over 50 percent in the 1780s and 1790s and continued upward thereafter. By the 1810s, nine out of every ten adults—both men and women—could sign. (See Appendix 1.) Literacy, however, was still closely associated with being a member of the Wampanoag elite and being a Christian.[141]

An Evaluation of Massachusett and Wampanoag Literacy

The conversions of the Massachusetts on the mainland stemmed from somewhat different roots from those of the Wampanoags on Martha's Vineyard. The Massachusetts attracted by John Eliot's message were in a much weaker state, psychologically and numerically, than the Wampanoags. Furthermore, for the Massachusetts, Christianity was tied more closely to the continuing presence of a particular English individual, John Eliot, who imposed on them Puritan modes of hairstyling, dress, and habitation. In contrast, for the Wampanoags, after the death of the younger Thomas Mayhew, Christianity became an indigenous feature of their culture that they promoted and continued themselves. In addition, the Massachusett Praying Indians were so devastated by King Philip's War that many of the survivors melted into their surrounding English communities, leaving relatively few viable Indian Christian communities, such as Mashpee and Sandwich, whereas the Wampanoags of Martha's Vineyard have retained their identity in Gay Head to the present day.[142]

While it is easy to identify these differences between the Christian Indians of the mainland and the off-shore islands of Massachusetts, it is less easy to see how such differences affected the native Americans' adoption of Christianity and, in turn, their acceptance of literacy. Some generalizations, however, can be made. First, the initial motives for teaching and learning reading were very largely religious. Natick's schoolmaster Monequassun, for one, fully appreciated the relationships among reading, religious indoctrination, and acculturation. In the Vineyard, where the acquisition of literacy required less cultural transformation, those who read resembled other Christians in other cultures. Several Indian women, for instance, drew consolation and strength from books during difficult marriages. Intensive reading of scriptural and devotional texts was a hallmark of devout Congregationalists in the English community. Indeed, Mayhew's description of the Wampanoags' reading, which he compared to that of poor Englishmen, fits the profile of "traditional literacy" sketched by David Hall of readers who approached print with reverential deliberation. They valued reading over writing and had access to only a few books, almost all of which, in this context, were scriptural or devotional.[143]

A second point is that the availability of texts in Massachusett, first for reading instruction and then as reading material, was crucial. Virtually everyone who cared about the missionary effort, from John Cotton to Experience Mayhew, complained about the lack of texts in the Indians' own language. At least primers, which all involved in the literacy effort considered essential to instruction, were usually in print. John Eliot's monolingual *Indian Primer* was first published in 1669. A new version was printed in 1699 or 1700 and a final version in 1720, this time with a parallel English translation. To judge from the commissioners' stocks, plenty of copies still existed in 1724 of this last edition. Access to these last primers may have been more a problem of distribution than production.

The availability of other texts in Massachusett actually declined over time. The book in shortest supply was the Indian Bible. For a variety of reasons, the stock was radically reduced by King Philip's War. Although John Eliot had been able to get a second edition published in 1685, once he was gone the emphasis of the Indian Library unquestionably changed. After the turn of the century, a new attempt to reprint the Indian Bible was in effect sabotaged by Cotton Mather. Instead, the texts printed in Massachusett were now shorter ones, heavily reliant on translations of sermons and homilies. The only scriptures still in print in the early eighteenth century were the Psalms and the Gospel According to John, published together in the *Massachusett Psalter* of 1709. Even the traditional devotional staples, such as *The Practice of Piety* and *Call to the Unconverted* were not reprinted after Eliot died in 1690. This surely contributed to what we would call "restricted literacy."

The striking lack of commitment to presenting the Bible in Massachusett, along with the new insistence after 1700 on bilingual texts of Massachusett and English, is symptomatic of a change in the official attitude toward native Americans. Indians were increasingly expected to conform to English ways, including learning English. The opinion that the Indians could not lose their aboriginal "savagery" without also losing their aboriginal language was not held by Cotton Mather alone. The English colonists were clearly losing confidence in a missionary enterprise that was conducted wholly in the language of the natives. Even the 1720 version of the *Indian Primer* betrayed a change in attitude. Unlike the 1669 primer, which presented Christian texts such as the Lord's Prayer without any evaluation of Indian character, almost every page of the new version of 1720 fairly oozed with anti-Indian prejudice and negative stereotyping. In contrast, the *Massachuset Psalter* of 1709 was a useful text in every way: it provided a book each from the Old and New Testaments and filled a gap in the reading instructional sequence by becoming the book to be taught next after the primer.

A third point, for both the Massachusetts and the Wampanoags, is that schooling was seen by all concerned, whether English or Indian, as the key to literacy instruction. Both John Eliot and Thomas Mayhew ensured that schoolmasters were hired to open schools for the Indians. Monequassun's and Peter Folger's initial efforts were crucial because they offered the first instruction in literacy to communities that lacked any previous experience with it. Monequassun's contribution was the more remarkable, in that he had acquired his own literacy with great pain. In the Vineyard, as successive generations passed, schooling became more prevalent, although it waned in the early years of the eighteenth century. The principle of schooling, however, became so widely accepted by Vineyard Indians that even parents who were not religious sent their children to be educated at what were, in essence, religious schools.

By the time, however, that literacy had become well ingrained in the native Vineyard population, there was another option to schooling: reading instruction that originated from the home. A fourth point, then, is that, just as the English could, Indian family members could impart reading instruction. In the absence of schools, parents and neighbors sometimes substituted for schoolmasters. Literate mothers, in particular, taught their daughters to read from the few texts available. For devout Vineyard Christians, such as the Hannit family, literacy was one of the features of their culture that they were usually able to pass down from generation to generation.

Finally, the evidence from written Massachusett suggests that the writing component of literacy played an increasingly important part, at least among the Christian Indian elite. The political control of Massachusett communities by the English government brought in its train the requirement of careful record keeping, in effect enlarging the scope of Indian literacy well beyond the religious. Besides keeping town records, recording wills and transfers of land, and writing court briefs, literate native Americans used their writing skills in a range of other ways. Whether it was recording the date of the death of a beloved family member, taking notes on a sermon, or even sending threats to the enemy, the Indians made writing their own. Through their acquisition of this skill they transcended the narrow religious context within which literacy had initially been introduced.

In sum, the literacy experiences of the Wampanoags, in particular, serve as a useful corrective to Jill Lepore's concerns about the negative role Indian literacy played in New England as an agent in compromising Indian culture. In Martha's

Vineyard, the Wampanoags absorbed literacy into their own culture rather than permitting it to absorb them. Indeed, literacy did not displace oral modes of communication but contributed, in the words of Kathleen Bragdon, to "the development and preservation of a distinctive native way of life lasting well into the nineteenth century."[144]

3

Books Read by Children at Home and at School

In a letter to the New England Corporation dated September 1655, the Commissioners of the United Colonies of New England listed the goods they wished to have sent to them for John Eliot's work among the Indians. Along with their requests for locks and canvas, scythes and nails was one for the least expensive of all the items they were ordering: hornbooks and "old Common primers" worth three pounds.[1]

The English hornbooks and primers that John Eliot needed in order to introduce the Massachusetts to literacy were, as we have seen, the first two elements of the traditional reading sequence that culminated in the Bible, as children trod "the ordinary Road of the Horn-Book, Primer, Psalter, Testament, and Bible." It is crucial to examine this sequence in order to understand the content and methodology of seventeenth-century reading instruction. Such instruction was universally believed to transmit much more than a skill: it transmitted the cultural, ethical, and spiritual values of the community. A close look, then, at the texts involved can tell us much about the value system of seventeenth-century and early eighteenth-century America.

The religiously linked texts of the "ordinary Road," however, were not the only books available to children before 1700—at least in Boston, the most important site in New England for the importation and printing of books in the seventeenth century and the hub for disseminating books to other colonies. The spelling book, already an identifiable genre in England, began to make inroads into the American colonies at the end of the century. Books that targeted children as their audience are also visible in the mid 1680s. And books that were not designed for children but, for a variety of reasons, read widely by them appeared in Boston. These included both "godly" and "ungodly" imprints.

The "ordinary Road" of Reading Instruction

The first text in the traditional sequence, the hornbook, was a little paddle of wood usually measuring less than three inches wide by four inches high.[2] To it was glued a single page that was covered by the transparent sheet of horn that gave the hornbook its name. A thin strip of brass secured both page and horn. The hornbook would be popular not only in the seventeenth but the eighteenth century. In

1784, the English poet William Cowper succinctly summarized the form and function of the hornbook:

> Neatly secured from being soil'd or torn,
> Beneath a page of thin translucent horn,
> A book (to please us at a tender Age
> 'Tis call'd a book, tho' but a single page)
> Presents the prayer the Saviour deign'd to teach,
> Which children use, and parsons—when they preach.[3]

The hornbook's "single page" presented the alphabet in lower- and uppercase forms. (These were colloquially known as "little" and "great" letters.) Next came the first three lines of the syllabary, a table of nonsense syllables organized alphabetically not only by their initial consonants but by the immediately following vowel. This was symmetrically placed in parallel columns:

a e i o u	a e i o u
ab eb ib ob ub	ba be bi bo bu
ac ec ic oc uc	ca ce ci co cu
ad ed id od ud	da de di do du

The rest of the page was devoted to the invocation ("In the Name of the Father . . .") and the Lord's Prayer (which Cowper calls "the prayer the Saviour deign'd to teach").

The only explicitly instructional material in the hornbook, therefore, is the three lines of *ab*s and *ba*s of the syllabary. They suggest a great deal more than appears at first glance. First, they imply the existence of a complete syllabary, extending down the alphabet to *az ez iz oz uz* and *za ze zi zo zu*. This two-letter syllabary was very ancient. Quite apart from any evidence in manuscript form, snippets of it had appeared in print early in the sixteenth century. A Latin-English ABC book published in London around 1538 included the syllabary up to the letter G.[4]

Second, the presumed usefulness of these two-letter nonsense syllables is intelligible only in the context of the methodology they imply: that children learned to read by spelling out syllables and words orally. Children, when told to read *ab, eb* . . . *ba, be*, pronounced aloud, "Ay, Bee, *ab*; Ee Bee, *eb* . . . Bee, Ay, *bay*; Bee Ee, *bee*."[5] Third, the parallel columns emphasize one of the many difficulties of the English graphemic system: there are at least two regular pronunciations for each vowel. The letter *e*, for instance, is pronounced quite differently in *eb[b]* (a "short" vowel") from the way it is pronounced in *be* (a "long" vowel). Finally, the truncated syllabary suggests the enormously important role that the syllable played in literacy instruction.[6]

The most famous reference to the hornbook in early America is that in Samuel Sewall's diary. Sewall, whom we met earlier as a staunch supporter of the third edition of the Indian Bible, was a devout Congregationalist and a successful Boston merchant who became a judge in the Massachusetts General Court in 1683. In a diary entry for April 1691 he recorded that he had sent his little son off to his

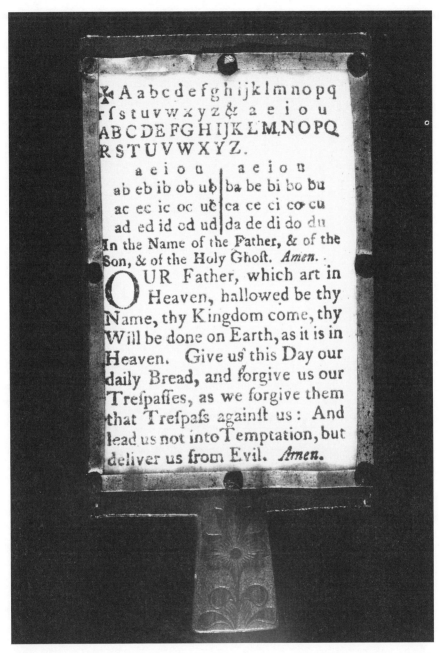

FIGURE 3. A hornbook. This hornbook shows the cross, which Puritans found abhorrent, placed just before the "Great A, little A" (upper- and lowercase *A*) of the first of the two alphabets. The alphabets, the truncated syllabary, the invocation, and the Lord's Prayer were all standard features of the hornbook. This one, with a leather backing, is much fancier than most. (Courtesy, Newberry Library, Chicago)

dame school, clearly for the first time: "This Afternoon had Joseph to School to Capt. Townsend's Mother, his Cousin Jane accompanying him, carried his Horn-book." Joseph was then aged two years and eight months. Sewall himself imported hornbooks: an entry in his letter book for 1700 mentions his ordering a gross.[7]

Hornbooks were not restricted to New England. Merchants' inventories show their occasional presence, along with primers, in stores in Middlesex County, Virginia, and in St. Mary's County and York County, Maryland, in the last third of the seventeenth century. Many other stores in the Chesapeake region, however, did not stock either text. Hornbooks are documented in Philadelphia in 1706.[8]

The text that followed the hornbook in the reading instructional sequence was the primer. In London, John Bunyan, author of *Pilgrim's Progress*, issued a work for children in 1686 titled *A Book for Boys and Girls; or Country Rhimes for Children*. One verse identifies the progress from hornbook to primer and psalter while at the same time bestowing some encouraging words on late bloomers:

> Nor let *them* fall under Discouragement,
> Who at their Horn-book stick, and time hath spent
> Upon that A, B, C, while others do
> Into their Primer, or their Psalter go.
> Some Boys with difficulty do begin,
> Who in the end, the Bays, and Lawrel win.[9]

The original meaning of a "primer" was a prayer book or devotional manual for the laity. Its secondary meaning of an introductory reading text evolved very early. As someone said of it in 1539, it was "Called the prymer, because (I suppose) that it is the fyrste boke that the tender youth was instructed in."[10]

After King Henry VIII broke with the Roman Church and created the Anglican Church, he attempted to control the publication of doctrinal texts and ordered that his authorized primer be the only one printed. Successive monarchs published primers that conformed to the Book of Common Prayer, the work that prescribed the form of Anglican services, but by the time the first settlers landed on American shores the English church had long since lost control of religious printing, with the exception of the Book of Common Prayer and the Bible. Primers were therefore published in England in some variety.[11] The "old Common primers" requested by the United Colonies Commissioners on behalf of John Eliot were these old primers that conformed to the Book of Common Prayer.

Unlike the single-paged hornbook, the primer was a real book, so the choice of a primer was crucial, theologically speaking. All Christian denominations had their own versions and considered those of others dangerously misleading. Thomas Shepard, teacher of the church of Charlestown, Massachusetts, and one of the translators of works for the Indian Library, made this point in a Boston election sermon in the spring of 1672, when he attacked imported Anglican primers for including pictures of Christ, which Puritans considered idolatrous: "the very primmers for children," he thundered, "whereby they may even suck in poison in their tender years" were being "sold in shops or brought over among us." He regarded them as a potential "Introduction to Popery it self," and expressed the wish that they might be "crushed in the egg."[12] Nonetheless, as Samuel Eliot Morison points out, we do not know which primers were used in New England schools (or, as he might also have said, in the home setting) until American printers began to publish them.[13]

The next book in the traditional sequence after the primer was the psalter. The first extant imprint of the Cambridge, Massachusetts, press, in 1640, is what is now known as the "Bay Psalm Book"—a verse rendering of the Book of Psalms composed chiefly by Richard Mather, John Eliot, and Thomas Welde.[14] This, however, was not the psalter used in schools but a hymnal for the meeting house. The school text was the prose Book of Psalms, which it was legal to print separately from the Bible. Indeed, in 1682 New Englanders could have a home-printed edition. John Usher of Boston announced that "The Psalter . . . which Children so much wanted, is in part printed, and will shortly be finished." The *New-England Psalter*, as it was titled, would be regularly reprinted throughout the eighteenth century.[15]

From the psalter, children proceeded to the New Testament and to the entire Bible. British law forbade the printing of Bibles outside Britain: the printing of the Indian Bible was an exception because of its unusual circumstances. But testaments and Bibles were imported regularly and would eventually become omnipresent in stores throughout the colonies. Moreover, many of the early immigrants had brought one with them.[16]

The New England preference for the "ordinary Road" is further supported by the inventory of Michael Perry. Perry was a Boston bookseller who died in 1700 at the young age of thirty-four, leaving a widow and a mountain of debt. At his damp little shop tucked under the steps of the Exchange, he had sold both imported books (purchased from Boston merchants) and locally printed ones. Listed in the inventory of his goods are close to 700 hornbooks: of these, 222 were "gilt," at one penny each, and 468 "plain" at a halfpenny. (Did gilt hornbooks have the brass rim over the transparent sheet, while plain ones just have a hornless page glued onto the little paddle?) In addition, for twopence each, Perry had 856 copies of the *New-England Primer* stacked up in piles in his rented house as well as in his store. He also had 124 copies of the *New England Psalter*, specially printed for children. Even some of his much smaller stock of Bibles look as though they were aimed at schools: he had 18 duodecimo Bibles, at three or four shillings each—the price depended on the quality of the binding—and 11 copies of Bibles half that size. In short, from Perry's bookstore one could have purchased every material component of the traditional reading sequence.[17]

It is paradoxical that, while all this evidence unequivocally supports Locke's "ordinary Road," there were in fact two other texts habitually invoked in the context of reading instruction, one religious and the other potentially secular: the catechism and the spelling book. The catechism was that sequence of questions and answers that instructed a child in the basic doctrines of Christianity. In the catechetical format, an adult posed the questions and the child provided predetermined answers. The Shorter Westminster Catechism, for instance, so often printed as an addition to the core text of the *New-England Primer*, begins with the question, *"What is the chief End of Man?"* The printed answer is, "Man's chief End is to Glorify God, and to Enjoy Him for ever." The contrast between the Bible and catechisms, in terms of existence in print, is striking. The Bible was considered unalterable and unique, apart from shades of translations. Yet catechisms, which expounded the doctrine embodied in the Bible, were invented and printed by the dozen, particularly in New England. They reflected how each author believed central Christian truths should be transmitted to children.[18]

The perceived need for yet another catechism clearly galvanized ministerial creativity. Cotton Mather, minister of Boston's North Church, was proud of the efforts made by New Englanders in this regard. "Few pastors of mankind," he declared, "ever took such pains at *catechising*, as have been taken by our New-English divines." He reeled off a list of those who had published them: Mr. Norton had published a lesser and a larger; so had Mr. Mather (Cotton's father); Mr. Cotton (Cotton's grandfather) had written several, as had Mr. (John) Eliot; Mr. Davenport had written one, Mr Stone another, and so on.[19]

In some ways, the catechism logically preceded every other text in a child's education, and at least one author of an educational treatise in the late sixteenth century identified it as the child's first book, preceding the primer. As we have seen, a catechism was the first text composed for the Indians, both by John Eliot and the younger Thomas Mayhew. Neither man, however, expected his Indian students to be able to read it immediately. In this context, as in the broader context of New England education in general, the catechism was a text that the child had to learn by heart with the help of an adult. It was implicitly acknowledged that it was too difficult for a beginning reader; instead, the child's reading ability would catch up with it. Being able to read made learning the catechism easier, as "excerising reading to the advancing of Catachising" (as the Watertown selectmen put it) implied. By the seventeenth century, therefore, although the catechism was a text that had to be learned by heart sooner or later, it stood outside the traditional reading sequence.[20]

It is understandable why Locke omitted the catechism from his list of books to be trudged through but not why he omitted the spelling book. Spelling books had been around as reading instructional textbooks even before *The English Schoole-Maister* by Edmund Coote, first published in 1596. Coote's clearly organized text remained a model throughout the following century.[21]

A spelling book was printed in America at a very early date. It was one of the earliest texts to come off the press of the English printer Stephen Daye after he arrived in Cambridge, Massachusetts, in the summer of 1638. We know of its existence only because a "Spelling Book"—its title was not identified—was included in a listing of seven works that he printed between 1639 and 1648. It is perhaps to be dated 1644.[22]

At least four crucial differences between spelling books and primers can be identified. First, the purpose of each book was radically different. In the sixteenth and seventeenth centuries, the primer was a devotional work to which reading instructional material—such as the addition of syllables—was ancillary. In contrast, the spelling book was designed to teach reading, and the meaningfulness of the content took second place. Spellers provided long lists of syllables and words to be spelled out and pronounced (later known as "tables"), which were interspersed with short passages of connected text to be spelled out and read aloud. These passages were composed only of the words introduced to that point; if they did include words not in the tables, they hewed to the principles (such as being restricted to up to words of two syllables accented on the first) that had been embodied in the tables. Because spelling-book authors almost universally equated word difficulty with word length, their books, like the hornbooks and primers, began with the syllabary and, as the tradition developed over the seventeenth century, presented words of an increasing number of syllables in each successive chapter. These tables of syllables and words formed the heart of any spelling book.

A second difference was related to the first: spelling books were, in theory if not always in practice, potentially dramatically more secular than primers. This secularity could be seen very early: Coote's first reading material (in monosyllables of no more than four letters) had been: "Boy, go thy way vp to the top of the hill, and get me home the bay nag, fill him well, and see he be fat." Once an author focused on method over content, the possibility that the quality of the content would be compromised was ever present. Coote himself had felt constrained to apologize: "This speech is made onely of the wordes taught before, where you are not to regarde the sence, being friuolous, but onely to teach distinct reading." So, in 1596, did Coote encapsulate the potential for a conflict between, on one hand, a sequential approach that used words consisting only of the elements already taught and, on the other, the meaningfulness of what was read. It is a conflict that is still alive today.[23]

Third, unlike authors of primers, authors of spelling books all displayed a fascination with the relationship between letters and sounds. In the simplest of orthographical systems (if not necessarily the best), one letter would represent one speech sound.[24] In English, however, phonemes exceed letters by a proportion of well over forty to twenty-six. Explaining the vagaries of English spelling therefore gave spelling-book authors plenty of grist for their linguistic mill. The result was the generation of "rules" that were intended to cover all the oddities of English orthography—rules for pronouncing letters such as *c* and *g* according to the following vowel; rules on the effect of a silent final *e* on a preceding single vowel; rules for dividing polysyllables into syllables, and so on.

A fourth difference was the natural result of the third: the audiences for each genre, primer and speller, were potentially not identical. The spelling book contained so much dense material that a small child (aged three or four, say) could not be expected to understand much of it, as Coote acknowledges at the end of his speller: "If thou thinke me either for hardnes of rule, or length of matter, vnfit for children: plentifull experience in very young ones, (beleeue him that hath tryed) doth dayly confute thee."[25] Nonetheless, of the two genres, primer and speller, it was the latter that had the potential for evolving into a text aimed at youth rather than small children. Even in Coote, the two young scholars "opposing" each other in a dialogue in the second part of his book seem to be at least seven or eight years old, as they challenge each other to spell *people* and *might* and identify what consonants are permissible after the letter *b*.[26]

The Indian Primer and the Spelling-Book Tradition

The constantly evolving spelling-book tradition was potentially available to John Eliot when he sought to create a reading instructional text for Massachusett-speaking native Americans of all ages. As described earlier, with the aid of one of his Indian interpreters, Cockanoe-de-Long Island, Eliot composed the *Indian Primer*, which was printed by the Cambridge, Massachusetts, press in 1669. It is by far the earliest colonial text for reading instruction extant, predating the first available edition of the *New-England Primer* (a 1727 imprint) by well over fifty years. It is therefore an extremely important work and key to discovering whether Eliot chose to take advantage of the spelling-book tradition.

In his *Indian Grammar*, published three years earlier, in 1666, in response to a request for a description of the Massachusett language, Eliot gives some idea of how he created its graphemic system. Although he did not identify Cockanoe-de-Long Island by name, he paid tribute to a "pregnant witted young man" with a good knowledge of his own language, who had been his interpreter and later his translator.[27]

In the early pages of the grammar, Eliot covered much of the same ground as others who described the writing of English, particularly spelling-book authors. He made some innovations to both the alphabetical letters and their names, introducing the "letter" *CH* after *C* in the alphabet, calling it "chee," and adding both *J* and *V* to the alphabet, calling them "ji" (as in *giant*) and "vf" ("*uph*"). Eliot was therefore one of the first authors to introduce *J* and *V* into what was still a twenty-four-letter alphabet, although he treated *v* as a vowel rather than the consonant it would become. He also renamed *W* "wee," making a clear distinction between the name of a letter and its sound: "We call w (wee), because our name ["double-you"] giveth no hint of the *power* of its sound." The speech sound represented by the *oo* in *moody* and *book* (which today are distinct sounds) was printed as *oo* with no space between the two letters.[28] In addition, Eliot also introduced accents to assist pronunciation, such as a circumflex to indicate a nasal *a* or *o*—sounds in the Indian tongue that are not part of the English phonemic system.

Eliot described the structure of Massachusett as a language that "doth greatly delight in *Compounding* of *Words*." The result was that the Indians spoke "*much* in *few words*, though they be sometimes long." Words were inflected by the addition of syllables, including those added simply for the sake of euphony. Possessive personal pronouns were prefixed to nouns ("Nuttah, *my heart*; Kuttah, *thy heart*); there were five different suffixes that had to be added to an active verb, depending on whether the object was animate or inanimate, and so forth. (The fifth suffix was the "in stead" form, "when one acteth in the *room* or *stead* of another." It was of great use in theology, according to Eliot.) The Massachusett for "I wish he did keep me" is *Noowaadchanukqunaz-toh*, while *nuppapaumukqunaz-toh* means, "I wish he did pay me." In the latter, Eliot says, "(Paum) is the radical word [root] and all the rest is grammar."[29]

With a language so grammatically dependent on syllable accretion, it is not surprising that Eliot used the syllabic unit as the key to his reading and writing instruction in Massachusett, just as all his predecessors had done for English. He declared that the formation of syllables in Massachusett was the same as in English. He taught adult Indians to divide a spoken word into its constituent syllables, use the vowel as a focal point, and then, if necessary, add the appropriate consonants before and after the vowel. "They quickly apprehended and understood this *Epitomie* of the *Art of Spelling*," Eliot reports, "and could soon learn to *Reade*." The men, women, and young adults, he said "thus rationally learn to Reade: but the *Children* learn by *rote* and *custome*, as other Children do."[30]

The *Indian Primer* of 1669 embodies Eliot's thinking not only about his orthographic system for the Massachusett tongue but about the very purpose of literacy instruction. The relationship between reading and religion is succinctly expressed by the book's title: *The Indian Primer; Or, The way of training up of our Indian Youth in the good Knowledge of God, in the Knowledge of the Scriptures and in an ability to Reade.*[31] It is significant that, even though the bulk of the text is doctrinal, set squarely in the primer tradition, the introductory pages reflect several of the aspects of reading and spelling instruction that most intrigued the authors of spelling books. First, of course, comes the alphabet. It puts *Ch* after *C* and adds *V*, but—surprisingly, in view of Eliot's discussion three years earlier—omits *J*, even though j is included later in the syllabary. After the vowels and diphthongs, Eliot introduces the syllabary, beginning "*ab eb ib ob ub alb*," and continuing with "*ba be bi bo bu bab dab*" and "*fab fap lab leb lib lob lub*."[32] Apparently Eliot was including only those syllables that were permissible in Massachusett—unlike some spelling-book authors, who listed the most unpronounceable syllables with abandon.[33]

The text of the *Indian Primer* then moves into its first reading lesson. Words are separated from each other by periods; polysyllabic words are subdivided into syllables by hyphens.

Wa-an-tam-we. us-seonk. og-e-
tam-un-at. Ca-te-chi-sa-onk.
　Ne-gon-ne. og-kee-tash. Pri-
mer.
　Na-hoh-to-eu. og-kee-tash.
　Ai-us-koi-an-tam-o-e. weh-
kom-a-onk.
　Ne-it. og-kee-tash. Bi ble.

Eliot used this first lesson to propose a sequence of instruction. The text translates, "Wise doing to read Catechism. First, read Primer. Next, read Repentance Calling. Then read Bible." ("Repentance Calling" was Eliot's translation of Richard Baxter's *Call to the Unconverted*.)[34]

Next comes a brief dialogue between a schoolmaster and his scholar.

    Noh. School-mas-ter-eu-uk.
a-se-ke-suk-ok-ish. woh. nee-sit.
nompe. pe-an-tam.
    Ne-gon-ne. puh-she-quad.

Overall, Eliot devotes a total of a page and a half to dividing words into syllables.

After the syllabary and the schoolmaster-scholar dialogue, the contents of the primer become entirely religious and syllable division vanishes. The primer includes the Lord's Prayer in English and Massachusett, the Lord's Prayer Expounded (in Massachusett), and the creed in English and Massachusett. The remaining pages are in Massachusett only, except for their titles: "Degrees of Christian Duties for Several Estates," the large catechism, a short catechism, the numeral letters and figures used for locating biblical texts, and the names and order of the books of the Old and New Testaments.[35]

The inclusion of two versions of the catechism at the end of the primer is paradoxical. This location suggests that Eliot regarded the catechism as an advanced text that children had to work their way up to. Yet, in his initial paragraphs, he seems to be recommending that the students read the catechism first—presumably because they had previously learned it by heart. Nor does he follow Locke's "ordinary Road" completely: he advises reading a devotional work, *Call to the Unconverted*, before the Bible, presumably because he needed a work of intermediate difficulty, and at this point there was no separate Indian edition of the psalter.

It is not difficult to demonstrate that Eliot was aware of the spelling-book genre, in general, by now familiar for almost three-quarters of a century, and of Coote's *English Schoole-Maister*, in particular. Like Coote's spelling lists, Eliot's lists consist only of monosyllables, not polysyllables, even though the latter appear everywhere in the running text.[36] Also, Eliot's handling of consonant-vowel-consonant words is identical to Coote's: he treats them as an extension of consonant-vowel syllables.[37] Again, for running text, Eliot divides polysyllabic words into syllables for a short time, then abandons the practice, just as Coote does. In addition, Eliot even uses, briefly, Coote's instructional format of a conversation between a schoolmaster and a scholar.[38] As in the grammar, he also, like Coote, distinguishes between the "power" and "sound" of letters, renaming the letter *W* "wee" to reflect the letter's "power" better.[39]

This analysis of Eliot's work reveals that as early as 1669, admittedly in an alien setting, Eliot made use of a body of knowledge that was unique to spelling books. Although his primer, in its content, hewed squarely to the primer tradition of a Christian devotional text, Eliot availed himself of the discussions of letter-sound relationships that could be found in the work of Edmund Coote and others. To Eliot and Coote alike, pronouncing words correctly was the key to reading and understanding them.

you put (e) in the end, which is not foun-ded?

Mai. This letter (e) in the end of a word not foun-ded   (e) Not foun-
hath two prin-ci-pall v-fes. The firft and chie-fest is to draw   ded.
the fyl-lable long, as he is made mad

A mill dam: A fhrewd dame.

My man hath cut my horfe mane.

A great gap: gape wide.

Spare this fpar. Be-ware of war.

*Feed vntil thou haft well fed.

You feele not my paine. A wafp is fell.   *In this found
                                                          when (e) is

He hid the ore hide.   long, it is com-

It is a mile to the mill.   monly doub-

A little pin: my flefh doth pine.   ked and made

A branch of fir, good for the fire.   a diphthong.

A dor fitteth on the dore.

Tos the ball: Tofe the wooll.   Make your

You haue a Dot on the nofe: and you dote.   Scholers very

Rud is not rude.   perfect in thefe,

A tun of wine: the tune of a fong.   therefore you
                                                          may try them

Scho. What is the fe-cond vfe?   in other like.

Mai. It chan-geth the found of fome let-ters: but this vfe
with the fur-ther de-cla-ra-ti-on of this let-ter, be-caufe it
is har-der, then you will at the firft ea-fi-ly con-ceiue, I will
re-ferre vn-to a-no-ther place.

Scho. Are no o-ther let-ters not at all, or but lit-tle pro-
noun-ced?

Mai. Yes. Uery ma-ny: as (a) is not pro-noun-ced in earth,   Letters not
goat: nor (e) in Georg: nor (i) in briefe: nor (o) in people: pronounced.
nei-ther is (u) pro-noun-ced in guido: all which words
of all forts, I will fet downe af-ter-ward, when I haue gi-
uen you more ne-cef-fary rules in thefe three firft chapters,
and you bet-ter able to vfe them.

                                                             CHAP.

FIGURE 4. A dialogue between a master and his scholar in Edmund Coote, *The English Schoole-Maister* (London: Widow Orwin, 1596; facsimile, Menston, Yorks.: Scholar Press, 1968), pt. 2, p. 15. This page from the second part of Coote's spelling book demonstrates the contemporary fascination with letter-sound correspondences. The "scholar" is engaging in a dialogue with his master, who is answering his question about why there is a final silent *e* at the end of so many words. Why, asks the student, do "you put (e) in the end, which is not soun-ded?"

Early Spelling Books on American Presses

In England, the 1670s and the following decades saw a dramatic increase in the rates of publication of works intended to introduce children to reading and, in some instances, writing instruction. We know of six new English spelling books in the 1650s, four in the 1660s, and thirteen more in the 1670s. In the 1680s, the rate mounted, with twenty new spelling books. The decade of the 1690s saw another dozen. Meanwhile, the most popular of the older ones were still being reprinted—including, of course, Edmund Coote's. Clearly, neither the restoration of the monarchy in England in 1660 nor the accession of William III to the throne in the Glorious Revolution of 1688-89 did anything to dampen enthusiasm for spelling books.[40]

When instructional books printed on American presses, other than those for the Massachusetts and Wampanoags, finally appear, it is late in the seventeenth century. Of course, schoolbooks had been imported all along, but until the advent of newspapers in the early eighteenth century, it is hard to know which they were. One sign of their popularity was their reproduction by an American printer. It was standard practice to let imported copies test the market and to go to the expense of reprinting them in the colonies only once the viability of the imported version had been firmly established. Schoolbooks printed on American presses, therefore, nearly always imply earlier sales of imported English copies, usually over a period of several years. Local production was assisted by the absence of any kind of copyright protection. Even for American imprints, there was no protection until the first state law of 1783 and the U.S. national copyright law of 1790. International copyright protection would be a product of the nineteenth century. American printers therefore freely reprinted imported works without any financial or ethical obligations to their English or Scottish authors.

Several spelling books and primers were printed on American presses at the end of the seventeenth century and the beginning of the eighteenth, and for the first time they were being published in cities other than Boston and written by men who, although Protestants, were not Congregationalists. The earliest American-written and American-printed speller was that of the German immigrant Franz Daniel Pastorius, a devout Pietist whose *New Primmer or Methodical Directions to Attain True Spelling, Reading and Writing of English* was printed for him in New York by William Bradford in 1698. (Learned and multilingual, Pastorius was a founder of Germantown, Pennsylvania, where he taught school.)[41] Another spelling book was printed in Philadelphia: a reprint of a work by a Quaker, indeed the founder of the Society of Friends, George Fox. It was initially published in London in 1670 under the title *A Primmer and Catechism for Children or a Plain and Easy Way for Children to Learn to Spell and Read Perfectly in a little time*. It was surely a sign of the changing times that only three years later it was reissued in London with a revised title patently aimed at the spelling-book market, *Instructions for Right-Spelling, and Plain Directions for Reading and Writing True English. With several delightful Things, very Useful and Necessary, both for Young and Old to Read and Learn*. In 1702 it was reprinted under the 1673 title in Philadelphia by Reynier

Jansen, who did printing work for the Philadelphia Friends.[42] Yet another spelling book was that of Nathaniel Strong, whose religious affiliation is not known. His *England's Perfect School-Master: or, most Plain and Easie Rules for Writing and Spelling true English* was first printed in London in 1674 and imported into New England for many years. Its earliest American reprint was a Boston one by Bartholomew Green in 1710, and it was reprinted at least once more in Boston in 1720.[43]

Unlike Strong's work, Pastorius's and Fox's texts are at heart doctrinal works, as their use of the word *primer* in the titles indicates. Pastorius's is devoted almost entirely to providing snippets of scripture, fully referenced ("they are troubled, because of their Transgressions, *Psalm* 31.9 ashamed *Rom.* 6.21 mourning, *Matt* 5.4"); Fox's offers lengthy expositions of Quaker doctrine. The printers of these texts must have felt that large swathes of text devoted to this kind of material would not attract enough buyers because both schoolbooks have additional material, probably inserted by their printers, that were already standard features in spelling books: a list of homophones, a short dictionary, and a gloss on scriptural names.

In a context where so much learning involved repetition and memorization, it is important to note that many of these features were aimed at helping children understand what they were reading by providing explanations of the meaning of words. In Pastorius's book, the list of homophones, described as words "alike in sound, yet unlike in their signification," begins with "Accidence, accidents . . . Acts, ax, ask," but the version in Fox's text helpfully provides some context: "*ASK* the Carpenter for his *Ax* / Since I learn'd my *Accidence* / there have been strange *Accidents. . . .* If he leave not *Coughing*, he / will soon be put in a *Coffin.*" Strong even put his homophones into verse, always assumed to be an added attraction: "I saw one sent unto the Hill's ascent, / Who did assent to me before he went. / As I perceiv'd his Gloves did leave a scent."[44]

The short dictionaries also fostered comprehension. Pastorius's "Explanation of some difficult words" begins with "*Abreviate*, to abridge or make short." Sections in Pastorius and Fox offer glosses on scriptural names: "Aaron, a Teacher"; "*Sa-mu-el* signifies, *heard of God.*" Pastorius also explains the names of the books of the Bible. The bulk of Fox's speller is devoted to a question and answer section reminiscent of the one in Edmund Coote in that the young person (the "scholar") asks the questions and the schoolmaster responds. But whereas the student in Coote's spelling book sought clarification of the relationship between print and speech, in Fox's version the scholar is asking about matters that relate to the Friends and to their belief in the inner light of revelation:

Sch. *Who are true* Christians?
Mast. Such as believe in the Light of Christ, and are led
    and guided by the Christ Jesus.
Sch. *Why are the true* Christians *called Quakers in this*
    Age?
Mast. It is in Scorn and derision that they are so

called, to render them and the Truth odious to the
People, that so they might not receive the Truth
and be saved.[45]

This question and answer format, with the child asking questions of the master, differs significantly from the set of questions and answers in catechisms, where the master is in essence testing the child to see whether he or she can respond with the correct memorized answer.

The first major difference among the three works involves their degree of secularity. While Pastorius's and Fox's works (at heart primers) are steeped in Christian devotional material, the brief religious content appearing at the end of Strong's work (a speller), such as the Lord's Prayer, the Ten Commandments, and graces for before and after meals, seems simply a sop to convention.

The second difference relates to the primary purpose of spelling-book authors: to teach the young how to attain a spoken pronunciation from the printed word. It involves lists of words divided into syllables and a formal discussion of the relationship between letters and their speech "sounds." Fox's treatment of the division of words into syllables is cursory compared with that of Pastorius and Strong, as well as with that of John Eliot in the *Indian Primer*, printed only a year before Fox's first edition. Fox's *Instructions for Right Spelling* in fact offers very few instructions for correct spelling. It presents *Ab ac ad . . . az*, and *Ba, ca da . . . za*, but not *eb ec ed* or *be ce de*. It provides polysyllables, divided into syllables by spaces, but in an offhand way, horizontally and with no regard for the number of their syllables. Even Pastorius's text is better organized: although he devotes only four pages to his word lists, the words are arranged by the number of syllables, rising from words of two up to words of seven syllables. Pastorius also pays more attention to rules that guide how a word is to be pronounced. He devotes several pages to examples of the different pronunciations of vowels, consonants, and diphthongs. For the letter *o*, for instance, he contrasts "Both, ghost, most" with "son, come, done" and "do, two, who."[46]

Nonetheless, both Pastorius and Fox give much less emphasis to these aspects than does Strong. In the true secular spelling-book tradition, Strong provides rules to explain why letters receive different pronunciations under varying circumstances. His sixth rule, in verse, discusses the final silent *e*:

6th   True
    E at the end must written be, from whence
    Words are made long, and so preserve their sense.[47]

Syllabic division also plays a prominent role in Strong's book. His tables of words rise from monosyllables in an ascending number of syllables to words of six syllables, such as *u-ni-ver-sa-li-ty*. The words are presented twice: once divided into syllables and again, in a parallel column, as wholes. This practice was not original to Strong—indeed, Ian Michael sees his work as the "final stage" of a slowly evolving process of dual presentation of words for spelling and reading.[48]

In still other respects, Strong's work separates itself from the other two works that have their roots in the primer tradition: it focuses on tips for writing. Both Pastorius and Strong offer hints on punctuation,[49] but Strong provides ten pages of a kind of early spelling demon list: "Back, not bak / Bald, not bauld" and ten pages of "pieces for writing schools"—copies for the beginning writer. He also adds mathematical material. Pastorius, it is true, had also included similar sections—or, more likely, his printer had included them to enhance the work's dubious marketability—dealing with numbers, time, weight, measures, money, and the multiplication tables. Strong, however, has a lengthy section on mathematics: he provides a numeration table, discusses addition and subtraction, particularly that of money, shows how to state accounts, and gives examples of receipts and invoices, such as a shopkeeper's bill.[50]

A major consequence of all this additional material on learning writing and mathematics was that it rendered the text much less suitable for a beginning reader and correspondingly more suitable for a student who already knew how to read. Indeed, the kind of spelling book represented by Strong's *England's Perfect School-Master* was clearly a textbook for young men, whom colonials called "youth," rather than a beginner's text for children. Like Edward Young, whose *Compleat English-Scholar in Spelling, Reading and Writing* (1682) was imported from London but not reprinted in America, Strong set his sights on the bevy of young men preparing themselves to be clerks in Britain's expanding commercial empire. Because writing instruction was begun so late, any text that featured the word *writing* in its title was aimed at children of at least seven, the age at which writing instruction usually began.[51] Strong's work is not a complete self-instruction manual for an aspiring clerk, because it includes no explanations of how to hold the pen or form letters, but it is very close to being one. However, the field was still wide open for a spelling book geared to the needs of beginning readers.

All of this suggests that, even before the close of the seventeenth century, mundane concerns (such as attention to homophones) were infiltrating conventional reading instruction. The primer continued its role as a devotional text that paid minimal attention to reading methodology—with Eliot's primer the exception—while the speller emerged as the vehicle for a much sharper focus on methodology and the link between letters and speech sounds, presaging the far greater role it would play in this regard in the following century. The spelling book, however, had split into two traditions, one still aimed at the beginning reader and the other at young men ready for more advanced instruction. Except for Pastorius's unusual and ultimately unsellable work, the American booksellers, dependent as they were on reproducing imported works, simply mirrored this division of audience along with some of the interdenominational, pedagogical, and practical contentions of the mother county.

John Lewis's *The Church Catechism Explained*

A text of a rather different kind was also available to children after 1700: John Lewis's *The Church Catechism Explained*, in its second edition by 1702. Of all the works discussed so far that sprang from a particular religious orientation, this is the first to come from the Anglican tradition. The other explicitly religious texts, such as the New England catechisms and Eliot's *Indian Primer*, were written by Congregationalists, and Fox's *Instructions for Right Spelling* was written by the founder of the Society of Friends. Pastorius, author of the *New Primmer*, was a Pietist (Pietism began as a movement within the Lutheran Church). In contrast, Lewis was the Church of England minister of Margate (a market town located in Kent, southern England), and his explanation of the catechism was rooted in mainstream Anglicanism in England.

Probably because of the hostility of many early Boston printers to Anglicanism, the *Church Catechism Explained* was not, as far as we know, reproduced in the American colonies until 1748, when Benjamin Franklin and David Hall apparently printed a copy in Philadelphia.[52] However, it was available as an imported text. Lewis did not write the work originally with a philanthropic organization in mind, but in time his treatise would become a routine adjunct to Anglican philanthropic efforts abroad. At this point its chief interest for us is that it was an attempt to teach reading comprehension: his text was an explication of the Church of England catechism.

An early taste of the approach Lewis would take was published in London anonymously in 1709 as *The Church Catechism Broke into Short Questions, with an Explanation of some Words, for the Easier Understanding of it*. The book volleys questions at its readers on the answers they have just given to the catechetical questions. The author explains his rationale: "The use of these Questions, is to try whether Children repeat their Catechism by rote, to engage their attention, and to imprint the sense of it on their minds."[53]

The Church of England required the young to learn the catechism before they could be confirmed. (Confirmation was a sacrament that could be administered only by an Anglican bishop, and thanks to Congregational and other opposition, no bishop was countenanced in America until after the American Revolution.) The catechism, in Lewis's view, was the work "wherein are taught you all Things a Christian ought to know and believe, in order to his eternal Salvation." (No Congregationalist would have made such a sweeping claim.) His book was an attempt to make explanations that "should be more useful to the younger Sort of my Parishioners, than those I have yet seen." Lewis had therefore tried to make the answers "plain and short, that they may be sooner learned and more easily remembered." He had also placed the scripture proofs in such a way that "the meanest Capacities may know what it is they [the scripture proofs] are brought to prove." The ensuing text was a twelve-week course in explaining the catechism.[54]

Lewis provides a series of questions that ask for summaries or elaborations of the catechetical text. In his answers, he offers recapitulations, provides glosses on unfamiliar vocabulary, explains relevant concepts, and then ties them all together with an explanation. For example, one of the opening questions of the Anglican catechism asks what the child's godparents have done for him. The child's formal catechetical response is:

They did promise and vow three Things in my Name. First, That I should renounce the Devil and all his Works, the Pomps and Vanity of this Wicked World.

Lewis asks what the child has promised to renounce, and in his own answer, he uses the child's answer to summarize and explain the original response.

I promise to renounce the three spiritual Enemies to my present and future Happiness; which are the Devil, the World, and the Flesh.

Lewis's next question seeks to clarify difficult terms.

What is it to renounce them?

The definition that Lewis provides is couched in language simple enough for a child to understand, and the key point is indicated by a different font.

It is inwardly to hate, and actually to *reject* them, so as not to follow, or to be led by them.

After an explanation of the word *devil*, Lewis asks the child to put the two terms, *renounce* and *devil*, together. To the question, "What is meant by renouncing him?" the child is to reply:

The refusing all Familiarity and Contracts with the Devil, whereof Witches, Conjurers, and such as resort to them, are guilty.

The heart of Lewis's approach—as with every attempt to justify the doctrines of a catechism, no matter which denomination the learner belongs to—lies in the scriptural proofs. Lewis's work obligingly provides not only the scriptural references but the actual text. When the child is asked to give proof of his or her obligation to renounce the devil and all his works, the answer is:

[The proof is] [f]rom 1 John iii.8. He that committeth Sin is of the devil; for the devil sinneth from the beginning.[55]

Lewis's approach, however, has limitations. Witches and conjurers, for instance, are new concepts added to an equation that has supposedly just been solved. Furthermore, the answers Lewis provides as "explanations" of the catechetical answers are themselves supposed to be reproduced verbatim, just like their catechetical models. This could lead to the same perils that the catechism itself was prone to—the child's parroting of answers, with no accompanying comprehension.[56]

The *New-England Primer*

Spelling books such as Strong's and Young's were not widely imported or frequently reprinted, and Lewis's catechism was generally used only by Anglicans.
But there was one book in the reading sequence, a primer, that was a uniquely
American product: the famous *New-England Primer*. Because of the frequency of
its publication and the multiplicity of its places of publication, children had access
to it not only in New England but increasingly in other colonies, which imported
it from New England. The oldest surviving text is a Boston imprint of 1727; this
sets the work at the far end, chronologically, of the texts discussed so far. But the
importance of the *New-England Primer* derives more from the messages and metaphors it offered to its young readers than for anything that it contributed to reading
pedagogy. Correctly titled a primer—given its doctrinal content—rather than a
spelling book, the *New-England Primer* was in fact a compendium of Puritan
theology. Reprinted over and over again through the entire eighteenth century, it
is nonetheless in spirit the schoolbook of the seventeenth. Indeed, in some sense it
was outdated even before it was in print. While it never teaches comprehension
explicitly, it is rich in metaphorical meaning.

The first hint of the existence of the *New-England Primer* is in 1690, when it
was advertised under that title in an almanac. The primer, "now in the Press," was
already in its "Second Impression" and had been "*enlarged*": "to which is added,
more *Directions for Spelling*: the *Prayer of* K[ing] *Edward the 6th.* and *Verses made
by Mr.* Rogers *the Martyr, left as a Legacy to his Children.*" It was sold by its printer,
Benjamin Harris, "at the London Coffee-House in Boston." Harris had arrived in
Boston in 1686 in a hurried departure from England and various brushes with the
authorities over his virulent anti-Catholicism. He is considered to be the primer's
compiler, and he had previously published, in London, several other little books
for children.[57]

By 1715, the *New-England Primer* was already being purloined by other printers. An advertisement of that date for a New London, Connecticut, imprint reads,
A Primer for the Colony of Connecticut, *or an Introduction to the true Reading of*
English. *To which is added, Milk for Babes*. The addition, *Milk for Babes*, was a
catechism written by the Boston minister John Cotton (the full title referring to
milk being drawn from the breasts of both testaments). It was one of two catechisms considered most suitable for children, for it was shorter than its rival, the
Westminster Catechism. Later versions of the *New-England Primer* would invariably add one or other of these two catechisms to their texts. The presence of the
catechism strongly suggests that the primer was aimed at parents as well as schoolmistresses or masters.[58]

The title of the oldest surviving edition of the *New-England Primer*, that of
1727, puts it firmly in the camp of reading instructional material: *The New-
England Primer Enlarged. For the more easy attaining the true Reading of ENGLISH.
To which is added, The Assembly of Divines CATECHISM* (that is, the Westminster
Catechism). After the introductory alphabets and the syllabary, it disposes of the
remainder of the pedagogical content in three pages. It presents words of one

syllable chosen for their familiarity rather than organizing them by spelling simi-larity: "child" and "face," "peace" and "pence." The following pages offer words in an increasing number of syllables, rising to words of five syllables, such as "For-ni-ca-ti-on" and "Ex-hor-ta-ti-on."[59]

One explanation for this mishmash is that this portion of the text was not in the original version. In fact, the next portion of the text is the famous picture alphabet, which by any logic should have preceded these spelling lists, not followed them. If the syllabary is a late addition, however, it is not very late: it seems highly likely that the spelling lists were already being printed in the 1690 edition, advertised as containing "more *Directions for Spelling.*"

By far the largest proportion of the primer is biblical or doctrinal. The practical section of the text, which lists the roman numerals as an aid to finding one's way around the Bible (a feature found in Eliot's *Indian Primer*), was dropped by half of the later editions of the *New-England Primer*. The catechism was always re-garded as an addition to the main body of the text. When all this is discounted, the remaining material is of most interest, for surely it is what made the *New-England Primer* the extraordinary publishing success that it would later become. Press runs could be huge: over the course of their partnership from 1749 to 1766, Franklin and his partner, David Hall, printed 37,100 copies. (Not one of them has survived.) Estimates of overall production vary, but some have suggested a figure of 3 million or more by the early nineteenth century.[60]

The best remembered feature of the *New-England Primer* is the picture alphabet. Each letter, illustrated by a crude little woodcut, is accompanied by a rhyming couplet. The picture alphabet follows the tradition of emblem books, in which a picture illustrates the literal aspects of some metaphorical point. Many of the images associated with the picture alphabet, however, as Patricia Crain has astutely pointed out, derive as much from the secular and market world as from a religious one, for their source is street and tavern signs. The picture that accompanies the letter *C*, for instance, is of a cat fiddling to three tiny mice, an image found in the late 1580s as the Cat and Fiddle inn sign. The Bible and Heart (linked together, by implication, in the primer's alphabet verses for the letter *H*) was another com-mon tavern sign in London, as were the Lion and the Lamb, the Royal Oak, and several others. Indeed, mid-eighteenth-century evangelicals found these images so crude that they were banished from later versions of the primer and replaced by clearly religious pictures and rhymes.[61]

Although the purpose of the images, Crain argues, is to cloak the inherent meaninglessness of the alphabetical letters on their own, the succession of words and images, she suggests, offer what might be called "an inventory of our sin-filled world." She also points to the oral aspects of the primer alphabet: children could not read the verses at this stage; instead, they would learn them by heart, associat-ing rhyme and image orally as well as visually in a culture that was primarily oral.[62]

Nonetheless, if we see the words as anchoring the image, rather than, as Crain suggests, the image anchoring the words, the effect of the alphabet within the overall context of the primer is not as frivolous as these images could have sug-gested on their own. Indeed, David Watters has maintained that the primer overall provides the "root metaphors of Calvinist theology": the angry father and the forgiving son, obedience and constriction, limitation of the self, and the dangers of disobedience to a father, all of which define a child's place in the world.[63]

Several themes run through the alphabet verses of the oldest extant edition of the *New-England Primer* of 1727: a Calvinist theology, the savagery of the natural world, the brevity of human life, the harshness of schooling for the young, and the theme of obedience.

The letter *A* presents the theological doctrine of original sin. In the illustration, a naked figure stands by a tree entwined by the serpent of temptation: "In *Adam's* Fall / We Sinned all." But the next letter immediately offers a path to redemption, through literacy: "Thy Life to mend / This *Book* Attend." The child is left with no doubt about which book is meant: it is pictured open, with "BIB" on one leaf and "LE" on the other. The concept of redemption through literacy is repeated in the woodcut for *H*, in which the cover of a closed book (clearly the Bible) is set side by side with a valentine-shaped heart: "My *Book* and *Heart* / Shall never part." The shifting use of personal pronouns highlights the importance to the child of reading. *We* all sinned with Adam (the child is part of the erring human race); *you* can mend your life with the Book (the adult reasserts authority, addressing the child in the second person); but *I* love to read (the restoration of the first person to the child intensifies the personal and emotional aspects of reading). If any child were tempted to ignore the importance of reading, the italicization of the word "Book" reinforces the point.

The natural world is savage at worst, indifferent to humanity at best: cats play then slay; dogs bite thieves at night; and as the eagle soars out of sight its savage intent is implicit. Lions, lambs, and nightingales are lit by the moon. Yet even the largest of the creatures is subject to God's awesome power: the letter *W* informs the child, "*Whales* in the Sea / God's Voice obey."

Human life is fragile. Children are constantly reminded of the inevitability of death and the brevity of life. The letter *G* depicts an hourglass: "As runs the *Glass* / Mans life doth pass." The illustration for *T* shows a skeleton holding a scythe in one hand and an hour glass in the other. Wealth and fame are no protection: "*Time* cuts down all / Both great and small." *X* illustrates the same message, but here it is brought far closer to the reading child: "*Xerxes* the great did die, / And so must you & I." Then the letter *Y* drives the point home: "*Youth* forward slips / Death soonest nips." A skeleton holds an arrow—symbol perhaps of death by accident or willful intent—directly at the head of a small figure that can only be a child.

In keeping with this grim view of life, and perhaps reinforcing the comfort attentive children can get from reading the Bible, the letter *F* is accompanied by the verse, "The Idle *Fool* / Is whipt at School."

Another theme is disobedience and its dangers. Watters interprets the last half of the alphabet as a litany of acts of disobedience against authority of all kinds— political, as in *O*, where King Charles II is saved from his disobedient subjects by a leafy oak tree, and religious, as in *P*, where the woodcut shows a cock crowing and Peter's terrible realization that he has betrayed Jesus. It is the first reference in the picture alphabet to the New Testament, and again, man is sinning. By the letter *U* we are back to sin, this time the sin of coveting your neighbor's wife: David sought to kill Uriah because of the latter's beautiful wife.

Biblical allusions are overwhelmingly to stories in the Old Testament. Not until the last letter is there another reference to the possibility of Christian salvation, and even this is veiled. A little head pokes out of the leafy crown of a tree: it is Zacheus, who, as short as any child, has climbed up a tree in order to see Jesus. Other pictures of trees occur in the alphabet, but the depiction of Zacheus's tree resembles the oak that saved King Charles II; just as that tree saved the king, so does the Christian tree, or cross, save Zacheus, who "sees" Christ in a spiritual as well as literal sense. The alphabet, then, has run the gamut from the apple tree of Adam and original sin to the tree of the cross and redemption.[64]

Despite the gentler tone of the verse for the last letter of the alphabet, the overwhelming impression conveyed by the alphabet verses is that of danger and death. Animals may indulge their wild nature, but man does so at his peril. Virtually the only ray of hope emanates from reading the Bible, which is also pictured as the only legitimate source of pleasure (unlike, say, David's lust for Uriah's wife).

The next entries in the primer follow this introduction with a certain grim logic. The "Dutiful Child" promises to honor the king and his (or her) parents. In the first person, he undertakes to obey his superiors and submit to his elders; to love his friends and hate no man. "I will learn my Catechism. / I will keep the Lord's Day Holy." The promises end with a vision of God's omnipotence and perhaps an allusion to hell made more potent by its being italicized: "I will reverence God's Sanctuary, For our GOD is a *consuming Fire*." Not until the Alphabet of Lessons for Youth does the primer present Christ again, with the letter *C*: "COme unto CHRIST all ye that labour and are heavy laden, and He will give you rest." But allusions to the hope of redemption, such as "SAlvation belongeth to the Lord," alternate with allusions to God's angry punishment: "LIars shall have their part in the lake which burns with fire and brimstone." Furthermore, children are naturally irrational but may be improved by corporal punishment: "FOolishness is bound up in the heart of a Child, but the rod of Correction shall drive it far from him." The author hints that as the child grows older he will grow spiritually stronger: "YOung Men ye have overcome the wicked one." Feminine pronouns or references to young women never appear.

After a section of doctrinal content—the Lord's prayer, the creed, and the Ten Commandments—there follows yet another set of instructions on dutifulness, this time specifically toward one's parents. Scriptural quotations support the point. It is pleasing to the Lord that children should obey their parents; ravens pluck out the eyes of those who do not. The obligation of childhood is a lifelong experience: when parents are old and frail and vulnerable, children are still to look up to them: "My Son, help thy Father in his Age, and grieve him not as long as he liveth. And if his Understanding fail, have patience with him."

Then comes another verse, again in the first person of the child. Reminding children that their youth is no protection against death, it is set in the ancient fourteen-syllable ballad meter of the Bay Psalm Book: "I in the Burying Place may

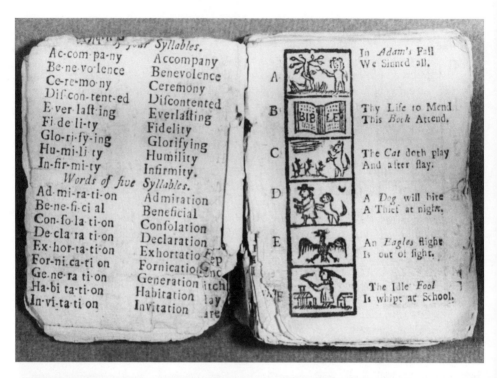

Words of four Syllables.

Ac-com-pa-ny	Accompany
Be-ne-vo-lence	Benevolence
Ce-re-mo-ny	Ceremony
Dif-con-tent-ed	Difcontented
E-ver-laft-ing	Everlafting
Fi-de-li-ty	Fidelity
Glo-ri-fy-ing	Glorifying
Hu-mi-li-ty	Humility
In-fir-mi-ty	Infirmity.

Words of five Syllables.

Ad-mi-ra-ti-on	Admiration
Be-ne-fi-ci-al	Beneficial
Con-fo-la-ti-on	Confolation
De-cla-ra-ti-on	Declaration
Ex-hor-ta-ti-on	Exhortation
For-ni-ca-ti-on	Fornication
Ge-ne-ra-ti-on	Generation
Ha-bi-ta-ti-on	Habitation
In-vi-ta-ti-on	Invitation

A — In *Adam's* Fall We Sinned all.

B — Thy Life to Mend This *Book* Attend.

C — The *Cat* doth play And after flay.

D — A *Dog* will bite A Thief at night.

E — An *Eagles* flight Is out of fight.

F — The Idle *Fool* Is whipt at School.

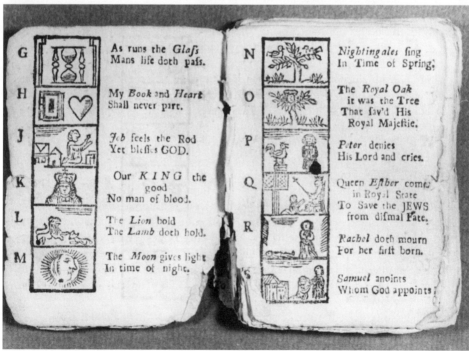

G — As runs the *Glafs* Mans life doth pafs.

H — My *Book* and *Heart* Shall never part.

J — *Job* feels the Rod Yet bleffes GOD.

K — Our *KING* the good No man of blood.

L — The *Lion* bold The *Lamb* doth hold.

M — The *Moon* gives light In time of night.

N — *Nightingales* fing In Time of Spring.

O — The *Royal Oak* it was the Tree That fav'd His Royal Majeftie.

P — *Peter* denies His Lord and cries.

Q — Queen *Efther* comes in Royal State To Save the JEWS from difmal Fate.

R — *Rachel* doth mourn For her firft born.

S — *Samuel* anoints Whom God appoints.

FIGURES 5–7. Word lists, picture alphabet, and verses, from a 1727 edition of the *New-England Primer* (Boston: S. Kneeland and T. Green). OPPOSITE, TOP: *A* through *F*. The page preceding the alphabet lists words of four and five syllables, both divided and undivided. Five is the highest number of syllables reached by the primer. OPPOSITE, BOTTOM: *G* through *S*. ABOVE: *T* through *Z*, and facing page. (Courtesy, American Antiquarian Society)

see / Graves shorter there than I." The "I" in the first two lines stand like gravestones, David Watters suggests, at the head and foot of the grave in which self is obliterated.[65]

Yet another verse reinforces the concept of the brevity of life and the urgency of finding a road to salvation. When the child awakes, he is to be aware of the acute fragility of his life; as he lies down to sleep, this slumber could be his last. Trees figured in the picture alphabet; now the metaphor for a child's life is that of a leaf falling from a tree in a blast of wind. In Watters's interpretation, the verse "compresses the root metaphors of life and death, day and night."

> Awake, arise, behold thou hast
> Thy Life a Leaf, thy Breath a Blast,
>   At night lye down prepar'd to have
> Thy sleep, thy death, thy bed, thy grave.[66]

The exhortation of John Rogers to his children, billed as an "addition" in the 1690 advertisement of the *New-England Primer*, appeared in virtually all subsequent editions. Also written in the ballad form, the poem was originally printed in John Foxe's *Book of Martyrs*.[67] The exhortation is accompanied by a picture of Rogers at the stake, with his wife and ten children ("one at her Breast") looking on.

The father leaves a list of instructions for his children that are perfectly in tune with the earlier ones in the primer. The children are to keep God always before their eyes; to abhor the "Whore of Rome" (Catholicism); to honor their dear mother, "Be always ready for her help, / and let her not decay." They should feed the poor, clothe the naked, and avoid lust and pride, "But always have before your eyes / that you are born to die." Rogers explicitly says that he hopes to be saved by the sufferings of Christ and offers more hope than the childish reader has received so far: "Why then should I fear Deaths grim look, / since Christ for me did die?" Here, then, is an image of a father willing to sacrifice himself just as Christ sacrificed himself for others.

> Come welcome Death, the end of fears,
>   I am prepar'd to die
> Those earthly Flames will send my Soul,
>   up to the Lord on high.

Rogers offers the hope of a reunion in heaven and a defense from helplessness on earth:

> Farewel my Children to the World,
>   where you must yet remain,
> The Lord of Hosts be your defence
>   till we do meet again.

The metaphor of consuming fire that has been associated with God earlier in the primer is transmuted to a means of deliverance. The fiery image is reversed: flames would send this father to heaven, not to the furnace and brimstone of hell.

Ironically, then, John Rogers's exhortation, despite its images of physical torment, actually offer some consolation and hope to the unrelieved oppression of the rest of the *New-England Primer*. Fatherhood has become sacrifice; redemption is foregrounded. Moreover, childhood is being redefined. The dependency promoted so intensely by the early portions of the primer is replaced in this poem by responsibility, as the children are asked to protect their mother and take their father's place in charitable endeavors. The metaphors in the poem suggest that one generation is bequeathing to the next not only its duties but also its autonomy, with the passage of time. All this was part of the Congregational values that parents wished to transmit to their children.[68]

Godly and Ungodly Books for Children

By the close of the seventeenth century, schoolbooks were not the only books available to young New Englanders. The anonymous *Protestant Tutor for Children*, another Benjamin Harris imprint, was reprinted in Boston in 1685 (a year before Harris arrived) from its English original of 1679. This tiny book is a Protestant catechism, teaching children to avoid such Roman Catholic practices as abstaining from meat on Fridays. It invokes scriptural justification for all its pronouncements. One of the questions and answers encapsulates the Protestant approach toward reading the scriptures:

> Q. *Is it for the common People to read the Scriptures?*
> A. Yes, Act. 17.11, 1 . . . they searched the Scripture, whether those things were so.

In an attempt to make the work more appealing to children, the printer, Samuel Green, had also added the verses attributed to the martyr John Rogers that would reappear in the *New-England Primer*.[69]

In contrast, Benjamin Keach's *Instructions for Children, or the Child's and Youth's Delight*, published in London in 1693 and reprinted by William Bradford in New York two years later, actually contains material of the kind found in spelling books. Its three pages of reading instruction include "Easie Syllables" and pronouncements on the impossibility of isolating the sound of a consonant: "Consonants, without Vowels, will make no sound, nor can they be pronounced." A short dictionary appears at the end of the book. The bulk of the text, however, is on how children should behave. Girls make a rare appearance in this book, and it is immediately linked to their sexuality and their propensity to read the wrong kind of book: the Devil, they are told, teaches them "to get Rowling Eyes, to cast amorous Glances, to read Love-Romances."[70]

Other works in print before 1700 held a particular appeal to the young even though they were aimed mainly at adults. Chief among these was Michael Wigglesworth's poem the "Day of Doom." Wigglesworth had served as the minister of Maldon, not far from Boston, from 1655 until his death in 1705. As Cotton Mather remarked in his funeral sermon on Wigglesworth, Wigglesworth wrote several works for the "Edification of such Readers as are for Truth's, dressed up in a *Plain Meeter* . . . and one of them, *The Day of Doom*, which has been often Reprinted in both *Englands*, may perhaps find our children, till the Day it self arrive."[71] The "Day of Doom" portrays the final Day of Judgment. Christ's coldly analytical reasoning presented in the poem made it intellectually challenging to its seventeenth-century readers; its vivid portrayal of hell fire made it compelling; and, it must be added, its meter and the preponderance of monosyllables made it easier for children to read aloud.

Wiggleworth's work (printed from 1662 on) is written in the fourteen-syllable ballad meter that was most familiar to New Englanders as the meter of the Bay Psalm Book and that would be used in the *New-England Primer* in the poem attributed to John Rogers. Within the traditional *a / a / b / b* rhyming structure,

Wigglesworth had added an internal rhyme, effectively tripling the number of rhymes—and adding a wealth of monosyllables. The esthetic result, as the rhymes and rhythms accumulate over the stanzas, is a kind of unrelenting drum roll, as if for mourners marching somberly in a funeral procession.

The "Day of Doom" opens: "Still was the night, Serene and Bright, when all Men sleeping lay; / Calm was the season, and carnal reason, thought so't would last for ay." The almost elegiac quality of the opening lines swiftly turns sinister, as a dazzling light turns night into day. Appalled, men realize that this is Christ's final coming: "Before his face the Heav'ns gave place, and Skies are rent asunder. / With mighty voice, and hideous noise, more terrible than Thunder."[72]

Christ sits in judgment over the living and the dead, dividing the saved from the damned. He permits a spokesman for each group of the wicked, despite their being already condemned, to offer an argument in his group's defense, an argument that Christ then demolishes by merciless logic. Several of these arguments relate to literacy. One sinner offers a kind of plea of idiocy: that the Bible was too difficult to understand and that therefore he and others like him should be held blameless: "How could we fools be led by Rules, so far beyond our ken, / Which to explain did so much pain, and puzzle wisest men?" Christ makes short shrift of this defense. In fact, he suggests, the sinners could have read portions of the Bible on the run.

> Was all my word abstruse and hard?
>> the Judge then answered:
> It did contain much truth so plain,
>> you might have ran and read.
> But what was hard you never car'd
>> to know, nor studied.
> And things that were most plain and clear
>> you never practised.[73]

The clear message is that the Bible is accessible at some level to all.

One further, and prosaic, point must be added about the "Day of Doom." To those who believed that longer words were harder words, the vocabulary, if not the concepts, of the "Day of Doom" was ideally suited to readers at a fairly early stage in their development. Because of the constraints of the fourteen-syllable metrical form, intensified by the restrictions of Wigglesworth's internal rhymes, the work is composed largely of monosyllables and bisyllables. (About 84 percent of the first ten stanzas, for instance, are in monosyllables.) Since monosyllables were the first kind of syllables that children were taught in the reading instructional sequence, few children would have had trouble pronouncing the text.

Another poem, addressed explicitly to young men, was Benjamin Keach's *War with the Devil or the Young Man's Conflict with the Powers of Darkness . . . To which is added, An Appendix, containing a Dialogue between an Old Apostate and a Young Professor . . . chiefly intended for the Instruction of the Younger Sort*, imported into Boston from the 1680s on.[74] *War with the Devil* skillfully leads its readers through the classic steps of conversion: conviction of sin, false hope of salvation, despair, and finally complete submission to the Savior. This lengthy poem has a happy ending, but added to it was another poem that does not: a dialogue between an "Old Apostate" and a "Young Professor" (presumably the newly converted youth of the preceding poem). Not until this second poem is there a reference to the role literacy plays in conversion. The apostate claims that the convert is foolish to trust scriptures that have been translated into English. "Thou art unlearn'd," he charges, "the Scriptures dost not know, / But wrestest them unto thy overthrow." Using the first three letters of the alphabet as a metaphor for entrance into book learning, the young professor identifies the latter as valueless if it does not include the fundamentals of Christianity. He redefines what it means to be "unlearned":

That man's unlearn'd, who never learned hath
The *A B C* of the true Christian Faith."

By the end of the dialogue, the apostate is inconsolable. If there is indeed a God, he will never show him mercy. The sinner is doomed to "lie / Broyling in flames to all Eternity."[75]

The "Day of Doom" and the *War with the Devil* were both among the steady sellers of the late seventeenth century and available to the young, at least to the young of Boston. A similar poem, the "Dialog between Youth, Christ and the Devil," would be included in some late editions of the *New-England Primer* after 1760.[76]

A few books were addressed directly to children. The most important of these was James Janeway's *Token for Children*, published in two parts in London in 1671 and 1672. An immediate publishing success in England, it was probably exported to New England soon after its appearance. Increase Mather (father of Cotton Mather), in the course of a sermon to his Boston congregation in 1677, mentioned *A Token* as a book "which many of you have in your houses." In 1700 Cotton Mather added a supplement, which he titled *A Token for the Children of New-England.* The two parts and their New England supplement were published together in Boston in 1700. The work was an archetypal steady seller: Sarah Osborn, a devout Congregationalist who lived in Newport, Rhode Island, read aloud from it in 1766 to the black and white children gathered at the large revivalist prayer meetings she held on Sundays in her home; and it was still being printed in Boston in 1771, by then with additional New England children.[77]

Janeway's book followed the well-established tradition of didactic works that were, in essence, conversion manuals for children. (Experience Mayhew had undoubtedly drawn on them or on Janeway's work itself in his portrayal of the converted Indian children of Martha's Vineyard.)[78] Its topic is the uplifting example of children who died young but convinced of their salvation, and it presents brief biographies of thirteen such children, six girls and seven boys, who died between 1632 and 1670. Janeway addresses his young readers directly: "Would you not do any thing in the World rather than be thrown into Hell Fire?" He explained the purpose of his book. "You may now hear (my dear Lambs) what other good Children have done. . . . May you not read how dutiful they were to their Parents? How diligent at their Books? how ready to learn the Scripture, and their Catechisms?" His book is designed to tell "how ho[lil]y" these children lived, "how dearly they were loved, how joyfully they died."[79]

The thirteen children in *A Token*, all aged between four and fourteen when they died, are portrayed as models of the young Christian reader. Every child over five was not only a reader but a reader who chose books over play, just as Janeway enjoins his young readers. Anne Lane "could not endure the company of common Children, nor play, but was quite above all those things which most Children are taken with; her business was to be reading, praying, discoursing about the things of God."[80]

The messages conveyed in Janeway's descriptions are perhaps not always quite what he intended. True, pious children were early and good readers, who learned "quickly" and "exactly," often at an unusually early age. Nonetheless, there is more than one suggestion that some carried their reading to excess. John Harvy, for instance, was "able to read distinctly, before most Children are able to know their Letters." When he developed sore eyes at the age of six, he was forbidden to go to school and ordered by the doctor to stop reading. John refused and stood by the window to get enough light to read the Bible and "good Books." He was "so greedy of reading the Scriptures and took so much delight in them," that he would scarcely leave himself enough time to get dressed.[81]

Reading, then, was not a passionless affair for these children. Because of their involvement with the subject matter, reading caused both joy and grief. Significantly, Janeway mentions these two emotions in almost the same breath. For one little girl, "Her Book was her Delight . . . and many Times she was so strangely affected in reading of the Scriptures, that she would burst out into Tears, and would hardly be pacified, so greatly was she taken with Christ's Sufferings." For John Sudlow, a similar absorption in what he read was accompanied by an urgent wish to comprehend what he was reading. "He could not endure to read any thing over slightly, but whatsoever he read, he dwelt upon it, laboured to understand it throughly and remember it." If he failed to understand a passage, he would ask one of his parents to explain it to him.[82] Absorbed in their reading, identifying with those they read about, struggling to understand what they read—these children are portrayed as regarding reading as an activity that held intense personal meaning.

Janeway recommends another work about godly children: Thomas White's *A Little Book for Little Children*. Reproduced in Boston in 1702, it is an advice book that also includes exemplary young lives. Many of them, however, are from ancient times, and some of the stories include descriptions of torture. The work never matched Janeway's success in the colonies, nor did it deserve to. Like Janeway, White included advice on reading: "When thou canst Read, read no Ballads and foolish Books, but read the Bible." He provided a reading list of other books, such as Arthur Dent's *Plain Mans Pathway to Heaven*, Lewis Bayly's *The Practice of Piety*, and Foxe's *Book of Martyrs*, all of them designed for adults.[83]

By the second decade of the eighteenth century, another genre had made its entrance into New England: pious autobiographies of young converts, published posthumously. New England sons could be given imported copies of books such as *The Life of Mr. Tho[mas] Beard*, who had died in 1710 at the age of seventeen, leaving an autobiography that was published by a family friend. From the age of three to twelve, Beard remembered, "there was little or nothing but Vanity." He had "Books more for a Shew, than Service; I was covetous of Books, but seldom read them"—a tantalizing glimpse of books as trophy objects. All this had changed by the time of his death.[84]

Or a parent wishing to give his daughter a book had recourse to Thomas Reynolds's *Practical Religion Exemplify'd in the Lives of Mrs. Mary Terry . . . and Mrs. Clissould*, reprinted in Boston in 1712 only one year after its appearance in London. Mary, like Thomas Beard, died in her seventeenth year. She learned to write at the age of eleven and jotted down the main points of sermons. Later she learned shorthand for the same purpose. She also wrote extracts from scripture under headings like "God's Covenant Promises" and "Of Humility and Meekness." Here was an exemplary girl who used not only her reading but her writing in the service of piety.[85]

These works, however, were not the only ones available to the young who liked to read. Already, in Boston, there was a subversive counterculture: books that were far from spiritual in intent had been creeping into the Boston marketplace. In England, the Restoration of the monarchy in 1660 had reintroduced much of the frivolity that had been stamped out under the Protectorate, and this change in society was reflected in English publications. Those in control of the New England presses could prevent the domestic publication of these romances, jestbooks, and chivalrous tales but not their importation.

Once again, the 1700 inventory of the stock left by the Boston bookseller Michael Perry is informative. In addition to the copies of the *New-England Primer* and the hornbooks, there were five copies of one title and three copies of another, both priced at eight pence. (This was twopence more than Latin schoolbooks, such as Johann Amos Comenius's *Janua Linguarum*, and the same price as an edition of *Sententiae Pueriles* or Ovid's *Tristia*.) The two titles are those of "histories": *Fortunatus* and the *Seven Wise Masters of Rome* (also known as the *Seven Sages of Rome*).[86]

Publications of the American presses give no hint that New England children or young people at the close of the seventeenth century could possibly want, or be permitted to purchase, any publications other than religious ones. Yet their Old England counterparts were able to buy, very cheaply, a mass of material that was aimed at those who were unsophisticated readers, young or old.

"Chapbooks," the nineteenth-century term for books described in contemporary broadsides or advertisements as "chapmen's books," were little unbound books that peddlers hawked around the English countryside throughout the seventeenth century from village to village along with ribbons and pins, brooches and gloves.[87] A London trade-list published in 1689 categorized them as small godly books, small merry books, double-books, and histories. They ranged in price from twopence for the "small godly" or "merry" books to sixpence for the much longer histories.[88] How many of these reached the American market and were reprinted on American presses is not clear. One "penny godly" that did unquestionably penetrate New England culture was the tale of Francis Spira. Spira was a Catholic living in early sixteenth-century Venice who was attracted to the message of free grace preached by Martin Luther. When his family put tremendous pressure on him to recant his conversion to Protestantism, he did so, but until the day he died he was tormented by the memory of an inner voice at his recantation telling him he was damned for denying Christ. The universal appeal of this tale is suggested by Pastorius's having a copy in his library.[89]

Other chapbooks known to reach New England included both steady sellers and contemporary imprints. Benjamin Franklin, born in 1706, enjoyed John Bunyan's *Pilgrim's Progress* (one of the few books children were encouraged to read that had a plot and adventures), and the first books he bought with his own money were Bunyan's works "in separate little volumes" (clearly chapmen's books). He sold these to finance his purchase of Richard Burton's *Historical Collections*: "small chapmen's books, 40 or 50 in all." "Richard Burton" or "R.B." was the pseudonym of Nathaniel Crouch, a London printer who published much material in the 1680s and 1690s aimed at a popular audience. He had a series on the history of Britain, with titles such as *England[']s Monarchs* and *Historical Remarks of London* (the latter presumably Franklin's purchase). His *Youth's Divine Pastime*, in its third edition in London in 1691, consists of stories taken from the Bible: as Gillian Avery remarks, they seem to be as salacious as he could find, ranging from the Levite's dismemberment of his concubine to the incest of Lot.[90]

"Histories," stories such as *Fortunatus*, unquestionably reached the American market in small quantities, as the inventory of Perry's stock shows. Madam Knight, who described her hair-raising journey in 1704 from Boston to New York on dreadful roads, showed an easy familiarity with such tales. Of her guide, who regaled her with stories of the dangers he had escaped, she remarked that "Remembring the Hero's in Parismus and the Knight of the Oracle, I didn't know but I had mett w[i]th a Prince disguis'd." These stories had universal appeal: children, Cotton Mather conceded, "are naturally taken with Histories."[91]

Perhaps even a few "merries" crept in, despite their often scatological content, for in 1722 Cotton Mather felt obliged to warn young women that there were "bad" books being sold openly in Boston:

> Books . . . seen and sold at Noon-day, among us; which I cannot be faithful unto GOD, and unto you, if I do not forewarn you against the Reading of them. There are Plays, and Songs, and Novels, and Romances, and foolish and filthy Jests, and Poetry prostituted unto Execrable Ribaldry.

Boston, in short, was bustling with ungodly books.[92]

But how much access did urban children have to this alternative culture? And did they take from the *New-England Primer* and similar "godly" books the lessons that adults intended them to take? To answer these questions we have to turn to the literacy experiences of actual children. Two deeply devout fathers—one of them Cotton Mather himself and the other Samuel Sewall—documented in their diaries the literacy experiences of their children. They reveal how their children reacted to the messages of damnation and salvation that the *New-England Primer* and other texts promulgated, and they permit us to learn how, as parents, they mediated between messages of despair and Christ's promise of eternal life.

4

Death and Literacy in Two Devout Boston Families

At noon in Boston, on a January Sabbath in 1690, Samuel Sewall informed his young son Sam that their nine-year-old relative, Richard Dummer, had just died of smallpox. Sam's father told him that he needed to prepare for death and that he should "endeavour really to pray when he said over the Lord's Prayer." Eleven-year-old Sam, munching an apple, "seem'd not much to mind." When, however, he came to say the Our Father, he "burst out into a bitter Cry, and when I askt what was the matter and he could speak, he burst out into a bitter Cry and said he was afraid he should die." His father tried to console him as best he could. They prayed together, and "read Scriptures comforting against death, as, O death where is thy sting, &c."[1]

Several years later, again in an icy January, Samuel Sewall returned home late one evening from a trip to Cambridge. He was met in the entry hall by his wife, Hannah, who told him that their daughter Betty (who had just passed her fourteenth birthday) had taken the family by surprise. Earlier she had appeared dejected, but then "a little after dinner she burst out into an amazing cry, which caus'd all the family to cry too: Her Mother ask'd the reason; she gave none; at last said she was afraid she should goe to Hell, her Sins were not pardon'd." When her parents tried to track down the reason for this outburst, Sewall pinpointed a sermon that he had read aloud to the family a week earlier. Its text was John 7.34, "Ye shall seek me and shall not find me." It was hearing this that had first "wounded" her, he realized. A verse in the sermon also taken from John, "Ye shall seek me and shall die in your sins," her father said, "ran in her mind, and terrified her greatly." Betty had stayed home the day before her outburst, and her fear had increased when she read a sermon by Cotton Mather, "Why hath Satan filled thy heart." She was in a state of such distress that the family summoned their minister to pray with her.[2]

Only a month later, Betty came to her father, as Sewall reports, "almost as soon as I was up and tells me the disquiet she had when waked; told me [she] was afraid should goe to Hell, was like [Francis] Spira, not Elected."[3] The grim tale of Spira, the Protestant convert who renounced his faith and believed himself damned for doing so, was clearly haunting her. Her father sent her away to relatives in Salem for a three months' change of air, and he visited her while she was away. Her spirits were not much better. "I set Betty to read Ezek. 37." ("The hand of the LORD was upon me . . . and set me down in the midst of the valley which was full of bones.")

112

This renewed reference to death, even though it also contains a message of resurrection, caused Betty to weep "so that [she] can hardly read." "I talk with her," Sewall says, "and she tells me of the various Temptations she had; as that was a Reprobat, Loved not God's people as she should."[4]

At the heart of all these scenes lay two realities: death and literacy. Sam was frightened by the death of his young relative; Betty's fears of death and hell occurred within a year of two deaths, that of the children's maternal grandmother, Hannah Hull, in whose house they all lived, who had died unexpectedly the preceding June, and that of Dame Walker, an old family friend and the children's teacher, who had died in December. The second reality was the children's ability to read: with Sam, his father turned to scriptural text for messages of consolation; for Betty, reading the Scriptures and sermons had actually been the cause of her distress.

Betty's despair used to be cited by scholars as the quintessential example of the dire effects on children of Puritan belief: an unnatural terror of death and damnation. She was certainly not the only child to be so affected. Elijah Corlet, born in 1609, remembered how at the age of four or five his father used to ask him "whether I went alone and prayed to God to bless me and to pardon my sins and save my soul from hell; and I sadly remember how . . . I loathed to hear of such things."[5]

More recently, however, other scholars have suggested that it was not unreasonable for devout parents to remind their children of the possibility of early death. According to Calvinist orthodoxy, all humans are sinful, including children, because of the original sin of Adam. Yet—notwithstanding the examples of converted children in James Janeway's *Token for Children*—it was unusual for a child to experience conversion, so Puritan parents might well have been haunted by the possibility of their children's dying early and unconverted. Anxiety for one's children, as well, of course, as for oneself, was made the more acute by the doctrines of divine election and the inscrutability of God. The first holds that God has predetermined which souls will be saved and which damned; the second that one can never be sure which category one belongs to, because God conceals his divine plan.[6]

These parental fears were intensified by the high rate of child mortality. Although those living in rural areas in seventeenth-century New England could expect to lose fewer children than those living in England or in the disease-prone Chesapeake area of the southern colonies, up to three children out of ten died in colonial New England before reaching the age of one, and nearly one in three before reaching twenty-one. During the eighteenth century, these figures changed for the worse. Mortality in towns was always higher, and large seaports like Boston were especially vulnerable. As trade increased, diseases borne across the water multiplied. Boston was particularly susceptible to successive epidemics of diseases such as measles and smallpox, both of which were usually fatal to infants and young children.[7]

Schoolbooks and the scriptural texts that formed the bulk of the reading of a godly household continually reminded New England children of the dangers of dying young and unregenerate, as we have just seen. But the books themselves can never really tell us how their young readers reacted to them. We must turn to diaries, therefore, for glimpses of how children responded. Two diaries written by Bostonians, spanning roughly the last quarter of the seventeenth century and the first quarter of the eighteenth, illuminate children's reactions to print and, more generally, the role that literacy played in the heart of a devout Puritan family. These same diaries also enable us to reexamine some of the assumptions commonly held about how orthodox parents used print in talking with their children about aspects of their faith, particularly those that related to death.

The diaries were written by two of the most eminent men in turn-of-the-century Boston. One was written by the merchant, later judge, Samuel Sewall, and the other by Cotton Mather, who became minister of the North Church in 1685. (Sewall, as we saw earlier, had supported a third edition of the Indian Bible; Mather had sabotaged it.) Sewall, born in 1652, kept his diary from the age of twenty-two until a few months before his death on the first day of January 1730. Cotton Mather, eleven years younger, wrote his diary from 1681 until 1725. Some gaps exist in the surviving diaries of both men.

Samuel Sewall and Cotton Mather shared the same intellectual and mental worlds. Both men were Harvard graduates, both kept up-to-date with British publications, both remained fluent in Latin. (They even both resorted to Latin in their diaries for their most private comments.) They were equally committed to the Congregational way. Mather's faith led him to practice it professionally as a minister; Sewall's remained personal and much more private. Both saw a direct link between their own sinfulness and family tragedy. Both were skilled at interpreting happenings metaphorically, as divine signs. In this they resembled all devout Puritans, who constantly attempted to decipher the meanings of natural and man-made events.[8] And both, along with other Congregationalists, interpreted the Old Testament as prefiguring the New and believed, above all, that the Bible offered lessons that were immediately applicable to their everyday lives.[9]

The two men also had much in common in terms of their family life. Both loved their first wives deeply and suffered when they were widowed. Both men fathered large numbers of children: Samuel had fourteen, all of them by his first wife, Hannah; Mather had fifteen: his first wife, Abigail, bore him nine and his second wife, Elizabeth, six. Of these children, only six, for each man, lived much beyond the age of two. The six Sewall children who survived their infancy were Samuel, or Sam (born 1678), Hannah (1680), Elizabeth, always called "Betty" as a child (1681), Joseph (1688), Mary (1691), and Judith (1702). Surviving children born to Mather and Abigail were Katharin ("Katy") (1689), Abigail ("Nibby") (1694), Hannah ("Nanny" or "Nancy") (1697), and Increase ("Creasy") (1699). Those born to Mather and Elizabeth who survived infancy were Elizabeth ("Liza") (1704) and Samuel ("Sammy") (1706).[10]

There, however, the resemblance ends, even apart from an eleven-year difference in age. Although both kept diaries, their diary-writing and their literacy in general took different forms. Mather was the author of hundreds of books; Sewall the author of one, along with a pamphlet on slavery, and a few broadsides and elegies.

The two men moved in slightly different social circles. Mather was occupied with a myriad pastoral obligations and many others of his own devising. His few forays into public life were intermittent and unsuccessful. Sewall, in contrast, was closely involved with the political and juridical events of Boston until his death.[11]

The differences in the two men's diaries reflect the differences in the men. Sewall's diary is about the external events in which he took part; Mather's is about his own interior life. Two excerpts from entries made on the same day give a glimpse of how the diaries differ in tone and content. On Saturday, March 14, 1702, Sewall wrote: "*at 5 p.m.* Capt. John Alden expired; Going to visit him, I happened to be there at the time." Mather's lengthy entry for the same day begins: "It was my Purpose to have sett apart this Day, as I did one the last Week, for Prayer, praeparatory to the Celebration of the *Eucharist*, which is to morrow, by my vile Hand to be adminstred. But because I preached Yesterday, and was afraid of over-doing, unto a Trespass against the sixth Commandment, I omitted it." But perhaps the contrast between the two diaries is best illustrated by the number of times each man mentions the other. Mather appears in Sewall's diary almost three hundred times; Sewall appears in Mather's diary only three.[12]

Another difference between the two men that is revealed in their diaries involves their approaches to educating their children. Sewall left education to the schools. Mather, who also sent his children to various schools, took a keen interest in their education at home and taught them literacy himself.

Both diaries, however, make clear the vital role of literacy in the transmission to their young of the two men's religious beliefs and ethical principles. They also reveal how the Sewall and Mather children interpreted texts and applied their messages to themselves. Every child we meet in these two families was an active reader and constructor of meaning, just like his or her father.

Literacy in the Sewall Household

Samuel Sewall cherished books. His diary entries are replete with examples of his reading and of his gifts of books to others. As David Hall has suggested, for Samuel, books "acquired ritual significance in a complex web of mutual caring and protection." His diary writing was part of this ritual, an attempt to order what he experienced.[13]

By the time Sam emerges in his father's diaries, he could read well. His father made a note, in May 1686, of the first time that Sam, then not quite eight years old, read aloud from the Bible during the family's twice daily prayer sessions: "My Son reads to me Isa. 22 in his course this morning." (Reading "in course" meant reading the portion of scripture that was set for that day. Reading "out of course" occurred when the father or master of the family wished a particular text to be read for some special reason.)[14]

Betty was also eight when she was called upon to read Isaiah 24 during family prayers. It is a chapter of dire predictions: "Behold, the LORD maketh the earth empty, and maketh it waste, and turneth it upside down, and scattereth abroad the inhabitants thereof. . . . All joy is darkened, the mirth of the land is gone. . . . Fear,

FIGURE 8. Portrait of the Boston merchant and judge Samuel Sewall (1652–1730). (Courtesy, American Antiquarian Society)

and the pit, and the snare are upon thee, O inhabitant of the earth." It upset her enough for her father to remark on it and on his own reaction: "It falls to my Daughter Elisabeth's Share to read the 24. of Isaiah, which she doth with many Tears not being very well, and the Contents of the Chapter, and Sympathy with her draw Tears from me also."[15]

Joseph was nine when we first learn of his taking part in reading aloud at the family devotions. He did so on Christmas, a day that caused tension between Anglicans and Congregationalists. Like all good Congregationalists, Sewall deplored the Anglican celebration of Christmas as a festival. The family read "in course" the fourteenth, fifteenth, and sixteenth Psalms. The fourth verse of Psalm 16 reads, "Their sorrows shall be multiplied that hasten after another god." Sewall seized the occasion to discourage his children "from Christmas-keeping, and charged them to forbear." "Joseph tells me," the diary records, "that though most of the Boys went to the Church yet he went not." This instance of resistance to peer pressure and of loyalty to the family's beliefs was rewarded. Joseph now finally took his turn at psalm reading (previously the prerogative of Sam). Here, Sewall was enlarging upon the significance of the scriptural reading for the benefit of his entire family. He was treating a particular verse as if it were a text for a sermon and showing his children its practical application.[16]

Family prayers and readings were a daily routine, yet these entries about the three older children are almost the only notations that Sewall makes of his children's participation in the family's devotions. The exceptions are the family prayers that immediately preceded the funeral of the six of his and Hannah's children who died in infancy. For almost all of these, Sewall recorded with great precision which child read, and what passage each read. That he did so is highly significant. In this context, the family routine was transfigured into an intensely meaningful ritual.

In general, the Puritans had deliberately rid themselves of much of the ritual practiced in the Anglican Church: there were no set forms of prayer printed in any prayer book, no celebration of Christmas, and no marriage sacrament. The only two sacraments of the Congregational Church were baptism and the Lord's supper. Perhaps the starkest break with mainstream Anglican practice had occurred in the context of death. The fate of the soul, in Calvinist doctrine, had already been determined, according to the concept of election. Puritans had of course rejected as idolatrous all Roman Catholic doctrines of purgatory, the state believed to precede God's final allocation of the soul to heaven or hell. As a result, holding a service in a church for the dead, offering up prayers for the soul of the dead (which continued to be the practice of the Anglican Church)—these, in the Puritan view, were heathenish customs, in that they presupposed that human prayers could alter God's judgment upon the soul once it had parted from the body. Once a person had died, the only prayers appropriate were those for the living. Funeral sermons, where the deceased was important enough to warrant one, were also initially aimed only at the living. They were preached not at the graveside but at the next Sabbath or the Thursday lecture. Similarly, funeral expense was decried as a form of idolatry.[17]

The human result, however, was that families were deprived of ritual at a time of bereavement when virtually all cultures have found a need for such ritual. The Puritans of New England had not, in fact, been able to do without it themselves for long. By the end of the seventeenth century, a variety of customs had emerged—such as sending gloves to invite mourners and giving funeral rings with stones of elaborately carved death's heads—that would have dismayed the Puritans of old England. For the funeral of any well-known adult, six of the more prominent men of the community were invited to be pall bearers. They carried the black pall (property of the community) over the coffin, which was itself borne on a bier, by friends or porters, from the house to the grave. On the pall might be pinned a few handwritten elegies. For the really eminent, a procession of townspeople would form. Later, the grave would often be marked with an elaborately carved tomb-stone. A funeral sermon might be preached at the next meeting, and published, along with the elegies. Ritual was restored to death, and the printed word became an ever more important part of that ritual.[18]

For the funeral of children, however, these elaborations were often missing. The younger the child at death, the simpler were the arrangements. Gloves and rings might be given for a two-year-old, but not for an infant. The child's small coffin was carried by friends from the home to its resting place, accompanied by the immediate family in a little procession. As was true for funerals of adults, no prayers were said over the grave, nor scriptures read.[19]

When Samuel Sewall records which of his children read and what each read at the family's prayers just before they all followed another little coffin to its grave, he is acknowledging—in his writing, which was itself part of his personal ritual—that the family reading had attained the status of a private family rite. Death, as Charles Hambricke-Stowe has put it, was an event within the devotional matrix, not external to it. In the context of loss, the bond between reading and devotion emerged stronger than ever. Sewall's account of the family's successive experiences with bereavement does not merely reveal that he drew lessons from the scriptures to apply to his own and his children's lives. It also discloses his assumption that, as the children grew older, their reading from the scriptures within the setting of the family's prayers would help them to confront their own loss and their fears of death.[20]

Sewall began keeping records of the family readings in the context of death when he was still doing all the reading and, in a sense, transforming routine into ritual for himself. He made one such entry in the winter of 1685. When the moans of the newest infant, Henry, barely two weeks old, awoke him at four one morning, Sewall arose to pray for him. He had already sent notes to Mr. Willard and his colleague at the South Church to ask them to pray for his child at the meeting house. Very early the next morning, before dawn, the family reading included the fourteenth chapter of John: "Let not your heart be troubled: ye believe in God, believe also in me. In my Father's house are many mansions: if it were not so, I would have told you." In his diary Sewall wrote:

> Child makes no noise save by a kind of snoaring as it breathed, and as it were slept. Read the 16th of the first Chron. in the family. Having read to my Wife and

Nurse out of John: the fourteenth Chapter fell now in course, which I read and went to Prayer: By that time had done, could hear little Breathing, and so about Sun-rise, or little after, he fell asleep, I hope in Jesus, and that a Mansion was ready for him in the Father's House. Died in Nurse Hill's Lap.

Two days later, Sam, aged seven, attended the first of the funerals of his brothers and sisters, as his father led him to Henry's grave in the family plot.[21]

Sam was spared the next funeral, that of his little brother Hull, who died and was buried in Newbury, where he had been sent for his health. Although the town turned out in force, the only member of his immediate family at the funeral was his father. The following year, however, in July 1687, another little brother, a much-beloved son named Stephen, died at the age of six months. This time the entire family was at the funeral. Sewall led his wife, Hannah, one of his brothers led his widowed mother-in-law, Judith Hull, Sam led his seven-year-old sister Hannah, and another boy named Billy Dummer led five-year-old Betty. This was the first funeral Sewall's daughters had attended, and it was a harrowing experience for them. "Sam. and his sisters cryed much coming home and at home, so that could hardly quiet them. It seems they look'd into Tomb, and Sam said he saw a great Coffin there, his Grandfathers."[22]

Three years later, in the September of 1690, the family escorted the coffin of five-week-old Judith to her grave. Sewall led his wife, Sam (now twelve) accompanied his grandmother, Hannah escorted Betty (soon to turn nine); and Jane Toppan, a young relative who was living in the family as a mother's helper, "managed" Joseph, who was not yet three. Now other children in addition to Sam were old enough to read. "Before we went, Children read the 18. 19. and 20th Chapters of John, being in course for family reading." Sewall himself, who normally read as a matter of course, did not read. This same ritual was repeated three years later for Jane, an infant who died "much as Henry did, in neighbour Smith's lap, Nurse Hill and I being by." All the children attended the funeral, accompanied by their grandmother, except Joseph.[23]

The sixth funeral reveals most clearly how Samuel viewed the relationship between scriptural reading and bereavement. This reading took place before the burial of Sarah Sewall, who died at the age of two on December 23, 1696. Sam was by this time nineteen, Hannah sixteen, and Betty about to turn fifteen. Only a month earlier, Betty had returned from Salem, where she had wept as she read the passage in Ezekiel about dry bones. Joseph, at eight, had already taken his place in the family's readings. A two-year-old is very much a part of any family, and this was a significant loss. As her father put it, "Thus this very fair day is rendered fowl to us by reason of the general Sorrow and Tears in the family." He had read Deuteronomy 22 on the day that Sarah died. It is a text about responsibility, about bringing your brother's straying sheep back to him. It had made him reflect that he had not been as "tender of my daughter, nor so effectually carefull of her Defence and preservation" as he should have been. "The good Lord pity and pardon and help for the future as to those God has still left me."[24]

The funeral took place on Christmas. The day was clear but the ground was covered with snow. "We bury our little daughter. In the chamber, Joseph in course reads Ecclesiastes 3d a time to be born and a time to die." ("To everything there is a season, and a time to every purpose under the heaven: A time to be born, and a time to die.") Betty then read the twenty-second chapter of Revelations, still in course: "And he shewed me a pure river of water of life, clear as crystal, proceeding out of the throne of God and of the Lamb." Hannah then read Psalm 38: "O LORD, rebuke me not in thy wrath: neither chasten me in thy hot displeasure. For thine arrows stick fast in me, and thy hand presseth me sore." Their father made comments: "I speak to each, as God helped, to our mutual comfort I hoped." He then "order'd Sam. to read the 102. Psalm." This was a special selection, "out of course." It is the prayer of the afflicted: "Hear my prayer, O LORD, and let my cry come unto thee." Every living Sewall child had now had his or her turn in reading to the entire family. To each child, or to each text—in this context, both became one and the same—their father had spoken words of explication and application in comfort.[25]

There were no outbursts by the children on the way home from the grave. Was it because they were older now and inured to these occasions, or did these scriptural readings, along with their father's interpretive comments, indeed enable them to put this new death into a religious and consolatory framework? It is not possible to be sure. What can be said, however, is that Sewall regarded their reading of sacred text as a core aspect of their sense of family. He had not previously asked any of the living to read "out of course" before the funerals of those of his children who died as infants. By introducing a specific text here, when he had not done so on other occasions, Sewall was both acknowledging the loss that his children had experienced and providing an example of how they should respond to it—which was, indeed, how he responded himself, by mining scriptural texts for their relevant messages. Family reading had become a ritual of consolation.

We may leave Samuel Sewall and his children reading—never does he mention his wife's doing any reading—toward the end of December, two years later. This image neatly summarizes his reasons for reading the Scriptures: the Bible offered calls for action in the political and personal realms. "I had the pleasure this day to read in course the 37. of Ezekiel." (This was the very text that had caused Betty to weep so bitterly.) "I could not but think of the Expedition of the Scots. Hannah read the 4th of Ephesians" (a letter of Paul that counsels long suffering and meekness). "How hard it is," Sewall wrote, "to practise the duties here laid down, especially about Anger and Malice. Betty read the 20th of Revelation, all in course."[26]

Literacy in the Mather Family

Cotton Mather was born into a highly literate family, where his father and grandfather both kept records of their lives.[27] His father, Increase Mather, ordained as minister of Boston's North Church in 1664, delighted in books to an excess. He would spend as long as sixteen hours a day in his book-lined study, emerging only for meals and family prayers.[28] Cotton Mather grew up in this bookish and hot-

FIGURE 9. Engraving of a portrait by Peter Pelham of Cotton Mather (1663–1728), minister of the North Church of Boston. (Courtesy, American Antiquarian Society)

house religious atmosphere. Maria Mather played her part in her children's religious upbringing, reading the Bible with them in its entirety twice a year, and making sure they had learned their catechism thoroughly. Cotton composed prayers spontaneously as soon as he was able to talk, learned to write before ever attending a writing school, and while still too young to take notes during sermons, remembered them well enough to write summaries of them as soon as he returned home. He also, he recalled, read the scriptures "with So much Ardour, that for one while nothing less than *Fifteen Chapters* a Day, divided into three Exercises, for Morning, and Noon, and Night, would suffice me."[29]

Cotton Mather attended Boston's grammar school, becoming so fluent by the age of eleven in Latin that he would take notes in Latin on sermons delivered in English.[30] He began to attend Harvard six months later, the youngest student Harvard ever had, and was graduated in 1678 at the age of fifteen. Overcoming (or perhaps just masking) a debilitating stutter to a considerable extent, he aided his father at the ministry of Boston's North Church. He was ordained there as a pastor in May 1685. John Eliot, now over eighty, attended the ceremony and, as Samuel Sewall recorded in his diary, offered Mather the traditional right hand of fellowship on behalf of the church elders, calling him "a Lover of Jesus Christ." A little over a year later, Mather married Abigail Phillips. She had yet to pass her sixteenth birthday.[31]

Mather's own reading at this time was as prolific as ever, but it was still the scriptures that afforded him the most satisfaction. He used the Bible as a source of insight and prayer. It was his custom, he wrote in his diary, to make "one *Observation*, and one *Supplication*" out of every verse.[32]

Mather's involvement with the literacy education of his children can be understood only within the context of his own literacy. He himself read much and speedily. He was skilled at skimming. As a contemporary put it,

> In two or three Minutes turning thro' a Volume, he cou'd easily tell whether it wou'd make Additions to the Store of his Ideas. If it cou'd not, He quickly laid it by: If otherwise, he read it, passing over all those Parts which contained the things he had known before, perusing those Parts only that represented something *Novel*, which he Pencil'd as he went along, and at the End reduc'd the Substance to his *Common Places*, to be review'd at Leisure; and all this with wonderful Celerity.

These novelties were pressed into service for his "Biblia Americana," a gigantic manuscript he was working on that was intended to provide a wealth of illustrations from learned works for the Bible.[33]

In writing, Mather was adept at summarizing and paraphrasing. He composed as rapidly as he read. For instance, he completed *The Religious Mariner*, a booklet of forty printed pages (described by him as two and a half sheets long in its manuscript form), in only "one little Part of a Day."[34]

Mather repeatedly looked to books for his own support. In 1685, as a newly ordained minister, he had felt that—like Jesus himself at the beginning of his ministry—he would be exposed to many temptations. His response then was to seek help in print: "I would Immediately go read a profitable *Book* or two, concerning *Temptations*."[35] He also used books as a means for improving the spirituality of others. By 1700 he was regularly leaving books as gifts to members of his congregation on pastoral visits. Six years later he was claiming that he gave away some six hundred of his own books a year.[36]

Writing was also supremely important to Mather. He used composition as an aid to spiritual healing for himself even more than he used it for others. Publication of his works mattered deeply to him, and he was bitterly disappointed that his monumental manuscript, "Biblia Americana," forever languished unpublished in his study. While pursuing his many schemes for its publication, he made it ever more unpublishable by adding further annotations to it almost daily.[37]

The act of composition, then, and its resultant physical object, the published book, offered him an assuagement of his many griefs and were a source of pride—so much so that he was forever berating himself for the sin of vanity. Indeed, he had something to be vain about. He published at a breathtaking rate, sometimes at the speed of almost a book or pamphlet a month (many of them were his sermons). By the age of fifty he had published 205 books, and by another six years nearly 280. By the time he died he had published close to 450.[38]

Mather's publications included a number of books that were specifically aimed at children. Perhaps the best known of these was his addition to James Janeway's *Token for Children*, a supplement called *A Token for the Children of New-England*, first published in 1700. Another publication, six years later, was an introductory reading text for children, in verse, titled *Good Lessons for Children*. (Although a second edition was printed, no copy has survived.) By that time Mather had also adapted two of the major New England catechisms, the "New English" catechism and the "Assemblies," or Westminster, catechism, so that they might be "more easily conquered by our Children." He later published other books for children and young persons. One of them, invoking the beginning of the alphabet as a metaphor for an introduction, was titled *The A.B.C. of Religion*, which Mather hoped to distribute among schools as well as families. In describing the level at which it was aimed, Mather revealed his awareness of the wide range of literacy abilities among the general public. He designed the book, he said—lumping adults and children together—for "Children, and People of the lowest Capacity."[39]

Numerous as Mather's publications are, a catalogue of these works underestimates the extent of his writing. Much that he wrote, including the "Biblia Americana," was never published. Furthermore, he was a prolific correspondent. His 569 surviving letters alone outnumber those of any other colonial Puritan, and he may have written as many as 5,000 to correspondents in places as far flung as Holland and the West Indies. His diaries, to which he devoted daily attention, preserve much of his writing that was not published in his lifetime.[40]

Mather's first extant diary is that for 1681, when he had just turned eighteen. Since he started every new diary with his birthday, February 12, each one coincides roughly with the calendar year. His diary keeping was, at least initially, an exercise in spiritual improvement rather than a record of events. In this, Cotton was following a well-established devotional tradition of using writing as a spiritual exercise.

Because he was monitoring his spiritual development, he took notes throughout the year and until 1711 transferred the main events of the year into the separate diaries that have come down to us. Each of the earliest extant diaries, therefore, is a retrospective on a year rather than an ongoing record. Mather also kept a separate list of what he called his "Contrivances to do good," and condensed and transferred these, too, to his main diary at the end of the natal year.[41]

Although the possibility of distortion exists in all journal keeping, including Mather's (one critic, for instance, has claimed that Mather was unduly harsh toward his third wife, Lydia), there is no reason to disbelieve the diary evidence on literacy. In general, Mather recorded his children's failures as well as their triumphs. His elder son Creasy was the prime example of a child who successfully avoided living up to his father's expectations, yet his wayward behavior appears regularly in the diaries.[42]

After Mather became a parent, he began to keep his diaries for the spiritual benefit of his children, who he hoped might profit from these accounts of his pilgrimage on earth. At one point in 1697, for instance, he records a heart-to-heart conversation with his eldest daughter, Katy, then eight. "I write this, the more particularly," he explained, "that the Child may hereafter have the Benefit of read-ing it." He also used the diaries as sources for his private autobiography, "Paterna," which he began writing for Creasy.[43]

The conversation with Katy that Mather recorded reveals that he was not reluc-tant to involve his children in his own writings. He warned her (inaccurately, as it turned out) that he was to die shortly and asked her to remember everything he had told her once he was gone. He had written a book, Cotton said, about ungodly children; in its conclusion, he had said that "this Book will bee a terrible Witness against my own Children, if any of them should not bee *Godly*." In effect, through the medium of print Mather had publicized what was to be expected of a Mather child.[44]

Reading aloud was an ingrained part of the household from the earliest days of Mather's marriage, although at first it was Mather who was doing all the reading. Just as it was in the Sewall household, reading the scriptures was a standard practice at the family's morning and evening prayers, attended by Abigail and the servants and later by the children. Mather described his approach to these readings not long after his marriage. At morning prayers, he read part or all of a chapter from the Bible to the "Family" and composed a prayer from what he had read. (In so doing, he was following the prescription for "Supplication" that he had set himself on his wedding day.) The evenings were a little different: then he selected a scriptural text and made a short "Meditation" (a very brief sermon) on the text, before beginning the prayers. Occasionally he read from a treatise that he considered suitable.[45]

In March 1702, Mather made a change in how he conducted the evening prayers. Since the family had already gone through the whole Book of Psalms and several other books in the scriptures, listening to a meditation on each, he now decided to start on the "Scotch Commentators" and read through them for their explications of the texts. He began with George Hucheson's expositions on the Book of Job.[46]

The trials that followed would make this choice harrowingly appropriate. Early in July 1702, Boston was seized with smallpox. His wife Abigail was already unwell. She had often suffered from a violently sore throat and breathless coughing and was now distressingly weak. On the last day of October Nibby was the first of her children to come down with smallpox. November came and went, while Mather's study was turned into a hospital as one child after another was smitten by the disease. The affection of the children for their father was revealed in their demands for his attention, couched in a form he could not refuse: "The little Creatures keep calling for me so often to pray with them, that I can scarce do it less than ten or a dozen times in a day."[47]

But his worst trial was "the Condition of my lovely Consort. It now began to be hopeless." In his diary, Cotton transferred his account to the present tense, as he reconstituted the chain of events. "At last, the black Day arrives: Tuesday, the first of *December*. I had never yett seen such a black Day, in all the Time of my Pilgrimage. The *Desire of my Eyes* is this Day to be taken from me. Her death is lingring, and painful." Conscious until the end, Abigail was able to tell her husband how serviceable he had been in drawing her closer to God. Her last words were, "Heaven, Heaven will make amends for all." She had lived with Mather for sixteen years, "just as many Years" her sorrowing husband wrote, "as she had lived in the World, before she came to me." She left behind her four living children: Katy, Nibby, Nancy, and Creasy. Five others had died as infants.[48]

Nowhere is Mather's use of composition as consolation more visible than in his response to death. He composed an elegy for Abigail, had it printed, and pasted it into the books that he gave in appreciation to the scores of persons who had attended the family during her consumption and the smallpox epidemic. The first four lines run:

> Go then, my DOVE, but now no longer *mine*;
> Leave *Earth*, and now in *heavenly Glory* shine.
> *Bright* for thy Wisdome, Goodness, Beauty here;
> Now *brighter* in a more *angelick Sphaere*.

The elegy closes:

> Thy *Prayers* are done; thy *Alms* are spent; thy *Pains*
> Are *ended* now, in *endless* Joyes and Gains.
>   I faint, till thy last Words to Mind I call;
>   Rich Words! HEAV'N, HEAV'N WILL MAKE AMENDS FOR ALL.[49]

Over three years later, as he began his forty-fourth year in February 1706, Mather took stock of his life. (He had married Elizabeth Clark Hubbard less than a year after Abigail's death. She had borne him a daughter, Liza, in July 1704; she would bear him a son, Sammy, the following October.) Mather jotted down his daily schedule. He revealed that he wrote before he read, for after rising at seven or eight o'clock—hours that he considered slothfully late—he sang his morning hymn, then wrote a short paragraph on whatever he had been thinking of as he was rising. Next, he wrote some more, transferring to his "Biblia Americana" (his massive manuscript on the Bible) some choice quotations from his "blank" books. These were the commonplace books that he called his Quotidiana, into which he copied or condensed passages that he culled from his omnivorous reading.[50]

Now his day began to include his children. After his own morning prayers in his study he would go down to lead Elizabeth, his children, and his servants in a familiar routine: "I *read* a Portion of the sacred Scriptures, and fetch a *Note* out of every Clause, and then *pray* with them, turning what I had read, into *Prayer*." Then he worked in his study until the midday meal, when he would join the family for dinner. He rarely sat down at the table "without relating to the Children some *Story* out of the Bible," from which he drew appropriate lessons.[51]

The next time father and family had a scheduled meeting was as the evening drew in, when they all gathered for evening prayers. He listened to his children reciting part of the catechism, read two or three verses from a Psalm, commented on every clause, and then sang the Psalm, and prayed with his family.[52] He acted, in short, as a teacher in his emphasis on explicating the texts being read. By showing his children how to transform their reading into praying, just as he himself did, he was building bridges between the texts and their own lives.

At about the same time Mather made some notes in his diary under the heading, "SOME SPECIAL POINTS, RELATING TO THE EDUCATION OF MY CHILDREN." His remarks fall under ten headings, most of which are devoted to his family's spiritual development. He urged secret prayer on his children and encouraged them to be kind to each other. As befitted the grandson of Richard Mather, who had suffered grievously from physical abuse during his schooling in England, Cotton Mather resorted to physical punishment only in cases of obstinacy or "some gross Enormity." He considered "the *slavish* way of *Education*, carried on with raving and kicking and scourging (in *Schools* as well as *Families*)" to be an abomination. He wanted so to conduct his instruction that being chased out of his presence would be the worst punishment of all; he wished his children to count it a privilege to be taught.[53]

The linguistic and literacy education of Mather's children was also important to him. He reiterated as part of his "SPECIAL POINTS" his attempts to entertain the "Olive Plants about the Table" with "delightful Stories, especially *scriptural* ones," and their corresponding lessons. In addition, "As soon as tis possible, I make the Children learn to *write*. And when they can *write*, I employ them in Writing out the most agreeable and profitable Things, that I can invent for them." (In other words, in the tradition of all writing masters, he wrote out some sentences for the children to copy.) Interestingly, he does not mention reading at all. This was just a slip, of course, as the children had all learned to read before they wrote, but its omission points to his primary interest in writing.[54]

Mather also consistently involved himself with the formal schooling of his sons. In the spring of 1706, Creasy was in his seventh year and was learning to read at school. For several months his father wrote out, in a straightforward script, a lesson in verse that Creasy was read and learn by heart. Mather intended to have him "improve in *Goodness* at the same time, that he improv'd in *Reading*." Underlying this approach was the widely accepted belief that imprinting a sentence on the mind also imprinted it on the heart. Hoping as always to do good in a more general way, Mather gathered these verses together and had them published under the title *Good Lessons For Children; Or, Instructions, provided for a little Son to learn at School, when learning to read*. Five years later, when it was time for Sammy, aged four and a half, to go to school to learn to read, Mather kept an eye on the future in his choice of a dame school: "It may be much for Interest of my little Son *Samuel*, if I send him to learn to read, with the Wife, of him that is Master of the Grammar-School, and then the Master of the School may take all Opportunities to forward him in further Learning."[55]

The elderly Increase Mather was also involved with Creasy's education: the boy used to go to his grandfather regularly for Latin instruction. On one such occasion, Creasy received an indirect lesson on family literacy and the power of the written word, in the form of a parental note. Creasy had run an errand for his father to someone who had detained him far longer than he should have. As a result, Creasy arrived so late at his grandfather's house that Increase angrily canceled the lesson. The boy came weeping to his father, who wrote a note to his own father, taking the blame on himself and promising that this tardiness would never occur again. Creasy was restored to his grandfather's favor, and Cotton was able to muse on a spiritual parallel—the reconciliation to be obtained by the advocacy of the Son to the Father.[56]

Throughout the year 1709, Mather made specific plans for his children's spiritual improvement. All of them involved literacy. Now aged between three (Sammy) and twenty (Katy), the children were to read Richard Baxter's *Mother's Catechism*. Mather also decided that they should each have a Bible in their hands during the daily prayers, so that they could read the verse as he made his observations on it. (By implication, they had not had individual copies earlier.) Moreover, he planned to have their rooms suitably fitted out for reading, writing, and praying; those who were old enough to write should now and then write out a prayer, which they would show him. (This seems to be the first instance in Mather's diaries of his requiring composition from his children.) He would, in addition, devote Saturday evenings to private talks with each family member.[57] A slight shift can be discerned in the power relationships in the family: Mather was no longer to be the sole authority over the Word, but was diffusing some of his control among his children.

In February 1711, as he entered his forty-ninth year, Mather reorganized the way he kept his diaries. Up to this point, he had kept a separate list of what he called his "Contrivances to do good" and had condensed and transferred these plans for the future to his annual diaries, just as he had done with his entries of the preceding year. Now, however, he condemned this procedure as too time-consuming and began to enter his plans for improvement as part of a daily diary-keeping routine. He dubbed these "GOOD DEVISED." From this point on, virtually every diary entry begins with his abbreviation, "G.D." The G.D.'s took the form of answers to a series of questions, and each day of the week Mather focused his intentions on a different group. The question for each sabbath, for instance, was how he could render service to his flock. The question for each Monday was, "*What* [*is*] *to be done in* MY FAMILY?"[58]

With the introduction of G.D.'s, Mather's diaries instantly become more immediate, because Mather was now writing daily entries rather than making annual summaries. In contrast, the entries now focus more on what Mather planned to do than on what he had actually done. This change poses a problem, for we do not know for sure how far Mather translated his G.D.'s into action. At least once, on one of his birthdays, he vowed to look back at his diary to check that he had accomplished everything he had set for himself. In the few instances when we can confirm his good intentions, we see that he did indeed carry them out. At one point, for example, he promised his children bookshelves, and the shelves were apparently in place soon after because he talked about the children's putting on them the books that he was going to give them. The fact, however, that he even contemplated certain literacy interactions with his children is as significant as whether he actually carried them out. His G.D.'s can therefore be viewed as a kind of series of lesson plans.[59]

In the first of his Monday G.D.'s under the new approach of 1711, Mather jotted down his plans to involve his children in reading aloud from a nonscriptural text during the evening prayers, in an enrichment of their literacy diet. Each of his "capable Children" should "take a Book of Piety, and . . . read some short pungent Passage in the hearing of all that are present." Mather would then "apply it, firstly to the Readers, and also to all the Hearers; that they may be taught the Way of Life, with a most awakened Attention unto it." Once again, he was teaching and interpreting text. Two years later, he planned to have two of his younger children (the youngest of whom, Sammy, was by then six and a half) read aloud each night before the evening prayers. They would each read a paragraph, in turn, from a poetical history of the Bible, until they finished it. He, of course, "would make still some agreeable Remarks upon it, for their Instruction."[60]

Mather exploited writing as a tool of devotion as soon as a child had mastered the skill. He valued copying as a vehicle for instruction and on one occasion decided that those of his children who could write should make copies of a "*Deed of Betrustment*" that he had prepared for them. This was a kind of spiritual will couched in the form of a letter to his Savior—a prayer that committed his children to the care of divine hands, once their earthly father was gone. At another point he resolved to exert greater control over the children's own private prayers: he wanted to know not only that they prayed but what they were praying for. He decided that they should write down the general tenor of their prayers and that he would also "assign" them several subjects for prayer and have them write out their petitions for each one.[61]

On several occasions Mather assigned his children the equivalent of essays. In August 1711 he planned to ask the four of his children who could write (these were presumably the four oldest, Katy, Nibby, Nancy, and Creasy, now aged from almost twenty-two to twelve) to retire to their rooms and write an answer to the question, "*What will be the best Manner and Method of my spending my Time in the*

World." Their answers would serve as a plan for their own lives, and, Mather wrote, "I will as far as I can oblige them to conform unto it." One of his G.D.'s for Katy, the oldest, was to have her write "brief Essayes of Piety, on such agreeable Subjects, as I may from Time to Time assign unto her." On other occasions, short answers were acceptable. Creasy, by far the least malleable of the children, was to receive a whole series of questions on the meaning of his life, for which he was to write "as distinct Answers as he can," and show them to his father.[62]

Mather's Monday G.D. in January 1712 was to revive a habit that seems to have fallen into disuse, that of having his children enter "agreeable and valuable Things" into the blank books that each had. He would undertake to provide them with appropriate reading material that would include scientific as well as devotional texts. Around the same time, he decided that his daughters should learn shorthand, which was valued by the devout because it aided in the recording of sermons.[63]

In August 1711 a literacy activity for Mather's wife is mentioned for the first time. Abigail, who may have been too busy with pregnancy and childbirth to have had any time for literacy activities, barely appears in the diaries until her lingering and painful death. Elizabeth, however, emerges into view from time to time. Mather's G.D. for her that August was that it would be to her advantage, and set a good example for others, if she would take notes on the sermons she listened to. Even he seems to have had qualms about this suggestion, however, because he qualified it with "if she would be prevailed withal." Later that same year he planned to search out "Books of Piety" for her with the suggestion that she read from them or the scriptures before beginning her private prayers and then transform her reading into prayer, as he did.[64]

As another birthday approached in February 1712, Mather as usual reevaluated his life. This year he reproached himself for his past "Remissness about the education of My Family." While we need not take this too seriously, since Mather was wont to upbraid himself for those very sins that he had least committed (such as sloth), his diary for 1712 does contain the most detailed descriptions up to this point of his literacy plans for his children.[65]

Creasy was now thirteen. Two years earlier, his father had written ominously that his son was already old enough to "know the Meaning of *Consideration.*" Mather's concern had heightened, if anything, in the intervening period, and he now felt that it would be fruitful to have Creasy read aloud to him on Sunday evenings from the Paterna—the autobiography that Mather was creating for him from his diaries. Mather seemed less concerned about Sammy, whose progress was beginning to afford him much pleasure. Sammy's reading had improved "mightily," and in an unusual move Mather decided to "Reward" his little son for his success in mastering what Mather had set him to read and learn. Later in the year, Sammy was similarly rewarded for learning rhyming couplets in both English and Latin. Mather's qualms over giving his children rewards of money, or some other small gift, were allayed by his promising himself that every time he gave a child something, the "Maxim of Piety" that he would let fall simultaneously from his lips would surely be "of much more worth and use unto them, than that Little Thing which I now bestow upon them."[66]

As for his three elder daughters (Katy, Nibby, and Nancy, who that year turned twenty-three, eighteen, and fifteen, respectively), Mather continued to see that they read and wrote in the service of piety. He still felt that copying was useful, and one of his G.D.'s was to have them transcribe into their blank books a description of "Virtuous and Gracious Women" from a book he had recently published. They were to study this and discuss it with him later. They were also to read carefully a sermon addressed to young women by "Mr. Vincent" and give their father an oral account of what they found there. Apart from this exercise in oral summary, Mather's most ambitious plan for them was to have them taught Hebrew.[67]

Along with all this spiritual sustenance, Cotton decided to provide two material additions to his family to promote literacy skills. He planned to give the younger children blank books, in which they were to write, for once, something that they had chosen for themselves, rather than what their father chose for them: they were to transcribe passages from their reading that had "most affected" them. They would show him their blank books every Sunday evening. In addition, every week he would give the children books, particularly those written by himself or his father. The price to be paid for this new book was that the recipients would have to write, in their blank books, a passage that Mather would assign from it. Those of his children too young to write—he could only have meant Liza (seven) and Sammy (five)—would learn something from the new book by heart.[68]

Besides these individual activities, father and children continued to share books by reading them aloud together. When Mather received from a London friend a new book titled *Practical Religion Exemplify'd in the Lives of Mrs. Mary Terry . . . and Mrs. Clissould*, he resolved to sit with his children and listen while they each read a paragraph aloud from it in turn, and to comment on passages that he thought they should particularly notice. On other occasions, he simply talked about his own reading.[69]

Writing, if it could not be communal, was at least to be used in the service of "Doing Good." One of the goods it could do was save Mather from vexation. The younger children were home from school during the equivalent of the spring vacations, and Mather, who worked at home, clearly found their presence trying. Instead of devoting their holiday "Entirely to play," which he felt made them unwell, Mather planned to assign them some writing in the morning. Four years later, he would perfect this approach by assigning Sammy, during a "Week of many Play-Dayes," the task of translating into Latin some sentences of Mather's own devising on "the true and right Intent of Play."[70]

In the evenings, the status of writing in the household was well spelled out. Each child was to respond to three questions before going to bed. The first was whether he or she had prayed privately that day. The third was what "Good" the child had put his or her time to. The middle question was, significantly, "*Have you used your Pen for any Good Purpose today?*" These questions had changed in one important respect from those Mather had determined to ask when his children were all a year younger. Then they were also to give an account of how they had spent their time that day, and what good they had done, but the literacy question had been different: "*Child, have you sought the Face of God, and read His word, this Day?*" We can detect here a switch in Mather's emphasis from reading to writing as the key literacy skill: from putting reading to good use to putting writing to good use. Mather himself, of course, was "Devising Good" with his pen every day of the year. Even so, he reproached himself, a year later, for having allowed some "Points of polite and pious Education" in his daughters to languish, particularly in the use of their pens.[71]

As his fiftieth birthday arrived, in February 1713, Mather decided to weave the family's "domestic Occurrences" into his remarks, in an attempt to make the family's evening prayer meetings yet more meaningful. When the newest accession to the family, his "pretty little Daughter" Jerusha, was being weaned, he resolved to make this the occasion of discussing, in his prayers, the character of a child weaned in true Christianity. As time went on, this approach evolved to include the most mundane events. When Mather realized how often he had to mend his pens, he observed that in future he would make it his custom to cry out, each time, "*Lord, Mend me, and fitt me for thy Service.*" This continual spiritualizing of the mundane encouraged his children to think as metaphorically as he did.[72]

In October of that same year, 1713, a measles epidemic hit the city of Boston. Mather braced himself for the worst, for Elizabeth was once again near her term. When all his children came down with the disease, one after the other, Elizabeth's tender care for her stepchildren proved her undoing. She delivered twins early, and her fever began to mount. Within the space of two weeks in November, five members of the family were dead: a maid servant, Elizabeth herself, her premature twins, and Jerusha.[73]

Jerusha was two years and seven months old when she died. Mather's fervent prayers for her had not been heard. "I begg'd, I begg'd that such a bitter Cup, as the Death of that lovely child, might pass from me. *Nevertheless!*" Young as she was, Jerusha had absorbed her father's lessons well. A "marvellous witty, ready, forward Child," she had been so precocious in talking that two months earlier her father had urged her siblings to teach her "Sentences of Piety" for her edification. Now measles rendered her speechless. Shortly before she died, her speech returned to her. She asked her father to pray with her, and her last words were that "*she would go to Jesus Christ.*"[74]

Mather happened across a manuscript that Elizabeth had written before she died. He added this lengthy "self-examination" of hers as an appendix to *The Religion of the Cross*, his funeral sermon and memorial to her that he now published. For Jerusha, he printed a brief memorial and put it into copies of his book *A Christian Funeral*, which he presented to well-wishers. Once again, writing—in this instance the writing of another as well as his own—proved a support and comfort to him.[75]

An unnatural quiet descended on the house, after what Mather described as a "*Month* which *devoured* my Family." He threw himself into his children's education once more. With no infants or young children, he wrote, the "quiet and easy and unhurried Condition which my Family (by sad Things) is bro't unto, gives me new Opportunity," to look out for the children's spiritual welfare. Creasy was the particular target of his concern. Now aged fourteen, he was proving remarkably resilient to his father's religious indoctrination. Mather himself could see that this "ungodly Son" was hopelessly unfitted for the ministry. Bowing to reality, he had already decided that Creasy should enter a secular business, and was altering the boy's education so that he could have "his Writing and Cyphring perfected." (Ciphering was computation using simple arithmetic, a skill essential to any commercial activity.)[76]

No matter what the crises of the moment were, Mather did not lose his faith in the potency of reading and writing as tools for Creasy's reformation. About three months before the measles epidemic, someone had given Mather a biography of a young man named Thomas Beard: before his untimely death at the age of seventeen, Beard had written down the "Experiences of his Piety." Mather seized the chance to show the work to Creasy. "I will oblige my Son *Increase* to read this Composure; and I will confer with him upon it." Even in the midst of the measles conflagration, Mather was still looking to literacy to aid his son's personal growth. Creasy had caught the measles like everyone else in the household (other than Mather himself), and Mather viewed his son's sickness and recovery as a lever for improvement. Creasy was to make it his first task, once he was well again, to "draw up in writing, some special Resolutions, for the future Conduct of his Life." A week later, Mather jotted down a new G.D. for Creasy: he would teach him and the other children his special technique of reading a verse in the Bible and turning it first into a lesson and then into a prayer.[77]

A month after the measles epidemic of 1713, Cotton added yet another "edifying Addition" to the evening prayer routine. Before the psalm and prayers, Liza and Sammy were to answer a question in the catechism "and have their Leaves ready turned unto the Proofs of the Answer in the Bible; which they shall distinctly read unto us; and show what they prove." The children were expected to be as adept as their father at invoking scriptural authority in support of doctrine by identifying the appropriate text.[78]

Mather's enthusiasm for education during this period of bereavement extended beyond his children to his servants. Although the Mather family, like any other professional family of the period, had many servants and enslaved Africans at any one time, they rarely appear in his diaries. He does, however, mention his African slave Onesimus, a young man who was purchased for him by members of his congregation in 1706. Onesimus was clearly able to read but not write, because now Mather decided that he should be paying more attention to his "Instruction and Management," and that Onesimus was to "be sure to read every Day. From thence I will have him go on to Writing."[79]

In July 1715, less than two years after Elizabeth's death, Cotton married a widow named Lydia George. In a letter to a friend he hailed her as one who "shines forever with a thousand Lovelinesses," and in his diary records offering prayers of thanksgiving in the family for the "excellent Mother" his children had acquired. Since Lydia, who had a married daughter of her own, was past childbearing age, this was the first union Cotton had experienced that was unencumbered by pregnancy or young children, and at first the marriage was intimate and happy.[80]

On his next birthday, as he began his fifty-fourth year, Mather altered his mode of keeping his diary slightly. He moved his family G.D.'s from Mondays to Tuesdays, perhaps in recognition of the fact that his children were less in need of him: his youngest child, Sammy, was now over nine. On the first Tuesday under this new system—February 14, 1716—he records, "G.D. Unto each of my Children, present my *Utilia* [his latest publication], with my Charges unto them, to make the Book very much their Companion and Counsellor." The G.D. for the second Tuesday under the new procedure involved Lydia: "G.D. It may not only be a Service to myself, but also greatly serve the Interests of Piety in my excellent Consort, if I should use, every Morning before I rise, to read a Chapter of my dear Arndt; and communicate unto her the principal Thoughts occurring on it." Since John Arndt's book was a devotional work written in Latin, Mather was proposing to communicate its main ideas, in translation, to Lydia as he read in bed. Other morning reading in bed took place over the following months. Because Lydia was perfectly capable of reading books in English herself, Mather singled out books written in Latin as candidates for being a "Bed-Book" to be read in translation as "Entertainment for my Consort" before he rose in the morning.[81]

The sunniness of this domestic coziness was overshadowed by a new trial: Katy, now aged twenty-seven, was showing every sign of consumption. By September of 1716, the "Angel of Death" was standing over her "with a drawn Sword." She died "gloriously," as her father put it, three months later. Once again, Mather turned to his pen for solace. He preached Katy's funeral sermon a few days later, as he had after the deaths of all the other members of his family. Katy had made a special request, before she died, for the topic of the sermon, and her father published this request together with his own memorial of her, titled *Victorina*. Through this publication, he believed, she would "outlive her Death, and continue gloriously to do good among the living."[82]

This published account of Mather's eldest daughter allows us a rare chance to compare his "Good Devised" with what he actually achieved in relation to his children's education. Katy, it turns out, was well educated; in fact, she had skills that went far beyond those mentioned in the diaries. She was, as her father put it, "happy in an Education, that was polite and agreeable to the Circumstances of a Gentlewoman." She was said to be a good needlewoman, to be dexterous with her pen, knowledgeable about the preparation and presentation of food, and skilled in both vocal and instrumental music. She learned Hebrew in her childhood; her brother Sammy later corroborated this fact and added that she also understood Latin. She had a good knowledge of Biblical geography as well. She clearly gained from her father's many lessons on literacy: Mather describes how she copied into her blank books quotations that struck her as spiritual "Treasures." In her reading, too, her father's influence was palpable. She had used her skill for the public good; for example, she spent several afternoons visiting an illiterate woman condemned to be executed for murder in order to read aloud to her. According to her father, her favorite book at the time of her death was a new translation of his beloved John Arndt.[83]

If Mather had been called upon to lose his oldest child, he was at least able to draw consolation from his youngest. Sammy proved to be the son that Creasy was supposed to be but never was. He was very quick as a student, so that his father was constantly jotting down G.D.'s about insisting that his grammar schoolmaster find more work for him to do at school, because he finished so much faster than his schoolmates. Mather also kept asking himself what he should do "for the raising of *Sammy*'s Mind, above the debasing Meannesses of Play!" He had Sammy translate from Latin to English and vice versa and allowed Sammy and Liza to learn French at their own suggestion. He also sent them both back to their writing school to perfect their script when Sammy was in his twelfth year. He made plans to introduce Sammy to geography and astronomy. He taught Sammy to read the scriptures and turn text into prayer as he himself did. He also gave him, as he grew older, a large number of books. By the fall of 1718, when Sammy, at twelve, was within a year of going to Harvard College (and Mather was contemplating raising "Certain Points of *Manliness*" with him), Mather decided to talk with him in Latin daily. By the time Sammy became an adult, his father was suggesting a wide range of theological works for him to read.[84]

Creasy, in contrast, was a continuing trial. He had been sent to England at the age of sixteen to stay with an uncle and had returned the following year, in May 1716, "much polished, much improved . . . and, which is wonderful, with an excellent Business prepared for him immediately to fall into." Creasy's ability to make a living, however, did not prevent him, a year and a half later, from making "a worse Exhibition of himself" than Cotton had "ever yett mett." He had brought disgrace upon his family by making a Boston prostitute pregnant.[85]

Yet again, Mather seized on literacy activities as a means of reformation. "Among other Methods of bringing my son *Increase* home unto GOD," he wrote, he would assign him sermons, which he was to read and then turn their main ideas, or "Principal Points," into prayers. Creasy was to write these in his diary. Five months later, Cotton was still looking to reading as a safeguard. He recommended that his sons read aloud to their sisters books by James Janeway: "G.D. Be not satisfied until *Increase* be prevailed withal, to read more, and spend his Evenings to better Account." A son who was poring over a book would not be able to engage in less desirable activities, and his reading aloud a Janeway book to the rest of the family, of an evening, would permit his father to monitor his activities satisfactorily.[86]

Even after the older of his children reached adulthood, Mather's confidence in the power of the printed word to alter their lives never faltered. He gave each child books that he considered timely. He decided, for instance, that Nancy, who at twenty-seven was unmarried and living at home, was to read "the Experiences of a young Gentlewoman, published with the Life of Mr. *Gearing*." (He himself had enjoyed the biography of Gearing.) She should also read Richard Baxter's *Poor Man's Family Book*. To Liza, who at seventeen was full of fears for her safety as another smallpox epidemic threatened Boston, he planned to give "the little Book, which relates the Death of a young French Lady." Clearly, Mather viewed the work as a model of how to face death when young. To Creasy and Sammy, he prescribed *The Young Man's Call to His Brethren*. Nibby does not appear as a book recipient, for she had married in 1716 and moved out of her father's household.[87]

If Mather's involvement in literacy assignments for his children was a constant, his marital happiness was not. He had been married to Lydia for less than three years when, in May 1718, his family G.D.'s begin to hint at discord: he noted the need for "exquisite Wisdom and Patience." By the end of July, instead of a G.D., he was writing the few words, "My GOD, My GOD!" At a period when he was beset with acute financial worries, Lydia had begun to display extraordinary emotional outbursts. Her relationships with her stepdaughters, particularly with Nancy, also deteriorated dramatically. In the margin of his diary, alongside the rapturous comment of "excellent Mother" that he had written when he was first married to Lydia, Mather added the comment in Latin, "*Ah! quam deceptus!*" (Ah! How I was deceived!) Ironically, the language that he had shared with Lydia earlier in their bed-book reading was now being used as a shield.[88]

Lydia, who was perfectly capable of interpreting Mather's comments, cryptic or otherwise, seized and hid the diaries of the four or five previous years, threatened to destroy his current diary, and ripped seven pages out of it. As ever, Mather sought relief in writing. "For fear of what might happen," he recorded in another, secret, diary, hidden where she could not find it, "I have not one disrespectful Word of this proud Woman, in all the Papers [his regular diary]. But this Week, she has in her indecent Romaging found them." His offer to strike out any passage that displeased her did nothing to mollify her. He was in despair but, as ever, spiritually resigned: "My glorious Lord, will have me dy to every thing: and so I must be Dead, even to those Papers, which are of more value to me, than any temporal Estate I can pretend unto."[89]

Lydia relented, however, and returned his diaries, although those for 1719 and 1720 are missing. By the time we can return to Mather's family G.D.'s the following year, domestic tranquility has apparently been restored. In fact, early in the year 1721 Mather's chief family anxieties, apart from his own poverty, were over Creasy, who continued to behave in a way very unbecoming to a minister's son. Even now that his sons Creasy and Sam (now at Harvard) were aged, respectively, twenty-one and fourteen, Mather persisted in using literacy for their spiritual improvement. He planned to write questions—the equivalent of a test—about "several Chief Actions" of human life, for in answering these questions correctly lay "the Skill of living unto GOD." His sons, as usual, were to answer these questions in writing.[90]

The last of Mather's surviving diaries is that for the natal year that began in February 1724. It was a difficult spring for Mather: his father had died the year before, and he felt deserted by his father, abandoned by his congregation, and reviled by Boston at large. His situation at home did not help. No doubt fearful of Lydia's rummaging, he had not mentioned his wife in any diary since her initial outbursts other than to voice occasional expressions of concern over her health. But in April he wrote of the "unreasonable and implacable Aversion" that she had for his "dear, dear *Nancy*." Characteristically, Mather sought comfort in reading and writing. A book titled *Divine Contemplations* by Major Henry Dorney proved helpful. "Never have I any where found vital Piety operating and exhibited more unto the Life, than in those precious Papers." Turning reading into writing, as was his wont, he proposed, he said, to "make an Extract with my Pen" of the book's most affecting and impressive passages. He had need of emotional support: in August, after months of alternating between towering rages and passionate reconciliations, Lydia left, taking with her, her niece and her niece's maid.[91]

Creasy had been living elsewhere for some years now. He had continued to upset his father, at one point contriving to take part in a riot at night with some "detestable Rakes in the Town." Mather had then been so angered that he had banished Creasy, temporarily, from his sight. He promised himself that he would write Creasy a "tremendous Letter," telling him that he would disown him until he showed himself to be penitent. The rift between them did not, however, prevent Creasy from leaping passionately to his father's defense when a naval officer insultingly named his slave "Cotton Mather." Despite all this, and despite his father's hand wringing over his son's "sloth," Creasy seemed to be settled well in business. Shortly before Lydia left the family, Mather noted that Creasy had boarded ship in Barbados to sail to Newfoundland. Now he received terrible news. The ship had miscarried. "I am advised, that my Son *Increase*, is lost, is dead, is gone. . . . My Head is Waters, and my Eyes are a Fountain of Tears!"[92]

Mather's anguish over this loss was made more acute by his anxiety over Creasy's spiritual fate: "But, the Soul of the Child!" There was only one ray of comfort. Much as he had done after his wife Elizabeth's death, Mather came across some penitent writings that Creasy had left on the table in his father's study. Mather added these to some sermons and published them in the forlorn hope that the child "who did so little Good" during his life might yet do some after his death. Of Creasy's writings, Mather wrote, poignantly, "If the Papers which he left in my Hands, were sincere and His Heart wrote with his pen, all is well! Would not my GOD have me to hope so?"[93]

Literacy still remained to Mather as a force for good in his diminished family, but now he shifted the burden to his surviving son. A few months before Liza married, Mather had asked Sammy, as part of his plan to have his children be blessings to each other, to persuade Liza to write down "the Desires of a Soul returning to GOD." Now, several months after Creasy's death, Mather's plan for Sammy, at eighteen, was that he should supply Nancy (almost twenty-eight) with appropriate material for her to read and write. He also wished that his servants, particularly their African slave Ezer, would learn to write. "*Sammy* shall do the Kindness of teaching them."[94]

The remaining years of Mather's life were clouded by further griefs. He had already lost his married daughter Nibby during a smallpox epidemic in 1721. Liza, also married, died at the age of twenty-two. Lydia, however, perhaps as a result of the news of Creasy's death, was reconciled to Mather. Nancy remained at home, unmarried. Samuel continued the Mather tradition of entering the ministry and eventually became one of the pastors of Boston's North Church, preaching where his father and grandfather had preached.[95]

But we learn of this from elsewhere than Mather's pen, for the last surviving diary closes at the end of his sixty-second year, in February 1725, three years before his death. His final diary entry, other than his annual list of sermons that he had preached, once again refers to the consolations of literacy and the crucial importance to him of composition. "When I sitt alone in my Languishments, unable to write, or to read, I often compose little Hymns." Usually he forgot them, he said, as fast as he composed them, but now for the first time he wrote one down:

> O Glorious CHRIST of GOD; I live
>   In Views of Thee alone.
> Life to my gasping Soul, oh! give!
>   Shine Thou, or I'm undone . . .
>
> My glorious Healer, thou restore
>   My Health, and make me whole.
> But this is what I most implore;
>   Oh, for an Healed Soul![96]

Like Samuel Sewall, Mather interpreted text for his children. Like Sewall, he used the scriptures to comfort and support them in the face of death. But Mather's interventions in his children's literacy went further. Three salient aspects of literacy in the Mather family, all orchestrated by Mather himself, emerge from his diaries: the capacity of literacy to foster interaction among family members, the communal nature of literacy within the family, and Mather's role as a teacher of literacy.

The cozy "Bed-Book" reading that Mather shared with Lydia, translating for her from his beloved Arndt, was the most spontaneous instance of interactions promoted by literacy. Mather, predictably, guided (or manipulated) all such interactions, but he encouraged his sons to instruct their older sisters or the family servants, and a grandfather to tutor his grandson. In fact, one of his own principal ways of interacting with his children, no matter what their age, was in the context of assigning literacy activities. The second aspect of literacy was a direct consequence of the first, with oral reading occurring in communal settings: at daily prayers, at the table, or when father and children shared books in the evening.

A third aspect of literacy in the Mather family was Cotton Mather's role as teacher for his children. He provided models of oral and literate activities; he set assignments; he taught his children how to comprehend text, with explanation or examples; and he constructed bridges between life, language, and literacy.

Mather constantly provided models of oral reading in the family's twice-daily prayers, and he would often share with his children the books he had written, offering them concrete models of his own writing. He also taught the children how to turn reading into prayer, and how any text could be applied to individual spiritual needs.

Some of the literacy assignments Mather gave his children involved merely the repetition that was a characteristic feature of colonial education: he had the children learn the catechism by heart (repetition from a book in the oral mode), and he had them copy texts, such as his "Deed of Betrustment" or passages from his own books or those of others (a form of repetition in the written mode). Sometimes his assignments were clearly make-work, as when he had Sammy write on the proper use of play during time off from school, or when he tried to influence his sons' evening occupations by insisting that they read aloud to their siblings. Here, literacy appears to have been used in the service of control rather than for any more elevated purpose. Some of Mather's other assignments, however, appear less restrictive and more open-ended. When he chose a book individually for a child, or asked the children to write down their prayers, or had a child write an essay on a topic of his choice, or insisted that the children record, in their blank books, whatever had struck them as important in their own reading, he at least opened the door to more individual responses from each child.

Mather appears to have diverged most sharply from the stereotypical view of colonial literacy instruction as restricted to rote learning in his teaching of comprehension (albeit always on his own terms and in the service of his own interpretations). Perhaps in part because he was a minister who spent his professional life explicating scriptural text from the pulpit, Mather appears unmatched in his eagerness to explain text—at least in the many examples he offers in his diaries. His explanations take several guises. Most often he explained a text himself, particularly at the evening prayers, in his "meditations." He also looked to professional exegeses of the sacred texts, such as the ones by George Hucheson, although these were no doubt beyond the understanding of several of his listeners at the daily prayer ritual. He was probably more successful on the many occasions when he himself interpreted texts for the children as they read books aloud, paragraph by paragraph.

Mather was also adept at using one text to expand, explain, or confirm another. He himself was embellishing the Bible by adding explanatory examples (culled from his omnivorous reading) to his unpublishable "Biblia Americana"; and he encouraged his children to prove the tenets of the catechism by using specific scriptural texts as their evidence.

The bridges Mather constructed to foster his children's literacy development linked spoken language and life, written language and life, and spoken and written language.

When he treated Jerusha's weaning as a metaphor for the Christian weaned in true Christianity, he moved from the concrete to the abstract, from a homely happening to a spiritual metaphor, and so from life to language. When he told stories from the Bible at the dinner table to his "Olive Plants" and drew appropriate lessons, he was linking the told story to his children's real lives.

Mather also often connected life—which he conceived of in deeply religious terms—with the written language, as he did when he gave to Liza, fearful over the possibility of her own early death from smallpox, a book relating the death of a young French woman, or when he showed his sons how to turn their reading of the scriptures into a prayer. Similarly, when he had Creasy draw up a blueprint on how to spend his life, or when he asked his children whether they had used their pens for any good that day, he was connecting books and reading to life, and life to writing.

Finally, when he asked Creasy to find the "Principal Points" of a printed sermon, turn them into a prayer, and write them in his diary, Mather was drawing together reading and writing. He was doing the same thing when he required the children to copy, from books, the passages that "most affected them" into their own blank books. He himself did this all the time, as he read through books, penciling new information and later condensing it for his "Quotidiana."

This said, it is important not to exaggerate Mather's role as a teacher of comprehension. His interactions with his children were highly controlling, and the textual interpretations he gave were not intended to be challenged. He was certainly not teaching comprehension in any modern sense. Nonetheless, his focus on textual explication, even though he defined it for his own ends and on his own terms, was the teaching of meaning.

It is proper to ask about the fruits of literacy in the two families. What form did literacy take for the children of Samuel Sewall and Cotton Mather, each of whom cultivated literacy in their families in different ways, and who wrote daily, or almost daily, in their own diaries? Both used literacy to a striking extent in the service of religion; but what was the overall effect on their children?

Perhaps inevitably, none of Mather's children turned out to be his match as an author. Sam did publish a few sermons—the first of which was the funeral sermon he preached for his father—but his lengthiest work was a life of Cotton Mather. It offered little independent evaluation and instead leaned heavily on his father's unpublished autobiography, "Paterna."

Nonetheless, certain members of Mather's family clearly came to share his views on the importance of literacy, and particularly of writing, as they moved into adulthood. Katy showed herself to be a true child of her father in using her literacy to do good by reading aloud to a convicted felon in the Boston jail and in copying down "treasures" from her reading into her blank book. But the most vivid testimony to the ultimate importance of literacy in his life is that of Creasy. This "ungodly Son" left behind on his father's desk—surely intending that his father should find it—his testimony to a repentant and contrite heart. Whether or not Creasy's "Heart wrote with his pen" we shall never know, but Mather's son had certainly internalized his father's emphasis on writing as a crucial mode of communication and self-expression within the family.

If the Sewall daughters kept diaries, they have not survived. The sons, however, of the Sewall family used their pens both to record and order their lives. Young Sam Sewall did not publish any books, but he did keep a diary, which informs us today that he was not happy in his marriage to Rebeckah Dudley, the daughter of the Massachusetts governor. Joseph Sewall, whose literacy began with his hornbook, became a published author. He had gladdened his father's heart by becoming a minister of the Old South Church. He published close to forty works, nearly all of them sermons. Nonetheless, the most eloquent witness to the literacy and devotional lessons he had learned from his family and his formal education is a journal that he kept during the seven months that immediately preceded and followed his graduation from Harvard in 1707. It is written in the classic mode of Puritan self-scrutiny, alternating between certainty and appalling doubt about his experiencing saving grace.[97]

The question with which this chapter began can now be answered. It does not, within the Puritan context, seem irrational for parents to have reminded their children of the possibilities of early death. Of Samuel Sewall's fourteen children, only three—Samuel, Joseph, and Judith—outlived their father. Of Cotton Mather's fifteen children, just two, Nancy and Sammy, survived him.

THE ANGLICANS AND
THE ORDINARY ROAD, 1701 TO 1776

5

The Literacy Mission of the S.P.G.

The most important evangelical organization in provincial America was the London-based Society for the Propagation of the Gospel, known by its initials as the S.P.G. This was not a descendant of the old organization that had sent horn-books and scythes to the Commissioners of the United Colonies of New England in the seventeenth century for the missions of John Eliot and Thomas Mayhew but one organized in 1701 by the Anglican Church. The efforts mounted by the S.P.G. in the eighteenth century, and by its sister missionary organization, the Associates of Dr. Thomas Bray, to convert and educate the poor, the native, and the enslaved, allow us to see literacy instruction through a different lens. Theologically far less demanding than the Congregationalists and far more confident that salvation could be won by faith, decent behavior, and steady church attendance, the Anglicans brought a new vision of what literacy was to accomplish.

Like the Congregationalists, Anglicans firmly believed that religious instruction included the teaching of literacy. Also like the Congregationalists, Anglicans followed the "ordinary Road" of imparting literacy instruction. Yet the value of literacy within the rubric of Anglicanism has a different resonance from its value within a Puritan context. It is hard to read the Anglican literature of the early eighteenth century without concluding that literacy for poor children, enslaved children, and native Americans was just one more component of a rigidly hierarchical structure, in which Christian belief was mediated by the clergy of a formal religious establishment with a strong liturgical tradition. The most challenging reading text to which children within the Anglican community could aspire was not so much the Bible as the Book of Common Prayer.

In the American colonies in general at the beginning of the eighteenth century, Anglicanism enjoyed the status of being an established church only in Virginia, Maryland, and South Carolina. Everywhere else, Anglicanism had to compete with other state churches and sects. In those parts of New England where Congregationalism was the established church (Massachusetts, Connecticut, and New Hampshire), Anglicanism frequently drew the ire of other Protestant sects as well as the Congregational orthodox for trying to establish a bishop in America. Thanks to local opposition from virtually every quarter, the Anglican Church did not achieve this ambition until after the American Revolution and had to settle for sending commissaries (bishop's agents) instead.

The promotion of Anglicanism was therefore heavily dependent on missionary activity financed by the Church of England. The organization that controlled this activity was the S.P.G., for which the Archbishop of Canterbury served as ex officio president, and which paid the salaries (always inadequate) of its missionaries and schoolmasters. From its foundation in 1701 until 1783—when Ebenezer Street, the society's New York Charity School schoolmaster, drew his last half-year's salary—the S.P.G. financed a major missionary effort in every British colony except Virginia and Maryland, where Anglicanism was already legally established. The society paid, in part or whole, for the support during that period of 329 Anglican missionary clergymen, 18 catechists, and 82 schoolmasters. The reach of the society spread from Brunswick, Maine, in the northeast down through the bustling ports of Boston, New York, and Philadelphia in the middle provinces to Augusta and St. George's, Georgia, in the south. The targets of its proselytism were not only white settlers and their children but indigenous Indians and enslaved Africans.[1]

While it never funded more than seventeen schoolmasters in America in any one year, the S.P.G. must nonetheless be regarded as a key player on the literacy instructional field in colonial America. Some of its schoolmasters served for over two decades. From the years 1714 to 1763, sixty-five of them in all taught in the American provinces: thirty-seven in New York, eleven in New England, six each in New Jersey and Pennsylvania, three in South Carolina, and two in Georgia. Most of the S.P.G.'s schoolmasters imparted nothing fancier than the basic elements of literacy (and, to boys only, of numeracy), accepting poor children into their classrooms without fees.[2]

A major emphasis of many of the spokesmen for the S.P.G., as John Calam has shown, was on subordination, a notion assumed to be of particular importance for the poor. While other organizations on both sides of the Atlantic at various times discussed and extolled the importance of knowing one's place, Calam has suggested that the S.P.G. was unique in the consistency of its approach toward the theme of subordination. The S.P.G. espoused good Christian behavior, within the established church and in the service of British imperialism. Its view on America as a whole was that of a parent reaching out to a somewhat wayward child in considerable need of education and civility. Its watchwords were obedience and deference, fidelity and dependence. In the annual sermons that the society instituted in London to spread its message, its preachers in the early years had pitying words for the "many Thousands there in our Plantations" who have become "almost as rude and ignorant as to Religion, as the Very Heathens [Indians] themselves."[3]

In general, men in the field echoed the society's convictions on the roughness of the American diamond, educationally speaking. John Thomas, an S.P.G. missionary in Hempstead, Long Island, New York, observed rudeness and ignorance first hand. The children of the people, he averred in 1712, "run about, for Want of letters and education, as wild, uncultivated, and unimproved as the Soyle was when their forefathers first had it."[4]

With this kind of challenge to face, the S.P.G. had already, in 1706, laid out a set of rules for its schoolmasters that inadvertently highlight the relationships among authority, subordination, and literacy, and between literacy and Anglicanism.[5] The S.P.G. schoolmasters were given a set of fourteen printed instructions. The first states their function: they were employed by the society to "[instruct] and dispos[e] Children to believe and live as Christians." To this end, second, they were to teach their scholars to "read truly and distinctly, that they may be capable of reading the Holy Scriptures, and other pious and useful Books, for informing their Understandings, and regulating their Manners." (Correct Christian behavior received more emphasis in these two regulations than the salvation of the soul.) Third, schoolmasters were to instruct their children thoroughly in the church catechism (that is, the Church of England catechism). They were to teach them to read it "distinctly and exactly" and then have them learn it by heart. The instructions did not ignore comprehension: the schoolmasters were to endeavor to "make [the children] understand the Sense and Meaning of it, by the help of such Expositions as the Society shall send over." (In fact, the society would rely very heavily on one key text: John Lewis's *The Church Catechism Explained*, which, perhaps in deference to this wording, was often referred to on both sides of the Atlantic, inaccurately, as Lewis's Exposition.)[6]

The fourth injunction turns to the other two Rs, succinctly encapsulating the pragmatic relationship linking writing and arithmetic to business: masters were to teach children "to write a plain and legible Hand, in order to the fitting them for useful Employments; with as much Arithmetick as shall be necessary to the same Purpose."

The next few rules turn from curriculum to the schoolmasters' relationship with the institutions of school and church. Masters were to be constant in their school attendance; morning and evening they were to use the S.P.G.'s prayers that accompanied the rules and to insist that their scholars attend church twice on Sundays, carrying their Bibles and prayer books with them so that they could be shown how to use them. (Knowing how to turn to the right page was an indication of how well a scholar knew these texts.) Again the "reverent and decent Behaviour" of the children is emphasized. The masters were to examine their scholars after the service on what they had learned. As soon as any scholars were suitably prepared, they should be recommended to the minister of the parish to be publicly catechized in the church.

The ninth injunction focuses on manners, both in and out of school. Children were to be warned against the vices to which they were most prone, such as lying, and encouraged to love truth and honesty. They were to be "modest, gentle, well-behaved, just and affable, and courteous to all their Companions." Moreover, they were to be "respectful to their Superiors," particularly the clergy. Their "Sense and Fear of Almighty God" should be a ruling principle that would govern their lives.

Schoolmasters were not to be as fearsome as the Almighty: in fact, they were to be gentle in their approach to discipline "that they may be loved as well as feared." "Correction" (that is, physical punishment), when it was applied, should be undertaken in such a way that children would understand that it was done "out of kindness, for their Good." Schoolmasters were to consult frequently with their ministers about their schools, and be examples of piety and virtue themselves.

The thirteenth rule implicitly acknowledges that all the preceding instructions are aimed at white children. But the S.P.G. was ecumenical in its reach, and it ordered that masters should be ready, "as they have Opportunity, to teach and instruct the Indians and Negroes and their Children." The regulations end on a practical note. Every six months, schoolmasters were to send an account of their schools to the secretary of the society, specifying the number of their scholars and the methods and success of their teaching. In 1738, this last procedure was formalized: a special form was sent out, called a "Notitia Scholastica," which schoolmasters were to use to report their numbers and methods.

Since the society was paying money, raised with difficulty from philanthropists, to men whom it often never met, it created a way of monitoring its employees: schoolmasters were to have their biannual reports certified by an S.P.G. clergyman in the neighborhood. This prudent move did indeed ensure some kind of quality control, and Anglican clergy were not reticent about informing the society of their opinions. When they approved of the schoolmaster, they could be very helpful by sending overseas a note in support of his plea for a higher salary; when a man was failing to fulfil his mission, they informed the society so. After 1738, when the notitia scholastica system was introduced, it was usually the clergy who had to sign off on the document, allowing for some useful maneuvering on the society's behalf. A rector could, and did, exert pressure on a schoolmaster by refusing to sign his notitia until he had improved in the area in which he was deemed deficient.[7]

Nonetheless, numerous problems intervened from the beginning. The first of these was the difficulty of attracting good men. It was not that qualifications for a schoolmaster position were particularly stringent. Once the society had figured out that the more qualified a man was, the less time he would stay in schoolteaching en route to the ministry, it was inclined to throw its support to men who were literate themselves but not much else.

Thomas Fiswicke provides us with a glimpse, from the perspective of an applicant, of what he, at least, considered an appropriate background for the position of schoolmaster in America. He applied to the society at its London headquarters in 1711, admitting that he was no great linguist: his education in Latin was meager, he explained, because he had been taken from school early. However, the little Latin that he had been taught enabled him to "spell true English, and know how to divide the sillables of Words." He thought that these skills would be adequate for "a People, who (as I may say) knows not their ABC." While his view of colonial educational attainment and even his view of his own qualifications did not diverge too sharply from those of the society, his promise to "willingly Offer my body to persecution, and martyrdom" may have struck a wrong note, for there is no evidence that the society ever engaged his services.[8]

Indeed, not much time passed before the society began to employ, as schoolmasters, men who were American born and recommended by an S.P.G. parson of a local church. This system had the great advantage of avoiding the homesickness that, as we shall see, was experienced by men like Benjamin Dennis. Only nine men seem to have been sent from England to the American colonies by the S.P.G., and after 1731 no one even applied to be sent over. Nonetheless, although recruiting local men seems not to have been too difficult, keeping good men often was.[9]

The biggest problem with keeping a man in his post was that his salary was so small. S.P.G. emoluments were never intended to offer complete financial support for a master; they were, instead, envisioned as a base salary that would allow the schoolmaster to teach poor children for nothing while he augmented it by an income from fee-paying parents of private pupils. Salaries therefore fell within a small range of fifteen to twenty pounds, and occasionally thirty pounds.[10] Men with large families proved to be a liability: unless they were supported financially by the local residents, the S.P.G. salary was doubly inadequate. William Leahy resigned in 1770, after less than two years as an S.P.G. schoolmaster in Hempstead, Long Island: he had been lured away to a better-paying school located among some wealthy farmers. The rector of his church, Leonard Cutting, attributed Leahy's defection to his large family of young children and a sickly wife. Writing to the society about a replacement, Cutting said, "we shall endeavour to get a single Man, or one with a small and active Family."[11]

Nonetheless, even a small salary seemed better than nothing in hard times, and sometimes the parishioners of an Anglican church would spontaneously request aid from the society for a man under just those circumstances. Twenty-eight inhabitants of Eastchester, New York, for instance, petitioned the S.P.G. in 1733 for a schoolmaster, explaining that Francis Chubb had settled among them and that he was a man of "great sobriety and integrity, who for his family sake which is numerous" would be willing to undertake a school. They had even built—with much difficulty, they said—a schoolhouse for him.[12] Their appeal was the more poignant because that very same year, in neighboring Westchester, William Forster, who was already receiving an S.P.G. salary, had proven a sad disappointment. Besides neglecting his school for other business, he was notorious for cursing and swearing and was frequently seen drunk. He even held the wrong political views: he favored the Pretender to the British throne. All of this was the more unfortunate because Forster had apparently been employed by the society since at least 1717.[13]

Other men, too, had such an "Affection for strong Liquour" that they could no longer be countenanced by the society. In fact one of them who had been teaching in Hempstead abandoned his school and opened a tavern. (The opinion of the local clergy was that tavern-keeping was incompatible with schoolkeeping.)[14] Others simply became too old. Poor old Thomas Gildensleave was really past it in 1729, and to judge from his spelling had probably never been up to it in the first place, when he reported of his scholars that he was teaching them their "Catechism reading writing and aRefmatick," and that he had "sum reeders sum Righters and sum sypherers." He complained of his age, his infirmities, and in particular of his failing eyesight. His pastor recommended him to the charity of the society in preference to their continuing him in responsibilities that he was no longer able to discharge.[15]

Strokes of misfortune befell schoolmasters of all religious convictions, of course, but one of the greatest challenges for the S.P.G. schoolmasters was the considerable hostility toward Anglicanism that could be found almost anywhere other than in the south. At one level, this meant that the "dissenters," as non-Anglicans were invariably called in the correspondence, were often reluctant to have their children learn the Church of England catechism, which was used as an instructional book by virtually every S.P.G. schoolmaster.[16]

A yet more serious obstacle, and one that cut at the heart of the society's effort to win the souls of black and Indian slaves, was the issue of baptism. Time and again in the early decades of the century, the fear of the Americans that baptism would somehow lead to emancipation was cited by slaveholders as a reason for refusing to allow slaves to attend the classes offered by the S.P.G. catechists. So seriously did the S.P.G. regard this refusal that its representatives were as vocal as any in lobbying for legislation that would divorce baptism from any notion of freedom. In fact, a succession of laws passed in the southern colonies had already effectively severed any possible connection between conversion and emancipation.[17] Even so, problems persisted. One was the reluctance of slaveholders to act as godparents, a necessary feature of the church's ordinance of baptism, leaving missionaries with the option of either refusing baptism to a slave or allowing his fellow slaves to act as godparents, which "most of us think improper."[18]

Doctrinal differences also affected S.P.G. schools by offering the possibility of competing sectarian schools. If a rival school were taught by a woman, it proved an added attraction for parents, for her fees were lower. As Samuel Purdy, the S.P.G. schoolmaster in Rye, complained in 1739, a Presbyterian woman had "set up Teaching Small Children, about a mile from my School, which takes off Several that used to Come to me."[19]

In addition to functioning in an often semi-hostile environment, the S.P.G. schoolmasters faced a problem familiar to their dissenting colleagues: spotty school attendance. In winter, many parents were unable "to furnish their Children with proper Cloathing to support the Inclemency of the Weather . . . [and attendance in] every School in the County, is extreemly thin for two Months in the Winter," one Long Island minister wrote in 1770.[20] In the spring and summer, parents removed the older children from school for just the same reasons that English and Indian parents had removed their children in the seventeenth century: they needed their help with farming. Basil Bartow, a schoolmaster of Westchester, New York, reported an annual total of forty-two students for the year 1745, although the most he had had at any one time was twenty-three in winter, some of them grown men who left for farming work when spring came. "[T]hen there came in a set of Small Schollars (who by reason of the cold and snow were not able to come in the winter)." These familiar problems were exacerbated by the fact that the target of the society's efforts were poor children, those who already had most difficulty attending school.[21]

Even once an adequate number of children reached the classroom safely, the difficulties of the schoolmaster were not over. The chief obstacle was a lack of books. Parents were normally expected to purchase the required school texts for their children, but, as William Huddlestone pointed out at the start of his stint as the S.P.G.'s New York city schoolmaster in 1711, poor children could not provide themselves with the "Books that's necessary for their instruction." He asked the society for a supply. Successive New York schoolmasters, including Thomas Huddlestone (William's son), Thomas Noxon, and Joseph Hildreth, requested and obtained schoolbooks. Hildreth complained in 1766, "the greatest dificulty I meet with, is the want of School Books, Writing paper and Lewis's Catechisms."[22]

Over and over again, throughout a period of some seventy years, requests for books, urgent and insistent, reverberate through the records of the S.P.G.[23] The first and crying need, common to missionaries as well as schoolmasters, was for church catechisms. Because no American printer published a Church of England catechism until the 1790s, these catechisms had to be imported from England.[24] At first the S.P.G. secretary saw to it that they were sent out directly from London. But there were instances of books that went astray, and in time the secretaries were presumably able to take the simpler and safer route of ordering books from New England booksellers who had already imported them.[25]

When the schoolmasters did beg for books, the society's secretary usually honored their requests. Grateful thanks for books received are recorded from many spots. In Rye, in 1710, the schoolmaster Joseph Cleator acknowledged the "Noble" present of books he had received from the society. In 1770, Joseph Hildreth wrote about the safe arrival of his own parcel of books in New York, when laws prohibiting the importation of British products had made it particularly difficult to obtain Anglican books: "nothing could be more acceptable, as they were very much wanted, and not a prayer book to be bought in this City (occasioned by the non importation)."[26] After the first decades, however, parents were usually expected to pay for their children's books, and parcels of books sent to schoolmasters included doctrinal works but not necessarily school texts.

When S.P.G. did provide schoolbooks, we are given a chance to see the texts that were considered essential for teaching reading at that time. In the early decades they follow, almost exactly, the "ordinary Road" delineated by John Locke. In 1709 Cleator, aged fifty-five, who had been the society's schoolmaster in Rye and Mamaroneck for the preceding two years, had begged the society for books in the letter that resulted in his "Noble" present. It would do him a great kindness, he wrote, if the society would bestow on him three or four dozen texts— "primers, psalters, Testaments, Bibles and Catechisms." The only "book" missing from Locke's list is the hornbook, never considered a text for schools run by schoolmasters.[27]

The books reached Cleator in August 1711, seven months after the secretary had notified him that they were being sent. Their numbers tell us what the society believed a school needed in the way of textbooks and how they fitted into the sequence of the curriculum. Cleator received twenty Bibles, thirty copies of the Book of Common Prayer, fifty psalters, two hundred primers, and two hundred catechisms. (He noted that he was supposed to have received forty testaments but had in fact received none.) The curriculum runs in the direction of the quantity of texts requested, from many to few: catechisms and primers first for the youngest children (two hundred), then psalters (fifty), followed by testaments (forty), copies of the Book of Common Prayer (thirty—this was an Anglican addition to the curriculum that Cleator had not even thought to request), and finally, for the most advanced students, Bibles (only twenty copies). "I have already distributed 3 or 4 Dozen of Psalters and primmers among my Scholars," Cleator wrote, "but we wanted Testaments very much, and a little writing paper wou'd do me a great kindness." (He received a ream of paper and another batch of catechisms the following May.)[28]

The Book of Common Prayer was the only text that distinguished the books in this curriculum from those of schools taught by other denominations. It was authorized by the king of England, who was the head of the Anglican Church. Faithful Anglicans had their own copy of the prayer book, but copies were also provided in churches, for the Book of Common Prayer prescribed the content of the liturgy in minute detail. (It was this reliance on set forms of prayer that had so repelled the Congregationalists and other dissenters.) Similarly, there was only one official Church of England catechism, whereas dissenters were always writing new ones. The practical effect of this Anglican prescriptiveness, in pedagogical terms, was an enhanced emphasis on the authority of the Church within Anglican schools and a strong affirmation of the one "right" way for children to practice their religion.

When the schoolmasters or clergymen requested copies of the Book of Common Prayer or psalters, they increasingly specified that they wished to have those with the Brady and Tate psalms. First printed in London in 1704, *A New Version of the Psalms of David* was available in a Boston edition nine years later and would be a steady seller for the rest of the century. Its charm lay in its revised wording (Nahum Tate was the English poet laureate), and the fact that the new wording fit established church tunes. (The storm of controversy it aroused among Congregationalists did not, of course, affect Anglicans.)[29]

Cleator's request for psalters and other books in 1709 reflected his needs as a schoolmaster. His experiences were probably typical of other S.P.G. schoolmasters in the early eighteenth century. Instructing girls as well as boys, Cleator conducted a moving school in 1709, teaching eighty children at three schools for four months each. Two years later he was down to two schools, and shortly after that he was in Rye, able to concentrate on one school only of thirty-five students, later moving his school to a little house he purchased for himself near the church. Initially he won praise for being "indefatigable" in instructing children entirely to their parents' "wonderful satisfaction and content."[30]

In October 1717, Cleator sent the Society a classic description of his school day. He catechized his scholars on Thursdays and Saturdays and (also in faithful compliance with the society's instructions) conducted morning and evening prayers. "My method of Teaching is that after the Children do very well know the Alphabet to Teach them to spell in their Primmer Twice over and Third time to read it perfectly[,] to say and answer to the whole Catechism, and after to read the psalter Testament and Bible, with writeing and arithmetick so much as I am able procuring Copies of better writting than I can pretend too." Cleator even provided a glimpse of his students' progress. Of boys who could "say and answer" the whole catechism perfectly, there were twenty-one who could, and twenty-seven who could not; and there were fifteen girls who had memorized the catechism, and eleven who had not.[31]

We could hardly hope for a more succinct description of elusive early eighteenth-century (and, by implication, late seventeenth-century) methodology. Cleator taught the children the alphabet; then, as soon as they knew their letters, he had them spell their way aloud through the primer twice and finally read it for the third time without the crutch of spelling. His students next proceeded to the church catechism, which presupposed the ability to read, at least in part, and to the rest of the curriculum—the Psalter, Testament, and Bible. Success was measured in doctrinal terms, tied to the mastery of the catechism.

Despite this self-assured description, only a month later Cleator's parson dispatched an angry letter to the S.P.G. secretary complaining that Cleator was neglecting his classroom for lengthy periods, failing in his task of preparing his children for public catechism, and far too ready with excuses for why his pupils could not attend church services. Nonetheless, Cleator continued to teach for the next fifteen years even though his eyesight was failing and he eventually went blind. With the help of a volunteer, he struggled through the school day until his death in 1732 at the age of seventy-seven. The oral nature of reading instruction certainly helped him.[32]

The Book of Common Prayer does not appear in Cleator's classroom as a school text, but it does in the same year that he gave his account, 1717, in a classroom not very far away. William Forster (destined to lose his position as S.P.G. schoolmaster because of his alcoholism and foul mouth) gave an overview of his Westchester school and its thirty-three scholars. One of the local Anglican minister's sons was learning Latin grammar, six scholars were taking lessons in arithmetic ("whereof one [is] in Practice three in Reduction [fractions] one in Multiplication and the other in addition"), nine were learning to write, and the other seventeen learning to read and spell. "The Books I use for the Children to spell and read are the Primmers (when be got) with the Church Catechism in them, Psalter, Common Prayer Books, Testaments, and Bibles." Children who were either spelling or reading used to "say" four lessons a day in one of these texts; those who were writing or casting accounts read in them twice daily.[33] The oral nature of reading instruction emerges vividly once again, as does the inviolable instructional order of the three R's. What is not clear, however, is whether girls were included in William Forster's school. It is probably safe to assume that they were, because charity schools were open to both sexes. The larger question is whether girls, at this early date, were being taught to write. They probably were not.[34]

The S.P.G. showed little sign of keeping up with the times, educationally speaking, and when spelling books appear in the S.P.G. records, they do so thanks to the initiative of schoolmasters in America, not clergymen in London. The speller, which was, as we shall see, the most important addition to the "ordinary Road" of the eighteenth century, surfaces as a desirable text for the S.P.G. provincial classroom in the early 1730s. In 1733, Edward Davies, who was keeping a school in Southampton, Long Island, asked to be sent some of Thomas Dyche's spelling books, "to Enable me to Instruct the Children committed to my Charge in the

True rules of Spelling." (This request underscores the vigor of transatlantic communication: Dyche's work would not be advertised by name in the *South Carolina Gazette* until 1735, or in the *Pennsylvania Gazette* until 1737.) In 1743, when the society was embarking upon its "Negro School" in Charles Town, South Carolina, the Charles Town clergyman organizing it locally asked the S.P.G. secretary to send spelling books for the school. They were in use the following year. In New York, moreover, spelling books were given by the Trinity Church vestry to the society's charity school in 1747.[35]

Writing instruction in the early decades of the century continued in the time-honored tradition of setting copies for the students to emulate. When the schoolmaster's own penmanship was poor, as Joseph Cleator admitted his was, he was particularly motivated to use commercially printed copies as Cleator did. A decade and a half later, in 1733, when Samuel Purdy wrote from Rye to describe his school, he mentioned the same practice. He taught as much writing and arithmetic as "may serve the Common occasions of vulgar People, which is the most our Countrey People will aspire after; I could heartily wish myself better qualifyed for all those but Cheifly for writing in which my weakness will discover it self." For children who were advanced in writing "my method is to procure Copies writ by the best masters and I find it answers the End very well."[36]

The inroads that arithmetic had made in the curriculum is well expressed by Rowland Ellis, writing from Burlington, New Jersey, a few years earlier. He had seventeen young male apprentices in the winter who attended fairly constantly, to whom he taught the usual subjects: "writing and Cyphering being what the people in these parts Especially here inclined to bring their children up in order to fit them for Trades and Employments."[37] His report confirms that the S.P.G. and its schoolmasters were in full accord on the commercial value of writing and mathematics.

The most extensive description of an early eighteenth-century classroom is provided by another Rowland, Rowland Jones, in June 1730. Because Jones was applying for an S.P.G. position rather than reporting on one already held, he treated the secretary to a much more extensive description of his methods than did schoolmasters already engaged by the society.[38] For children just starting to learn to read, he wrote, he preferred primers "well furnished with Syllables," particularly those that had tables of syllables running from one syllable up to eight. (As we will see, it was the inadequacy of most primers in this regard that paved the way for spelling books.) He took the children over the tables of syllables several times until they were perfect. Then he would move forward in the primer, and, every two or three pages, have the children repeat the content there.

When the children "get the Primer pretty well," he moved them up to the Psalter. Some editions of the Psalter had the proverbs at the end, and these Jones would assign to be learned by heart, "the which I take to be very agreeable." Once children had mastered these, through repetition, then, he reported, "I move 'em into such Places as I judge they are fit for either in the New or Old Testament." Rather than have his pupils start reading at the beginning of the Bible (as was the usual practice), he moved them "where I think they may have Benefit by: So making of 'em perfect in their Vowels Consonants and Dipthongs." Then, "when they go on their Reading clean, without any Noising, Singing or Stumbling, with deliberate way, then I set 'em to begin the Bible in order to go throughout." The definition of "good" reading as accurate oral reading emerges clearly from this account.

Jones's approach to writing instruction was equally systematic. He began by teaching his students one letter after another, "till they come to cut pretty clean letters." Then he taught them to write words of one syllable, two, and so forth, "and so to the longest words, and when they joyn [their letters] handsomly, I give 'em some sweet pleasing Verses [as copies], some perhaps on their Business, some on Behaviour, some on their Duty to Parents etc." Once they had "come to manage double Copies readily I give 'em some delightful Sentences or Proverbs, or some places in the Psalms, or any part of the Bible . . . and also to other fancies that may be for their Benefit." (It is not quite clear what "double Copies" means— perhaps parallel texts on a single vertically oriented page.) The texts children were to write, in short, were mainly moralistic or religious.

Jones described his mathematical instruction in similar terms: "I find no way that goes beyond that Way of Repeating both in Spelling, Reading, Writing and Cyphering." He clearly treated spelling as a subject that was separate from its uses in learning to read (spelling-for-reading), for he put his students to spelling twice a week (spelling-for-spelling, which entailed moving from speaking the whole word to pronouncing its alphabetical letters). He also conducted catechizing lessons twice a week.[39] Jones neatly encapsulated the theory that *repetitio est mater studiorum* (repetition is the mother of learning), the methodology so deeply entrenched in colonial literacy and numeracy instruction.

Although the methodology was standard, the experiences of the various S.P.G. schoolmasters who used them were in no sense uniform. Benjamin Dennis and four schoolmasters of the New York Charity School, William Huddlestone, his son Thomas Huddlestone, and his successors, Thomas Noxon and Joseph Hildreth, provide examples of those who tried to inculcate literacy and Anglicanism into the young, despite a variety of obstacles that ranged from hostile Indian attacks and schoolhouses in flames to hopes for local financial support that never materialized. In these accounts, the "ordinary Road" emerges again and again as the route the S.P.G.-supported schoolmasters followed in their pedagogy.

Benjamin Dennis was originally from Clerkenwell parish in London. The S.P.G. committee decided in the fall of 1710 that he was "well qualified for teaching Children to read and write and the Church catechism" and sent him out to Goose Creek, South Carolina, with the promise of an annual salary of twenty pounds.[40] Dennis's minister was Francis le Jau, who had been sent to Goose Creek himself as an S.P.G. missionary four years earlier to serve as the parson of the parish of St. James.[41]

Goose Creek was a tough place for the society's servants. Disease was rampant— Le Jau's predecessor had died of a fever—and newcomers were particularly susceptible. Moreover, all the problems, denominational, political, and financial, that beset missionaries and schoolmasters seemed to fall with especial weight on the Goose Creek enterprise. The community of about one hundred families that Le Jau and Dennis were, respectively, to minister to and instruct did not appear to be particularly interested in either church or school. Two and a half years elapsed before Le Jau could move into his house, which was supposedly being financed by his parishioners (poor themselves), and even then it was far from being finished.[42]

Le Jau himself was a difficult man, according to some. The local commissary, Gideon Johnston, maintained that Le Jau quarreled with anyone who held opinions that differed from his own and was "an odd sort of Man, and as to his temper, one of the most unfit persons in the World for being a Clergyman."[43] Be that as it may, Le Jau was consistently kind to Benjamin Dennis from the moment Dennis arrived in Goose Creek in the fall of 1711. After staying with Le Jau for a few weeks, Dennis moved to the house of a man named Captain Davis. He would have to teach there, Dennis reported back to the S.P.G. secretary, since the school-house that was being built was not yet ready. He was taken to see a village of local Indians and was fascinated by the painted chests, stored under the thatch, in which the Indians preserved the bones of their ancestors.[44]

The charm of his new surroundings soon waned. First he became ill in a general sickness that took some four hundred lives. No sooner had he recovered than he fell from a horse and broke his thighbone. Meanwhile his wife and children had traveled from England to Maryland, then to Virginia, and embarked on a sloop for South Carolina on the final leg of their long journey. As the sloop was sailing toward Charles Town, it was attacked by a privateer. The passengers were robbed of all their possessions, and the sloop had to turn back to Virginia. It was, remarked Le Jau, "a sad accident considering how hard it is to Provide oneself with Necessarys in this country." It was August 1712 before Dennis was reunited with his wife and two children and moved to a borrowed house.[45]

Meanwhile, Dennis had begun his school. In obedience to the society's instructions for schoolmasters, he wrote a series of letters to the S.P.G., usually more often than the required once every six months, and did not hesitate to complain about his lot. From our point of view, it is unfortunate that he interpreted his instructions to describe his methods of teaching as restricted to his catechetical instruction and never discussed the rest of his teaching. In a letter sent in February 1712, he gave a quick, if incomplete, review of his instructional methods, mentioning that he had begun to catechize several blacks, but had to give up because of the recent sickness. "I have at present 18 Scholars four of which are Blacks." Two of these four were children and the third was a man born and baptized in Portugal, a churchgoer who wished to learn arithmetic. The fourth was a young woman who wished to be prepared for baptism. Dennis catechized "the ignorant" twice a day, and the "more perfect" twice a week.[46]

By December Dennis was asking the society for an increase in his salary and muttering that he would not have gone through this for twice the salary. The following March he was somewhat more explicit about his teaching. He now catechized twice a day and expounded twice a week, out of Lewis's exposition. He felt that he had had good success: whereas only a few children could say the catechism when he arrived, now "most of the Children . . . can not onely say their Catechise now but also are able to pass through a good part of their Exposition." Parents were sending their children to him because they liked his approach, but those in his own parish were not contributing anything to his salary. He now had thirty scholars: twenty-seven whites, one black, and two Indians.[47]

When Dennis reported his progress the following year, in May 1713, he noted that none of the (free) Indians had yet sent their children to his school, even though they often promised him that they would. Meanwhile, his financial situation had eased somewhat, since the South Carolina assembly had made a settlement on schoolmasters.[48]

The next February, Dennis had some drama to report. He and his family had been forced by a violent hurricane to "quit the house naked, and shelter our Selves in a Nigroe hut." His books were spoiled, and his house too damaged to live in. He had been unable to repair the house, partly because of a lack of workmen and partly because of a lack of money. His school was low in students.[49]

In this same letter, Dennis made the standard schoolmaster's plea for books. Predictably, he had had trouble obtaining books from the first. The society's secretary had sent parcels of books, to both him and Le Jau, but Dennis's had not arrived.[50] Now he asked for some copies of the Book of Common Prayer, a few copies of the *Whole Duty of Man*, and some Bibles. The secretary responded by sending him, care of Le Jau, eighteen Bibles, a bundle of prayer books, and six copies of the *Whole Duty of Man*.[51] Dennis's request is a good example of the enormous time lag between a letter and its response. Separated by a vast ocean, Dennis asked for books in February and the secretary wrote that he had dispatched them in July.[52]

In April 1714, Dennis gave another report. His school had increased to twenty-three students: twenty of them were white, two were half Indian, and one was black. His class now included two children whose parents were noncomformists. He continued to catechize twice a day and "twice a week expound out of Mr. Lewis's Catechise by heart, and some have proceeded a great way therein."[53] In August, while complaining that "every thing is so prodigious dear here that it is almost impossible to live," he noted that he was now teaching three children of Baptists and two more of Presbyterians. Their parents had protested against his using the Anglican catechism, but he had remained firm, and they had given in. "I find no small trouble with 'em," he wrote, leaving it unclear whether he was referring to the dissenter's children or the dissenters themselves, "but shall not begrudge my labour." Le Jau bestowed his blessing on this principled stand: "I have praised his conduct."[54]

When Dennis wrote again, in September 1715, it was to report that he had been engaged in an activity very different from schoolkeeping. Because of an Indian uprising—the Yamasee War—he had had to take on garrison duty. Although the numbers in his school were slowly picking up again, his circumstances were exacting a price. "I have sufferred enough," he wrote, "for the Service of this Place." In November, Le Jau told the secretary that Dennis had "been reduced to Low Circumstances by this miserable Warr, where for a long time he has done the duty of a Souldier with great Zeal." Despite everything, "he continues to be[have] himself very well and carefully in the Station the Society had put him in."[55]

Dennis put up with his unhappy situation a little longer, then begged the society to recall him. The secretary wrote in August 1716 to give him permission to do so. Dennis responded that he was "mightily Oblig'd." He could see no prospect of either the church being completed or a school properly supported in the parish: "indeed the miserable State of the Province at this Juncture, both by war and sickness will (I fear) rather destroy both than give life to either." Even his friends were at risk: Le Jau, he said, was reduced to a "very low Condition." He felt that he had faithfully carried out the society's instructions, despite "hardships, losses, disappointments, fatigues, sickness and unjust dealings."[56] Benjamin Dennis, consistently praised by Francis Le Jau for his unwearying labors for his school, now vanishes from the S.P.G. records.

If Dennis exemplifies the conflict between society expectations and their fulfillment, William Huddlestone of New York is an example of the poverty endured by some of the S.P.G.'s best men. More important, his experience illustrates a quiet revolution that occurred at the beginning of the eighteenth century: the inclusion of girls in previously all-male schools and their introduction to writing instruction.

A cousin of Joseph Cleator, Huddlestone was recommended to the S.P.G. as a schoolmaster for poor children in New York city several years before Benjamin Dennis began his ill-fated mission in South Carolina. In 1705, the Reverend William Vesey, the Anglican rector of Trinity Church, New York, wrote to the society's secretary to suggest that Huddlestone be given an allowance. Huddlestone had been teaching at a private school in New York for over fifteen years and had conducted classes in the church catechism for Dutch, French, and English children. A devout Anglican, he was almost continuously elected a vestryman at Trinity Church and had served as the church's clerk since the church was chartered in 1697, for which he was now receiving a stipend of thirty pounds. Since he had a large family, his private fees and the clerk's stipend failed to support him adequately, and he was, according to Vesey, indigent.[57] Huddlestone received what was, in effect, a handout the following year, as well as some books from the society, but he was not formally appointed as an S.P.G. schoolmaster until the summer of 1710. The school itself had been opened three years earlier as a charity school for "poor boys and girls."[58]

In his first letter to the society in his new post, Huddlestone asked for an addition to his salary of ten pounds and would continue to ask for a raise in almost every subsequent letter that he wrote.[59] He based his request on the number of boys that he taught: his terms of employment stipulated that he teach forty "poor Children of this City." Forty boys, he said, was "a great Number to teach," and he only had eight boys left whose parents paid him. Predictably, he asked the society to send him books; the last batch sent had never arrived. The boys' parents, he said, "are so miserable poor that they are not able to provide them Books that's necessary." (In another letter he claimed that they could not even provide their children with adequate clothing.) He requested the new Tate and Brady psalters and "the Bible of large Print with the same Psalms and Common Prayers in it for my own use in my School."[60] Six months after that, in January 1711, he issued his first progress report. He had received the list of boys from the mayor of New York. The boys themselves, when they came to him, "were altogether ignorant, rude and unpolished." A year later, seven of these same boys had done well enough to be put out to trades and business, having learned to read, write, and cast accounts. The school may have been founded for both sexes, but clearly only boys were attending.[61]

At the same time, the loss of private pupils was taking its toll financially. Huddlestone was now reduced to seven such pupils, the victim of local snobbery: "The People of Fashion in the Town haveing taken their children from him out of a sensless notion that they will not send them to a charity school," as some of his supporters put it. As a result, they said, his numerous family was in a desperate state.[62] Although the society finally relented and in December 1713 promised Huddlestone an additional five pounds, Huddlestone apparently had to keep his school that winter in City Hall itself, since he could not afford to rent a house. It was only the charity of Reverend Vesey, who had taken up a collection for him, he wrote, that prevented him and his family from perishing.[63]

Huddlestone's financial difficulties never deterred him, he claimed, from being "an instrument of doing good to these poor creatures under my care."[64] He continued to teach forty children at a time; a list of their names in 1713 confirms that they were all boys. Two years later, however, in July 1715, the mayor of New York certified that there were still forty poor children at the school—but this time the accompanying list includes the names of two girls, Mary Finney and Elizabeth Cranell. (Elizabeth was probably the sister of William Cranell, whose name also appears on the list.)[65] While girls had already been included in other S.P.G. schools, such as those of Benjamin Dennis and Joseph Cleator, this was the first time in the history of the New York charity school that girls received educational support from the S.P.G. From that point on, girls were regularly included in the school. As early as 1722 there were fourteen girls along with thirty-two boys.[66]

In the fall of 1716, William Huddlestone wrote an impassioned plea for yet another raise, pointing out that, unlike other schoolmasters, he did not get "the value of a Shilling save my Salary of £15." (Since he was drawing a salary from the Trinity Vestry as the church clerk, he was being a little disingenuous.) He turned from this painful topic to his teaching methods. In the morning he taught his scholars to "Spell read & write till Eleven a clock. At which time the Bell calls us to Prayers, where we daily appear to the great Growth and Encouragement of that Infant Church." In the afternoon, the children spelled, read, wrote, and "cypher[ed]" from one o'clock until five, when he read the psalms for the day. Everyone who could read made the responses. "And then we sing a Staff or two of the psalms we have read, and soe conclude the Day." He taught the church catechism three times a week.[67]

Sunday was just as much a school day as the rest of the week. The children started the day by learning by heart the appropriate graces and prayers. Then they trooped off to Trinity Church, returning to school after the sermon, where the readers among them repeated the text of the sermon to Huddlestone and identified biblical passages that supported the text. (This, of course, was the classic approach to "verifying" the tenets of the catechism. Cotton Mather had been among those who used it; John Lewis based his exposition of the catechism on it.) Those who could write reported on "what little" they had got out of the sermon. Finally, those in the top class gave the answers from a chapter or two of Lewis's *Church Catechism Explained*. The other children were dismissed after repeating the church catechism, singing a psalm, and reciting some prayers. "As for my Success in teaching," Huddlestone reported, "I have taught a Considerable Number who knew not a Letter (when they came to me), [but who] can now read write & Cypher through the Rule of Three." Some of these had now gone to sea, others to trades. He reiterated his need for an increase in salary, because his wife, Sarah, was also teaching at his school: "my Wifes time being Likewise wholly spent in that Service."[68]

By the end of August 1723, Huddlestone was dead.[69] His son Thomas, who been acting as an usher for his father, was recommended by both the mayor and church officials and duly appointed in his father's place in the spring of the following year. When he sent in a report on his teaching methods, it resembled his father's to a high degree. The only difference from his father's description of his day was that Thomas Huddlestone did not mention spelling, and the morning school closed at half past eleven rather than eleven o'clock. He did, however, issue a plea for the usual books—copies of the Bible and the Book of Common Prayer with the new version of the Psalms (the Tate and Brady version), a few testaments, psalters, and primers and some copies of Lewis's *Church Catechism Explained*. These, he said, "are very much wanted and would add much to the carrying on that good and charitable work we have now in hand."[70] Since he was reluctant to turn away needy children, his school grew in numbers, and in the spring of 1730 it included sixty-eight children, of whom twenty were girls. Were it not for the society's charity, Huddlestone wrote in May of that year, "a great many hundreds [of children] might be brought up without knowing whether there is a God or not, and indeed as it is there's too many running about the Streets like lost sheep going astray."[71]

Six months later, in the fall of 1730, Thomas Huddlestone, too, died. If he and his father exemplified schoolmaster hardship, what ensued with the choice of his successor was a striking example of the political passions that literacy instruction could evoke, and of the importance the Trinity Church charity school had assumed in the eyes of church members. Thomas's mother, Sarah, who had continued to help in the school, not only had to confront her "almost Insupportable grief" but was deprived of her major source of income.[72]

Sarah Huddlestone now took an extraordinary step: she attempted to win the S.P.G. position for herself. In October of the following year, she wrote a letter to the society asking to be allowed to continue the school. She based her claim on the grounds that she had spent about thirty years, first with her husband and then her son, "in teaching and instructing young Children to Spell read & write the English Tongue and in keeping them under such a due and regular Occonomy as might best Enduce to their Improvement as well in learning, as in the Principles of Religeon and Vertue." She adduced financial reasons as well as her skill at classroom management. Thanks to the society's bounty, she said, and to the income her son derived from the clerkship of Trinity Church, supplemented by the needlework of her four daughters, her son had been emboldened to pay for the addition of a room to their house (which functioned as the schoolhouse) by taking out a mortgage on the existing structure. Thomas had reasonably expected to pay it off quickly by his "Prudent and frugall" management. But now, she said, that God had taken away her "chief Pillar, the only Support and Comfort of her Self and Family," she feared destitution. She added a point that actually weakened her case: she said that most of the children now being accepted into the school were barely capable of reading or writing; others had either been removed by death or put out to trade.[73] By implication, she was admitting that she was unqualified to teach arithmetic or bookkeeping.

Sarah Huddlestone bolstered her cause by appealing to the leading citizens of New York. Enclosed with her letter was a petition, a large sheet of paper signed by a remarkable galaxy of sixty-nine notables, headed by the Reverend Alexander Campbell and including the mayor, the city council, several aldermen, a justice of the supreme court, an attorney, seven vestrymen of Trinity Church, and twenty-two "principal merchants." The signers added their own supporting comments to her pleas, attesting that she was a "prudent, carefull, and virtuous woman," but they weakened their claim by appealing to the society's compassion rather than stressing Sarah Huddlestone's experience. They asserted that she was responsible not only for her four daughters but in addition for two orphaned nephews. Moreover, "Her being so long accustomed to a school, gives her some claim to that office." Were she granted the position, the attestation continues, coming to the crux of the matter, it would be discharged as faithfully and "as well as if given to a Man." The attestation ends with a practical consideration: the clerkship, for which neither they nor Sarah Huddlestone thought a woman qualified, could be split off from the schoolteaching.[74]

The one name that did not appear on this attestation was the only one that mattered: that of the rector of Trinity Church, William Vesey. (The signature of Alexander Campbell was a drawback: the man was widely rumored to be a rogue.) Vesey was unalterably opposed to Sarah Huddlestone's appointment and made his position known to the society. His selection was Thomas Noxon, a long-time vestryman of the church. Vesey's choice was supported, as the minutes of Trinity Church Vestry show, by others in an official position in the church as well.[75] The S.P.G. of course heeded Vesey, whose advice they had been taking for almost thirty years, and appointed Noxon in February 1732, at a salary of twenty pounds. They did, however, give Sarah a "reward" of fifty pounds "for her late husbands Service in Catechizing the Negores and Indians."[76]

Passions rose so high on the subject of Sarah Huddlestone's quest that leaflets were printed up locally and sent off to S.P.G. headquarters in London. One such leaflet, dated August 1732, exclaims, "How basely Mr. Vesey has behaved towards Mrs. Huddlestone, is very well known, for he obliged her to take out the Society's [fifty-pound] Bounty in Goods, from Hucksters and Shop-keepers with whom Mr. Vesey dealt," to the loss, the leaflet claimed, of some third of its value. Moreover, Vesey was said to have employed Thomas Huddlestone without recompense to write out his accounts, sometimes "till the Ringing of the last Bell on Sundays." His mother was, the leaflet continued, ten times more qualified to teach than Thomas Noxon. "It is a matter of wonder," proclaimed another published pamphlet, "to the Privy Council, the Magistrates of the City, the Judges of the Province & to all sensible & disinterested people of this place, who have recommended Mrs. Huddlestone . . . how Mr. Vesey could so impose upon his Lordship [the Bishop of London] & Soc. against plain reason . . . or how the recommendation could prevail against that of so many worthy gentlemen & the united voice of the people."[77]

The writer who accused Vesey of impoverishing Sarah Huddlestone through making her use his favorite storekeepers also had a few choice, and clearly exaggerated, words to say about Thomas Noxon. "He is a strange-out-of-the-way Clerk who cannot sing by Note, and a most unaccountable Schoolmaster who can neither read nor write." Furthermore, he was unfit for his office and blundered almost daily in front of the whole congregation. He was indeed "altogether unqualified" for his post. Thomas Noxon defended himself against these attacks by writing a response that was also printed and circulated.[78]

So much civic resentment persisted against Thomas Noxon that the following spring the mayor refused to give him a certificate in attestation of the reports Noxon sent the society about his school. Instead, officials of Trinity Church appointed a committee to visit the school once a month, apparently in response to a suggestion by the S.P.G., which was probably nettled by the unseemly controversy over Noxon's appointment. From then on, a church committee regularly visited the charity school and certified the information on student numbers and other details required by the society.[79]

Noxon taught for eleven years, but there may have been some truth to all the charges of incompetence leveled at him, for he gave up the clerkship, a lucrative position, two years after he was awarded it. The letter he sent to the society's secretary in 1742 to report that he had "no Negroes, or Indian Children sent to me by their Masters—by reason they don't incline to have them Instructed in Reading" was written by someone else, and his own signature was shaky. In June 1743, the society secretary accepted his resignation.[80]

The man chosen by William Vesey and his vestry to succeed Noxon was Joseph Hildreth. He began to teach the school without a formal acknowledgment from the society under the assumption that it would soon be forthcoming. The S.P.G., however, had other ideas. The secretary wrote to inform Vesey that, "after mature consideration," because of the number of schools already available in the province of New York (nine English schools, one Dutch, one French, and one Latin), the society was giving preference to men who planned to take holy orders, of whom there were several in New England. They would therefore discontinue the New York charity school.[81]

By this time, however, the school had a significant role to play in the life of the church and even of the city itself, and Vesey wrote back in some alarm. While it was indeed true, he said, that there were nine English schools, there was only one, the charity school, that was taught by a Church of England schoolmaster. He conceded that there were "some School Mistresses who teach little Children to reade, but it cant be Expected that they will teach the Children of the poor gratis, since they want Charity to Support themselves." He appealed to the society's compassion and religious convictions alike. The school had been a "constant Nursery for above Forty Years" to the Anglican Church, he argued, and its disappearance would result in depriving "the Children of the Poor, who's Parents can hardly give them bread . . . of the opportunity of Learning to Read" and of being instructed in the principles of Christianity.[82]

Vesey prevailed once again, as he had done so often in the preceding decades, and the society provided a rather grudging support to the schoolmaster of ten pounds a year (increased to fifteen pounds a few years later). But Vesey himself did not live to see it. He died at the age of seventy-two—"our own almost irreparable loss," his churchwardens and vestry called it—in July 1746. Rector of Trinity Church from its charter of 1697 until the day of his death, he had performed the duties of his office, according to a notice in the press, "with unwearied Diligence and uncommon Abilities."[83]

Hildreth, like other masters before him, was soon able to enjoy the fruits of the clerkship for the church, and by the 1750s the vestrymen of the church were providing substantial assistance to the school in a variety of ways. Not only did they augment Hildreth's salary from 1754 on, first with bonuses and later with a regular supplement of forty pounds, but they regularly raised money for the school itself by tapping charitable bequests and donating the church collections on those Sundays when charity sermons were preached. In this way, the charity children were provided with clothing over the years, as needed, and the school with necessities such as wood for the fire and, on one occasion, spelling books. Other organizations in the city also helped: theatrical companies in the 1760s, for instance, were able to overcome the distaste of some of the citizenry for their productions by designating their performances "For the Benefit of the CHARITY SCHOOL." Support for the school was becoming institutionalized: the church was not just supporting a charity school but "Trinity School," as Hildreth addressed his letters from 1763 on.[84]

The vestry's support also extended to the construction of a new school building, for which they successfully solicited contributions from public-spirited citizens of New York. Hildreth himself was instrumental in persuading the church to construct it when church officials were deciding to build a chapel near the existing church. The schoolhouse was a splendid structure, two stories high, fifty feet long by twenty-three wide, with a "Wing" of eighteen square feet; in Hildreth's eyes, it was "one of the most beautiful edifices in this city." Completed by November 1749, this "handsome, large" building was designed to house the school on the second floor and the schoolmaster's family on the first. Alas, while Hildreth was staying overnight with a friend, and his wife and children were out of town, a raging fire of unknown origin reduced it to ashes; the church, although some distance away, narrowly escaped the same fate as burning cinders were blown onto its steeple.[85]

The schoolhouse was rebuilt, and in the 1760s the Trinity Church committee was still visiting it on the first Monday of every month. The vestry was paying for a schoolmistress to instruct the girls in reading and needlework, while "those that can Read," Hildreth reported, "come to me an hour in a day to be taught to Write." His students now numbered forty-eight boys and twelve girls, the total mandated by the vestry, and included the children of both Anglican and noncon-formist parents. The routine continued much the same as it had under William and Thomas Huddlestone. The children attended the church services on Holy Days and on Wednesdays, Fridays and, of course, Sundays. Hildreth dispatched similar descriptions of his school day throughout the 1760s.[86] He was relieved of some of the catechizing duties that had so burdened some of his predecessors: the children attended catechetical instruction with the Reverend Samuel Auchmuty, who had been appointed the church catechist, successor to the Reverend Richard Charlton.[87]

In April 1765 Hildreth was more forthcoming than usual in his report about his methods of instruction. He revealed that once the boys had mastered spelling out words from a text and were beginning to read without spelling, he introduced them to writing: "of the Boys," he said, "18 are learning Arithmetic and accompts several of which will be fitted for any kind of business in a little time, 20 are learning to write, and 10 to spell, it being my constant method as soon as they begin to read to put them to writing." (He was therefore introducing penmanship instruction a little earlier than was the usual custom.) Of the girls, the fourteen who could already read were coming to him every afternoon for writing instruc-tion. In addition, every Sunday afternoon in the schoolroom, he taught large numbers of black catechumens to sing psalms. On one topic he differed not at all from his predecessors. His salary was not enough, he wrote, even with the addition of thirty pounds for his clerking duties, to support his wife and their four children, and "altho' my Duty in this School greatly exceeds that of any other School in this place, yet my pay is much less, which is extremely discouraging."[88]

A striking consistency may be seen in the curriculum of the New York Charity School from the early decades of the eighteenth century to the American Revolu-tion. Successive schoolmasters used the same texts and followed the same proce-dures, decade after decade. It is only possible to detect three curricular changes of any substance during this period. First, the decade of the 1740s saw the introduc-tion of spelling books as an instructional tool. All the schoolmasters—the two Huddlestones, Noxon, and Hildreth—used primers, psalters, testaments, the Book of Common Prayer, and the Bible in their classrooms, but it is not until Hildreth's classroom that spelling books are mentioned. They were provided not by the S.P.G. but by the vestry of Trinity Parish, in 1747.[89]

Second, only once did any of the schoolmasters (again, it was Hildreth) suggest that their students could profit from reading something other than the traditional doctrinal texts, or that the children actually wanted to enlarge the scope of their reading. In a request to the S.P.G. for some books in October 1769, Hildreth asked for the usual Bibles and prayer books. He added a request for "a few small religious Tracts, I make no doubt but 'twould have a good effect on the minds of the poor Children, many of whom are inclined to read."[90] The society, as usual, responded favorably to this appeal, and by the time of his report a year later Hildreth said he had received the books and distributed most of them, adding, "the rest I shall give out occasionally for their encouragement." Three years later he made the connection more explicit. He said he had now distributed all the tracts "as Premiums among my Scholars, and found it to have a good effect." He asked for a fresh supply.[91] This faint hint that children were eager to read something other than the familiar religious texts suggests that youngsters might have welcomed a richer reading diet than the one they were given.

The third innovation was again Hildreth's, although it had been begun in a small way by William Huddlestone. Hildreth taught children "psalmody," how to sing the psalms. He first mentions it in 1768 and specifies that he taught only "those who are capable." His success was such that not only could many of the scholars "join with great decency in singing the Psalms in Church" but they could entertain the congregation with a hymn at festivals or at the Charity sermons. (Although he never said so explicitly, the singers were undoubtedly the boys only, as was the custom in Anglican churches everywhere.)[92] Like reading tracts, psalmody enhanced the children's skills, for it involved reading the music as well as the words.

The last innovation was by far the most important, because it reflected a major cultural shift that was duplicated throughout the American colonies. It took place in two stages. The first was the admission of girls to the school, which we have been able to date very precisely to 1715. The second was the girls' access to the schoolmaster for writing instruction. The schoolmasters' wives took care of their reading instruction. In May 1762 Joseph Hildreth noted that the girls came to him for an hour each day for writing instruction. Hildreth had succeeded Thomas Noxon when the latter resigned in 1743, and it is therefore tempting, although there is no hard evidence, to date the teaching of writing to the girls in Trinity School from that point on. Just how far the female sex still had to go, however, was well exemplified by the failure of Sarah Huddlestone to take over the school herself.

The history of the New York Charity School, "Trinity School," affords us a rare chance to look at the literacy education of the poor at its provincial best, particularly under Hildreth's regime, when earlier problems of inadequate financial support had been resolved. The school had many advantages over its rural counterparts. The very fact of its being an urban school forestalled children's seasonal disappearance to help out with the family farm, and the financial support given the school by the Trinity vestry meant that problems such as inadequate clothing and shortages of firewood were alleviated. After 1749, the school was housed in a good building. Moreover, the initial stigma attached to the school of its clients being charity children, in a city that had all too many of them, was unquestionably overcome. By 1760 both Anglican and nonconformist parents were sending their children there, and the disappearance of nonconformist children in 1764 (they had previously represented about two-thirds of the intake) suggests that the school was now sufficiently sought after to be restricted to the children of Anglican parents. Apparently, the school had a waiting list throughout its history, allowing the school to dismiss children whose attendance was poor and substitute others in their place.[93] Finally, the schoolmaster was not overburdened, despite the large numbers: the Huddlestones and Hildreth both had female help to teach the girls reading and sewing, and a male assistant for the boys. The only serious obstacle to a good education was a continuing shortage of books.

The numbers of children served by the school increased steadily, with only an occasional retreat. William Huddlestone had forty children in his school in 1710, but in 1730 his son Thomas actually taught, with his mother's help, sixty-eight children, the highest total up to that time. When, however, Hildreth took over the school from Thomas Noxon in 1743 he had only fifty-six students—forty boys and sixteen girls. During the 1740s and 1750s, the number of children in Hildreth's school ranged between forty-eight and sixty-one. In December 1761, Hildreth began to provide the S.P.G. with statistics that identified his students by sex: he now had a school of sixty children, forty-eight boys and twelve girls. This proportion of four boys for every girl was permanently abandoned three years later, when twelve girls were added for a total of seventy-two children. The new ratio of two boys to one girl continued until 1767, when two orphaned boys were added. The following year saw an increase to seventy-five children—fifty boys and twenty-five girls. In 1770 the enrollment grew to eighty-five (fifty-five boys and thirty girls). These numbers were too great for two people to teach, and at this point the vestry of Trinity Church hired an assistant for Hildreth, "a Lad brought up at my School," he wrote in 1772, "who has been a great help to me in forwarding the Children in their learning." The school continued to grow, reaching eighty-six children in 1775.[94]

It is possible to estimate the turnover in the school—and so the number of those judged successfully taught—by looking at the numbers of children who left each year, when known. As we saw earlier, the names of forty children were listed by William Huddlestone in 1715, and they included, for the first time, the names of two girls, Mary Finney and Elizabeth Cranell. The mayor's certificate in the fall of 1716 showed forty-eight children, of whom now six were girls. Mary and Elizabeth were still in school, and Mary had been joined by her sister Dinah Finney. The other three girls were Sarah Wheeler and Mary Jones, both of whom had male siblings, and Deborah Sympcampe. By the time of the September 1717 list, Mary Finney and Elizabeth Cranell have vanished, as have their siblings, but Sarah Wheeler, along with her brothers, and Deborah Sympcampe are still at school. The name of Anne Prosser appears for the first time.[95] The girls, in other words, were in school for only two years. It is highly probable that, at this early date, they were not being taught to write.

Given that the inclusion of girls in the 1710s was still something of an innovation (though a permanent one), a better test is the number of boys who continued their enrollment. Of the forty-two boys in school in the fall of 1716, twenty-four (57 percent) were still there the following year. By 1725, only one boy from the

1717 list, Joseph Paulding, was still a student.[96] These numbers suggest a relatively rapid turnover.

The interpretation of these numbers, however, is complicated by the fact that we do not know why the children left. The figures cannot distinguish between attrition (sickness, moving, and so on) and success. A better gauge of successful literary acquisition is the number of children who left the school because they had, essentially, obtained from it all they were assumed to need: that is, the number of boys who were "put out" to trades annually, and of girls identified at the same time who did not enter a trade but who presumably left to enter domestic service.

Hildreth provided precise statistics on qualified school leavers from 1764 on, when he informed the society that in the preceding year thirteen children (eight boys and five girls) had left the school from a pool of seventy-two children. This proportion grew as the school grew, and by the time the school had an enrollment of eighty-six children in 1775, the number of children leaving over the course of the year had reached thirty. The turnover rate was such that a child entering one year could expect to be literate enough (and, if male, numerate enough) to leave after three years, and often before four complete years, of schooling. The rate of leaving was much the same for both sexes, except that girls, for the last years of Hildreth's school (after 1769), could expect to leave within three years. By the time four full years had passed, the turnover of students, both male and female, was complete.[97]

The crucial question, frustratingly hard to answer, concerns the quality of the children's literacy. We may reasonably infer that they could read aloud familiar religious texts, up to and including the Bible; that they could answer by heart questions posed to them from the catechism; that the girls were able to sew and the boys knew enough arithmetic to identify a missing term in a set of proportions (the "rule of three"). How well they understood what they read we cannot know, but they satisfied the minimal literacy requirements of the prerevolutionary period.

A larger question is also unanswerable: how much was Anglicanism, with its emphasis on obedience within a rigidly hierarchical structure, imbibed by these students? Certainly their S.P.G. teachers for the most part would remain unalterably Anglican and Loyalist when their particular brand of faith was put to the test in the crucible of the American Revolution.

6

Literacy and the Mohawks

The frontispiece to the third edition of the Mohawk Book of Common Prayer, printed in London after the American Revolution, in 1787, is a fitting metaphor for how British rulers viewed their relationship to their Mohawk subjects, who were by then living in Canada. The scene is set in the interior of a church. At the back, a window reveals clouds in the sky. At the right, but still in the background, is a (white) minister preaching from the pulpit to a shadowy mass—the church is packed—of Indians. In the foreground, the scene shifts to a kind of interior court-yard with a projecting carved canopy, under which are seated, on a dais, a man and woman, each of whom extends a book to two of the three Indians kneeling at the foot of the dais. The British king and queen, for this is who they must be, are flanked on either side by clerics, bewigged, white-bloused, and black-robed, behind whom stands a figure in a tail coat. (Is he a servant, a politician, or a missionary?)

Facing this group, mostly with their backs to us, and in the right foreground, are eight more Indians, this time standing. They are decently clad but of a fierce aspect; their hair is pulled back in a high pigtail. Long earrings dangle from their ears and thongs cross over their shoulders, implying quivers. They too (perhaps sharing the same tailor as the clerics) have short, muttonchop sleeves on their white blouses. Blankets cover the legs of them all, knotted around the waist to leave their bare legs exposed in the front, in sharp contrast to the tight leggings of king and courtiers.

The graciousness of the royal pair bestowing the books, the submissive humility of two kneeling Indian converts receiving the books—one of whom looks across at the group of unconverted Indians standing aloof and suspicious—aptly symbol-ize the cultural transformation that the books were intended to effect. As befitted a state religion, the Anglican Book of Common Prayer, printed bilingually in English and Mohawk, comes straight from the hands of the ruler and his consort. Also fittingly, books are the tools that the converts will use to transmit the faith to those who have so far resisted it. The Mohawk Book of Common Prayer, the illustration implies, will bridge the divide between Indians, just as it has bridged the divide between English and Indian cultures.[1]

Not included in the portrayal is the fact that in this edition—the third in a series that began in 1715—the vital assistance of a native American is at last acknowledged. His contribution is indicated in the work's title: *The Book of Common Prayer, and Administration of the Sacraments . . . A New Edition: to which is*

FRONTISPIECE

FIGURE 10. Frontispiece to *The Book of Common Prayer . . . Translated into the Mohawk Language* (London: C. Buckton, 1787). In this frontispiece to the Mohawk prayer book, the king and queen of England are graciously bestowing the fruits of Anglican philanthropy on the Mohawks—a prayer book in their own language. (By permission of the Syndics of the Cambridge University Library)

added the Gospel according to St. Mark, Translated into the Mohawk Language, by Captn. Joseph Brant, An Indian of the Mohawk Nation. It is the linguistic achievement of the Mohawk leader T'hayendanegea. For the first time, a native American had made a complete chapter from the New Testament available in print to his fellow speakers of Mohawk.

The eighteenth-century mission of the Anglicans to the Mohawks is the focus of this chapter. It was just one of many denominational missions that took place in the eighteenth century, most of which included the opening of schools for the Indians. Indeed, Jean Fittz Hankins has calculated that, in New England and the province of New York alone, in addition to instructors of European origin, 222 Indians, nearly all of them men, taught in Indian schools between 1698 and 1776.[2] The Anglican mission to the Mohawks, however, was one of the very few to issue books printed in an Indian language other than Massachusett.[3] Given the central importance to Anglicanism of the Book of Common Prayer, it is perhaps not surprising that the first translations consisted mainly of excerpts from this liturgical text.

The Mohawk mission echoes several themes familiar from the preceding century. The first is the agency of the native Americans themselves. In no sense was Anglicanism imposed on them by the British: those Mohawks who chose to accept it did so for their own reasons. Other themes include the contradiction between the religious tenets and the actions of Europeans who were, at least nominally, Christians; the disastrous effect of the sale of rum to the Indians, often in defiance of laws banning the practice; the rational fear of the natives that European settlers had designs on their land; and the malignant effect of European microbes. In some instances, disease or war so devastated the Mohawks that they were receptive to a different belief system.

Some themes relate directly to efforts to teach the Mohawks to read and write. Of crucial importance to the British conversion effort in the province of New York was the presence of certain native Americans who, for a variety of reasons, became deeply committed to the particular brand of Christianity that was bringing literacy in its train. Their role was not quite the same as that of a "cultural broker," to use Margaret Szasz's term—that is, a native American who managed to negotiate both cultures successfully—although such persons often became that as well.[4] Rather, it entailed being a committed convert, for whom literacy was one of the several compelling attractions of Christianity. To effect the general adoption of the new religion by his or her tribal group, these committed converts also needed to be people of influence—or somehow acquire their influence through conversion, as Hiacoomes did among the Wampanoags.

Other themes weave through the Mohawk experience. As always, it was essential for the missionaries to find an interpreter—not someone who would interpret the native culture to the missionaries (a topic in which they generally had little interest) but someone who could convey the missionaries' beliefs to the native American community concerned. This required a speaker of the Iroquian language, Mohawk, either a native informant or a European who had learned the language. Yet another familiar theme is the question of which language would be used in Christian instruction. When the mission to the Mohawks began, the English were so outnumbered by the native Americans that there was little doubt that the texts of Christianity, in this instance the Anglican liturgy, would have to be provided in Mohawk, a language that had never previously been written down.

One of the startling aspects of the Mohawk mission is that none of the English missionaries ever voiced any concern about writing Mohawk. It seems to have been the least of their problems, presumably because it had been solved by Dutch missionaries before Englishmen arrived on the scene. Nor, in the majority of the discussions on Mohawk during the early eighteenth century, does anyone comment on its syntax or phonology. The missionaries, most of them mediocre linguists, simply complained loudly about how hard Mohawk was to learn.

Finally, there is the role played by literacy instructors. But first Mohawk men had to be found, despite long periods in which there was virtually no missionary activity in the community, who were able to serve as schoolmasters to the young and continue the transmission of literacy in the Mohawk tongue.

In one respect, however, the Anglican missions to the Mohawks differed sharply from those to the Massachusetts. Unlike the Congregationalists, the Anglicans saw no need to "civilize" the Indians as part of their conversion procedures. They were content simply to "gospelize" them—to bring them the "good news" of Christianity without requiring any radical change in their way of life. No villages like Natick would be created under this approach.[5]

The First Mission to the Mohawks

The motives of the members of the London-based Society for the Propagation of the Gospel (S.P.G.), who had kept the conversion of the "heathen" in mind ever since they founded the society in 1701, were largely philanthropic. Fortunately, these motives meshed nicely with what the English government wanted in its seemingly endless series of conflicts with France: Indian support in any future contest against the French in North America. The English were already concerned that French Jesuits, whose aim was to convert the Indians to Catholicism, had made significant progress with the Iroquois tribes on the southern borders of Canada.

Five Indian tribes known as the "Five Nations"—the Mohawks, Oneidas, Onondagas, Cayugas, and Senecas—covered a vast expanse of territory in what is now the state of New York. The Mohawks lived on the eastern edge of the confederacy, the Senecas on the western. Members of the Five Nations spoke languages that had evolved from a common proto-Iroquoian language, and they functioned politically as a loose confederacy of independent tribes known as the Iroquois League or the Iroquois Confederacy. The confederacy controlled the forests for hundreds of miles all the way west from the Hudson River (home of the Mohawks) to Lake Ontario and north to the borders of the French in Canada at the Saint Lawrence River.

The confederacy had enjoyed a prolonged period of peace and prosperity from the mid 1670s until 1689 (the onset of King William's War), thanks to the "Covenant Chain" its members had forged with the English. The chain was a political and military alliance between the Five Nations and the English that guaranteed the nations security and better trading terms for their fur pelts at Albany. The Dutch residents of Albany had thrown in their lot with the English and had prospered in their turn.[6] The war, however, which lasted until 1698, brought disaster to Iroquois warriors when they supported the English against the French. The Mohawks alone lost 60 percent of their fighters to war wounds and disease. By 1700, in short, a cultural crisis was looming, and the surviving Mohawks sought, in the words of William Bryan Hart, "sacred solutions to social strain."[7] They also sought practical solutions. In 1701, the same year that saw the creation of the S.P.G., leaders of the Iroquois Confederacy signed away eight hundred square miles of their hunting grounds to William III in the hope of counteracting territorial intrusions from the French. Their Mohawk representatives included Theyanoquin, a sachem born in about 1676 who was called "King Hendrick" by the English.[8]

It was universally agreed among leaders of the English government that if the natives were to be converted to Episcopal Protestantism (Anglicanism), the interests of the crown would be much enhanced. Indeed, the progress the French Jesuits had made in converting the Iroquois to Catholicism was such a cause for concern to the English and Americans alike that in 1700 the New York Assembly passed a law banning Jesuits and priests from the province of New York. For several reasons, geographic as well as political, the Mohawks were the most promising targets of Anglican proselytism in the contested region. They were, thanks to their superior skills as warriors, the acknowledged leaders of the Iroquois Confederacy. They were also the nation that was closest in proximity to Albany, the farthest navigable point up the Hudson River from the city of New York and the focal point for the lucrative fur trade. Moreover, a key Mohawk sachem, King Hendrick, had conducted the initial land transaction with the British.

When, therefore, a mere three years after its foundation, the officials of the S.P.G. expressed an interest in bringing the consolations of Anglican Christianity to the Mohawks, they had no trouble in convincing the English government of the worthiness of their cause, or in squeezing from it some additional financial support. Their first missionary was the Reverend Thorogood Moor, who departed from London for Albany with a young kinsman in 1704. Albany was then a township of about 250 families, most of them Dutch, situated on the west bank of the Hudson River 145 miles upstream from New York. Stockaded and manned by two companies of British troops, it was the unquestioned gateway to Iroquois territory and the headquarters for a group later called the Commissioners for Indian Affairs. The commissioners were local Dutch residents (including the fur trader, landowner, and mayor Peter Schuyler) who were charged with conducting all negotiations with representatives of the Five Nations. [9]

Moor was attempting to convert a people who, thanks to the efforts of the Jesuits and a few Dutch ministers during the previous century, already had some familiarity with Christianity. Yet Moor left this remote outpost only a year after he had arrived, disillusioned by his lack of progress with the Mohawks. It is a failure he may have brought on himself, since he apparently made no attempt to preach sermons with the help of an interpreter, let alone to learn the language, which he hoped his young relative would do on his behalf. (The Mohawks refused to allow the young man to settle with them.) Moor himself, however, blamed other factors for his failure: the behavior of the New England Christians, who had taken away the Indians' lands without purchasing them; the deplorable behavior of local Christians, particularly the soldiers at the garrison at Albany, who were the only Englishmen the Mohawks encountered; and the continual misrepresentation of the British by the local Dutch who traded with the Indians. He also believed that the Indians were dying out. Whether it was from rum or from "some new Distempers we have brought amongst them," he wrote, they were wasting away, in their own words, "like Snow against the Sun."[10]

After a three-year gap, the S.P.G. appointed Thomas Barclay as the missionary to the Indians. Barclay was already serving as the chaplain to the two English garrisons at the forts of Albany and Schenectady. Since he had plenty to do without preaching to the Mohawks, the appointment seems to have been in name only.[11]

Yet Moor's earlier assessment of Mohawk receptivity to Christianity turned out to be too gloomy. As it had elsewhere, the waning of the Indian population made the Indians receptive to new ideas and alternate world views. Indeed, two Dutch Reformed ministers in Albany and Schenectady were already ministering to Mohawks interested in Christianity. The Reverend Bernardus Freeman, the Schenectady minister, became the first Protestant to learn Mohawk enough to figure out a way of transcribing it into selected letters from the Roman alphabet. (Independently and earlier, Jesuits had already done so.) As a result, its vowels correspond to continental, not English, pronunciations. With the help of an unidentified Mohawk and a Dutch interpreter named Lawrence Claessen, Freeman translated portions of the Bible, extracts from the Book of Common Prayer, and certain Dutch Reformed texts into Mohawk. They remained in manuscript form for the time being.[12]

Meanwhile, the English governorship in New York had changed (Lord Cornbury had been removed), and the new governor was instructed from England to carry out the so-called Glorious Enterprise of conquering New France (Canada) by means of coordinated expeditions from land and sea. The Iroquois were a key component in the force that was to attack by land. The initial effort of 1709 was a disaster. The English and their Iroquois allies were left stranded on the banks of Lake Champlain, lacking food, let alone materiel, because the ships intended to resupply them from England never arrived. Against a backdrop of Iroquois anger and shame, Colonel Peter Schuyler, then the second-in-command of the Indian forces (Francis Nicholson was the commander), stepped up his appeals to the Iroquois to ally themselves more firmly to the English cause. His plan was to get a leader from each member of the Iroquoian confederacy to come to London. Unable to persuade anyone but four Mohawks and one adventurous young Mahican to make the sea voyage, in 1710 he and Colonel Nicholson accompanied them to England. One of the Mohawks died en route, but the remaining four were touted in London as the Kings of the Five Nations.[13]

The Mohawks King Hendrick (a signator of the 1701 treaty), his brother or colleague Ohneeyeathtonnoprow (John, as he was known to the English), and Sagayeanquaprahton (Brant, a grandfather of Joseph Brant), along with the Mahican Elowohkaom or Etcwa Caume (Nicholas), were received royally in a visit that was designed to impress them with British might. They were taken to dockyards and arsenals, driven around London in coaches, escorted to specially staged plays and cockfights, and—creatively dressed for the occasion by a theatrical dressmaker—graciously received in a royal audience by Queen Anne herself. They also presented their concerns in person at a meeting of the S.P.G. When they departed for the voyage home, they each held the products of literacy in their hands: a quarto Bible and a handsome copy of the Anglican Book of Common Prayer, bound in red Turkey leather.[14]

The native Americans had been left in no doubt about the awesome power that lay on the other side of the ocean from their home. With the guiding hand of either Schuyler or Nicholson, they sent a letter to the S.P.G. expressing their satisfaction at the response to their request for English assistance in "the thorough Conversion of their Nations." The letter is signed with the sachems' beautifully sketched totem marks—a horse, a horned animal, and a tortoise. It hints that the Indians had their own agenda: they hoped that their newly converted subjects would "convince the Enemies to saving ffaith that the only true God is not amongst them." If faith in (Protestant) Christianity and power did indeed go hand in hand, they would have a clear advantage over their enemies. This voyage to England and back would eventually prove to be a turning point, despite the fact that Brant fell ill and died within a few months of his return.[15]

The excitement of meeting real, live native Americans led the society to focus with renewed energy on its mission to the Indians in general and the Mohawks in particular. In an effort toward the latter, its members passed a resolution authorizing the translation of the scriptures into Mohawk and offered to pay the salaries of the ministers they planned to send out; however, they requested royal aid for building the missionaries' houses and a chapel, to be constructed within a fort for security. Queen Anne responded by commissioning a set of communion silver inscribed with her name for the next S.P.G. missionary to bring with him, and by authorizing a small protective force. In October 1712, the society's next full-time missionary to the Indians, the Reverend William Andrews, reached the port of New York, carrying the queen's silver, an altar cloth, an ample tasseled cushion for the pulpit, two copies of the Book of Common Prayer, and four oil paintings of Her Majesty's Imperial Arms. (One was for the chapel; the others for the Mohawk Castles.)[16]

The Mohawk leaders met Andrews in Albany, and by November he was ensconced in his log house within the "Queen's Fort," forty-four miles distant from Albany along a rough Indian path. From there, he was able to report back to the S.P.G. on his splendid welcome from the Indians. The "Lower Castle" of the Mohawks, Tiononderoge, was close by; the "Upper Castle," Conajoharie, lay nearly twenty miles up the river Mohawk. (A later missionary would put the distance at thirty-eight miles.) Altogether some 580 Mohawk men, women, and children lived in these and another couple of settlements. Andrews's chapel was named the "Queen's Church" by the society, in a tribute to their monarch.[17]

William Andrews's Mission to the Mohawks

Conditions at the fort were miserable. "[I]n the winter season for 4 or 5 months we can scarce stir abroad by reason of the Extream Coldness of the Weather and deep Snows," Andrews wrote to his sponsors, "and in the Summer tormented with fflyes and Muschetoes, and can't stir abroad without being in danger of being stung with the Snakes, here are so many of them, Especially the Rattle Snake."[18]

Andrews received linguistic assistance from two translators, Lawrence Claessen and John Oliver. He needed it, for he found that the "Mohocks Language is Extream hard to be learnt." Claessen, who spoke little English, translated from Mohawk to Dutch. He had been kidnapped by the Mohawks as a child of eleven, and by the time he was restored to his Dutch kinfolk at the age of about twenty-one, he was fluent in all five Iroquoian dialects. Oliver, in turn, translated from Dutch to English, in a three-man translation effort that must have been cumbersome indeed. He was parish clerk for the Reverend Thomas Barclay, who served as the chaplain for the garrison stationed in Albany. Claessen confirmed the difficulties that Mohawk presented: he considered it "almost imposible for any to learn it perfectly except they begin with it when Children." Andrews was so concerned about the possibility of losing the indispensable Claessen, who acted as interpreter for the entire province, that he tried to teach English to two Mohawk boys. But he prudently desisted when he met with their resistance: "they soon grew weary on't and if I had not laide it aside they would not learn to read their own Language."[19]

In November 1713, Andrews issued a report on the formal education of the Mohawks. The Indians were enthusiastic about their children's learning to read and write: they had built a large school house "& are very forward to Send their Children to School." He hoped the society would encourage the undertaking by making an allowance to a schoolmaster. He recommended Oliver, who would do the job for twenty pounds a year. Clearly, Oliver's mastery of Mohawk was improving.[20]

The missionary effort was conducted entirely in Mohawk, Andrews wrote from the fort to his employers. But the circumstances required much writing of Christian texts: "We write what we teach the Children at present. They are very apt to learn most of them, but would learn much better if we had printed Books for them. We teach them in their own language, for they [the adult Indians] are not willing their children should learn any other, and if they should be Thwarted by attempting to teach their children what they do not Approve of, may spoil all." He expressed a preference for keeping this a Mohawk-only mission: he believed that if the Indians learned English or Dutch they would be corrupted by the vile language of the twenty or so English soldiers manning the fort or by the Dutch inhabitants (most of whom were tough trappers and traders).[21]

Andrews had already taken the first step toward providing the Mohawks with

instructional texts. In the fall of 1713 he reported sending the society two manuscripts (which he identified as Claessen's translations) in Mohawk. The longer
contained extracts from the Book of Common Prayer: it included the church
catechism, morning and evening prayers, the litany, "Several Psalms and Chapters
of the old and New Testament, some other Prayers & Graces before and after
meat, and some Singing Psalms, for they'l sing Psalms very well." The second and
much shorter one was that earliest and most familiar of instructional texts, "a Copy
for some Horn books in the Indian Language to be printed if the Honorable
Society pleases."[22]

The Mohawk version of the Book of Common Prayer was published in July
1715 by William Bradford in New York under the title *The Morning and Evening
Prayer, the Litany, Church Catechism, Family Prayers, and Several Chapters of the
Old and New-Testament.* Andrews spent several weeks in New York—a welcome
respite from his hardships up north—seeing the work safely through the press.
Apart from its overall title and the titles of its subsections, the prayer book was
entirely in Mohawk. The translator was identified as "Lawrence Claesse, interpreter
to William Andrews, missionary to the Indians."[23]

This Mohawk prayer book, covered in soft brown leather and printed in unusually large type for the period, devotes most of its 115 pages to excerpts from the
Anglican Book of Common Prayer and to a variety of prayers, including some
clearly tailored to their unique audience. A prayer for rain, for instance, precedes
one for fair weather; "A Morning Prayer for the Master and Schollars" is soon
followed by "A Short Prayer for Every Child when they first come into the seats at
Church." The "several chapters" of the Bible announced in the title are few in
number: they consist of three psalms, the first three chapters of Genesis describing
the creation, and excerpts from three chapters of Matthew that relate the birth of
Jesus and the Sermon on the Mount. Additional scriptural material consists of
sentences selected from all parts of the Bible to support different themes, such as
"Of the dutys of Husband and Wife." These excerpts are scrupulously documented
by references to the Bible, a text that was wholly inaccessible. As another translator
said of it decades later, this "probably was all that could then be procured."[24]
Procurable or not, the choices made vividly highlight how differently Anglicans
and Congregationalists approached conversion: the focus of the former was on
translating the Book of Common Prayer whereas one of the first decisions of the
latter, in the person of John Eliot, had been to translate the entire Bible.

The Mohawk prayer book presupposed that the art of reading had been mastered. The text Andrews had intended for instruction was the hornbook, but no
copy of a Mohawk hornbook is extant. Indeed, it may not have been printed, for
although gilt hornbooks and primers were sent to Andrews in June 1714 and
arrived the following January in a package from England that also contained penknives, inkhorns, and paper, they were presumably printed in English. But it
turned out that Andrews had not limited his creation of instructional texts in
Mohawk to hornbooks. As he reported in the summer of 1715, he had printed
200 of the Mohawk prayer books, 150 catechisms, and "a small Spelling book for

the Children [to] learn before they have their larger books to prevent their spoiling them to[o] much at their first Entrance."[25]

In the same letter of July 1715, Andrews reported on school attendance. He told the society that some twenty children were attending school "pretty constantly"—but that he had to be constant himself in providing them with food, or they would not attend. The Indians were very poor, he said, especially in the summer when their only food was a root they dug from the ground, some Indian corn, and dried fish. At least he could hope for better things now they had some books printed in their own tongue. It is not clear how much teaching Andrews was doing himself. Oliver was still there, but he was eventually found unsatisfactory: three years later he would be dismissed by Robert Hunter, the governor of New York and New Jersey provinces, for incompetence.[26]

Andrews also evaluated the overall progress of the students in literacy. Some of the children, he reported, "begin to read pretty well." One young man was outstanding: he could "read extrordinary well any of the Sermons and prayers we have in Indian and begins to write a good hand." Andrews explained that the "reason he has so much out Script the rest" was that the lad was lame, with one leg shorter than the other; he was therefore incapable of hunting and so he was "most of his time in the house," unlike the others, who were "as much abroad as home." But Andrews and Oliver were glad to have the Mohawks whenever they could spare the time to come "to learn their books," Andrews said, articulating the perceived indissoluble link between literacy and religion, "for it will be the principle means of laying a good and lasting Foundation of Religion amonge them."[27]

One aspect of Andrews's missionary work was reminiscent of the work of the Mayhew family among the Wampanoags: Christianity had a special appeal to Mohawk women. Well before any texts in Mohawk were available, Andrews had reported in October 1714 that he had taught most of the children of the Lower Castle their prayers, adding, "many of their Parents are very carefull in keeping them to their Duty every morning and evening as well as themselves. Here are a great many very good Women . . . [who] can give a good Account of their ffaith." After listening to a service at the chapel, the women would gather together at one of their wigwams, and those with the best memories would rehearse what they had just heard. Some prayed for an hour. Like Wampanoag women, they may have been motivated by the abusive behavior of their husbands when intoxicated. Very few of the men, Andrews wrote, were "so good." When they were sober, they were "orderly and civil," but under the influence of drink they were "like so many mad distracted Creatures, run about Starke naked the wretchedest Spectacle in the world & are for doing any mischeife[:] some are for burning their houses others for killing their wives and Children"—a possibility that their wives tried to forestall by burying their guns and hatchets.[28]

Andrews labored on at the fort, in a community of rough soldiers, their captain, and Claessen and Oliver. Members of his Mohawk congregation must have compared favorably with some of the Europeans. The behavior of Captain Charles Huddy was such that Andrews refused to give him a certificate of good character—

an act of probity that caused Huddy to harass him by dispatching scurrilous reports about him to the S.P.G. Not until Governor Hunter fired Huddy for, among other offenses, selling rum to the Indians (prohibited by the colony of New York), did Andrews have any relief.[29]

Occurrences elsewhere in the colonies were also beginning to take their toll. The Five Nations had already expanded to the Six Nations with the addition of the Tuscaroras, who had moved out of North Carolina to Iroquois territory after their defeat in the Tuscarora uprising of 1711–13. Now the Yamasees were on the attack in South Carolina, slaughtering hundreds of colonists; this was the conflict that had interrupted the schooling provided by the S.P.G. schoolmaster in Goose Creek, Benjamin Dennis. Andrews blamed it on the colonists who had cheated the Yamasees in trading and land purchases: "These base practices and wicked Examples of Christians are the great obstacles of the Conversion of the Indians." Andrews himself was sometimes in peril. He had been warned not to go among the Oneidan Indians because they blamed him for the deaths of some infants he had baptized. He had a brush with death in his own fort. Only thanks to the intervention of the soldiers in the fort did Andrews escape being attacked by a Mohawk who had entered the chapel with a hatchet in his hand and murder in his heart while Andrews was reading prayers.[30]

As happened with such painful regularity in missions to native Americans, the rosy promise of the summer of 1715 was not sustained. By the fall of that year, Andrews was disconsolate. Some of the Mohawks had gone over to the Catholics, who were much more lavish in their gifts than he could afford to be. He was drained financially by entertaining Iroquois visitors who dropped by him en route for Albany and expected food and drink, pipes and tobacco. He did what he could, he said, for twenty aged Mohawk widows at the Lower Castle, bringing a half dozen of them back to dinner every Sabbath for a meal, but he had no salary to spare to buy them blankets, or food to encourage the children to keep coming to school.[31]

The following spring brought no relief. The Mohawks were still resolutely opposed to learning English. Andrews had actually offered to teach English himself to "two or three girls, who can Read pretty well in their owne Tongue, but they would not Learn." Much more disappointing was the number of children who were no longer interested in learning to read their own language. School attendance had dropped to six or seven, and even these children "come so seldom that they make but little Thing on it." Ironically, the number of texts potentially available to the Mohawks, although as yet only in manuscript, had greatly increased. Claessen had completed his translations of an exposition of the Creed, the Ten Commandments, and the Lord's Prayer; he had also translated St. Matthew Gospel and some sermons and instructions for adult Mohawks. He had even produced translations of some of the historical passages in the Old and New Testaments "for the Use of the Children" and was close to completing a translation of one of the expositions of the Anglican catechism. But none of these would see print. Indeed, Andrews canceled an earlier request to England to have the catechism and "vocabulary" printed.[32]

By spring of the following year, 1717, Andrews was close to despair. Attendance at the school had fallen away to only four or five children: "These Indians have but little Esteem for Learning," he wrote. Even attendance at the Indian chapel had sunk to a low point. He had had to refuse communion to some of his converts because of their scandalous lives, which had alienated them from him. In this context, the gift of five English Bibles sent by the Archbishop of Canterbury for the Indian chapel must have seemed derisory indeed. In October 1718, Andrews asked the society to relocate him.[33]

The S.P.G. understood the dedication Andrews had shown and acquiesced to his request. The following June, Andrews entrusted the furnishings of the chapel, including the precious silver plate, to Huddy's replacement, sent the society's books and schoolbooks to the Reverend Robert Jenney in New York, and left his Mohawk mission forever, heading for Virginia. He died a little over two years later.[34]

Andrews's mission foundered, as William Hart has suggested, on a failure of communication. Neither side of the linguistic and cultural divide met each other's expectations. From the Mohawk perspective, schooling failed to provide enough of the food or material items such as scissors, rings, and buttons that the Mohawk parents had anticipated in exchange for allowing their children to be absent from their duties at home. Another obstacle was that Oliver, the schoolmaster, knew no Mohawk and Claessen, who did, was present only once every two weeks. From the Anglican perspective, Mohawk parents really had no love for learning and their motives for supporting the school initially were based solely on their wish for material gain.[35]

Nonetheless, literacy for a few Mohawks survived, along with the Anglicanism that brought it. The unexpected long-term impact of the literacy instruction offered by the unsatisfactory Oliver would be revealed as time passed. For eight years the Indian chapel had no missionary, although the fort continued to be maintained. Then, in 1727, the society sent the Reverend John Miln to live—in much greater comfort than Andrews had done—in Albany. (He was a replacement for Thomas Barclay, who many years earlier had become deranged.) But Miln's health failed after four years, and he left Albany for England.[36]

The S.P.G. finally decided to send a full-time missionary to the fort once again. They selected Henry Barclay. The son of Thomas Barclay, he was born in Albany and grew up there in the proximity of native Americans. In this respect he resembled Experience Mayhew on Martha's Vineyard, although he seems to have been far less skilled than Mayhew in the local language. He was fluent in Dutch, thanks to his Dutch mother. A graduate of Yale, he began his work in 1735 as the society's catechist at Fort Hunter.

Henry Barclay's Mission to the Mohawks

Like Andrews, Barclay lived at Fort Hunter, but unlike Andrews, he taught the school himself. Again in contrast to Andrews, who had lacked transportation, Barclay visited the Upper Castle of the Mohawks on a horse he had bought for the purpose. He was therefore able to preach to a larger number of Mohawks than had his predecessor. Throughout this period, the Mohawks received him warmly.

In June of the following year, 1736, in a letter to a fellow schoolmaster and missionary, John Sergeant in Stockbridge, Massachusetts, Barclay made some comments on his experiences. He labored, Barclay wrote, under great disadvantages for the lack of a translator. Even if he acquired one, he thought it would take him two or three years to master the language. Nonetheless, he said, "I am almost amazed at the Progress the Youth make in Reading, and Writing their own Language." All the young men, aged from twenty to thirty, "constantly attend School when at Home, and will leave a Frolick rather than miss." Several of them wrote as "good a Hand" as he himself did.[37]

That August, Barclay reported to the S.P.G. on his progress at Fort Hunter. He had by now made himself "master of the Pronunciation of their Tongue," and took the service in Mohawk at the chapel every Sunday. He taught a catechetical class in the evenings to young and old alike, and he was in school every day. In his school he had over forty young men and children whom he was teaching "to read & write their own Tongue, most of whom make vast Progress." Every Sunday he read the exposition of the catechism that Claessen had translated years earlier for Andrews. But all this reading in Mohawk concealed an unfortunate truth: Barclay could pronounce Mohawk from a text but not speak it or understand it orally. "I find their Language very Difficult to attain without the Assistance of an Interpreter, by reason of their Verbs, which I find are varied and their Conjugations very numerous."[38]

In the fall of 1737 Barclay voyaged to England for ordination as an Anglican minister. Upon his return in April of the following year, he was told by the society to split his time between Fort Hunter and the Albany mission (whose congregation had been augmented by some very respectable Irish Protestants). This new arrangement left the fort without schooling, and in the fall of 1740 Barclay made an innovative request: he urged the society to fund two native schoolmasters, explaining that the society's bounty would not have the "good effect which they hope for unless some means could be found to instruct the Youth (upon whom my greatest hopes are Built,) to read their own language." Several Indians, he said, were well qualified for the task and could be prevailed upon to undertake it. His own mastery of the language, meanwhile, was improving. (He painted a less rosy picture to his friend John Sergeant, writing that he would have had much greater success if he had had the services of a translator and a schoolmaster.)[39]

Here was the proof that Andrews's efforts had not been in vain. Despite the lapse of time between Andrews's departure in 1719 and this call for help in 1740, there were still literate men in the community. True, these might have been the twenty- and thirty-year-olds that Barclay had just been teaching, but it seems more likely that they had become involved with literacy during the first mission and were now grown to adulthood. The S.P.G. granted his request, and Barclay hired two Mohawk sachems for the job, Cornelius for the Lower Castle and Daniel at the Upper. He also requested and received S.P.G. funding for using the services of the indispensable Claessen, now very elderly. Barclay needed him to translate into

Mohawk one of the gospels and a couple of Christian texts, including Bishop Man's *Instruction for the Indians*.[40] Meanwhile, the chain of covenant between the English and the Six Nations had been renewed, and a bill was passed by the New York Assembly that authorized the construction of a stone chapel at Fort Hunter, since the earlier chapel was in ruins.[41]

In the fall of 1742, Barclay reported on the death of Claessen. He informed the society that the two sachems, Cornelius and Daniel, were teaching school at the Lower and Upper Castle, respectively, for ten pounds a year. (As in every other instance in which native Americans undertook to teach, their salary was half or less of what was offered to an English schoolmaster.) Cornelius, in particular, was "very faithful and Diligent and vastly successful." Barclay said that there was a fifteen pounds surplus from the society that he planned to spend on paper and ink. He was realistic about the practical needs of the Mohawks: he gave permission to the schoolmasters to leave their schools to go hunting during the two hunting seasons each year. (Since they took their entire family with them, he had little choice: there would have been no students anyway.)[42]

The society's secretary, Philip Bearcroft, professed himself delighted with Barclay's "Prudence & Integrity" and gave him permission to spend the surplus (which he set at seventeen pounds ten shillings) as Barclay wished. Bearcroft had dispatched a parcel of books: two dozen each of the Book of Common Prayer and the Bible, fifty of the Bishop of Man's *Instructions for the Indians*, and a slew of pamphlets he had pulled out of the society's stores. These were intended for Barclay's Albany congregation.[43]

What was desperately needed, however, was not devotional texts in English but reading instructional texts in Mohawk. Even though some of the 1715 Mohawk prayer books might still have been available, none of the spelling books Andrews had written and printed could have survived, victims of the ephemerality of introductory reading textbooks. The result was that literacy instruction demanded extraordinary dedication. As Barclay reported in May 1743, "The Children Attend the School very Steadily and make very great Proficiency; The School Master [Cornelius] is also very Diligent and takes great pains, Being obliged to write Manuscripts to Instruct them by having no Books printed in the Indian Tongue proper for that Purpose." Barclay certainly appreciated the need, for he said that he was still looking for an interpreter to do the translations for the schoolbooks. He unwittingly revealed that he had an odd reluctance to dispense the society's money to those who had earned it: not knowing the society's wishes, he wrote, he had not yet paid the schoolmasters' salaries. (It was a trait that would come back to haunt him.)[44]

Cornelius instructed several young adults, women as well as men, in addition to the children at the Lower Castle. He also served at the chapel when Barclay was absent in Albany and read prayers there. He was, according to Barclay, "much beloved by his Countrymen." Barclay had at last, he informed the society in November 1743, paid their stipends to both schoolmasters. He acknowledged to the society his deep gratitude for a fifty pounds gratuity, but another twenty pounds intended for the Indians as a bounty remained out at interest. Once again,

Barclay was finding it hard to part with the society's money entrusted to him for the Mohawks.[45]

In the spring of 1744, France and England declared war. (King George's War would last from then until 1748.) Inevitably, the war made itself felt in the forests of Iroquoia. Barclay reported to the society the following spring that he had just passed the preceding two months at the fort in a "very disagreable Manner." Half a dozen Mohawks returning from Schenectady had spread the rumor that a huge force of white men was coming to destroy them all. Many of their countrymen panicked and fled into the woods. Barclay managed to calm most of them down, but the rumors persisted. The most damaging was one directly related to the printed word—not to the literacy that Barclay had instituted but to what he had not—literacy in English. Barclay had been accused, he wrote, of being "the Chief Contriver of the Destruction intended against them, That Notwithstanding my Seeming Affection for them, I was a very bad Man and in League with the Devil who was the Author of All the Books I had given them." (Since there were still no new schoolbooks in Mohawk, and it was most unlikely that Barclay was in a position to give away any of the earlier Mohawk prayer books that had survived, the books in question can only have been copies of the English Book of Common Prayer or the Bibles sent by the S.P.G. and its well-wishers.) The Mohawks of the Lower Castle were not inclined to believe this tale, "But the Upper Town [Castle] was all in a Flame, Threatning to Murder the Inhabitants setled about them, And had Sent Expresses to all the Six Nations."[46]

Everything eventually settled down and the French were said to be at the back of it all. The major culprit was identified as a trader who did business with both the Mohawks and Indians allied to the French, but the episode had a most unfortunate side effect. The trader had succeeded in making Barclay's life uneasy, as Barclay himself reported, "By persuading the Schoolmaster of the Lower Town that the Society allow'd him Twenty Pounds Sterling a Year, and that I defrauded him of the Greatest Part." Barclay's defense had proved unconvincing. Cornelius had left the school, gone to hunt at a great distance, and would not return until spring. The Upper Castle school had also "gone to wreck since this alarm," according to Barclay, "so that I have not had occasion to Draw for the Stipend allow'd them this year." By the next year, the accusation against Barclay had been magnified into the rumor, he wrote, that he had received "£100 in goods to be distributed among them, which I had converted to my own use."[47]

For the loss of confidence in him by Cornelius and Daniel, Barclay had himself to blame, at least in part. He had received a handsome increase to his allowance of fifty pounds, none of which he had shared with the hardworking schoolmasters; he had left a bounty for the Indians somewhere to gather interest instead of disbursing it; and he had declined to pay either Daniel or Cornelius for the past teaching they had done before the collapse of both schools.

The alarms and excursions continued. The French and their Indian allies laid waste to a frontier settlement, took more than a hundred prisoners, and kept Barclay and his neighbors "in a continual Alarm by Sculking Parties" that murdered and kidnapped the local inhabitants around Albany. The "Lately Populous and Flourishing County of Albany," Barclay wrote from the safety of New York city, "is become a Wilderness." The Mohawks, instead of joining the English, as the English felt they had every right to expect, remained nominally neutral.[48]

The death of William Vesey, rector of Trinity Church, in July 1746 in New York, offered Barclay an escape from these miseries. The vacancy of Vesey's pulpit was an opportunity that would not occur again. Barclay wrote to the society from New York, that same December—so it was already a fait accompli—that after several months of heart-searching he had decided to accept the living of Trinity Church. He mentioned the suspicions he had incurred from the Mohawks over the one hundred pounds' worth of goods that he had supposedly failed to distribute. He could see, he said, "no Prospect of being serviceable to the Indians, amongst whom I could no longer reside with Safety." Now "agreably settled" in his new incumbency, his mission to the Mohawks was at an end. So, too, were the services of the Commissioners for Indian Affairs. From 1746 to 1751, William Johnson would negotiate with the Mohawks on behalf of the province of New York as the sole Indian commissioner.[49]

John Ogilvie's Mission to the Mohawks

Once the peace treaty of Aix-la-Chapelle was signed by France and England in October 1748, the path was cleared for the S.P.G. to renew its mission to the Mohawks. The society's next missionary to the New York frontier was John Ogilvie, who had been recommended to the S.P.G. by Barclay. Born in New York and a graduate of Yale College, Ogilvie was influenced in his Anglicanism by the Reverend Samuel Johnson, who was to become the first president of King's College, New York. Ogilvie returned from England and his ordination there in the fall of 1749. He stayed with Barclay briefly to convalesce from an illness on the sea voyage and began to learn Mohawk from his host. By the following June Ogilvie was at Fort Hunter. His reports to the society were full of references to the moral degeneracy of the Indians, who, he said, "Since the war . . . are intirely given up to Drunkenness." He set his hopes, like others before him, on the "Rising Generation," claiming that the children were "universally disposed to learn."[50]

Ogilvie had the help of an unidentified interpreter at Fort Hunter, and some of the earlier prayer books left printed in Mohawk must have survived—perhaps the special chapel copies—because in the first of two services held at the Indian chapel each Sunday he read most of the service himself in Mohawk. He delivered his sermon, however, in English, and his interpreter translated it.[51]

Ogilvie was initially less sympathetic than any of his predecessors to the Mohawk language. Like John Eliot, he believed that the Mohawks needed to be formed into a "civil Industrious People," but, like Cotton Mather, he took the view that English should be introduced so they would use it "instead of their own barbarous Dialect." Nonetheless, when Eleazar Wheelock surreptitiously sent a letter to the Mohawks inviting them to send their children to him in Connecticut to learn English, Ogilvie was outraged at what he considered poaching on Anglican territory and refused his permission for the children to be sent.[52]

He let the S.P.G. know that the Mohawks had requested a schoolmaster. In fact, he said, there was a need for one for the non-Indian inhabitants—particularly, by implication, for the Dutch. (Many English families had fled to New York city during the war.) "The [European] children here have no Education, but the Little they receive from their Parents, & even many of them not able to read, & very few who understand the English language." Since he had to split his time between Fort Hunter and Albany, he hoped that a young Yale graduate would materialize to help him with the schooling. Meanwhile, he took on the responsibility of teaching the Mohawk children himself: "I act as Schoolmaster myself, and every Day I have near twenty Indian Children to teach reading b[e]sides some of the Young Men who learn to write."[53]

As was always true when a conversion effort by Europeans or descendants of Europeans in America took root, there was a committed Indian convert at hand. On a trip to the Upper Castle, Ogilvie met Abraham, brother of King Hendrick, the Mohawk who had voyaged to England forty years earlier. Abraham was such an enthusiast of Christianity that he had neglected his hunting in order to hold services for his fellow Mohawks and instruct them in the principles of religion. Barclay wrote from New York that he could corroborate the hardships that Abraham's dedication had brought him: "I am a Witness of his Zeal & his Poverty in good measure."[54] Barclay's assessment of the elderly Abraham was confirmed by Colonel William Johnson, who wrote to George Clinton, governor of New York, to ask for some financial acknowledgment of Abraham's work and that of Paulus (son of King Hendrick), who "has made it his Study to teach the Mohawk Children to read, and has been of great Service to them." Johnson asked that Paulus be salaried as a schoolmaster.[55]

The S.P.G. appointed an assistant to Ogilvie in the summer of 1751. The elderly Reverend John Jacob Oel was to serve as the pastor of the Upper Castle, Conajoharie. Ogilvie "put him into a method of instructing the Indians at Canijohare as far as his Age & Infirmities will admit." But help was still needed for the Lower Castle, now known as the "Castle at Fort Hunter." Ogilvie was reluctant to appoint a Mohawk as schoolmaster, citing the Indians' supposedly "Strong Inclination" to have their children taught English. Colonel Johnson, however, used his influence with the S.P.G. to again recommend Paulus (whose Mohawk name was Sahonwadie) as the schoolmaster. By the summer of 1753 Sahonwadie was performing double duty, teaching the children at Fort Hunter and acting as a clerk and lay reader there during the times that Ogilvie, now a married man, was in Albany.[56]

An incident that occurred at Fort Hunter before Sahonwadie took over as the lay reader may have precipitated his service there. Just after Easter in 1751 and shortly after Ogilvie had returned from Fort Hunter to Albany, some Mohawk men "fell to drinking in the excess, [and] barbarously murdered" the wife of one of the sachems. Citing alcohol as "the most fatal obstruction to the Progress of the glorious Gospel of Christ," Ogilvie lamented the death of the "worthy woman who officiates as reader in Church, during my absence." This casual reference to continuing literacy among Mohawk women suggests, once again, how piety motivated female reading acquisition and practice.[57]

Fighting between the English and French now flared up more fiercely than before, as the Seven Years' War reached a critical phase in North America. Already a leading figure among the Iroquois, William Johnson, who was an adopted Mohawk, persuaded the Six Nations to join the English cause. At the ensuing battle near Lake George, which ended in a victory for the English, King Hendrick, leading his warriors into battle astride Johnson's horse, was bayoneted when the horse was shot dead beneath him. In a later battle, Johnson was wounded but survived. Sahonwadie, who was now the schoolmaster of the Upper Castle, succeeded his father as sachem.[58]

The tumult of the times must have caused Ogilvie to question the wisdom of sending a non-Indian into the area to keep school. He had been invited by the Mohawks to accompany them on their expedition to Lake George as their chaplain but had declined; he clearly preferred to stay in Albany and minister to the wounded soldiers at the army hospital there. "Good Old Abraham," King Hendrick's brother, had served in his stead, performing divine services every morning and evening, Ogilvie told the society at the close of 1755. At the Upper Castle, Sahonwadie was teaching forty children a day: several were beginning to read and some of them to write. They were learning the Anglican catechism and the tunes to several psalms. There was therefore a renewed need for a schoolmaster at Fort Hunter. Ogilvie wished to appoint the man himself: according to the S.P.G. Journal, "he knows an Indian well qualified for this Service, but he is much addicted to strong drink, & therefore should be employed only upon condition he keeps himself sober."[59]

Texts in any language, during the war, were in short supply. Ogilvie sent out a plea to the S.P.G. to send him copies of the Book of Common Prayer, the *Soldiers' Monitor*, and any "practical Tracts" for the use of the hospital. In 1756 and again in early 1757 Ogilvie had to leave his mission to the Indians to serve as the chaplain for the Royal American Regiment. He conducted services for the Mohawks and Oneidans on the force while also looking after the spiritual needs of the other soldiers. Even so, he managed to spend two months in the winter of 1758 at Fort Hunter and pay a visit to the Upper Castle to administer the sacraments. Under the circumstances, he was teaching Mohawk children at Fort Hunter himself. Paulus (Sahonwadie), he wrote later, was so caught up the war that he had neglected his teaching duties sadly. Sahonwadie was, of course, now fulfilling his duties as sachem in the wake of his father's death in battle.[60]

Ogilvie left Fort Hunter and Albany again to accompany the Royal American Regiment on their assault on Niagara in 1759. He was with the army when Montreal fell to the British in September 1760 and was instructed by the British to go to Montreal for the winter to attend to the needs of the Protestants there. His mission to the Indians was effectively at an end.[61]

From the perspective of the S.P.G., its mission to the Mohawks was at a standstill. For many years, no satisfactory replacement was found for Ogilvie. The

Reverend Thomas Browne, a former army chaplain, served at the Albany mission until 1767, but missionary work among the Indians was not part of his job.[62] Remarkably, during this lull in missionary activity, Sir William Johnson (knighted for his exploits at Lake George and his ability to keep the Mohawks loyal to the British) renewed the quest for providing the Mohawks with a text in their own language. He sought the assistance of Daniel Claus, a German immigrant who had recently arrived in Mohawk country to study the language, and who had been the guest of Joseph Brant. (Claus would later marry one of Johnson's daughters.) Claus was in Montreal when Johnson first wrote to him, early in 1761, to ask him to correct the old Indian prayer book and produce an improved translation.[63] Its publication in New York was overseen by Henry Barclay, who reported in the fall of 1763 that the printer, William Weyman, had lost his best worker and the project had been stalled for two months. Perhaps Johnson took matters into his own hands at this point, for a much abbreviated edition of the Mohawk prayer book, titled *The Morning and Evening Prayer, the Litany, and Church Catechism . . .* , was printed in Boston in 1763. The book is only twenty-four pages long, saving space by combining the morning and evening services into one but retaining the litany and church catechism. It does not credit any organization with its publication and can only have been issued under the auspices of Johnson himself. From late 1763 on, therefore, the Mohawks again had access to a freshly printed Anglican prayer book in their own tongue. [64]

During this period of missionary inactivity, Johnson had persisted in his requests for schoolmasters for the Indians. He was made a member of the S.P.G. in 1766, an honor that gave his requests added importance, and within a few years obtained two schoolmasters, both white—Colin McLelland for Fort Hunter and Edward Hall for Johnson's own community, Johnstown, where white and Indian students attended school together. (McLelland began teaching in April 1769 and had thirty Mohawk students by December.) Johnson also oversaw the publication, in 1769, of a much expanded version of the Mohawk Book of Common Prayer, generally identified as the second of the Mohawk prayer books. (Its New York printers complained that Mohawk had so many additional *g*'s, *k*'s, and *y*'s that they had to borrow them from their colleagues.) Johnson ordered an edition of four hundred copies, with twenty of them adorned with gilt lettering as gifts for the sachems. This time the British government paid for the printing.[65]

The new prayer book of 1769 dropped the prayers to be read by children upon first sitting down, a distinctive feature of the 1715 edition, and rearranged the order of a few other prayers but otherwise reproduced the entire content of the edition of 1715, adding translations of the rites of communion, baptism, matrimony, and burial. All three of the earlier missionaries—William Andrews, Henry Barclay, who had died before the book was out, and John Ogilvie—are credited in the title with the work's preparation. However, the names of Lawrence Claessen and Daniel Claus are absent.[66]

Meanwhile, the man who would make the greatest contribution to the third and last eighteenth-century edition of the Mohawk prayer book was in the process of being educated by Sir William Johnson. T'hayendanegea, known to the English as Joseph Brant, was the step-brother of Johnson's common-law wife, Molly Brant, herself a granddaughter of the Brant who had visited London. At the age of seventeen, Joseph had accompanied Johnson on his 1759 Niagara campaign. Two years later, Johnson sent him to board at Eleazar Wheelock's Moor's Indian Charity School in Connecticut to perfect his English and receive an English education.

Brant would prove to be one of the school's few successes. Between 1764 and 1772, Wheelock—a Congregationalist whom Johnson steadfastly barred from operating in Anglican territory—sent out twenty-two former students from the Indian Charity School as schoolteachers to the Iroquois: eight white missionaries, thirteen Indian schoolmasters, and one Indian schoolmistress. The project was doomed from the start not only because of Wheelock's insensitivity to the vast linguistic, cultural, and social differences that separated the acculturated Algonquian schoolmasters from their Iroquois students but also because of his insistence that the instruction be carried out in English. The Mohawk students did not understand English and their teachers could not speak Mohawk. One of the two who tried to teach the Mohawks was a Delaware Indian, Hezekiah Calvin. Calvin, only sixteen or seventeen at the time, taught at Fort Hunter in the winter of 1765 and again in 1766. He found Mohawk impossible, describing his experience as a non-speaker as that of "a dumb stump that has no tongue to use." The Mohawks thought very poorly of him, complaining that he would "come into their Houses and go out with out saying how do you do." He was mercifully recalled by Wheelock in the fall of 1766.[67]

As early as the 1760s, the Mohawks had made many changes to their way of life. They had sold, given away, or been cheated of much of their land. Although they still hunted for two months a year, many now lived in sturdy houses. They owned horses, sleighs, and wagons. They had adopted many European customs, such drinking tea, and from Albany stores they bought English goods that ranged from women's stocking to padlocks and knee buckles. By the end of the decade, however, they were suffering yet again from population loss and disorientation. Many Mohawk leaders had been killed at the battle of Lake George; others had succumbed to disease and alcoholism. Sachems no longer commanded the respect they once did. Once again, Mohawks looked for spiritual solutions to stem a cultural decline, and once again they looked to the religion of the English for help.[68]

In September 1770, the S.P.G.'s resident missionary in Albany, the Reverend Harry Munro, paid a visit to Fort Hunter, which had been without an S.P.G. missionary since Ogilvie's departure. He sent back the kind of report that was dear to the society's philanthropic heart: "The schoolmaster [McLelland] is universally beloved by the Indians, & their Children are making considerable Proficiency under his Care, both in Reading & Writing."[69] Munro did not identify the language in which instruction was being carried on, Mohawk or English. It must, however, still have been Mohawk, in defiance of a ruling by the S.P.G. that instruction was to be in English, because the next missionary sent to Fort Hunter by the society would be anxious to learn the language and to create reading instructional texts in Mohawk.

The Christian Mohawks themselves had reactivated the search for a missionary. They were led by Little Abraham, who was now the leading sachem. (He was related by marriage to the Brant family.) He and eight other Mohawks from the Lower Castle had come to Johnson Hall, Sir William's residence, in May 1770 to meet with the Reverend Charles Inglis, assistant curate of Trinity Church, and the Reverend Miles Cooper, President of King's College, New York. The two men were visiting Johnson to discuss the Mohawks and potential missions. The Mohawk deputation, citing their loyalty to the church and crown and voicing their amazement that a Catholic missionary had recently been authorized by the government to begin a mission to their tribe, requested new Anglican missionaries for both castles. Inglis seconded this request, pointing out to the S.P.G. that in addition to the Catholics' posing a religious threat, the missionaries sent out by Wheelock—Inglis referred particularly, without naming him, to Samuel Kirkland and his work among the Oneida—were a political threat. Indeed, as political passions rose after the passage of the infamous Stamp Act, the "dissenting" missionaries heavily favored the American cause over the British. The result was a new search by the S.P.G. for a suitable missionary. The man selected was John Stuart. A graduate of Philadelphia College, Stuart made the obligatory trip to England for ordination. Scottish by descent, he was a commanding figure of six foot four inches and was reportedly "of a robust Constitution, a good Scholar and of unblemished character."[70]

The Mohawk Mission of John Stuart

By December 1770 Stuart was in Fort Hunter. He made the usual trip to the Upper Castle, where he preached with the aid of an interpreter (presumably Oel) on Christmas Day. But while the Upper Castle had an "elegant little Church with a Cupola & Bell," which Johnson had built for the Mohawks there, Stuart found the chapel at Fort Hunter in disarray. It no longer had glass in the windows, a reading desk, or a communion table, and the pulpit was made only of rough boards. Moreover, "the Books belonging to it are all lost, except the Bible." Particularly disturbing was the loss of the Mohawk prayer book, printed only a year earlier.[71]

Fort Hunter was no longer the remote outpost of former years. While Stuart put the Indian population at 170, the growing white population at Fort Hunter could on occasion generate close to 200 worshippers at the Indian chapel for the Sunday evening services, which Stuart conducted in English. He claimed that he conducted the services on Sunday mornings in Mohawk, but it is difficult to see how, in the absence of the Mohawk prayer book. Meanwhile, he struggled to learn the language, for "none of them understand English even tolerably." Mastering their language would take a long time, he wrote, "partly from the Difficulty of articulating their peculiar Sounds; and partly from the total want of the necessary Helps [a grammar and dictionary] for I have no other Way of acquiring it but Viva Voce."[72]

But help was at hand: in July 1772 Stuart reported that he had hired a young

Mohawk "(who understands English) to reside with me as a private Tutor, & public Interpreter." He was not sure how long he could keep him, however, since he could not afford to pay him enough to ask him to neglect his hunting and live there permanently. The young Mohawk tutor was probably not Joseph Brant, for he had returned from his stint at Eleazar Wheelock's school in 1763 to be groomed for leadership.[73]

Now receiving aid for acquiring the language, Stuart also obtained assistance for the church building. Johnson used his own funds to spruce up the chapel by installing a new floor, adding a pulpit, a desk, and a communion table, putting panes of glass into the windows, and having a belfry constructed with its accompanying bell. When Johnson wrote to the society in the fall of 1772, he was able to report that Stuart was "much esteemed" and that the "School is very promising."[74]

But one feature of missionary work had not changed. "The Indians frequently complain of the want of Books in their own Language," Stuart wrote, voicing the complaint that cut across both time and denominational boundaries. Now, however, he had an assistant who was the best possible choice, Joseph Brant. With Brant's indispensable aid, Stuart was trying to get some more texts translated: an abridgment of the history of the Bible, some chapters selected from the Gospels on the birth, life, and crucifixion of Jesus, and a "large and plain Explanation of the Church Catechism." All of these would be "small tracts," and Johnson had promised to finance their publication. Interestingly, the Mohawks themselves were pushing for the translation of the entire New Testament. It was a hope that would remain unfulfilled when Johnson died suddenly, in the middle of a conference with the Iroquois, in July 1774. His will did not include any mention of funding the publications, which were left without financial backing.[75]

The following year, Stuart was more candid about Joseph Brant's contribution to the proposed edition, which now included not only an exposition of the catechism and a "compendious History of the Bible" but a complete translation of the Gospel according to St. Mark. By the time Stuart wrote in October 1775, Brant had left for Canada with Johnson's nephew Colonel Guy Johnson to prosecute the war there. (The younger Johnson had succeeded his uncle as the commander of the British forces.) The translations could not be completed without Brant, Stuart wrote, "and perhaps he is the only Person in America equal to such an Undertaking."[76]

It would be six years before the S.P.G. heard from Stuart again. His mission to the Indians was about to be overtaken by larger events that would find him on the losing side in the conflict between Britain and her American colonies.

An Assessment of Mohawk Literacy

Like the Wampanoags, many Mohawks found literacy a valuable addition to their culture, and like them, they embraced it (if they did) for different reasons. Two sachems who taught it—Cornelius and Daniel—worked hard at their instruction, despite their lack of teaching tools, and only when they came to believe that

Barclay was swindling them out of their salary did they abandon their posts. For them, literacy may have been most valuable in providing them with an income.[77]

Other Mohawks surely viewed literacy, which was offered only in the context of Anglicanism, as a crucial aspect of their new beliefs. "Good old Abraham," for instance, was wholly committed to the rituals and texts of Anglicanism. Similarly, the women who read at the church in the absence of a minister appear to have been deeply committed to Christianity.[78]

Other Mohawks absorbed literacy along with some aspects of Christianity. (How closely they adopted, syncretized, or alternated Christian beliefs with their existing belief system lies beyond the scope of this study.) For many Mohawks, literacy was just one of the spiritual and practical advantages that Christianity offered, along with survival goods and the sacraments.[79]

In contrast, T'hayendanegea (Joseph Brant) became a devout convert to Anglicanism and a culture broker between the English and the Mohawks.[80] His translation of the Gospel of St. Mark into Mohawk proved to be the only complete book of the Bible that would be available to the Mohawks in the eighteenth century. By the time T'hayendanegea saw the published product of his translation as part of the third version of the Mohawk Book of Common Prayer, he was in Canada, where he had led the Mohawks after the British defeat in the American Revolution.

Decades of Transition, 1730 to 1750

PRELUDE TO PART TWO

As the evidence presented in Part I suggests, the "ordinary Road" of literacy instruction—the hornbook, primer, Psalter, New Testament, and the entire Bible—was followed by Congregationalists and Anglicans alike. Of all the settings and organizations discussed so far, only the Society for the Propagation of the Gospel in its mission to the Mohawks failed to offer the full course of reading instruction culminating in the Bible. Everywhere else, instructors followed the teaching sequence, essentially offering their students a course in Christianity.

While schoolmasters and missionary societies stuck to the traditional texts, the world around them was changing. The advent of newspapers introduced an important addition to the stock of print available for reading in the early eighteenth century. The advertisements that all newspapers carried from their first issues are a valuable source of information on the world of letters after about 1730.

A review of advertisements run in the *Boston Weekly News-Letter* from 1730 to 1750 reveals that the quantity of reading possibilities was growing during those two decades. Among the advertisements for the entire year 1731 only six notices appeared of books for sale, two of which related to books printed by subscription, including an essay by Cotton Mather's son Samuel. In contrast, forty-one of the fifty-two issues of 1742 ran advertisements for books. By 1750, few issues lacked them.

The increase in the number of book titles in the eighteenth century can also be demonstrated by production and importation figures. After an initial modest rise between 1700 and 1730, the publication of domestic titles (see Appendix 3) and the trade in imported books (see Appendix 4) seemed to stagnate in the decade of the 1730s. (Note, however, that through the quantity of his productions, Cotton Mather had single-handedly skewed production figures upward for nearly three decades until his pen was silenced in 1728.) From the 1740s onward, however, the trend turns up, with the exception of a slight and brief decline in imports in the late 1740s caused by a depression related to the War of the Austrian Succession. True, the white (and so potentially literate) population of the American colonies nearly quadrupled between 1710 and 1760, with raw numbers rising from some 286,800 persons to 1,275,400, suggesting a population increase that far exceeded the rise in book production. But since we know only the numbers of titles being printed domestically, not the size of each edition, these figures should be interpreted not as a proportionate reduction in available print but rather as an increase in reading choices.[1]

One factor that contributed to the increase in the number of books and pamphlets that were being imported and published in the American provinces (as we term the colonies in the eighteenth century) after 1740 was a series of visits by the Anglican minister George Whitefield, who first came to America in the winter of 1738–39. His arrival heralded what has become known as the "Great Awakening," in which "New Lights" (Whitefield and his followers) were pitted against "Old Lights," who rejected the emotionality of his appeals for conversion. In the fall of 1740, a journal of Whitefield's voyage from England to Savannah and then on to Philadelphia and back to England, written by a companion of Whitefield's, became the eighteenth century's version of a best seller.

The strong sales of the journal signaled the beginning of a rage for works by or about the preacher. Even a favorable mention by Whitefield was enough to cause a book to be reprinted in America. Cotton Mather's *Ornaments for the Daughters of Zion*, for instance, out of print for a year shy of half a century, was reissued in 1741 by Boston printers as now "Recommended by the Rev. Mr. Whitefield in his New-England Journal." By 1747 works by and about Whitefield were such sought after items that new books on him were being sold straight off the ships at the Boston docks. According to the printer Isaiah Thomas, Whitefield was "like a comet [who] drew the attention of all classes of people. The blaze of his ministration was extended through the continent, and he became the common topic of conversation from Georgia to New Hampshire. . . . [T]he press groaned with pamphlets written in favor of, or against, his person and ministry." Even Whitefield's critics agreed on his influence on printing and literacy: "Books of this un-happy tendency, books Calvinistic, enthusiastical, and antinomian do abound," the Old Light rector of Yale College, Timothy Cutler, complained. "The press here never had so full employ before, nor were people ever so busy in reading." People would travel long distances to hear Whitefield's sermons and those of other evangelicals read aloud.[2]

George Whitefield, along with the publications he wrote or inspired, features in several of the accounts of literacy education in Part II, which include the experiences of a school for orphans that he opened in Georgia. The disparities in the provision of elementary education in provincial America were closely tied to the regional, religious, and ethnic differences among the provinces. A brief review of literacy education from about 1700 to 1750 in provinces from New England, the middle region, and the south—Massachusetts, Pennsylvania, and Virginia—gives some idea of the multiple forms of education across the English-speaking American continent.

The orthodox colonies of Massachusetts Bay and Connecticut—which by this time had annexed Plymouth and New Haven, respectively—and, by the first decade of the eighteenth century, New Hampshire, all required children to learn to read. Townships in many of these colonies supported schoolmistresses to teach children to read in the summer and schoolmasters to teach writing and advanced reading in the winter.

In the larger towns of Massachusetts, as elsewhere in much of New England, public schooling opportunities for boys continued to improve: by 1720 Boston had two Latin grammar schools and three writing schools. In the cities, curricular offerings expanded gradually for boys whose parents could afford to send them to private schools. By 1750, private schools in Boston, for example, were offering classes in mathematics (from arithmetic to trigonometry), in astronomy, navigation, merchant's accounts, and gauging and surveying, thereby providing theoretical perspectives that were not included in any apprenticeship. In addition to lessons in the three Rs, private instruction was available to boys in history, geography, Latin, French, Greek, and shorthand, among other subjects. The appeal to parents of a "polite Education" led to the encouragement of activities that would have been banned in Boston in the preceding century, such as dancing, as well as the more acceptable subjects of instrumental and vocal music.[3]

Girls were not wholly excluded from this curricular expansion, although they rarely attended a school at the same hours as their brothers. They were able to learn "all sorts of Needle Work, Tapestry, Embroidering and Marking," as a woman advertised in 1739. By the late 1740s, women entrepreneurs were offering to teach other female artistic skills, such as painting on glass, waxwork, and japanning. Instruction in musical instruments such as the flute, violin, and spinet had long been considered acceptable for girls. By the 1740s, both sexes could join in learning "vocal psalmody." Girls as well as boys could take the language lessons, most often French, that were offered in Boston and other major colonial cities well before 1750. (Liza as well as Sammy Mather, it will be recalled, took French lessons.)[4]

Outside the cities, the small towns and villages of Massachusetts continued to offer district schooling to their young. As towns grew larger, the "moving school" was introduced: a system in which one schoolmaster taught in two or three different locations for months at a time each year. Dissatisfied with this arrangement, parents often sought permission from the authorities to set off their quarter of the town as a separate village where they could open their own school.[5]

Educational provision was very different in the south. No southern colony passed the "apprenticeship" legislation, the adaptation of the Poor Laws that required parents and masters to teach children to read and specified penalties if they did not. Elementary education in southern colonies, in particular, lacked governmental provision. Secondary education fared better: several southern colonies passed legislation sponsoring Latin grammar schools in key towns.

Despite Virginia's legislative disregard for elementary schools, many Virginian colonists of small means appreciated the importance of education and made sacrifices to open schools themselves. As Thomas Bullock has documented, education in the rudiments in Virginia during the eighteenth century was more general than many have supposed. By the middle of the eighteenth century, education had evolved into several forms, including community schools organized by parents and "free-schools," such as the Symes and Eaton Schools, endowed by bequests of land in 1643 and 1659, respectively. Over ten such schools were endowed (if not necessarily opened) by 1750. Since free schools were usually designed to educate poor children, their curriculum was often initially little more than the three Rs. Another form of education was offered by the private tutor—always male—hired by the head of a household, who would house and feed him, provide him a schoolroom, pay him a small stipend for teaching the children of the family, and permit him to take local children as fee-paying pupils to boost his income. The final form of nonpublic education was the purely private school, run with an eye for profit by an entrepreneur and likely to be located in towns such as Williamsburg, within easy reach of their clientele or offering room and board. The widespread existence of private schools is confirmed by a report on education by 29 Anglican clergymen living in 18 different Virginian parishes in 1724. The report reveals that no minister had a "free" school in his parish, but almost all could attest to private schools. One typical response came from the clergyman of a parish in Gloucester County: "There is no publick school in this Parish but there are several private ones, where Children learn to read English & to write."[6]

In the middle colonies, denominational education was the norm. New York and New Jersey relied almost entirely on schools sponsored by different denominations and on private schooling, and Pennsylvania did the same. The Pennsylvania government was the only one to issue laws on literacy. In 1683, its version of the Poor Law had required that, besides teaching children a skill or trade, the parents and masters of all children should have them "instructed in reading and writing, so that they may be able to read the Scriptures and to write by the time they attain to twelve years of age."[7] This acceptance of writing as a minimal educational requirement for girls as well as boys set the tone for the decades that followed: Pennsylvania was outstanding in its acceptance of the need to educate both sexes in both literacy skills.

Schooling in Philadelphia, dating from the hiring of Enoch Flower in 1683 to teach the three Rs, proceeded apace, with the Quakers at the forefront.[8] The Friends' Meeting in Philadelphia created a school in 1690 that was open to both sexes, and nine years later hired schoolmistresses to teach girls and young boys. The wealthy paid by subscription for their children while poor children were admitted free. As Carl Bridenbaugh has noted, girls of the lowest social class probably had better educational opportunities in Philadelphia than anywhere else in the colonies.[9] The city also increasingly provided an abundance of private schools, which were advertised in the *Pennsylvania Gazette* from 1728 on.

The wealth of schools available in Philadelphia was not mirrored in the villages of rural Pennsylvania. But here, too, individual denominations started schools, with the Quakers again leading the way. As in Philadelphia, it was characteristic of Quakers to offer comparable schooling to girls and boys, often in single-sex schools. The fact that Quakers held separate men's and women's meetings allowed women to use their literacy to gain authority as they served as clerks, treasurers, elders, and ministers in Pennsylvania and New Jersey.[10]

Despite these disparities in education by region, one instructional innovation was common across geographical boundaries: the general adoption of the spelling book. The increasing use of the speller across the American provinces is the most significant feature of the 1730s and 1740s, decades of transition that saw the introduction (or, from another point of view, reintroduction in a new form) of the spelling book. From now on, the speller would be the book used in schools across the American provinces to teach children to read. Inserted into the reading sequence after the primer and before the Psalter, it was to become the most widely imported and domestically printed reading instructional schoolbook of its time, with the possible exception of the primer. Spellers would be bought in addition to, not instead of, primers. The latter would continue to be used as the first real book that the child would meet (since the horn book had only one page), but they would be as likely to be found in the home as in the school. However, the unflagging use of primers, particularly of the overwhelmingly popular *New-England Primer*, in schools taught by women can be still documented at the end of the century.

The use of spelling books toward the end of these transitional decades emerges in the last two of four descriptions in Chapter 7 of children and adults involved in literacy education. We begin with Benjamin Franklin, whose formal education was over well before 1730 and who therefore provides a point of comparison, an example of the limited education, with its restricted access to books, that was all that children could obtain in the early decades of the eighteenth century. The next three examples—taken from rural Virginia, Georgia, and rural Pennsylvania—are of children and adults learning and teaching reading and writing in the transitional decades of the 1730s and 1740s. These examples permit us to look at instruction at a time when, in many schools, literacy instruction was changing. While Devereux Jarratt of rural Virginia in the 1730s exhibited the disadvantages of learning only by taking the "ordinary Road," literacy was on the brink of becoming more systematic and, at least for some, more enriched. The new systematization offered by the spelling book affected reading instruction by providing ample practice in learning the relationship between letters, syllables, and their pronunciations. At the same time, writing was enriched—at least in a few settings—by a new focus on communication in the form of letter writing. This focus emerges in the 1740s in the letters written by children in the Bethesda School for Orphans in Georgia and in Christopher Dock's little German-speaking schools in Pennsylvania villages, where Dock encouraged his students in different schools to write to each other. Moreover, although the use of literacy in the service of religion, the key feature of Part I, is as strong as ever in these two decades, the reading instructional road was being widened to permit more secular and expansive uses of literacy, foreshadowing the significant features presented in Part III. For the moment, we look first at teaching and learning literacy in individual classrooms (Chapter 7) and then at the rise in popularity of the spelling book as a reading instructional text (Chapter 8).

7

Schools, Schoolteachers, and Schoolchildren

By 1730, Benjamin Franklin had long since finished his formal education, and his experiences form a backdrop to those of the other learners discussed in this chapter. Born in 1706, the same year as Cotton Mather's younger son Samuel, Franklin had served only part of his apprenticeship as a printer with his half-brother James before he smuggled himself out of his home town, Boston, to escape from the apprenticeship. He had then worked as a printer in Philadelphia and, for two years, in London, and in 1730 he was about to become the owner and editor of the *Philadelphia Gazette*. Under his insightful and frugal management, the newspaper would be a commercial success.

Franklin provides what is perhaps the eighteenth century's most vivid example of the brief and interrupted schooling that was available to most children in the early decades, and yet Franklin's story reveals how much could be wrung from that education by someone with his ingenuity and perseverance. Scholars have often extolled Franklin as the archetypal self-made man, but it is important to note that the formal aspects of his early education, which he recounts in detail in his *Autobiography* and which totaled perhaps four years of noncontinuous schooling, gave him the tools to teach himself.

In a busy Boston household bursting with children, Benjamin, the youngest son in a family of seventeen children, stood out for his quickness in learning to read. He accomplished it so early that, he said, "I do not remember when I could not read." He may well have first learned at home from his siblings before attending Sarah Kemble Knight's little reading school, which Sammy Mather also attended.[1]

Although all of Franklin's brothers had been apprenticed to various trades, Franklin's intelligence convinced his father, a devout Congregationalist, that this son should be educated for the church. When Franklin was eight years old, therefore, his father, Josiah Franklin, sent him to one of Boston's two free grammar schools. He did well there, rising in just under a year from the middle of the class to its head. As Josiah looked ahead, however, to the expenses of college and the poor salaries of the college-educated, he changed his mind, removed his son from the grammar school, and sent him instead to "a School for Writing & Arithmetic." It was "kept by a then famous Man, Mr Geo[rge] Brownell," Franklin recalled, "very successful in his Profession generally, and that by mild, encouraging Methods." Under Brownell's kindly regime, Franklin "acquired fair Writing pretty soon," but made no progress in arithmetic. When Franklin was ten his father removed him from this school, too, to assist him with his trade of candle and soap making.[2]

The single most important feature of Franklin's education, once his formal schooling ended, was his determination to read as much and as widely as possible. His father's library, in Franklin's view, was far too narrowly focused on books of "polemic Divinity." It did include Plutarch's *Lives*, Daniel Defoe's *Essay on Projects*, and Cotton Mather's *Bonifacius: An Essay upon the Good*, the last two of which "perhaps," Franklin says, "gave me a Turn of Thinking that had an Influence on some of the principal future Events of my Life." Franklin read most of the theological works anyway, but he often regretted that "at a time when I had such a Thirst for Knowledge, more proper Books had not fallen in my Way."[3]

His love of reading, which of course was aided by his precocious skill at it, made book ownership a priority, and he spent any money he acquired as a child on purchasing books. He had enjoyed John Bunyan's *Pilgrim's Progress* (one of the few books that adults encouraged children to read that had a plot and adventures), so his first purchase was of Bunyan's works "in separate little Volumes" (clearly chapman's books). He sold these in order to finance his purchase of Richard Burton's *Historical Collections*, "small Chapmen's Books, 40 or 50 in all." His reading of these cheap little booklets from the chapman subculture, aimed not at children but adults, highlights the lack of appropriate secular reading material for children in the second decade of the eighteenth century.[4]

At the age of twelve, Franklin was contracted to serve his half-brother James in the printing business until the age of twenty-one. His new career as a printer's apprentice greatly increased his access to books. He befriended the apprentices of booksellers and was able to borrow a new book overnight, "which I was careful to return soon & clean," and he sometimes stayed up in his room reading for most of the night to be sure he could return the book early the next day. His apprenticeship was also helpful to his literacy in more conventional ways: he was forced to pay more attention to spelling and punctuation, and he improved in both.[5] A tradesman who was a frequent visitor to the printing house took an interest in Franklin and gave him access to his own library, which was much better stocked than Josiah's. When Franklin wrote a ballad about a recent drowning, it was printed by his brother and hawked around Boston to much acclaim. His father, however, discouraged him from further flights of poetic fancy by warning him "that Verse-makers were always Beggars."[6]

Franklin now switched to writing prose. He was clear-sighted about its value, both intellectually and commercially. "As Prose Writing," he reminisces in his *Autobiography*, "has been of great Use to me in the Course of my Life, and was a principal Means of my Advancement, I shall tell you how in such a Situation I acquir'd what little Ability I have in that way." The account that Franklin gives is the more impressive because he invented his own training in written composition, a subject that was not being taught in any reading or writing school at the time. Instead, "writing" was defined by teacher and student alike as penmanship.[7]

Franklin's self-education as a prose writer began with his love for argumentation, which he would later condemn as "a very bad Habit." He and his friend John Collins took to debating on a variety of topics, one of which was whether the female sex could and should be educated in "Learning." (Collins maintained that girls and women were "naturally unequal to it"; Franklin took the opposing position, "perhaps a little for Dispute sake.") Collins was swift in repartee, and Franklin began to suspect that he was being outwitted in argument not so much by the strength of Collins's positions as by his dexterity with the language. He therefore started to write down his own arguments, and he and his friend, now at a distance from each other, entered into a series of letter exchanges. Once again, Josiah Franklin had an impact on his son's career. Happening upon this correspondence, he pointed out to Benjamin that, whatever the merits of his arguments, he fell "far short in elegance of Expression [style], in Method [organization] and in Perspicuity [insightfulness]." Young Franklin saw the justice of these comments and was determined to improve.[8]

The chief vehicle for his self-improvement proved to be a copy of the *Spectator*. The *Spectator* had gone out of publication as a London journal long since, but it was still available as an imported reprint. Franklin, who had never come across a copy before, seized upon it as a model of good writing. He devised three approaches to capitalizing on its literary felicities. First he took notes (he called them his "Hints") on a particular passage. He let these rest for a few days and then tried to recreate the original from them. The ensuing comparison between his own effort and the original revealed some of his faults, which he then corrected. He is not specific about what he considered his faults to have been, but they certainly included the meagerness of his vocabulary. He even regretted having given up writing poetry, thinking that the discipline of finding rhymes, and synonyms with the appropriate meter, would have supplied him with a larger selection of words.

Franklin's next self-imposed exercise, therefore, was to turn selected passages into verse, and then again, after an appropriate gap, recreate the prose. These exercises focused on enriching his style, but his third practice was designed to improve the organization of his prose. He used to take his notes and shuffle them. Later, he would again try to recreate the original, after reorganizing his notes into a logical order. Once again, he learned much from a comparison with the original. He was even gratified to find that "in certain Particulars of small Import, I had been lucky enough to improve the Method or the Language." By physically manipulating his notes, he was mentally teaching himself how to arrange his thoughts, exploiting the relationship between thinking and writing (in this case, printed writing) to model the act of thinking. All these exercises in mental self-improvement had to be undertaken at night or on Sundays, a day when he skulked alone at the printshop to avoid attending religious services with his father.[9]

Franklin's next attempt at composition is well known. Several men in James's circle of friends wrote pieces for James's iconoclastic newspaper, the *New England Courant*, and often visited the printing office. Their conversations about the approval their essays had evoked inspired Franklin to write a piece himself. He disguised his handwriting and slipped his essay under the door of the printing house at night. The next morning, as it was read aloud to members of the group, he had the "exquisite Pleasure, of finding it met with their Approbation," and of hearing that their guesses about its authorship were all of men with a reputation for learning.[10]

Years later, these early, successful approaches to self-instruction in composition, which took place with virtually no assistance from formal instruction, led Franklin to include them in his plans for an English school in Philadelphia. In *Proposals Relating to the Education of Youth in Pensylvania* [sic], published in 1740, he described a practical curriculum, designed to inculcate the "*most useful* and *most ornamental*" subjects. In their pursuit of successful literacy acquisition, students of the academy were to be taught to write swiftly as well as legibly and to read the "best" writers, such as Addison and Pope, recommended as models of good writing. Students were to form their own style by writing letters to one another and by "making Abstracts of what they read; or writing the Same Things in their own Words," and by retelling or paraphrasing in writing what they had just read. Unlike Franklin himself, they would have a teacher to aid them: their work was to be "revis'd and corrected by the Tutor, who should give his Reasons, explain the Force and Import of Words, &c." Far too canny to support these radical suggestions by alluding to his own experience, Franklin, in bulky footnotes, bolstered them with references to the words of the British philosopher John Locke.[11]

Franklin's deliberate efforts to teach himself how to write prose provide a backdrop to another rare eighteenth-century instance of treating writing as composition, a series of letters written by children to their benefactor, George Whitefield, at the Bethesda School for Orphans that he founded in Georgia.

One of George Whitefield's earliest accomplishments as he traveled around the American colonies, beginning in 1738, was to establish this boarding school for orphans just outside Savannah. The school became an object of keen interest back in England, where Whitefield and his supporters promoted it by publishing tracts about it. One of the tracts included the letters, all dated March 24, 1741, composed by ten children, who ranged in age from ten to seventeen; their anonymity was preserved in the printed version by publishing only the first and last letters of their first and last names.

A few days before these letters were written, a miniature revival had occurred among the younger children at the school. As their superintendent remarked, there was much weeping and begging of God in "Scripture-Language" to have compassion upon them, to pluck them "as Fire brands out of the Burning."[12]

Three days after this experience, which was known to all the children whether they had taken part in it or not, the older children were asked—it is hardly possible that they undertook this outpouring of prose spontaneously—to write to their benefactor. Not surprisingly, many of them mentioned this episode. "The little Children are coming to Christ; for indeed there appares [sic] a visible Concern in the whole Family, but especially among the Boys," one twelve-year-old girl wrote. A fourteen-year-old boy invoked a phrase from Ezekiel to describe the same phenomenon, alluding to the very passage that had once made young Betty Sewall weep so much that she could barely read:

The Spirit of the Lord, I hope, is beginning to blow among the dry Bones here. The House was never since I came liklier to answer the End of its Institution than now: Little Boys, and little Girles, at this and that Corner crying unto the Lord, that he would have Mercy upon them.[13]

Several of the letters refer to the writer's own sense of being saved. As the same twelve-year-old girl phrased it, "I am fild with Wonder and Admiration when I think that I am out of Hell. . . . O Wonderful Love! Well might one say, Eternity is too short to utter all Thy Praise." A ten-year-old boy began his letter convention-ally, but immediately swung into spiritual self-examination:

Dear and Reverend Sir,
This is to let you Know that I am in good Health, hoping that you and all your Friends are the same. I heartyly bless God, that he has been pleased to let me see a little of my wicked Heart; and I hope he will be pleas'd to carry it on untill it ends into a sound and thorough Convertion.

A girl of ten, probably named Rebecca, also wrote about her sense of sin and her hope for salvation, before shifting into a brief comment on her health:

Dear and Reverend Sir,
    I have found great Concern about my poor Soul since your leaving us, God has shown me more and more of the Hardness and Wretchedness of my Wicked Heart. Indeed I have great Reason to bless God for my coming here, for I enjoy many Blessings spiritual and temporal; God has been wonderfully good to me, but I have slighted his rich Mercies. O! It fills me with Wonder and Amazment to think God has not cut me off long ago and sent me to Hell, for I am sure I have deserved it: For O it greves me to think I have been sinning against so good and gracious a God; but God has promised that those that seek him early shall find. I have not been well, but I am now better, blessed be God. Dear Sir, I hope God will strenghen you to go out into the Highways, and to entrete poor Sinners to come to Repentance.
    O may the Lord contineu the Concern that we are all under, till it ends in a thorough and sound Convertion. . . .
                    Your dutifull and unworthy child
                    R——a B——n.[14]

From the perspective of a modern writing instructor, Rebecca shows a firm grasp of topic: her introductory topic is the salvation of her own soul. She links her concern over it to the departure of her addressee, which, she implies, is related to her growing awareness of her own sinfulness. Then she shifts to her many blessings at Bethesda—a shift that leads her to reproach herself for neglecting God and her corresponding amazement that he has not abandoned her long ago. She continues the contrasting parallelism between what she deserves and what she receives: she talks of her grief at her sin on the one hand and the merciful goodness of God on the other. Only then is there an awkward jump to the issue of her own health. She then reverts to speaking directly to her addressee: she prays that God will give Whitefield the strength to keep up his work of entreating sinners to repentance. She ties this wish neatly back to her original topic of her concern over herself, this time enlarging it beyond herself to sinners in general: she prays that the Lord will continue the concern until all are converted. Except for the sidetrack over her health—and even that is connected to God, who is said to have restored it—the letter has a beginning, a middle, and end that are satisfying even to the modern reader.

The content in this letter derived, of course, from the religious education the children had received, and Rebecca must have been reiterating statements heard many times from her teachers; but she had, nonetheless, also learned the concept of taking a topic and exploring it to its limits.

By the standards of its founder, the Bethesda School has to be judged a success. If the ten children who wrote these letters are representative of the students as a whole, the spiritual messages that Whitefield wished to impart had been thoroughly absorbed. On the basis of these same letters—surely among the earliest written by children living in America ever to appear in print—the school also has to be judged a success in terms of its academic ambitions. If we can assume that the letters were not doctored or corrected in any way by the Bethesda schoolmasters—and Whitefield claimed that the letters were "spell'd precisely as [the children] wrote them"—they provide us with a window on literacy in action. They display a good grasp of conventions in all senses: the conventions of letter writing, of the literary requirement of remitting a central message, and of the mechanics of spelling and punctuation.[15]

The formulaic beginnings and endings appropriate to letter writing all appear here. The children start their letters with salutations such as "Dear and Reverend Sir," and end them appropriately: Rebecca even links her closure to her relationship to Whitefield by calling herself his "dutifull and unworthy child." She and other children use the common convention of discussing their health and that of their correspondent. The ten-year-old boy begins his letter by reporting on his own, then enquires about that of Whitefield and ends by asking Whitefield to write to them all, "to let us Know how you and all your Friends are." These children had clearly been taught the structural components of a letter and conventional ways of opening and closing a correspondence.

Moreover, many children had mastered, to a great extent, the concept that a well-written letter should focus on one or more clearly delineated topics. Rebecca's letter is a particularly fine example of a topic—the salvation of her soul—that is addressed, explored, and left but returned to again at the end of her letter. The fourteen-year-old boy focuses on the topic of the spirit of the Lord blowing through the school, first describing it and then detailing its effects.

Finally, the children had successfully acquired most of the conventions of the written language in terms of the mechanics of capitalization, punctuation, and spelling. In the eighteenth century, nearly all writers habitually capitalized important words, particularly nouns; the children follow this convention. Their punctuation shows a fair grasp of the correct use of exclamation marks and semi-colons (unless these were inserted by the printers). Rebecca uses a comma in her first sentence to unite two coordinating clauses without a conjunction; today she would be charged with a "comma splice." The children's spellings are by no means always correct, but their misspellings are illuminating. Most of them are phonetic: that is, although the spelling is incorrect, the misspelling would generate a pronunciation of the target word that would be correct. Misspellings like "greves" for *grieves,* "entrete" for *entreat,* and "contineu" for *continue* (all products of Rebecca's pen), "fild," "heartyly," "convertion," and "ungreatfull" all display a solid grasp of some of the rules of the English sound-to-spelling system. Other mistakes (such as the failure to produce the possessive *their* in "there Concern") are familiar to any teacher of English composition today.[16]

These young Georgia children were receiving what was, at the time, a good grounding in the basics, and even though they were orphans, Bethesda School was conducted as if they were of at least middling social status. Devereux Jarratt's story, in contrast, provides an example of the literacy education that a parent of only modest means in Virginia could afford in the late 1730s and 1740s. Despite minimal formal education, Jarratt, through self-education, attained a level of literacy that enabled him to jump from one social class to another, from the "simple," as he called it himself, to the gentry. His experiences, like Franklin's a generation earlier, also reveal the widespread lack of appropriate reading materials for the young before the half-century mark, the difficulty of acquiring consistent schooling in the countryside, and the continuing reliance on doctrinal material as the texts of instruction. More important, they give us insights into how many children must have learned to read—by memorization—before the introduction of the rigorous methodology supplied by the spelling book.

Access to literacy instruction in Virginia was unquestionably affected by a child's social class. Of all the colonies, Virginia came closest to replicating the rigid English class system. The social differences between settlers were heightened by the advent of tobacco farming as the colony's major crop. Labor intensive and very hard on the soil, tobacco farming promoted both a need for a great deal of land, because fields became depleted within a few years of cultivation, and a vast number of laborers. The need for cheap labor to work the tobacco fields encouraged the African slave trade, and the tempo of importing enslaved Africans quickened in the 1670s. Political positions were held mainly by men whose families owned the great plantations. But the situation reversed itself after the turn of the century with the introduction of wheat farming and increased interior settlement. By the mid-eighteenth century, yeoman farmers had begun to grow prosperous, as indicated by the fact that more of them than ever now owned slaves.[17]

Jarratt, who was born in 1733, had the advantage of being a member of a family that owned some land. He was the youngest child of a carpenter, "a mild, inoffensive man, and much respected among his neighbors," he recalled. Jarratt had two older brothers and a sister. His grandfather, who was English, had acquired twelve hundred acres of land in Virginia. Thanks to this small plantation, Jarratt's family was "free from real want. . . . They always had plenty of plain food and raiment, wholesome and good, suitable to their humble station." All their food came from the family plantation, with the exception of sugar, and the family's clothing was made by his mother. The only articles of clothing purchased were hats and shoes.[18]

Even as a child, Jarratt was intensely aware of the prevailing class system. As he recorded in his autobiography, "We were accustomed to look upon, what were called *gentle folks*, as beings of a superior order. For my part, I was quite shy of *them*, and kept off at a humble distance. A *periwig*, in those days, was a distinguishing badge of *gentle folk*." In fact, whenever he saw a man sporting a wig riding along the road near their house, it would give him such a "disagreeable feeling" that "I would run off, as for my life. Such ideas of the difference between *gentle* and *simple*, were, I believe, universal among all of my rank and age."[19]

His parents' aspirations for this much loved youngest child were modest. They "neither sought nor expected any titles, honors, or great things, either for themselves or children. Their highest ambition was to teach their children to read, write, and understand the fundamental rules of arithmetic. I remember also," Jarratt wrote, "they taught us short prayers, and made us very perfect in repeating the *Church Catechism*." By the "Church Catechism," Jarratt meant the Anglican catechism, for the Jarratts were members of the Church of England, the established church of Virginia.[20]

This statement once again illuminates the contrasts, particularly relating to their motivation for literacy instruction, between the adherents of the established Church of England and nonconformists. For Anglicans, the Anglican catechism played almost as important a role as the Bible itself, and because the clergy were the interpreters of the Bible, Anglicans did not necessarily feel the compelling need that nonconformists did to teach the young to read it themselves. Nonetheless, this family read the Bible aloud. Jarratt happened to have an extraordinarily retentive memory. "Before I knew the letters of the alphabet, I could repeat a whole chapter in the Bible, at a few times hearing it read, especially if the subject of it struck my fancy. The 16th chapter of Judges, and some other parts of the history of *Samson*, I soon learned to repeat; because I was so much taken with his strength, exploits, and vengeance on the *Philistines* for his *two eyes*."[21]

His was an unusual memory: "I had indeed an aptitude in learning several things, but more especially those, in which the memory was mostly concerned. I have never conversed with any person in my life," Jarratt recalled, "whose memory seemed equal to mine. Nor did I ever know one, who could repeat so many lines, in an English, or Latin poet, as I could, in the same space of time." Since he also had a good ear for music and a pleasing voice, he could remember and sing songs of almost a hundred verses long, such as "Chevy Chase," after hearing them only a few times.[22] His good memory, as he was only to discover much later, would prove to be a hindrance to him when he was introduced to reading.

Jarratt's father died very suddenly before Jarratt reached the age of seven. His widowed mother still managed to send him, at the age of eight or nine, he records, "to an English school in the neighbourhood:—and I continued to go to one teacher and other, as opportunity served, (though not without great interruptions) till I was 12 or 13. In this time I learned to read in the Bible, (though but indifferently) and to write a sorry scrawl, and acquired some knowledge of Arithmetic." His mother now died, leaving him to the care of his older brother Robert, and his formal education ended.[23]

Although it is not possible to reconstruct the sequence of literacy instruction from this brief account, it seems most unlikely that Jarratt was taught to read through a spelling book. Here, as elsewhere, the Bible was the apex of the reading curriculum, and no doubt the primer, the Psalter, and New Testament were the routes that led up to it.

Under Robert's indulgent supervision, Jarratt's jobs consisted of exercising race-horses and preparing game-cocks for matches, as well as plowing, harrowing, and other field work, which he enjoyed much less. He did, however, decide that he needed to improve one aspect of his education, arithmetic. "I borrowed a plain book, in manuscript," he writes, which he studied at noon while the horse that he was using to harrow or plow was grazing. He learned more in a month than he had in his several years of disrupted schooling. "I was so well skilled in the *Division of Crops*, the *Rule of Three*, and *Practice*, that, you may be sure, the fame of my learning sounded far."[24]

When Jarratt talked about the "fame" of his learning, he was being factual as well as ironic. A man named Jacob Moon heard of Jarratt's prowess and invited him to become a schoolmaster in Albemarle County. He assured Jarratt that he would be able to attract enough pupils to make the move worthwhile. In 1751, equipped with that indispensable attribute of a gentleman, a wig—which he had acquired from a slave, who had himself received it as a discard from his master—Jarratt rode off on a borrowed horse and saddle.[25]

It did not take long for Jarratt to encounter the difficulties of maintaining himself as a schoolmaster when his only income was the fees of his students. "We soon entered on the business of raising a school. But I quickly discovered the number of pupils would be far short of what I had been made to expect." Moon was pleased with the instruction his schoolmaster provided, but Jarratt was not able to make inroads among the young in such a new and raw settlement. Albemarle County was "nearly a frontier county," he remembered, so "the manners of the people were generally more rough and uncivilized than in the more interior parts of the country."

At some point during that year, however, a significant event occurred that would have more meaning in retrospect than it did at the time. Jarratt came across a published collection of sermons by George Whitefield. "Mr. Whitefield's eight sermons, preached in *Glasgow*, were left, by some one, at Moon's. This being the first sermon book I ever had seen, or, perhaps, heard of, I had the curiosity to look into it. I was but a poor reader, and understood little of what I did read. And what I did understand, in those sermons, had no effect—supposing I had no concern in the contents, as the *author*, I was told, was a *New-light*, and consequently what he said was nothing to *Churchmen*."[26]

A year of teaching while living at Moon's house netted Jarratt only nine pounds. It also, because the house was situated on the banks of the James River, exposed him to malaria, which attacked him regularly. So he began another school, boarding with the parents of his pupils, for a length of time that was in proportion to the number of their children that he taught. He began at the house of Abraham Childers, where the family was as keen on "*merriment, banter, buffoonery* and such like" as he was. He left this pleasant situation with considerable reluctance to live with the next set of parents of his pupils, the daughter and niece of the Cannon family.[27]

Now, for the first time, he was living among gentlefolk. Cannon "was a man of great possessions, in lands, slaves, &c. &c." Even more daunting, his wife was a "New-light," a devotee of George Whitefield who reportedly would not tolerate any ungodliness in her household, let alone levity. Upon his first entrance into this household, he found Mrs. Cannon reading a religious book. He said little the entire evening. "I was truly out of my element, and was glad, when the morning arose, to get off to my little school, that I might, once more, be from under the eye of restraint."[28]

Anxious not to lose his room, board, and pupils, Jarratt now began hypocritically playing the role of the devout believer. It was Mrs. Cannon's practice "to read [aloud] a sermon, in *Flavel*, every night—to which she wished me to attend." He obliged her by being present for this reading, and although "I had, indeed, little relish for such entertainment, yet, agreeable to my purpose of playing the hypocrite, and gaining a favourable opinion, I affected a very close attention." He even asked her—despite the length of the sermon—to read aloud a second one, "though, probably, I understood not the tenth part of what was read." (John Flavel's sermons were too "experimental and evangelical," he said, for "one, so ignorant of divine things, as I was, to comprehend.") When Mrs. Cannon became tired, she would ask Jarratt to take a turn in reading. It was now that Jarratt's quick memory proved a disadvantage. As his account unfolds, it exposes the gulf between his ability to read material already familiar to him from hearing it (the Bible) and his ability to read entirely new material. His vocabulary was not up to the task, nor, one suspects, his ability to pronounce the words he met. Certainly, his efforts at reading were an embarrassment: "so poor a hand did I make of the business, that reader and hearer were rather abashed, than edified." Mrs. Cannon soon refrained from asking him to take his turn, and for weeks he sat there listening to her each evening, battling a strong urge to sleep.[29]

Then came an epiphanal moment. The text of the sermon she was reading to him one night was "*Then opened he their understanding.*" Somehow it spoke to the crux of what was blocking Jarratt from intellectual as well as spiritual progress, as he saw it: his lack of comprehension of what was being read. Although the topic, Jarratt explains, was "as dark to me, as any of the former," he was able to apply the text to his own situation: "I felt myself imprest with it, and saw my personal interest in the solemn truths." He was now emotionally engaged with the text. To the great joy of his landlady, he began to show a genuine interest in religion and since he was the first member of her family to do so, she persuaded him to stay for the remainder of his year.[30]

Jarratt had to return, however, to the Moon family the following year to open his school there again because his total income over the past year had been a mere seven pounds and promised to deteriorate further. The Moons were not happy with the change that had come over him: he was now earnestly urging them to look out for their own souls. "*But they made light of it*—turned all off with a laugh—imputing the whole to *new-light cant*," which church people needed to have nothing to do with. Jarratt persevered on his own. He did not "understand the meaning of many scriptures" that he read, he explains, "but I understood enough to know, that except we *repent*, we must perish."[31]

Jarratt sensed that he needed an instructor, and he looked for books to aid him. His efforts offer a striking example of just how difficult it was to obtain books in the Virginia hinterlands in the 1750s. "I had not a single book in the world, nor was I able to buy any books [because of his lack of cash], had I known of any for sale." But somehow he got his hands on an old, "smoky" copy of Robert Russel's *Seven Sermons on Different Important Subjects*. He used an approach that would today be called "repeated readings" to help his comprehension. "I borrowed the book, and read the sermons again and again." The old story of Francis Spira, the one that had so distressed young Betty Sewall, also made an impression on Jarratt. "But I still wanted help in understanding the scriptures."[32]

Jarratt had never heard of an expositor, a work that explicated scripture, "yet I thought it necessary there should be a book of that sort." Someone told him about "a very large *book*, belonging to a gentleman, about five or six miles distant across the river, *which* explained all the New Testament." Emboldened by his lengthy stay at the Cannon house, during which he had "worn off some of my clownish rusticity, and had become less shy of persons in the upper ranks of life," he called on the owner and asked him if he could borrow it. The book was William Burkitt's exposition of the New Testament. Here, for the first time, Jarratt had an aid to comprehending the Bible. Along with exhortations to "Observe" and "Learn," Burkitt provided below each scriptural verse or group of verses some background to help unpack their full meaning. He related them to other passages in the Old or New Testament, guiding his readers to draw conclusions about what course they should take in their own lives.[33]

Because Burkitt had been a clergyman of the Church of England, Jarratt hoped that this book would prove acceptable to the Moons and that they would listen to the parts of it that he selected to read to them. But they were not interested. Undeterred, and lacking a candle, he sat on the hearth with Burkitt propped up on the end of a nearby chest and "by the light of the fire, read till near midnight. It pleased God mightily to improve my understanding, by these means—and I soon became, what was called a good reader, and my relish for books and reading greatly increased."[34]

Jarratt now moves beyond our interest in his acquisition of literacy. After a vacation with one of his brothers that nearly undid his new-found religion, he returned to Moon's and was then invited back by Mr. Cannon to teach his young son, this time at a salary of fifteen pounds. He was later aided by the generosity of his employer to take lessons in Latin and Greek and prepare for ordination. In the fall of 1762 he voyaged to England to be ordained and subsequently became the rector of the Anglican church of Bath Parish, Virginia. He had already made a major transition from "the *ax* to the *quill*" but now went one step further, from the quill to the pulpit and the Book of Common Prayer.[35]

While Jarratt in rural Virginia was acquiring such poor literacy skills that we wonder how well he could teach others, schoolmasters in Pennsylvania were beginning to use an instructional text that would prove of great service in both reading and writing instruction. A German spelling book surfaces in an unusually rich description of literacy education in a rural Pennsylvania setting: in two little country schools where Christopher Dock, a Mennonite, taught for many decades in the first half of the eighteenth century. The instruction in reading and writing in German offered by Dock illustrates the consistency of the literacy curriculum across linguistic boundaries.

Dock, a devout Mennonite, emigrated to Pennsylvania from Germany at some point between 1710 and 1714. He then spent ten years teaching literacy, in German, to children in Skippack, a village some sixty miles northwest of Philadelphia. During the next ten years he farmed a tract of a hundred acres that he purchased from the Penn family, spending four summers teaching in Germantown. In 1738, however, he returned to his teaching mission full-time: he opened a school in Skippack once again, and another in Sollford. On alternate weeks, he taught for three days a week at one school, and then another three days at the other.[36]

One of his students had been Christopher Saur, who attended Dock's Germantown school during at least one summer. After Saur became the leading printer of works in German in the colonies, he wished to publicize his master's gentle pedagogy and prevailed on Dock—with some difficulty—to describe his teaching methods. Dock handed Saur his manuscript *Schul-Ordnung* (*School-Management*) in the summer of 1750 but modestly insisted that it should not be published until after his death. Saur died long before Dock; Saur's son, also named Christopher, prevailed upon Dock to let him publish the work in 1770. It is arguably the first "methods" text printed in America.[37] Although Dock is far from methodical in presenting his approach (he himself called it a "piecemeal" account), and although he reveals as much about his Christian beliefs as about his teaching, he nonetheless presents an invaluable portrait of a small, mid-century rural Pennsylvania school that aimed only at teaching the three Rs.

Several features in Dock's account can be generalized beyond his own school. The equipment, for one, had improved by the middle of the century. Each of his schools had a blackboard, which Dock used regularly for teaching arithmetic; crayons that he also used (if only for writing a commendatory "0"—meaning zero mistakes—on the hands of students who knew their lessons);[38] and slates that the children employed for their writing practice. One piece of equipment is instantly recognizable today: a wooden tag on a nail that children had to take when they needed to leave the classroom for the outhouse. Coeducation was completely accepted. (The boys sat on one side and the girls on the other, a practice that would continue in most schools late into the nineteenth century.) The scriptures were used in reading instruction, and a spelling book is mentioned. Dock was an exceptionally devout man, but this characteristic probably did not set his school apart from most other Pennsylvania schools of the time—or, indeed, of schools anywhere. Most intriguing of all is that Dock's literacy instruction in German was virtually indistinguishable, other than linguistically, from that in English.[39]

Dock's gentle methods arose from his affection for the young. "First I owe God particular thanks," he wrote in *School-Management*, "because besides calling me to this profession He has given me an extreme love of children. For if it were not for love it would be an unbearable burden to live among children. But love bears and never tires." It was said that tears would come into his own eyes if they started to glisten in those of a reprimanded pupil. Like Cotton Mather, Dock used the withdrawal of his approval as his most powerful weapon of discipline.[40]

A new child, he reports, was welcomed into the school by the other children, who would hold out their hands to him. After newcomer was asked whether he intended to be diligent and obedient (unsurprisingly, the answer was always yes), Dock continues, "he is told how to behave; and when he can say his A B C's and point out each letter with his index finger, he is put into the Ab." As in English instruction, the first step was to identify the letters by name. This step proceeded without the aid of writing: the child had to point to the letters. Moreover, just as in English instruction, the syllable (the vowel-consonant combinations familiar from the hornbook, such as *ab*) was a key unit of instruction.

Dock was a believer in tangible rewards, some of which were literacy-related. A child who progressed far enough to join the *Ab* class was told that his father owed him a penny and that his mother should fry two eggs for him. His parents should do the same for successive promotions, "for instance, when he enters the word class." Dock's own rewards consisted of samples of his own beautiful penmanship: if children hesitated to volunteer to look after a newcomer, Dock would offer "a bird or a writing-copy." On other occasions he promised a sketch of a flower.[41]

Dock used literacy activities to fill up the time of waiting at the start of the school day, exercising leniency about punctuality because some children came from such a distance: "when a few children are present, those who can read their Testament sit together on one bench; but the boys and girls occupy separate benches." They were given a chapter from the Testament, which they read aloud in turn ("round robin" reading, it is called today), while Dock wrote out their writing copies for them. Reading—ever defined as oral—was judged to be successful if it was accurate. (Dock, of course, was so imbued with the scriptures that he did not need to have the text in front of him to identify mistakes.) Those who gave an error-free performance went to their place at the table and began copying texts onto their slates. Those who made mistakes had to sit at the end of the bench; the last child on the bench was called "a 'lazy pupil,'" never "stupid," which suggests a lack of capacity to learn; the term "lazy" implied that improvement was up to the child. Anyone could try harder.[42]

Three major divisions of students were apparently under the same roof: the children learning the alphabet, those in the spelling book (which Dock calls the "Ab" class), and those in the Testament class, who read the Bible (mostly, but not exclusively, the New Testament). Dock outlined the task of the children in the spelling class: "In spelling, when a word has more than one syllable, they must repeat the whole word, but some, while they can say the letters, cannot pronounce the word, and so cannot be put to reading." (They had not mastered the crucial leap from spelling out the letters individually to pronouncing a whole word.) One strategy Dock used to help the unsuccessful members of this class was to take the book, spell out the word himself, and have the child pronounce it. What we would today call peer teaching and modeling now came in handy: "If he is slow, another pupil pronounces it for him, and in this way he hears how it should be done, and knows that he must follow the letters and not his own fancy."[43]

Those who were judged ready for the Testament class, the third group, also profited from peer teaching: the new member was handed to a veteran, who helped him or her read a verse or two. For one week, these children kept a foot in both classes: "they must learn their lesson in the speller with the small pupils and also their lesson with the Testament pupil." Once they reached a certain level of accomplishment, they became full-time Testament pupils and "they are also allowed to write" (an activity clearly regarded as a privilege). Other advanced children read the newspaper (printed in German by Christopher Saur), wrote letters to their peers in the other school taught by Dock, or did sums.[44]

A mark of what Dock called "intelligent reading" by the children was their respect for commas, signaled by their pausing briefly when reading aloud. He therefore devised a system to monitor this. If a Testament pupil stopped reading before reaching a comma or period, he received a "one-fourth failure." Reading straight through a comma earned another quarter-point failure. Repeating a word twice was penalized by half a point. After each child had read in turn, those with demerits had to stand in a row according to the total of their demerits. Those with the most had their places in class taken by those with none.[45] Once again, "good" reading was equated with accurate pronunciation rather than comprehension and by the children's compliance with that age-old command, "Mind your stops."

Nevertheless, Dock did not ignore comprehension. Because children from different denominations attended his class, he felt he could not use any one catechism and left the teaching of a catechism up to the parents. But he used a catechetical approach to teaching the comprehension of Christian beliefs. Children were expected to find passages in the Bible that provided an answer to the questions he posed. He focused on the human qualities that led to spiritual life, such as faith and justice, and those that led to death, such as faithlessness and injustice. "Whoever finds a passage," he explains, "steps forward, the next follows, and so they form a row, boys and girls separately, as each finds some passage of Scripture until they are all in a row. Then the first reads his passage." For example, if the question was "What is faith?" one child might respond by reading aloud the verse, " 'The substance of things hoped for, the evidence of things not seen. Hebrews xi.1.' " If another child happened to have selected the same text, he had to step back out of the row and find another text. The more passages the children found, "the more clearly does the truth of the same appear. In this way one passage of Scripture serves not only to fix another one in memory, but also to elucidate and explain it." A variation on this practice was to have the children sit "very still" and as soon as a passage occurred to them, to stand up and read it.[46] This locating of biblical evidence to support doctrine was another feature of Protestant education that crossed denominational and linguistic boundaries.

Writing at Dock's schools served two purposes, calligraphic and communicative. The chief patron of its calligraphic aspects was Dock himself, who, as noted earlier, drew quick sketches of birds or flowers to use as little bribes or gifts for his students. He also gave lengthier and more complex pieces as awards (*Schriften*) that were widely admired in his own time. Some twenty-five of them adorned the walls of the school, and his pupils used his gifts as wall decorations in their own homes.[47]

Dock's teaching of communicative writing took the form of requiring his students at the Skippack and Sollford schools to write letters to each other, which he carried from school to school himself. He tried to match the members of each pair, two boys or two girls, according to their level of ability. "When one became his correspondent's superior, he wrote to another whose equal he tried to be." The letters began with, "My friendly greeting to N.N." The children were asked to include a short verse or a scriptural text and then write about their school exercises, such as their motto for the week, or pose the kind of question that Dock asked them—to be answered by a scriptural quotation. Although the format was fairly restrictive, it did allow for some individual expression.[48]

We have several examples of Dock's own writing for communication. Despite his reluctance to have the *School-Management* published, in his later years he was less shy about appearing in print and published a letter, two hymns, and an essay on rules for children, which were printed in various issues of the younger Christopher Saur's *Geistliches Magazien (Spiritual Magazine)*.[49] Several of Dock's rules for school relate to literacy: "58. If you are to recite your lesson, open your book without noise, read loudly, slowly and distinctly, that every word and syllable may be understood"; "63.—Keep your books clean inside and out; do not scribble or draw in them; do not lose or tear them"; "64. In writing do not soil your hands and face with ink, and do not spatter the ink on the desk on your or other children's clothes." The last school rule is still appropriate: "65.—When school is out do not make a clatter. In going down stairs do not jump two or three steps at a time, lest you hurt yourself. Go quietly home."[50]

The portrait of literacy instruction that emerges from these three accounts in the first half of the eighteenth century is complex and uneven. Access to education and the quality of literacy instruction was influenced by numerous factors. Geography played a large part—the town schools of much of New England were unachievable in Virginia, with its dispersed population. At the political level, motivation for literacy instruction varied widely across the colonies, from the legislative mandates of Massachusetts and Connecticut to the virtual absence of literacy legislation in Georgia. Religion continued to play a crucial role: education in schools sponsored by different denominations was key to many a child's instruction all over the colonies. The urban-rural divide was important. So was the wealth of one's parents.

But there had yet to be, before the middle of the eighteenth century, one common denominator. Absent from the accounts of the Bethesda School (although it might have been there) and Jarratt's schools is the work that would be hailed as an educational innovation for the most elementary stages of literacy instruction; that would be integrated into the "ordinary Road" as a school text; and that would dominate the second half of the eighteenth century as the most indispensable of all reading instructional texts in schools: the spelling book. Dock's use, after 1738, of a German spelling book in his two little schools was a harbinger of things to come.[51]

8

The Rise of the Spelling Book

The use of a spelling book in Christopher Dock's little German-language schools was a sign of changing times. By 1750, the spelling book was emerging as an introductory reading instructional text that had already appeared in classrooms across the American colonies; by 1760 it was firmly established, and by 1770 it was an indispensable text. It would continue to be so for the following four decades.

In England, enthusiasm for publishing spelling books had continued unabated since the turn of the century. In the first decade of the eighteenth century, authors—one of them Thomas Dyche—produced some 15 new titles. In the 1710s, a half dozen more titles appeared; in the 1720s, another 8, which included the speller of Henry Dixon; 3 more in the 1730s; 16 in the 1740s, one of them the work of Thomas Dilworth, and from the 1750s to the 1770s, 13, 13, and 11 new spellers, respectively, were published each decade. Meanwhile, many of the older ones were still being reissued, including the venerable *English School-Master* by Edmund Coote, which reached its fifty-fourth printing in 1737, 141 years after its first publication.[1]

"Spelling" was consistently defined as naming the letters of a word aloud in their correct sequence. This process was used in the service of all three literacy activities, reading, writing, and oral spelling. As the British hymn writer Isaac Watts remarks in *The Art of Reading and Writing English*, published in London in 1721, spelling is "the Art of composing Words out of Letters and Syllables, either in Reading or Writing."[2] In both, the process was similar: for each word, the reader or writer identified (aloud) the letters of the first syllable and then pronounced it as a unit. The learner repeated this process, accumulating syllables until he or she had pronounced or written the entire word. An example of this cumulative spelling technique is provided in one of the spelling books: "D, o, x, Dox; o, doxo; l, o, lo; Doxolo; g, y, gy; Doxology."[3]

The Uses of Spelling for Writing

The role that spelling books were to play in American reading instruction (spelling-for-reading) can be understood only in relation to another kind of book that focused on the uses of spelling for writing instruction: the "secretary" books that began to be printed in Boston as the seventeenth century turned into the eighteenth. Good spelling was viewed, as it is today, as important to good writing. American imprints—all of them copies of imported English works—reflected this emphasis in the publication of books aimed at clerks ("secretaries"), who, it was assumed, had already learned to read. The intellectual progenitors of what we might call these "secretary" books were authors such as Nathaniel Strong, whose *England's Perfect School-Master* had first appeared in London in 1674 (and was still being reprinted in Boston in 1710), but their instruction was far better suited to the intricacies of the legal world than his.

The "secretaries" of the time were invariably men working for other men, and the titles of these books usually indicated that their target was young men. The use of the word *secretary* in the title of T. Goodman's *The Experienc'd Secretary*, published in Boston in 1708, implied a male readership. This text for the experienced includes some examples of nonbusiness correspondence (termed "Familiar Letters," and written mostly by men to other men), a recherché discussion of rhetorical tropes, and a short dictionary. But its chief value was as a source of information on legal forms. Because the author assumed that the purchaser would have fully mastered the basic features of the written language, the book contains no information on letter-sound correspondences.[4]

A Boston product of the preceding year, *The Young Secretary's Guide*, had also offered its readers models of letters and a dictionary along with legal forms. But it had apparently been compiled from various sources by its printer, Bartholomew Green, and it soon had to compete with the authentic *Young Secretary's Guide*, attributed to Thomas Hill, whose fourth edition was reprinted in 1713 by yet another Boston printer, Thomas Fleet—without the dictionary.[5]

The publications of only a few years later, however, show a marked increase in their interest in the structure of the English orthographic system. *The Young Man's Companion* (with no author identified in its American version) was reprinted by William and Andrew Bradford of New York in 1710 from its second London edition. It begins its four-part volume with a brief examination of the spelling system from the perspective of both reading and writing. It includes rules for the pronunciation of words, such as "Letters that are writ, and not sounded," as well as hints for writing, such as "points" (punctuation). It even includes a few tables of syllables, "both whole and divided." Significantly, these began with words of three syllables: the absence of monosyllables identifies the work as an advanced text. The remaining three parts of the work are devoted to arithmetic, letter writing (the models have been copied from Hill's work), and the usual legal forms. When William Bradford, now in Philadelphia, published the work again eight years later, he preserved its spelling-book features: "(B) is not sounded after M, yet we write, dumb, thumb." He also kept the portions on punctuation. The question mark is explained: "This note [?] is put when any Questions made . . . *Qu. What shall I do? Whether* [sic] *shall I flee?*" The age-old rules for syllable division popularized by Edmund Coote are still in evidence, as are Coote's explanations of such matters as the final *e* and even paraphrases of his examples, as in "*It made me Mad.*" [6]

In 1737, Andrew Bradford, William's son, also in Philadelphia, published a fifth edition, "greatly Enlarged and carefully Corrected" and now titled *The Secretary's Guide, or Young Man's Companion*. The four-part division remains the same, but the initial discussion of the written language has all been rewritten and is more detailed than ever. Although a guide to pronunciation is still included, more emphasis has been given to correct spelling: "Of *Letters* sounded *alike* [such as *c* and *k*], and how to avoid Mistakes, in writing *one* for the *other*." The second part now features "Letters of Compliment [and] Friendship," as well as business letters, and even includes letters where women are correspondents. The generalist turn that this sort of work was taking can be seen in other additions that include monthly notes on gardening and another entire book, *The Family Companion*, which has instructions for wine making at home and "choice and safe" remedies for illnesses and injuries.[7]

Among those alert to the usefulness of the "secretary" books was Benjamin Franklin. His 1748 reproduction of the ninth British edition of George Fisher's *The Instructor; or Young Man's Best Companion*, retitled *The American Instructor*, offered "Spelling, Reading, Writing, and Arithmetick in an easier Way than any yet published; and how to qualify any Person for Business, without the Help of a Master." Like Bradford, Franklin provided two texts for the price of one, adding a treatise for the home, the *Poor Planters Physician*, which ran the gamut from how to mark table linens to pickling fruit. This last, unlike virtually all of the rest of the book, was addressed specifically to young women. Franklin had put his inimitable stamp on the whole project: "In the British edition of this Book, there were many Things of little or no Use in these Parts of the World." He had omitted those and inserted what was useful "to us Americans."[8]

Given Franklin's background and his own arduous self-education, it is no surprise that he, too, believed that elucidating English orthography was a crucial part of the book. While the bulk of this lengthy book is devoted to instruction in business matters, the first fifty-six pages, or about 18 percent of the book, relate to literacy. The treatment of letter-sound correspondences is more complex than ever. That spelling-book staple, a list of homophones, "*A Scent*, or Smell/*Ascent*, a going up/*Assent*, Agreement," is longer. Moreover, the *American Instructor* is the first English book printed in America to discuss the details of learning penmanship (such as how to hold a pen) and to give not only model sentences but entire paragraphs for reproducing in writing—"copies"—in both prose and verse. Franklin was even able to include pictures of the secretary and roundhand scripts. The difficulties of producing woodblocks of script, when no American yet had the skill or materials to attempt copperplate engraving, were so great that Franklin was the first American printer to do so.[9] The practical, do-it-yourself *American Instructor* enjoyed considerable success. Franklin soon reissued it, and the New York printer Hugh Gaine felt impelled to publish his own version in 1760.[10]

For all their emphasis on letter-sound correspondences, none of the self-help books printed on or after 1748 included "tables"—those lists of words, categorized by the number of their syllables, that lay at the heart of the speller. For by this time, these lists had become the sole province of the spelling book.

The Uses of Spelling for Reading: The Alphabet Method

Spelling was considered vital in the service of reading acquisition as well as writing acquisition. In a chapter titled "Directions for Reading" in his *Art of Reading and Writing English*, Watts gives us a glimpse of how spelling-for-reading aided the identification of words:

> If you do not certainly know any Word at first sight, do not guess at it, lest thereby you get a Habit of miscalling Words, and reading falsely; but be sure to spell every Word and Syllable before you pronounce it, if you are not acquainted with it.

Watts was sensitive to the potential embarrassment of calling out letter names during reading:

> I confess, it does not appear so well when you are reading in Company, to spell Letter by Letter; therefore spell any strange long Word you meet with in your Mind, Syllable by Syllable, and pronounce it slowly, step by step.[11]

Key to the spelling book was the appreciation that, in English as in all alphabetically represented languages, letters represent speech sounds. With varying degrees of success, spelling-book authors tackled the vexing nature of the English orthographical system and tried to explicate it.

For every spelling book, the individual letter of the alphabet was the starting point. As the English schoolmaster Thomas Dilworth explained in 1740, in the preface to his *A New Guide to the English Tongue*, "As to *Letters*, we are to observe that they are the Foundation of all Learning, as being those *Parts* of which all *Syllables, Words, Sentences*, and *Speeches* are composed." This conflation of the written and the spoken language represents a misunderstanding, shared by all who discussed the subject, that would not be completely cleared up until the growth of linguistics at the end of the nineteenth century. Letters are the basic units of written English, not of spoken English. The basic unit of spoken English, and all other languages, is the phoneme.[12]

While British spelling-book authors in the seventeenth and eighteenth centuries all labored under the same linguistic misapprehension, there was no comparable unanimity among them, as Ian Michael has made clear, on what children should be doing as they tackled reading. The authors of spellers disagreed even about what names to give the letters of the alphabet (for example, *j* was usually written out as *jay* or *jea*, but was also spelled *je, jee* or even the Hebrew *jod*). They differed about the treatment of the consonantal *i* and *u* (which eventually became the *j* and *v* of the modern alphabet) and about the usefulness of teaching the "powers" ("sounds") of the letters—half of them not even discussing the issue. They could not agree on the rules for syllable division or on what a diphthong is and how many there are.[13] That they disagreed on so many issues, however, is probably of less significance than the fact that they all agreed that these issues were crucially important.

Moreover, what spelling-book authors did agree on outweighed those issues on which they were at odds. Like Coote, they all assumed that reading instruction was conducted orally, without any writing, and they were united in their assumption that, after the letter, the syllable was the next appropriate unit of instruction. They also all invoked principles of length and alphabetization to organize this syllabic material. They agreed that monosyllables are "easier" than polysyllables and that the learner should therefore proceed from the one to the other. As we have already seen, successive authors had expanded on Coote's practice of presenting only lists of monosyllables: they now offered lists of words in an ascending number of syllables. Within the overarching category of syllabic length, they arranged their lists in alphabetical order.[14]

All authors also agreed that the correct separation of a word into its syllables, usually indicated by a hyphen or a space (as in "Ho-li-ness" in the *New England Primer*), was the key to its pronunciation. A cluster of rules, all present in the work of Edmund Coote, was associated with this belief. The first rule was that every syllable must begin with a consonant. The second was a function of the fact that in English each of the letters for the vowels (*a, e, i, o, u*) regularly represents two phonemes. (The same is true of *y*, but not all spelling books recognized it.) So a vowel that comes at the end of a syllable is pronounced "long" (like the *e* in *be*), while a vowel followed by a consonant within a syllable is given its "short" sound (like the *e* in *bed*). (The hornbook, it will be recalled, had implicitly acknowledged this distinction, with its introductory *ab*s and *ba*s.) The authors of spelling books did not necessarily call the phonetic differences in the vowels *long* or *short*, but the terms *long* and *short*, used by reading teachers even today, can be found in texts for teachers as far back as 1587. They were present in Coote's work of 1596 when he had his schoolmaster explain that an *e* at the end of a word was "to draw the syllable long, as he is *made mad*"; and Isaac Watts assumed in 1721 that he would be immediately understood by his young readers when he explained that "Every Vowel has a long and a short Sound."[15]

A third rule of spelling division was that if a consonant cluster (as we would term it today) can begin a word, it must begin a syllable. For instance, the word *astray* was to be divided *a stray*, not *as tray*, because *str-* is a permissible beginning consonantal cluster. Conversely, the syllable division would be *re con cile*, not *re co ncile*, because *nc-* cannot begin a word. There was a hitch to all this: authors often encountered words for which the second and third rules clashed. The rules worked for *cho sen* and *ci der* but not for *go blet* or *flu ster*, where the division indicates that the vowels in each of the first syllables are long, whereas in fact they are short. How authors approached this problem often defined their text.[16]

As the decades passed, the contents of spellers became more and more similar. They all began with the alphabet, printed in three fonts, roman, italic, and old English (gothic). Each of these alphabets was immediately followed by the so-called double letters, ligatures of two or more letters printed with a single piece of type, such as *fl* and *ct*. Then came the "tables" of words: the syllabary, monosyllables and polysyllables, grouped by syllabic length. They were interspersed in most texts with "lessons," which were short passages of connected prose that supposedly exhibited words presented in the preceding tables, or at least were restricted to words of the number of syllables presented to that point.

A central feature of the true spelling book was a lengthy discussion of letter-sound correspondences, often in the second part of the text, which offered a variety of rules on how to pronounce words. Additional features were ever-expanding lists of the homophones and rudimentary dictionaries seen in earlier spelling books, together with explanations of the meanings of biblical names.

Spelling Books by Dyche, Dixon, and Dilworth

Many of these characteristic features appeared in three spelling books that were, among them, to blanket the American colonies in imported and local imprints until after the American Revolution. Works by Thomas Dyche, Henry Dixon (as part of a compendium), and Thomas Dilworth were a significant presence in eighteenth-century America after 1730. They differed in their aims from the semi-commercial texts of Nathaniel Strong and Edward Young in that they all geared their works toward teaching young children to read. And they differed from the doctrinal works of Franz Daniel Pastorius and George Fox, let alone primers and psalters, by including secular text. It says much for the colonials' enthusiasm for devotional and scriptural material that it would be Dilworth's text that would eventually conquer all its rivals by the time of the American Revolution—in part because he pleased his customers by writing a speller that avoided secular texts and adapted scriptural ones.

The earliest of these three schoolbooks was *A Guide to the English Tongue*, written by the London schoolmaster Thomas Dyche (pronounced "ditch") and first published in that city in 1707. Dyche published several other works, including a Latin school "vocabulary," *The Youth's guide to the Latin Tongue*, and an English dictionary. While all of these works went into at least four editions and his English dictionary into seventeen, none was as popular as his reading instructional text, *A Guide to the English Tongue*. Over fifty English editions are documented by 1800, and that number is certainly an underestimate of the total output. One London printer alone, Charles Ackers, printed thirty-three editions between 1733 and 1747, averaging nearly eighteen thousand copies annually.[17]

Dyche's *Guide to the English Tongue* is divided, as Edmund Coote's had been, into two parts. In the first part of his original London edition of 1707, Dyche begins with the syllabary and works his way through tables of some twenty-two hundred monosyllables. His first table of words runs from *blab crab drab* to *shy sky fly*; his second deals with short vowels in words of four letters (*back hack jack*); and so forth.[18] The net result is a procession of monosyllables that rhyme by eye as well as ear. Dyche himself thought that this "gingling of the Words," as he called it, would aid the young reader's memory. It could also prove troublesome for the instructor. According to a 1734 comment by Henry Boad, a schoolmaster in Colchester, England, and the author of a rival spelling book, the "jingling syllables . . . in schools among boys, are apt to create too great a mixture of mirth and folly . . . which, let [the master] do his best, he cannot prevent in some waggish boys, when they study *hiss, kiss, miss,* &c." (The ribaldry lay in the "&c," where the rhyme now shifted to the letter *p.*)[19]

For the polysyllables that followed, an innovation that would prove of great durability and copied by all subsequent authors of spellers was Dyche's recognition of syllabic stress. His *Guide to the English Tongue* presents words of two syllables, accented on the first (*turt-le*); followed by words of two syllables with an accent on the second (*pre-pare*); and he works his way up through the polysyllables in this fashion. This was a practice, as Michael has observed, that "set the pattern for the rest of the century." By chapter 7, Dyche is presenting hyphenated lists of words of six and seven syllables, and, like Strong, offering parallel lists of words without syllable division. The second part of Dyche's *Guide* provides a very clear discussion of the rules of pronunciation.[20]

The most striking feature of Dyche's book is how little connected reading material it offers. One of the few pieces of connected text he provides occurs in conjunction with his table of words of two syllables, which is also the last piece of reading practice until almost the end of the book. Alphabetically organized by the first letter of the first word, the disjointed sentences sound more like copybook maxims than reading material: "Always begin, go on, and end with God. / Be slow to promise, swift to perform. / Custom in sinning takes away Sense of Sin . . . / Vouchsafe no leisure Hours to sinful Sports. / Utter no Secrets to abuse your Friend . . . / Yield your self a Captive to mighty Reason."[21] They suggest the themes of rationalism that would characterize Enlightenment texts.

At the end of the work Dyche turns to writing instruction, to which he devotes five pages. He includes two pages of illustrations of different scripts: round hand, italic, and secretary. Given its lack of reading material, its chief value to its purchasers presumably resided in its systematization of reading instruction, its model scripts, and its copybook maxims for writing instruction. Overall, *A Guide* is a book in which content has been sacrificed to methodology and comprehension to what reading teachers today would term "word attack skills." The contrast between Dyche's spelling book and the richly metaphorical, heavily doctrinal *New England Primer*, its predecessor by less than two decades, is stark.

Stark or not, Dyche's speller was soon being imported. The southern and middle colonies showed a decided preference for it. Although Hugh Gaine produced an edition in New York in 1753, Dyche's speller was rarely reprinted in the colonies—probably because its copperplate engravings of scripts were beyond the skill of colonial printers to reproduce. The work was already known in the colonies by the early 1730s, because in 1733, as we have seen, it was requested by a schoolmaster in Bridgehampton, Long Island, for the school he taught under the auspices of the Society for the Propagation of the Gospel. It was for sale in South Carolina by 1735, when the first advertisement for it appeared in the *South Carolina Gazette*, founded three years earlier. Between then and 1767, some sixteen advertisements in the same paper specified it by title. Dyche's spelling book also found favor in Pennsylvania, where it was advertised in the *Pennsylvania Gazette* a dozen times from 1730 to 1750, when its importance declined and it was advertised only six more times up to 1761. When the *Georgia Gazette* was launched in 1763, it, too, advertised Dyche's speller, while a copy of the work was sold to a customer for one pound six shillings by a general merchant in Virginia in 1758.[22]

Henry Dixon's Spelling Books

Although Dyche's book was popular in the southern and middle colonies, the New England colonies turned first to Henry Dixon's *The English Instructor,* originally published in London in 1728. Dixon was the master of a charity school named St. Albans, in Holborn, London. His was the earliest of all the spelling books discussed so far to state forthrightly that it was designed to be used by young children. The *English Instructor* was, its title page proclaimed, "a more plain, easy, and regular METHOD of Teaching young Children, than any Extant." Dixon also asserted that it was designed to instruct children in "*the Duties of Religion.*" It was an almost immediate success in England. It reached its twenty-third edition in 1760 and would be reprinted on that side of the Atlantic at least sixty-nine times up to 1823. An advertisement for imported copies of the speller was placed in the *Pennsylvania Gazette* in 1739.[23]

Only three American reprints of the *English Instructor,* Boston editions of 1736, 1746 (a reproduction "with Additions" of Dixon's eighth edition), and 1750, seem to be extant.[24] Indeed, Dixon's *English Instructor* did not find favor with New Englanders in precisely that form for very long. It was soon superseded by a work that maintained much of the content of its two parts but added a third: an American compilation titled *The Youth's Instructor in the English Tongue* that came to be called the "New England Spelling Book." The name of the compiler is not known, but Daniel Henchman, one of the publishers of Dixon's *English Instructor,* brought out an edition of the *Youth's Instructor* in 1757.[25] Another edition was printed a couple of years later, also in Boston, by the partners Samuel Draper and Zechariah Fowle. Fowle's apprentice at the time was Isaiah Thomas, born in 1749 and apprenticed to Fowle as a six-year old. Thomas recalled that the *Youth's Instructor* was "in great repute, and in general use for many years." The work had been printed at least twice in the 1750s before 1757, the date of our first extant copy, and the next decade saw another ten editions, all from Boston. Some editions of the *Youth's Instructor* were very large: the one Thomas mentions was of twenty thousand copies. It is symptomatic of the ephemerality of children's schoolbooks that not a single copy of this particular printing has survived.[26]

The *Youth's Instructor* of 1757 bills itself as "Collected from Dixon, Bailey, Owen, Strong and Watts," in three parts. Its sources include four British spelling books: in addition to Dixon's *English Instructor,* it draws on Nathan Bailey's *An Introduction to the English Tongue* (1726), John Owen's *The Youth's Instructor in the English Tongue* (1732) (from which it borrowed the title, Owen's only contribution), and Nathaniel Strong's *England's Perfect School-Master* (1674), already discussed. The acknowledgment of Isaac Watts's part in the collection refers to the inclusion of sections of his *Art of Reading and Writing* (1721). Watts was already so well known for his *Divine Songs Attempted in Easy Language for the Use of Children* (1715) that simply invoking his name made the book more sales worthy.[27]

Of all these sources, Henry Dixon's was still the major contribution. The thrust of the revision of Dixon, however, which excluded some material and added others, is in almost every instance in favor of a yet more elaborate presentation of the tables—and so of exemplars of the relationship between letters and sound—at the expense of connected text. The revision therefore continued a trend begun in the Boston *English Instructor* of 1746, which had also adapted the original of 1728 by cutting reading material and expanding the word lists.

The strongest impression provided by the *Youth's Instructor*, as had been true of the earlier *English Instructor*, is of rampant inconsistency. There is no uniform tone to the book: it is an uneasy mix of the sacred and profane. The introductory portion of Henchman's 1757 edition of the *Youth's Instructor* is identical to that in his 1746 edition of the *English Instructor*. The lessons in monosyllables that follow are uniformly religious: "Thus a good Child will call on God. . . . He will hate sin, and strive to please God."[28]

A sharp difference in tone can be detected between these lessons and a poem that was featured in the London 1728 and the Boston 1746 versions as well as the Boston edition of 1757. Written entirely in monosyllables, it is one of the most long-lasting of all spelling-book poems and may be of greater antiquity than Dixon's particular text: the word *eye* still rhymes with the name of the letter *A*, and *J* and *Z* are named *Jod* and *Zod*.

As far as discipline is concerned, a "spare the rod and spoil the child" approach is paramount. In terms of pedagogy, few texts so well express the importance of the alphabet and the child's conviction that once he has mastered the letter *A* in its capital form by pronouncing its name (by "say[ing] great A"), the rest of the alphabet, and indeed, all learning, must ineluctably follow.

A Boy that once to School was sent,
On Plays and Toys was so much bent,
That all the Art of Man they say,
Could not once make him say great A.
His friends that saw him in these Fits,
Cry'd out, for shame, leave of[f] thy Tricks;
Be not so dull, make it thy Play
To learn thy Book; come say great A.
The Dunce then gap'd, but did no more,
Great A was yet a great Eye-Sore.
The next Boys jog him; sure say they,
'Tis not so hard to cry great A.
No, no, but here's the Case, says he,
If I cry A, I must cry B,
And then go on to C, and D,
And that won't do, but still there's Jod,
Lurks in the way with X, Y, Zod.
And so no End I find there'll be,
If I but once learn A, B, C.
But as Things stand I will not do it,
Tho' sure I am one Day to rue it.

The boy's schoolmaster muses on how to cure this dangerous disease. He knows of a healing plant in the woods.

> This Plant, adds he, will clear his Sight,
> And with a Touch make him grow Bright.[29]

The moral at the end of the prose version of this cautionary tale (found only in the 1728 edition) puts the matter more bluntly. It reads, "He that will not learn by fair Means, must be whipt." The plant that has the magical property of clarifying the schoolboy's vision is, of course, the birch.[30]

The first significant change in the *Youth's Instructor* from the earlier *English Instructor* is the inclusion of a table of words in which "*Spelling* may be either divided according to the general Rule, or as they are pronounc'd." In a footnote, Dixon (if it is Dixon and not the compiler) suggests that syllables might be divided in a way that would lead the child to pronounce the vowels more accurately: it is, he writes, "more natural and agreeable to the Pronounciation to divide the Word Master" (which was subject to the rule that initial consonant blends might not be divided) "*Mas ter* than *Ma ster*, or Sister, *Sis* ter than *Si* ster." But this, the author adds, in a rare acknowledgment of the role of the teacher, he submits to the "Discretion of the judicious Instructor."[31] (It would take the spelling-book author Noah Webster, after the American Revolution, to convince the public that this radical change was an improvement.)

The next change from the 1746 text is the excision of all the connected text composed of two-syllables words. The tables of three-syllable words are intact, but only the first three of the lessons are retained. One of them proclaims, "You have now, my good Child, in some Measure, been taught your Duty." Missing in the *Youth's Instructor* is a lesson in the 1746 edition on the importance of being content with one's station in life: "No Station in this World can afford us unmixed Pleasure. . . . [T]he Head that wears a Crown, is fill'd with more Disquiet, than the Breast of a Commoner." The lesson closes with a prayer asking God to grant "the Blessing of Sedateness in Mind" that would guarantee happiness "in every Circumstance of Life." Is there a political significance in the abandonment, by Boston printers with strong egalitarian beliefs, of a lesson that so well conveyed approval of the social immobility beloved of the upper classes in Britain? The new material warns the young to avoid their peers who take the name of the Lord in vain: "Hence, where such Children meet, a dreadful Thing! The Streets with Oaths and horrid Speeches ring."[32]

The tables of four-syllable words in Dixon's 1746 edition are preserved in their entirety in the 1757 *Youth's Instructor*, as are the "Cautions and Directions against the Vices incident to Children." Activities that invite a parental spanking include both the wish to get above one's station and the desire to lord it over the poor:

> *Crimes for which Children ought to be Corrected.*
> If it be ask'd, what Faults, what Crimes demand
> A Punishment from Parents dreaded Hand?

Mark well, observe, reflect, and take due Care,
The chief are Lying, and Neglect of Prayer,
Omission of your Book and School Affair,
Taking God's Name in vain, excessive Play;
Envying those whose Dress appears more gay;
Contemning and pursuing him with Scorn,
Whose tatter'd Rags confess him more forlorn.[33]

At this point the *Youth's Instructor* of 1757 drops any further four-syllable material and moves into the scriptural names (duly sorted by length and syllabic stress), homophones, and abbreviations of titles that had appeared in Dixon's *English Instructor*.

One new feature in the 1757 compilation is an emphasis on writing instruction. The edition includes pithy sentences as well as longer selections to serve as "copies" in writing schools and even poems on the art of writing.[34] Yet another addition, and one that would endure in other spellers, is an increase in the number of fables that close the first part of the book, a feature of Dixon's original 1728 edition. Fables, though mostly in Latin, had been part of the instruction of the young for centuries. The Boston version of Dixon's speller in 1746, however, seems to have been the first school text in English in the American colonies to include fables. One of these, reprinted in the *Youth's Instructor*, is the story of a condemned youth who, at the gallows, under the pretext of whispering a last word to his mother, uses the opportunity to bite her ear "clear off." When horrified bystanders ask him the reason for this extraordinary act, he explains that his mother deserved it, "for if she had but whipt me soundly for the Book I stole when I was a Boy, I should never have come to the Gallows for pilfering, now I am a Man." It is another example of the inconsistency of tone. It is the ultimate incongruity that it was by stealing a book, presumably in order to imbibe its knowledge and virtue, that the youth has come to such a horrid end.[35]

The new fables in the *Youth's Instructor*, rather than preaching the value of virtue for its own sake, praise qualities that are important within a social context. The added fables extol the importance of choosing companions with care; caution against the dangers of pride in one's socioeconomic status (exemplified by a prince's horse with his embroidered saddle, golden curb and purple reins, who is reduced to the level of a beast of burden, just like the lowly ass he has mocked), and warn of the hazards of envy (displayed by the turkey and goose, whose resentment of the peacock for his "gorgeous Train, and . . . heavenly Plumage" is deemed self-destructive). Set within the context of reading instruction, these are hints of a trend that would appear with much greater visibility in writing instruction, where texts set for students to copy would laud virtues with a public face over those with a private one.[36]

The second part of Dixon's *English Instructor* of 1746, the section that had tackled the "decoding" of English, is preserved almost intact in the *Youth's Instructor* of 1757. It involves a lengthy dialogue in which a child questions his master on letter-sound correspondences. A typical exchange focuses on the *gh* combination in English:

Q. *How is* gh *sounded?*
A. Sometimes as in the Word *Ghost,* sometimes as in *laugh, cough,* &c.
Q. *Where is* gh *writ and not sounded?*
A. In high, nigh, might, night, bought, nought, caught, taught, &c.[37]

If greater attention than ever is paid to letter-sound correspondences in the *Youth's Instructor,* there is also a new emphasis on comprehension. A section that appeared for the first time in the *English Instructor* of 1746 and was preserved in its 1757 version presents a discussion on how to teach the Bible. It is an early and important instance of the teaching of comprehension and it addresses the teacher rather than the child. Dixon highlights what today we would call the importance of background information to textual understanding. He suggests that in order to initiate children into the knowledge of the scriptures it may be appropriate for the instructor to acquaint them with the major events of the Bible, such as the Creation, the Flood, the building of Solomon's temple, and the coming of Christ in the flesh. These historical events should be used as platforms for a discussion of God's wonderful goodness to mankind. The teacher is to explain the grounds for believing in their historical truth—that they were written at the time they happened, or soon after, by persons of unimpeachable character, chosen by God to propagate his message.

Dixon warns the instructor against getting himself involved in anything but the simplest passages and suggests that he stick to the "practical points of Christianity: and raise the Affections of Children to an Imitation of those Virtues recorded in the Life of our blessed Lord." These virtues are identified as patience, humility, and doing good to the souls of men.[38]

If this approach turns out to be too difficult, Dixon has another suggestion. It is strongly reminiscent of the efforts John Lewis makes in his *Church Catechism Explained* to help the young understand what they are reading. The instructor, Dixon says, should choose an easy verse from the scriptures and ask his children to "read it over and over, 'till they are well acquainted with it, and are almost able to repeat it by Heart." Then the subject matter of the verse should be turned into questions that can be answered from the text. A child might be asked, for instance, to read *Ecclesiastes* 12.1:

Remember now thy Creator, in the Days of thy Youth,
while the evil Days come not, nor the Years draw nigh,
when thou shalt say I have no Pleasure in them.

The instructor would ask the following questions:

Quest. *WHom ought you to remember?*
A. My Creator . . .
Q. *When ought you to remember your Creator?*
A. In the Days of my Youth.

These answers evince what reading professionals today would term "literal comprehension," because they are derived directly, some might say parroted, from the text.

Other questions demand a deeper level of understanding, a paraphrased reply rather than a verbatim repetition, and an awareness of how the text fits into a broader theological context, the familiar one of dying young and unrepentant.

Q. *Why ought you to remember your Creator so soon?*
A. For two Reasons.
First, For fear I should die young and unprepared for want of remembring him.
Secondly, Because it will be much harder for me to remember him when I am grown up, and old in Sin.

When the child is asked if the passage expresses this "Caution," he or she responds that it does and quotes the original text, which begins, "While the evil Days come not." The child has therefore, in Dixon's representation, employed the classic approach to supporting an opinion, that of quoting scripture as evidence.

Dixon then suggests a third possible approach to teaching reading comprehension: the identification of key features, or main ideas, of a text. The child was to read and reread two or three chapters of the Bible, from either the Old or the New Testament. The instructor would then point out the most important features of these chapters, such as the story of the Creation in the Book of Genesis. He would test the child's literal comprehension with questions such as, "Who created the World?" and "In how many Days did God create the World?"

By this point in the text, the printer of the *Youth's Instructor* had reached the end of part two and needed some filler to reach the bottom of the page. It was perhaps a sign of changing times that the text he chose consisted not of the proverbs that had ended the 1746 edition ("A Cat may look upon a King") but of two pieces of correspondence. One of them, paradoxically bearing the date 1720, was a student's letter to his parents expressing the hope that the excellent progress he was making in his studies would be a worthy compensation for their care.[39]

Dixon's contribution to the *Youth's Instructor* ends with the second part. The third part of the book displays the value publishers set on secular concerns. Lifted wholesale from the work of Nathaniel Strong, it covers rules of arithmetic, along with forms of bills, bonds, releases, bills of sale, and so forth.[40] The contribution of Isaac Watts to this part of the book is a discussion of reading verse drawn from his *Art of Reading and Writing*. It explains the distinctions between meter and rhyme, gives examples of the most common English meter in which every second syllable was accented (citing the first lines from Sir Richard Blackmore's *Prince Arthur*, "I sing the Briton and his gen'rous arms"), and presents two kinds of uncommon verse. One of these "has a quick and hasty Sound, and must have the Accent placed on every third Syllable." It was used for matters of "Mirth and Pleasantry." The example given is more familiar to us from Lewis Carroll's parody (" 'Tis the voice of the Lobster: / I heard him declare / 'You have baked me too brown, I must sugar my hair' ") than from this original by Watts himself:

'Tis the Voïce of the Slúggard: I heár him complaín,
You have wák'd me too soón, I must slúmber again.

(Watts's instructions for reading verse would reappear, without attribution, in later reading instructional texts, such as a 1760 *New-England Psalter.*) The third part of the *Youth's Instructor* closes with Watts's conclusion to his own book, a brief paean to the "unspeakable" advantages of reading and writing. Letters, we are told, "give us a Sort of Immortality in this World, and they are given us in the Word of God to support our immortal Hopes in the next."[41]

In sum, Dixon's work, as it appeared in its final form in the *Youth's Instructor*, was a clear advance on Dyche's from the perspective of contemporary standards. Despite its considerable unevenness of tone, it explicated letter-sound correspondences as well as or better than Dyche, included much more connected text than Dyche did, and even gave suggestions on teaching children how to understand the Bible, still the apex of the reading sequence.

Dilworth's *A New Guide*

Despite a good run, after 1760 the *Youth's Instructor* began to lose its supremacy to a text whose reading lessons were much more scripturally based: Thomas Dilworth's *A New Guide to the English Tongue*, first published in London in 1740. Dilworth (who was a schoolmaster in Wapping, a mile east of London's Tower Bridge) worded his title to capitalize on Dyche's earlier success while at the same time promising an improved version. The work found a ready audience in Britain, where it was printed 127 times by 1800.[42]

Dilworth's *New Guide* also pleased Americans, from the south up through the middle Atlantic provinces to New England. Within a year of its publication it was being imported into South Carolina: the first advertisement for the book appeared in the *South Carolina Gazette* in January 1741. Five years later an advertisement was placed in the *Pennsylvania Gazette*, along with one for Dyche's speller. In 1747, Benjamin Franklin began to advertise his own edition of Dilworth. Dyche's book continued to be advertised, but now as the second of the pair "Dilworth's and Dyche's spelling books." It vanished from advertisements in the *Pennsylvania Gazette* after 1761 even while it continued to be advertised in the southern colonies.[43] From the 1750s on, the *Pennsylvania Gazette* advertised Dilworth's speller extensively. From 1752 to 1776, only two years produced no advertisement for the speller. Some years saw repeated notices: six in 1760, nine in 1761. In the southern provinces, after a curious twenty-four year gap in the *South Carolina Gazette* (beginning in January 1741), advertisements for the *New Guide* appeared there again in June 1765 and June and July 1767, and in 1768 they began to be published in the *Virginia Gazette*. Storekeepers often kept more copies of Dilworth's speller on their shelves than they did of testaments and psalters.[44]

The first extant American reprint of Dilworth's text was issued by the ever watchful Benjamin Franklin in 1747, who issued a copy of the eighth British edition. (Seven years earlier, Franklin had compiled his own spelling book from those of other authors, but it had apparently not caught on.)[45] The next known American reprint of Dilworth's *New Guide* was that of James Parker, in New York, in 1754, where it was advertised as a reproduction of Dilworth's fifteenth edition. An additional two editions appeared in 1755 and 1757. Between 1761 and 1765, inclusive, the work was reissued five times—in Philadelphia as well as New York, and for the first time in Wilmington (Delaware) and Boston. After that, not a year passed up to, and including, 1775 that lacked a new domestic imprint of the text. In some years there were several. In 1772 alone, Dilworth's speller was printed in the colonies three times—once in Philadelphia and by two different publishers in Boston. By the time of the American Revolution, different domestic reprints of the *New Guide* totaled at least twenty-six editions, of which seventeen are extant. (See Appendix 3.)

The success of the *New Guide* in the American colonies was due, in part, to the quality of the work itself, as judged by the standards of the time. In his preface dated 1740, which reappears in the five-part eighth edition—the one reproduced by Benjamin Franklin in 1747—Dilworth stakes out his claim to originality. He is, he correctly says, providing more careful gradations of difficulty for the learner than any of his predecessors, "For tho' it be true that other *Performances* of this Nature have pretended to proceed *Step* by *Step*; yet it is true also that none of them have provided those gradual *Paces* for their *Scholars* to ascend by, till they arrive at the Perfection of *Spelling*." He believed that earlier treatments of monosyllables had been particularly faulty. His solution was to subdivide monosyllables, providing children with words of two letters, followed by words of three letters, four letters, and so forth, offering "short easy *Lessons* between each *Table* of Words, adapted in such a Manner, that no *Lesson* contains any one *Word* which does not belong to a preceding *Table*." Dilworth is apologetic about the results that such an approach created:

> It must be acknowledged that the first *Six Lessons* do but just make *English*: Yet, I hope, whoever considers the Difficulty of composing *Sentences* to be read in *Lessons*, wherein each Word is confined to *three Letters*, will readily overlook the Baseness of the *Language*.[46]

He also avoids, he says (surely with a jab at Dyche's inclusion of rhymes such as *hiss* and *kiss* that had aroused schoolboy snickers), "all such *Words* . . . which might tend to excite loose and disorderly Thoughts, or put Youth or Modesty to the Blush." His tables, Dilworth says, are filled only with words that "even such as a Child may have some *Idea* of at the first Pronunciation." Practice was the great medium of instruction, he maintains, and masters should, on one hand, encourage their scholars to read, along with his first part, the texts of the "best" English authors, those in English journals such as the *Spectator*, *Tatler*, and *Guardian*. On the other hand, instructors should banish from their students' eyes all "*idle Pamphlets, lewd Plays, filthy Songs*, and *unseemly Jests*, which only serve to corrupt and debauch the *Principles* of those, who are so unhappy as to spend their Time therein."[47] (Dilworth provides us here with a glimpse of a healthy counterculture of reading material thriving in its British setting.)

Dilworth confronted two problems of pronunciation that many other authors had failed to address. First, words that matched in spelling but not in pronunciation were invariably included in the same tables because of their visual similarity. He had continued this practice, he said, but had indicated differing pronunciations by parentheses, with breves over the vowels, as in "(dŏne) (gŏne) (nŏne)." The second problem was the familiar one of words like *bri-stle* and *co-py* in which the division of syllables indicated a long pronunciation for the first vowel, when in fact the vowel was short. Dilworth used a solution that he had borrowed from Dyche: he put a quotation mark after the offending vowel, as in *bri" stle*, *co" py*, and *ad mi" ni" stra tor*. His preface was followed by two and a half pages of names: those of over six dozen British schoolmasters who had endorsed his book "as the best of its Kind, that hath yet been made public."[48]

As a consequence of this approach, Dilworth hones the alphabetical and numerical aspects of a spelling book to a new art form. "*Words of Two Letters*, viz. *one Vowel and one Consonant*, Am, an, as . . . *Words of three Letters*, viz. *one Vowel and two Consonants*. Dab nab. Web. Bib fib . . . *Words of Five, Six,* &c. *Letters*, viz. *One Vowel, and the rest Consonants* . . . Scrub shrub." It is a system that is so wedded to individual letters that, in common with other spellers, it makes no distinction between digraphs (such as *sh*) and consonant blends (*scr*).[49]

Another major difference from Dyche's work—and Dixon's—is that Dilworth greatly increased the number of lessons that now regularly followed the tables, providing, as he had promised, "six short Lessons at the End of each Table." Dilworth's first lesson, coming after the last of his tables of three-letter words, was one that became universally regarded as the first "real" reading that children encountered in the work. It is not a trivial one:

NO Man may put off the Law of God.
The Way of God is no ill Way.
My Joy is in God all the Day.
A bad Man is a Foe to God.

The profoundly theocentric world view that this suggests is characteristic of what follows. Indeed, the lessons for Dilworth's tables of disyllables are all based on the psalms. One reads: "Unto thee, O Lord, will I lift up my Soul: My God, I have put my Trust in thee." The first part of the *New Guide* continues with alternating tables and lessons, employing the by now standard technique of subdividing polysyllables by syllabic stress. His tables reach words of five syllables with the accent on the fourth (*ex pe" ri ment al*). His table of British place names, such as "Stone henge" and "Strat ford," was faithfully reproduced in all the American editions. But more important than all these innovations is Dilworth's consistency of approach. Unlike his predecessors, he overcomes technical problems, such as syllabic length, to offer a consistent and coherent Christian message to his young readers.[50]

The second, and shortest, part of Dilworth's *New Guide* is the traditional table of homophones. His third is an "English Grammar" in the customary format of question and answer that dated back to Edmund Coote. Like the treatments in both Dixon's *English Instructor* and the compendium *The Youth's Instructor*, the so-called grammar involves a detailed discussion of letter-sound correspondences. It covers all the rules on syllabic division that had been the bread and butter of spellers since Coote's time. But it also moves into what is recognizably "grammar" in the modern sense:

Q. *WHAT is* Syntax?
A. It is the disposing of Words in their right *Case, Gender, Number, Person, Mood, Tense* and *Place*, in a Sentence.
Q. *Give an Example.*
A. *Good Boys are not beaten*; here the Words are placed according to *Syntax*: Whereas should I say, *Beaten not are Boys good*, it would be unintelligible; because there is no *Syntax* in this Sentence.[51]

This kind of material had already found its way into schoolbooks actually titled "Grammar" and would eventually be dropped by spelling books altogether as they ceded the subject matter to grammar books.

In his fourth part, Dilworth has a *"useful Collection* of Sentences, *in* Prose and Verse, Divine, Moral and Historical" designed to be potential copy material. This portion of the text closes with a selection of Aesop's fables, illustrated with wood-cuts. The fifth and last part of Dilworth's spelling book provides standard forms of prayer for children.

It is not difficult to identify the features of the *New Guide to the English Tongue* that made it such a successful rival to the *Youth's Instructor*. First, Dilworth was aware of the importance of the child's understanding what he or she was reading. While it is in fact unlikely that every child would have had "some Idea of" the meaning of all the words that Dilworth included in his tables, he at least paid attention to this aspect of the speller. He was recognizing the fact that the purpose of a reading instructional text is to enable children to decode words from print into the form of language with which they are already familiar, speech. In contrast, all too many earlier British authors had assumed that, just as an introductory Latin text taught children an unknown language, an introductory English text had to teach children English as if it, too, were an unknown language—which, given their esoteric choice of vocabulary, it in effect became.

Second, Dilworth introduced a tight measure of vocabulary control. His lessons did indeed draw only on words he had introduced in previous tables. The mismatch between, say, the few syllables of the *New-England Primer* and the text that followed does not occur here. A third feature, and the one that may have been crucial from the New England perspective, was Dilworth's theocentric view. Unlike the Dixon spellers, there is complete consistency in Dilworth's work in tone and content. His texts are virtually all based on the scriptures. To New Englanders who had experienced a renewed interest in religion after the Great Awakening (the religious revival of the 1740s), the text must have seemed tailor-made.

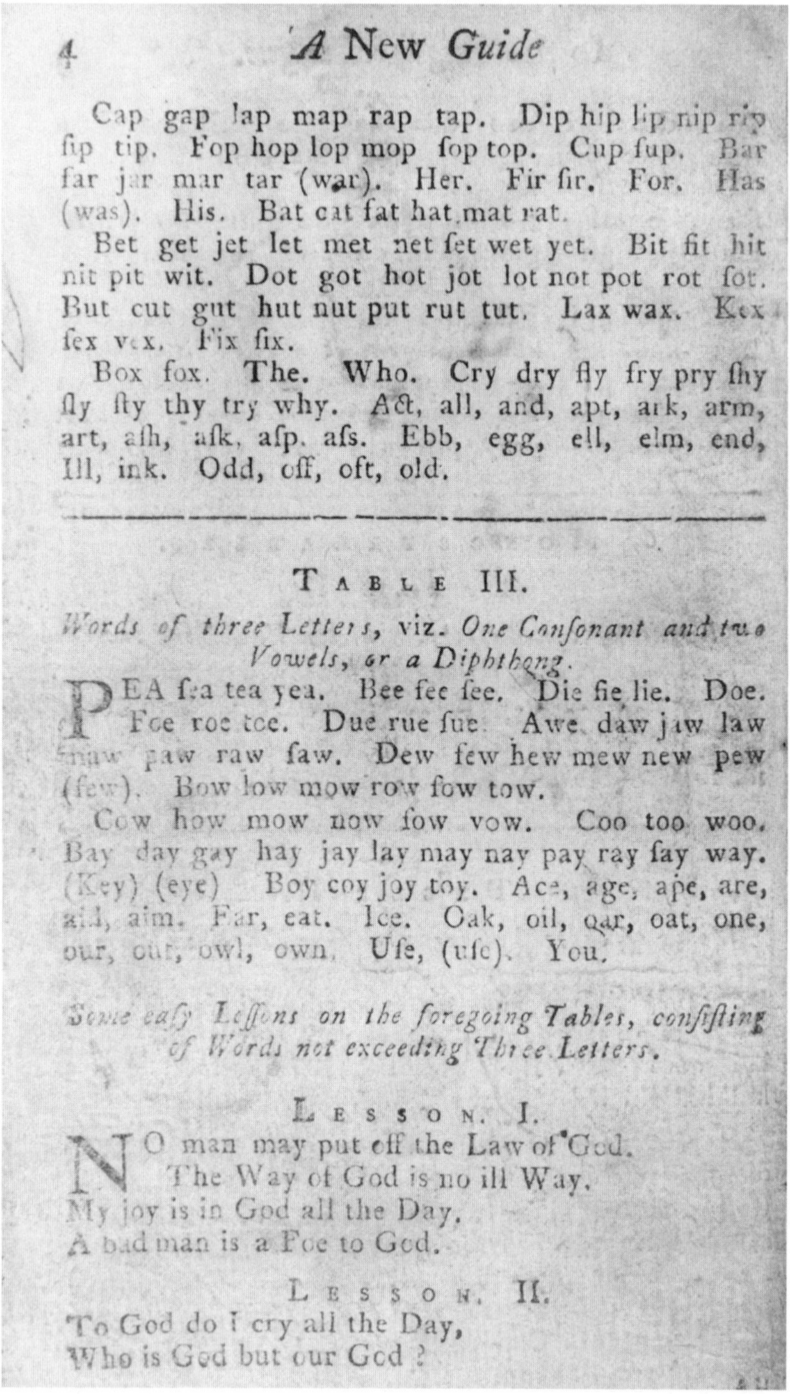

Cap gap lap map rap tap. Dip hip lip nip rip
fip tip. Fop hop lop mop fop top. Cup fup. Bar
far jar mar tar (war). Her. Fir fir. For. Has
(was). His. Bat cat fat hat mat rat.

Bet get jet let met net fet wet yet. Bit fit hit
nit pit wit. Dot got hot jot lot not pot rot fot.
But cut gut hut nut put rut tut. Lax wax. Kex
fex vex. Fix fix.

Box fox. The. Who. Cry dry fly fry pry fhy
fly fty thy try why. Act, all, and, apt, ark, arm,
art, afh, afk, afp. afs. Ebb, egg, ell, elm, end,
Ill, ink. Odd, off, oft, old.

TABLE III.

Words of three Letters, viz. One Confonant and two
Vowels, or a Diphthong.

PEA fea tea yea. Bee fee fee. Die fie lie. Doe.
Foe roe toe. Due rue fue. Awe daw jaw law
maw paw raw faw. Dew few hew mew new pew
(few). Bow low mow row fow tow.

Cow how mow now fow vow. Coo too woo.
Bay day gay hay jay lay may nay pay ray fay way.
(Key) (eye) Boy coy joy toy. Ace, age, ape, are,
ail, aim. Ear, eat. Ice. Oak, oil, oar, oat, one,
our, out, owl, own. Ufe, (ufe). You.

Some eafy Leffons on the foregoing Tables, confifting
of Words not exceeding Three Letters.

LESSON. I.

NO man may put off the Law of God.
The Way of God is no ill Way.
My joy is in God all the Day,
A bad man is a Foe to God.

LESSON. II.

To God do I cry all the Day,
Who is God but our God ?

FIGURE 11. The first reading lesson from Thomas Dilworth, *A New Guide to the English Tongue* . . . (Boston: William M'Alpine, 1771), p. 4. The words in the tables and the lesson at this early point in the speller have only three or fewer letters. Even within these constraints, Dilworth offers a strictly theocentric message. (Courtesy, American Antiquarian Society)

Finally, a distinctive and appealing feature of the *New Guide*—new, at least, to an American audience—was the illustration of the fables. The *New-England Primer* had always had woodcuts illustrating its introductory alphabet, along with a picture of the martyr John Rogers at the stake. No locally printed spelling book up to this point, however, including the *Youth's Instructor* (which had also included fables), had ever had any illustrations. In fact, the inclusion of pictures in the British version may have been a hindrance, initially, to its republication on an American press. The fidelity of an American reprint to its original was such that American printers felt obliged to find someone who could create woodcuts to reproduce the pictures—something that was much harder to do than merely copying the text. (This was a dedication to fidelity that arose from necessity: their imprints were competing against imported copies, all of which had illustrations.) Benjamin Franklin seems to have solved the problem with his characteristic ingenuity. His Philadelphia edition of 1747 has an illustration for each fable, and he is believed to have made these woodcuts himself.[52]

Dilworth's speller supplanted the earlier works by Dyche and Dixon, and from the mid-1760s on was the favorite of American printers. Even booksellers who advertised the other spelling books that they continued to import rarely omitted to inform their customers that they had Dilworth's on hand as well. Advertisements appeared occasionally in the *Pennsylvania Gazette* in the late 1740s and 1750s for spellers by Richard Browne, John Owen, and William Markham, and in the mid-1760s for those by John Deane, John Palairet, and Daniel Fenning, but Dilworth's headed the list. The printer David Hall stood out, in 1761, for the richness of his imported offerings, but even he emphasized Dilworth above all others: "Wholesale or Retail, DILWORTH's, Dyche's, Markam's, Young's, Dixon's, Sproson's, Watt's, Boad's, and other Spelling Books."[53] Storekeepers, unlike booksellers, were much more likely to stock just one speller: they would advertise Dilworth alone, in company with the other books of the reading sequence. Typical were the offerings at the store of William and Joseph Trimble, who ran a notice in the *Philadelphia Gazette* in 1761 for "testaments, psalters, Dilworth's spelling books, trader's sure guide, primers, hornbooks."[54]

By the 1750s, then, imported and domestic imprints of spelling books were available. By the following decade, they could be obtained in some variety. By the 1770s, the genre had firmly established itself as the first book that children would meet after the primer. Spelling books forthrightly declared that a mastery of letter-sound correspondences was the route to successful literacy acquisition. But their authors had not neglected meaning: in the later spellers, children were expected to read meaningful text. All in all, the importance of spelling books in teaching children to read in provincial America can hardly be overestimated.

PART THREE

New Paths to Literacy Acquisition, 1750 to 1776

PRELUDE TO PART III

Different American colonies, originally wholly disparate in their designs and aims, were drawing closer together, linked in their political, economic, and social structures by their common emulation of British models. This process accelerated after 1750, and from about the middle of the century it is possible to perceive a growing consensus among the American elite on the materials suitable for their children's literacy development. This phenomenon, which falls under the rubric of what Jack Greene calls the stage of *social replication*, affected many folks of the "middling" sort as well as the elite.[1]

Literacy in the American provinces was still on the rise. It was one of the reasons why provincial Americans (unlike the French, who rioted) were able to accept calendar reform with such equanimity: when eleven days were dropped from the calendar in September 1752, they had been prepared for over a year by widely circulated reproductions of the 1751 British act authorizing the change and by discussions in colonial almanacs and newspapers. Americans had read about the act and understood it.[2]

In Great Britain, the year 1730 had, for a variety of reasons, already "marked a turning point in the history of the English book trade," as John Feather puts it. The continued expansion of the trade up to the last quarter of the eighteenth century included a vigorous expansion of its provincial market—the flow of books from London to major county centers that ranged from Exeter in the southwest to Newcastle in the north. A national interest in education was a key element of this British expansion, along with increased literacy (even without any kind of state support) fostered by various philanthropic societies.[3] Unsurprisingly, the expansion of the book trade was felt not only within the British Isles but in the trade between London ports and the provincial markets of America.

As far as books were concerned, after 1750 exports from London to North America and the British West Indies grew at an even higher rate than American production until, now at historically high levels, they reached a temporary plateau in the 1760s, picking up again in the early 1770s. Only after the revolutionary years would exports to North America begin to decline (see Appendix 4).[4] In addition, partly because new newspapers were being published as well as new books, print production increased on American presses, beginning in the mid 1750s and reaching a peak in the years of the American Revolution. From 1754 on, the number of titles of books, newspapers, and pamphlets printed every year in America never fell below two hundred; and in the 1760s, as more towns printed their own newspapers, the median number of titles for that decade was comfortably over three hundred. From 1770 to 1775, even the lowest annual number of titles for that six-year period was only a little shy of four hundred, while the single year 1775 produced approximately a thousand (see Appendix 3)[5]

Newspapers made a significant contribution to these numbers. Eighteen newspapers were being published in 1760, weekly or bi-weekly, at printing offices in 10 port cities, and between 1763 and 1775 newspaper titles nearly doubled in number. Although these figures would pale in comparison to the 99 newspaper titles published in 1790 in 62 places, they were an ever more important component of a communication network that still relied heavily on face-to-face encounters and manuscript correspondence.[6]

The vigor of the expansion of reading material can be detected from yet another source: American newspaper advertisements for books. In the 1750s, the median number of advertisements listing five or more titles printed in any newspaper in any one year stood at 25. (This was already an increase over the median of 20 for the 1740s.) But in the 1760s the median rose dramatically to over 60. The single year 1762 demonstrated a unique spurt of newspaper advertising for books, exhibiting more than 110 advertisements for five books and over.[7] In short, from about 1750 on, more print was ever more available to those who could afford it.

The increased production of reading instructional texts was part of this printing boom. As we have seen, the availability of spelling books across the American provinces accelerated after 1750. Increasingly, it was the same spelling book at any given time that appealed to the public: by the 1770s, Thomas Dilworth's *New Guide to the English Tongue* would enjoy popularity throughout the provinces. A measure of how it compared with other spellers can be gauged from the sales of Jeremiah Condy, a Boston bookseller, who between 1759 and 1768 dispatched 499 copies of Dilworth's speller to stores and individuals across New England while selling only 43 copies of Dyche's speller and 22 of *The Child's New Play-Thing* during the same period (ratios of 23 and 12 to 1). Indeed, after 1762, Condy sold no copies of Dyche's speller (see Appendix 3)[8]

If books were a feature of the second half of the eighteenth century, so was education. In general, most of the expansion of the curriculum at the elementary level had already occurred before 1750. After about the late 1740s, we can see more elaboration than innovation. For example, by far the most favored foreign language had been French, and it continued to be so, but other languages were now offered occasionally, such as Italian, Spanish, and even Portuguese. History was offered in Boston at least once in the 1730s, but after 1750 notices for it occurred occasionally across the provinces. The most important change was the introduction of English grammar as a separate and identifiable subject, defined by one Boston schoolmaster in 1774 as "the Art of Reading, Speaking and Writing the English Language with strict Propriety, and Elegance."[9] Advertisements for that and even for English grammar schools were much in evidence in the 1770s.

The reading instructional books mentioned earlier continued to hold sway. The *New-*

England Primer kept up with the times in a modest way by adding new material. By the 1770s, it included several of Isaac Watts's hymns, such as the much-loved cradle hymn. Some editions catered to customer choice by including both catechisms—John Cotton's *Milk for Babes* and the Westminster Catechism. The *New-England Primer* enjoyed an almost mythic status among New Englanders, remaining a book that was extensively used in families. One New Englander gave a copy to his young nephew, and in his inscription begged him to remember "when he looks into this little Book . . . that his Uncle upon a Bed of dangerous Sickness Warns Him—to remember his Creator in the days of his Childhood—To love his Book." At school, as we have just seen, Dilworth's spelling book, *A New Guide*, went from strength to strength.[10]

The second half of the eighteenth century also witnessed a growth in schooling opportunities for girls—minimally in the public sector, substantially in the private one. A key factor that influenced children's access to literacy instruction, public or private, was of course location, whether they lived in a city, small town, or a purely rural setting. In New England, the moving school was still one of the forms town schooling took, an unsatisfactory compromise conceived to cope with town growth. By this time many town-supported schools were "generalist" schools, still restricted to boys, where boys were introduced to the A B C's by the town schoolmaster. Future U.S. president John Adams, who "kept school" briefly at the Center School in Worcester, Massachusetts, in 1756, mentions the *New-England Primer* in his school and children who "rattle[d] and Thunder[ed] out A, B, C."[11]

Most children who lived outside cities were at a disadvantage for schooling opportunities. Yet it was not a straightforward equation. While private schooling was much more readily available in cities after mid-century, girls who lived in a small Massachusetts or Connecticut township and who could attend the town school were actually better placed for receiving a subsidized education than their counterparts in Boston. The less ambitious a school was (in the sense of having no desire to offer a classical education) and the later it was founded, the better the chances girls had of attending a free school. In the town of Kent, Connecticut, for example, founded in 1740, all those who had to subscribe their names to documents could sign their names, whether they were male or female. In contrast, Boston's town educational system targeted only boys; girls had no opportunities for town-funded schooling until 1789, when primary schools were instituted.[12]

Educational opportunities for girls, even in provinces committed to education, such as Massachusetts and Connecticut, could vary substantially. In Sutton, Massachusetts, where male power and money was widely distributed, religion was decentralized, and there was no tradition of grammar schooling, girls had access to summer schools taught by town-salaried dames from at least 1767 on. In contrast, in Northampton, also in Massachusetts, wealthy, elitist, and politically powerful men living in a single-church community succeeded until the next century in steering all the school funds toward the support of the town grammar school to the exclusion of providing any schools for girls.[13] Girls living in Connecticut towns were probably at an advantage over those living in

Massachusetts in terms of access to free schooling because Connecticut, after 1700, dropped the number of Latin grammar schools the province expected to maintain to four: in New Haven, Hartford, New London, and Fairfield. After 1755, when Fairfield was unable to support its grammar school, the number of these high-cost schools was reduced to three, freeing up money for regular town schools.[14] Even in New England, in short, girls' access to town-funded schooling remained problematic and idiosyncratic.

The situation for girls able to take advantage of private schooling was very different. Many of the offerings aimed at them were artistic or musical. Instruction in drawing and painting was common, implicitly or explicitly aimed at girls. Classes for girls taught by women instructors from the 1740s on became increasingly diverse in their offerings, which included such decorative activities as gold, silver, and silk embroidery, sprigging, tapestry, quilting, knitting, waxwork, and painting on glass.[15]

Nonetheless, after about 1750 schools of all kinds were being opened across the American provinces. A few towns in Rhode Island, which had never passed a single law mandating any kind of literacy obligation on the part of its townships, nonetheless maintained publicly supported town schools. Some of these were the result of the province's territorial enlargement in 1747, when several towns, such as Bristol, were transferred from Massachusetts to Rhode Island and continued an existing tradition of grammar school support. Others, such as Whipple Hall in Providence, founded in 1768, were basically elementary schools for reading and writing instruction. Whipple Hall was built and financed by a group of wealthy citizens led by Moses Brown. Its design reflected the advances that girls had made by the late 1760s in coeducational schooling: the first floor was divided into a "Children's Apartment" on one side, to be taught by a mistress, and a "Young Gentlemen and Ladies Apartment" on the other, taught by a schoolmaster.[16]

Another gauge of the improved educational climate for schooling for both sexes is the number of newspaper advertisements placed each decade for private schools that promised every kind of instruction from Greek to moral philosophy to needlework. In both the *Pennsylvania Gazette* and the *South Carolina Gazette*, the decade with the highest number of such advertisements was the 1760s, when over sixty of them were placed in each paper. Yet another feature of this period is the increasing importance, throughout the provinces, of writing, as reflected in the growing number of advertisements for writing equipment.[17]

The broader context for this expansion of choices in literacy-related items and offerings was the increasing affluence of Americans after the half-century mark. Even rural southern New England and the Chesapeake showed a steady improvement in living standards as the eighteenth century progressed.[18] Commerce expanded in the form of increased importation from Britain of consumer goods. From roughly 1740, as Timothy Breen demonstrates, an unprecedented consumer culture developed in provincial America. The general prosperity of the times permitted those of the middling sort and even the lower sort, as well as the gentry, to aspire to household goods that indicated gentility. Newspaper advertisements in all the major ports had always listed domestic goods, but now they promised luxury versions, such as "beautiful China Ware" and a huge variety of fabrics (linens and lawns, taffetas and silks).[19]

After 1760, the quantity and quality of imported goods grew. Whereas New York merchants of the 1730s had rarely advertised more than 6 different British items in a single issue, those of the 1770s could list no fewer than 350 and even as many as 1,000 different items. Mere "satin" fabric had been advertised in New York in 1733; in 1763 eight different kinds of satin could be purchased. Novelties appeared, such as Wilton carpets and ivory stick fans. The range of choice was impressive in its pricing, variety and color. Customers could choose from "superfine" to "low-priz'd lawns and cambrick," between "rich green and brown damask," among "rich flower'd silks of different figures," from scarlet, crimson or blue broadcloth, white and scarlet or white and blue lace. Specialty items such as "Decanter Labels, Decanter Corks with Silver Tops" epitomize the genteel products dangled before the eager consumer. Children were included as potential consumers. In 1756 children's eating utensils were advertised as pocket knives and forks; by 1765 they were available in ivory and bone, with their own sheaths.[20]

Other items were for sale in the second half of the eighteenth century, just as they had been in the first half: men, women, and children with dark skin—the enslaved. In the following chapters, we look first at their experience with literacy, in the rare cases when they had access to it (Chapter 9), then at writing instruction itself (Chapter 10), at the new world of books for children, those "pretty" books published by the London printer John Newbery and his successors (Chapter 11), and finally at the literacy instruction, formal and informal, taking place within three elite families during the 1770s—one in Massachusetts and two in Virginia (Chapter 12).

9

Literacy Instruction and the Enslaved

In the fall of 1745, Joseph Hildreth of the New York Charity School, appointed its schoolmaster a year earlier, reported that he had other pupils than the forty poor white children who were attending his school in the daytime: "12 Negroes" who did not attend his regular school but came in the evenings to learn how to sing psalms. A few years later, Hildreth noted that he had fifteen Negroes in the evenings, to whom he was teaching not only psalm-singing but reading the Bible.[1]

By treating "Negroes" as educable human beings, Hildreth was ignoring the laws of the land, which treated them as chattel. Their status appears vividly in advertisements. One such advertisement, as unexceptional as the scores of others like it that ran in every paper, appeared in the *Boston Weekly News-Letter* on May 19, 1737, placed there by Thomas Fleet, the newspaper's printer. It was for an auction, and among the property to be auctioned, human beings are jumbled in with books and dishes:

> This Afternoon, will be sold by Thomas Fleet, at the Heart and Crown in Cornhill, by Way of Auction or Vendue, the best Part of the Books which should have been Sold last Night, together with Two likely young Negro Women, in good Health, and most Sorts of Houshold Goods.

The term *Negro* in colonial America denoted, specifically, an enslaved African. In fact, the word *free* had to be added to denote an African who was not enslaved. By the beginning of the eighteenth century, the enslavement of Africans in the American colonies, whether in the northern, southern, or middle regions, had solidified into an institution bolstered by legislation of all kinds. Between 1680 and 1710, in particular, almost every English colony promulgated laws that attempted to define the status of the enslaved as human property and enshrine measures that addressed the contradictions inherent in treating a person as a thing.[2]

One of these contradictions was the status of the enslaved soul. Samuel Sewall had raised the question in 1700 when he wrote that holding one's neighbors under perpetual bondage "seems to be no proper way of gaining Assurance that God has given them Spiritual Freedom." Those who believed that at the spiritual level, at least, every man and woman was created equal and that it was their duty to promulgate the Christian message to life's downtrodden could not ignore their obligation to offer that message to the enslaved. This obligation was reinforced by a letter sent to the colonies in 1727 by Edmund Gibson, Bishop of London, who was also the head of the Society for the Propagation of the Gospel. In it, he urged masters and mistresses of the enslaved to "encourage and promote the Instruction of their *Negroes* in the Christian Faith."[3]

Two kinds of action were possible for the devout: individual and group. A look at individual conversion efforts involving literacy instruction provides glimpses of the consequences of literacy for the enslaved; an examination of institutional activities shows how slave literacy was viewed by religious groups. The explorations reveal a striking dichotomy between reading and writing instruction. As was true in other contexts, reading instruction was heavily favored as the vehicle for transmitting Christianity; however, in the context of slavery, writing instruction was avoided at all costs by all the slaveholding groups that could have provided it. Individual slaves, however, were sometimes able to learn to write, and this acquisition became a crucial part of their self-definition.

While some groups of West Africans lived on the "margins of literacy," thanks to their contact with Muslim traders who were literate in Arabic, most Africans who were kidnapped in their own country and exported by violence into an alien one had not encountered literacy before.[4] They reacted to books on their first exposure to them in much the same way as native Americans initially did. Indeed, the trope of the "talking book" is a common one in African American lore. Olaudah Equiano, kidnapped from Benin in the late 1750s, first encountered books after he was sold to the owner of a trading ship heading for England. When he heard his young master or his friend Dick reading, he thought they were talking to the books. (His experience reemphasizes the oral nature of personal and private reading.) When alone, he would pick up a book, talk to it, and then put his ears on it, "in hopes it would answer me; and I have been very much concerned when I found it remaining silent."[5]

As they had with native Americans, the supposedly magical qualities of books quickly dissipated with a second generation of American-born slaves, who learned English and rapidly came to appreciate that understanding print was something one could learn to do—if taught. The conviction of the enslaved that literacy could bring power, that illiteracy was one of the factors that whites exploited in order to maintain their dominance, and that writing was the literacy skill that could aid self-definition would become, from the early eighteenth century to the end of the Civil War, an underlying theme of African American identity and aspirations for freedom.[6]

In the early stages, however, when so many Africans were newly imported from the West African coast or the West Indies and had no knowledge of English, attempts to teach literacy—always conducted in English—foundered on linguistic barriers, among others. Unlike John Eliot, the younger Thomas Mayhew, and the Anglican missionaries who tried to convert native Americans, those who taught enslaved Africans never once attempted to learn, let alone analyze, African languages.

A series of related events that had an important impact on many of the enslaved was the revivals of the Great Awakening. When the British evangelist George

Whitefield crossed the Atlantic for the first time in the spring of 1738, his mission was just one part of an evangelical movement sweeping the colonies. Nonbelievers were drawn to believe as never before; those who were already Christian were split between the "New Lights" and "Old Lights" in a fervent reexamination of their faith. The New Lights emphasized the emotional aspect of faith and welcomed all to their meetings, black and white, young and old, male and female, slave and free.[7] In this ecumenical context, many of the enslaved experienced conversion and with it an urge to learn how to read the sacred scriptures. Successive missions by Presbyterians, Baptists, and Methodists drew Africans to their congregations, and in several cases ministers or church members offered reading instruction.[8]

Also important was the literacy instruction offered to the enslaved by individual white Christians. Legally, there was nothing to stop slaveholders anywhere in the colonies from teaching their slaves to read. Writing instruction was banned by South Carolina and Georgia (in 1740 and 1755, respectively), but reading instruction was still so closely linked to Christian indoctrination that it remained immune from repressive legislation throughout the colonial period. Private attempts to teach reading may have been more widespread in the colonies than we have thought, for devout Protestants should not have been able to escape their moral obligation to teach their household slaves to read so that they could read the Bible. Household slaves, however, were far outnumbered by those on large plantations, who had no opportunity to learn other than from a fellow literate slave.

The efforts of a few of the enslaved to acquire reading and even writing themselves should not be overlooked. Advertisements for runaway slaves throughout the colonies give hints of those—always a handful of those sought by the advertisers—who managed to acquire some form of literacy in spite of their bondage.[9]

One striking example is provided in a letter by an enslaved mulatto, who in 1723 smuggled out from Virginia a poignant appeal to Edmund Gibson, Lord Bishop of London, begging the bishop to "Releese us out of this Cruell Bondegg" and permit his children and those of his fellow slaves to be brought up as Christians and "be putt to Scool and Larnd to Reed through the Bybell." While his plea for the end of slavery went unanswered, his request that enslaved children be brought up as Christians might have spurred Gibson to action: four years later, as we have seen, the bishop published and widely circulated a letter instructing Anglican masters and mistresses to give their slaves a Christian education.[10]

In the southern colonies, there are a few documented instances of individuals providing reading instruction to their domestic slaves. In Goose Creek, South Carolina, in 1706, some slaves had been taught to read several years before Benjamin Dennis arrived there. In 1739, sixteen-year-old Eliza Lucas began to look after the family's six-hundred-acre plantation in Wappoo, South Carolina, when her father went abroad. Two years later, she gave daily reading lessons of up to two hours to at least two young slave girls. Philip Fithian, a tutor on a Virginia plantation in the early 1770s, offered a few reading lessons to a young slave named Dennis. Sarah Osborn of Newport, Rhode Island, took scores of slaves into her house for family prayers in the 1760s, but she appears not to have taught them to read.[11]

In Philadelphia, where Quakers were opposed to slavery on both religious and ethical grounds, many enslaved and free African children had access to the school for blacks taught by the dedicated Anthony Benezet. Benezet and his French Huguenot parents had emigrated from France to London in 1715 when he was two years old, and from London to Pennsylvania when he was seventeen. He first taught in Germantown, succeeding Francis Daniel Pastorius. Three years later, in 1742, Benezet, who had become a Quaker, was accepted as a teacher at the Friends' English School of Philadelphia. He remained there for twelve years, becoming famous for his refusal to use harsh discipline. He then moved on to a Friends-supported morning school for girls in Philadelphia, resigning because of ill health in 1766. Only nine months later, he returned once again, this time to keep a morning school for poor girls only, with a reduced number of pupils.[12]

Two causes animated this gentle and kindly man, of whom a visitor from France once said, "he carries his love of humanity to the point of madness." They were, in Benezet's own words, "The right education of our youth, in a manner consonant to our Christian calling & profession; & the Abolition of the Slave Trade." Among his almost forty publications were his indictment of slavery as wholly incompatible with Christianity, his depictions of slavery's horrors, and his urgent appeals for the abolition of the slave trade. As early as 1754, he had convinced the Yearly Meeting of the Philadelphia Society of Friends to declare the practice of slavery and slave-holding to be inconsistent with Christian principles.[13]

Benezet's evening school for Africans united his two great educational causes. He opened the school in 1750, teaching the children in his own home at night because his mornings were entirely taken up by his girls' school. In 1770, he raised enough money from home and abroad for a school to be built and a schoolmaster paid. The curriculum included reading, writing and arithmetic. When the school was in danger of being closed, in 1782, after the resignation of its master, Benezet laid aside the girls' school and taught the Negro school himself, moving it to his own home for his convenience. He was a firm believer in black aptitude. The notion, he said, that "blacks are inferior in their capacities, is a vulgar prejudice, founded on the pride or ignorance" of arrogant masters.[14]

In New England, as in the middle colonies, slaves were usually treated less harshly than in the south. Cotton Mather, for one, honored his Christian obligation to introduce his slaves to Christianity. Within his own household, two of his slaves—Onesimus, bought for Mather by his congregation in the mid-1700s, and Ezer, a servant in the 1720s—knew how to read, although we do not know who taught them. Mather even set up and paid for an evening school for blacks and Indians that lasted from at least January 1718 to the end of 1721. Significantly, Mather offered no writing instruction at this school (even though he envisioned such instruction for his own domestic slaves): the school was to instruct its students only in reading the scriptures and learning the catechism.[15]

Other individual slaveholders went further and taught writing as well as reading. One slave who was fully literate was Pompey Fleet, whose master was Thomas Fleet of Boston, printer of the *Boston Weekly News-Letter*. Not only was Pompey Fleet employed at the press and at setting type but he carved the woodcuts that decorated the ballads and small books printed by Fleet, such as the *Prodigal Daughter*. Better known is "Newport Gardner," as his admirers dubbed him. He was brought in 1760 as a youth named Occramer Marycoo to Newport, Rhode Island, where he was taught to read. He was accepted as a devout Christian who became well known for speaking French and writing poetry. He composed his own songs and ran a singing school in Newport.[16]

The most remarkable instance in colonial America of an enslaved person who acquired literacy is that of Phillis Wheatley. Kidnapped in West Africa and transported on a schooner named Phillis, Wheatley was about eight years old when she reached the port of Boston in July 1761. Susanna Wheatley, wife of the wealthy Boston merchant John Wheatley, purchased her to be her personal servant. From the start, Phillis was treated as a member of this devout Congregationalist family. (Susanna, in particular, was an enthusiastic supporter of George Whitefield.)[17]

Also in the household were the eighteen-year-old Wheatley twins, Mary and Nathaniel. True to the colonial convention of women as reading instructors, Mary rather than Nathaniel decided to teach Phillis to read. Phillis learned to do so "Without any Assistance from School Education, and by only what she was taught in the Family," according to a published letter from John Wheatley. Within sixteen months of her arrival in Boston, Phillis had so well mastered English in its written as well as oral form that she could read "the most difficult Parts of the Sacred Writings, to the great Astonishment of all who heard her." John Wheatley also reveals that Phillis's refusal to be constricted by the racial and gender stereotypes of the day showed itself in another way: "She has a great Inclination to learn the Latin Tongue, and has made some Progress in it."[18]

Phillis also insisted on learning to write. "Her own Curiosity," according to John Wheatley, "led her to it." Her first known letter, addressed to the Congregationalist minister Samuel Occum (a Mohegan Indian converted to Christianity), was written when she was thirteen. By this time she was already writing poetry. She was clearly familiar with translations of the classical poets, for her poems contain numerous references to persons and places of the classics as well as allusions to other eighteenth-century poets and biblical texts. She became a devout Christian, finally joining the Old South Church in 1771.[19]

Phillis Wheatley had probably been writing poetry for a couple of years by the time she wrote her earliest known poem at the age of fourteen, in 1767.[20] It was addressed to the students of Harvard College. It has a wistful tone, for she was writing to boys of her own age who were receiving a college education that her sex, let alone her race, categorically denied her: "Improve your privileges while they Stay: / Caress, redeem each moment." Two years later, she wrote an elegy for Joseph Sewall, who had died at the age of eighty-one. He had been pastor of the Old South Congregational Church for the previous fifty-six years. "I too, have cause this mighty loss to mourn / For this my monitor will not return." In one of history's pleasing twists, the son of the author of America's first antislavery tract was thus celebrated by a slave.[21]

The first of Wheatley's poems to be published appeared in December 1767 in the *Newport (Rhode Island) Mercury*. Another poem was printed in 1770 in Boston

FIGURE 12. This portrait of Phillis Wheatley appears as the frontispiece to Wheatley's *Poems on Various Subjects, Religious and Moral* (London: Printed for A. Bell, and sold by Cox and Berry, Boston, 1773). Engraved at the insistence of the Countess of Huntingdon, Wheatley's patron, the portrait accentuates the publishing novelty of a black woman as an author. (Courtesy, American Antiquarian Society)

as a broadside: Wheatley's elegy to the Reverend George Whitefield, who had died of an asthma attack that September while on yet another New England tour. Wheatley's poem was reprinted in newspapers around the colonies as well as in broadsides in other towns.[22] In it, she alludes to Whitefield's broad ecumenical appeal, to Jesus's colorblindness and to his promise of spiritually empowering the politically powerless:

> Take HIM, [Christ] "my dear AMERICANS," he [Whitefield] said,
> Be your complaints in his kind bosom laid:
> Take HIM ye *Africans*, he longs for you;
> Impartial SAVIOUR, is his title due;
> If you will chuse to walk in grace's road,
> You shall be sons, and kings, and priests to GOD.[23]

Although Boston printers declined to publish Wheatley's poetry in book form, these and other poems were revised and first published as a book in London in 1773. Wheatley's London publishers sought to forestall skepticism about the work's authenticity by printing, in addition to John Wheatley's letter, an attestation signed by some of Boston's leading citizens, including John Hancock and a bevy of ministers. Among the latter were Cotton Mather's son Samuel, still minister of Old North Church. Rather than using the euphemism "Negro Servant," which was how Wheatley was identified on the title page after her name, the signers referred to her legal condition in blunt terms: the author, they said, was "a young Negro Girl" who was "under the Disadvantage of serving as a Slave in a Family in this Town."[24]

An assessment of Wheatley's poetry lies outside the scope of this study. What is important is that Wheatley had a brilliantly clear conception of what the skill of writing could do for her. She turned writing into creation, and through it she created herself. She had the support and understanding of her white Christian family, who aided her search for publication, the most public form of identity construction. In the fall of 1773, John Wheatley formally emancipated her. By the time of the American Revolution, Phillis had transformed herself from "slave" and "Negro servant" to "the famous *Phillis Wheatley*, the African poetess," as the *Pennsylvania Magazine* dubbed her in 1776.[25] Her literacy and fame could not save her, however, from the poverty engendered by the racism of her time.

While individual efforts to teach literacy to the enslaved were important, we know more about institutional efforts. Just as had been the case in attempts to convert native Americans, English organizations rather than American ones took the initiative in converting the enslaved. During the eighteenth century, two pious organizations based in London instituted formal instruction designed to bring the enslaved into the fold of the Anglican Church: the Society for the Propagation of the Gospel (S.P.G.) (which, as we have seen, was already active in evangelizing poor whites and native Americans), and the Associates of Dr. Thomas Bray, created in 1724. In this context of organized philanthropy, the choices that were made— teaching reading but not writing, preferring a schoolmistress to a schoolmaster, and in one instance an enslaved over a free person—shed light on the relationship between humanity and race, literacy and gender, autonomy and obedience, slavery and freedom.

These themes were played out in New York city; Savannah, Georgia; Charles Town (later Charleston), South Carolina; Philadelphia, Pennsylvania; Providence, Rhode Island; and Williamsburg, Virginia. In some of these the S.P.G. was the prime mover, in others the Associates of Dr. Thomas Bray; and in yet others the two associations each provided a small salary to the same man.

The slaveholders' fear of slave insurrection, created by the very institution of slavery, threatened to poison all attempts to introduce religion, let alone literacy, to the enslaved population. It immediately confronted and hindered the philanthropic organizations that attempted to introduce religion—and with it literacy in reading—to the enslaved, despite their acceptance of slavery itself with very little demur. Although the Englishmen sent out by the S.P.G. often voiced their distress at the treatment of the blacks they witnessed there, particularly in the southern colonies, it was a rare man who so much as hinted at any disapproval of the institution of slavery itself. As for the organizations, the S.P.G. early joined the ranks of slaveholders, first by the acquisition of the Codrington estate in Barbados in 1710, and later by purchasing blacks in Charles Town, South Carolina.[26]

Like all other literacy efforts, schooling for the enslaved was based on the premise that reading instruction promoted Christianity. The S.P.G. classrooms, as we have seen, often included a few blacks (as well as Indians) from time to time, who were taught in the same room as white children. But occasionally the S.P.G. ventured into educational experiments that specifically targeted enslaved Africans as the objects of its philanthropy. Its catechists, in particular, considered the enslaved a group well suited to their attention.

The first S.P.G. evangelical work with slaves occurred in New York city, beginning only a couple of years after the S.P.G. was created in 1701. It was a modest effort, involving only catechetical instruction. The society supported Elias Neau, a French Protestant who had suffered much in his native, and Catholic, country for his faith. After several years of imprisonment and service in the galleys, he had emigrated to New York city, where he became a successful merchant and a vestryman of Trinity Church, committing himself wholeheartedly to Anglicanism. Overcoming the objections of the Reverend William Vesey, minister of Trinity Church, who considered Neau's English too poor for him to serve satisfactorily, Neau soon became a catechist for the S.P.G. at a salary of fifty pounds a year.[27]

The enslaved population in New York at this time was considerable and would grow larger over the coming decades. Once the English took over New Amsterdam from the Dutch and renamed it New York in 1664, the slave trade began a rapid expansion, and the following year the New York laws formally recognized slavery as an institution. From 1701 to 1726, 1,570 enslaved Africans were imported into New York from the West Indies, and another 802 directly from Africa. By 1746 there would be more than 9,000. No other colony north of Maryland would hold more of the enslaved.[28]

Neau's attempt to convert enslaved Africans to Anglicanism came, therefore, during a period in which the number of enslaved Africans in the city was expanding rapidly and the edginess of slaveholders was already apparent. Even though teaching reading was not part of his mission, Neau used books as quasi rewards. Among his pupils in 1705 were a mixed blood "mulatress" from the house of the governor, Lord Cornbury, two enslaved African women from the house of Reverend William Vesey, and four Indians. He gave books to all of them, even though they presumably could not read, parting with forty-six books altogether. Some of the Negroes, he wrote six months later, came only two or three times, but "they keep the Books notwithstanding." Books held symbolic meaning to the enslaved.[29]

Slaveholders remained reluctant to send their slaves to Neau even though New York passed a law in 1706, stating that baptism did not change the condition of servitude of the baptized. (Five other colonies, Maryland, Virginia, North Carolina, South Carolina, and New Jersey, had already passed such legislation.)[30] Nonetheless, the number of Neau's pupils increased. His mission even survived a slave uprising in 1712 that many slaveholders blamed on his school. Until his death in 1723, Neau kept up his catechizing with great devotion, visiting the slaves in their own homes when they were sick and continuing to dispense small tracts. As a local clergyman put it, "his Resolution and perseverance in the work has been truly wonderful."[31]

While the S.P.G. viewed schooling for slaves as just one of many components of its mission, the other orthodox Anglican organization based in London, the Associates of Dr. Bray, dedicated its entire philanthropic schooling efforts to that cause alone. Like the S.P.G. correspondence, the letters from men in the colonies back to the secretary of the associates evince a clear understanding of what the latter would like to hear. Nonetheless, these letters also include so much that was unwelcome that they may be trusted, in general, for the truthfulness of their portrayals. They show a discrepancy, from the very first, between how the associates expected Christian men and women to treat their slaves and how the slaves were actually treated.

At the genesis of the associates was Thomas Bray himself, who had been instrumental in founding not only the S.P.G., in 1701, but the Society for Promoting Christian Knowledge two years earlier. In 1723, Bray received a bequest from an old friend, whose will stipulated that a tenth of his English estate should go to "Dr. Thomas Bray & His Associates" as capital for a charitable fund. The income from this fund was to be used for setting up schools dedicated to "Instructing in the Christian Religion Young Children of Negro Slaves," as well as any of their parents who wished for such instruction. Bray soon named four of his friends as associates.

The income from the legacy was at first so small (about forty pounds) that Bray and his colleagues used it initially to send books out to the colonies for the use of missionaries, catechists, and their pupils. Bray died in 1730, but a month before his death he had reconstituted the associates into a much larger group of men. Between then and 1733, the associates became involved in setting up Georgia as a charitable (and slave-free) colony, for reasons that related to another, but much larger, charitable bequest that had provided the motive for Bray's enlargement of the group of associates. So it was not until May 1733, when the Georgia Trustees split off from the Associates of Dr. Bray, that the new group of associates again looked for ways to implement the original legacy. The associates now had the additional charge of carrying out the terms of Bray's own legacy, which he had dedicated to establishing denominational libraries.[32]

For the first decade or so after Bray's death, the associates concentrated on sending out books to Anglican missionaries and other Protestants to create such libraries.[33] But they also continued Bray's earlier practice, dispatching in 1735 instructional books to laymen and laywomen as well as missionaries for their use in teaching their African slaves. The content of the boxes that the associates sent to Charles Town, South Carolina, that year (by way of Savannah, Georgia), reveal that they were texts designed for reading (but not writing) instruction, and not merely for catechetical instruction. The box provides further evidence that, as early as the mid 1730s, the spelling book was already being accepted as a new but vital component of the "ordinary Road." Each of three boxes contained three Bibles, 30 primers, 30 "small" spelling books, 30 hornbooks, 20 testaments, and 30 psalters. One of the boxes was directed to Lilia Hague. Known to have owned thirty-one slaves nine years earlier, she is said to have taken considerable pains over her slaves' education. Another Charles Town recipient was Mrs. Anne Drayton. In her letter of thanks, she said that "all her negroes were instructed in the Christian religion, some of whom could read and instructed others."[34]

A few years later, in the fall of 1742, while the associates were attempting to broaden their mission in the southern colonies, they received a letter from the Reverend Alexander Garden, who was serving as commissary (representative) of the Bishop of London for South Carolina.[35] Garden thanked the associates for his own parcel of their books, which had contained fifty copies of a work popular among proselytizing colonists, Thomas Wilson's *The Knowledge and Practice of Christianity Made Easy to the Meanest Capacities; or, An Essay towards an Instruction for the Indians,* first published in London in 1740.

The title of this work text reveals an attitude toward the "heathen" that was characteristic of virtually every hierarchically organized society, a category that certainly embraced Great Britain. Any culture that believed in social ranking also believed in intellectual ranking. The implication was that Indians were possessors of the "Meanest Capacities" and therefore required religious materials deliberately written down to their intellectual level. This notion of inferiority was not restricted to any particular ethnic or racial group. It was widely held of all non-European races, and especially of the enslaved Africans. This bias reappears time and again in the correspondence of the Associates of Dr. Bray, particularly in letters from the American side of the Atlantic.[36]

Some of these letters came from Joseph Ottolenghe, the catechist supported by the associates in Savannah. It was ironic that Ottolenghe should send them his impressions of slavery, because Georgia was a special case in the history of British colonization: in 1735, it had become the only British colony to prohibit the importation or use of "Black Slaves or Negroes." It was governed by the trustees, twenty-one men based in London who had split off from the Associates of Dr.

Bray. They were led by James Oglethorpe, a Member of Parliament who would become the only trustee to voyage to Georgia. The trustees, a body that periodically changed its membership, never opposed slavery as immoral in and of itself or for its consequences for the enslaved Africans; instead, they attacked it for its deleterious effects on the morals of white slaveholders. Georgia was created primarily as a buffer between South Carolina and the Spanish to the south, and secondarily as a catchment area for honest debtors who could not achieve a decent living back in Great Britain. Charity was to be combined with practicality: the immigrants were to add to Britain's wealth by producing such high-quality products as wine and silk. But their way of life was to be "Christian, moral and industrious." In addition, the possibility of slaves escaping southward to the Spanish in Florida was believed to be incompatible with Georgia's military purpose of guarding the colonies' most southern flank.[37]

It did not take long for the trustees' vision of industrious colonists plucking a good living from fertile soil to become untenable. The land was not as fruitful as its boosters had made out and restrictions on the titles and size of landholdings were slowing development. As a result, a vocal group of immigrants soon began to press for the repeal of the prohibition of slavery as an answer to their economic hardships.[38] The military arguments against slavery effectively vanished when Oglethorpe defeated the Spanish decisively at Bloody Marsh in 1742. Six years later, the trustees began formulating a slave code. Three years after that, slavery was legalized.[39]

In January 1751, the month that slavery was legalized, the Associates of Dr. Bray chose Joseph Ottolenghe at their London meeting to be their Georgia catechist. His salary was supplemented by a smaller one from the S.P.G. An Italian by birth, Ottolenghe had come to England two decades earlier and had converted to Anglicanism from Judaism. He reached Savannah in July and was not short of potential pupils. Despite the earlier prohibition against slavery, as many as a thousand slaves were already in Savannah, introduced from South Carolina under the pretext that they were hired laborers. (The white population numbered about forty-two hundred.)[40]

Two months later Ottolenghe sent a report not to the associates but to the S.P.G., his other employer, on the obstacles to the pious designs of his benefactors. The pastor of Christ Church (Savannah's only Anglican church), Reverend Bartholomew Zouberbuhler, had given notice in church that Ottolenghe would instruct slaves on Sundays, Tuesdays, and Thursdays, "in the Evening at a Time when their Owners can best spare them." Ottolenghe instructed those who were advanced in years, and not capable of learning to read, he explained, "in as plain a Manner as I can, in such Principles as suits best with their Condition & Capacity." He had a different explanation for why the enslaved Africans were "slow of Apprehension, of a dull Understanding, & soon forgetting what they have learn'd": their unhappy condition. But that idea, he said, was "a String not to be touch'd upon by so unskilfull a Finger as mine is."[41]

In December, Ottolenghe brought the associates, too, up-to-date on his progress. He continued to include reading instruction in his catechetical efforts in the hope that the Africans "may be able in Time to comfort themselves in reading the Book of God." After his reading lesson, he made his students repeat the Lord's Prayer, the Creed, and a short portion of the catechism. This last he then explained to them, "in as easie & Familiar a Manner as I can." Before the slaves left, he gave a brief sermon on some aspect of Christianity, introducing a biblical story to support his point. He was particularly careful to "use them with all the Kindness & endearing Words" that he could.[42]

The following year, in June 1752, Ottolenghe was optimistic. Many of his catachumens had gone through the entire church catechism, "& several [had begun] to read tolerably well." All of them could repeat prayers by heart.[43] Like other catechists, Ottolenghe had to contend with objections raised by slaveholders against the conversion of their slaves. The slaveholder, he wrote, "would be a greater Gainer . . . for in such a Case, he would have instead of an immoral dishonest Domestic a faithful Servant."[44] The argument that Christianity would make slaves more obedient and trustworthy, and so better as slaves, was used again and again in Anglican arguments for conversion.[45]

Meanwhile he believed his little house was the only place where the slaves were "civily used." He now sang Psalms with them, and, he reported in November, "several of them who have really good Voices, having learn'd the Words & Tune at Schole, join the Congregation at Church." He was also teaching whites at night. Those who came were mostly apprentices, who were "miserably ignorant of their Duty, & not able to read [their Duties] in the Book of God." The previous August, the associates had dispatched a box of useful books and pamphlets to Ottelenghe. It presumably arrived after he had sent off this letter, since he did not mention them. The box included hornbooks, primers, fifty copies of Henry Dixon's spelling book *The English Instructor*, and a few psalters and testaments. [46]

Despite all these aids to reading instruction, a year later, in the fall of 1754, Ottolenghe sounded less hopeful and more aware of the difficulties of what he was attempting to do. For the first time, he voiced the insight that religious belief could be valid only if it were based on genuine understanding. Language differences were proving to be a serious obstacle. "[O]ur Negroes are so Ignorant of the English language, & none can be found to talk in their own, that it is a great while before you can get them to understand what the Meaning of words is, & yet . . . without such a knowledge Instructions would prove Vain . . . for how can a Proposition be believed, without first being understood? And how can it be understood if the Person to whom it is offer'd has no Idea even of the Sound of those Words which expresses the Proposition?" Ottolenghe repeated his earlier insight. "Slavery," he said, "is certainly a great Depresser of the Mind, which retards their learning a new Religion, propos'd to them in a new & unknown Language." Another obstacle to be combated was the superstition of their old religion. He had not even offered any of the Africans for baptism, for those who were most advanced had been removed to remote plantations. The "best Harvest," he continued, would be from the "Infants that encrease daily upon us."[47]

The next letter from Ottolenghe, after a four-year gap, was written in July 1758. It was a reply to charges by the associates of neglect. (By this time word had got out the Ottonlenghe was spending most of his time as a government employee, collecting taxes for the silk business.) He defended himself by saying that his yearly letters had been lost in the war (the Seven Years' War that was pitting France against England over much of the globe), and that he had been suffering from blinding headaches, which reading and writing exacerbated. He now described his classroom. Sometimes he had fifty Negroes at one time, and at others fewer than ten. Some attended for six months and then disappeared for as many months or a year before they reappeared. He reminded his correspondent that their movements were "guided by the Dispotic will of their owners and have no other Leizure but what is allowd them." They had also been needed for road and fort building.[48]

Ottolenghe was at pains to show how faithfully he had tended his charges. "I have built a Large Room with a large Chimeney for the Use of these poor souls the Latter extremely necessary for them who are of a Chill Constitution, ill fed and worse cloathed, that many are not fit to be seen by a modest Eye; and while in Summer we're ready [to] faint with Heat, they solace themselves round a large fire." He provided candles, purchased at his own expense, so that he could teach them by night. To the question about what fruit his method had produced, he responded, "as much as I could reasonably expect" under the circumstances. He waxed eloquent on the miseries of the slaves: "ill fed, ill cloathed; cruelly corrected [punished] & barbarously treated . . . reduc'd to a most deplorable & cruel Slavery!" Dogs and horses were treated better, he said.[49]

Nonetheless, Ottolenghe maintained, those who attended constantly were able to say the catechism by heart and repeat simple prayers. Some could read "but in general poorly." He then showed a rarely voiced appreciation of the importance of comprehension, noting that simply calling words off a page did not necessarily equate with understanding them. The slaves were not ready for baptism yet, he said, because although they were able to repeat everything that he had taught them, "I have reason to believe that they . . . yet have very little Notion or Idea of what they thus repeat, and consequently a Parrot might as well be baptiz'd as any of them." He himself had had two slaves, a young man and his wife, for the past four years, but although he had treated them more like children, their progress in learning had been slow indeed. The office of catechist, he summed up, is "not so easy as it may be imagin'd." He asked for the associates' compassion, as his difficulties had been greatly increased by a fire in Savannah that had consumed the silk storage house, and with it all his letters and several sums of his own money.[50]

All the objections to instruction Ottolenghe voiced had in fact been answered by an experiment that was unique at the time in the annals of bringing literacy to the enslaved and would continue to be so. This was a day school for young Africans in Charles Town, South Carolina, organized by Alexander Garden, the Charles Town commissary.

Unlike Georgia, South Carolina had been open to the slave trade since its planting. Slaves are documented as early as 1670, and in the late 1730s the importation into the colony of captured and enslaved Africans was on the rise. Between 1734 and 1737 alone, nearly 10,500 were imported. Except for the years in which prohibitive duties discouraged importation, the documented number of Africans imported annually up to 1765 would rarely fall below 1,500 and would twice rise over 3,500. It did not take long for the numbers of blacks in rural areas, where they were sent to work on the indigo and rice plantations, to far exceed those of whites. In addition, the number of "home-born" slaves was on the rise.[51]

In South Carolina in 1739, the enslaved rose against their enslavers in a revolt known as the Stono Rebellion. By the time it was all over, forty-four blacks and twenty-one whites were dead. The following year, the South Carolina legislature responded with comprehensive legislation designed to exert tighter control of its slave population. One of its sections was an antiliteracy provision that prohibited anyone from teaching a slave to write, or causing a slave to be taught to write, or employing a slave as a scribe. The penalty for violating the law was £100. The reason provided in the preamble was that "the having of slaves taught to write, or suffering them to be employed in writing, may be attended with great inconveniencies." (Writing would permit such "inconveniencies" as communication and the forging of passes.) South Carolina thereby became the first of only two colonies to prohibit writing instruction for the enslaved. (Georgia used South Carolina's code as its model for similar legislation in 1755.) Reading instruction, however, was implicitly still permitted by the law.[52]

In contrast to the rural plantations of South Carolina, Charles Town, its leading city by geographical location and political importance, was thoroughly cosmopolitan and much more racially balanced—almost half white and half black. The town had had a long relationship with the S.P.G.: an S.P.G. missionary, the Reverend Samuel Thomas, had taught twenty Africans to read in 1704 while ministering to the white Anglican population.[53] The more benign environment of urban servitude may have contributed to a relative openness, on the part of white residents, to the notion that African children could be released from their chores to be sent to a day school for literacy instruction. Nonetheless, schooling for enslaved blacks was not to embrace total literacy. Only reading could legally be taught.

Alexander Garden, the prime mover and organizer of the scheme, was a Scot who had arrived in South Carolina in 1719 in his mid thirties; he had become the rector of St. Philip's Church in Charles Town that same year. Eight years later he was appointed a commissary by the Bishop of London, representing the Anglican Church in North and South Carolina and in the Bahamas. He was thus the leading Anglican minister of the southern colonies.[54]

Garden directed his proposal for a school to the S.P.G., which ultimately financed it. A man renowned for his orderliness and his fidelity to his own routines ("methodical" was the adjective others liked to use of him), he articulated his vision of the school to the S.P.G. secretary in a letter dated May 1740.[55] He had come to his conclusions, he said, after a great deal of thought, and he numbered them as he wrote. First, he said, there was no virtue in attempting any kind of wholesale instruction of Negroes and Indian slaves (initially targeted for instruction). Their ages, nations, and languages were far too diverse. His second point arose from his first: the students should be taken only from the "Home-born," under the age of ten. Third, he believed that their instruction would never work out at the hands of white instructors. So, fourth, he envisioned "Negro Schoolmasters, home born,

& equally Property as other Slaves, but educated for this Service & employ'd in it during their Lives, as the others are."

He had tried for a long time, he said, to persuade every owner of eighty or a hundred slaves to pay for one boy from among the children under the age of ten to be educated for such a position, but no owner had been willing to give up the slave's labor. His new idea, therefore, was that the S.P.G. should purchase one or more male slaves, home born, and between the ages of twelve and sixteen. They would be "forthwith instructed in the Principles of the Christian Religion as contained in the Church Catechism, to read the Bible, and to make use of the Book of Common Prayer." (As in other cases of Anglican evangelism, the Anglican prayer book featured as a school text.) Garden was confident that this plan could be managed in two years. Usually, adults passed on their religion to their children; here his object was to reverse these roles. Slaves lived together "in contiguous Houses" and conversed almost solely among themselves, so that "if once their Children could but read the Bible to them, and other proper Tracts of Instruction" during the evening and their other spare time, "this would bring in at least a Dawning of the blessed Light among them." He envisioned the light spreading among their relatives, "daily Teaching and learning of one another."[56]

Despite the visionary elements of the plan, Garden was strictly practical when it came to implementing the first step, the purchase of two suitable young male slaves. With the approval of the S.P.G., in April 1742 he purchased a fourteen-year-old named Harry and a fifteen-year-old named Andrew from the estate of the late Alexander Skene for the price of £56 9 3 ½. At the time of their purchase, both boys had been baptized and could say the church catechism, but neither knew a letter of the alphabet. "They have been ever since under my Roof, and sent daily to School." Garden himself was undertaking all the expenses involved in their maintenance and education.[57]

That September, Garden reported to the S.P.G. that Harry was "of an excellent Genius, & can now (in the space of 8 months) read the N. Testament exceeding well." (Once again, accurate oral reading was being used as the criterion of excellence.) Harry would be completely qualified in another six months, by which time Garden would have the schoolhouse ready. Andrew, however, was of "a somewhat slower Genius, but of a milder & better Temper." His education would take perhaps three or four months longer, but Garden reckoned that he would need the less supervision of the two.[58]

The school opened on Monday, September 12, 1743. Some "good Christians of this place," according to Garden, had raised funds to build the school building near the parsonage. Garden had earlier announced the school's opening from the pulpit and inserted a notice in the newspaper. By October the school had thirty pupils, and as the number was increasing daily, Garden planned to use Andrew as an assistant for the time being until he had learned enough to be ready to teach alone in another parish. Garden said that he would pay for the schoolmaster's maintenance as long as he lived. Once he himself was gone, he was confident that the masters and mistresses of the slaves would be willing to contribute the trifle that the school cost, while the parents of the slaves "wou[l]d gladly do it, though they should pinch it off their own Backs & out of their own Bellies." (This was touching testimony to the importance the slaves themselves attributed to this educational experiment.) Garden's only difficulty was a familiar one: he was short of books. He begged the society to send him one hundred spelling books, fifty psalms with the Common Prayer Book (in the edition printed by March for Staners), fifty testaments, and fifty Bibles. Here, for perhaps the first time, we see the effect of the speller on the traditional reading instructional sequence in an Anglican context: the spelling book actually displaced the hornbook and primer, while the Psalter, another feature of the "ordinary Road," was offered only within the context of the Anglican prayer book. [59]

The S.P.G. obliged with the books, although it was a long time before they arrived, and the school proceeded to grow in numbers.[60] "The Society's Negro School, under my Care, succeeds even beyond my first Hopes or Expectation," Garden wrote the following year. It had sixty children being taught the principles of religion and how to read the scriptures. Fifteen of them, he said, "are now capable to read the Testament very well, & 20 more are in Psalters, & the rest in the Alphabet and Spelling Books." His only disappointment was in Andrew, "an exceeding good nature'd & willing Creature, yet [who] proves of so weak an understanding, that I'm afraid he will not be soon Qualified to Teach alone." He asked the S.P.G. for authorization to sell him and get a youth of "better Genius" in his place.[61]

The society's response to this last request was that Andrew, rather than being sold, should be sent over to Barbados for the use of the manager of the Codrington plantation. The utter lack of compassion that this decision evinced, even within the context of a general acceptance of slavery, moved Garden, on a visit to London in the summer of 1746, to request that Andrew be sold to someone locally, rather than be separated from his South Carolina family. (Four years later, Andrew was sold in Charles Town for the equivalent of £28 11 5d sterling.) While in London, Garden made a presentation to the members of the S.P.G., reporting that the school, then open for two years and eight months, had sent out twenty-eight children as sufficiently instructed and had grown to seventy in number. Fifty-five of these were children, taught during the day, and the other fifteen were adults who came for instruction at night. Garden "plainly perceives," the printed report of this meeting declares, "a very general and earnest Desire among Negroe Parents of having their Children instructed, and also an Emulation among many of them that are capable of Instruction."[62]

Since the number of children were, in Garden's words, "rather more than one School Master can teach," it is not clear why Andrew was not kept on as an assistant. Presumably he was not literate enough to be helpful, or perhaps Garden was feeling the financial strain of paying for the food and clothing of two teachers. No record exists of the purchase or education of another African in his place.[63] School reports continued to be favorable over the next few years, and the book shortage was eased by a second packet of Bibles, Common Prayer Books, testaments, and spelling books, this time with the addition of the S.P.G. staples, church catechisms and John Lewis's exposition, *Church Catechism Explained*.[64] In February 1751 Garden wrote to the S.P.G. with unabated enthusiasm for the school. He wished the society could see how it was "spreading the light of the blessed Gospel among the poor heathens," he said, "and how much they rejoice in it." He reiterated an earlier request for books, "only taking leave to observe that Dyches spelling books are much more proper and useful than those which were last sent." (His is the first reference to Thomas Dyche's speller, *A Guide to the English Tongue*, imported into South Carolina since 1735, as a reading instructional textbook of acknowledged value.) A hurricane in Charles Town in 1752 blew down the school, but within a month Garden had it rebuilt and running again.[65]

Garden died in 1756, but the supervision of the school, and presumably the expenses, were continued by his successors as rector of St. Philip's Church: first by the Reverend Richard Clarke and three years later by the Reverend Robert Smith. (When Smith took over, he asked the S.P.G. for primers, common prayer books, and Bibles. Was he not aware of the newly perceived importance of spelling books?) The school continued with apparent success, despite being battered in 1760 by smallpox and the Cherokee war. But in 1768 Harry, who had been teaching in the parsonage of St. Philip's Church, became insane and was consigned by the parish vestry to the madhouse. The S.P.G. made no attempt to replace him, which would have involved the purchase of another slave, and the school closed.[66]

The well-publicized success of the Charles Town school and its slave instructor was frequently mentioned in the S.P.G.'s published annual abstracts of their proceedings. It is noteworthy, therefore, that the experience was ignored by the Associates of Dr. Bray in 1760, as they sought, in their turn, to create schools for the enslaved. (One of the reasons may have been the cost of purchasing a slave to be trained as a teacher—the associates were operating on a low budget.)[67] Opening schools was an expansion of the associates' goals: formerly, as when they were helping to support Ottolenghe in Savannah, they had aimed only at providing catechetical instruction with perhaps some reading instruction.

The associates' change of approach dates back to January 1757, when John Waring, their secretary, wrote to Benjamin Franklin asking for his advice about schooling slaves. Presumably influenced by Ottolenghe's earlier comment that the "best harvest" would be children born in America, Waring suggested to Franklin that the school be aimed at just such a clientele. Aware of the great success that the Society for the Propagation of Christian Knowledge was having in Wales, with its circulating charity school movement that sent itinerant schoolmasters all over the country (reaching over ninety-eight hundred pupils in 1757), Waring questioned whether something comparable could be begun in the American colonies. He did not take into account, however, the vast difference in geographical scale between Wales and Pennsylvania.[68]

The slave population of Pennsylvania was concentrated in the port of Philadelphia. By the late 1750s the city had been importing the enslaved for over seventy years, although on a far smaller scale than in the southern colonies. The involvement of the city with slavery, as Gary Nash has demonstrated, was far greater than was once thought. Roughly one in every fifteen families was a slaveholder around the end of the seventeenth century, but thanks to high import duties on slaves after

1712, imports slowed markedly until the abolishment of duties after 1731. They then picked up again, only to decline once more until the onset of the Seven Years' War in 1756. When the white indentured servants of Philadelphia were pressed into military service by the British government, the need for labor drove up the demand for slaves significantly. Between 1758 and 1766, imports ranged annually from 100 to a peak of about 500 slaves in 1762. The total slave population of Philadelphia in 1757 is not known, but ten years later there were 905 slaves between the ages of twelve and fifty in the Philadelphia area, and perhaps another 270 younger than twelve.[69]

Benjamin Franklin was a slaveholder himself, and at the time of his correspondence with Waring he held a boy named Othello. Aged fifty-three and financially independent, Franklin had just accepted the invitation of the Pennsylvania Assembly to act as its agent in London to address various political grievances. His response to Waring's letter is full of insights. By implication he rejected the notion of an itinerant schoolmaster and recommended a separate school for blacks. If it were under the care of someone whom people could trust to "imbue the Minds of their young Slaves with good Principles," such a school might have a number of such children sent to it, he wrote. Franklin recommended the Reverend William Sturgeon as a good man to supervise such a school. (Sturgeon was the S.P.G. catechist for enslaved Africans in Philadelphia and an assistant minister of Christ Church, the leading Anglican church.) Franklin went on to explain why so few masters currently educated the slave children in their families. It was "partly from a Prejudice that Reading & Knowledge in a Slave are both useless and dangerous" and partly because the masters and mistresses of what he called "common Schools" were reluctant to take black children, lest the "Parents of the white Children should be disgusted & take them away, not chusing to have their Children mix'd with Slaves in Education, Play &c."[70] In these few words, Franklin succinctly summarized two conventional arguments against educating slaves. The first was that slaves' acquisition of reading (Franklin took it for granted that writing was not to be taught) was not the benign activity its Christian promoters believed. As the master of the enslaved Frederick Douglass would say much later, education would make Douglass "unfit . . . to be a slave . . . unmanageable . . . discontented and unhappy." The second argument pinpointed one of the social consequences of slavery: white parents did not wish their free children to mix with those in bondage.[71]

The associates adopted Franklin's suggestion and also acquiesced to a later suggestion of his: that if the children "were taught some useful Things besides Reading it might be an Encouragement to Masters and Mistresses to send them." Having already remarked that one schoolmaster could teach up to forty Negro children to read without needing an assistant, Franklin wrote: "I think a Mistress might be best to begin with, who could teach both Boys & Girls to read, & the Girls to knit, sew & mark [embroider]." In effect, this suggestion made the school more attractive to the masters and mistresses of girls than of boys, and on the few occasions when the sources reveal the sex of the students, girls outnumbered boys by two to one.[72]

The Negro Charity School at Philadelphia, the first-ripened fruit of the Associates' pious designs, opened in November 1758, once the batch of 192 books sent by the associates for the school's use had arrived safely. (The most useful of these, pedagogically speaking, were the forty copies of the *Child's First Book*, which seems to have served as a primer and introduction to the spelling book, along with the same number of Dixon's speller, *The English Instructor*.)[73] "Many of the Scholars are very young," Sturgeon reported, but several of them could already say the Creed, the Lord's Prayer, and parts of the catechism. They attended church every Wednesday, and he examined them in their catechism once the service was over "and explain[ed] such Parts of it as they are capable to comprehend."[74]

Franklin and his wife, Deborah, provided eyewitness accounts of the school's pupils. Deborah Franklin did not visit the school itself, but she did go to hear the children being catechized by Sturgeon at his church in the summer of 1759. She reported to her husband, still in London, that seventeen of the children responded to the questions of the catechism "very prettily indeed." Five or six were too little to do so, but "all behaved very decently" and the experience had given her a great deal of pleasure. She said that she intended to send Othello to the school. Four years later Benjamin Franklin looked in on the school himself and was impressed by what he found. The children had made considerable progress in reading, he informed the associates, in relation to the time they had spent there. Most of them could answer the questions of the catechism readily and well. They also "behav'd very orderly, show'd a proper Respect & ready Obedience to the Mistress, and seem'd very attentive to, and a good deal affected by, a serious Exhortation with which Mr. Sturgeon concluded our visit." Franklin pronounced himself on the whole much pleased, and added a comment that revealed that stereotypes about black native intelligence were by no means confined to the southern colonies. On the basis of this experience, he said, "I . . . have conceiv'd a higher Opinion of the natural Capacities of the black Race, than I had ever before entertained. Their Apprehension seems as quick, their Memory as strong, and their Docility in every respect equal to that of white Children. You will wonder perhaps that I should ever doubt it," he added, "and I will not undertake to justify all my Prejudices, nor to account for them."[75]

Between the time the school opened and 1770, the salary provided by the associates for successive schoolmistresses of the Negro Charity School at Philadelphia remained at twenty pounds. In terms of enrollment, between November 1758 and June 1759 the school admitted thirty-six students, but some of them may have left within the year, and later the number was consistently restricted to thirty. By 1770 the school had many more applications than places for any vacancies that occurred.[76]

Four schoolmistresses in succession staffed the Negro Charity School at Philadelphia between the school's opening in 1758 and the last report from the school to the associates in 1774. The first of the schoolmistresses was an experienced teacher whose name is never mentioned. She had to be dismissed for falling under the sway of a clergyman, the Reverend William McClenaghan, who displeased the Anglican hierarchy, and for consequently neglecting her school. Before she was obliged to leave in May 1761, she was teaching eleven boys and twenty-four girls to read. In addition, she was teaching fifteen of the girls to "sew and work with their Needle." Her successor was Elizabeth Harrison, a woman in her mid-forties who was the wife of Richard Harrison, the S.P.G.'s schoolmaster of the charity school of the Academy of Philadelphia.[77]

The third schoolmistress, Mrs. Ayres, took over in November 1764. During the nearly four years of her instruction up to her retirement to the country in the spring of 1768, 59 Africans were admitted to the school; 27 were in attendance when she left. Of these, 19 were slaves and 8 free. The report of these last students was that "Three are in the Bible, One in the Testament, Two in the Fables Nineteen in Spelling and Two learning the Alphabet." This report demonstrates how entrenched the spelling book, an innovation in the 1730s, had become in the reading sequence by the 1760s. Moreover, Mrs. Ayres had expanded the standard sequence by adding Aesop's *Fables* as a school text between the speller and the New Testament.[78]

Mrs. Ayres was succeeded by Sarah Wilson, who taught at the Philadelphia Negro Charity School for the final years of the prerevolutionary period. A report made of the school in May 1774 suggests that she offered a fairly rich curriculum, at least for the girls. Thirty children were attending the school. Of the younger children, both boys and girls, ten were said to be "in" the alphabet, another three in their primers, in accordance with the customary sequence, and seven in the spelling book. But then the instruction was differentiated by sex. It was presumably a boy who was "in [Aesop's] Fables," another boy who was in the Psalter, and three more boys who were reading the Testament (the entire Bible is never mentioned, probably because none of that particular group of children had yet reached that level). In contrast, girls who had already learned to read added sewing and then knitting to their lessons, which ran in parallel to their continued reading instruction. In the year of the report, two girls were spelling and sewing, another was sewing and reading the Testament, a fourth was knitting and sewing as well as reading the Testament, and a fifth girl, in addition to reading the Testament, was embroidering a sampler. Embroidering a sampler was clearly the apex of the sewing curriculum, and only one girl is known to have reached that level. (A girl was at the sampler stage a year later, but there is no way of knowing whether she was the same girl.) Notably absent from the school's offerings is any mention of writing instruction. The sole girl who was embroidering a sampler may have been the only child in the school to form letters, in thread, as well as read them.[79]

Franklin had proved to be so helpful in setting up the Philadelphia Charity School that the Associates of Dr. Bray turned to him again to inquire of other locations for schools and for the names of local Anglicans to supervise them. Franklin suggested New York city; Newport, Rhode Island's major port; and Williamsburg, in Virginia. He also provided the names of appropriate supervisors. The New York city and Williamsburg schools were open by September 1760. The Rhode Island school took longer, because the minister Franklin recommended left Newport before he could set it up. It too, however, was functioning by November

1762. The grateful associates unanimously voted Franklin in as one of their members as of January 1760.[80]

The most successful of these new schools, in the sense of attracting the most consistent attendance by the children, was the school in New York city, opened, at Franklin's suggestion, by Reverend Samuel Auchmuty, who had been serving as the S.P.G. catechist for enslaved Africans in New York city since 1747. (He was also an assistant minister to Henry Barclay, rector of Trinity Church and former missionary to the Mohawks, and his signature occasionally appeared with Barclay's on S.P.G. certificates for the Trinity charity school taught by Joseph Hildreth.) In September 1760 Auchmuty advertised in the *New-York Mercury*:

> a Free school is opened near the New-Dutch-Church for the instruction of 30 Negro Children, from 5 years old and upwards, in Reading, and in the Principles of Christianity, and likewise sewing and knitting; which School is entirely under the Inspection and Care of the Clergy of the Church of England in this City. . . .
>
> N.B. All that is required of their Masters and Mistresses, is that they find them in Wood for the Winter. Proper Books will be provided for them gratis.[81]

Four months later, the school was full, having received sixty applicants. In August of the following year the school remained full, the schoolmistress, Mrs. Lourier, was reportedly "very industrious," and the older scholars were importuning Auchmuty for testaments and Bibles. In October, Auchmuty reported that he was not yet requiring the schoolmistress to bring her pupils to church on prayer days, he said, "for, after the School is out, she has her self & Children to take care off, & Victuals to prepare, which she can'ot do, while the Scholars are about her." In addition, some of the older children were needed at home by their mistresses to "lay a Cloth, & wait upon Table; therefore should I detain them till Prayers are over at Church, I fear it would occasion some uneasiness and grumbling, which I would chuse to avoid."[82]

The list of students that Auchmuty enclosed with his October report provides the most detailed look available at any of the schools funded by the associates in the American colonies. Along with the name and age of each child and the date of admission, he passed on what was presumably Mrs. Lourier's report card on the student's "Improvement." The thirty pupils detailed range in age from five to nineteen, with the girls greatly outnumbering the boys by twenty-one to nine. The boys spanned the ages of five to ten with a median age of six; with the exception of the one nineteen-year-old, all the girls were aged between five and eleven, with a median age of seven. The tendency was, as time passed, for masters to send younger children. All but four of the students were in the stages of initial reading instruction categorized as "Learning to spell &c." Of the four more advanced students, the nineteen-year-old Isabella could already sew as well as read. Of the remaining three, the eight-year-old Hannah "Reads very well," while of Judah, aged nine, it was also said that he "Reads well &c." The biggest surprise was five-year-old Mary, who was categorized as "Reads well &c." and had presumably been taught at home. Of the entire group, three children were denoted "free," while twenty-seven of the children, including all of the free Africans, had been baptized.[83]

As Auchmuty himself pointed out, the large number of baptized African children indicated how far sentiments in New York about the baptism of the enslaved had evolved since Elias Neau's day. He was at pains to counter the opinion of John Waring, still the associates' secretary, that "too many both of Masters & Slaves are possessed with a groundless perswasion that Baptism breaks asunder the bonds of Slavery." Despite the uprising of 1712 that had proved so harmful to Neau's endeavors and the occurrence of the "Great Negro Plot" of 1741, baptism of the enslaved in New York city, at least of those owned by professed Christians, had become accepted as the norm. Auchmuty reported that he had for several years past baptized between eighty and one hundred slave children annually, as well as a few adults, as had the ministers of the Dutch churches and the Congregationalists. "[A]nd yet," he said—with a throwaway sentence that showed how well he understood the situation—"they continue peaceable Slaves."[84]

For more than a decade before he was called on to supervise and promote the work of the associates' New York Negro School, Auchmuty had been teaching and lecturing on the catechism to adult enslaved Africans by virtue of his position as the S.P.G.'s salaried catechist. By the early summer of 1762, he reported to the S.P.G. secretary, some sixty to seventy adults were attending his classes regularly, learning both the church's and Lewis's catechism. In addition to these, he wrote, "there are many more that come occasionally; and, tho' they ca'not read, are well pleased & pay great attention to, my Lectures on the Catechism." Auchmuty's description of the handful of enslaved Africans whom he felt able to admit to communion is eloquent of the links that Anglicans felt obtained between reading, Christianity, and deference. That January, he had allowed two of his adult African catachumens to receive communion. Their characters, he said, were "unexceptionable, and their knowledge of our most holy Religion, and their duty, very considerable for People of their Colour." Furthermore, "[t]hey read well." Auchmuty's interpretation of Anglicanism as a religion of obedience to authority was still a perfect representation of the view of the S.P.G. itself. It gave him, he wrote a couple of years later, "no small pleasure to reflect, that not one single Black, that has been admitted by me to the Holy Communion, has turned out bad; or been, in any shape, a disgrace to our profession."[85]

As far as the associates' school was concerned, Auchmuty continued to send encouraging reports back to London. In the fall of 1762, he reported that the school was in a "very flourishing Condition"; that all the children attended the Sunday services and that he catechized them between services; that some of them were advanced enough for him to teach them Lewis's *Church Catechism Explained*; that the S.P.G. schoolmaster of Trinity School, Joseph Hildreth, had consented— just as he had done almost twenty years earlier—to instruct them, along with adult blacks, in psalmody; and that he intended to admit no children unless their masters undertook to keep them at the school until they were "perfectly instructed, in the principles of our most holy Religion." By the following spring Auchmuty had overcome his scruples about keeping Mrs. Lourier after school in order to bring her class to his weekday lectures, and he reported that the students now attended these as well as, of course, going to the services held at Trinity Church every Sunday.[86]

Mrs. Lourier was clearly an exceptional person. Auchmuty himself called her "faithful" and "diligent," "careful" and "industrious." When he was planning to be away, he detailed someone else to look in on the school but admitted that it was really unnecessary: the mistress was "so good a Woman," he said, "that she may very well be trusted." She was good at what she did—"very clever at her bussiness," as Auchmuty put it—and enjoyed teaching: she "seems to be very happy with her employment," he said. But she was clearly more than just a good teacher: she was also dedicated to the principle of instructing the enslaved. She persuaded Auchmuty to allow her to admit more children than the limit permitted rather than turn them away, arguing that some of the older children would soon be leaving anyway. At times, therefore, such as in the spring of 1765, she was teaching thirty-seven children instead of the requisite thirty.[87]

In the fall of that same year, Auchmuty sent the associates a plea for more spelling books: "[Mrs. Lourier] is as careful of their Books as possible: but, still Children will destroy them." By this time, Auchmuty had succeeded to the pulpit of Trinity Church and resigned his post as catechist for the S.P.G. Despite his new responsibilities, he continued to keep an eye on the school for the associates. In September 1774, he reported that though Mrs. Lourier was in declining health, she "continues her usual diligence." She died the following month. By then, the turbulence of the times precluded a replacement for her.[88]

The success of the New York Negro school was not replicated in Newport, Rhode Island, where the school for African children opened in 1762. Both cities were ports for the importation of the enslaved, but while enslaved Africans were a considerable element in New York City, they were an even larger element in Newport, which was, as one scholar has put it, "the capital of North America's trade in slaves."[89]

One factor that militated against the school's success was that its chief promoter and supervisor, Reverend Marmaduke Browne, was a newcomer to Rhode Island who lacked the reputation and respect Auchmuty had enjoyed for so long in New York city. The son of an Anglican New Hampshire clergyman and a graduate of Trinity College in Dublin, Browne had arrived in Newport only recently, becoming the S.P.G.-supported minister of Trinity Church in December 1760.[90]

A second factor was what we would call today the racism and classism of the Newport slaveholders: even the churchwardens with suitable children were not sending them to the Negro school. As Browne put it, their neglect was "in some measure owing to the contempt incident to the colour & slavery of the Blacks." He ascribed the resistance of Newport slaveholders to Christian conversion efforts to the religious climate of Rhode Island itself, home to a hotchpotch of religions where fewer than a third of its forty thousand inhabitants, he claimed, had been baptized themselves.[91]

The third and most disastrous handicap to the success of the Newport school was an ineffectual schoolmistress. Mary Brett was the wife of Dr. John Brett (a highly respected community member it would be unwise to offend), and she taught the school in her own house for an annual salary of twenty pounds. Unlike the dedicated Mrs. Lourier, she was early the subject of complaints of "negligence" that were "not altogether ill-founded," according to Browne, who also found her "too much disposed to earn her money without exertion."[92]

In July 1766, Browne confirmed that the school was finally full and the mistress was more diligent, that several of the blacks read "tolerably," and that the girls had made some proficiency in sewing and knitting. In his next letter he reported that he continued to visit the school frequently to check on the schoolmistress, "who I fear without constant inspection would not so conscientiously discharge her duty as she ought." He also asked for an additional supply of books, identifying them as the "childs first book" (the A B C book) and Dixon's *English Instructor* (which by now had already been replaced in most of the colonies by Thomas Dilworth's speller).[93]

Browne died at the age of forty in March 1771 and was succeeded by the Reverend George Bisset, who had been serving as the assistant minister of Trinity Church and was also master of a local grammar school. He was dismayed by the state of the associates' Negro school when he took over its supervision in the fall. Mrs. Brett had been ill and only two or three children were attending regularly. Threats of replacing her (which would have been hard to do, "as the teaching of blacks is not here reputed very creditable") improved her performance, but it was more difficult to overcome the apathy of slaveholders. Bisset advertised the school in the *Newport Mercury* that August, and by October 1772 the school had seventeen or eighteen children in regular attendance.[94]

Enrollment continued to improve, aided by Bisset's well-publicized threat, in March 1773, of closing the school down altogether unless more students were enrolled. But disillusionment for the entire enterprise was creeping into Bisset's letters. Whereas Marmaduke Brown had spoken glowingly, at least for public consumption, of the "exalted pleasure" and the prospect of a "glorious futurity" to be obtained by those who worked on behalf of the young enslaved, Bisset declared in the spring of 1775 that until "Masters are realy in earnest about the Instruction of the Young Blacks" and until a schoolmistress could be found worthy of her salary, he despaired "utterly" of "seeing Effects worthy of the Generosity of the Associates."[95]

The fourth school for enslaved Africans to be funded by the Associates of Dr. Bray was the school at Williamsburg, Virginia. Virginia had been familiar with indentured Africans since 1619, but the Africans' slippage into lifelong bondage in this colony was a slow process, not fully completed until the Virginia Assembly passed a law, in 1705, that defined them as real estate. Concurrently with this definition, a massive importation of Africans began that was to radically change the face of Virginia. By the midpoint of the eighteenth century, the number of blacks, through both importation and natural increase, had come close to equaling the number of whites in Virginia. In the town of Williamsburg, renamed as such and newly laid out as the colony's capital in 1699, the ratio of blacks to whites was almost equal.[96] There was no shortage, therefore, of potential pupils for the associates' Negro school.

As before, the associates took Franklin's advice about whom they should ask to undertake its creation and supervision. Franklin had recommended William Hunter, the postmaster and the publisher of the *Virginia Gazette*, and the Reverend Thomas Dawson, rector of Bruton Parish Church, commissary to the Bishop of London, and president of the College of William and Mary.[97]

The school opened in the fall of 1760, with Mrs. Anne Wager as its schoolmistress and an initial enrollment of twenty-four children. (That number, Hunter wrote, was "as many I think as one Woman can well manage.") Since Dawson thought that the twenty pounds allocated by the associates for all the school's expenses was too low, he planned to give Mrs. Wager the entire amount and raise an additional ten pounds through local subscriptions to finance the rent for the schoolroom. He died, however, before he could raise any of the money, and the associates' unexpected commitment to a thirty-pound annual payment in a province in which the exchange rate favored the American side would prove to cause a strain in transatlantic relationships. At this point, however, John Waring left the question of salary to Dawson's discretion but insisted that the enrollment be raised to the usual thirty.[98]

Waring was well aware the new school's need for books. He had already sent one package, and in June 1761 he sent another. With one exception, Waring labeled the contents of the second "for the Use of the School"; the exception was the twenty Common Prayer Books that he designated, "to be given to the Children when qualified to use them at Church." The texts in this second box, then, comprise the backbone of the associates' reading curriculum. When books with the same titles from the first box are added to them, they give us an overview of the number and kinds of texts that the associates thought were essential to the inauguration of a school for young enslaved Africans. The combined shipments included 90 copies of that introductory A B C, the *Child's First Book*; 50 of Henry Dixon's speller, *The English Instructor*; 25 of *The Church Catechism Broke into Short Questions* (a work similar to John Lewis's *Church Catechism Explained*); 25 testaments; 25 psalters; 20 copies of the *Christian Guide*; 15 of *An Easy Method in Instructing Youth in the Principles and Practice of the Christian Religion*; 13 of Wilson's *Knowledge and Practice of Christianity Made Easy* (invariably dubbed the "Indian instructed" in the associates' inventories), ten of William Burkitt's *Help and Guide*; five of the *Church Catechism with Texts of Scriptures*; and five Bibles.[99]

The quantities suggest, like others before them, the order of the curriculum: the larger the number of texts, the younger the age of the children who were presumed to need them. The sequence ran, then, from the A B C through the Psalter and New Testament, culminating in the Bible. The important addition to a sequence that in most respects was identical to that in New England schools in the preceding century was, as with the other schools funded by the associates, the spelling book. In this mid-eighteenth-century setting in Virginia, orchestrated from afar by British Anglicans, the reading sequence also included a few additional titles, two of which related to the catechism of the Anglican Church.

Although William Hunter died before he could contribute further to the cause of the Williamsburg school, the associates had already, at his suggestion, written to ask both the Reverend William Yates, who had succeeded Dawson to the presidency of William and Mary College, and Robert Carter Nicholas, a prominent lawyer in Williamsburg, to manage the school. Nicholas, who took over the responsibility for keeping an eye on the school and paying Anne Wager's salary, had graduated from the College of William and Mary and was just completing a five-year stint as a burgess for York County. He was a committed Anglican, a friend of Thomas Jefferson, and a slaveholder.[100]

Nicholas wrote to the associates in the fall of 1761 that although he had "no very sanguine Expectations of the School's answering the Design of the pious Founder," no endeavor of his would be found wanting. Disturbed by this pessimism, John Waring responded the following April that "in a Little time You will find Reason to alter your Opinion."[101] Nicholas's reply, in June 1762, did not assuage Waring's concerns. The schoolmistress was "very diligent," Nicholas reported; he had drawn a salary for her of twenty-five pounds, and he was hopeful of giving a good report of the school soon. But he made it clear that his expectations were still low: "I must own to you," he wrote, "that I am afraid the School will not answer the sanguine Expectations its pious Founders may have form'd; but we will endeavour to give it a fair Trial."[102]

In September, Yates and Nicholas sent off a list of the names, along with those of their owners, of the thirty African children now attending the school; of these, three were free—a seven-year-old named Mary Anne, and Elisha and Mary Jones, almost certainly siblings. The ages of the students, "as nearly as can be judged of," as Nicholas put it, ranged from four three-year-olds to one ten-year-old. Five of the children were thought to be six years old, ten were aged seven, and four were eight years old. The median age was seven. Unlike the sex ratio in the associates' other schools, in Williamsburg boys had the edge on girls by sixteen to fourteen.[103]

Yates and Nicholas also enclosed in the September 1762 letter several pages of a document they called "Regulations."[104] As it turned out, these rules were unenforceable, and indeed Nicholas had to back down almost immediately because they gave offense to the masters of potential students—they were "not well relish'd," as he put it.[105] Nonetheless, the regulations offer valuable insights into the expectations that the "Trustees," as Yates and Nicholas called themselves, held for the school, for those who were likely to send their enslaved Africans to it, and for the schoolmistress.

The first rule is aimed at the slaveholders. Since the school was already full, owners of eligible children were asked to give their names to the trustees so that any vacancies could be filled at once. They were also to undertake to keep the children in school for a minimum of three years. They were to send them to school properly clothed and clean: in fact, the trustees would prefer a uniform. Owners were also to send the children regularly and punctually, and they were to permit them to be "Chastized for their Faults without quarrelling or coming to School on such Occasions." Owners who had complaints, however, should lay them before the trustees. Moreover, the slaveholders were expected to give a Christian example themselves, catechize the children frequently, and in general be supportive of the schoolmistress's efforts.

The rules for the schoolmistress are even more explicit and numbered tidily. The first specifies school hours: from seven o'clock in the morning in the winter and six in the summer. The second relates to reading methodology: "She shall teach her Scholars the true Spelling of Words, make them mind their Stops & endeavour to bring them to pronounce & read distinctly." This is, in effect, a synopsis of the alphabet method of reading instruction in its eighteenth-century format. The reference to the "true Spelling of Words," it should be noted, occurs in a context in which written spelling was never taught, although oral spelling probably was. In this context, therefore, the "true Spelling of Words"—unless Yates and Nicholas were writing carelessly—must be an allusion to the ever growing importance of the spelling book in reading instruction: it would provide the children with the "true Spelling" of words at the same time as they learned to pronounce them by spelling them out, letter by letter. Attention was to be paid to punctuation during oral reading (the children were to "mind their Stops"), and a high value was placed on accurate oral reading. Implicit in these rules is the assumption that reading aloud without mispronouncing any words would fulfill the goals of reading instruction.

The third rule focuses on the content of such instruction. The schoolmistress's main charge is to teach the children "to read the Bible, to instruct them in the Principles of the Christian Religion according to the Doctrine of the Church of England, [and to] . . . explain the Church Catechism to them by some good Exposition." The Bible was therefore the ultimate goal of reading instruction, just as it had been in its Congregationalist counterpart in seventeenth-century New England. Special to the associates' brand of sectarian instruction, however, was the key role of Anglican doctrine, particularly as embodied in the Anglican catechism. Significantly, the children's comprehension was not ignored. As we have seen, the rules put a paradoxical and dual emphasis on, on one hand, rote learning of texts, and, on the other, the schoolmistress's using "some good Exposition" to help the children understand those texts—which, like the catechism itself, was apparently also to be learned by rote. That is, the memorization of doctrinal texts extended to memorizing published expositions of doctrine such as the *Church Catechism Broke into Short Questions*.

The next rule relates to the children's being taught precisely those religious doctrines that were most useful for their "private Life, especially such as concern Faith & Good Manners." The fifth paints a vivid picture of the decorum expected of the children as they attended church services. The schoolmistress was to escort her students to the church from the schoolhouse "in a decent & orderly Manner" before the service begins. They would join in the service fully, repeating what the minister said as directed, but "in such a Manner as not to disturb the rest of the Congregation." Their teacher was to take care that as soon as they were able to use them, the children would carry their Bibles and prayer books into the church with them. (From the children's point of view, the ownership of these religious texts represented the tangible rewards of their education.) To prevent idleness on the Sabbath, the schoolmistress was to assign "some Task out of the most useful Parts of Scripture, to be learnt on each Lord's Day . . . & shall require a strict Performance of it every Monday Morning." (Cotton Mather would surely have approved.)

The sixth rule focuses on prayers. The schoolmistress was to use appropriate prayers every morning and evening and teach the children how to say grace before and after their meals. This was the only occasion in which the teaching of comprehension was mentioned without invoking a publication designed to teach it. The schoolmistress herself was to explain to the children "the Design & Meaning" of saying grace. In the seventh rule, the relationship between Anglicanism and social control emerges all too clearly. The schoolmistress was to take particular care of the children's manners and behavior. She would oblige her students to learn by heart all those parts of the scriptures "where Christians are commanded to be faithful & obedient to their Masters, to be diligent in their Business, & quiet & peaceable to all Men." These were the scriptural passages that would be invoked for a century by Southerners seeking biblical support for the institution of slavery.[106] The last rule turned to the nonliteracy portions of the curriculum and noted that the girls were to be taught knitting and sewing. The schoolmistress was to keep a close watch on the children between school hours, lest they fall into "any indecent Diversions."

The primary author of this document was probably William Yates, whose name precedes that of Nicholas as joint signer of the letter. Its attention to decorum in church, for one, suggests an interested party. Its precision about the curriculum also implies someone knowledgeable—and Yates, who, like Nicholas, was a native son of Virginia and a graduate of the College of William and Mary, had been the principal of the Peasley School in Gloucester County, Virginia, before becoming college president.[107]

The "Regulations" for the Williamsburg school have two main implications. For one, they suggest that the expectations for enslaved Africans, as far as reading instruction was concerned, were no different from those held by other men for other targets of philanthropy, such as the children taught in the charity schools funded by the S.P.G. They also suggest that neither Yates nor Nicholas questioned the implicit prohibition against writing instruction for the enslaved. No slave child was to be taught to write, but a school that taught such a child to read did not, in theory, present a problem.

Yates died in the fall of 1764, and Nicholas carried on the correspondence after the fancy flourish of the regulations. There was, however, an eighteen-month gap between that effusion and Waring's letter to Nicholas of March 1764 in which he reiterated his request for details about the school.[108] And then it was December before Nicholas responded. He informed Waring of Yates's death and voiced his opinion on his task of school supervisor. He called it a "very difficult Business," adding, "I find it necessary to manage it with great Delicacy." The mistress continued to be diligent, but he was having a hard time finding her a room to rent for the schoolhouse.[109]

Not until his letter of the following December did Nicholas finally include another list of schoolchildren.[110] This time he did not even guess at the ages of individual children, recording only his assumption that they ranged between four and ten. Mrs. Wager had not kept an account of their dates of arrival and departure "with any scrupulous Exactness," but he thought that they had been there from six months to two and a half years. As for the rules, he had had little success. "[T]he Masters & Mistresses were so averse to every Thing that lookt like Compulsion," he wrote, "that I thought it most adviseable to relax a little in hopes that Things might be put upon a more agreeable Footing." The enrollment was currently up to thirty-four. Because the children had no control over whether they could attend ("they only attend, when there is no Employment for them At Home"), the schoolmistress was willing to instruct any child who turned up.

Few of the children were allowed to stay as long as the three years stipulated by the regulations. Those who did so, "generally learn to read pretty well, & learn their Prayers & Catechism." He was afraid, however, that the good principles they learned at school were all too soon effaced, when the children went home, by the bad examples set them there. As for the schoolmistress, she was elderly and he was afraid that teaching would soon prove to be too much for her. Nor was he hopeful about replacing her. She continued, nonetheless, he said, to take great pains with the children.

The list of children, dated November 1765, that Nicholas enclosed in this letter may be compared with his earlier list of September 1762. It is a frustrating comparison, in that if the children had actually fulfilled their minimal three years of attendance, they would presumably just escape appearing on the second list anyway. Nonetheless, it is possible to make some inferences about the schooling the children received. In the new list of 1765, the sex ratio is even more in favor of boys, by nineteen to fifteen. Only three of the children on the first list were still in school three years later. Two, John and Doll, now aged about ten, were owned by John Blair, whose superior status was denoted by "Esquire." (He was probably the John Blair born in 1689 to a prominent Virginia family.) The third, named Roger, was now also aged about ten; he was the property of Peyton Randolph, Esquire. There is no clear reason why some children stayed and others left. Randolph, for instance, had had another seven-year-old enslaved African, named Aggy, at the school in 1762. Yet Aggy, unlike his age-mate Roger, was no longer at school in 1765. Not one of the four children who were aged three in 1762 had continued, although they might be expected to have done so, given their extreme youth. Even the slaveholders had changed. Seventeen families had sent children to the school in 1762; eighteen did so three years later. But only seven of those eighteen families appear on the earlier list.

Those of the slaveholders who appear on both lists perhaps offer the most revealing insights of all. Mrs. Campbell had sent three boys in 1762, aged six and seven: London, Aggy, and Shropshire. In 1765 she was still sending children, but now it was Young and Mary. Similarly, Dr. Carter's George, aged six, has been replaced by Nancy. George Davenport and his wife had sent three children in 1762: three-year-old Dick, six-year-old Anne, and eight-year-old John. Now, in 1765, not one of these remains; instead, Mrs. Davenport has sent a child named

William. Anthony Hay's Rippon, aged three, has now been replaced by Jerry. We can only speculate about whether the children had completed, in contemporary terms, their education in reading.

Out of all the slaveholders, only Blair showed a continuing commitment to the education of his slaves. In 1762 he had sent seven-year-old Doll and John, together with nine-year-old Jane; three years later he was still sending Dolly and John, along with five more children—Elizabeth, Catherine, Fanny, Isaac, and Johanna. For the other slaveholders, the school served their needs rather than the children's.

In a third list provided by Nicholas in February 1769, girls predominate by eighteen to twelve. Only four children appear on both this list and that of 1765. Two of them were again the slaves of John Blair. A third child, Mary Ashby, was free, and her brother John appears for the first time. Once again, there has been a considerable turnover of slaveholders: only six on this list were also on that of 1765. The slaveholders on the 1769 list represent the wealthier inhabitants, who owned more than just a handful of slaves: as well as Blair and Robert Carter Nicholas himself, now treasurer to the colony, they included the commissary to the bishop and some prosperous craftsmen, innkeepers, and shopkeepers.[111]

The warm relationship between Nicholas and Waring had cooled by the time Nicholas sent his last list. The high cost of renting a room for the school, the salary of twenty-eight pounds for Mrs. Wager (more than any other of the associates' schoolmistresses was receiving), and above all, the vagaries of the exchange rate between England and Virginia all combined to make the Williamsburg enterprise by far the most costly of the associates' schools. It clearly engendered some resentment among the associates' donors, who were well aware of the great wealth that many Virginia planters enjoyed. According to Waring, himself a regular contributor to the associates' funds, "it might have been reasonably expected that such a Scheme would have met with liberal Encouragment on the Spot, without being indebted to Strangers for its Support."[112] Nicholas corresponded once a year and stayed within the new limits of twenty-five pounds that the associates set in 1769. In one of his last letters to the associates, in December 1772, he reiterates the obvious, that there was "far from being a general Disposition" to promote the school's success. The reasons, he wrote, "which I first foresaw & mention'd to you, will forever work an Indifference in the Generality of the Owners of Negroes as to the Education & Instruction of their Children."[113]

In fact, Nicholas had never detailed the reasons for the general indifference of Virginia gentlemen to the education of enslaved children. We can assume, however, that these men held the same prejudices as those whom Franklin described as believing that "Reading & Knowledge in a Slave are both useless and dangerous." The only real impetus, therefore, to sending the enslaved to school was the Christianity of the slaveholder. But a great many slaveholders were either not Christians themselves or were Christians unconvinced of the need to offer much in the way of instruction to their slaves. Only men like Robert Carter Nicholas or John Blair, deeply committed to their faith and determined to propagate it, undertook to support education in reading with any seriousness.

It is impossible to know how much progress the children who attended the

Negro schools funded by the associates or the S.P.G. made in reading. In 1819, a church historian of Charles Town noted, there were still "coloured persons now living here, who were taught by [Harry and Andrew] to read."[114] But whatever progress the enslaved made, the paradox of their situation remained the same: they were being educated, but for servitude alone. Their literacy was designed to confirm their condition, not relieve it. Reading instruction was subsumed to their hoped-for conversion to Anglicanism, a denomination that at the time saw no incompatibility between Christianity and slavery. The double message sent to the children would be articulated many decades later by other, adult, slaves who embraced reading as their key to freedom but found it a double-edged sword. In the words of Frederick Douglass, who was able to read antislavery arguments, "I would at times feel that learning to read had been a curse rather than a blessing. It had given me a view of my wretched condition, without the remedy."[115] Was it this anguish and torment that drove Harry, the enslaved schoolmaster at the Charles Town Negro School, to the madhouse?

It is striking how universal the assumption was, even among those prepared to offer their enslaved Africans some education, that it was legitimate to teach reading but not writing. This assumption illustrates the unstated but deeply held belief among colonists that writing acquisition was somehow the hallmark of the free. Quite apart from its potential for forging a pass, it marked a person's identity in a way that the skill of reading did not. And it did so in a context in which writing was viewed, pedagogically, as just another vehicle for conveying the ideas of others by copying them. This impression is reinforced by a look at apprenticeship indentures for free Africans in Williamsburg. Where educational provisions are made, they include the familiar ones that male apprentices should be taught both to read and to write.[116]

In contrast, reading was permissible for slaves because it allowed them access to scriptural doctrine. In a letter to the S.P.G. in 1716, Francis Le Jau, the South Carolina missionary who befriended Benjamin Dennis, sketched the ideal vision of the slave as a reader: "Our Baptized Negroes . . . have behaved themselves very well upon all occasions. . . . [T]hey prayd, and read some part of their Bibles in the field and in their Quarters, in the hearing of those who could not read; and took no notice of some Profane who laught at their Devotions."[117]

This comforting vision of the consequences of reading acquisition—devout and trustworthy slaves—was not, however, the whole story. In another letter to the secretary of the S.P.G., written in 1710, Le Jau also suggests that reading acquisition by the enslaved was fraught with potential problems. In his letter he recounts the story of an enslaved African in his Goose Creek parish in South Carolina, whom he describes as "the best Scholar of all" and a "very sober and honest Liver." This man had acquired a book in which he had read a description of the judgments that would chastise men on the last day. It had made a deep impression on him, and he warned his master of the coming of "a dismal time [when] the Moon wou'd be turned into Blood."[118]

Le Jau summoned the man, who told him that he had read about the judgments in a book. But when he refused to show the book, Le Jau "charged him not to put his own Constructions upon his reading after that manner." Some other slaves, however, had overheard the booklover's conversation with his master, and rumors began to circulate that an angel had come and spoken to the man, and that "he had seen a hand that gave him a Book, he had heard Voices, seen fires." Le Jau did his best to tamp down this wildbrush blaze, taking care "to undeceive those who asked me about it." But the warning was obvious: "I fear that those Men have not judgment enough to make a good Use of their Learning," he wrote; "and I have thought most convenient not to urge too far that Indians and Negroes shou'd be indifferently admitted to learn to read." He even extended the dangers of reading to a more general audience: "I have often observed and lately hear that it had been better if persons of a Melancholy Constitution or those that run into the Search after Curious matter had never seen a Book." Reading, in short, could lead to misinterpretation, could arouse the imagination to a fever pitch, could even drive a man mad.[119]

Perhaps the important point to note is that the "book" that led to all this could only have been the Bible. Le Jau admitted as much in his next letter: "our best Negro Scholar . . . put his own Construction upon some Words of the Holy Prophets which he had read; the thing indeed is inconsiderable in itself, but I fear the Consequences." The source was probably the Book of Revelations. Angels feature largely therein, while the twelfth verse of the sixth chapter reads: "And, lo, there was a great earthquake; and the sun became black as sackcloth of hair, and the moon became as blood; And the stars of heaven fell unto the earth." If the Bible could be misinterpreted, no text was safe from the constructions—or, rather, the misconstructions—of the unlearned.[120]

Once again, the word *inconveniences* occurs in the discussion. In another letter Le Jau commented on "the inconveniences which I perceive . . . to arise from the bad use some Slaves make of their reading, so as to discompose their heads, and do some harm to their fellow slaves; I forbear urging too far the exercise of reading among them."[121] Only previously sanctioned interpretations, in short, were permissible in a culture of bondage.

Instruction in reading the scriptures, therefore, was not the safe activity that its supporters once supposed, and the day would come when southern states in a young United States would prohibit it with as much ferocity as they prohibited writing instruction.[122]

10

Writing Instruction

The notion that the ability to write was an essential part of what it meant to be free is not easily inferred from historical discussions of writing. In eighteenth-century America, writing was lauded for its extraordinary benefits in equipping the novice to participate in society rather than for its value to the writer. Indeed, as I argue in this chapter, there was an inherent contradiction between the formal properties of writing instruction and its subtext. The former stressed self-control, discipline, submission to the desires of another (writing was presumed to occur in a work setting), and laborious work; the latter viewed writing as a gateway to self-expression and self-identification. Once children had practiced the disciplined aspects of writing, their wish to express themselves emerged as they heeded the more subversive subtexts of writing instruction in unauthorized marginal notations in their copy books, in diaries, and in "familiar" letters of their own composition.

A second argument made in this chapter is that writing instruction reflected, and was a part of, the wider world of commerce and culture, which was becoming increasingly more complex, more elaborated, and more similar to its counterpart in England. In this sense, writing was a reflection of changes in the society at large, and the elaboration, expansion, and replication of the tools of writing instruction were just one manifestation of this tendency.

We begin with the actual process of writing instruction. Like those who taught reading, American writing masters depended heavily on books imported from England for both the form and content of their instruction. When they looked for content alone to obtain "copies," as they were called—those sentences they could set their students to copy—they turned to English spelling books or to what we would term self-help manuals. Most of these provided several pages of printed maxims and poems suitable for the novice penman. The *Youth's Instructor* of 1757, the spelling book known as the "New England Spelling Book" compiled from several imported English spelling books, contains many such "copies." Because such texts were designed to be written on a page line by line, without spilling over onto the line below, they were most often either snappy sentences, brisk imperatives, or poems—which by definition had lines of roughly equal length. Some of the sample one-line copies in the *Youth's Instructor* contain every letter of the alphabet, such as, "A dazzling Triumph quickly flown, is but a gay Vexation." (This omits the letter *J*, a symptom of its still shaky status as an independent letter.)[1] This was the eighteenth-century equivalent of the typist's "The quick brown fox jumped over the lazy dogs."

Another single-line copy, which also appears in the 1757 *Youth's Instructor*, is a poem that covers all the features of penmanship the young writer must learn. Self-restraint and control are involved in all that he (for the poem appears to be directed solely at boys) is to do. Because the initial letters of each line of the poem are in alphabetical order, the text jumps around in its topic selection. Nonetheless, the poem's series of imperatives can be seen to cluster around several themes. The learner is instructed on preparing his writing materials, on maintaining a proper posture, ruling lines, holding his pen, and cleaning up after himself. Hints are given on improving the look of his piece (regularity is key) and on measures to take in emergencies, such as blots. His relationship with his schoolmates is speci-fied: he is urged to assist younger boys, yet compete with his peers. He is never to play or quarrel in school time. Predictably, he is informed that practice makes perfect.

> All Letter ev'n at Head and Feet must stand;
> Bear lightly on thy Pen, and keep a steady Hand.
> Carefully mind to end in every Line.
> Down Strokes make black, and upward Strokes make fine.
> Enlarge thy Writing if it be too small.
> Full in Proportion make thy Letters all,
> Game not in School-time, when thou ought'st to write,
> Hold in thy Elbow; and sit fair to th'Light.
> Join all thy letters with a fine Hair-stroke.
> Keep free from Blots thy Piece and Writing-Book.
> Learn the Command of Hand by frequent Use:
> Much Practice doth to Penmanship conduce.
> Never deny the lower Boys Assistance:
> Observe from Word to Word an equal Distance.
> Provide thy self with All things necessary:
> Quarrel thou not in School tho' others dare thee.
> Rule straight thy Lines, be sure to rule them fine;
> Set Stems of Letters fair above the Line.
> The Heads above the Stem, the Tails below.
> Use Pounce to Paper, if the Ink go thro',
> View well thy Piece: compare how much thou'st mended;
> Wipe clean thy Pen, when all thy Task is ended.
> Young Men your Spelling mind; write each word true and well;
> Zealously strive your Fellow to excel.[2]

The emphasis that these instructions laid on the definition of writing as pen-manship and learning as self-discipline was characteristic. Those who wrote about writing discussed it as the formation of elegant alphabetical letters. In this "Poem on Writing," written some time before 1712, the London writing master George Bickham identifies the virtues of the written word. It allows men to communicate across vast distances, whether to conduct business or maintain friendships: "For by this Art with distant Worlds they dealt. . . . And all the Joys of absent Friends they felt." Furthermore, writing "supports our Learning, Merchandize, & Arts, / Religion, Hist'rys of the World & Men." Bickham's final tribute to writing sits solidly within the tradition of the dedicated penman. Mere men are not qualified to sing its divine praises.

> Writing! O Heav'nly Art! W[ha]t skill can raise
> An Earthly Voice so high, to sing thy praise?
> Thy Merit is above our mortal Lays.[3]

What Bickham omits from his poem is as informative as what he includes and appears to reflect how the writing masters of the eighteenth century conducted their classes. Nowhere does Bickham mention the role that writing plays in composition, literary or otherwise. True, men and women compose whenever they write letters to their friends, but there is no hint in the poem that new genres of composition, writing designed to charm or amuse—such as the essays published in the *Spectator*—are of any consequence. Rather than teaching a child to express himself, the writing masters focused on those aspects of writing instruction that looked to its form, its purely visual properties. The job of the writing master was to teach a variety of scripts, and the fundamental task of the student was to learn how to represent the words of others in these scripts.

Bickham also alludes tangentially to another crucial aspect of writing instruction: its use in "Merchandize." Writing, as we have seen, was the indispensable prerequisite to mathematics instruction, and it is joined with accounting in the earliest of our records. In 1645 in New Haven, it will be recalled, Mr. Pearce had offered to teach children writing and arithmetic; in 1667 in Boston, Will Howard was given permission to "keep a wrighting schoole, to teach childere to writte and to keep accounts." The link between writing instruction and the teaching of mathematics and bookkeeping was very strong: many of the late seventeenth-century and early eighteenth-century London writing masters who published copybooks also wrote business texts. (George Bickham was one of them.)[4]

It may seem odd to postpone a discussion of writing instruction until the tenth chapter of a book on literacy instruction. It is not until the eighteenth century, however, that we have any evidence of *how* writing was taught in the American colonies. The seventeenth-century sources, as we have seen, frequently mention the teaching of writing in the context of town schooling and colonial legislation, but they focus on the fact of instruction, not its methodology. What evidence we have for that century is indirect: the fruits of instruction that appeared in the scripts of adults.

The eighteenth century saw major changes in writing instruction. The change did not occur in the discipline itself—writing masters had always viewed writing instruction as an exercise in fine handwriting and would continue to do so—but in the world served by this penmanship and the clientele that penmanship would now reach. The increasing secularism, commercialism, and affluence of eighteenth-century America proved a boon to literacy in writing. The altered climate fostered a movement toward a practical, commercially relevant education, which enhanced the prestige of the writing masters. At the same time, the relative affluence of Americans permitted an increasing number of the "middling" sort to desire education in penmanship for their daughters as well as their sons. And, finally, the new climate promoted the increased importation of the materials required for writing. As a result, writing instruction became more valued and more available in the American provinces than ever before. Provincial lawmakers would reflect—and promote—this change by enshrining it in their revisions of the Poor Laws, eventually requiring girls as well as boys to learn to write. Parallel to this change would run a new enthusiasm for letter writing. Particularly after 1750, as Konstantin Dierks has documented in some detail, letter writing would become more popular among all classes and ages than it had ever been.[5]

The first external change that had beneficial consequences for writing instruction was a growing interest throughout the American provinces, most easily seen in New England, in an education that was considered more attuned to the commercial job market than was the traditional classical curriculum of the Latin grammar schools, which still served as the preparation for the ministry and law. As Jon Teaford has documented, from the 1670s on, even wealthy Massachusetts townships became more reluctant to support grammar schools. Some outlying townships could genuinely argue that Indian attacks made school attendance dangerous. Both the county courts and the General Court became correspondingly averse to presenting such towns for noncompliance, either ignoring violations of the law that required townships of over one hundred families to support Latin grammar schools or hesitant to impose fines on the towns that were presented. After 1700, Connecticut restricted its town-funded grammar schools to four, one for each county seat: New Haven, New London, Hartford, and (but only until 1755) Fairfield. New Hampshire, which split off from Massachusetts in 1679, maintained grammar schools regularly in only a few townships.[6]

As New England's town system of schooling evolved, it was initially the town schoolmaster, as we saw earlier, who was expected to instruct boys in penmanship. Recall that Jeremiah Peck at the colony of New Haven in 1661 had hoped to dodge the chore of teaching writing at his ambitious Latin grammar school but was ordered to do so by the colony anyway. In the seventeenth century perhaps only in Boston, because of its size and its sponsorship of a Latin grammar school, was a writing master salaried to aid the grammar school master, and even that arrangement did not last long. Private writing masters filled the gap.[7]

The turn of the seventeenth into the early eighteenth century saw a decided shift by several New England townships in favor of separate, town-funded schools actually designated "writing schools." In Connecticut, several small towns sponsored writing masters, while the number of the province's grammar schools decreased. The creation of writing schools was a response to a transatlantic movement that was growing in force by the end of the seventeenth century, favoring a business education over a classical one. So powerful was this movement, designed to equip clerks for the expanding needs of international commerce, that in 1699 Samuel Pepys could count sixty-four private writing masters residing in the cities of London and Westminster. The changes in Boston provide the clearest example of this trend in provincial America. As early as 1682 the city voted that there should be "one or more Free Schooles" for the "teachinge of Children to write & Cypher within this towne." The Writing School in Queen Street was opened in 1684, followed by the North Writing School in 1700 and the South Writing School in 1720. Meanwhile the opening of a second Latin grammar school in 1712 did not redress the growing imbalance between the number of students pursuing a classical education and those pursuing a technical one in favor of the latter.[8]

The effects on attendance are visible in Boston: the writing schools rapidly overtook the Latin schools in terms of the numbers of pupils they attracted. While numbers varied considerably from year to year, in 1740, 145 boys attended the two grammar schools and 406 attended the three writing schools (270 of these at the North Writing School); two years later the grammar schools enrolled 159, while the writing schools enrolled 376. (The population of the city was over 16,300.) In 1755, the count of boys attending two of the three writing schools was 453: 216 boys at the South Writing School and 237 at the North.[9]

A second factor in the increasing importance of writing was the enhanced prestige of writing masters and of the profession as a whole. Whereas in reading instruction the book was the crucial element, in writing instruction what mattered most was the master. Professionalism reached new heights in eighteenth-century America. Boston, once again, provides the most vivid example of the writing master's enhanced status. Although the city voted annually on schoolmasters, appointments were normally for a lifetime. (Only one dismissal in Boston for incompetence is recorded.) Such was the distinction of the job and so sought after were teaching positions at its three town-funded writing schools that from 1733 to 1775 the schools fielded only eight writing masters among them, because the same man would often move from one school to another as he advanced through the system, rising from usher (assistant) to master (in one school) to senior writing master. All positions drew town salaries.[10]

As was often true with crafts, the position tended to run in families. Abia Holbrook senior, for example, a kegmaker and sometime gravedigger, produced three writing masters. Two of them were his sons, Abiah Junior, born in 1718, and Samuel, born in 1729; the third was a grandson, also Abiah, the child of yet another son, Elisha. Samuel served as usher to his brother Abiah at the South Writing School until he left to become a junior master for a year at the Writing School in Queen Street. This sharing of power with the senior master seems not to have suited him, and he taught in the private sector for the next fifteen years, until he was chosen to succeed his brother upon Abiah's death, at the age of fifty in 1769. Samuel took over the South Writing School until the war closed it six years later. Similarly, the youngest Abiah Holbrook became an usher at the Queen Street school in the fall of 1773, a week after the premature death of John Proctor Jr. The latter was another example of familial craftsmanship: his father, John Proctor senior (a teacher legendary for his severity), had been master of the North Writing School from 1731 to 1743.[11]

This record of climbing the professional ladder in town-funded positions obscures an important fact: the years of training that had already taken place before a young man was qualified to get his foot on the lowest rung of the salaried ladder and become an usher. Abiah Holbrook Jr., who would eventually exceed all his peers in reputation, had begun to learn his craft as a young man apprenticed to John Proctor at the North Writing School. In May 1741, by then twenty-three, he invoked his experience in a petition to the town to permit him to open a private school "to teach Writing and Arithmetick (he being bro't Up thereto by Mr John Proctor and by him Recommended)." He taught at this private school in Boston for a year, leaving it for the position of usher to Proctor when that job opened up in August of the following year. Eight months after that, Holbrook became the master of the South Writing School. Similarly, his nephew Abiah Holbrook had an extended period of training at his uncle's hands at the South Writing School before he was appointed usher to James Carter at the Writing School in Queen Street in 1773.[12]

By the middle of the eighteenth century, as Ray Nash has noted, the Boston writing masters were at their apogee of prestige and material success. Their salaries varied according to the demands of their position, but from 1750 on, masters of the North and South schools were paid £100 a year, while the two masters teaching together at the Writing School in Queen Street were paid £80 each from 1755 until 1762, when the salary for the senior of the two was raised to £100. Sporting wigs, armed with ferules (canes), and enjoying high community visibility, they were a commanding presence on the Boston scene.[13]

The number of professional books that writing masters could use for their craft grew in number in England during the early eighteenth century, aided by the invention of copperplate engraving and printing, which had transformed the publication of copybooks in Europe as early as the sixteenth century. Copperplating would not, however, have an impact on printing in the American colonies until after the American Revolution. Rare was the American who had the technical skill and financial capital to print writing copybooks in domestic versions.

The most inhibiting factor was cost. Even copperplate copies for students—those printed slips that the "scholars" could use as models to spare the writing master the repetitive task of setting copies individually—were expensive. When, in the early 1750s, Anthony Benezet was asked by a young schoolmaster friend to purchase some copies for him to use with his students, Benezet refused to do so because of their price, saying that twenty-four copperplate copies alone cost two shillings and sixpence. We do not have sales figures for the set of text copies that William Thorne, a Philadelphia writing master and accountant, advertised in the *Pennsylvania Gazette* in 1763 as executed in the "large modern Round Text, for the Use of Schools." But we do know that the copybook composed by Thomas Powell, master of a boarding school in Burlington, New Jersey, and engraved in copperplate did not do well. He published *The Writing Master's Assistant* in 1764, with its subtitle announcing "a concise and practical System (in Copper Plate) for teaching to write" and accompanied by directions on "how to hold the Pen, how to sit, and how to use the Plates." Benezet bought four of Powell's copybooks at five shillings each but had to return the remainder to their author, "as I cannot persuade People to purchase them, other Books of that kind being to be had, of our Booksellers at a lower Price."[14] The very few domestically engraved and printed copybooks, in other words, proved to be even more expensive than imported ones.

The only examples of copies readily available to an American student—and no professional writing master would have considered them adequate—were those made by being engraved on wood. Benjamin Franklin, with his keen eye on what was needed by the young in literacy acquisition, included some of them in his *American Instructor* of 1748 (his slightly Americanized version of that quintessential self-help book, Fisher's *Young Man's Best Companion*). The work contains some instructions on how to hold and make pens, and the copies include the Italian and secretary hands, a print script, and "An easy Copy for Round Hand," which the engraver had based on Franklin's own handwriting. Students wishing for models of German scripts could also find some: Christopher Saur featured four pages of woodcuts displaying the German running gothic in his German-American calendar for 1754.[15]

Most American writing masters, therefore, had to acquire copybooks either by bringing them over in person, if they had immigrated from Britain, or by purchasing imported copies. The copybooks in the possession of the Abiah Holbrook who taught at Boston's South Writing School from 1743 until his death convey an idea of their number and their extent. Holbrook's collection of twenty copybooks includes one that dates from before the turn of the century (John Seddon's *The Pen-mans Paradis Both Pleasant and Profitable*), but the remainder were printed— all of them in London—between 1700 and 1726. George Bickham was represented by his *Round-Text* and *Round-Hand*, John Langton by copybooks on the round hand and small Italian hand, and Charles Snell by his *Art of Writing in It's* [sic] *Theory and Practice*. Holbrook was also able to consult, among others, three titles by George Shelley (one of them his *Natural Writing in All the Hands*), William Brooks's *Delightful Recreation for the Industrious*, and an arithmetic text by Thomas Weston. By 1750, dozens of additional copybooks were available in London for potential export to America. Twenty-eight different copybook titles were advertised in 1750 by J. H. Overton of London, with prices ranging from six shillings for George Bickham's *United Pen-men* to one pound five shillings for Bickham's complete *Universal Penman*.[16]

Of all the texts used by American writing masters and their students, the *Universal Penman* was probably the most important. The work's originator and engraver, George Bickham, whose "Poem on Writing" is quoted above, was a London writing master who began to collect samples of penmanship from his colleagues in 1733. He engraved their contributions and issued his compilation of their work in fifty-two irregular installments over the course of the following decade. *The Universal Penman* was designed to display the range of contemporary talent on hand around London: twenty-six writing masters, including Bickham himself, contributed to it.[17]

Imports of Bickham's work were not restricted to Boston, although advertisements for it in other provinces were relatively rare. A couple of notices for it appeared in the *Pennsylvania Gazette* in 1751, and the work was purchased for the use of Alexander Seaton's school at Philadelphia in 1762. Other imported copy-books were advertised over the years, none of them frequently: because they were aimed at instructors rather than students, they were expensive items that attracted only a small clientele. William Milne, who ran a night school in Philadelphia, inserted a notice in the *Pennsylvania Gazette* in 1751 that he was selling some "curious Copper-plate books" that included, in addition to copybooks by Bick-ham, works by Charles Snell, Thomas Ollyffe, and Edward Cocker. Cocker was in his prime in the 1660s and 1670s, Snell and Ollyffee in the early 1700s. (Works by Bickham and Snell had found their way into the collection of Abiah Holbrook.) The *South Carolina Gazette* ran a notice in the summer of 1767 for Joseph Cham-pion's copy books "in all the various hands of Great Britain, with the Greek, Hebrew and German characters." (Champion had contributed over forty pages to the *Universal Penman*, one of them an internal advertisement for Bickham's work that declared, written in a beautiful round hand, that nothing, in Champion's opinion, could be "more Advantageous to the Publick than the Work" in which Bickham was engaged.) The *South Carolina Gazette* advertised Champion's *Pen-man's Employment* the following year.[18]

A third element that contributed to the popularity and importance of writing instruction was the increased desire among middling folk for gentility. From the middle of the century on, as Richard Bushman has documented, the aspiration to gentility in all aspects of life, from one's dwelling place to one's household goods, animated many who formerly had neither the time nor the money, and perhaps not even the inclination for it. Only in the eighteenth century did the writing desk made its appearance as a genteel addition to the household, eloquent of business and social correspondence alike.[19]

Aspirations to gentility were accompanied by, and in part the result of, a general growth in prosperity, which featured an increasing number of servants and slaves whose toil spared slaveholders from the grinding chores of earlier times. The skill of writing had long been considered a necessity for boys but a suitable activity only for elite girls. Now, as the notion of gentility spread down the social scale, writing instructors were able to capitalize on a view of penmanship that placed it in the forefront of the genteel arts that girls should acquire.

English writing masters had experienced a major change of heart about the desirability of courting female pupils. At first, early seventeenth-century English writing masters had followed the example of their continental predecessors by promoting the notion that young women should be taught a particular script, the Italian hand. The rationale was that because women are naturally flighty, they need a script that is quick to execute and easy to learn. As Martin Billingsley, author of the *Pens Excellencie* of 1618, phrased it, women "(having not the patience to take any great paines . . .) must be taught that which they may easily learne . . . because their minds are (upon light occasion) easily drawn from the first resolution."[20]

Writing masters of the following century, in contrast, realized how important a female clientele was to their financial stability and were much less inclined to alienate their potential pupils. They began to couch their promotion of instruction in terms that stressed women's beauty and delicacy, not their flightiness and inability to concentrate. In 1717 William Brooks designed and published, in London, a copybook expressly for the "Ladies of Great Britain," calling it *A Delightful Recreation for the Industrious*. (A copy found its way into the professional collection of Abiah Holbrook.) "As I have largely provided for the instruction of those of my own Sex, in the Art of Fair Writing," he wrote—using the Italian script to do so— "so I esteem it my duty to endeavour ye Perfection of your Qualifications, by presenting you with an imitable Specimen of the Italian Hand, which, as your own, I recommend to your choice and practice, being full of Beauty, Ornament and Delight, & invented for the Sole use and Embellishment of your fair Sex." (No example of girls or women using the Italian hand in eighteenth-century America seems to be extant. Busy writing masters offering girls private instruction used the standard round hand.)[21]

The same motif is continued in the poem "The Penman's Advice . . . To Young Ladies" by the London writing master Samuel Vaux, dated 1734, which appears in Bickham's *Universal Penman*. It draws parallels between the skills young women demonstrate in embroidery (that is, nonfunctional sewing) and those needed for writing (implicitly identified as nonutilitarian penmanship).

> With Admiration in your Works are read
> The various Textures of the twining Thread.
> Then let the Fingers, whose unrivall'd Skill,
> Exalts the Needle, grace the Noble Quill.

Poor writing, the poem continues, is a disgrace to the beauty of the writer:

> An artless Scrawl ye blushing Scribler shames;
> All shou'd be fair that Beauteous Woman frames.

Calligraphy may even have a role in nourishing an incipient romance:

> Strive to excell, with Ease the Pen will move;
> And pretty lines add Charms to infant Love.[22]

Vaux's poem is representative of appeals by writing masters for female pupils based on the propriety and genteel advantages of their learning to write a fair hand. Penmanship was, just as it had been earlier for Cotton Mather's daughter Katy, a key marker of the young gentlewoman.

A fourth factor that both promoted, and was affected by, the eighteenth-century emphasis on the craft of writing was an expansion in the availability of writing materials and stationery. The expansion occurred at different times in different provinces at their respective stages of development, beginning in the 1730s. After the end of the Seven Years' War in 1760, luxury items of stationery began to appear and from the early 1760s on, there was no newspaper printed in a port city that did not advertise a full range of imported stationery with all the newest and trendiest items. By the 1770s, all provinces were importing similar stationery items. This is hardly surprising: to a very great extent, the items advertised had been loaded onto ships headed to different destinations but originally moored to the docks of the same British port of origin.

Newspaper advertisements for writing implements reaffirm the argument that, in the area of writing, the 1730s and 1740s were decades of transition, while the 1750s and 1760s represented what Jack Greene calls *social elaboration*.[23] The earliest advertisement to be specific about the tools of writing and writing instruction, rather than just the vague "all Sorts of Stationery," was placed by William Parks in October 1730 in his own newspaper, the *Maryland Gazette*, which he had launched three years earlier. Parks, who had been involved in at least three provincial newspapers in England and had just returned from a trip to London, felt confident about what provincial southerners would buy: "Large and small Copy-Books, with Copies ready wrote in several curious Hands, for Youths to learn to write by; Blank Copy Books; School-Boys Peices, Pen-knives, Quills, Pens, Ink-Horns, Ink-Powder." It would be thirteen years before any Boston paper would be so specific. In December 1743 Joshua Blanchard placed a lengthy advertisement in the *Boston Weekly News-Letter* specifying writing equipment: "Paper of all sorts; Books for Accounts and Records; Blanks; Ink-Stands, Ink-Powder; Sealing-Wax; Slates; Spectacles; black-lead pencils; Ivory-Books."[24] In Blanchard's list, slates and sealing wax are new refinements, and slate pencils would be advertised a few years later. By 1755 slates and slate pencils had appeared in the *South Carolina Gazette*, and they were soon being advertised across the colonies.[25]

Paper, by far the most common surface on which all this equipment would be used, was also featured in advertisements. From an early period, paper had been manufactured in England in a small range of qualities and sizes. In 1660, for instance, when the British Parliament issued its list of rates on imports, paper was categorized into "Blew, Browne, Cap, Demy[,] Ordinary printing & copy paper." In colonial newspapers, the earliest advertisements simply list "Paper of all sorts," as did Blanchard. The first American paper mill was not built until 1691, outside Philadelphia, and the construction of other domestic mills followed. By the early 1750s, the variety of imported writing paper (more likely to be used for writing than the cheap newsprint produced locally) was already considerable. In the *New-York Mercury*, its printer, Hugh Gaine, advertised "cut Post, and common Writing Paper, by the Sheet or Quire," in the fall of 1752, but by the next summer the choice was far broader: "Imperial, Medium, Royal, Demy, Post, and common Writing-Paper." Less than a year later, New York residents could purchase gilt and black-edged paper, marble paper and ruled paper for music.[26]

A refinement already advertised by Parks was unquestionably powdered ink. Ink could be made at home, and it indeed was, not only in the early decades of colonial settlement but presumably much later in any home far from a country store. Young Harry Willis, a schoolboy at Nomini Hall in Virginia with plenty of access to ready made ink, made a "red Ink or Liquid" for fun in 1774 by boiling up a concoction whose main ingredients were pokeberries, vinegar, and sugar. Recipes for making ink continued to be a standard feature in certain books, from spelling books to almanacs, well into the nineteenth century, while bottled ink would not be man-

ufactured in the United States until 1825.[27] Nevertheless, imported ink in powdered form was available at least as early as 1730, when Parks advertised it in the
Maryland Gazette. It was a common product by the 1750s and 1760s, when it was
offered for sale in the south, the middle colonies, and New England.[28]

Ink powder did not come cheap. Jeremiah Condy, a Boston merchant, was
selling packets of an unidentified brand of ink in the 1760s for ten shillings a
dozen, or ten pence each. In Virginia, the retail price ranged from one to two
shillings each. In Charles Town, South Carolina, James Poyas was selling ink
packets at the same period for £1-2-6 for a half dozen. Even accounting for the
vagaries of intercolonial currencies, these were not prices within reach of the poor.
The great charm of ink powder, and one that justified its cost for those who could
afford it, was that all one had to do to produce liquid ink was to add water.[29]

From the mid 1740s, inkpots were being advertised all over the Atlantic sea-
board, in brass, leather, and horn. By the early 1750s they could also be purchased
in pewter and flint glass. Inkstands to support the inkpots soon evolved from the
prosaic wooden ones advertised in 1751 to pewter ones with their matching inkpots a mere three years later.[30]

Besides paper, ink, and an inkpot, the prospective writer needed a pen. Quill
pens were made, as the term suggests, from feathers plucked from birds, ideally
from large ones such as geese or swans. (Primary wing feathers were still much
preferred for their strength, just as they had been in the late sixteenth century.)
They needed to be treated with heat as well as sharpened. As it had been for
centuries past, the quill pen was still the standard writing implement of the eighteenth century. It would remain so until a way was found to produce flexible steel
nibs by machine, as late as the 1820s. A fountain pen was advertised in Philadelphia in 1749 but seems not to have caught on; tin pens were advertised in Savannah, Georgia, in 1763, alongside brass fountain pens, and steel pens in Salem,
Massachusetts, in 1809.[31] Quill consumption at a writing school could be very
high. In September 1765, John Tileston, master of Boston's North Writing
School, bought ten thousand quills for his own school from the captain of a newly
arrived ship at the cost of forty-five shillings per thousand and purchased another
four thousand for his colleague John Proctor Jr., one of the two masters of the
Writing School in Queen Street. Tileston needed eleven hundred more only a year
later.[32]

Although Parks in Maryland had specified quills as one of his imports in 1730,
quills do not appear in advertisements in Philadelphia until they are identified by
brand as "Dutch quells" [*sic*] in the *Pennsylvania Gazette* in the fall of 1749, and
in New York as "very good Dutch Quills" in Hugh Gaine's *New-York Mercury* in
the summer of 1753. They had been imported into the colonies all along, but their
mention on these dates suggests a specialization of product: "Dutch" quills were
considered high-quality instruments worthy of advertising space.[33] (From the first
entries in his account book in the spring of 1759 up to the last entries in 1770,
Jeremiah Condy sold Dutch quills for a shilling for every twenty-five.) Similarly,
imported "black-lead" pencils were being advertised in the 1740s and "Cedar
Pencils" by the early 1750s.[34] Penknives, although mentioned by Parks in 1730,

also only make their appearance en masse in advertisements from 1753 on, from South Carolina to Boston.[35] A powder for blotting appeared in the form of "Pounce and pounce-Boxes" in advertisements of the mid 1750s. (Pounce could also be made at home by pulverizing chalk and rosin.)[36]

If these stationery items were used in the service of letter writing, another product was needed in order to seal the letter. (Envelopes were not invented until after the close of the colonial period.) The most commonly used was sealing wax, which had been advertised in Boston since the early 1740s. And an alternative product was offered that was faster to use and did not involve melting any wax, a messy procedure at best: wafers. These begin to appear in advertisements for imported wares in the mid 1750s. Wafers packed in at least two different sizes of boxes were obtainable in New York by then, while red and black wafers make their appearance a few years later.[37]

The specification of a product by a brand name was another aspect of the increasing elaboration of writing materials. "Dutch quills" and "Holman's Ink-Powder" were usually advertised in tandem. Dutch quills were promoted in Philadelphia and elsewhere from 1749 on. Similarly, Holman's ink-powder made its first advertised appearance in 1755 and by the mid-1760s was being hawked in newspapers from Providence to New York. The attribution "Dutch" seemed to have selling power, as Dutch sealing-wax was featured in a Virginia newspaper in 1770.[38]

As imports from Britain picked up their pace after the close of the Seven Years' War, one improvement after another could be seen in imported writing materials. Increasing luxury in stationery items appears in the advertisements of the 1760s, often printed in newly founded newspapers that were themselves an indication of changing times. When William Goddard began printing the *Providence (Rhode Island) Gazette: and Country Journal* in October 1762, he wasted no time in running his own advertisement for stationery. He listed account books, "pocketbooks" (a combination of a letter case and a wallet), and "Writing Paper of all Sorts," together with sealing wax, wafers, pencils, and steel cases. (Something to hold pencils in was a new convenience.) A few months later, in April 1763, when James Johnston, proprietor of the printing press in Savannah, Georgia, started the *Georgia Gazette*, he too was quick to advertise the stationery at his printing office. By November, he was selling not just black but now red ink powder, tin pens, brass fountain pens (both novelties), red pencils as well as black, pocket-books and letter-cases, along with quills, sealing wax and wafers. Penknives "of various kinds" were now available.[39] Other advertisements promoted named brands: Clark's leather inkpots, Jones's best penknives, and "supersuperfine Sealing Wax."[40] Writing equipment had entered the luxury market even while the simpler forms were still readily available.

A companion to all these improvements in writing equipment was a new emphasis on the range and number of scripts that a good writing master was able to teach. Advocating the learning of a variety of scripts was not, in itself, an innovation. Since the first printed professional copybooks of the sixteenth century, writing masters had displayed their skill with a range of scripts. What was new from about the 1740s on was that writing masters explicitly advertised their command of a large number of scripts, most of which had no utilitarian value. As James Hovey informed his public in 1742, he was prepared to teach "Arithmetick, and divers Sorts of Writing, viz. English and German Texts; the Court, Roman, Secretary & Italian Hands." (The Court was Elizabethan in age and to modern eyes is wholly indecipherable.) Or, as James Carter put it thirty years later in an advertisement for his Boston evening school, "Such as are curious may learn, besides the usual Hands, Roman, Italian Print, all the black Hands; as old English, German-Text, and every other, even to old Court Hand."[41]

Other advertisements promised the opposite of a wide range of scripts, emphasizing instead a speedy approach to learning the first and most important aspect of writing, legible handwriting. An advertiser in a 1755 Boston newspaper promised to teach "persons of both sexes from twelve to fifty years of age, who never wrote before, to write a good hand in five weeks, at one hour per day." (The notice incidentally revealed how late writing instruction could begin.) Another reminded potential writers of the prerequisites for instruction. Samuel Giles of New York, advertising his New York evening school for writing and arithmetic, in 1762, observed that teaching the rudiments took up too much of a teacher's time, so "for the Future, no Children will be taken but such as have already been taught to Read, and are fit for Writing."[42]

The suggestion that writing could be taught in a few weeks relates to another feature of writing instruction that actually militated against total reliance on a writing master: the importation of copybooks with engraved writing samples for students. William Parks had advertised "Large and small Copy-Books, with Copies ready wrote in several curious Hands, for Youths to learn to write by" as early as 1730 in the *Maryland Gazette*. He seems to have been far ahead of his time, for it is not until the 1750s that we see consistent advertising for "Copy Books for School Boys" in newspapers in Philadelphia and New York. Perhaps deference to its three writing schools kept such advertisements out of the Boston papers, but copybooks were certainly available in Boston by the early 1760s: Condy sold three sets of "Copper Plate copies" then to a customer at a shilling each.[43]

The rise in demand for writing implements and materials may be seen most clearly in Virginia, which had lagged quite dramatically behind the other provinces in advertising stationery. Although the *Virginia Gazette* was first published in 1736 and included advertisements from the beginning, merchants placed only one advertisement for books and stationery before 1760. The decade of the 1760s produced another ten merchants who paid for advertisements—six for both books and stationery, and four more for stationery by itself. Yet during the following decade, the 1770s, nine merchants advertised stationery and books together while an astonishing fifty-two (90 percent of all the stationery advertised between 1736 and 1780) placed advertisements for stationery alone. During that decade, writing apparently assumed an importance for Virginians that it had never reached before.[44]

All of these factors—the movement toward a practical, technical education rather than a classical one, the enhanced prestige of the writing masters, the relative affluence and desire for gentility that enabled American fathers to afford writing instruction for their daughters, and the increased importation of the materials required for writing—promoted writing and benefited from it. The increasing importance of writing instruction for both sexes was reflected in provincial legislation. Around 1750, many provinces made key changes to their Poor Laws that enshrined a major societal shift. Virginia revised its Poor Laws in 1748 to mandate that girls as well as boys be taught to write; New Jersey's new Poor Law of 1758 required both sexes to be taught both literacy skills, and North Carolina's did the same in 1760. In 1771, Massachusetts finally made a long overdue change to its Poor Laws. It had issued a supplement in 1703 and then a clarification in 1710 that specified that boys apprenticed under the law had to be taught to write and read, but girls still only to read. The legislative change in 1771 at last required apprenticed girls to receive writing instruction. New York did not yield until after the Revolution, but in 1788 it, too, required writing of both sexes of poor children.[45] Since these legal modifications reflected societal change rather than promoting it, and since the relevant laws dealt with the bottom of the social heap, better-placed girls were even more likely to be introduced to writing instruction than the children for whom the laws were designed.

The reasons for this change were never articulated in the laws in the relevant legislation, but they were presumably a function of several factors, social as well as economic. From a young woman's perspective, the usefulness of being able to write was undeniable. As young women increasingly found socially sanctioned ways to earn money—not only as teachers of reading and sewing, but as housekeepers, storekeepers, market gardeners, haberdashers, milliners, and midwives—it was crucial for them to be able to write in order to keep records. Advertisements reflect the importance of a woman's being able to write and figure. "A Young Woman," an advertisement in a 1762 Boston newspaper states, "that can be well recommended, can write, cypher, & tend a Shop, or would go into a Gentleman's Family as a House-keeper, wants Employ."[46]

So far in this chapter we have looked at the tendency toward the elaboration, expansion, and replication of the tools of writing instruction from the viewpoint of those who taught it and the materials they used to do so. Another perspective is that of the pupils. The development of children's prowess at calligraphy can be seen from a remarkable collection of manuscript "pieces" penned by boys taught in the three writing schools of Boston in the second half of the eighteenth century and preserved at Houghton Library, Harvard University. Written with quill pens on large foolscap pages, the pieces in the collection offer a unique look at the products of New England's most highly regarded schools of writing instruction.

The entire collection consists of 188 manuscripts written by 117 different boys (many boys wrote more than one piece). Not all manuscripts are dated, but those that are span the years 1748 to 1782. The spacing in time, however, is not uniform: more pieces are preserved from the decade of the 1760s than from any other. Each of the Boston writing schools is represented in the collection: of the 89 pieces that mention their school, 10 were written at the Writing School in Queen Street,

20 at the North Writing School, and 59 at the South Writing School. (During most of the years the South pieces were written, Abiah Holbrook was the master.) Only a minority of the pieces include their authors' ages, but those that do reveal an age range from nine to sixteen years old. The pieces are examples of the boys' best work, which they would have prepared for display at the annual inspections of the school by the Boston school committee each June. School committees consisted of the selectmen and Boston notables. (In 1738, for instance, the inspection group included the two clergymen sons of Samuel Sewall and Cotton Mather, Joseph Sewall and Samuel Mather.)[47]

Higher standards were required of these exhibition pieces as the decades passed. Up to 1757, many of them consisted of what were really beginners' efforts: they are single sentences set by the master at the top of the page and reproduced six times by the student. Their chief claim on the reader's attention is the swirls and birds added by the master for decoration. But from the 1760s on, the quality of the pieces improves dramatically. The better students were expected to produce a dazzling array of scripts, fitting their writing into ever smaller spaces.

The curriculum itself moved in the direction of increasing complexity, but not—at least according to the dated manuscripts in the collection—until 1760. Before that, the only script displayed by the manuscripts is the basic round hand, which had become the standard business hand of the eighteenth century. From 1760 on, students added successive scripts in a set order. The first script, round hand, was learned when they entered the school at the age of seven or so. William Palfrey displayed his efforts at this at the age of perhaps seven or eight.

Learning round hand took several years, and during this time the student might well be exposed to, without being expected to be fully master of, italic print and roman print, and use these for the title of his piece or for his signature. At the age of perhaps ten, he was introduced to the second script, German text, the easier of two gothic scripts. Growth in skill seems to have accelerated now for some boys. The next year the student would perfect his third and fourth scripts, roman print and italic print. If he had the ability, at the age of thirteen or fourteen he would be taught his fifth script, the more difficult gothic known as Old English print. Soon thereafter, by now an accomplished penman, he would add other scripts, such as the Italian script once reserved for women, up to a total of perhaps eight. By this time, his control over spacing and the size of his letter formation was so secure that he was able to write a range of scripts in small geometric spaces. From struggling to imitate the script as well as the words set by his master (as in figure 13), the student had matured to confident mastery of many scripts, now imitating only the words and layout of the "copy" set him (as in figure 14). William Palfrey, aged perhaps thirteen or fourteen, shows how much progress he has made over the course of six years in a dazzling effort penned in 1754. All three writing schools produced examples of this piece, which was clearly the apex of the writing curriculum. His and the other pieces in the collection were indeed a "form of self-presentation but not self-expression," as Tamara Plakins Thornton puts it.[48]

If the curriculum displayed internal elaboration, yet another elaboration within the collection as a whole, and one that meshes well with the increasing amount of

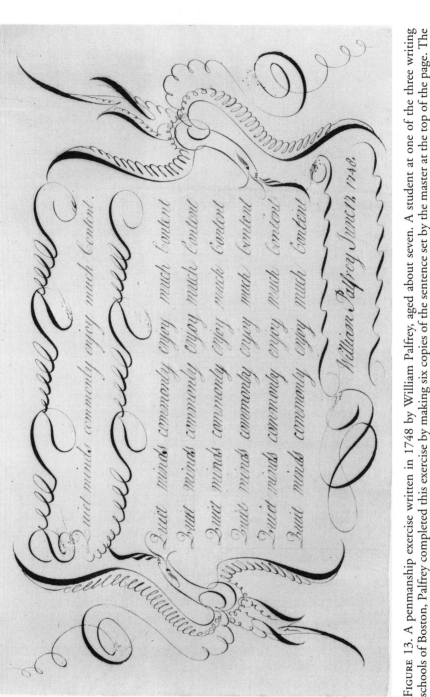

FIGURE 13. A penmanship exercise written in 1748 by William Palfrey, aged about seven. A student at one of the three writing schools of Boston, Palfrey completed this exercise by making six copies of the sentence set by the master at the top of the page. The master added the ornamental birds to spice up the interest of this beginner's piece. (By permission, Pf MS Typ 473.2 UWS [91], Department of Printing and Graphic Arts, Houghton Library, Harvard College Library)

FIGURE 14. A penmanship exercise written in 1754 by William Palfrey, aged about thirteen, now a masterful penman. In his octagons, the central script is German text; from top, clockwise, the scripts are round hand, Old English print, round hand, secretary, round hand, Roman print, round hand, and German text. (By permission, PfMS Typ 473.2 UWS [102], Department of Printing and Graphic Arts, Houghton Library, Harvard College Library)

choice in stationery items during the 1760s, is the use of colored ink. Red ink appears on 104 manuscripts, but never earlier than 1759, when the date is given. In 1763, a third color, blue, appears. On two pieces, green or gray appears as well as black and red. The trend is particularly noticeable in the South Writing School, where Holbrook used all these colors for his "Writing Master's Amusement," a gorgeous manuscript interpretation of the alphabet that devoted a page to each letter. He seems to have permitted boys aged thirteen and older to indulge in new ink colors, obviously a privilege and perhaps an added motivation for a boy who was repeating a piece.

The importance of George Bickham's *Universal Penman* in its American setting emerges clearly from the Houghton manuscript collection. The pieces written by the 117 boys who took classes at the three writing schools of Boston during the 1760s and 1770s show their indebtedness to the plates in Bickham's *Universal Penman*: if we ignore the twenty-five beginners' single-sentence pieces—such as "Quiet minds commonly enjoy much Content"—the original texts of almost two-thirds of the remaining pieces can be found in Bickham's book. While the boys have not always followed the scripts used in a particular piece (some, for example, have substituted round hand for the Italian script in Bickham), they have always followed the wording of the texts with scrupulous fidelity.

Manuscripts found elsewhere in the colonies reveal the continuing emphasis on the value of mastering a range of scripts—only a couple of which, the round hand and the easier gothic, served any utilitarian purpose. James Brown Mason of Providence, Rhode Island, for instance, in his writing book of 1771, wrote alphabets in round text, German text, the old-fashioned secretary hand, Italian, Old English print, and italic print. George Bickham's name appears in an invoice copied by Mason.[49]

If mere students could reach such heights of calligraphy, the skill of their writing masters, who had trodden the path their students trod, could reach far greater heights. The writing master Richard Rogers of Oxford (near Worcester, Massachusetts) wrote a fine piece in August 1759. He used the roman print script and Old English black letter on a one-page manuscript featuring the "Twelve good Rules found in the Study of King Charles the First of Blessed Memory," such as "Prophane No Divine Ordinances . . . Pick No Quarrells . . . Reveal No Secrets." These ancient pieces of advice would have served the decorative function of a picture mounted on a wall, with their bold lettering emphasized by Rogers's stark black vertical braces.[50]

At this level of accomplishment, penmanship enhanced the meaning of the text in a striking way. The finest example is the work of Abiah Holbrook. His masterpiece has survived, a manuscript dubbed "The Writing Master's Amusement." It is a treatment of the letters of the alphabet, one to a page, which Holbrook said in his will he did "only for my amusement" (hence the modern title), "though seven years in compleating them." Although time has dimmed some of its colors—black, red, blue, and olive-green—the beauty of his manuscript remains. Holbrook used Thomas Watson's *Copy Book Enriched with Great Variety of the more Usefull and Modish Hands* (published around 1690) as his major source. But Watson's huge roman capital letters are the only part of the older text that Holbrook has reproduced closely. The remainder of each of his pages is devoted in turn to all the other scripts—italic print, round text, and round hand from the Latin scripts; German text, English text, and the secretary, chancery, and engrossing hands from the gothic scripts. Holbrook begins his manuscript with the Ten Commandments and proceeds alphabetically: The letter *L* intones, "Lying Lips are an Abomination to the LORD." "Xalt the LORD," in red, is the treatment for *X*. The whole manuscript is a testimony to the continuing power of orthodox New England belief.[51]

Language clothed in calligraphy was—or could be—language pregnant with meaning and rich with aesthetic pleasure. The pleasure that penning a piece of this caliber brought the penman could be experienced even at an elementary level. Lindley Murray, who would become the most widely sold author of schoolbooks of different kinds in the first four decades of the nineteenth century, remembered a piece he had penned at his school in New York city around 1753, executed when he was eight years old. He was asked by his instructor, he recalled, to "exhibit a specimen of my best hand writing" on a sheet that was decorated with "a number of pleasing figures, displayed with taste and simplicity." His task was to transcribe, in the center of this (presumably printed) piece, the New Testament account of the angels' salutation to the shepherds, who were tending their flocks by night, near Bethlehem. Almost sixty years later he still vividly remembered the pleasure it gave him.

> The beauty of the sheet; the property I was to have in it; and the distinction which I expected from performing the work in a handsome manner; prepared my mind for relishing the solemn narrative, and the interesting language of the angels to the shepherds. I was highly pleased with the whole. The impression was so strong and delightful, that it has often occurred to me, through life, with great satisfaction; and, at this hour, it is remembered with pleasure.[52]

Murray had experienced the emotional power of calligraphy: its ability to enhance the meaning of what was penned.

Yet for all the pleasure that beautiful handwriting could produce for writer and reader alike, there was an inherent contradiction in the products of the writing schools: the more beautiful the student's script, the longer, in general, it had taken the writer to produce. The overall purpose of the writing schools, after all, was economic—a preparation for the mercantile world. The writers of professional books for writing masters in the eighteenth century tried to straddle both sides of this gulf by proclaiming, as George Bickham did in his introduction to the *Universal Penman*, that "Usefulness and Beauty are the Excellencies of Writing." The bulk of the texts in Bickham's collection are penned in that useful business hand, the "round hand," which had, as early as the 1730s—although it was still being billed as a "Modish" hand then—already become the prevailing business script of the eighteenth century. This revolutionary script, an adaptation of the older italic, was the product of English penmen. It was designed to be simple, legible, and swift, because the business of British commerce, reaching ever farther around the globe, required such a script of its clerks. So successful was it that other countries adopted it: the French called it *lettre anglaise* and the Italians *litera anglese*. (The fact that round hand is as legible today to us as it was to its eighteenth-century users is a tribute to its longevity: we still use a form of this script.) The round hand is much in evidence in the second of the three parts of the *Universal Penman*, which is devoted to "Various Forms of Business, Relating to Merchandize, and Trade." Probably sensing a need for a less expensive book that focused only on business, Bickham excerpted all the business-related pieces in the *Universal Penman* to issue another publication in 1743, *The United Pen-Men for Forming the Man of Business*. Subtitled *The Young Man's Copy-Book*, it includes such pieces as tradesmen's bills, promissory notes, bankers' notes, acquittances and receipts, and business letters.[53]

Yet even in this context a voice was raised that challenged the value of the round hand. A few of the business pieces included in both the *Universal Penman* and the *United Pen-Men* demonstrate a smaller and more fluid version of the round hand known as "running hand." One of Bickham's contributors, John Bland, had urged its inclusion for merchants and tradesmen, because, he said, it was a style "most proper for the ready Dispatch of Business. . . . And I think that a Running Hand of this Nature is better adapted, and has a more Natural tendency to Expedition than that which is commonly written after a formal Roundness [round hand]." "Expedition," or speed, was the key word here.[54]

Later writers would be much more openly critical of the consequences that traditional writing instruction had on speed of execution. B. F. Foster, for example, published a system of penmanship in 1835, subtitling it *The Art of Rapid Writing*. He asserts that the three qualities needed in writing are legibility, expedition, and beauty. However, he says, the pupil taught by the old system, "attains *legibility* to perfection," as long as the writing is performed slowly, "*beauty* of character, to a surprising degree—and of EXPEDITION, not even the name." Faced by the reality of the countinghouse, Foster claims, the young penman would be told that "it will never answer to write so slow." He then "sacrifices all to expedition, and, nine times out of ten, his writing degenerates into a mere scrawl." Foster blamed this lapse into illegibility on the technique of the old system, which required a student to write with his fingers alone, resting his arm as he did so and therefore having to reposition it for each new section of text.[55]

Foster had articulated a simple truth: from the perspective of the real world, the emphasis by writing masters on beautiful calligraphy and the control of a range of scripts was, frankly, almost absurd. A youth needed only to "write a fair hand" in order to obtain a job, and he needed to be able to write quickly. In addition to round hand, lawyers might need to master the easier gothic script for such legal adornments as titles for wills, but most job seekers needed only one script, the round hand. No wonder the writing masters were so careful to keep the secrets of the trade within the professional community. As soon as a book was published, as it was in 1791, that revealed to the novice how a script could be broken down into just a few key strokes for mastery of the entire alphabet, the control held by traditionally trained writing masters over instruction and its income would be at an end. Indeed, John Jenkins's heretical claim in the third edition of his *Art of Writing, Reduced to a Plain and Easy System* that young gentlemen and ladies without access to a writing master could, thanks to his system, acquire penmanship so successfully that they might "immediately become, not only their own instructors, but instructors of others" in effect sounded the death knell for the apprenticeship approach to becoming a writing master. If penmanship could be learned from a book, not a man, the profession of writing master was in serious trouble.[56]

Our view of what went on in writing schools in terms of subjects other than penmanship is in danger of being distorted by the examples of beautiful penmanship that have survived from such schools. Once again, our best evidence on the rest of the curriculum of the writing schools is from Boston. The requirement that children had to be able to read before they could be admitted was enforced. When John Proctor, master of the North Writing School, was accused in 1741 of discriminating against boys who came from "Families of low Circumstances in the World" by refusing to admit them, he responded that he had "refus'd none of the Inhabitants Children but such as could not Read in the Psalter." The lack of action taken by the Boston selectmen confirmed his right to do so. Nonetheless, if masters hewed to a set of instructions handed down to them by a 1719 Boston town meeting, oral reading was practiced and spelling instruction initiated in some form. The instructions stipulated that scholars were to read from the scriptures every morning and evening, and masters were to ensure that "proper Seasons be Stated & Sett a part for the Encourageing of good Spelling."[57] (This would have been a version of the oral spelling contests that became so familiar in the nineteenth century.)

While spelling received some attention, the most important job of the writing schools, other than teaching fine penmanship, was the inculcation of mathematics—at the very least, that part of mathematics that was necessary for business, arithmetic and bookkeeping. The alliance between penmanship and mathematics emerges clearly in surviving manuscript arithmetic books. Manuscript arithmetic books fall into several groups. Some are copies of printed texts; others are copies of manuscript texts that may themselves be the copies of printed text; others may be unique to the writing master who wrote them; yet others are notebooks into which students transcribed, as fair copies, the problems and their solutions that they had worked out somewhere else. It is by no means always easy to identify who the author is—the master or the student. Manuscript arithmetics, therefore, are either doing service as a textbook or are the student's final copy of sums worked out on scrap paper or perhaps a slate. Either way, they are largely devoted to explaining commercial arithmetic. The theory behind manuscript arithmetics was presumably that mastery can come only from reproducing a model. This, after all, was one of the key assumptions made by penmanship instruction.[58]

One arithmetic manuscript book that vividly shows the relationship between arithmetic and penmanship in its most calligraphic form is clearly the work of a writing master, not a student, because the embellishments are far beyond the capacity of a beginner yet are integrated into the text rather than added for effect later. Penmanship and sums combine to produce a dramatic, even messy, impression on some pages. On one, the headings are decorated with vicious-looking fish, human heads in profile, and the birds so dear to the hearts of writing masters. Squiggles emanating from titles such as "Sundry Methods of Reducing Sterling Money into Currency" turn themselves into more fish. The heading "Addition of Vulgar FRACTIONS" shudders beneath a fierce bird seemingly about to duke it out with a predatory carp, beak to jaw. Student illustrations were naturally less showy, and most are simply the bored doodlings of the young—such as the ship in a 1710 manuscript by Henry Flowers—that are common to all periods.[59]

In addition to presupposing the mastery of writing, arithmetic books also presupposed the complete mastery of reading. When the manuscript was a "cyphering" book rather than anything more ambitious, it was restricted to arithmetic, and all the sums set were based on real life, or at least quasi-real life, objects and situations. In a cyphering book the student would typically work his or her way through number placement, addition, subtraction, multiplication, division, "reduction" (fractions), perhaps including avoirdupois weight, up to the calculation of ratios by what was known as the rule of three. Items covered might include, as did Mary Clough's manuscript of 1762, calculations about pounds of sugar, yards of cambrick, ounces of silver, and barrels of molasses, along with sums involving shoe buckles, penknives, stockings, pepper, currants, and figs.[60] These homely examples were assumed to be comfortably within the understanding of the young mathematician.

More advanced mathematical operations could invoke a more theoretical approach and require a higher level of reading skill. "Geometry," for example, the thirteen-year old George Washington wrote in 1745, was "a very useful and Necessary Branch of the Mathematick; whose Subject is greatness: for as Number is the Subject of Arithmetick, so that of Geometry is Magnitude, which hath its beginning from Point, that is a Thing supposed to be indivisible, and the Original of all Dimension. By it is explained the Nature, Kind and Property of continued Magnitude that is a Line, a Superficies and a Solid" Carefully copied from some source, these and similar definitions were left for the pupil to decipher as he could.[61]

The climax of the cyphering book, and of the arithmetical portion of any manuscript that tackled advanced mathematics such as geometry, was the "golden" rule of three. Alice Chase explained this nickname in her 1755 arithmetic book:

> The Golden Rule or Rule of Three
> This Rule is Termed Golden from the Excel=
> =lency of it for as Gold Excels all other
> metals so doth the Rule all others
> in Arithmetick.

The rule of three was a system for working out a fourth and missing item, given the other three; we would call it a problem of proportions or ratios. Samuel Coates drew ladders of sums in his cyphering book of 1724 to work out his answer to one such a problem:

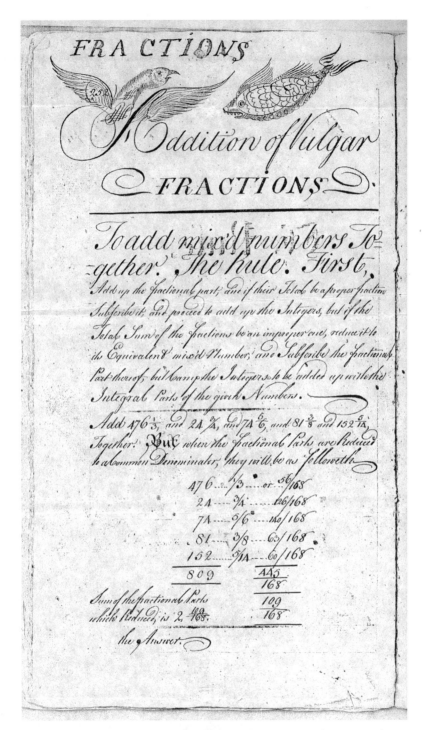

FIGURE 15. A page on fractions from a Virginia tutor's "Arithmetic Book, 1751–1766." The writer of this manuscript arithmetic book added decorative touches to the chapter titles. (Photocopy of a manuscript in a private collection)

Admit a man Dying left his Estate amongst his 3 Sons and one Daughter to his Elde[s]t Son he gave £500 to his middlemost £400 to his youngest son £300 & to his Daug[h]ter £200 but being Dead his Estate is found to be worth but £800 how much must each child have in proportion to what was Left him.[62]

In his ciphering book of 1749/50, John Brown had a mathematically more complex example that harked back to the early years of colonial settlement:

If 12 Pioneers make a Trench 40 Foot Long 4 Foot Wide and 6 Foot Deep in 24 Days, In How Many Days will 48 Pioneers make a Trench 60 Foot Long 6 Foot Wide and 12 Foot Deep
    Ans—54 days—[63]

For girls, the rule of three was the farthest they would advance in mathematics. For young men, surviving manuscript books show the most intricate of calculations. Examples include William Collis's approach to finding the solidity of a cone and Andrew Lamb's "new Rules for finding Longitude," which he wrote in 1754 at the age of seventy, after forty years of being a teacher of navigation.[64]

The disparity between the number of newspaper advertisements for printed "Arithmeticks" (as they were called) and the substantially higher number of times a teacher of arithmetic is mentioned in advertisements for private instruction suggests that learning arithmetic, like learning writing, was still highly dependent on a person. This dependence was true even though arithmetic had long had its own schoolbooks, all initially printed in England. The most venerable of these was James Hodder's *Hodder's Arithmetick*, available in London since 1661 and still popular at the turn of the century in its revision by Henry Mose. Another was the *Arithmetick* of the English writing master Edward Cocker, published posthumously in 1678 by John Hawkins.[65]

Not until the mid eighteenth century, however, were arithmetics advertised as such in American newspapers. They were available long before, then, of course: recall that Benjamin Franklin had improved his grasp of the subject by working his way through Cocker's *Arithmetick* on his own. But only in the 1750s with the publication of many more newspapers, do we begin to see merchants advertising the arithmetics of George Fisher, John Hill, James Hodder, and Edward Cocker, the last of which was now available in a revised edition by Fisher. And even then, it is quite striking to see how many more newspaper advertisements there were for reading instructional texts, such as primers, spelling books, and even dictionaries than for arithmetics.[66]

Another factor that may have contributed to this low volume of printed arithmetic texts was the amount of arithmetic included in such standard self-help books as Franklin's *American Instructor: Or, Young Man's Best Companion* (his slightly Americanized version of Fisher's *Young Man's Best Companion*). This work, together with imported copies of Fisher's original *The Instructor; or Young Man's Best Companion* and the *Young Secretary's Guide,* continued to be available for decades.

Composition

The eighteenth century saw a marked expansion of literary culture as well as learned culture in the American provinces. Since the works in manuscript and print that resulted were largely the products of adults, they lie beyond the scope of this book. But a couple of instances of writing poetry deserve comment because their authors were young women. Phillis Wheatley, the "African poetess," won a reputation for herself across the colonies for her elegies, as we know. Jane Turell, daughter of Benjamin Colman (minister of Boston's Fourth, or Brattle Street, Church and a rival of Cotton Mather), was among the first generation of American girls to read widely in English poetry and prose—thanks to her father's library and encouragement. In 1718, at the age of not quite eleven, she wrote her first poem, a hymn.[67]

Like poetry, prose composition was initially the perquisite of the grammar schools. The boys were introduced there to composition instruction—but in Latin and Greek. Instruction in composing English, as Benjamin Franklin noticed in the 1710s, was rarely to be obtained.

A handful of schoolbook manuscripts provide a glimpse of copying model letters, a practice that would eventually lead to composition rather than penmanship. One schoolbook of 1710 offers "The form of a letter to request a kindness." Another, copied into a schoolbook by R. Paine in 1757 and purporting to be from one sister to another, uses the formal phrasing of the eighteenth-century polite letter. It includes the sentences, "We have long expected yr return with great Impatience" and, "I entertain some small hopes of being bless'd with yr company." In a 1771 writing book, James Brown Mason used an old text for his model son-to-father school letter. Inattentive, perhaps, to the content, or misinterpreting its import, he left out a key negative:

> London May 10th 1711
> Honoured Father
> In obedience to your command I send this to inform you what advance I have made in my Writing. I find now by experience, that to write a bold face hand correctly requires [no] small care and application—but this is no Discouragement to me since you have frequently told me, that to write a good hand would be more serviceable to my Design than any.[68]

More to the point in terms of composition are the occasional unsanctioned additions to a schoolbook, where students gave vent to their opinions and emotions. Expressions that identified the connection between the book and its owner were popular. Four months before his seventeenth birthday, John Gorton wrote:

> John Gorton his book God
> gave him Grace thereinto Look
> April the 8th Day, 1770
> Warwick [New England]

But more evaluative comments could intrude. A month later, he was tackling multiplication. After inscribing, "Multiplication . . . is that by which we Multiply / Two or more Numbers the one into / The other to the End that Their product may be Descovered," Gorton added, in small and hurried writing, the classic complaint:

> Multiplication is Vexation Division is as Bad
> the Rule of three Doth puzzle me and
> practice makes me mad—
>   This is rit with a very Bad pen
>   JG[69]

William Collis had a few kind words to say about the female intellect:

> On Female Education
>   In Education all the differa[n]ce Lies.
> Women if Taught would be as brave, as Wise,
>   As haughty Man, improv'd by Arts and Rules

Valentines were popular. Benjamin Carr in 1768 wrote down one that he had obviously committed to heart after hearing it recited, as his rendering of "carnation" suggests:

> A heart of gold a friend of mine
> I chuse you for my volentine
> I first cast lots and then I drew
> And fortain [fortune] said it must be you
> Drew you out from all the Rest
> The Reason was I love you best
> Shure as the grape grose on The vine
> So shure you are my volentine . . .
> for lilys white and vilots blew
> Crown Nation Sweet and so are you
> Remember what their is to pay
> A pair of gloves on yester day[70]

These juvenile attempts at self-expression point to a crucial element lacking in writing instruction: the teaching of composition. Not until the early 1770s would composition appear in advertisements for schools as a subject for instruction.[71]

Letter writing, the most important addition to writing instruction in general and to composition in particular, lies beyond the scope of this book. Konstantin Dierks has demonstrated that interest in the publication of manuals dealing with personal letter writing (the so-called familiar letter), as opposed to writing letters for business, received a large boost in 1741, when Samuel Richardson completed his manual, *Letters Written to and for Particular Friends, on the Most Important Occasions*. (Richardson had laid the work aside temporarily to write a novel whose plot and characters were displayed entirely through their letters: parts 3 and 4 of *Pamela; or, Virtue Rewarded* were published shortly after his manual on letter writing appeared.) The introduction of this new emphasis on letters as the conveyors of feeling and sentiment went hand in hand with the popularity of the new epistolary novels. Dierks points to a dramatic increase in writing "familiar" letters, gaining tempo from mid-century to the end of the century, as new letter writers used this format to redefine gender and class boundaries, reevaluate their self-identity, and link themselves through their letters to the happenings in their own lives and the lives of distant friends and family members. As they did so, the social circle of letter writing was greatly enlarged, reaching more of the "middling" sort than ever before and expanding the ages of potential letter writers. An appreciation for letter writing was occasionally visible in school settings, as we saw at George Whitefield's school for orphans, Bethesda, in Georgia, and at the two schools of Christopher Dock in the 1740s.[72]

It took much longer, however, for familiar letter writing to enter the formal writing instruction of children. Business manuals had long contained a few familiar letters, as we have seen.[73] But, as Dierks points out, it was not until 1750 that the author of the twenty-fourth Boston edition of John Hill's *Young Secretary's Guide* would self-consciously address his "Epistle to the Reader" to "the Younger Sort of either Sex" and acknowledge young people's need for instruction in composing letters. Hill's book includes a series of exemplary letters targeted at both sexes, although those aimed at young men in the business world far outnumber those aimed at girls or boys.[74]

Letter-writing manuals aimed solely at children would not appear in England until the 1780s or be reprinted in America until the 1790s, but in the 1770s writing masters began to advertise such instruction, as John Druitt did in Boston in 1774 when he promised to teach young ladies "Epistolary-writing."[75] More children were apparently writing letters, although most of the surviving evidence of children's letter writing dates from the 1770s on.[76]

Examples of what writing instruction did for its pupils should appear in the spontaneous letters of the young. But these are not easy to find, and when they are preserved, their relationship to any formal writing instruction is cloudy. R. Paine had practiced writing a letter by copying a model of one supposedly written by one sister to another. But when the time came, in 1757, for him to write a real letter to his own sister, he was far breezier than any model would have been: "Our fish is in Town, I believe I must send him to court you, his infinite good humour will suit you to a Notch," he wrote, playfully addressing her as "The right hon[ora]ble The Lady Eunice[,] Dutchess of Weymouth and Mistress of the Navy." His own careful instruction in penmanship is revealed on his envelope, where the address shows a fine mastery of the round hand, accompanied by a small flourish.[77]

Diary evidence gives some idea of pre- and postinstructional experiences. A journal kept in 1772 by a ten-year-old Virginian, Sally Fairfax, demonstrates the freedom with which children spelled and wrote. Her handwriting is terrible and her spelling would today be called "invented." At one point in her diary she virulently condemns an enslaved African who had killed a cat of hers: "that vile man adam at night kild a poor Cat of [illegible] gest because she eat a bit of meat out of his hand and scrached it. a vile wreach of new negrows if he was mine I would cut him to peices a son of a gun a wiced negrow he should be kild himself by rites." A letter she wrote almost six years later demonstrates the difference that years of schooling have made. The handwriting of the letter is amazingly altered for the better, and her spelling is regularized.[78]

The phonetic spelling that Sally displayed earlier is characteristic of the young or the minimally taught. Diaries of the early to mid-eighteenth century display a range of spelling variation, but those written by men or women who had received only a little education in their earlier years are consistent in their use of phonetic spelling and their lack of concern with grammar, punctuation, and spelling "correctness," a notion that would solidify only later.

An example of adult spelling in the 1750s is suggestive. The spelling in the diaries kept by New England soldiers who left their farms to fight in the Seven Years' War is often, even by the standards of the time, aberrant. Indeed, when Fred Anderson began to mine the diaries for their views of the war, he quickly concluded that he would have to transliterate them into conventional orthography to make them intelligible. For example, the orders against bad language issued to soldiers in 1759, as recorded by a diarist from Deerfield, Massachusetts, run:

> General orders—it is vary Nitoriously tru that profane cosing & swaring praules [prevails] in ye campt; it is vary far from ye cristian solgers Deuty; it is not only vary Displasing to God armeyes, but dishonorable before men. it is theire fore Required & it will be expected that for ye futur ye odus sound of cosing & swaring is to be turned in to a prefoun silence.[79]

Somewhat better spelling might be expected from those whose professional training presupposed some formal education. And, indeed, we have an example of better spelling in a diary kept by John Thomas, a surgeon who was called on to perform several amputations during an expedition against the Acadians of Nova Scotia in 1755. In his entry for June 4 Thomas describes a British attack led by Captain Adams. The British forces suddenly came into full view, across a large salt marsh, of a French blockhouse and barricades:

> Now we hear the Indians [allies of the French] begin to make thare most Hideous yells & a Large Numbers of the Enemy Appearing Redy to Ingage us our troop keep on thare march & when we have Got within musket Shot we Recived the Fire of thare Swivel Guns with Partrige Shot which seemd to come very thick wounded several of our men but None killed.[80]

This kind of literacy was functional literacy: it accomplished what the diarists wanted of it. But increasingly, it did not conform to what was becoming a prescriptive approach to spelling, with only one "correct" spelling for each word. Whereas, in the seventeenth century, little if any disgrace had been attached to inconsistent spelling, in the eighteenth new standards were evolving. Among the upper classes in England, good spelling was being associated with good breeding. "Orthography is so absolutely necessary for a man of letters," Lord Chesterfield wrote to his son in 1750, "that one false spelling may fix a ridicule upon him for the rest of his life." (The printed version of his letters, published posthumously, was available as an import in the colonies in the 1770s and would become very popular among the colonial elite.)[81] The colonies had far to go before accepting such an extreme position, but that was the direction spelling would take. Spelling books played a key role in this, for they were regularizing spelling as well as teaching reading.

The single most important change in the eighteenth-century, however, was not the standardization of spelling but the gradual abandonment of gender as the basis for deciding which children should receive writing instruction. After about 1750, the acceptance of the desirability of such instruction for girls of all social classes grew steadily. As we have seen, the change was legislated in Poor Laws across the colonies, which now required that poor girls apprenticed under the laws, just like poor boys, be taught to write as well as read. What was acceptable in principle, however, did not necessarily translate immediately into practice. Rural living, low social standing, and the entrenched values of those in power over school spending would continue to militate against the provision of publicly funded writing instruction for girls in many towns until well after the American Revolution.[82]

For the African-American community, the situation was very different. Enslaved, and eventually even free, blacks would see a steady erosion of their chances to become literate. Before the American Revolution, writing had already been banned in Virginia and Georgia; after the war similar legislation would be passed in other southern states. By 1834, five such states would pass laws prohibiting the teaching of writing and even reading to the enslaved in any venue for any reason; three of these would prohibit such instruction to free Africans, and a sixth would define any school for blacks as an unlawful assembly.[83] The writing of others, in the form of legislation, was used as an instrument of control, and writing instruction was withheld from the enslaved lest it should empower them.

11

The New World of Children's Books

A depiction of a penman serves as the frontispiece for a little American book for children titled *The History of the Holy Jesus*, first published in 1745: it is a woodcut ostensibly depicting the anonymous author. Like the masters of Boston's three writing schools, he sports a wig, but in other respects his portrayal is as far removed from the formidable appearance of, say, John Tileston as possible. His wig, it is true, ends in a roll of six soft curls, but his demeanor befits one who has written for children a verse account of Jesus's "Birth, Life, Death, Resurrection and Ascension into Heaven; and his coming again at the great and last Day of Judgment." He is clad in a Puritan-style jacket and neckcloth; his right hand, extending beyond a white ruff, holds the quill he has used to pen this work, as he pauses momentarily from its composition, lost in thought.[1]

The *History of the Holy Jesus* is an exemplar of the shift in reading instruction and the availability of books to children that was occurring, at least in some parts of the American provinces and for some children, during the transitional decades of the 1730s and 1740s. Of the eight genres into which scholars have traditionally divided so-called children's books (a term used loosely here to indicate not only books designed for children but those read by them despite their intended adult audience), the seventeenth century had seen only two of them: religious works and chapbooks. Now, from the 1730s on, many exemplars of the remaining six genres would appear: fables, courtesy books, schoolbooks, works of advice, a group of related books that includes fairy tales, nursery rhymes, and the *Arabian Nights*, and, lastly, works designed deliberately to amuse children. One additional source has often been overlooked by scholars: the texts used in penmanship instruction. Books in all of these categories were imported into America in the eighteenth century (at different times and with varying degrees of enthusiasm), and many of them were also reprinted on American presses.[2]

The availability of a wider variety of reading material for children was related to the increasing number of books printed in, and imported into, America during the eighteenth century. Even as the volume of American book production rose, so did that of importation, which outstripped domestic production for the entire century. After 1750, the rates of increase of both local and imported imprints rose to ever new heights with each succeeding decade until the years of the American Revolution. During the four years from 1771 to 1774 alone, some 60 percent of Britain's total export of books was being shipped to the American colonies, averaging an

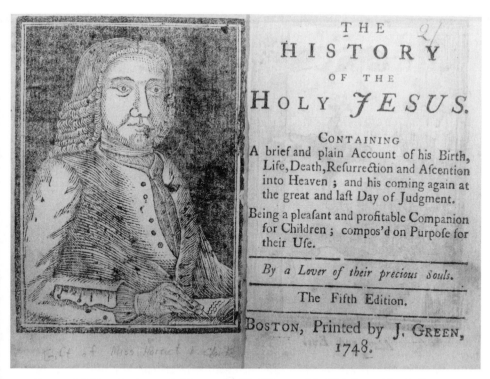

FIGURE 16. Frontispiece and title page of *The History of the Holy Jesus*, 5th ed. (Boston: J. Green, 1748). The familiar portrayal of a writer holding his pen depicts the act of authorship here, rather than of penmanship. The author of this popular children's book is identified only as "a Lover of their precious Souls." (Courtesy, American Antiquarian Society)

estimated 120,000 items (including pamphlets as well as books). The growth was such that from roughly 1750 to 1775 the increase in books was larger than the increase in the American population (see Appendix 4).[3]

In this chapter I argue, however, that the broadening of children's reading material was not just a matter of the growing availability of all books: it was, to some extent, the product of an alternative view of children. In England, profound shifts were occurring in cultural perceptions of childhood that affected the content of books for children. In America, the new material would not supplant the old but would run parallel with it or change it. This shift in how children were viewed in the English context can be traced, in part, to the profound and enduring influence of the British philosopher John Locke. As we saw earlier, Locke had advocated a gentler view of childhood. He believed in a tabula rasa, a clean slate, ethically as well as epistemologically. Children were not, in his view, tainted with original sin but morally neutral, although they had a natural tendency to try to dominate. He had recommended an education that took advantage of children's malleability and trained them to good habits rather than bad. In his view, the desire for esteem and fear of disgrace were the most powerful factors motivating children's behavior.[4]

Locke's views on reading instruction, articulated in his *Some Thoughts Concerning Education* (1693), were brief. He believed that the child "may *learn to Read*, without knowing how he did so." He rather regretted the "ordinary Road of the Horn-book, Primer, Psalter, Testament, and Bible" and explicitly condemned the conjunction of learning with compulsion: "I have always had a Fancy, that *Learning* might be made a Play and Recreation to Children." Children could learn the alphabet, for instance, he suggested, through playing with dice that had letters pasted onto them. "Thus Children may be cozen'd [tricked] into a Knowledge of the Letters; be *taught to read*, without perceiving it to be any thing but a Sport, and play themselves into that which others are whipp'd for." With these views, Locke cleared the way to a view of literacy education that would be pleasurable rather than punitive.[5] As the decades passed, Locke's ideas had gradually become incorporated into the conventional child-rearing wisdom of many in Britain. By the second half of the eighteenth century, according to Samuel Pickering, his influence was "monumental." Locke's *Some Thoughts* was imported occasionally into the American provinces, but his chief influence was indirect.[6] His new vision of childhood lent itself readily to a new definition of the purposes of children's reading, which for so long had been focused on their salvation.

This gentler view of the child coincided with other changes that were economic rather than ideological. If ideology had a major impact on materials used in reading instruction or on reading within a family setting, commerce affected texts for writing instruction. As Britain's wealth became ever more linked to her overseas trade in the eighteenth century, the importance of correct behavior in a commercial context was reflected in the content of copybooks. Printed copybooks (and their manuscript reproduction by writing masters) represent a ninth genre of the new or altered forms of material for children's reading and writing instruction.

Chapbooks

Chapbooks were the least expensive form of reading matter and, because very few copies have survived, certainly the most difficult to document. Cheap paper and an enthusiastic readership have played a part in their physical destruction.[7] As we have seen, the few seventeenth-century chapbooks that were imported into New England were apparently the "histories," those tales of derring-do and romance that traced their origins back to medieval times. The appellation "history," however, was not necessarily restricted to such tales: a 1771 New York catalogue advertising a "Variety of small Histories, commonly called CHAPMEN'S BOOKS" includes works that range from *Pilgrim's Progress* to the *Life of Dean Swift* and a cookery book.[8] Evidence of the existence of eighteenth-century chapbooks comes almost entirely from similar publishers' catalogues, diaries and autobiographies, and advertisements in books and newspapers.

The earliest published mention of a bookseller's involvement in chapbooks occurs in 1728. An advertisement at the end of a book printed in Newport, Rhode Island, by Benjamin Franklin's older half-brother, James, recommends Bibles, schoolbooks, and "Chapmens' History Books and Pamphlets."[9] By the early 1750s, chapbooks were being advertised regularly in newspapers from major ports, such as Boston, New York, and Philadelphia. Hugh Gaine, in his own paper, the *New-York Mercury*, advertised, without specifics, "A good Assortment of Chapman Books" in 1754, but in June of the following year he listed forty-four "Chapmen BOOKS" separately by title. The list is a wonderful hodge-podge of the books and pamphlets light enough to be hoisted around the countryside by the peddlers. Several of the old religious steady sellers are represented—the seventeenth-century *Pilgrim's Progress* of John Bunyan (abridged to a chapbook format), Benjamin Keach's *War with the Devil*, and the *History of Francis Spira*. Also included is Robert Russel's *Seven Sermons*, one of the books that Devereux Jarratt had used to improve his reading comprehension. But the preponderance of the list is designed to entertain rather than convert. Such entertainment was not necessarily contemporary. On the list are the older "histories": *The History of Parismus* and *Valentine and Orson*, tales that originated in the fifteenth century—and that had been imported into Boston since the 1680s—the much newer *Fairy Tales*, and an abbreviated version of *Robinson Crusoe*. Schoolbooks for literacy instruction are not forgotten: Gaine offers both Thomas Dyche's and Thomas Dilworth's spelling books to help with reading, together with *The Young Secretary's Guide* as an aid to writing. Perhaps the distinguishing feature of these works is that they were considered a basic set of works for those who had little chance to get into a town to purchase books.[10]

Advertisements appearing in a 1760 Philadelphia almanac published by William Dunlap and in a catalogue issued by the Philadelphia bookseller William Bradford at about the same time also show a preponderance of the chivalric romances. They include *The Seven Champions of Christendom*, *Valentine and Orson*, and *Guy of Warwick*, along with *Fairy Tales* and such clearly adult works as *Pleasures of Matrimony* and *Female Policy Detected*. Yet another Philadelphia bookseller, Andrew Steuart, who had moved from Belfast, Ireland, to set up a printing press in Philadelphia in 1758, was actively involved in the chapbook trade. In 1763, he included an advertisement for chapbooks at the end of one of his steady sellers. Like Gaine's list, Steuart's list promoted, along with the standard medieval romances, the *Arabian Nights*, novels such as *Robinson Crusoe* and *Gulliver's Travels* (clearly all in abbreviated editions), and Aesop's *Fables*.[11]

How much of this chapbook fare reached the hands of children remains problematic, since virtually none of the "histories" portion of it is extant and we do not even know how much reached adults. What is certain is that the imported chapbook market had expanded by the close of the 1760s, with Philadelphia, New York, and Boston leading the way. Booksellers who immigrated into the American provinces from Britain were the most attuned to the potential profitability of chapbooks. Henry Knox, an immigrant from London, provides an example of such booksellers, as well as of the sheer quantity of chapbook material. He imported thousands of chapbooks from London into his London Book Store in Boston in the 1770s, paying a wholesale price of only two pennies each for them. In general, chapbooks were within the financial reach of most Americans.[12]

Domestic chapbook publication appears to have been small—or equally ephemeral. However, two little works produced on American presses fall into a new subcategory of the chapbook market, chapbooks aimed directly at children: *The Prodigal Daughter* and *A New Gift for Children*. The *Prodigal Daughter* was first advertised in 1736 by Thomas Fleet in his *Boston Evening-Post* as a "small BOOK in easy Verse, very suitable for Children." Its chapbook status was evident from the discount for bulk purchase at four pennies a copy as opposed to sixpence for a single copy. The title character of *The Prodigal Daughter*, available in a 1767 imprint, is a girl from Bristol, England, who is rendered so obnoxious by her parents' indulgence that her father finally turns on her, cuts off her overly generous allowance, and confines her to her room on a diet of bread and water. In revenge, she bargains with the devil to poison both parents, who are saved only by being warned by an angel in a dream. When they accuse their child of intended murder, she falls into a deathlike trance for four days. She repents and is saved, but not before her burial and miraculous revival allow her to bring back titillating tales of the "burning Lake of Misery" from her brief foray into death. The story, in rhyming couplets, is reminiscent of Benjamin Keach's *War with the Devil or the Young Man's Conflict with the Powers of Darkness*, but its sensationalist aspects outweigh any serious call to repentance, and no account in the preceding century would have permitted the girl to escape eternal punishment.[13]

The second chapbook, *A New Gift for Children: Delightful and Entertaining Stories For little Masters and Misses*, is a tiny Boston imprint. Although the work, as was common with chapbooks, is undated, the place of publication is identified as Boston and the printer as D[aniel] Fowle. It was probably issued between 1750 and early 1755.[14] Paper-bound and poorly printed, it is important for two reasons. It may be the first surviving storybook for children to be printed in America, as Gillian Avery suggests. And it includes stories that treat children as children.[15] Indeed, children are its main characters, and the attention it pays in its subtitle to little "Misses," as well as "Masters," suggests the authorship of the English printer John Newbery (discussed below). Its dialogues, one of which shows "how a little Boy shall become a great Man," had already become so popular that it had been added to the 1743 spelling book *A Child's New Play-Thing*. Girls are included in other stories. Polly Smith is praised and kissed by both parents for wanting to "make a poor man glad" through her charity. With blithe inconsistency of tone, the stories also include grim verses from the British hymn writer Isaac Watts, who warns children to watch their lips in order to keep from lying and going to hell.[16]

Both of these chapbooks for children include illustrations, by now the hallmark of a work for children. The woodcuts in *A New Gift* are quite detailed but not particularly relevant to the text. In contrast, those for an early edition of the *Prodigal Daughter* printed by Thomas Fleet were executed for that particular text. Pompey Fleet, an enslaved African with a gift for illustration and one of the workers in the printing shop of his master Thomas Fleet, carved his initials on several of the pictures in a Fleet imprint (probably to be dated 1768). Isaiah Thomas later used these as his model, carving them himself with far less skill.[17]

Fables

Aesop's Fables were included in the wares hawked around by chapmen who bought them wholesale from Andrew Steuart of Philadelphia in the 1760s. Of all the genres of books read by children, fables were the most ancient. The *Fables* of Aesop (the Greek credited with composing them in the sixth century B.C.E.) were a staple of the Latin grammar school curriculum and were assigned to schoolboys, either in Latin alone or in bilingual versions, throughout the seventeenth and eighteenth centuries. Locke, in his *Some Thoughts Concerning Education*, had recommended them as the best "easy pleasant Book" suited to a child's capacity, regarding them as a vehicle for moral education. He had particularly encouraged the use of those with illustrations. But these secular tales, in which the speech and actions of anthropomorphized animals provide morals for human beings, had not been included in works designed to teach children to read English in the seventeenth century.[18] Henry Dixon's spelling book of 1728 was one of the first spellers to feature fables, and from then on the inclusion of a few fables in spellers was taken for granted. The illustrations of the fables in Thomas Dilworth's speller of 1740 initiated another trend.[19]

Courtesy Books

Until the eighteenth century, courtesy books, addressed only to men, had concentrated on the manners needed to make one's way in the world in contexts in which etiquette was all important. In these manuals, courtesy and virtue are intertwined: they are guidelines on becoming a gentleman.[20]

A courtesy book of longstanding that made its way into the American provinces was *The School of Good Manners*. While its fourth London edition of 1701 was in both Latin and English, its American versions used only the English portion, and someone added a lengthy religious section, which had the effect of steering the work away somewhat from its original focus on the manners of a gentleman. (Later printers liked to ascribe this addition, erroneously, to a Boston schoolmaster named Eleazar Moody.) A steady seller beloved by printers at the low-quality end of the market, it was published in a New London, Connecticut, edition in 1715 and intermittently thereafter and reprinted in Boston in 1732. The first surviving edition is one put out by Thomas and John Fleet in 1772. George Washington spent much time as a youth copying out its instructions.[21]

The School of Good Manners consists largely of imperatives issued in support of 163 numbered rules: "Decently walk to thy Seat or pew. . . . If thou canst not avoid Yawning, shut thy Mouth with thine Hand or Hankerchief before it. . . . / Come not near when another reads a Letter or any other Paper." In the religious material added later, Puritan orthodoxy appears and the importance of reading the scriptures is stressed: "If God do open your Eyes and bring you to Salvation, it will be by light let in by the Word. . . . Therefore read it, and muse upon it, and never read it without looking up to God to speak somewhat to you out of it."[22] To this, however, the printers of a Boston edition in May 1732 had elected to introduce further additional material. The eighth chapter of the work, according to their advertisement, included "Good Thoughts for Little Children, A compendious Body of Divinity, an Alphabet of useful Copies" (that is, texts, arranged alphabetically by their initial letter for copying as a penmanship exercise) "& Cyprian's Twelve Absurdities, all in Verse." When this last frivolity for the mind could be added to a book as dedicated to external forms of behavior as the *School of Good Manners*, something was changing in the way children's books were being conceptualized. The desire to amuse children had already become a market consideration.[23]

Religious Books

The traditional forms of religious books continued to be marketable, and older works were given a boost by the Great Awakening of the 1740s. Michael Wigglesworth's *Day of Doom* was republished intermittently right through the middle of the eighteenth century. Inspirational biographies of devout, but dead, children remained popular. In February 1741, for instance, an advertisement in a Boston newspaper listed the fourth edition of *Early Piety, exemplified in Elizabeth Butcher of Boston*. It had first appeared in 1718, the year that this eight-year-old had died. That most long-lasting of Puritan works, John Bunyan's *Pilgrim's Progress*, was still being imported into the colonies in various formats in the 1770s.[24]

Early in the eighteenth century, however, the Bible was rendered more appealing to young children by being printed domestically, as well as imported, in a "thumb," or abridged and miniature version. In addition, the *Holy Bible in Verse* was first put through the press in 1717 in Boston by Benjamin Harris (presumed author of the *New-England Primer*). Harris was responsible for the halting and enigmatic verse of this edition. Like the primer, it was illustrated.[25]

The English nonconformist theologian and hymn writer Isaac Watts (1674–1748) is probably best understood not so much as a transitional figure in the competing views of the child that evolved over the eighteenth century but as one who straddled them both. On one hand, he upheld an orthodox view of the child that warned of the possibility of early death. On the other, he stressed the redemptive love of Christ and the beauty and glory of God. He also used language that was immediately intelligible to a child. He wrote a large number of works in both prose and poetry, drawing on the works of John Locke for both.[26]

Watts's works were hugely popular in the American colonies from the first. His *Hymns and Spiritual Songs* for adults was not only imported into the colonies but soon printed on American presses. His earliest hymns for children, *Divine Songs, Attempted in Easy Language for the Use of Children*, were first published in London in 1715. The earliest extant American edition is dated 1730 (a Boston edition of the seventh edition), but it has been calculated that the work was reprinted sixty-six times in America between that date and 1819.[27]

Judged by an eighteenth-century yardstick, the vocabulary of *Divine Songs* is easy, in that the hymns are composed mainly of monosyllables; polysyllabic words do not, for the most part, exceed two syllables. The identification with the child's viewpoint is fostered by a simple but effective technique: nearly all the verses are written as if they were addressed by the child directly to God. (This technique was not unique to Watts: the *New-England Primer* had used that very strategy in its "I in the Burying Place may see / Graves shorter far than I.")

The content of *Divine Songs* deals primarily with the majesty of God and with children's duties to God and themselves. The first song seeks to dispose of the child's doubts that he or she has anything worthwhile to offer God: "Th' Eternal God will not disdain / To hear an Infant sing." Nonetheless, Watts presents, with great fidelity, the dangers of dying unconverted: "A thousand Children, young as I, / Are call'd by Death to hear their Doom."[28]

Significantly, Watts's portrayal of literacy is identical to the one sketched in the *New-England Primer* and to that offered by James Janeway in his *Token for Children*: reading the Bible brings the child joy. In a poem titled "*The Excellency of the Bible*," the child is told that God is revealed most clearly in his "Book":

> Great GOD, with Wonder & with Praise
>   On all thy Works I look;
> But still thy Wisdom, Pow'r and Grace,
>   Shine brighter in thy Book.

Watts emphasizes the affective aspects of reading:

> Then let me love my Bible more,
>   And take a fresh Delight
> By Day to read these Wonders o'er,
>   And meditate by Night.[29]

Reading at an early age is considered a blessing, because it gives the child access to God's word all the sooner. Indeed, Watts's next poem is titled "*Praise to God for Learning to Read*." The child offers praises to the Lord, "That I was taught, and learnt so young / To read his holy Word." The Bible is a means to salvation: "this Book of thine / Informs me where to go / For Grace to pardon all my Sin, / And make me holy too." One exception to the equation of "Book" with the Bible is on those occasions when it means an account book. For God has another book besides the Bible. The verses titled "*Against Lying*" suggest its function.

> Then let me always watch my Lips,
> Lest I be struck to Death and Hell,
> Since God a Book of Reckoning keeps
> For every Lye that Children tell.[30]

Watts's most striking innovation in his poetry for children is the inclusion of a few poems that draw comparisons with the natural world. His "LET Dogs delight to bark and bite" and "Birds in their little nest agree," both of which enjoined children to be nice to their siblings, also indirectly suggested to children that poems need not always focus on the divine.[31]

Meanwhile, the work of Watts's Anglican contemporary John Lewis also flourished on both sides of the Atlantic. Lewis's *The Church Catechism Explained* reached its seventh London edition by 1714; it was in its twenty-seventh edition in 1759 when Lewis dedicated it to the Society for Promoting Christian Knowledge, the sister organization of the Society for the Propagation of the Gospel (S.P.G.).[32] As we have seen, a succession of S.P.G. employees used it in their teaching.[33] The work's appeal grew as time passed, at least among Anglicans. Benjamin Franklin, who always kept an eye out for a steady seller, printed it at Philadelphia in early 1751; he even advertised it ahead of those other steady sellers, Isaac Watts's explication of the Assembly's Shorter Catechism (one of the catechisms included in the *New-England Primer*) and Watts's *Divine Songs for Children*. In New York, pro-British and pro-Anglican Hugh Gaine printed *The Church Catechism Explained* in 1765, a few years after he had launched his newspaper there. As a religious instructional text for Anglicans that laid emphasis on understanding, it clearly filled a niche.[34]

If Lewis's *Church Catechism Explained* was a text that tried to teach comprehension while at the same time keeping children, socially speaking, in their place, several other religious texts for children also attempted to meet children on their own level, but in a more appealing way. Indeed, some of them struck a refreshingly new note for American children. One of these was the *History of the Holy Jesus*, with its pensive woodcut. It is of particular significance because, of all the texts discussed, it alone was an indigenous American product with no known British antecedent. Composed in verse by an author who has never been identified—other than as "a Lover of [Children's] precious Souls"—it would prove to be a rip-roaring bestseller as soon as it appeared in its first Boston edition.

The *Boston Weekly News-Letter* advertised it on January 31, 1745, as "a pleasant and profitable companion for Children" and as "Compos'd on purpose for their Use." The earliest extant edition, identified as a third edition, was published at Boston in 1746, but the work reached its sixth printing only three years later and was being printed at New London, Connecticut, within a few more years. It reached a twenty-fourth Boston edition in 1771.[35] Printers handed on to each other the "cuts" that illustrated it and that formed one of its principal charms: they show New Testament figures clad in traditional Puritan garb. When Zechariah Fowle put out an edition at Boston in 1766, he took advantage of his only moderately talented apprentice Isaiah Thomas, then aged fifteen, to produce a new set of cuts.[36]

The *History of the Holy Jesus* is written in the classic fourteen-syllable meter of the ballad, and its verses move along at a nice clip. The author, according to the 1746 edition, introduces his tale by delineating the joys of paradise and man's fall from divine grace: "A pleasant Paradise the Lord / Prepar'd with beauteous Trees, / And all the Fruits thereof to Man, / To eat whene'er he pleas'd." The account of

Jesus's birth, life and death is straightforward, emphasizing joy over grief and focusing on Jesus's power to save. It does not take the reader many verses to realize that a major reorientation has taken place since the seventeenth century. No longer are unbaptized children threatened with "the smallest room in Hell" as they had once been in Wigglesworth's "Day of Doom." This change is particularly evident when the young reader comes to the description of the Last Judgment. In the new version, the emphasis is upon God's mercy and redemptive love. Death is inevitable, of course, but Jesus the savior has softened its sting: while hellfire is still a reality for the wicked, it no longer seems to be a possibility for children:

> And now, dear Children, for whose Sakes
> 　　This little Book I've penn'd,
> O be entreated now to make
> 　　Your Judge your dearest Friend . . .
>
> Keep close to his most just Commands,
> 　　In all Things please him well;
> Then happy it will be with you
> 　　When Thousands go to Hell.[37]

In the seventeenth century, tributes to dead children, such as elegies, had expressed the hopeful view that the young were in heaven; but in works addressed to living children, this optimism was an innovation.[38]

Advice Books

Books of advice had abounded in the preceding centuries, aimed at a range of ages and offering hints on how to achieve worldly success. By the first half of the eighteenth century, however, the three genres of advice, courtesy, and religious books often blended, and it can be difficult to place a work neatly in any one category. One such example is the anonymous *Friendly Instructor*, an English import that was reprinted at Boston at just about the same time as the *History of the Holy Jesus*. It consists of a series of dialogues between friends, presented in a format of questions and answers that run like a series of scenes in a play. The debates, however, center mostly on religious topics, particularly on how to undertake religious duties. Presenting an even gentler view of childhood than does the *History* and a novel angle on girls, it offers examples of how to read the scriptures with understanding. Moreover, its clear message is that children can help one another in the search for Christian truth.

Its treatment of girls is undoubtedly related to the sex of its author. She was an unidentified British "Lady . . . who has long been employed in the Education of Children," as Philip Doddridge, the English nonconformist minister and hymn writer, notes in its preface. (This impeccable reference made the book immediately acceptable to the godly in New England and elsewhere.) The work's female slant is at once evident in its dialogues: all but one of them take place between two girls, without any boys present. Since the only other inclusion of girls in books for children previously had been as exemplars of pious deaths, this was a striking novelty.[39]

The first American imprint of the *Friendly Instructor* was issued by Benjamin Franklin, ever alert to publishing opportunities for children, in December 1745. It was advertised in the *Boston Weekly News-Letter* as "just published" by Joshua Blanchard only a month later. It was originally subtitled *A Companion for young Ladies and Gentlemen*, but when it was reprinted in 1749 by Rogers and Fowle, its printers suggested an even younger audience by changing the subtitle to *A Companion for young Masters and young Misses*. It was being imported into Charles Town, South Carolina, by 1747, but none of its domestic imprints for the next three decades, whether from Boston, from Philadelphia, or from Garrat Noel's bookstore in New York, have survived its enthusiastic young readers. The work continued in popularity throughout the remainder of the colonial period and beyond.[40]

The *Friendly Instructor*'s "plain and easy Dialogues" present problematic areas in children's lives, such as telling lies or the death of a sibling, and include several discussions of the actual process of reading and listening: "*On reading the SCRIP-TURES*"; "*On reflecting on what is read*"; and "*On remembering what we hear.*" In one of these dialogues, Charlotte and Olivia discuss reading the scriptures. Charlotte informs her friend that she does enough reading at school, so "I don't love to read at home too." "Not love to read the Word of God, *Charlotte!*" is Olivia's scandalized response: " 'tis sad indeed if you don't." She asks Charlotte whether her parents read the Bible. Charlotte replies that they do, but that they read it "to mind the Sense, which is none of our Business till we are bigger." Olivia counters that, young as they are, they are capable of getting some meaning from the scriptures, and she suggests that Charlotte has just been concentrating on pronouncing the words accurately, without attending to their meaning: "You mind [pay attention] to read the Words right, but I find not at all [to] what you are reading about." The notion that children should be actively seeking meaning from their reading was not new, but the contrast between reading aloud accurately ("word-calling," as reading teachers would term it today) and comprehension was rarely made so explicit.[41]

Olivia then shows Charlotte, using techniques of questioning that she had learned from her father, how to approach biblical texts. She gets Charlotte to summarize the account in the second book of Kings about how the prophet Elisha was mocked by children, forty-two of whom were subsequently torn to shreds by two female bears coming out from the woods. Why, she asks, did they suffer this fate? Charlotte ventures in response that it was because they were wicked children. Upon further questioning, she gains the insight that their wickedness lay not in their having called the prophet a "bald Head" (after all, he was indeed bald), but in venting their anger upon him by taunting him for a physical infirmity. "I did not think of this Use of the Story before; but, as you say, 'tis indeed a very common thing, when we would show our Anger, against any, to call 'em crooked, hump-back'd, bald-pated, one-eye'd . . ." Charlotte then goes a step farther and realizes that nobody should be mocked for an infirmity. The girls' interaction becomes a model, in short, of how to explore the implications of what one reads and make inferences from the text.[42]

A comparable emphasis on active intellectual participation is transferred to prayer: unless "your Thoughts go along with your Words," as another devout girl, Dorinda, puts it, true prayer is not taking place. Nor can one remember a sermon without paying attention: "how Shou'd [young persons] remember what the Minister says, when they are thinking on other Things most of the Time?"[43]

The religious slant of this little work is far more hopeful than grim. While the possibility of hell has not disappeared, the emphasis is overwhelmingly on faith as a determinant of salvation, and there is no discussion of predestination. Indeed, it is emblematic of the differences between this and earlier books that preach religious piety that Lemira, stricken by illness and convinced in the nick of time of her true repentance and faith in a merciful Savior, in fact lives to greet her friend again.[44] The entire tone of the *Friendly Instructor* is very different from that of, say, the *School of Good Manners*. Its young readers are not preached at; instead, they are instructed indirectly by the discussions between other children: the book is well named, for it is friends who are undertaking each other's instruction.

Other new books were appearing in the advice category. It was again a sign of changing times that Boston took to its heart two works addressed to older children, both printed by Rogers and Fowle, that concentrated largely on the practical and the secular. The first was advertised in May 1747 as *A Present for an Apprentice: Or, a Sure Guide to gain both Esteem and Estate, with Rules for his Conduct to his master, and in the World*. It discusses such matters as comportment after leaving an apprenticeship, choosing a wife, and the education of children. ("I recommend it to you, in the most earnest manner, not only to make them scholars, or even Gentlemen . . . but men of business too.") It emphasizes the traditional qualities expected of apprentices—honesty, industry, loyalty, and service.[45]

The second book, companion to the first, which was published in Boston a few months later, was praised even more extravagantly by its booksellers. Their advertisement heralded it as "One of the most useful Books of the kind extant" and "necessary to be had in all Families." Titled *A Present for a servant Maid, Or, the Sure Means of gaining Love and Esteem*, it had reportedly sold in large numbers in London. The book was full of practical hints on going to market, dressing fish, flesh, and fowl, and doing laundry. Despite the subtitles of these two books, their emphasis is more on caution and competency than material success. "Esteem," however, was a word now in high regard, thanks to the educational philosophy of John Locke, and the allusions to love, esteem, and estate invoked the approach of the British printer John Newbery.[46]

Booksellers in the middle colonies were quick to print the first of this pair of books themselves. By December 1749, David Hall's imprint at Philadelphia of *A Present for an Apprentice* was already in its fourth edition, reprinted twice within twelve months. It was later advertised in the *Pennsylvania Gazette* by Benjamin Franklin: he placed it seventh on a list of books that set—presumably in order of importance—*The American Instructor* in second place and John Lewis's explanation of the church catechism in fourth. As a reader commented, once he had overcome the unattractiveness of the "unpromising" title of *A Present*, he found there "such a system of morality and oeconomy as persons of all ranks might improve by" and a style that "the most accomplished readers might be delighted with." Retailed at one shilling, or nine pence a dozen, this pamphlet proved attractive to children and adults alike. For some reason, perhaps because "servant" had a different connotation in slave-holding America, its sister publication did not.[47]

Schoolbooks

A new work for reading instruction appeared in the mid eighteenth century that was markedly different from earlier and, indeed, from contemporary schoolbooks for children, *The Child's New Play-Thing*. This was the first spelling book to reveal that the influence of John Locke, who believed that reading should be an enjoyable activity, had now reached into texts for reading instruction.

The Child's New Play-Thing is anonymous, but it was printed and probably written by Mary Cooper, a printer's widow, in London in 1742. Its third edition, a Boston imprint, was advertised in January 1744 in the *Boston Weekly News-Letter*, with a subtitle that suggests the work lays its emphasis not on being instructive, nor even on being easy, but on actually being amusing: *Being a Spelling-book intended to make the Learning to read a Diversion instead of a Task*. It diverged dramatically from its predecessors by including the "romances," or histories, that Boston children had formerly been able to read only in chapbook form, and it offered "Scripture Histories, Fables, Stories, moral and religious Precepts, Proverbs, Songs, Riddles, Dialogues, &c." The usual claim was made that it was tailored to the young mind: "The whole adapted to the Capacities of Children, and divided into Lessons of one, two three and four Syllables." (Some things had changed, but the assumption that word difficulty was a function of syllabic length had not.) Dialogues had already been added to it since the first edition: "1. Shewing how a little Boy shall make every Body love him. 2. How a little Boy shall become a great Man." (These, as we have seen, were also published in chapbook form and were probably the work of John Newbery.) *A Child's New Play-Thing* is an exemplar of the new approach to children that was soon to be perfected by Newbery, which focused on their pleasure rather than their spiritual well-being.[48]

Another American imprint of *The Child's New Play-Thing* was published in Boston in 1750, and others in Philadelphia in 1757, in Wilmington, Delaware, in 1761, and at least once more in Philadelphia in 1765. It was imported occasionally into the south: Purdie and Dixon's *Virginia Gazette* advertised it in 1773. It did much better as an import in the middle and northeastern colonies: Benjamin Franklin was selling imported copies in Philadelphia in the summer of 1747. It was imported into, and sold in, New York by Hugh Gaine, who gave it a splashy quarter-column advertisement in December 1752 and for the next four years advertised it occasionally. These numbers pale when compared to those of Dilworth's *A New Guide*—over a ten-year period in the 1760s the New England bookseller Jeremiah Condy sold twenty-two copies of Dilworth's *New Guide* for

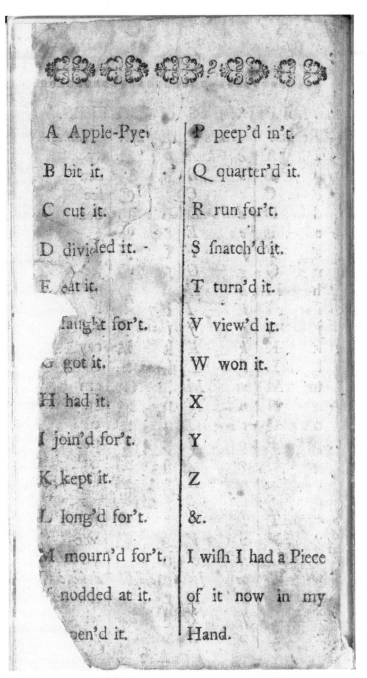

A Apple-Pye,	P peep'd in't.
B bit it.	Q quarter'd it.
C cut it.	R run for't.
D divided it.	S snatch'd it.
E eat it.	T turn'd it.
F faught for't.	V view'd it.
G got it.	W won it.
H had it.	X
I join'd for't.	Y
K kept it.	Z
L long'd for't.	&.
M mourn'd for't.	I wish I had a Piece
N nodded at it.	of it now in my
O pen'd it.	Hand.

FIGURE 17. The alphabet in *The Child's New Play-Thing* (Boston: J. Draper & J. Edwards, 1750). The motif of self-gratifying consumption presented here offers a striking contrast to the stern theological messages of the alphabet verses of the *New-England Primer*. (Courtesy, Rare Books Division, the New York Public Library, Astor, Lenox and Tilden Foundations)

every copy of *The Child's New Play-Thing*—but they do suggest a small but faithful audience.[49]

The first extant American edition of *The Child's New Play-Thing* is the Boston one of 1750, a reproduction of the London fourth edition. It opens with an alphabet that, far from confronting the child with original sin, as the *New-England Primer* does with its "In *Adam's* Fall / We Sinned all," brandishes consumption as the object of the child's interest. Childish aggression and the theft of desired objects are now depicted as understandable, even admirable: "A Apple Pye / B bit it / C cut it . . . R run for't. / S snatch'd it. . . . I wish I had a Piece of it now in my Hand."[50] Patricia Crain sees this mid-century publication as a turning point in presentations of the alphabet. Instead of the text dominating the illustrations, as I argue the alphabet verses did to the woodcuts of the *New-England Primer*, here the alphabetical letters become characters themselves in a tale of greed and consumption, serving as the subjects of attacking verbs such as "bit" and "snatch'd." From this time on, Crain argues, the alphabet would be "dressed up and decked out, animated, ornamented, narrated, and consumed."[51] Meanwhile, alphabet books, previously missing from the American experience, would become a much-loved feature of American childhood.

After this riotous introduction, the tables (called simply "WORDS") of the *Child's New Play-Thing* are, by the standards of rival spelling books, a hodge-podge, but they are grouped semantically—birds, fish, insects. After each set of words of a given number of syllables, the work is structured so that the child meets one lesson on moral precepts, another on religious precepts, then a fable, and finally a "history" on a scriptural topic (such as "Noah's Flood" or the account of Sampson).

Under this organizational scheme religious indoctrination has been reduced to a quarter of the whole, but the secular impact of the entire work is even stronger. The *Child's New Play-Thing* lauds virtues that allow the individual to navigate the shoals of a consumer society, as the late eighteenth century was fast becoming. Watch out, is the message: there are a lot of folks out there waiting to get you. Be prudent in choosing your friends. The first fable, accompanying the lesson on monosyllables, deals with a good dog who kept bad company: "*Tray* was a good Dog, and would not hurt the least thing in the World." His association with the aggressive and well-named Snap, however, leads him and his pal to be torn limb from limb by dogs whom Snap has alienated. "By this Fable you see how dangerous it is to be in Company with bad Boys," the moral counsels.[52]

The fable that accompanies words of four syllables focuses on true versus apparent value. As a stag drinks from a fountain, he admires his magnificent antlers reflected there but thinks poorly of his skinny legs. His opinion of his own attributes is altered radically when hounds pursue him and his antlers become fatally entangled in the branches of trees. His last words, as the hounds close in on him for the kill, voice his regret over his failure to appreciate what was really worthwhile about himself: "How foolish I was to depreciate those Legs, which alone could be serviceable to me, and admire these Horns, which have been accessary to my Destruction!"[53]

What these and other fables in the *Child's New Play-Thing* have in common is the notion that the individual is in control of his own fate: with a wise choice of companions and an intelligent assessment of one's own qualities, one can keep out of trouble. Almost stunningly absent in these tales is the earlier concept that one's material, let alone spiritual, well-being in this life and the next is wholly dependent on the divine will of the Almighty.

This approach to the individual as a social being is reinforced by the additions to the spelling book of dialogues that could well have been lifted straight from the work of Newbery. They focus overwhelmingly on being loved and depict the rewards to be gained by buttering up one's seniors. The first dialogue, which would be reproduced in the chapbook *A Child's New Gift*, purports to show how a little boy can make everybody love him. "Every Body is so fond of Master L—— . . . Because he is a good natur'd Boy, and loves to oblige every Body." The lad is cheerful, never peevish; he shares his possessions with his playfellows; and he has excellent manners. Having good manners means "to behave yourself prettily at all Times, especially amongst Strangers." Manners do not consist of being considerate to others but of formulas, of saying "yes Sir" or "no Madam" and "pray Madam give me such a Thing" and of bowing handsomely when entering or leaving a room. As for the boy's godliness and piety—not one word is said.[54]

In another dialogue, the boy is taught how to become a great man. He is to be very good, and he is told, "love your Book better than your Play, and keep company with none but such Boys as do the same." He should enjoy reading "Histories of great Men" and emulating them. He should furnish himself "with all Kinds of useful Knowledge." He needs to "write well, to read properly, to speak fluently, and to think with Judgment." The Bible has vanished as the one book worth studying. The book has been redefined as a book of secular instruction. The scope of reading now includes biography. A one-sentence summary at the end of the dialogue is telling: man and God are put on an equal footing as objects of admiration and emulation, while the wrath of God is no longer to be dreaded. What counts is how other people view what you do: "In short, you must love God and good Men, and fear nothing but to do an ill Action."[55]

While the worldly messages radiated by *The Child's New Play-Thing* represent a radical departure from those emitted by any other speller that had reached the American market, the work is also innovative in its choice of reading material. Along with rhymed riddles, it includes stories that had formerly been the province of the chivalric romance: the tales of Saint George and the dragon; of Guy, the Earl of Warwick; and of Fortunatus and the purse ever full of money. In short, a spelling book was daring to include forms of literature that had always been considered anathema by those who held to the old Puritan values.[56]

Of the three romances presented in *The Child's New Play-Thing*, Guy of Warwick was probably the best known. It had appeared in England in numerous guises, including that of a cheap chapbook.[57] In the version of Guy provided by the 1750 Boston edition of *The Child's New Play-Thing*, the story is reduced to a few pages, but the essential love story is preserved. Guy has to win the love of Phillis, the beautiful daughter of the Earl of Warwick, by some "noble Deeds of Arms." These include confronting a giant named Rumbo who was so tall that "he could step over a House with as much Ease as we step over a Kennel"; and he saves a lion from a dragon by thrusting his sword "under the Wings of the Dragon quite to his Heart."[58] All in all, *The Child's New Play-Thing* gives a glimpse of a very different world of reading from that of the seventeenth century. But the work was probably never adopted as a school text in the American provinces. Indeed, its title page recognized its potential for use at home by stating that it was designed "for the USE of SCHOOLS, or for Children before they go to School."[59]

Fairy Tales, Nursery Rhymes, and *The Arabian Nights*

The story of the swashbuckling Guy was a "romance" or a "history" rather than a fairy tale, but it was as close to a fairy tale as most American children would get before the 1760s. Although the French fairy tales written by Madame D'Aulnoy had been translated into English by 1700, they were not imported into the colonies until the 1750s. Indeed, discomfort with the genre continued well into the nineteenth century: Americans of all denominations were suspicious of fairy tales, whose stories of goblins, monsters, and magic violated the Protestant concept of truth. When fairy tales did appear, they were often in chapbook form. Unspecified "Fairy Tales" are mentioned, for instance, in the advertisements for chapmen's books Hugh Gaine placed in his New York newspaper in 1755, as well as in a Philadelphia almanac in 1760. In addition, there is some slender evidence by the late 1760s that these tales were being printed on a domestic press: an advertisement for *Robinson Crusoe, [Mother] Goose's Tales, Arabian Nights, History of Mother Bunch, Tom Thumb, Jack the Piper, Jack Horner,* and *Jack and the Giants* appeared at the back of *The Friar and the Boy,* published in 1767 by Andrew Barclay of Boston.[60]

The Arabian Nights is one example out of many (another being the new epistolary novels) of a work that would branch out into at least two formats: one high-quality edition and one chapbook version. It was on sale in an expensive edition, as a six-volume import, from the middle of the century on. But it had also made it into the chapbook market by 1763, when Andrew Steuart listed it among his books for chapmen, along with *Guy Earl of Warwick, Aesop's Fables, Valentine and Orson,* and *Gulliver's Travels.*[61]

Nursery rhymes fared only marginally better. Mary Cooper printed *Tommy Thumb's Song Book* in London in 1744. The work contains many of the old nursery rhymes and was obviously designed for children. It may well have been one of the imported "pretty books," discussed below, that were advertised throughout the colonies; it was on sale at Boston in 1767, but it was not widely printed in America until much later.[62] The entire genre was unsuited to Puritan sensibilities.

Copybooks and Writing Pieces

If nursery rhymes and fairy tales met with little success up to the American Revolution, another kind of text—one often overlooked by scholars—was common throughout the colonies: the texts that writing masters used for their students to practice their penmanship. In the eighteenth century, Britain's wealth was ever more linked to her overseas trade. Commerce was king, and commerce required an army of clerks to carry out the drudgery of record keeping and accounting of an empire. The effect commerce had on content may be readily seen in the content of copybooks. Because children inevitably read the texts that they were penning, they were being exposed to new, and vastly more secular, messages.

Here we turn again to the collection of the boys' penmanship examples, penned at the three writing schools of Boston between 1748 and 1782, this time to examine their messages. The Boston writing masters frequently used their own copy of George Bickham's *Universal Penman*, engraved in London by 1743, for a source for setting copies. Almost two-thirds of the longer pieces penned by the boys can be found in Bickham's work. Apart from two pieces that do not fall neatly into any category (1 percent), the remainder of the boys' 188 manuscripts can be sorted into nine categories: 80 moral and ethical pieces (43 percent), 28 business and commerce (15 percent), 17 aesthetic (9 percent), 17 penmanship (9 percent), 14 political (7 percent), 12 intellectual (6 percent), 9 religious (5 percent), 7 educational (4 percent), and 2 bookkeeping (1 percent).[63]

When these are compared with the books that children read in the preceding century, it is startling to find that only nine of the pieces, a mere 5 percent, deal with religious themes. More than 40 percent of the collection addresses moral issues. The one-liners are particularly suited to conveying such messages ("Sound not a trumpet in your own commendation"), but page-length pieces also hammer away at ethical themes, particularly those that relate to man's social relationships. These were directly relevant to the jobs that the boys of the writing school were expected to hold, where retaining the confidence of one's trading or business associate was essential.

Many of the one-sentence copies for beginners dwell on the importance of choosing friends wisely and avoiding the disastrous effects of a bad choice: "You may learn to know men by their company"; "Better to be alone than in bad company"; "Flattering friends are worse than enemies." Others warn against the dangers of boastfulness: "Nothing more recommends a Youth than Modesty." Still others frankly admit that a financial incentive is a potent one: "The hope of reward sweetens Labour"; "Money commands many enjoyments." Education is the key to worldly success and by implication permits one to rise above one's social class: "Education is that which makes the man." Religion receives only token acknowledgment: "Admire, adore and praise, the God that guides thy ways."[64]

The longer pieces in the moral category follow in the same vein, offering lists of instructions on how to foster and cement social relationships. The close relationship between personal discretion and financial reward is summed up in one of the titles, "Human Prudence, or, How to get Riches." Virtue is featured frequently. As John Molineux proclaims in his 1763 piece, "Virtue's the Friend of Life the Soul of Health / The poor Man's Comfort and ye rich Mans wealth." Nowhere in this text is the Deity mentioned. The commercial pieces in the collection bring the connection between prosperity and prudence into even sharper focus. They discuss the importance of reputation, quoting from Shakespeare's *Merchant of Venice*,

"Good name in Man or Woman, / Is the immediate Jewel of our Souls" in a piece titled "Reputation and the Credit of the Merchant." Andrew Cunningham's manuscript, which he penned in 1774 at the South Writing School, declares that "Merchants [are] of great Benefit to the Publick" because they spread around the wealth. Another piece, penned on ten different manuscripts, is titled "How to get Riches, Humbly inscrib'd to the British Nation." It unwittingly reveals how dependent American commerce was on the mother country.

The thrust of the fourteen political pieces is on extolling and protecting personal and political liberty. Apart from a fleeting reference to "princely order," only two of the pieces mention royalty, and both were penned early, in the 1750s. Ten of the others, in contrast, include the word "liberty" either in their titles, their opening lines, or both, and they emphasize that the duty of government is to protect the governed. A much repeated sentiment is, "The Love of Liberty with Life is giv'n." Liberty and Britain are linked, seemingly indissolubly: one piece, after apostrophizing Liberty as a goddess, continues, "From British Laws our choicest blessings come." These sentiments, all of which derived from Bickham's *Universal Penman*, convey the message that ordinary citizens on both sides of the Atlantic were believed to have, as early as the 1740s, what would later be termed "unalienable Rights." As the relationship between the colonies and Britain worsened, however, preceding the American Revolution, dissatisfaction with the British government found its way into one piece: in 1774, eleven-year-old James Thwing of the Queen Street school penned a piece subtitled, "Considerations on the destructive Spirit of Arbitrary Power." (It had no model in the *Universal Penman*.) The sole end of government, his piece proclaims, is the good of the governed. When the interests of the governed are not pursued, "we know what Opinion the people will have of their Governors."[65]

These are Enlightenment themes. Not a single piece speaks of Christian themes, such as Christ's redemption. Instead, religion is to be esteemed for its civilizing influence. These and the other texts, which focus on intellectual and aesthetic topics as well as the value of fine penmanship, reflect the secularism, rationalism, optimism, and materialism of the eighteenth century. If someone had deliberately chosen texts to educate young penmen in the rights of man, he could not have done a better job. There, inscribed in the penmanship copies of the writing schools of Boston, is a recipe for the declaration of American independence, once the mother country was perceived to have betrayed her trust.

The expansiveness of this vision in the penmanship copies does not extend to girls. Girls were not expected to work for a living—even though many young women did. Members of the female sex are barely mentioned, and when they are, the mention is unflattering, invoking them only in their relation to males. In one text, they are viewed as a sexual temptation to youth: young men are warned to keep away from "the harlot's door." Mothers, it is true, have an important role to play in guiding their children, but they are cautioned against overindulging their talented sons: "Nature appears profusely kind, / Trust not to that. Act you yo[u]r part: / Imprint just morals on their heart."[66]

Books for Amusement

The eighth and newest category of books for children, those designed to please them rather than instruct them, penetrated the American urban market most completely. The works of John Newbery, who is universally considered the originator of "children's literature," made their way across the seas to American bookstores and American children, at least in the major seaports. Newbery began his career as an apprentice to a printer in Reading, England. When William Carnan took over the business in 1737 and died the same year, Newbery continued it, married the widowed Mary Carnan two years later, moved to London, and by 1745 was installed at the Bible and Sun in St. Paul's Churchyard, where he purveyed fever powder as well as children's books.[67]

Apart from the very recent *Child's New Play-Thing*, which was ostensibly an instructional work, the only books that British children had been able to read purely for pleasure before Newbery published his *Little Pretty Pocket-Book* in 1744 were the romances and histories of the cheap chapbook market. Newbery's contribution was to distance himself from the chapbook trade and to create works for children that were superior, at least in terms of their physical production, to anything in the chapbook market. He deliberately made them alluring, with secular, child-oriented content and many illustrations. Small, with brightly colored book covers and often gilt-tipped pages, they were appealing both to sight and touch. The key word that summed up all these attributes was "pretty."[68]

Newbery's texts focus on children themselves as characters. (So, of course, had many religious works such as James Janeway's *A Token for Children*; but those accounts featured children whose lives had been devout but who were now dead.) Those in Newbery texts were alive and engaged in a variety of exploits. The tales were not realistic, but they mostly presented games, fun, and possibilities to children—particularly the possibility of material success, provided one adhered to a few carefully defined rules. Compared with the chapbook market, which endlessly recycled old tales, Newbery's publications struck refreshingly new notes.

Newbery invoked "The great Mr. Locke" in his *Little Pretty Pocket-Book* to justify these new kinds of books for children. He alluded to Locke's views on reasoning as the essential element of the educational experience. "Would you have a Wise Son, teach him to reason early. Let him read, and make him understand what he reads. No Sentence should be passed over without a strict Examination of the Truth of it." Discipline was also to be conducted along Lockean lines: children's passions were to be subdued, not by whipping, but by "Reasoning, and mild Discipline." But Newbery had other motives than educational ones in mind. The subtitle of the book, *Intended for the Instruction and Amusement of Little Master Tommy, and Pretty Miss Polly*, targeted girls explicitly as its audience as well as boys, for perhaps the first time in the history of British publishing. (A few books had earlier been addressed to boys and girls, but no prior work for children had mentioned a girl's name in its title.) Its price restricted it to a middle-class audience.[69]

Over the years, Newbery added more and more titles to his juvenile publications. In 1752 he published his *Lilliputian Magazine* for children. It was short-lived, but known to American children: it actually had forty-nine young subscribers from Maryland. Some of Newbery's books, such as *A Museum for Young Gentlemen and Ladies*, were openly didactic, but in a genial way; others tapped into Anglicanism, including *The History of the Life . . . of our Lord and Saviour Jesus Christ* and Newbery's child's companion to the *Book of Common Prayer*; yet others were instructional texts in reading. These included the *Royal Battledore*, an illustrated introduction to the alphabet (and a rival to the old hornbook), and *The Infant Tutor*, subtitled "an Easy Spelling Book." But yet others were openly entertaining, telling stories in which children were the leading characters. In 1761 Newbery published his *The Renowned History of Giles Gingerbread*, and four years later *The History of Little Goody Two-Shoes*. They were destined to become children's classics.[70]

Newbery's works for children, although they grew out of a nominally Anglican religious context, were replete with the materialism of the mid-eighteenth century. *A Pocket-Book* consists mainly of illustrated children's games (Thread the Needle, Blindmen's Buff, Shuttle-Cock); they accompany each letter of the alphabet, in upper- and lower-case, with verses and morals. The game for "little k," for instance, has a picture of a boy at bat and is titled "Base-Ball." (Confusingly, the illustrations in the accompanying text do not correspond to the alphabetical letters.) Once he has hit the ball, the boy flies off to "the next destin'd Post / And then Home with Joy." The moral is a comparison with British merchants: "Thus *Britons* for Lucre / Fly over the Main; / But, with Pleasure transported, / Return back again." The statement that joy results from returning home with new-found wealth, obtained overseas, is not far removed in spirit from some of the sentiments of the penmanship texts.

The "Great Z" (capital *Z*) introduces the fable of the shepherd who cries wolf. The moral is in the form of a letter from the children's "hearty Friend, Jack the Giant-Killer": "To Master Tommy, or Miss Polly. This Boy's Fate, my Dear, is a remarkable Instance of the Folly and Wickedness of telling Lies." Lying is not punished because it is an offense against God; rather, it brings its own judgment down on the head of the liar. Newbery's overall message is clear. Motivation is to be rooted in the desire for personal self-advancement, not by a fear for the fate of one's immortal soul. Boys are to be motivated by their desire to get ahead in the world; girls by their need to make themselves popular, presumably because popularity enhances their marriage prospects. All this is consistent with the message of John Locke that parental and public approbation or disapproval are the keys to controlling children's behavior.[71]

Toward the end of a 1767 edition of *A Little Pretty Pocket-Book*, on a page illustrated by a coach and six (always a Newbery metaphor for success), Newbery presents "a little Boy, who learned his Book to that surprising Degree, that his Master could scarce teach him fast enough." In this context, precociously early reading ability gets the attention of the adults in the child's life. Since the boy had the added advantage of being "dutiful to his Parents and obliging to his Playmates, every Body loved him. His Learning and Behavior purchased him the Esteem of the greatest People, and raised him from a mean State of Life to a Coach and Six, in which he rides to this Day." The word "purchased" is well chosen. In this view of the world, education serves as a down-payment for climbing the social ladder. The concept of "Esteem" is readily recognizable from the work of John Locke.

The female version of this exemplary boy child is "a little Lady . . . who has behaved so well that every Body is in Love with her." She, too, is dutiful to her parents, kind to her playmates, and obliging to everyone else. Like her male counterpart, she is rewarded for sticking to her books: "she learns her Book to Admiration, works well with her Needle, and is so modest, so willing to do as she is bid," that Lady Meanwell gives her a gold watch—no doubt to add punctuality to her many other virtues—and promises her a ride in her own coach. (Girls who were not members of the aristocracy, of course, could rarely aspire to owning a coach themselves, but a ride in someone else's, particularly one belonging to a titled woman, was a desirable substitute.) Newbery closes this letter to the imaginary parent with, " 'Tis this learning, Madam, and good Behaviour, that brings us the Esteem of the whole World."[72]

Many of Newbery's books contain references to learning to read that throw further light on just how far reading has been removed from its earlier religious moorings. In *The Valentine's Gift*, first published in 1765 and advertised in the *Virginia Gazette* three years later, Newbery paints a portrait of what reading instructional texts should look like. In this tale, a little boy is weeping because "they made him go to School, and he did not like to go to School." His "Valentine," Lady Lucy, demands to see the contents of his satchel. Evidently dissatisfied with what she finds, she opens her closet, "where all Mr. Newbery's little books lay in a window. . . . Bless me! says the little boy, I should like such books as these." He is enchanted by the sight of "Miss Friendly in the lord-mayor's coach" as well as by a pretty little Bible that makes him exclaim that he would "love to read in such a Bible as this." He is also very taken by the Newbery dictionary, "the size of a snuff box. This Dictionary won't come thump against my head like our great one at school." He admires the "pretty Little Fables, written by Abraham Aesop, Esq." and the *History of Little Goody Two-Shoes* (other Newbery imprints).[73]

Lady Lucy informs the boy that she is not keen on having her "books tumbled over in this manner; but if you will promise me to be a good boy, you shall begin with the first of them, and carry away as many as you can read. What, put them in my pocket, mame [ma'am]? says he. Yes, in your pocket." Off the child goes, and reads five books before dinner. Although he has the reputation of being "the dullest booby in town" who "cannot learn anything," he defends himself by saying: "Not in those dirty dull books . . . but I can learn any thing in such nice little pretty books as these."[74]

Side by side with this shameless internal advertising of other Newbery products, the account in the *Valentine's Gift* again emphasizes the pleasurable aspect of reading. It also offers a new angle—a comparison between school texts and Newbery texts that redounds very much to the credit of the latter. The message is that even dull children can learn from attractive books, and that adult dictionaries are too heavy, metaphorically as well as physically, for children. Books small enough to be tucked away in one's pocket have a special appeal. But the feature that is the most striking departure from earlier times is Newbery's treatment of the Bible. His "pretty little Bible" is to be preferred to the full version. To be sure, children's versions of biblical material had been available in chapbook form for decades, but the suggestion that the child ought to be reading a reduced version rather than the original would never have been countenanced by earlier authors.

In other works, Newbery presents highly fictionalized accounts of actual reading instruction. They are illuminating for what they reveal about motivation for reading, the child's responsibility for learning, and even reading methodology.

Giles Gingerbread is the young hero of Newbery's story of that name, first printed in London in 1764. (It was reproduced in Boston four years later, where it was retailed for two pence.) Giles is motivated to learn to read by hearing the tale of Toby, who through his literacy won his master's confidence, partnership, and eventually wealth and coach, because he revealed the dishonesty of a fellow servant by reporting it in an anonymous letter, disguising his handwriting. Giles's father, a baker, teaches his son the alphabet by giving him twenty-four gingerbread letters. (The letters *J* and *V* have still not made their way into the alphabet in this tale.) Giles uses them to spell the word *top* correctly, but when he tries to spell *goose* he spells it *guse*. "You Blockhead, is that your Manner of Spelling" is his father's unkind reaction to this effort in invented spelling. Giles is saved from a more physical manifestation of his father's wrath only because he has to chase after some geese and goslings. He returns in tears, complaining that the geese hissed and laughed at him. "Ah, that is because you cannot read, answered the Father. Come hither, *Giles*, says he, you must learn to know all the Letters, and the Sound they have, alone, and when joined to others, before you can spell and read."[75]

Giles proceeds to pick up each letter in turn and study it carefully. "A, A, A, says he, Ay, Mr. A, I shall know you again. Apple for that—B, B, B, you are not at all like A, Mr. B: I should be a Blockhead if I did not know you—C, C, C, I shall know you Mr. C indeed, and so will every Boy that loves Custard." His father, pleased with his son's progress, rewards him with one book that has lessons on how to be happy and go to heaven (a classic Newbery text used in many of his books for children) and by another that provides vivid examples of how those who ignore reasonable explanations will come to a bad end. The boy who flouts his father's injunction not to go near a lion certainly meets his: in the accompanying picture, the lion smirks at the child's lifeless body. Giles has done so well that his father bakes him a gingerbread book. Giles soon nibbles off a corner from it: "I always learn it before I eat it," is his defense, and "I am not the only Boy who has eat his Words." Relenting, his father bakes Giles a gingerbread book a day, "so that it may be truly said, he lived upon Learning."[76]

This little story has several features that are significantly different from those in older works. As in *The Valentine's Gift* that would follow it a year later, there is no suggestion that learning to read is valuable because it provides access to the scriptures. Instead, the motivation here is that Giles needs to learn to read so that he will travel about in a coach and other people will not make fun of him. His father assists him by making the letters, but Giles is essentially responsible for his own learning, teaching himself the discriminating features of each letter. In terms of content, the characters are mainly children and the setting is a farm, but the death and dismemberment that befall the disobedient, in a story within the story, presage similar Awful Warnings of the next century, in which children cause their own disasters. (Nonetheless, in this case, the warnings are softened by being distanced from the protagonist.)

The tale of Giles also offers an insight into reading instructional methodology. The "sound" of a letter is clearly distinguished from its name (a distinction that spelling-book authors also made), and the learning of a particular sound is reinforced by linking a particular letter to a word that begins with that letter: *A* for apple, *B* for blockhead, *C* for custard. (As in the alphabet of the *Child's New Play-Thing*, the key words are tilted toward the gustatory.) This approach was as old as the first alphabet verses, but it is unusual to find any description of what the child was supposed to do with it. One feature, however, did not differ from all that had gone before. The divorce of reading instruction from writing instruction was still a constant: Giles had to learn the letters by remembering their shapes, without once writing them down.

The History of Goody Two Shoes, which Newbery published a year after Giles Gingerbread, goes one step further and actually portrays the teaching of graduated reading lessons. Goody Two Shoes and her younger brother have been left alone in the world by the death of both parents. Convinced that a kindly man in the neighborhood is good because of his "great Learning," Goody is highly motivated to learn to read herself. (The copybook maxim "Learning makes a good Man better" comes to mind.) In the total absence, in England, of anything resembling the New England district school, Goody waylays little boys and girls as they return from school and borrows their books, which she reads until they come back for them. She progresses in this manner until she is fluent enough to teach others. Her instruction proceeds traditionally enough from letters to words to sentences, but her great innovation is to get the children to compose, even though they have not been taught to write. She achieves this by cutting out ten sets of wooden lowercase and six sets of capital letters and instructing her students to use them to write with: "And having got an old Spelling-Book, she made her Companions set up all the Words they wanted to spell, and after that she taught them to compose Sentences" on the lines of "*I will be good.*"[77]

She moves from child to child and house to house (in a chapter titled "*How Little* Two-Shoes *became a Trotting Tutoress*"), giving lessons. At each house she finds children who are reading at a higher level of accomplishment than the preceding one. Billy, her first pupil, calls her "doody Two-Shoes" because he is so young that he is "not able to speak plain." Despite the disadvantage of his extreme youth, he is able to identify the letters by name and set them out in alphabetical order. At her next stop, Sally Simpson (who, like Billy, is praised for having learned her previous lesson well) sets up the time-honored syllables, *ba be bi bo bu*, and gives them "their exact Sounds as she composed them." Goody, pleased with

Figure 18. A woodcut of "Goody Two-Shoes" teaching herself to read from books she has borrowed from schoolchildren on their way home, in *The History of Little Goody Two-Shoes* (New York: Hugh Gaine, 1775). In this American reprint of a Newbery children's book, Goody Two-Shoes learns to read so well that she becomes the teacher of other children. (Courtesy: American Antiquarian Society)

her pupil's progress, teaches Sally how to spell words of one syllable, such as *pear* and *plumb*, *top* and *ball*, *cock* and *hen*. These words, functional in a child's vocabulary, are reminiscent of similar semantic groupings in *The Child's New Play-Thing*.

Goody then trots off to her next clients, a family of poor children who live in Gaffer Cook's cottage. Goody asks one of the little boys what he had for dinner. When he responds, "bread," she says to him, "set the first Letter." He does so, and each child in turn contributes another letter until "*Bread*" is spelled. At her last stop, the children awaiting her eagerly are an advanced group, dealing "only in Sentences." One child sets up the letters to form the sentence—in, predictably, mostly words of one syllable—"*The Lord have Mercy upon me, and grant that I may be always good.*"[78]

Goody of course reaps the emotional and material rewards of prestige and employment for spreading the light of literacy across the countryside. Now called by her proper name, Margery, she is made the principal of what is grandly called "a Country College," where she continues her praiseworthy pedagogical work among the young. She holds her school in a large and spacious room and tries a kinesthetic approach to learning: the letters are placed around the room so that children have to get up and fetch them in order to spell words, "which not only kept them in Health, but fixed the Letters and Points firmly in their Minds."[79]

In a real sense, Newbery has been true to Locke's principles. Reading acquisition was enjoyable for these imaginary children; and they were reading and spelling only what they understood. Moreover, he invited the child into the world of literacy as an active partner with the characters he created. At one point in the *History of Goody Two Shoes*, after listing the mixed alphabet that Billy was to sort out ("B D F H . . ."), Newbery asks: "Now, pray, little Reader, take this Bodkin, and see if you can point out the Letters from these mixed Alphabets, and tell how they should be placed as well as little Boy Billy." The entire book was designed for a parent to read aloud to a child.

The New World of Children and the Expansion of Children's Reading

Newbery's publications in England occurred in a social context in which middle-class parents were treating children as special objects of affection and expense. In a sense, his work was a direct product of this context. The "new world of children" in the eighteenth century in England has been well sketched by John Plumb, who points to the features that transformed the lives of British children—at least those of the upper and middle classes—over the course of the century. Up to 1770, according to Plumb, the number of schools, particularly private schools and academies, increased steadily; after 1770 they increased sharply. The schools offered an ever-growing range of secular subjects designed to prepare boys for careers and equip girls with the proper social graces. At the same time, children were able to become spectators, along with their parents, at a host of novelties, such as zoos, puppet shows, and circuses. They could attend concerts, learn to play new instruments, draw and paint. They were taken on extensive tourist trips at home and even abroad. Card games, board games, and toys multiplied. The jigsaw puzzle, designed to teach maps in an amusing way, appeared in 1762. London clothiers designed special clothing for infants and children. Plumb argues that British middle-class children became "luxury objects" on whom their parents delighted to spend money.[80]

One of the purchases that British parents could make for their "luxury objects" was books—books, moreover, that sought to amuse children rather than instruct them. Newbery's publications were tailor-made for this aim. Their most salient attribute was their prettiness. Indeed, when the word "pretty" turns up in an American advertisement, it is usually a safe guess that a Newbery book is being advertised.

It did not take long for America, ever dependent on the culture of the mother country, to begin to enjoy its own consumer revolution. As Cary Carson, Ronald

Hoffman, Peter Albert, and others have demonstrated, the second half of the eighteenth century was the time of a major change in consumption in the America provinces, in which demand for items associated with refinement and gentility drove supply rather than the other way around. It has been said that books were not affected by these trends; whatever the case for adult books may be, America was certainly affected by the new market for children's books. At the same time, it should be borne in mind that more traditional reading material for children (for example, in the schoolbook category, Dilworth's spelling book) always held its own. But where Newbery books were concerned, they had no cherished titles to compete with or supplant; instead, they were a completely new addition to the market that could function alongside standard titles.[81]

The expansion of books designed to be read by children began tentatively in America in the 1740s, as we have seen, in the arenas of religious books, schoolbooks—even if these produced only one innovative imprint, *The Child's New Play-Thing*—and to a small extent, advice books. But from 1747 on, only three years after Newbery's first publication of *A Little Pretty Pocket-Book*, Newbery books became readily available in imported copies. With increasing frequency and in phrasing that identifies them with more and more certainty as Newbery books, newspapers in almost every major colonial port advertised imported children's books. Their advertisements appear in papers as far north as Massachusetts and as far south as South Carolina. Benjamin Franklin was the first to advertise what appear to be Newbery works in the *Pennsylvania Gazette* of July 1747, publicizing, side by side with the *Child's New Play-Thing*, "sundry pretty books for inticing children to read." Two years later, the *South Carolina Gazette* mentioned "new invented Books for Children" and advertised children's books regularly thereafter. In November 1750, imported Newbery titles were given a great deal of space in an advertisement in the *Pennsylvania Gazette*, and their contents listed. A June 1756 issue of the *Boston Weekly News-Letter* informed its customers that, "imported in the last ships from London," there were "all sorts Toys, a fine Assortment of pretty Books for Children." The conjunction between toys and books was highly significant. Both were for the child's enjoyment without any overtly didactic intent.[82] By 1772, Edward Cox and Edward Berry, two Londoners who had opened a store in Boston in 1766, were featuring sixty-nine "Little Books for the Amusement and Instruction of Children" in their catalogue as a firmly established separate genre.[83]

The first Newbery books extensively advertised for the American market were the products of his playful approach to reading instruction itself rather than his *Little Pretty Pocket-Book* and other works aimed more directly at children's amusement. Newbery promoted his instructional works in a lengthy advertisement that he placed in the *Pennsylvania Gazette* of November 1750. For a shilling, a parent could purchase *A Museum for young Gentlemen and Ladies: Or, A private Tutor for little Masters and Misses*. Aimed, for a British audience, at governesses and tutors in the home setting, this work ran the gamut of instructional subjects from "Directions for reading with Eloquence and Propriety" to historical and geographical descriptions of various countries and the dying words of great men. Two pennies would buy *The Royal Battledore: Or, First Book for Children*, which was Newbery's replacement for the old hornbook and intended as the first work to introduce a child to reading. It claimed to teach the alphabet (in twenty-four letters), in "a plain, easy, and entertaining Manner, in order to induce Children to learn their Letters." It also offered some first syllables, and—its only concession to religion— the Lord's Prayer. Every letter had an illustration, and the whole small work was "Neatly Bound, Gilt and Glaz'd."

For three pennies, Newbery offered *The Royal Primer*, the next step in his instructional sequence. The book after that, for six pence, was *The Pretty Book for Children; Or, An Easy Guide to the English Tongue*, which was another catch-all work, like the *Museum*. It was supposedly so well adapted to the capacities of children that it combined the contents of a spelling book, psalter, and history book, all in one.[84] The smaller of these books were modestly priced, and advertisements for imported books place at least one of them, the *Royal Battledore*, at Hugh Gaine's print-shop, the Bible and Crown, in New York in 1757. Newbery's *Pretty Book for Children*, however, seems to have fared poorly on the market, despite its being published by Hugh Gaine in a domestic edition in 1762. His *Aesop's Fables in Verse*, supposedly written by "Woglog, the great Giant," which Gaine published at the same time, enjoyed much greater popularity.[85]

It is appropriate to conclude this overview of children's books from the early eighteenth century to the mid-1770s with *The Royal Primer*. The earliest surviving copy of this Newbery imprint was printed in 1753 at Philadelphia in an "improved" edition. It was reissued occasionally in Philadelphia and reprinted in 1768, 1770, and 1773 by William McAlpine of Boston, a royalist, who is also one of the first known printers of the children's fairytale *The Famous Tommy Thumb's Little Story-Book*, published in 1768.[86]

Subtitled "An Easy and Pleasant Guide To the Art of Reading," this Newbery primer stands in stark contrast to the *New-England Primer*, its direct competitor. On a variety of levels, it exhibits how the very understanding of the nature and purposes of this new version of reading instruction differed from those still held so dear by most New Englanders. While it may not have been authored by Newbery himself, his hand is evident. Commercial considerations have transformed into a marketing tool a genre whose very title once indicated an introduction to prayer.[87] The frontispiece runs:

He who ne'er learns his *A*, *B*, *C*,
For ever shall a Blockhead be;
But he who's to his Book's inclin'd
Will soon a golden Treasure find.[88]

The most important difference between this message and those emanating from the *New-England Primer* is that, as in other Newbery imprints, the "Book" has lost its referent as the Bible. Instead, it stands for learning. What is more, a book is not to be read for its own merits but for the motive of money. A "golden Treasure" could, of course, be a metaphor for learning in general rather than tangible wealth, but the rest of the text suggests otherwise. Moreover, failure to tackle the alphabet does not put the child's immortal soul at risk; instead, it subjects him or her to the charge of stupidity, to the insult of being called a "Blockhead." (This name-calling would not have been countenanced by the author of the *Friendly Instructor*.) The only constant between the two primers is the overriding importance of the alphabet. Mastering the A B C still remains the entrance to all other learning.

Predictably, the alphabet is wholly different from that in the *New-England Primer* and, as does that in *The Child's New Play-Thing*, it concentrates on food and familiar objects: "A stands for Apple and Awl. / B stands for Book and for Ball. / C stands for Custards and Cream. / D stands for Dog and for Dream." Crain has called this the "alphabet array" or the "worldly alphabet," for it serves as a kind of gateway to the whole world, organizing objects by their happening to begin with the same alphabetical letter and alerting the learner to "the vast quantity of things in the world up for consumption."[89] It is as much an Enlightenment alphabet as the maxims for eighteenth-century copybooks are Enlightenment motifs: both serve to emphasize the attainability of worldly things.

This focus on concepts that are readily intelligible to the child is continued in the illustrated alphabet. The illustration for A is titled "*Apple*"; B depicts a "*Bull*," C a cat. The only similarity between this illustrated alphabet and the verses and woodcuts of the *New-England Primer* is the use of the words *Cat, Dog, King, Lion, Queen, Whale,* and *Xerxes.* Most of these, however, had already been removed from the *New-England Primer*'s alphabet verses by reformers after the Great Awakening, who considered them too frivolous.

The bulk of the text of the *Royal Primer* is conventionally religious but would never pass the test of New England orthodoxy. "O Come, let us sing unto the Lord, for the Lord is a great God; and a great King" runs the second lesson in monosyllables. A short scripture catechism for children provides another contrast to the *New-England Primer*, which always included either the Westminster catechism or "Milke for Babes." Instead of asking probing questions about God's relationship to man, this catechism is little more than a finding aid to biblical characters: "Q. who was adam? A. The first man that god made, and the father of us all. . . . Q. Who was noah? A. The good man who was saved in the Ark, when all the world was drowned."[90]

A section on the child's duty again provides a very different stance from that of the *New-England Primer*. The child is addressed directly, and a blueprint is proposed for a safe route to heaven:

> My dear child, if you would live happy in this world, and go to hea-ven when you die, you must,
> Ho-nour your fa-ther and mo-ther.
> Love your bro-thers[,] sis-ters, and friends.
> O-bey your su-pe-ri-ors.
> For-give your e-ne-mies, and pray for them . . .
> Be cha-ri-ta-ble to the poor.
> Be a good boy and learn your book.[91]

The pathway to heaven sounds none too exacting. (Methodologically, the splitting of words into syllables in a running text is an example of a path that the British would tread in their instructional works, but not the Americans.)[92] More traditional is the inclusion of the Ten Commandments and several of Isaac Watts's hymns for children.

The remainder of the *Royal Primer* is devoted to snippets about animals or biblical figures, with accompanying pictures and a brief elucidation of their meaning, in the time-honored tradition of the fable. The parrot "prates he knows not what, / For all he says is got by rote." He is compared to silly boys who have also learned by rote, "who prate with-out think-ing, and learn their les-son with-out look-ing at their book"—a brief reference to memorizing text masquerading as reading.[93] Moreover, unlike the *New-England Primer*, where girls are virtually invisible, this work is patently aimed at both sexes. Good girls as well as good boys are to kneel to ask God's blessing twice a day, girls and boys both bestow their charity, and when a final vignette expatiates on the rewards of virtue, its accompanying woodcut portrays a little girl decked out in a very fancy dress. However, the text informs the child that piety, modesty and generosity are greater ornaments than fine clothes and will bring a wealthy husband in their train.[94]

Close to the work's end, a woodcut exhibits "St. Paul's Church" (Cathedral) in London, which not coincidentally happened to be the site of Newbery's printing house. After a relation of its long history and of the Great Fire of London that destroyed it in 1666, the text continues: "it was soon rebuilt at a vast expence, by that great and justly admired architect, the late Sir Christopher Wren. No church (that of St. Peter's at Rome only excepted) can stand in competition with it."[95]

It is surely appropriate that this little book should close on this materialistic note. It makes a reference to the cost of Saint Paul's Cathedral, as if that were the most outstanding characteristic of this national treasure; it offers an ecumenical concession to the architectural superiority of a Roman Catholic cathedral, too far away to visit, in a spirit far removed from the old sectarian rancor; and it in essence skillfully packages an advertisement—for who could visit Saint Paul's without also noticing Newbery's bookstore?—in what at first glance seems only to be a paragraph from a tourist's guide. Whether authored by Newbery himself or not, it perfectly reflects his spirit.

The evidence suggests that the new "pretty" books reached the homes of the colonial elite with no difficulty, no matter where they lived. Their reach further down the social scale is much more problematic. In addition, the schoolbook market was particularly resistant to change: sales of the *Royal Primer* never came close to threatening those of the *New-England Primer*. For the years 1750 to 1759, for instance, one domestic imprint of the former has survived to six of the latter. The next decade saw one imprint of the *Royal Primer* (in 1768) to a dozen of the *New-England Primer*. Three more editions of the *Royal Primer* of 1775 have survived (two of them McAlpines's), compared with seventeen of its rival. (The *New-England Primer*, it should be noted, had itself modestly adapted to changing times by adding poems such as Isaac Watts's cradle hymn.) The American Revolution put paid to anything with the title "Royal" in it until 1787, when Isaiah Thomas printed a copy. Meanwhile, printings of the *New-England Primer* quickened, averaging about four editions a year in the decade of the 1780s and over six editions a year during the 1790s, with the last half of the decade averaging out at seven a year.[96] (See Appendix 3.) Editions that are documented but not longer extant raise the overall total yet higher.

Nonetheless, in the arena of books that did not explicitly seek to teach children to read, the stage had been set. Many of these recent texts, mostly authored by Anglicans in England, offered a new conception of childhood, an alteration in the importance of religion, and a portrayal of reading as an amusing and economically vital exercise rather than the gateway to salvation. It was a vision that would run in parallel with the older one, not supplant it, and it would extend its effects with the passage of time. Our touchstone for the popularity of a given work has been that it should be printed by an American printer. If that is our criterion, widespread acceptance of the new kind of children's books must be dated to the 1780s. That was the period at which the Worcester printer Isaiah Thomas would become America's leading publisher of John Newbery's little books, which aimed not to instruct children, let alone convert them, but to please them.

12

Literacy in Three Families of the 1770s

In Boston in 1772, twelve-year-old Anna Green Winslow wrote in her journal: "My aunt Storer lent me 3 of cousin Charles' books to read, viz.—the puzzeling cap, the female Oraters & the history of Gaffer too-shoes." Two of these imported publications, *The Puzzling Cap* and *The History of Goody Two-Shoes* (as Anna must have meant), were products of the Newbery house.[1]

If our generalizations about the availability and acceptability of books for the amusement of children are to find support, we must look at detailed descriptions of family and school reading provided in private journals. A close examination of three families in which literacy was taught and acquired during the 1770s will enable us to answer several questions that arise from earlier chapters. First, how far had the new "pretty" books for children, the publications of the Newbery firm in London, infiltrated the American market? We have seen that they were widely advertised in major American cities, but books promoted do not necessarily translate into books bought. Second, has the conventional sequence of reading instruction altered since the early days of settlement? Is the traditional "ordinary Road" of the seventeenth and early eighteenth centuries still in evidence as late as the 1770s?

This question relates directly to the third: is the spelling book, which I have argued is the great innovation in reading instruction from about the 1740s on, as indispensable as newspaper advertisements for spellers have suggested? The evidence in an earlier chapter has shown that spelling books were used in schools for poor children funded by the Society for the Propagation of the Gospel after about 1760, as well as in schools for enslaved children supported by the Associates of Dr. Bray. But how did the speller fare in the environment of three families—one in Boston, Massachusetts, and two in Virginia—that were among the most privileged in their respective communities? A final question relates to the uses of literacy. How did children use their literacy, and how did teachers teach it in the period leading up to the American Revolution? And how did both children and teachers deal with the craft of writing, taught for so long not as a vehicle for communication but as an exercise in the formation of beautiful lettering?

Our first witness, Anna Green Winslow, left Nova Scotia for New England to live with an aunt in the fall of 1770. Our second, Philip Vickers Fithian, became a private tutor to the wellborn Carter family at Nomini Hall in Westmoreland County, Virginia, in the fall of 1773, bringing his own sensibilities as a Presbyterian into an Anglican household. Our third witness, John Harrower, voyaged from Scotland the following spring as an indentured servant and began to serve out his indentures by living as a tutor with another Virginian family.

Anna Green Winslow was a child of privilege. Her mother, Anna Green, was the daughter of a wealthy merchant, Joseph Green. Her father, Joshua Winslow, was commissary-general of the British forces in Nova Scotia during and after the British expulsion of the French Acadians; he traced his ancestry to a brother of Edward Winslow, one of the founders of Plymouth Colony. Anna was the elder of two children, but her younger brother, John, stayed behind with their parents in Cumberland, Nova Scotia, when, in 1770, she was sent to Boston at the age of ten. She lived there with her father's sister, Aunt Deming, while she was attending what a later age would call "finishing" schools—a writing school, a sewing school, and a dancing school.[2]

Aunt Deming provided a congenial home for her niece. Anna noted that it was warm in even the coldest weather. Additional family members in the household were Aunt Deming's husband, John Deming, and Anna's cousin Sally Winslow, five years older than she. (Anna had other relatives in Boston, several of whom were within walking distance.)[3] The last member of the Deming household was an enslaved African. Much like Phillis Wheatley, Lucinda had been kidnapped and imported from Africa at the age of seven. No hint is ever offered in Anna's journal about whether Lucinda had been taught to read. She did, however, play the flute well: she served as the accompanist for the birthday party given by Aunt Deming, on the occasion of Anna's twelfth birthday, for the little girls who gathered at the house to dance in couples at an "assembly." Lucinda was one of the thousands of slaves who worked as domestic servants, a silent and barely visible backdrop, in Boston households.[4]

The Demings were devout Congregationalists and members of Boston's Old South Church. Joseph Sewall had only recently retired from its pulpit after serving the church there for fifty-six years, and he had been replaced by the Reverends John Bacon and John Hunt. Hunt was a favorite of Anna's: "I understand him better than any body else that I hear preach." As a matter of course, Anna went to the two services at the Old South Church on the Sabbath as well as the weekly evening lecture. When the ministers began a course of lectures every Wednesday evening on the catechism, she and her aunt attended those. These biweekly visits serve as a refrain to much of the diary.[5]

Anna's surviving journal begins on November 18, 1771, shortly before her twelfth birthday on November 29, and ceases a year and a half later. She wrote it in the form of a running letter to her parents, making entries in it at least once a week and often every few days. She also wrote letters to her parents and took pains not to reduplicate her remarks in the journal. At certain points she would pack up her journal pages and send them off to Cumberland—on one occasion she sent off forty-five. (At a later date someone stitched the seventy-two pages of the extant journal into a little book.) Anna's parents would respond and comment on the journal in their letters to her. Their daughter had a keen sense of audience.

When her father failed to make any reference to the journal, she was quick to scold him in an entry targeted at her mother: "My Hon'd Papa has never signified to me his approbation of my journals, from whence I infer, that he either never reads them, or does not give himself the trouble to remember any of their contents." She threatened to address future journal entries only to her mother.[6]

The best single characterization of the journal is perhaps that it was an open site for family communication. Its most important public function was to provide a place where the family members could draw closer and exchange news. This feature may be seen in the fact that the journal was readily available to all. Aunt Deming read it regularly and sometimes added pithy little remarks about its surface features, using Anna's voice to do so. One entry in adult handwriting reads, "N.B. My aunt Deming dont approve of my English, & has not the fear that you will think her concernd in the Diction." Visitors were treated to oral readings from it, occasionally to Anna's discomfiture: "I have just been reading over what I wrote to the company present, & have got myself laughed at for my ignorance." Visiting clergymen were informed of it. When Mr. Hunt was told how often his name and words appeared in her journal, "He laugh'd & call'd me Newsmonger, & said I was a daily advertiser."[7]

Anna's journal was indeed a conduit for messages and news: "I saw Mrs. Whitwell very well yesterday, she was very glad of your Letter." "Aunt bids me give her love to pappa & all the family & tell them that she should be glad of their company in her warm parlour." A long entry gives a vivid description of how her uncle Ned broke his leg when he was tossed out of his vehicle when the horse drawing it fell down an icy hill. Anna spent several entries keeping her parents updated on the scandalous activities of the notorious Betty Smith, a thief and frequenter of the workhouse, who would soon be in jail. Finally this newsworthy story came to a close: "Last Wednesday Bet Smith was set upon the gallows. She behav'd with great impudence."[8]

Anna also used her journal for entering poems that she would later share with others. She copied out one about the mayor of London and another that her aunt had found in a pocket book belonging to Anna's late grandmother. The latter begins, "Dim eyes, deaf ears, cold stomach shew, / My dissolution is in view / The shuttle's thrown, my race is run, / My sun is set, my work is done." The death of an acquaintance inspired the inclusion of the lines, "Stoop down my Thoughts, that use to rise, / Converse a while with Death."[9]

Anna's entries in her diary shed much light on how a highly literate twelve-year old used and improved her literacy for her own ends. One of the journal's most striking features is that Anna had remarkable control of biblical material and put both her writing and her reading to work in the service of her religion. She mentions several times that she was keeping a "text journal"—a list of the texts of the sermons she had heard and her comments on them. Sometimes she transcribed texts from sermons onto loose-leaf paper or wrote summaries in her journal of what she had learned from a sermon. Sometimes she skipped the exercise: "I remember a great deal of the sermon, but a'nt time to put it down," but at other times she gave extended summaries and even—apparently—verbatim reports:

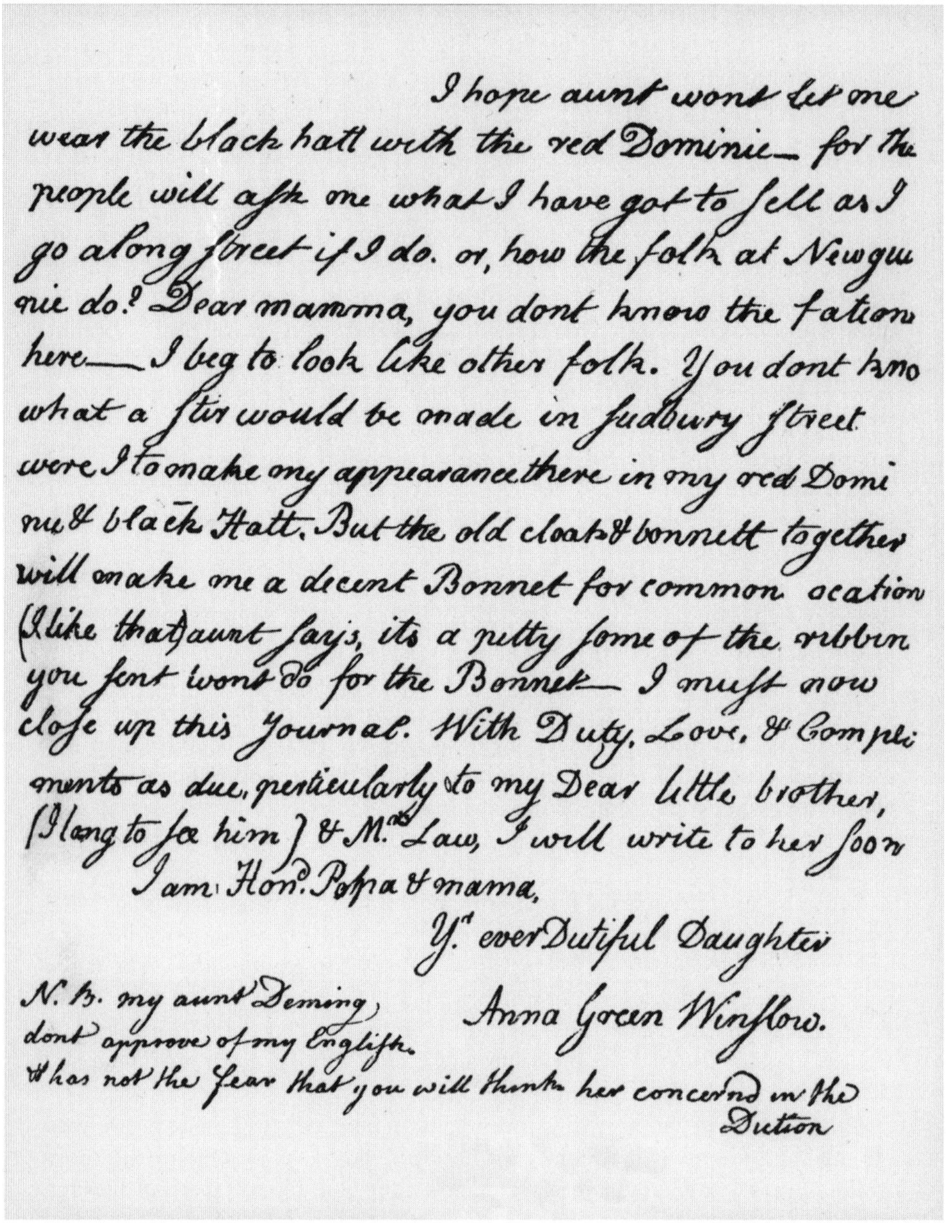

I hope aunt wont let one wear the black hatt with the red Dominie— for the people will afk one what I have got to fell as I go along ftreet if I do. or, how the folk at Newguinie do? Dear mamma, you dont know the fation here— I beg to look like other folk. You dont know what a ftir would be made in fudbury ftreet were I to make ony appearance there in my red Domi nie & black Hatt. But the old cloak & bonnett together will make me a decent Bonnet for common ocation (I like that) aunt fays, its a pitty fome of the ribbin you fent wont do for the Bonnet— I muft now clofe up this Journal. With Duty, Love, & Compli ments as due, perticularly to my Dear little brother, (I long to fe him) & Mrs Law, I will write to her foon I am, Hond Poppa & mama,

Yr ever Dutiful Daughter

Anna Green Winflow.

N. B. my aunt Deming, dont approve of my Englifh. & has not the fear that you will think her concernd in the Dutton

FIGURE 19. This excerpt from the diary of Anna Green Winslow, written on November 30, 1771, the day after Anna turned twelve years old, reveals the diarist's preoccupation with fashion, as well as her firm round hand. The comment in more mature script at the bottom of the page was added by Anna's aunt, Sarah Deming, in Anna's voice. *Diary of Anna Green Winslow: A Boston School Girl of 1771*, ed. Alice Morse Earle (1894; repr., Williamstown, Mass.: Corner House Publishers, 1974).

"Mr. Beacons text yesterday was Psalm cxlix.4. For the Lord taketh pleasure in his people; he will beautify the meek with salvation. His Doctrine was something like this, viz: That the Salvation of Gods people mainly consists in Holiness. The name *Jesus* signifies *a Savior*. Jesus saves his people *from their Sins*." Her sermon transcriptions ceased only after her aunt urged her not to "attempt a repetition of perticulars, that she finds lie (as may easily be concluded) somewhat confused in my young mind."[10]

More generally, Anna used her knowledge of the scriptures to draw lessons from them for her own use. One day, a heavy snowstorm followed by rain prevented her from her usual visiting. Anna was deeply disappointed. "Boast not thyself of tomorrow," she wrote, "for thou knowest not what a day may bring forth." This quotation from Proverbs, according to Aunt Deming, was "a most necessary lesson to be learn'd & laid up in the heart." Anna concurred: "I am quite of her mind. I have met with a disappointment to day, & aunt says, I may look for them every day." On other occasions, her scriptural references could be much more flippant: heavily bandaged because she was suffering from boils, she wrote that she was "swath'd hip & thigh, as Samson smote the Philistines." She also quoted her uncle's remark that clergymen who wore cassocks, as did the Congregational minister Dr. Pemberton, "all have popes in their bellys," and she then dashed off a relevant reference to a New Testament passage in which Peter urges the clergy to be humble examples to their flock.[11]

The oral reading that was such a feature of the colonial experience is much in evidence in this setting. Anna read the scriptures aloud. Usually she relayed them daily to her aunt, but she read aloud other books as well. "I have read my bible to my aunt this morning (as is the daily custom) & sometimes I read other books to her." "It's now tea time—as soon as that is over, I shall spend the rest of the evening in reading to my aunt." She also read out the letters she had received as well as parts of her journal.[12]

One of the books Anna read was the classic *Pilgrim's Progress*, but diary entries show just how far novels were infiltrating even the most devout of Boston's households. Secular books were now considered acceptable gifts to the young on New Year's Day, and Anna was delighted to receive "one very handsome one, viz. the History of Joseph Andrews abreviated." She added, with unconsciously Puritanical spelling, "In nice Guilt and flowers covers." The abbreviated status of Henry Fielding's novel *The History of the Adventures of Joseph Andrews* indicates that this was a chapbook version, but the quality of the binding and the gilt-tipped pages suggest a Newbery publication designed for children. (Aunt Deming had read Fielding, too: the sight of Dr. Pemberton wearing a cassock as he "roll[ed] up the pulpit stairs" had reminded her of Fielding's character Parson Trulliber—a very "unpleasing" image, she said.) The edition of *Gulliver's Travels* that Anna read later was also an "abreviated" version. It was lent to her by her cousin Charles Storer. Anna's aunt Storer—a more sophisticated woman than Aunt Deming—described it as a burlesque "which aunt says I may read for the sake of perfecting myself in reading a variety of composures." Clearly, Anna's aunts felt that monitoring and guiding their niece's reading was one of their responsibilities. At the age of twelve and a half, Anna and yet another cousin began to read aloud other novels together: "Very stormy. Miss Winslow & I read out the Generous Inconstant, & have begun Sir Charles Grandison." The latter, Samuel Richardson's novel, would also have been in abbreviated form, in an imported version of perhaps fifty pages. Advertisements for several of these novels had appeared in the *Providence Gazette* in 1762, while in the *Boston Gazette and Country Journal* in 1772 the abridgments were billed as "Little Books for the Instruction & Amusement of all good Boys and Girls."[13]

Anna did most of her reading at home. Her schools had other priorities, which were taken very seriously by all concerned. Only bad weather or poor health, such as boils on her fingers, prevented Anna from attending her classes daily. She took dancing lessons from William Turner, who instructed her in minuets and country dancing (the fact that Turner could ply his trade in a city that had once considered dancing an anathema was another sign of changing times); sewing lessons at Mrs. Smith's school, where she learned needlework; and writing lessons from Master Samuel Holbrook of the South Writing School. She would normally go to her sewing and writing classes twice a day, but in the winter Holbrook canceled his classes for girls in the late afternoon, so Anna stayed all afternoon at her sewing class instead.[14]

Anna's attendance at the South Writing School is in one sense an anomaly: her journal entries reveal she had been taught to write, in every sense of the word, perfectly well before she ever set foot in Master Holbrook's school. As Alice Morse Earle, the editor of Anna's journal, notes, "The writing is uniform in size, every letter is perfectly formed; it is as legible as print, and in the entire diary but three blots can be seen, and these are very small." Since calligraphy rather than composition was the focus of writing instruction, Anna's attendance at school can be explained only by the importance that genteel families attached to fine penmanship as one of the attributes of a gentlewoman. Anna's penmanship instruction was as nonutilitarian as the embroidery she learned at her sewing school: she had already learned to write and sew at home, where she used both skills for practical ends. At Aunt Deming's house, Anna used her writing functionally in her journal and letter writing, and her sewing skills functionally in making clothes. Her activities in the latter arena included sewing six "shifts" (slips) for herself, making several shirts for her uncle, spinning yarn, knitting new feet for Lucinda's socks, and learning to knit lace.[15]

Anna's formal writing instruction, in common with that of all other students at writing schools, involved her in penning pieces from a copy. She seems to have completed one or two of these a day, and if bad weather prevented her from going to school, she would pen a copy at home: "This day Jack Frost bites very hard, so hard aunt won't let me go to any school. I have this morning made part of a coppy with the very pen I have now in my hand, writting this with." The decorative value of copies is clearly indicated by her plans to use them as gifts: "This being a fine sun shine (tho' cold) day I have been to writing school, & wrote two pieces, one I presented to aunt Deming, and the other I design for my Honor'd Papa, I hope he will approve of it." A verse that she quoted from her copybook not only articulated the gratitude that the young were expected to feel because of the expense of their private education (the only one available to Boston girls) but emphasized that penmanship was an "art" that separated the well-bred from the common. It is a classic copybook piece that is also found among the collected pieces of the Boston boys:

"Next unto *God*, dear Parents I address
["]Myself to you in humble Thankfulness,
"For all your Care & Charge on me bestow'd;
"The means of Learning unto me allow'd,
"Go on I pray, & let me still pursue
"Those Golden ARTS the Vulgar never knew."

"The poetry I transcrib'd from my Copy Book."[16]

Anna's family completely accepted the prevailing concept that writing instruction focused mainly on penmanship. Her mother at one point complained of her daughter's "*terrible margins*" but expressed pleasure at her improvement in other respects. "I am glad Hond madam," Anna wrote in response, "that you think my writing is better than it us'd to be—you see it is mended just here . . . [and] I will endeavor to make my letters even for the future." Aunt Deming was in the best position to see how Anna's handwriting was progressing, and she had no qualms about expressing her views of it: "My aunt Deming says, it is a grief to her, that I don't always write as well as I can, *I can write pretily*." Yet Anna herself had a keen appreciation of the difference between form and function and could be airily dismissive of the former: "I have just now been writing four lines in my Book almost as well as the copy. But all the intreaties in the world will not prevail upon me to do always as well as I can, which is not the least trouble to me, tho' its a great grief to aunt Deming. And she says by writing so frightfully above."[17]

Anna seems, however, to have recognized that other aspects of writing instruction were useful. She had obviously been taught how to write a formal letter or note in the third person, because she plays around with the form with her friends. Her ten-year-old friend Caty Vans had promised to make her a nightcap in the latest fashion, and a misunderstanding had ensued. Anna sent Caty a "billet [-doux]" to clear the air, using her mother's maiden name for her last name:

Miss Green gives her compliments to Miss Vans, and informs her that her aunt Deming quite misunderstood the matter about the queen's night-Cap. Mrs. Deming thou't that it was a black skull cap linn'd with red that Miss Vans ment which she thou't would not be becoming to Miss Green's light complexion. Miss Green now takes the liberty to send the materials for the Cap Miss Vans was so kind as to say she would make for her, which, when done, she engages to take special care of for Miss Vans' sake. Mrs. Deming joins her compliments with Miss Green's—they both wish for the pleasure of a visit from Miss Vans.

Similarly, she helped a friend by penning formal invitation cards to an all-female party. She was fully aware of the social-class aspects of these notes, regarding them as well suited to the ensuing gathering, which she judged a "very genteel well regulated assembly."[18]

Occasionally Anna engaged in what we would today call metalinguistics—the conscious examination of her reading and writing as linguistic objects. All her remarks on her penmanship were of this kind. She termed her handwriting "pot-hooks and trammels," and after eighteen months of schooling she was still unrepentant about her supposed lack of progress in penmanship: "I have paid my compliments to messrs Holbrook & Turner (to the former you see to very little purpose) & mrs. Smith as usual." When she observed that an old cloak and bonnett could be altered into a "decent bonnett for common ocation," she immediately adds "(I like that)," in an apparently approving comment upon her choice of words.[19]

On several occasions Anna made a note of a linguistic feature. After remarking that she had attended her writing school that day with difficulty because of the mud, she put an asterisk after the word "aunt." Her note below reads, "Miss Green tells her aunt, that the word refer'd to begins with a dipthong." Her linking this to her attendance at Master Holbrook's school suggests that she had learned it there. On another occasion, she corrects her mother's spelling: "I went to Mrs. Whit-well's last wednessday—you taught me to spell the 4 day of the week, but my aunt says that it should be spelt wednesday." Her temerity at offering this unsolicited piece of spelling advice brought on a violent attack of the giggles: "My aunt also says, that till I come out of an egregious fit of laughterre that is apt to sieze me & the violence of which I am at this present under, neither English sense, nor anything rational may be expected of me."[20]

It is impossible to read Anna's journal without admiring her linguistic skill. Even when some vagaries of spelling are taken into account, it is clear that her literacy did for her whatever she needed it to do. It remains to ask how much of it Anna regarded as work and how much as play. She talked about reading and writing as if they were homework and linked them to her sewing "work" (as it was called throughout the nineteenth as well as the eighteenth century). For instance, a month after her twelfth birthday she reported that she had finished sewing a shift: "I began my shift at 12 o'clock last monday, have read my bible every day this week & wrote every day save one." Penning copies was certainly work, and work that Anna valued none too highly. Composition, in contrast, was closer to play: there is no doubt that Anna enjoyed writing her journal. Reading was work in the sense that reading the Bible was a Christian duty.[21]

But Anna also used reading and writing for recreational purposes, reading the new Newbery children's books, reading aloud shortened versions of novels, and expressing herself fully in her diary. She used her copying skills to good effect, copying newspaper articles that caught her fancy and keeping her parents up-to-date with the scandalous activities of the notorious Betty Smith. In one of her entries, she reveals how she integrated all the facets of her literacy, work and play, into a typical day. "I think this day's work may be called a piece meal for in the first place I sew'd on the bosom of unkle's shirt, mended two pair of gloves, mended for the wash two handerchiefs, (one cambrick) sewed on half a border of a lawn apron of aunts, read part of the xxist chapter of Exodous, & a story in the Mother's gift." And, of course, she wrote all this down in her journal. This juxtaposition of work and enjoyment, of reading for piety and reading for pleasure, is the mark of the new world of children that was being absorbed into the old.[22]

It would do Anna an injustice, however, to give the impression that her interests were confined to literacy and religion, assemblies and sewing. She had a keen sense of the ridiculous. (When she received her elaborate night cap from Caty Vans, the sight of it sent her into one of her "frolicks.") But her real passion was clothing and jewelry. The diary is replete with descriptions of marquesite and paste jewelry, of red cloaks and yellow coats, of black mittens and blue ribbon ("black & blue is high tast"), of pompadour shoes and fantastic hair treatments. In fact, Anna expended the little money at her disposal on clothing. When her paternal grandmother gave her some money as a New Year's gift, she combined it with her allowance to purchase an item that evoked her most lyrical writing: "a very beautiful white feather hat . . . with the feathers sew'd on in a most curious manner white & unsullied as the falling snow." Nowhere does she mention buying a book.[23]

From the perspective of a literacy learner who was so advanced that she discloses nothing about her earliest literacy instruction, we turn to that of a literacy teacher. Philip Vickers Fithian was twenty-six years old when he left the little town of Cohansie (Cohansey), New Jersey, on October 20, 1773, to ride south to Nomini Hall, Virginia, where he was to tutor the children of the wealthy Carter family. He had graduated from the College of New Jersey (Princeton) the previous September and since then had been taking Hebrew lessons from a clergyman in Cohansie, as part of his plan to take orders as a Presbyterian minister. This year of teaching in Virginia was to be an interlude between college and his chosen profession. Fithian had long kept a daily journal of his activities, and this continuing journal and his letters provide vivid glimpses of the life of a tutor on a southern plantation.[24]

Fithian had been told a little about his future charges in a letter that their father, Colonel Robert Carter, had written to the Rev. John Witherspoon, the president of the College of New Jersey. (Witherspoon was a dedicated Presbyterian whose religious preferences influenced many of the young men under his care.) Fithian knew that he was to "teach his Children, five Daughters, & three Sons [one was in fact a nephew], who are from five to seventeen years Old—The young Ladies are to be taught the English Language. And the Boys are to study the English Language carefully; & to be instructed in the Latin, & Greek." His salary was to be thirty-five pounds sterling, equivalent to about sixty pounds a year in New Jersey's currency. He was to have the "undisturbed use of a Room," access to Carter's extensive library, a servant (a euphemism for a slave), and free fodder for his horse.[25]

The stereotyped views of the south held by nonconformists in the middle and New England provinces almost prevented Fithian from going. They prompted his New Jersey friends and relatives (his parents had both died suddenly three years earlier) to issue many warnings about Virginia, where Anglicanism was the established church. They told him, Fithian recorded, that "Virginia is sickly—That the People there are profane, and exceeding wicked—That I shall read there no Calvinistic Books, nor hear any Presbyterian Sermons," and even that there would be such pressure on him to be sociable that he would spend more money than he earned. He had countered these cautions by convincing himself that he would have a better opportunity to find the time he needed to study for his ordination and that the experience would broaden his horizons. Nonetheless, he set off on his long journey by horseback with considerable trepidation.[26]

After traveling for eight days, Fithian arrived at Nomini Hall. As he approached the "great house" through the long avenue of poplars that led from the main road, he found it "most romantic" and "truly elegant." Set high on a bluff facing the Nomini River and visible from as much as six miles away, Nomini Hall was the hub of a plantation of twenty-five hundred acres and the nerve center of over sixty thousand acres scattered all across Virginia and Maryland. The estate required some six hundred enslaved Africans to keep it up. Most worked in these often isolated fields, but others, many of them descended from the ninety-four-year-old patriarch Gumby and his "wife" (marriage was forbidden for slaves), worked in the house and its related structures.[27]

The main building stood in the center of four other, much smaller buildings, each a hundred yards distant. The one at the northeast corner was "The Schoolhouse." Forty-five feet long by twenty-seven across, it was a story and a half high, with dormer windows on the second floor. Of the two rooms on this floor, Fithian had the one immediately above the schoolroom, which he shared with Benjamin Carter, the eldest of his charges at seventeen. (They each had their own bed.) The second room on that floor was the bedroom of Ben's brother, Bob Carter, aged fourteen, and his cousin Harry Willis, also fourteen. Below, the largest room was the schoolroom itself, while two smaller rooms were the lodgings of Colonel Carter's clerk and steward, Mr. Randolph. All the rooms, Fithian was careful to point out, had fireplaces.[28]

From the window of his room Fithian could see the "exceedingly beautiful Prospect of the high craggy Banks of the River *Nominy!*" Some of the rolling hills were covered with cedar and pine shrubs, while others were bare, "& when the Sun Shines look beautiful!" Only five miles away was the Potomac River, which marked the border between Virginia and Maryland. Fithian's eyes often turned in that direction, the direction of home.[29]

The school routine, as Fithian was soon to discover, was much interrupted by the midday "dinner," the most substantial meal of the day. The children gathered before breakfast in the schoolroom. (The fact that Fithian was often still dressing and not there to greet them was the source of many fights.) Once he was there, he listened to each of them say one lesson, in this setting where oral performance was still the most common mode. At eight o'clock, the Nomini Hall bell rang, at which point the children left the schoolroom. At the next bell half an hour later, Fithian walked over to the great house to join Colonel and Mrs. Carter for breakfast. (The children ate separately.) After breakfast was over at about half past nine, the school assembled until a bell rang at noon. An interval of rest ensued for all concerned until the dinner-bell rang at half-past two or three. After dinner, which could last over an hour if there were visitors, tutor and pupils reassembled in the classroom until another bell rang at five, and Fithian's duties were over for the day. The schedule therefore offered about five hours of instruction, and a little more when Fithian later extended the day to five-thirty.[30]

Fithian found that many occasions arose that took the children out of school. For one, the older girls had music lessons three times a week. Priscilla absented herself regularly from Fithian's class to take piano lessons from Mr. Stadley, the music master, who rotated among the plantation houses, staying at Nomini Hall from two or three days each month. By December, Nancy was missing lessons as well: she was learning the guitar from her father, since it was an instrument Stadley did not teach. Dancing classes, held at neighboring plantations as Mr. Christian, the dancing instructor, rotated among them, were another interruption. They regularly withdrew Bob and Nancy from their studies—an absence that Fithian would much later welcome. He was "rid of two *troubles* . . . for this hot weather," he wrote in July of the following year; "I can hardly keep them in the Room, much less to any useful business." In addition to these predictable absences, school would be canceled for a picnic on the river or perhaps a ball. As Fithian noted the following April, "It is with difficulty I am able to collect the members of our School together for Business. Holidays have become habitual, & they seem unwilling to give them over."[31]

On his first day as a teacher, however, all this lay ahead of him. He jotted down his initial impressions of the eight children in his charge. It was his first opportunity to evaluate the levels they had reached under the guidance of their former tutor, James Marshall.

Monday Novemr 1st [1773]
We began School—The School consists of eight—Two of Mr Carters Sons—One Nephew—And five Daughters—The endest [*sic*] Son [Benjamin] is reading Salust; Gramatical Exercises, and latin Grammer—The second Son [Bob] is reading english Grammar Reading English: Writing, and Cyphering in Subtraction—The Nephew [Harry] is Reading and Writing as above; and Cyphering in Reduction—The eldest daughter [Priscilla] is Reading the Spectator; Writing; & beginning to Cypher—The second [Nancy] is reading next out of the Spelling-Book, and begining to write—The next [Fanny] is reading in the Spelling-Book—The fourth [Betsy] is Spelling in the beginning of the Spelling-Book—And the last [Harriot] is beginning her letters—"[32]

This brief description is highly revealing. It shows the disparities between the education provided to boys and that provided to girls of the same family. Priscilla, then thirteen and the oldest of the five girls, was a year younger than Bob. But she was never going to be taught the classical languages. Moreover, she was only just being introduced to arithmetic, even though both Bob and Harry had been working with numbers for some time. One reason for this difference may have been her frequent absences for music lessons with Mr. Stadley. The boys received no formal instruction in music during Fithian's year in Virginia, but Ben had been taught earlier how to play the flute, which he did with some skill. Girls of this social class, which was as high as any in the colonial period, were traditionally taught different subjects from boys: they needed to perfect their English, learn to write, and be groomed in the genteel skills of music and dancing. The boys learned to dance (dancing was a crucial skill in this elegant Virginia context, and Fithian was constantly embarrassed by his own ignorance of the art), but, other than Ben's lessons on the flute, they apparently did not learn how to play any instruments. This lack of musical training is the more noticeable because Colonel Carter was himself an accomplished musician who often performed on the harmonica for his family in the evenings and kept a harpsichord, piano, guitar, violin, and flutes at Nomini Hall. He had even arranged for an organ to be made in London to his specifications for his Williamsburg residence.[33]

The second feature to emerge from Fithian's record of his first day is that the order of the curriculum was as unyielding as it had been a century or more earlier, with reading instruction preceding writing instruction. None of the three youngest girls who were learning to read (Fanny, Betsy, and Harriot) touched a writing instrument. Nancy, at eleven, was just "out of the Spelling-Book" and therefore qualified to begin penmanship. Writing instruction preceded arithmetic instruction. Priscilla, at fifteen, knew how to write and was just beginning her ciphering. In contrast, Bob and Harry, working at subtraction and fractions, respectively, were both practiced writers.

A third feature of Fithian's schoolroom, and the one that did distinguish it sharply from the schoolrooms of the preceding century, was the supremacy of the spelling book as the key text for introductory reading instruction. (Fithian never identifies which text was being used, but it was probably not Thomas Dyche's, which had receded from favor in the 1760s even in the south, but Thomas Dilworth's.) Except for Harriot, the youngest, the other three little girls were working, or had worked, their way through the speller. Nancy, at eleven, had actually finished with the speller. Fanny, who at nine was "the Flower in the Family," in her tutor's opinion, was "reading in the Spelling-Book" (as opposed to still spelling the words out orally, letter by letter). Betsy, aged eight (whom Fithian characterized as "young, quiet and obedient") was still spelling syllables out at the beginning of the speller. Five-year-old Harriot was not even up to the spelling book, because she did not know her letters.[34]

Another aspect of Fithian's first day is the enshrinement of English grammar as a formal subject of instruction, as worthy of attention as Latin and Greek. Both Bob and Harry were immersed in it, and Robert Carter later gave Fithian for the use of the school a textbook titled *The British-Grammar*. Fithian considered Carter himself, who had attended the College of William and Mary between the ages of nine and eleven, a "good scholar, even in classical learning, and . . . [a] remarkable one in english grammar."[35]

But perhaps the most intriguing glimpse Fithian provides is of Priscilla reading the *Spectator* in school. Whereas the aim of reading instruction, for so long, was held to be reading the Bible, here for the first time we see, in this sophisticated and highly literate family, a hint of the texts that children would read in its place, once they had left the spelling book behind them. The spelling-book author Thomas Dilworth had recommended the *Spectator* as suitable reading material, for the journal, still readily available in imported copies, provided models of well-crafted essays. Fithian himself read it regularly. The growing importance of composition may also be seen in another gift: some seven weeks later, Carter gave Fithian, for Nancy's use, a copy of the *Compleat Letter-Writer*, a work with samples of model letters. The implication was that now Nancy should both read formal letters and practice writing them herself.[36]

With his Presbyterian training, it would have been most unusual for Fithian not to have included the Bible somewhere in his instruction. Indeed, he reveals casually that the boys, at least, were reading through the Bible "in Course" in much the same way that the children of Samuel Sewall had, in another place and time.

One incident reveals that Bob, just like the Sewall children, understood perfectly well what he read while reading aloud, even if he occasionally misconstrued a passage. Bob was one of the most challenging of Fithian's students. (Nancy was another.) Mr. Marshall, Fithian's predecessor, had considered him "destitute of capacity." Fithian disagreed but thought him "extremely volatile & unsettled in his temper, which makes it almost wholly impossible to fix him for any time to the same thing." Bob much preferred shooting at ducks in a nearby pond to his school studies: "Bob seems sorry that he must forsake the Marsh & River when he is daily fowling, & never kills any Game." He had another enthusiasm: he liked to take his dog to bed with him.[37]

This particular morning, Bob's attention was, for once, fixed not on bagging ducks but on what he was reading. He and Harry were taking turns reading aloud the twenty-seventh chapter of Deuteronomy. It consists of Moses's charge to the people of Israel; after listing the penalties allocated to different sins, such as dishonoring one's father or mother, each verse ends with the words, "and all the People shall say Amen."

Bob [who had] seldom, perhaps never before, read the verse, at last read that "Cursed be he that lyeth with any manner of Beast, and all the People shall say Amen." I was exceedingly Pleased, yet astonished at the Boy on two accounts.—1st At the end of every verse, befor[e] he came to this, he would pronounce aloud, "Amen." But on Reading this verse he not only omitted the "Amen," but seem'd visibly struck with confusion!—2d And so soon as the Verse was read, to excuse himself, he said at once, Brother *Ben* slept all last winter with his Dog, and learn'd [taught] me!—Thus ready are Mankind always to evade Corection [punishment]!"[38]

Bob's spontaneous "Amens" show that he understood and was obeying what he considered the command in the verse, "and all the People shall say Amen." But he innocently misconstrued the carnal sense of lying with beasts. Indeed, his sleeping with his dog bothered him so much that a few days later he asked Mr. Randolph, the clerk, "if he thought *God Almighty* knew it!"[39]

Apart from asking them to read the Bible aloud, Fithian seems to have given the boys and Priscilla only a few other books to be read during schooltime. In June he required Bob and Harry to read Pope's Homer. This monumental verse translation of the Greek epic left them cold: "Homers inimitable fire cannot charm or move them!"[40] Additional opportunities to read in school, ironically, were provided to the older children by their mathematical studies. Wingate's arithmetic textbook was one of those used in the classroom—at least, Fithian mentions that he "met" a particular "merry Problem" in the book on a Thursday, which was of course a school day. The problem, as he quoted it from the book, was to "discover a Number which any one shall have in his mind, without requiring him to reveal any part of that or any Number whatsoever." The victim of this piece of magic was to think of any number, double it, add any even number, then divide the result by two and subtract the number he first thought of: "then you may boldly tell him what Number remains in his mind after that Subtraction is made, for it will be always half the Number which you assigned him to add."[41]

Fithian seems to have found his instruction of the older children more rewarding than that of the younger ones. Nancy, who had finished with the speller, was presumably reading and writing from the *Compleat Letter-Writer* that her father had introduced to the school, but Fithian does not say so. Nor does he mention the reading progress of Fanny or Betsy, both of whom were "in" their spelling books when his year began. Even by the end of his time there, he does not record whether Fanny and Betsy had completed their studies in the speller. Nor did he introduce either of them to writing, which was enough of a landmark for him to have recorded it. Fanny, ten by the time he departed in October 1774, was not yet learning to write. Almost the only time Fithian mentioned her at school was when she teased him to draw her the same picture on paper that he had drawn her earlier in the sand. Betsy is virtually invisible. She did not even join in with Fanny and Harriot when Fithian caught them stuffing rags into their dresses below their apron strings in order to look pregnant, like their mother.[42]

Of all the children, Harriot—described by Fithian as "bold, fearless, noisy and lawless; always merry, almost never displeased," and with a natural ear for music—was the only one who was instructed by no one but Fithian. On November 1, 1773, when Fithian began to teach, she did not know the letters of the alphabet. It took two months for her to learn them, in this one-room schoolhouse where she had to compete with seven other children for her turn to recite. On December 31, he recorded, "*Harriot* to Day for the first time said all her letters." It took her until March before she was "saying" such a "good lesson" that Fithian gave her a coin in appreciation; and not until June did he buy her her first actual book, a primer that cost him three shillings. From then until the time that he handed his charges over to his successor, John Peck, on October 17, 1774, he recorded no further literacy landmark. Harriot's experience is emblematic of just how difficult it was to master the letters of the alphabet without any associated motor movement. Children had to learn to distinguish the features that discriminate one letter from another by just looking at them.[43]

Because the boys slept in the same building as Fithian, he spent more time with them than with the girls. Indeed, part of his responsibility was to have guardianship over the boys, and he seems to have functioned more as a father to them than

Colonel Carter himself. Ben at least was given some responsibility by his father, who sent him off to the slave quarters to supervise the measurement of the slaves' corn allowance, but Bob did nothing but get himself into trouble. It fell to Fithian to "correct" (beat) Bob for his various misdemeanors.[44]

Outside the schoolroom setting Fithian displayed a less restrictive concept of literacy instruction. After school was dismissed, Benjamin's passion for horses ensured that he was always out riding until dark, but Bob would sometimes be in during the evenings. On these occasions Fithian might read to him. One of Bob's characteristics was his empathy for those less fortunate than he, or as Fithian put it, he was "pleased with the Society of persons much below his Family, and Estate." One March evening, Fithian was reading "to *Bob* in the Monthly Review the remarks on the Poetry and writing of *Phillis Wheatly* of Boston; at which he seem'd in astonishment; sometimes wanting to see her, then to know if She knew grammer, Latin, &c. at last he expressed himself in a manner very unusual for a Boy of his turn. & suddenly exclaimed, Good God! I wish I was in Heaven!" (This outburst perhaps stemmed from his conviction that in heaven all distinctions of gender, race, and class would be extinguished.) Ben also read more broadly outside the classroom. One evening Fithian went to sleep while Ben was still "poring over a History of England" by the fire in their room. His tutor thought up another way to get Ben to practice his literacy: in exchange for a small coin, Ben read to Fithian or played the flute for him for twenty minutes after Fithian was in bed.[45]

Bob had a similarly unrestricted view of literacy. One day Fithian found a book of Newbery's *Aesop's Fables* as told by the giant Wog-a-log. Bob had created his own kind of entertainment for the book. "On the writing-Table in the School-Room," Fithian recorded, "I found this morning an old Book of Esops Fables done into English Verse; in the Margins of this Book up & Down Bob had in his scribbling Way recorded the Names of several young Ladies of Westmorland & Richmond Counties." At the bottom of page 23 "his own Name is written at full length & in as elegant a hand as he is master of with a Dash below. *Robert Bladen Carter.*" Bob's signature adorned other pages, interspersed with his inscriptions of the names of eighteen young women:

In the Life of Woglog the great at the first page
Miss Lucy Carter of Sabine-hall.
   Page 3d at the Bottom of the Leaf
Miss Lettitia Turberville of Hickory Hill.

Fithian could not decide whether the ladies' names were intended to be a foil to Bob's, or vice versa. Theirs were designed to adorn his, one suspects, as he had made terse comments on some: "Miss Steerman is a beautiful young Lady." But "Miss Lydia Pettit had d——m'd ugly Freckles in her Face, otherways She is handsome & tolerable—"[46] The incident suggests how ubiquitous the works of John Newbery and his successors had become by the 1770s, at least among the gentry.

The association between women and reading (as opposed to women and writing) was still strong, and in this elite setting, since all the housework was done by slaves, reading was a major leisure-time activity for women. Women often had more time to pursue reading as adults than they had enjoyed when they were younger and their time was taken up by music and dancing lessons.

Frances Carter, the mother of Fithian's pupils, was a voracious reader. Fithian was astonished by how well informed she was. One afternoon at dinner, when the conversation turned to reading, Colonel Carter remarked that he "would bet a Guinea that Mrs Carter reads more than the Parson of the parish!" The relationship between reading and religion for women, however, was still intact, and even her husband's remark hinted that the reading interests of a woman and a minister were similar. Another dinner-time conversation focused on the topic of the soul: Frances Carter observed that she had heard that women had no souls. Priscilla responded in a flash, "if I thought so I would not have spent all this morning in Reading; nor would Women, (said the well discerning Miss) be careful to avoid any Shameful, or Sinful Action."[47]

Reading, in other words, could still be defined as a devotional act, despite the much larger range of books available to young women by this time. As Kevin Hayes has shown, by this point in the eighteenth century women had the opportunity to read books ranging from treatises on housewifery and household medicine to history, biography, travel, and science—and, of course, novels. Young men admired young women who read broadly. Fithian commented approvingly on the choice of a friend of his, who was soon to be married to "a Girl of Reading, Taste, & Delicacy." Reading and refinement went hand in hand.[48]

Fithian's own reading was transformed by his sojourn in Virginia. He had free access to Colonel Carter's extensive library, which he catalogued for posterity. It may have been the library's copy of Wingate's arithmetic that he quoted in his directions for numerical mind reading. Once he turned down the opportunity of seeing a cock fight in favor of reading Junius's *Letters* and Plato's speech on Alexander the Great. He borrowed from the library several volumes, such as Henry Hammond's annotations on the New Testament, to assist him with the essays he was preparing for his prospective ordination as a Presbyterian minister. By June, with the essays under control, he looked for lighter reading. "I took out of the Library to read for entertainment the 'Amusement of the *German Spa*[']; it is a well written piece—Designed entirely for Amusement." He took to reading Jonathan Swift and Laurence Sterne. "I begun to read the first Volume of Tristam-Shandy [*sic*]—He is droll in the account he gives us of his Birth & Family." He began to take a book along with him on his evening stroll, "musing & stumbling along." He once—but only once—became so engrossed in his reading that he made the grave mistake of missing dinner. Avid reader though she was, Frances Carter was not even faintly assuaged by his excuse. "I told her I was engaged in reading a pleasant Novel.—That I was not perfectly well—But She would not hear none, & said I was rude, & censurable." Fithian read magazines and newspapers whenever they came his way, from the *Gentleman's Magazine* to the *Pennsylvania Gazette*, the latter particularly welcome because it reminded him of home.

All the latest magazines and reviews were sent regularly to Colonel Carter from London, and their arrival was always hailed with pleasure. Fithian was particularly taken with a review of a new history of Great Britain and planned to buy it.[49]

Fithian's writing continued to be an essential part of his life. He kept his journal daily with great fidelity but also wrote letters frequently to Elizabeth Beatty (Laura) back in New Jersey, with whom he was in love. Previously he had had a very enjoyable "Litterary Correspondence" with a young woman named Belinda, now dead.[50]

From early April 1774 to the end of May Fithian took a break from his teaching, riding home to see his relatives and present himself for examination before the Presbytery. He went to the meeting house on the Sabbath ("How unlike *Virginia*, no rings of Beaux chatting before & after Sermon on Gallantry; no assembling in crowds after Service to dine & bargain; no cool, spiritless harangue from the Pulpit") and spent a great deal of time with Laura. After successfully passing his first examination at the Presbytery, he headed back to Virginia to find there a supper of crabs, strawberries, and cream and a "great welcome—*Ben, Bob*, Miss *Fanny* & *Betsy* came in to see me—The others in bed."[51]

"Our little beautiful Seminary collected," he recorded on his first day back teaching. "They seem all glad to see me, & willing to enter on business." At the end of June, Fithian gave a progress report.

My Charge seem rising slowly, & uniformly in their several Parts—Harry begun at Reduction & is now working Fellowship; he improves too in Writing. Bob began at Addition and is working Compound Division: he is the best writer in the School— Ben begun with reading Salust he is now reading Virgil & the Greek-Testament. He writes extremely bad—Priscilla began Addition & is working Division; She improves in writing, & reads tolerably—Nancy mends fast in writing, but reads carelessly thick & inaccurately.[52]

The progress of the younger students was apparently not worthy of comment.

A week later Fithian gives us a rare opportunity to hear the voices of an eighteenth-century one-room school. For a few days he changed his way of keeping his diary and jotted down verbatim conversations:

Well, Nancy, I have tuned your Guitar; you are to practice to Day with Priscilla, who is to play the Harpsichord, till twelve o Clock; You can repeat the Verses of the Funeral Hymn?—I can Sir—What, Harry, do you hesitate at that plain Sum in Arithmetical Progression? *Bob*, attend to your Business—When I am bedizen'd with these clamorous children, sometimes I silently exclaim—Once I was told, now I know I feel how irksome the Pedagoging Scheme is—Fanny—I say, Fanny, dont you hear me, Fanny, and Betsy, sit down—pray, Sir, must I multiply here by 32— yes, thick-Scull—But Mr Fithian, I dont know how to divide by 5 ½—Look, Sir [obviously a complaint by one of the little girls], do you see what Mouth's *Harry Willis* is making? I can say my Lesson—Buz, Buz,—To divide by 5 ½ you must double both your Dividend & divide.[53]

From this clamor, Fithian emerges as a good teacher of the older children within the confines of the oral tradition: "I can say my Lesson" is the refrain. Teaching children to remember and recite verse by heart was one of Fithian's techniques. He answered a question on mathematics by providing exactly the information needed to move the learner forward. He was probably less good in teaching reading than in any other subject. If Nancy's progress is any indication, he relied on the spelling book to do the job for him.

The very next morning Fithian spotted Bob and Harry skulking behind the writing table "with their Slates on their Knees, & their Faces close together, just as I have done a thousand Times, in our little School-house in *Greenwich*." The boys were gossiping about Fithian's love life: "I wonder Mr *Fithian* has not fallen in Love yet with some of our Nominy-Girls. . . . I suppose Mr *Fithian* never thinks of Girls—Indeed says *Harry*, drawing his chair clos[er] lowering his voice, I never in my Life saw a Man who thought so little of these things." Thus does Fithian inadvertently reveal his use of slates for writing instruction.[54]

On other occasions, his charges used paper. When, for instance, Harry and Bob wished for permission to go to the races, they wrote him a letter and Fithian responded in kind. His letter is a useful model of the persuasive letter that is not intended to fully persuade.

Nomini Hall Octr 6th 1774.

For masters harry & bob.

I approve highly of the method you have taken in asking for liberty to attend the race this afternoon, and think myself bound to give you an answer in the same manner.

This Race happening so soon after the other, which was at the same place, and so much like it seems to promise nothing that can require your attendance, it is therefore my *desire* and *advice* that you stay contented at home. But if your inclination be stronger than either of these, and you still choose to go, you have my consent provided you return by Sun set in the Evening.

Yours

Philip V. Fithian[55]

When Fithian was first inquiring about the conditions of his service, Colonel Carter had promised him a servant to wait on him. The name of this young enslaved African was Nelson, and he made up the fire first thing in the morning in all the rooms of the schoolhouse, blacked Fithian's shoes, tidied up, and generally made himself useful. (He was skilled at killing rattlesnakes.) Nothing suggests that Nelson thought of instruction for himself. But a young African, Dennis, who worked in the house, did receive some instruction. At one point Fithian recorded a horrible accident to the boy's hand, when the heavy front door slammed shut on it, taking off half a finger. In the September after Fithian returned from his visit to New Jersey, Dennis's father, whom Fithian never identifies, asked Fithian to teach his son to read. "*Dennis* the Lad who waits at Table, I took into the School to day at his Fathers request, He can spell words of one syllable pretty readily. He is to come as he finds oppertunity." In the six weeks that remained of Fithian's stay in

Virginia, Fithian never mentioned him again, other than tipping him on his departure. Presumably Dennis never again had the opportunity.[56]

This is not the only evidence, however, of an interest in literacy among the enslaved. For the benefit of Dennis's grandfather, the ninety-four-year old patriarch Gumby, Fithian wrote down "a List of his Children, & their respective ages." Gumby and his wife were touchingly grateful: "Thank you, thank you, thank you Master, was the language of the old Grey-headed pair.—Call on us at any time, you shall have *Eggs, Apples, Potatoes*—You shall have every thing we can get for you—Master!" It is most doubtful that they could read the list, but in a culture where dates of birth were deliberately concealed from slaves, Fithian's list provided a vital clue to their family history.[57]

In October, Fithian's year was drawing to a close. His replacement, John Peck, was a fellow college graduate, to whom Fithian had written a long letter of advice; his most practical hints on pedagogy had been to "go into the [local] school and acquaint yourself with the method of teaching, and procure some copper plate copies." Peck arrived at Nomini Hall on October 15 ("is he [as] grave as you?" Frances Carter had asked). He came within inches of finding the classroom a pupil short: Bob had been thirty feet up a chestnut tree and was unwisely sawing off the bough he was standing on. It split and fell, taking the entire branch and Bob with it; he had saved himself only by catching hold of a branch on his way down. The following Monday, Fithian relinquished his students to his successor: "Before Breakfast I heard all the School a lesson round[,] Mr Peck Present—After Breakfast I heard their Tables, Grammer &c & then in Spite of my resolution with great reluctance, I resigned up to Mr Peck my little much-loved Charge!" Ten days later, he was back in New Jersey.[58]

On January 26, 1774, the same day that Philip Fithian recorded running a foot race against Ben and Harry around the schoolhouse, stables, and great house (he won by a rod, but it nearly did him in), John Harrower, "being reduced to the last shilling I hade was oblidged to engage to go to Virginia for four years as a schoolmaster for Bedd, Board, washing and five pound during the whole time," selling his indenture for the price of his passage. Harrower had left his family behind him. His wife, Ann, two young sons, and a daughter were still in the windswept village of Lerwick on one of the Shetland Isles of Scotland. He had already been separated from them for seven weeks while he traveled south to London, sometimes on foot, in an attempt to find work. But England was deep in a depression, and there was no work to be had for a clerk without personal connections.[59]

A man of forty-four, Harrower quickly caught the attention of David Bowers, the captain of the *Planter*, the ship on which he and seventy-four other indentured servants were to sail for Fredericksburg, Virginia. While the ship was lying off the Isle of Wight, some of the other indentured servants on board, who had been complaining about their rations, threatened to mutiny. Harrower did not join in, and when the captain went on shore briefly for more supplies, he asked Harrower to assist the mate if trouble were to brew again. During the remaining twelve weeks that he spent on board, Harrower helped the captain and mate, both prostrate with fever, by nursing the first mate, keeping the ship's log up to date as well as the mate's and the captain's journals, and by making a fair copy of the names, ages, and occupations of all the indentured servants. In addition to himself, four others identified themselves as "Clerk & Bookkeeper."[60]

After a difficult Atlantic crossing, the *Planter* finally headed up the Rappahannock River in the second week of May for Fredericksburg, Virginia, its farthest navigable point. "All along both sides of the River," Harrower recorded, "there is nothing to be seen but woods in the blossom, Gentlemens seats & Planters houses." Harrower's usefulness to the captain now stood him in good stead: Bowers recommended him highly to William Anderson, the merchant in charge of selling the servants' indentures. Anderson saw to it that Harrower's indentures were sold to a man who would treat him well. Advising him that this was the best situation for him, Anderson contracted with a friend, Colonel William Daingerfield, for Harrower to serve for four years as the schoolmaster to Daingerfield's three schoolage sons.[61]

Harrower was, therefore, like Philip Fithian, although by a very different route, to become the tutor of children in a Virginia plantation. He must have seen Belvidera, the home of his employer, while the *Planter* was making her way up the Rappahanock. A handsome house built only a few years earlier on a thirteen-hundred-acre plantation, it looked down from a bluff onto the Rappahannock some seven miles below Fredericksburg. If Belvidera did not match Nomini Hall in size or elegance, it lacked none of its appurtenances. It too had a schoolhouse, twenty feet long by twelve feet wide, which stood "by itself at the end of an Avenue" right by the wharf. Harrower moved in there a few days later. The schoolhouse, he recorded, was so close to the river that he could "stand in the door and pitch a stone on board of any ship or Boat going up or coming doun the river." Like Fithian, he slept in the room above the schoolroom and took all his meals with the family.[62]

Again like Fithian, Harrower encountered a genteel way of life that was based on the toil of the enslaved. How many slaves there were "the Lord only knows," he wrote to his wife. He estimated there were about thirty laboring in the fields in addition to those in and around the house who worked as servants, gardener, seamstress, cook, pages, and so forth. Although slaves appear frequently in his journal, only one entry refers to his teaching them: one Sunday evening he taught the catechism to a group and then read to them.[63]

While he was waiting in Fredericksburg for the colonel to send for him, Harrower made his first purchases on behalf of his new job and his own recreational reading, spending five shillings that Daingerfield had given him. From vendors who boarded the ship with their wares, he bought the book he kept his journal in, to which he later transferred his earlier notes, and purchased "a small Divinity book called the Christian Monitor and a spelling book, both at 7 ½ [pennies] & an Arithmetick at 1/6d. all for my own Acco[un]t." Weeks earlier, as the *Planter* was preparing to leave its London mooring, he had bought a "penknife, a paper Book" (presumably the original repository of his daily record) "and some paper and pens." The speller and the *Christian Monitor* would prove to be the only books

Harrower purchased during the two and a half years recorded in his journal. His personal reading seems to have consisted of newspapers, which his employer would send up each week to the schoolhouse for him.[64]

A much less well-educated man than Philip Fithian, Harrower offers neither Fithian's telling insights into his students' characters nor his vivid depictions of the Virginia way of life. In spelling that betrays the rolled Rs of his Scottish ancestry, he gives more details of the clothing that he acquired and of the new wheat harvester that Daingerfield used than he does of his school. He does, however, reveal exactly how far children from the ages of four and a half up could progress in their reading acquisition when they were taught by a competent adult like himself. In fact, his students' progress in literacy acquisition compares most favorably with that of the Carter girls, whose education suffered from the attention Fithian paid to the educational needs of their older siblings. Notably, Harrower taught eight hours a day to Fithian's five and a half.[65]

Harrower's account, like Fithian's, again supports the central role of the spelling book in reading instruction. The journal documents the longevity of the late seventeenth-century reading sequence (aside, that is, from that eighteenth-century innovation, the spelling book): Harrower records the continued use of the texts John Locke had called the "ordinary Road": hornbooks and primers are not mentioned, but the children ascend from the speller to the Psalter and the New Testament, with the Bible as the pinnacle of the reading curriculum. Harrower also bears witness to the seemingly unbridgeable divide, even on the eve of the American Revolution, between reading instruction on the one hand—an oral activity—and writing and arithmetic instruction on the other, which used paper, ink and quills, and slates and slate pencils. Finally, it confirms, yet again, not only that children were expected to have mastered reading before they were introduced to writing, but that adults could be instructed in writing long after they had learned to read.

Harrower recorded his first meeting with his students.

FREIDAY 27TH [May, 1774]
This morning about 8 AM the Colonel delivered his three sons to my Charge to teach them to read write and figure. His oldest son Edwin 10 years of age, intred into two syllables in the spelling book, Bathourest [Bathurst] his second son 6 years of age in the Alphabete and William his third son 4 years of age does not know the letters.

The children had spelling books in the schoolroom already, it appears, because Harrower later sold his own newly acquired speller.[66]

Edwin progressed rapidly. He must have been a large lad, for Harrower later revised his age downward to eight years old. In June, when Harrower wrote a long letter to Ann about his new and genteel surroundings, he was able to tell her about the Daingerfield boys and say that although "the oldest just begun to syllab" when he first met him, "I have now . . . the oldest reading." In December, he wrote, "The Colls. Childreen comes on pretty well. The Eldest is now reading verry distinctly in the Psalter according to the Church of England. . . . The Col. and his

Lady being extreamly well satisfied with my Conduct in every respect." Edwin does not resurface, apart from cutting "one of his temples to the bone" in a fall from a grape vine, until January 23, 1776, when Harrower reported, "This day I entred Edwin into the Latin Gramer." Edwin, in other words, had become a proficient reader in just under twenty months.[67]

Bathurst was a couple of days from celebrating his seventh birthday when he first became Harrower's student in May 1774, still learning the alphabet. Six weeks later he was spelling from a spelling book (the title is never identified). Harrower pinpointed the two stages within the spelling book when he told his wife in June that "I have now the two youngest spelling and the oldest reading." Naming aloud the letters of the words in the tables and the lessons was the first step, called "spelling"; pronouncing the words without prior spelling was "reading." By December, Bathurst was ready to begin reading the Psalter. It took more than a year for him to reach his next important milestone. In mid February 1776 he began to learn to write; less than three weeks after that he completed his reading sequence: "Tuesday 5th [March 1776]. "This morning Bathurest Daingerfield got don reading through the Bible and the Newtestament." Harrower gave the whole school a holiday to celebrate. It had taken Bathurst only twenty-two months to grow from a nonreader to a good decoder of difficult material. (It is not possible to gauge how much he understood what he read.)[68]

William (Billie), the Daingerfields' third son, was four-and-a-half years old when he came under Harrower's tuition, not knowing his alphabet. By that June he was in the spelling book, and he proceeded to make as good progress as his older brothers, but at a much younger age. On May 7, 1776, Harrower recorded, "Billie ended reading through his Bible." He would not turn seven until October.[69]

Any opportunity that Harrower had to make money for his wife and children came from the other pupils whom he taught, for whom he was able to charge fees. (His indenture specified only five pounds for his four-year stint teaching the Daingerfield boys.) Once Daingerfield was confident about Harrower's skill, he rode around to his neighbors drumming up business. Since, in a few cases, this entailed the students living at his house, this was a real kindness. By the December after his arrival, Harrower had ten students in all.[70]

Two more students, James and William Porter, enrolled in the school at the end of the following month, January 1775. They had been removed from a school in Fredericksburg by their father, a merchant there, to be taught by Harrower. Porter was English and his wife Scottish, from Edinburgh, so they may have believed in the superiority of a British education. In April, the parents visited Belvidera to see their sons. A successful oral performance satisfied instructor and parents alike: "Mr. & Mrs. Porter [came] from Town, who heard their Eldest Son read and seemed verry well pleased with his performance since he came to me." Another visit in August reaped similar accolades: Mrs. Porter told him "that her sons did me great honour." The boys remained at Harrower's school for a year, and at the end Porter paid him not the contracted five pounds but six pounds. He had earlier presented Harrower with two silk vests and two pairs of cotton trousers, along with "a Gallon of rum at Christenmass, both he & Mrs. Porter being extreamly well satisfied with what I hade don to [their sons]."[71]

Other students included Sally (Sarah) Evans, a planter's daughter who attended for at least a year, and the Pattie and Edge children. William Pattie, and later John and Lucy Pattie, had spotty attendance, probably because their father, who was a carpenter, had a difficult time coming up with the fees. Philip and Dorothea Edge were the children of Benjamin Edge, a planter of modest means, and they were still in attendance in October 1775. By far the most challenging of Harrower's day students was their cousin, John Edge. John was the illegitimate son of Benjamin Edge's brother Samuel, an overseer at a nearby plantation. In June 1774, "This day Mr. Samuel Edge Planter came to me and begged me to take a son of his to scholl who was both deaff and dum, and I consented to try what I cou'd do with him." Harrower seems to have been genuinely creative in approaching the boy's disability. As he could not use the spelling book with him, he introduced him directly to writing and arithmetic, teaching him the words he needed for his immediate use: "he has been now five Mos. with [me]," he told his wife, "and I have brought him tolerably well and [he] understands it so far, that he can write mostly for any thing he wants and understands the value of every figure, and can work single addition a little. He is aboutt fourteen years of age." Young Edge attended school only until late November, and Harrower was unable to collect any of the money his father owed him, despite numerous requests in writing and in person.[72]

A more rewarding student, and one who paid him with great promptness, was Thomas Brooks, who worked as a carpenter at Alexander Spotswood's estate, Nottingham, located about four miles from Fredericksburg. Brooks came for instruction only in the evenings and on Sundays, starting in the August of Harrower's first year. Brooks, as Harrower described him to his wife, was "a young man a house Carpenter who Attends me every night with candle light and every Sunday that I don't go to Church for which he pays me fourty shillings a year. He is Carpenter for a gentleman who lives two miles from me." Brooks was there to learn writing and arithmetic exclusively. He left the following January only because he was obliged to go forty miles away on his job. But in October he visited Belvidera and joined Harrower, the new overseer, Anthony Frazer, and another schoolmaster named Mr. Heely for a very convivial evening of whist and dancing until midnight: "Mr. Heely playing the Fidle & dancing. We drank one bottle of rum in time. Mr. Frazer verry sick after they went home."[73]

Harrower had two other students whom he taught at their home. Once again, their experience emphasizes the gap between reading and writing instruction. He was asked to come to see the two daughters of a widow, Mrs. Lawrence Battaile, and "begin them to write." On a Saturday in June 1776, Harrower "went to Mrs. Bataile's and entred two of her Daughters to writting, Viz. Miss Sallie and Miss Betty & continued teaching them until night, when I agreed to attend them every Saturday afternoon and every other Sunday from this date untill 8th June 1777 (I[f] it please God to spare me) for four pound Virginia currancy." The Sundays were soon switched to Wednesday afternoons, apparently a school holiday at the Daingerfields'. Progress consisted to a certain extent of how much paper the girls could fill up as they practiced: "I . . . seed each of my Pupils write a page of (Quarto) Paper." He taught from noon to sunset.[74]

The young housekeeper at Belvidera, Lucy Gaines, was also new to penmanship, and Harrower helped her in an unofficial capacity. Lucy brought a letter for him to read from an old admirer from whom she had not heard for three years—not because she could not read it herself but because she wished to make fun of it. It is a classic example of the spelling most Americans used who had received only a modest amount of literacy education. It is also innocent of any punctuation.

> my deear love and the delite of my life very well remembur the great sattisfaction we have had in Each others Company but now is grone Stranger to Each other I understand you are a going to be marrid and I wish you a good husband with all my hart if you are ingaigd and if not I shuld think my self happy in making you mistress of my hart and of Evrething Els as I am worth if you culd have as much good will for me as I have for you we might live I belive very happy you may depend on my Cincerety If you think fit to Except of my offer I will make you my lawfull wife as sone as posoble if not I hope no harme don tho I can nevor forgit your preshus lips as I have Cist so offten and am very desiours to make them my one my Cind [kind] love and best respct to you my dove; this from your poor but faithfull lover till death PS pray let me no by the barer wheathar it is worth my while to put mysilf to the truble to com & see you or not
> Aadressed To Mrs. Lewse Gains

Lucy Gaines's ungrateful response to this marriage proposal was, according to Harrower, that "she does & always did hate him." (Her suitor would have done well to avail himself of the kind of service Harrower provided: on one trip to town Harrower had been asked to dictate and write a love letter for a shoemaker.)[75]

Lucy's unidentified admirer had chosen a poor time to approach her: she was romantically involved with the young overseer, Anthony Frazer. Harrower used delicate nautical metaphors to describe the progress of their relationship, which often took advantage of the empty schoolroom on weekends: "This [Friday] afternoon Lucy came home" (he usually designated her "Lucy friggat") "& was in school with the Anthony Man of War when I returned, & Moored there in Blanket Bay along side of him all night."[76]

Harrower's greatest contribution to Lucy (given that his fatherly reproaches to Frazer for his lack of commitment to marrying Lucy were producing only a frosty silence) was to help her to compose. A few days after they had both laughed at her admirer's letter, she needed to borrow a side saddle in order to ride to her mother's. She wrote a note to Frazer to ask if he would go over to Mr. Beck's to persuade Mrs. Beck to lend one to her. The splashes of ink all over her letter bear eloquent witness to just how difficult writing with a quill pen was for a beginner. As the request was actually a ruse for meeting Frazer, in the end Lucy decided not to send it. Harrower kept the letter and added his own comments to it, in which he distinguished penmanship from composition:

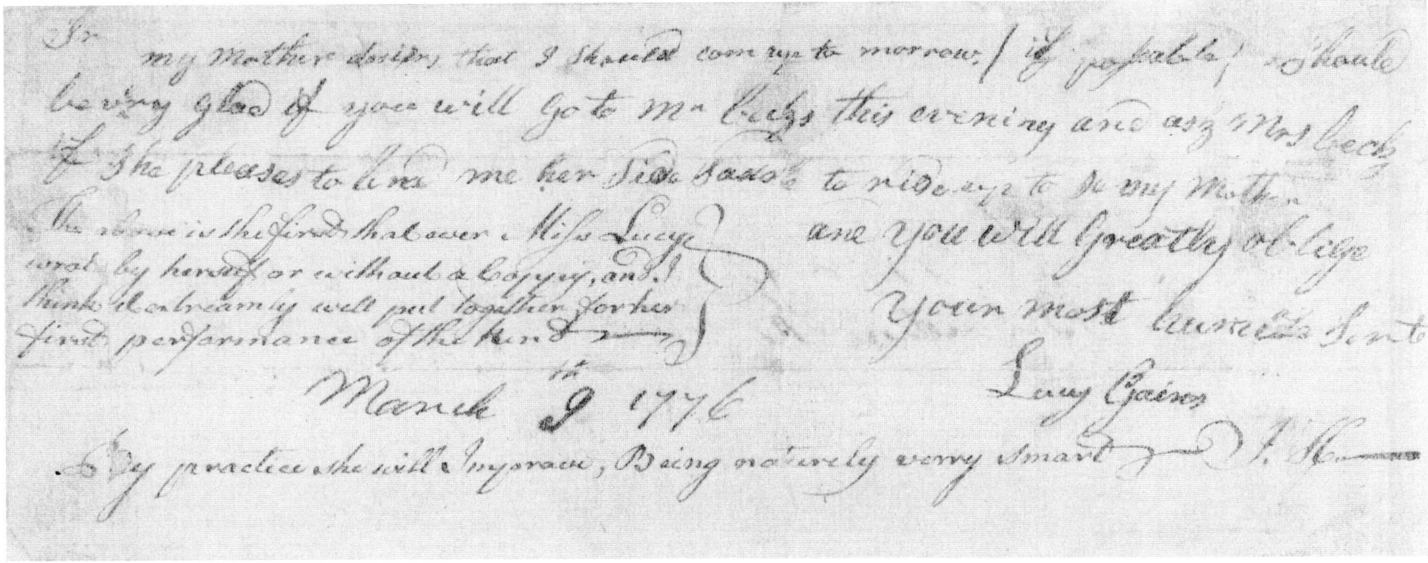

FIGURE 20. The first attempt at composition by Lucy Gaines, housekeeper to the family of Colonel William Daingerfield, written on a Virginia plantation in 1776. The family's tutor, John Harrower, thought highly of Gaines's effort. (Courtesy, Virginia Historical Society)

The above is the first that ever Miss Lucy wrote by herself or without a Coppy, and I think it extreamly well put together for her first performance of the kind.

By practice she will Improve, Being naturely verry smart. J.H.[77]

Harrower made an entry in his journal for every day, even if it was only to write, as he often did on school days, "Nothing remarcable." On Wednesday, July 10, 1776, however, there was definitely something remarkable enough to record. He had been at Mrs. Battaile's, where he taught the girls

until sunset and then returned home & soon after hea[r]d a great many Guns fired towards Toun. About 12 pm the Colo. Despatc[h]ed Anthy. Frazer there to see what was the cause of [it?] who returned, and informed him that there was great rejoicings in Toun on Accott. of the Congress having declared the 13 United Colonys of North America independent of the Crown of great Britain.[78]

Epilogue

The American Revolution directly affected a book trade that had been heavily dependent on importation. One immediate impact was that it sharply curtailed the importation of the new "pretty books" for children. In general, the booksellers and printers who were the most enthusiastic boosters of books published by John Newbery had only recently immigrated to America, bringing with them fashionable ideas from the other side of the Atlantic. John Mein had led the field in advertising the imported children's books for sale at his London Book Store in Boston. But his support of British policies in his weekly newspaper, *The Boston Chronicle*, made him so hated that well before the Revolution he had gone into hiding to wait for a ship back to England. In New York, Hugh Gaine, who had printed more Newbery books than any other American printer, also supported the British cause and had to abandon his newspaper. In contrast to Mein, however, Gaine redeemed himself after the war in the eyes of the public and began to publish Newbery titles again, reissuing *The History of Little Goody Two-Shoes* and publishing *The Mother's Gift*, both in 1785.[1]

The biggest postwar publisher of Newbery works became the printer Isaiah Thomas, who had retreated from Boston to Worcester, Massachusetts, before the siege of Boston and who remained in Worcester after the war. He thought so little of the children's books aspect of his business that he nowhere mentions it in his history of American printing. Historians of children's literature, however, would hail him, not quite accurately, as the first American printer to devote his attention to books for children.

Spelling books imported from Great Britain were similarly affected by the American importation embargo. Nor could American printers easily fill the gap: paper importation was also a casualty, and only a few local paper mills were operating. The net result was that overall American book production dropped steeply for several years, beginning in 1777 (see Appendix 3).

American dependence on imports was one of the many issues that citizens of the new United States had to ponder. This moment in history was a unique opportunity for Americans to begin writing their own spellers and grammars. Anthony Benezet, the Quaker humanitarian, became the first to write and publish a reading instructional text after the war. His little book, titled *A First Book for Children*, appeared in Philadelphia in 1778. Still using the alphabet method and beginning with the syllabary, Benezet nonetheless presented language that was easily understood by children: "Am I to go? . . . Is it an ax? Is it an ox?" Lessons in words of two syllables, dispersed among the word lists, reflect the author's piety, presenting a snapshot of the life of Jesus that includes verses from the Gospel according to Matthew. Offering the same messages as the *New-England Primer*, but less harshly, the primer closes with the verses of Isaac Watts that speak of death as a natural occurrence: "Why should I say 'tis yet too soon / To seek for heav'n or think of death? / A flow'r may fade before 'tis noon, / And I this day may lose my breath."[2]

The most important result of the Revolution, from the perspective of the history of literacy instruction, was its impact on young Noah Webster. Son of a Connecticut farmer who—disastrously for himself—mortgaged his farm to send his bright younger son to Yale College, Webster felt the repercussions of the war when he and other members of his junior class had to leave New Haven for a year for the safety of the interior. The experience left him an ardent patriot. He channeled his patriotism and a search for self-identity into the new country's own search for identity by conceiving a grand plan to reform the spelling and pronunciation of the English language. His overall aim was to create what he later called a "federal language" intended to unify the newly created country.[3]

In 1783, Webster published the first book of a three-part series titled *A Grammatical Institute of the English Language*, which was to consist of a spelling book, grammar, and reader. With considerable forethought, he had protected its copyright by registering it in the state of Connecticut, one of the few states then to offer such protection. The spelling book was designed, Webster wrote in his introduction, to "introduce uniformity and accuracy of pronunciation into common schools." Indeed, his work was the first ever to offer children a guide to pronunciation: with the aid of numerical superscripts, Webster devised a key to the pronunciation of all the vowels so that learners would know how to pronounce them correctly. The speller's first reading lesson, after lengthy lists of words to be spelled and read, begins, "No man may put off the law of God." This had been the first lesson of Thomas Dilworth's speller, the work that Webster was hoping his own book would replace.[4]

Revised and entitled *The American Spelling Book* in 1787, Webster's spelling book was eventually a dazzling success, soon outstripping its rival, Dilworth's *New Guide to the English Tongue*, in its sales (see Appendix 3). The reasons for its success include the improvements Webster introduced, such as his pronunciation key, his unremitting promotional efforts, and the appeal of the book to citizens of the new United States as a truly American product. Webster received additional financial protection for the work when a federal copyright law was passed in 1790. The *American Spelling Book* became the most widely used introductory reading text in the United States until its sales began to slip after 1816, when Webster sold its entire copyright to a single firm in order to focus on writing his monumental dictionary, *An American Dictionary of the English Language*. Once the dictionary was in print in 1828, he undertook a radical revision of the *American Spelling Book* with the aid of a New York educator named Aaron Ely. The revised speller appeared the following year, titled the *Elementary Spelling Book*, and soon superseded its predecessor in its sales.[5]

Despite the popularity of the "Ole' Blue-Back"—the *Elementary Spelling Book*—the role of the speller was to shift. Even before Webster died in 1843, the approach to American reading instruction had changed. New schoolbooks had been published to teach reading, and their content differed dramatically from the dreary lists of spelling words in spelling books. The appearance of works like the McGuffey *Eclectic Reader*, of which the first two books were printed in Cincinnati in 1836, was permanently transforming the literacy landscape.[6] From now on, children would be introduced to reading through carefully sequenced readers that featured stories about children, presented in large print and adorned with plentiful illustrations. Yet spelling books did not vanish from the educational scene. Far from it: they came into use as the spelling books that we recognize today—works designed to help children to spell rather than read. Webster's *Elementary*, which could be purchased at virtually every little country store across the nation, proceeded to beat out all its competitors as a spelling book in this revised sense.

For one special population, however, Webster's "Ole Blue-Back" speller retained its ancient usefulness as the pathway to reading acquisition: the enslaved and the newly freed. Both the *American Spelling Book* and the *Elementary Spelling Book* turn up again and again in the descriptions by enslaved Africans of how they tried to teach themselves to read before the Civil War, in defiance of a system that prohibited such instruction by brutality, intimidation, and legislation, and after the Civil War. In 1866, nearly six hundred thousand of the newly freed bought copies of the blue-back speller, which had attained a reputation of mythic proportions among African American communities for the role it played in teaching the novice to read.[7]

Conclusion

The first purpose of this book has been to identify what kind of literacy was taught, when, where, how, to whom, and why. In addressing these questions, this study has offered a series of vignettes on literacy instruction and acquisition in a range of contexts, from native American to immigrant European, from the impoverished to the elite, from the enslaved to the free, at home and at school.

Some practical questions may now be answered. What was a child's age when literacy instruction began in colonial America? Children could be very young when they were introduced to reading at home or school. Elizabeth Walker was only two and a half when she drowned, in 1664, on her way to her Plymouth dame school. Joseph Sewall was also under the age of three when he was first sent to his dame school in Boston in 1691. In the 1760s, masters and mistresses of slave children had no qualms about sending three-year-olds to the Negro charity school in Williamsburg funded by the Associates of Dr. Bray. While dame schools certainly served a caretaker function, the important point is not how much these young children could absorb of their instruction but the generality of the belief that they could and should be introduced to reading so young.

Writing instruction, in contrast, was begun much later: John Molineux, the youngest writer to identify his age on the exhibition pieces of the penmanship collection at Houghton Library, was nine; Rebecca, the youngest child at the Bethesda Orphanage to write a letter to George Whitefield, was ten. But these examples are misleading, for both children had clearly been introduced to penmanship, and in Rebecca's case to letter writing, at least two or three years earlier. Sam Sewall and Benjamin Franklin were ten and nine, respectively, when their fathers removed them from their Boston Latin grammar schools and sent them to writing schools; Philip Fithian's student Nancy Carter was just beginning to write at the age of eleven. (This seems unusually late: in fact, her father later taught her youngest brother to write at the age of six and a half.) Ray Nash's suggestion that writing instruction could be introduced at age seven seems plausible for boys. But the most striking feature of such instruction is that learners could begin at almost any age after six, provided they could read. Clients between the ages of twelve and fifty were the targets of an advertisement in a Boston newspaper in 1755. The carpenter Thomas Brooks was an adult and the Battaile girls were probably in their teens when John Harrower began teaching them to write. Indeed, until about 1750, for many girls late writing instruction was the most that they could expect.[1]

How long it took to complete writing instruction varied considerably. The same Boston entrepreneur of 1755 dared promise that novices could master a "good hand" in five weeks; yet, since instruction involved teaching ever more complex scripts, it could continue until at least the age of sixteen, as we know occurred at the three Boston writing schools. Liza and Sammy Mather were sent back to their writing school aged thirteen and eleven, respectively. Anna Green Winslow, already a good writer, was taking more lessons at the age of eleven. Only Benjamin Carter, about to turn seventeen, was beyond writing instruction when Fithian began his stint as the Carters' tutor; Bob, at fourteen, and Priscilla, at thirteen, still needed practice. Yet basic writing as well as reading instruction was completed in three years at Joseph Hildreth's Trinity School for charity children in New York. We have to conclude that the length of instructional time depended on the financial circumstances and ambition of parents and that even for the children of the elite instruction was spasmodic and attendance at school frequently interrupted.

How long did it take for a child to acquire reading literacy? The evidence suggests that Americans firmly believed that children could be taught to read in three years. This was the length of time William Yates and Robert Carter Nicholas, trustees of the Negro charity school in Williamsburg, believed was necessary for the young slaves to be sent to their school—where only reading was taught. (In fact, fourteen-year-old Harry, the slave being groomed to teach at the S.P.G. school in Charles Town, learned to read the New Testament in a mere eight months.) Three years, too, was the span that allowed children in Hildreth's Trinity School to learn enough to leave qualified for one of the trades. With a good teacher and a very small class, such as the one taught by John Harrower in Virginia, a young student could learn to read in a mere two years. Both Bathurst, age seven, and Billie Daingerfield, aged four-and-a-half, when Harrower first began to teach them, reached the goal of reading through the entire Bible in twenty-two and twenty-four months, respectively. This length of classroom stay is consistent with what Carl Kaestle reports on the length of school attendance in the early Republic: three years on average.[2] Such a brief (by our standards) length of time suggests that children had by that time been given the tools to continue learning on their own.

Here we must address the issue of the children's comprehension. Much of the Bible makes for difficult reading at any level, let alone for a six- or seven-year-old. The inescapable conclusion is that the alphabet method, embodied in the spelling book, produced very good "decoders"—children who became adept at pronouncing the long words facing them. It would be most unwise, however, to assume that these children understood all that they pronounced. This issue did not escape the attention of the single most influential spelling-book author of the early American Republic, Noah Webster. He addressed it in a four-page essay titled "Modes of Teaching the English Language," which he included in his last publication, a collection of essays published in 1843. "The opinion that the pupil should never pronounce a word which he does not understand is a great error. . . . When he is no longer perplexed with hesitation about the *pronunciation*, he proceeds with advantage to the tasks of *gaining ideas*, and learning definitions. *One thing at a time*."[3] Even his contemporaries did not agree with him, and the revolution effected by publications such as William Holmes McGuffey's *Eclectic* reading series, initiated in 1836, still reverberates today. McGuffey's child-centered stories, printed in large print and lavishly illustrated, set the tone for subsequent generations who believed, as we still do, that it is important for children at every level to understand what they read. I return to this issue in the Afterword.

American literacy in the colonial period was striking both for its constancy and, after about 1750, its change. We turn first to features that remained the same over some fourteen decades, and next to innovations in literacy.

Literacy Constancy

By the 1770s, many aspects of colonial literacy instruction remained remarkably unaltered. Whether we look at the definitions of literacy, at the order of instruction, the methodology of instruction, the religious (and, to a lesser extent, the social and political) underpinnings of reading instruction, the commercial presuppositions of writing instruction, or the gendered nature of literacy instruction, constancy is the watchword.

The first aspect of literacy constancy is that, for most of the colonial period, the definitions of the three literacy skills of reading, writing, and spelling were much the same as they had been at the beginning. Reading was conceptualized as a receptive tool—the vehicle for listening to the pronouncements, whether religious or secular, of one's elders and betters. Writing meant penmanship, a definition that excluded what we consider the primary purpose of writing—self-expression. When children wrote, they were supposed to focus on elegant and exact letter formation while they copied the precepts of others, and when they spelled, it was as if the sole function of spelling were to list letters in a predetermined order. This pedagogy treated writing as if its only purpose were to be the conduit for the thoughts of one's elders, with its chief virtue lying in the beauty of its presentation and the accuracy of its letter sequencing. Writing's continuing close links to commerce also fostered such a theoretical view, for clerks were employed not to express their own thoughts but to carry out the business of their employers.

Second, the order in which the skills were taught—spelling as the route to reading, reading before writing, writing before arithmetic—was seemingly inviolable throughout the entire period. Only a few instructors introduced writing early in their instruction (but never before reading instruction), such as Christopher Dock in his German-language classrooms in Pennsylvania and Hildreth in his Trinity School. This postponement of writing instruction was a direct consequence of using quill pens as the writing instrument and paper as the writing surface. Even when other implements and surfaces became available, as did slates and slate pencils in the 1740s, old habits persisted and the order of instruction showed no alteration.

Moreover, the methodologies for reading and writing instruction remained the same. Reading was taught through the alphabet method, using the alphabetical letter as the unit and proceeding from the letter to the syllable, from the syllable to the word, from words to sentences, from part to whole. Writing instruction was equally systematic, also moving from part to whole, from the formation of one letter to another, and then from one script to another.

A fourth area of constancy during the entire colonial period was that of the religious foundations of reading instruction. Even that little paddle of wood with the A B Cs and the Lord's Prayer—the hornbook—was still in evidence at the end of the colonial period, with hornbooks advertised in provincial newspapers as late as the 1770s.[4] With the exception of the hornbook, which was used at home or at dame schools, the other Christian texts of the "ordinary Road"—the primer, the Psalter, the New Testament, and the entire Bible—could be seen in all but the most sophisticated classrooms in provincial America. And even the few classrooms that eschewed the purely scriptural texts, like Philip Fithian's, used primers. The goal of reading instruction for virtually all children, in any region of the colonies, was to enable them to read the entire Bible.

This generalization about the "ordinary Road" requires some modifications: in English-speaking Anglican settings, the Anglican Book of Common Prayer was usually inserted into the instructional sequence before the Bible and occasionally even instead of it—although of course the children were reading their Bibles in church. Protestant missionaries by definition used Christian texts for reading instruction, although here a sharp difference may again be seen between denominations, a product of each denomination's attitude toward the scriptures. The Congregationalists—John Eliot and successive members of the Mayhew family on Martha's Vineyard—took tremendous pains to translate the scriptures into the Massachusett tongue. But the Anglican missionaries to the Mohawks showed a noticeable lack of interest in translating the scriptures, restricting translations to a few chapters from the Bible and paying much more attention to successive translations of the Book of Common Prayer. Other interdenominational differences may be attributed to how attuned the missionaries involved were to the demands of literacy instruction. John Eliot and his successors were keenly aware of the need to produce reading instructional texts translated into Massachusett, specifically Indian primers, while the Anglicans funding the Mohawk mission remained blind to the need, and only their first missionary, William Andrews, solicited such a text, a Mohawk hornbook.

Even after the introduction of spelling books, with their much greater potential for secular content, by far the most popular speller from the 1750s on was the one that offered its lessons as if it were a manual in Christianity—Thomas Dilworth's *New Guide to the English Tongue*. The lessons in his piously conceived work were based on scriptural passages, which he had carefully rewritten to include only words made up of the number of letters and syllables reached by that point. Spelling books in general were used as a stepping stone to the Bible. John Harrower, teaching the children of a Virginia plantation owner in the mid 1770s, moved his pupils from the speller directly into the Bible. Philip Fithian, instructing the children of another Virginia plantation owner, was one of the exceptions to the general rule: he expected his female students to turn from the speller to the *Spectator* rather than to the Psalter or New Testament. But Fithian still used the Bible as part of his communication with his students: the three boys directly under his care read the Bible "in course" as part of their daily prayer routine. The goal of reading the Bible, an oral goal attained by oral means, was in harmony with the lives of many families, such as those in orthodox New England, where the devout listened to scriptural exegeses from their minister at the meeting house. Bible reading continued to play a crucial role in pious family settings, from those of Samuel Sewall and Cotton Mather to those of Phillis Wheatley and Anna Green Winslow.

In addition to religious motivations, the social and political motivations for reading instruction remained important throughout the entire colonial period. Reading was still regarded as a bulwark against barbarism, and in principle children needed to learn to read so that they could read and obey laws as adults. The civilizing effect attributed to reading acquisition was believed to apply to children of every culture, European, Indian, or African.

A fifth area of constancy was the link between writing and commerce. The link was strengthened in early eighteenth-century America, which saw an increase in the number of, and attendance at, writing schools by boys eager for a practical, job-oriented education. The popularity of such schools waxed as that of the Latin grammar schools waned. The increasing number of advertisements for stationery—in Virginia, for example, in the 1770s—signaled the ever-growing importance of writing in a burgeoning consumer context.

Finally, the gendered nature of teaching the three Rs remained virtually the same through most of the colonial period. With the important exception of girls' improved access to writing instruction after about 1750, discussed below, the generalizations I made in my 1988 article about literacy instruction and gender in New England are supported by the additional evidence in this book.[5]

Women remained largely responsible for initial reading instruction, men for writing and mathematics instruction. As a judge put it at the close of the seventeenth century in a poem about schools in Philadelphia:

Good women, who do very well
Bring little ones to read and spell,
Which fits them for writing, and then,
Here's men to bring them to their pen,
And to instruct and make them quick
In all sorts of arithmetick.[6]

Reading was considered a job for an amateur, easy to teach. All that was required of reading instructors was their ability to read themselves. Reading methodology was unquestioned, and the texts used to teach reading were readily available for purchase for a moderate amount of money. Reading was therefore generally taught, unaccompanied by writing instruction, by women, who offered it at home or at school, with their low fees paid by individuals or towns. In contrast, writing instruction was considered a craft, like printing, and the province of men who had undergone a lengthy training under writing masters. The texts for writing instruction, purchased by writing masters for their own use, were rare, expensive, and imported; none was successfully reprinted on American presses until after the Revolution. The different fees paid for writing and reading instruction show that the former was valued more highly.

Men could, if necessary, lower their instructional goals and teach elementary reading. Southern tutors regularly did so; masters in grammar schools were often obliged to when boys arrived in their schoolrooms unable to read. But when townships sought to improve children's reading, they looked to women for help. Since women received salaries that were one-third of what their male colleagues received, their assistance was doubly attractive to towns. Women rarely taught writing, and when they did, it was to girls only. Job differentiation by gender was a major feature of colonial culture as a whole, and the teaching of literacy conformed to this division.

The differentiation between the sexes affected literacy learners as strongly as it did literacy teachers. Reading was required of all children for the reasons just given, but until about the 1740s writing was insisted on only for boys, who were expected to use it in their work. This was just one aspect of the broader pattern of educational discrimination by gender. Some girls in the eighteenth century received private instruction in Latin, as did Katy Mather. The father of Jonathan Edwards had his "sixty feet of daughters" (ten tall daughters) taught Latin so that they could teach their only brother when their father was away. Other girls, such as Jane Turell and, astonishingly, Phillis Wheatley, had access to major English literary works. A few women presided over literary salons in major American cities. But for the most part, even the children of the elite were treated differently according to their sex. In Philip Fithian's schoolroom in Virginia in the early 1770s, the Carter girls did not pursue arithmetic in any depth, nor were they taught Latin. As in the seventeenth century, girls and women in the eighteenth century were still defined by their relationship to men (daughter, sister, mother). Their personal goal was to make a good marriage, and their education was tailored to that end, emphasizing artistic skills, such as dancing, painting, and playing a musical instrument, as well as the homemaking skills of sewing, knitting, and embroidery. Well might Abigail Adams, whose education took place entirely at home, write to her husband, John Adams, in 1776, "If you complain of neglect of Education in sons, What shall I say with regard to daughters, who every day experience the want of it." It would take the American Revolution to raise the question of educational parity for girls, as Mary Beth Norton demonstrates, and even then it would mostly take the guise of training them, in Linda Kerber's phrase, for "Republican Motherhood."[7]

Literacy Change

Several striking additions, however, to the literacy landscape altered this portrayal of literary constancy, and we turn to these to address the second purpose of this book—to seek an explanation for the rising rates of signature literacy over the eighteenth century. With the exception of the spelling book, which made headway during the transitional decades of the 1730s and 1740s, all these changes occurred after the midpoint of the eighteenth century in a context of rising prosperity, commercialism, consumerism, and aspirations toward gentility. Every change detailed below promoted children's and adults' access to books and literacy instruction, laying the groundwork for the "reading revolution" of the new republic. Moreover, with only one exception, all these changes can be linked to Jack Greene's concept of cultural convergence, reinforced by Timothy Breen's documentation of a new consumer culture. By 1760 many aspects of colonial culture had converged, and the middling sort as well as the social elite emulated the refinements and innovations imported from Great Britain. Thanks to an increasing number of advertisements in a growing number of newspapers, consumers from all walks of life were able to indulge in the "creative engagement," as Breen terms it, of choice. All the innovations reviewed below occurred across the colonies.[8]

Literacy instruction needs equipment, but none of the technology involved in literacy changed in any dramatic way during the colonial period. Children continued to read books printed on hand presses and to write with quill pens.[9] What did change in the second half of the eighteenth century was availability. Books became cheaper and easier to produce. While the colonies continued to import paper from England long after the first colonial paper mill was built in 1690, paper, type, and presses were imported in greater quantities, and the cost of producing an imprint fell somewhat. Moreover, imports of books from Britain grew markedly in the second half of the eighteenth century. After a slump in 1756, the number of imported books rose significantly during the Seven Years' War (surviving a brief depression from 1762 to 1763). By the early 1770s, the British were sending 60 percent of their total overseas shipments to American ports, far exceeding both their shipments to Europe and the number of domestic imprints produced in America (see Appendixes 3 and 4). Evidence from newspaper advertisements confirms that imported schoolbooks were part of this deluge. Domestic production of schoolbooks also rose, especially of spellers. From 1765 to 1775, at least one American edition of Thomas Dilworth's *New Guide to the English Tongue* came out each year, printed in various American towns, and in 1772 as many as three editions came out (see Appendix 3). The net result was that, during the 1760s and 1770s, imported and domestic primers, spelling books, psalters, and testaments, the basic texts of reading instruction, were widely available and within the financial reach of all but the truly impoverished.[10]

Similarly, materials for writing instruction became easier to obtain in any city setting. The trend started around 1740 and spiraled upward in the 1760s, paralleling the increase in the availability of reading material. From the 1760s on, purchasers could buy writing implements of all kinds and at all levels of frugality or extravagance. The transformation was one of both quantity and quality. It led, on the one hand, to the democratization of writing, as what had been expensive (particularly paper) became cheaper; and on the other to the further consolidation of penmanship as a mark of gentility. The increase in advertisements for finely crafted writing desks was a mark of writing's progressively more genteel status. At the same time, slates became more common, useful for the beginning writer and for working out sums. With the advent of packaged ink and inkpots priced to suit all purses, it became easier to have instant access to ink at home. Writing was being demystified. Its final demystification would await the do-it-yourself books of the 1790s and thereafter that John Jenkins and other writing masters would publish to help novices teach themselves penmanship by breaking the art into small steps.

The changes in children's literacy activities during the second half of the century may be grouped into five areas, all of them set within the context of a general expansion of schooling: the acceptance of the spelling book as an introductory reading text; a new and gentler vision of the child that promoted new kinds of books for children; the commercialization of children's reading; a new focus on girls as the objects of educational attention in both reading and writing instruction; and even a tentative movement toward the redefinition of reading and writing.

The backdrop to these changes was the expansion of private and public schooling. In every context, white or black, slave or free, native or immigrant, the formal school setting emerges as the norm for literacy instruction throughout every generation except that of the first generations of settlers. Although much informal instruction no doubt took place in families, then as now, virtually every source that deals with literacy, other than the earliest New England laws relating to reading instruction, mentions schooling and schoolmistresses and schoolmasters. Moreover, even the early reading and apprenticeship laws assumed that deliberate teaching was involved: parents and masters were to "endeavour to teach, by themselves or others, their Children and Apprentices." And the literacy taught and practiced in the homes of Samuel Sewall, Cotton Mather, Phillis Wheatley, Anna Green Winslow, and others occurred against the backdrop of formal schooling. Although mothers still frequently taught their children to read, family members normally took over instruction only if schools were unavailable or children not well enough to attend them. Access to schools, school dames, and schoolmasters, therefore, was an important feature of access to reading and nearly always a critical feature of access to writing instruction.

The number, variety, and availability of schools, town-sponsored and private, day and evening, increased significantly after the midpoint of the eighteenth century.[11] In New England, all the provinces but Rhode Island mandated town-supported schools of some kind. In the middle provinces, schooling continued to be organized along denominational lines. The Quaker influence in Pennsylvania, in particular, ensured more equal educational treatment of girls and better access, in single-sex schools, for girls to writing instruction. In the South, some community schools teaching the basics were in operation, if communities were clustered close enough to make it practical and community enthusiasm for schooling was keen. On the estates of the gentry, private residential tutors continued to be the norm. By the 1760s, private schoolmasters and some schoolmistresses were advertising their literacy instruction in greater numbers than ever before. (We should, however, remember the large numbers of colonial children who had access to no schooling at all, particularly in cities where poverty was increasing.)

In terms of literacy instruction, the first and single most important innovation was one that affected reading primarily and spelling secondarily: the widespread adoption of the spelling book as a text for teaching young children to read. True, spelling books had been printed on a New England press in the early years of settlement, and spellers as a genre were older than Edmund Coote's *English Schoole-Maister* of 1596. However, when the first identifiable spelling books in America appeared at the end of the seventeenth century (such as those by Nathaniel Strong, Thomas Goodman, and Thomas Hill), they were aimed mainly at helping young men prepare for jobs as clerks. The new kind of spelling books, exemplified by Thomas Dyche's *Guide to the English Tongue* and imported into the colonies in the late 1730s, were different, because they were designed to introduce *children* to reading. From then on, spelling books gradually became the key reading instructional text in the schoolroom, inserted into the reading sequence after the primer. Often obviating the need for the Psalter (because the child who left the speller could pronounce words in any part of the Bible), spelling books such as those authored by Dyche, Henry Dixon, and Thomas Dilworth became entrenched in the educational landscape. Schoolmasters requested them as early as the 1730s for the schools for the poor funded by the Society for the Propagation of the Gospel (S.P.G.); they appeared at Anthony Benezet's schools in Philadelphia—indeed, Benezet composed one himself—and, in German, at Christopher Dock's little schools in rural Pennsylvania; they were the key instructional tool at Philip Fithian's and John Harrower's classrooms on Virginia plantations in the early 1770s; and a bilingual spelling book in Delaware and English was the only instructional text prepared for schools for the Delaware Indians by David Zeisberger, Moravian missionary to the Delawares, in 1776.[12]

Even those teaching the enslaved made use of spelling books. Spellers were packed in boxes that the Associates of Dr. Bray dispatched from London to Charles Town, South Carolina, in the 1730s; for the Negro charity school organized by Alexander Garden in the 1740s, also in Charles Town; and they were a key element of the Negro charity schools in Philadelphia, New York, Newport, and Williamsburg supported by the associates during the 1760s.

All in all, spelling books increased in variety, number, and pedagogical importance, whether imported or domestically printed. This was, of course, a transatlantic phenomenon. Even while a solid preference was emerging throughout the provinces in the 1750s and 1760s for Thomas Dilworth's *New Guide to the English Tongue*, other spellers, newly arrived from the mother country, continued to be advertised in every American port. Together with dictionaries, which received similar advertising space, spelling books had a profound influence on the regularization of spelling. As the quotations that appear throughout this book bear witness, the spelling of writers educated in the last half of the eighteenth century looks very different from the spelling of all but the elite of the seventeenth century, and increasingly similar to our own. (Town records show this contrast well.)

Reading methodology was not affected by the inclusion of the spelling book in the reading sequence. Far from it: spellers were the quintessential embodiment of the alphabet method. They brought a wealth of systematization and order to the approach, organizing words by syllabic length, by the syllable receiving the primary accent, and so forth, methodically matching their lessons to the tables preceding them. Spelling out words letter by letter, syllable by syllable, initially aloud and then, as the reader matured, silently continued to be the route to word identification.

Content, in contrast, had the potential to be deeply affected. For the first time, a book existed in the reading sequence that was neither part of the scriptures nor scripturally based: spellers were potentially vehicles for secularism. The cheerful poem in Henry Dixon's speller about the little boy whom no one could "make . . . say great A" was but one example of the direction spelling books could take. Authors could ignore this opportunity for secularism, as Thomas Dilworth did when he revamped scriptural material into words of the right number of syllables, but the very existence of spellers was an invitation to move outside the traditionally prescribed religious sequence. The anonymously authored *Child's New Play-Thing*, first published in the American provinces in 1743 and offering medieval tales such as that of Fortunatus, reflected the new conviction that reading should be pleasurable. Its radical challenge to the traditional texts showed just how far an author could take the genre.

The second major change of the colonial period, of which *Child's New Play-Thing* was itself a product, was the new vision of children promulgated by the English philosopher John Locke. Locke's view of children as malleable rather than innately sinful had pointed the way to a literacy education that offered children more pleasure than anxiety, one aimed to amuse rather than to convert them. The London printer John Newbery could, and did, invoke the name of "The great Mr. Locke" in support of the merit of his new "pretty books," little works designed to appeal to children by their attractive presentation, tipped with gold and rich with pictures. Locke had made another contribution, however: he had emphasized appealing to the child's reason and understanding, and his influence could be detected even in religiously based works for children. For instance, the *Friendly Instructor*, first advertised in America in 1746, made it clear that children should be actively seeking meaning from reading the scriptures.

It is important, however, to keep this innovation in perspective. The new "pretty books" were confined to those who could afford them—the eighteenth-century elite. Not until the 1780s would the Newbery books be published in large numbers by Isaiah Thomas and Hugh Gaine. Similarly, the lighthearted *Child's New Play-Thing* was never a threat to the sales of more traditional spelling books, particularly Dilworth's *New Guide*. It is safe to assert that most rural districts in the provinces were untouched by these developments—with one exception. The chapbooks that peddlers toted around the countryside reached many who otherwise had little access to books, and fairy tales would soon be included in the backpack.

A third change affecting literacy instruction and acquisition was directly related to the preceding one. The marketing of literacy equipment as expressive of taste as much as of utility, such a noticeable feature of the 1760s, was especially visible in the business of publishing books for children, where consumerism and gentility coalesced. Newbery's little volumes for children brought books into a market relationship with them. The child as consumer rather than the object of proselytization was a child whose wishes were being catered to even while he or she was subjected to manipulation. Once children were acknowledged to have tastes of their own, they were also open to Newbery's flagrant advertising of one book within another. So were their parents, to whom Newbery appealed by suggesting his pretty little gilded books as gifts for holidays such as New Year's Day.

The fourth change was an unexpected consequence of this commercialization of products aimed at children: for the first time in British and American history, girls were brought into the spotlight as consumers. The change affected both reading and writing instruction positively. As far as reading was concerned, the new "pretty books" made conscious attempts to appeal to the female sex. The title *Little Goody Two-Shoes*, with all the feminine implications of the appellation "Goody," was one of the first books designed for children ever to feature a female in its title. The *Friendly Instructor*, written by a woman, featured girls as the protagonists in conversations and as purveyors of insights into biblical reading (normally a male preserve). The Newbery books were fairly evenhanded in enticing both sexes to behave well in order to be rewarded by riding in a coach and six. In the seventeenth century, girls had been visible in print only after death, dying converted and confident in their salvation, as in James Janeway's *Token for Children*. Their introduction into the new books for children was a welcome departure from male pronouns.

In the arena of writing instruction, commercialism and a parental urge for gentility brought similar benefits to girls. Before the 1750s, the pupils most likely to have access to writing instruction (particularly free access because the town was paying for it) were white boys of the "upper" sort, followed by the sons of the white, middling sort. Gender, class, and race dictated who would be taught to write. After about 1750, however, writing masters actively wooed (white) girls as students, advertising the hours that were convenient for them (since convention prevented girls from attending school at the same time as boys). Indeed, the eighteenth century witnessed the gradual elimination of the earlier bias against teaching girls to write. Access to writing instruction had always been the prerogative of the daughters of the elite, through private writing masters. (Margaret Winthrop and Ann Yale Hopkins, who both became wives of colonial governors, are examples of elite women with fine writing skills in the seventeenth century; Jane Turell, daughter of one Massachusetts minister and wife of another, is an early eighteenth-century example.) But now such access was extended down the social scale, even as far as to poor girls. White girls were taught to write in the charity schools funded by the S.P.G. at some point after 1715, when they were first accepted into the master's school in Trinity School in New York, and certainly by 1761. Girls as wells as boys attended the Bethesda orphanage school in the 1740s, and like the boys penned letters to their benefactor George Whitefield.

The shift in sentiment in favor of teaching girls to write was reflected in legislation. Virginia was the first to mandate, in 1748, that both sexes must be taught to write as well as read. Later Poor Laws in other provinces continued the trend. (It should be noted, however, that this was a shift in principle, and not all practice would follow suit: the discrepancies between male and female signature rates continue to show well beyond the American Revolution) (see Appendix 1) Moreover, after the mid-century mark, young women as well as young men became part of the new culture of writing letters that Konstantin Dierks has described.[13]

Quantitative evidence reveals the growth of women's signing literacy. Signing rates in New England, whether male or female, continued to exceed those of other provinces. Joel Perlmann and his colleagues estimate that in the early decades of the eighteenth century 30 or 40 percent of New England women were signature literate; in the 1760s, 60 percent; and by the 1790s some 80 percent could sign their names (see Appendix 1).[14]

These quantitative data on girls' improved access to writing instruction are fleshed out by impressionistic evidence from the letters and journals they wrote as adults. Mary Beth Norton, who examined thousands of documents written by women for her study of the revolutionary experiences of American women, identifies three levels of women's writing ability, which I generalize here to both sexes.[15] The characteristics of the first level, "basic literacy," are phonetic spelling, poor grammar and punctuation, and insecure handwriting. The writings of Lucy Gaines's suitor, who claimed he could "nevor forgit" her "preshus lips," and of ten-year-old Sally Fairfax, furious with the killer of her cat and fuming that he "shoud be kild himself by rites," and of the man who issued the military order during the Seven Years' War against the "odus sound of cosing & swaring" all exhibit the features of level 1. At level 2, the "intermediate" level, writers write in coherent sentences, but nonetheless make some grammatical and spelling errors, and their manuscripts often shows blots and uneven lines—they are writers who write infrequently (or, to expand Norton's definition, who have received only a modest amount of education). Examples of level 2 are the diary of John Thomas, a surgeon who recorded in 1755 that "we Recived the Fire of thare Swivel Guns," and Lucy Gaines's blot-disfigured but well-phrased letter to the overseer Anthony Frazer. At the third and "advanced" level, writers have a good command of grammar and spelling, and although the penmanship of women is still generally inferior to that of men, both sexes reveal the influence of formal instruction and write frequently and easily. The journals of Philip Fithian and eleven-year-old Anna Green Winslow (with allowances made for her age) are examples of this level.

Of the few documents found by Norton written by white women between 1720 and 1760, all fall into levels 1 or 2. (Norton did not have access to the writings of learned women.) Between 1760 and the mid-1780s, the Revolutionary era, the number of white women's writings increased considerably, and Norton found examples of all three levels of literacy. From the mid-1780s on, however, women's writings, which increased dramatically in quantity, also improved noticeably in quality, with most writers attaining levels 2 or 3. Norton concludes that these last women had been able to obtain formal schooling more easily than had preceding generations. Since many of them were presumably taught to write in the 1760s or 1770s, their writings are evidence of an improved educational climate for girls' and women's writing instruction that developed some time after 1750, accelerating in the early 1770s. As Norton demonstrates, the American Revolution itself would inspire a radical rethinking of women's roles and so of their education.[16]

In addition to this major improvement in writing instruction for some girls, a fifth factor emerges as a novelty in literacy instruction in the eighteenth century, although tentatively. The conventional, if implicit, definitions of reading as the uncritical reception of the ideas of others and of writing as the uncritical reproduction of the words of others began to be challenged.

After about 1740, children were occasionally reminded to pay attention to the meaning of what they were reading. It would be a mistake to think that they had never been asked to do this before. It was thought that because reading meant oral reading, the act of performance would reveal whether readers had understood what they were reading. In the words of James Burgh, author of a popular rhetoric titled *The Art of Speaking*, first published in London in 1761, young people were to use the natural inflections of their voice in reading: "For *reading* is nothing but *speaking* what one sees in a book, as if he were expressing his *own* sentiments. . . . And hence it is that no one can *read* properly what he does not *understand*." But this blithe equation between the reader's emotive reading and his or her comprehension no longer satisfied all instructors. During the course of the eighteenth century several authors, whose works represented a variety of genres, attempted to foster children's reading comprehension. John Lewis's "Exposition" of the Anglican Church catechism is one example, but the same feature occurred in spelling books and children's books. In American reprints of 1746 and 1757 of his speller *The English Instructor*, and also in the *Youth's Instructor*, Henry Dixon suggested several ways for the teacher to elicit understanding of the scriptures. The author of the children's book *The Friendly Instructor* offered hints, through the characters in her stories, on the same topic. Her protagonist refutes the idea that it is acceptable for her young friend to wait until she is older to try to understand the scriptures. Other authors went further, demanding critical thinking in addition to understanding the author's message. John Newbery invoked "The great Mr. Locke" as his authority for declaring that every father should teach his son to read, "and make him understand what he reads. No Sentence should be passed over without a strict Examination of the Truth of it." Future president John Adams articulated this idea well in 1761. The English law, he claimed, "greatly favours Education. . . . Freedom of Enquiry is allowed to be not only the Priviledge but the Duty of every Individual. We know it to be our Duty, to read, examine and judge for ourselves . . . what is right."[17]

Moreover, also during the latter part of the eighteenth century, important hints surfaced that writing instruction might be redefined in the future as composition. Benjamin Franklin, innovative as always, was one of the first to voice this idea in his *Proposals Relating to the Education of Youth* (1749). Drawing on his own experience, where he had been obliged to cope with the absence of formal composition instruction by creating it for himself, he stressed the importance of using writing as a tool of thinking, for enhancing comprehension by summarizing and paraphrasing one's own thoughts and those of others, and for communicating with others, particularly by writing letters. By the 1770s, private schoolmasters were beginning to advertise instruction in "Epistolary-writing." Konstantin Dierks has documented the surge in letter writing in the second half of the eighteenth century and its ties to a new respect for "female" qualities of tenderness and regard. Writing, in other words, was in the process of being transformed from its definition as penmanship into something like our modern, multifaceted conception of writing. Previously a marker of gentility and professionalism, it was expanding to console and amuse, to socialize and inform. Except for the enslaved, writing was becoming democratized. Nonetheless, it would take until the early 1830s for young schoolchildren in the United States to have a textbook that explicitly taught them composition, as Lucy Schultz has shown.[18]

Another aspect of the redefinition of writing was subtler. The prohibition against teaching the enslaved to write, male or female, in the schools sponsored by the S.P.G. or by the Associates of Dr. Bray, reveals a problem with our accepting at face value the colonials' own definition of writing as penmanship and reading as the reception of adult values. The school texts that American children in general read (free as well as enslaved) were supposed to make them more "docile," to use Benjamin Franklin's adjective. Reading instruction for slaves therefore involved the same texts, including the spelling books, as those offered to free children. But in no instance was writing instruction offered formally by philanthropic societies to the enslaved—even though only two provinces during the colonial period, South Carolina and Georgia, legally prohibited it.

Those who discussed why slaves should not be taught to write, as did the authors of the preamble to the restrictive South Carolina and Georgia legislation of 1740 and 1755, referred obliquely to the "inconveniencies" of having slaves taught to write. They meant, of course, the opportunity it would give slaves to forge their own passes. But surely the larger issue was that it would treat the enslaved as if they were the free. In defiance of its definition as penmanship, writing allowed one to be free, for the freedom to express oneself in speaking and writing was, and is, an integral part of the concept of liberty.

One last characteristic of American literacy instruction should be noted, one that owed nothing to English imports: the light hand of the social class system in the colonies. It may be seen, ironically, in penmanship instruction. The scripts selected by British writing masters for their students reflected the rigid British eighteenth-century social structure by offering different instruction to different groups. Masters encouraged a "*free* and *easy*" script among gentlemen, a more precise, yet "*bold* and *masterly*" round hand from those aspiring to a commercial education, and a wholly different script, the delicate Italian hand, among ladies.[19] But in colonial America, little evidence exists to show that gender affected the choice of instructional script. Writing masters appear to have taught girls the usual round hand, as the handwriting of Anna Green Winslow suggests. The problem for women was not that they had been insufficiently instructed in the Italian hand but that they had barely been instructed at all.

Social distinctions were felt most keenly in the South, as Devereux Jarratt was all too well aware, but the conviction, well before the Revolution, that provincial Americans were a free people who should have free access to the printed word, was widespread. The New England experiment in education, in particular, was unique for its time. Back in Old England, it was fashionable for the genteel to question the wisdom of allowing the lower classes to learn to read, let alone write. The argument was that education would make them discontented with their lowly lot. Ignorance, one British commentator wrote in the 1750s, was the opiate of the poor, shielding them from the knowledge that there was any other way to live. Because the wealth of the nation depended on the working poor, another wrote in 1788, "there is a degree of ignorance necessary to keep them so, and to make them either useful to others or happy in themselves. What ploughman who could read the renowned history of Tom Hickathrift, Jack the Giant-Killer, or the Seven Wise Men, would be content to whistle up one furrow and down another, from dawn in the morning, to the setting of the sun?" This attitude still prevailed in some circles in Britain as late as the nineteenth century.[20]

While it is rare indeed to find the issue of restricting literacy framed in those terms in colonial American sources, when it was made, it was usually in the context of slavery. The Reverend Francis Le Jau raised it in connection with teaching slaves to read: he feared their misinterpretation of biblical text. But the issue was never once raised by the founding fathers. Just the reverse: because of reading's special relationship with religion, the founders of Massachusetts Bay colony passed their earliest piece of educational legislation in 1642, requiring that the parent or master of every child see to it that the child be taught to read. Five years later they legislated town support for writing and advanced reading instruction for boys. While other countries, such as Sweden, had mandated reading instruction for the same religious motives, no other region of colonial America in the 1640s passed laws requiring townships to institute town-supported schools to teach writing and reading. Nor, with the exception of Scotland, did any European countries. As the American provinces grew closer in culture, all benefited from a growing appreciation of the importance of literacy. Children of both sexes were the beneficiaries of this new understanding.

The Formation of Self

What the culture prescribed for children to do with their literacy skills and what children in fact did with them were by no means one and the same.[21] Given other options, including works aimed at adults, children did not necessarily restrict themselves to the "good books" they were expected to read. Benjamin Franklin used his small funds to purchase chapbooks that were very different from the polemical religious works on his father's bookshelves. Children born later in the eighteenth century had a wider choice, provided their parents had the means and will to buy them the new imported "pretty books" now on sale in city bookstores or the gentle advice of the *Friendly Instructor*.

Choosing a book was one way for children to express themselves, but print cost money, over which they had little control. Writing, when the materials had become cheaper and were at hand in one form or another, lent itself more readily to self-expression. Katy Mather kept a conventional commonplace book; Creasy Mather left his father a contrite note, expressing repentance to an earthly as well as a divine father. Novice readers of all ages used their pens to vent their feelings, often in the margins of the books they were reading. Massachusett and Wampanoag Indians expressed themselves in the margins of Indian Bibles. Children and adults alike scribbled marginalia on books or manuscripts such as hand-written arithmetic books. The irrepressible Bob Carter wrote a list of the names of the girls he fancied in the margins of a Newbery imprint, with withering comments on those at the bottom of his list. Children wrote down poems from memory, as did the author of "Crown Nation Sweet and so are you." And they kept, as did Anna Green Winslow for her parents, and Sally Fairfax for herself, journals and diaries. From the 1770s on, children who acquired literacy increasingly turned to the more personal form of letter writing to display who they were, how they fitted in with their families, and what they thought of the world. Benjamin Franklin went further, using his childhood experiences with literacy to promote the literacy acquisition of others. In his *Autobiography* he describes how he taught himself to compose, and in his plan for his "English" school he gives advice on how to teach composition. The self-help and schoolbooks he published also promoted literacy acquisition. His *American Instructor* helped youth to spell, while his Dilworth's *New Guide*—which he was the first American to print, years before the work caught on in America— helped young children learn to read.

We are therefore probably mistaken in trying to fix a label of "liberating" or "conservative" on the consequences for the young of attaining literacy. The young, like their elders, more often used their reading and writing as an "expansion of personal space," in the important formulation of Richard Venezky.[22] From the Wampanoags to Anna Green Winslow, from Creasy Mather to Phillis Wheatley, literacy formed an important part of their spiritual, affective, social, and personal lives.

For girls in particular, as they grew into women, the opportunities for self-expression provided by reading expanded greatly in the last half of the eighteenth century. Elite women—or any woman who could read well enough and was able to borrow or purchase a book—now had access to texts on managing their homes and health, as well as to works of science and the more familiar fare of religious and devotional books. They even had access to fiction. (To a lesser extent, children did too, although the full impact of children's literature would not be felt until after the American Revolution, when Isaiah Thomas began reprinting Newbery titles.) What is more, women would turn their facility with the pen to a new use: that of authorship.[23]

Support for a fully literate populace in which women wrote as well as men would be even stronger in the new United States, for now the preservation of the republic depended on an informed citizenry. The rise of private academies for both sexes after the American Revolution, the common school movement that followed in the nineteenth century, the creation of colleges for women as well as men—all these stemmed from this early colonial conviction about the crucial role to be played by literacy in the life of a child. It was a decidedly American contribution, and in the South in the antebellum era literacy would prove to be the single acquisition by the enslaved that their masters would view with most alarm, and one they would attempt to prevent by the most degrading of legislation. For all understood, as we do today, that literacy is the shining hallmark of the free.[24]

Afterword: The Lessons

The colonial approach to reading and writing instruction has been discarded today, and rightly so, for children lost much by having their writing instruction deferred for so long. The late introduction of writing instruction was a legacy that persisted for centuries after the initial rationale (the difficulty of manipulating and sharpening a quill pen, the cost of paper and ink) had vanished.[1] Even throughout most of the twentieth century, when children were being taught in first grade how to form their letters and copy their homework from the chalkboard, instruction in composition was routinely deferred until second grade at the earliest.[2] The single most important contribution of the whole-language movement of the 1980s was to unite reading and composition writing in the classroom from the moment children set foot in school.

Nor are we tempted to go back to the lengthy exercises in the pronunciation of lists of words, arranged mainly by syllabic length and stress placement, that were the backbone of the spelling book: they involved an excess of repetition and deferred meaningful reading far too long. Indeed, from the 1820s on, educational reformers initiated a quest to find substitutes for the alphabet method and devised several new approaches (the word, phonic and sentence methods) in attempts to improve beginning reading instruction.

Moreover, even if a teacher wishes to use a part-to-whole approach, of which the alphabet method is certainly an extreme example, the phonic approach is superior. Under the alphabet method, if students meet the word *leg* for the first time in a book, they have to make the linguistic leap from the letter names, "el, ee, gee," to the word's pronunciation, "leg." (Critics noted that the "el, ee, gee" would more likely be construed as *elegy* than *leg*.) Under the phonic approach, sounding and blending the letter sounds, "lll, eh, guh," is a somewhat better springboard to the pronunciation of "leg."

Nonetheless, some more useful lessons may be drawn from the literacy experiences of long ago. For one, the alphabet method drew attention at a very early stage, without necessarily announcing it, to some of the complexities of the English spelling system. Children in colonial and provincial America were exposed to alternative pronunciations of vowels from their first instructional text, for, while they were mastering the syllabaries of the hornbook, primer, and speller, they learned that the *e* in *eb* was to be pronounced differently from the *e* in *be*. These principles were reinforced throughout the spelling book.

Eighteenth-century spelling books, reviled in later decades, also remind us that teachers, if not necessarily students, should understand the rules of pronunciation. Because the popular whole-language movement of the 1980s de-emphasized phonics, most textbooks designed to teach novice teachers how to teach reading, and published for the first time between 1980 and 1994, contained few discussions of the relationships between letters and sounds. University teacher-training courses were similarly silent.[3] In contrast, an eighteenth-century teacher or student reading conscientiously through the grammar section of Thomas Dilworth's *New Guide to the English Tongue* of 1740 (or even the second part of Edmund Coote's *The English Schoole-Maister*, first printed in 1596) had access to detailed discussions of the vagaries of the English spelling system, such as the effect of a final silent *e* on a preceding *c* and *g*, or on the variant pronunciations of the letter-combination *gh* (in *ghost* as opposed to *cough*, or "not sounded" as in *high* and *bought*). While it is reasonable to argue that children's heads should not be stuffed with rules about the English phonological and orthographical system, it is much less convincing to suggest that teachers of literacy need not learn about the complexities of the system.

Moreover, our examination of eighteenth-century spelling books highlights the role of systematic instruction that builds on lessons previously taught. The spelling book was supremely systematic, proceeding sequentially from letter to syllable to word and presenting texts for reading (such as lessons in words of three syllables) only when children had already learned how to pronounce words of three syllables. (Today such texts are called "decodable.") Many children who were exposed to this instruction for only a couple of years ended up being able to pronounce any word they met. Even enslaved Africans who somehow acquired a copy of Noah Webster's *American Spelling Book* or his *Elementary Spelling Book* and obtained a few lessons from a sympathetic person were able to continue on to conquer reading.[4] In this respect, the alphabet method may be compared to systematic phonics today. The superiority of systematic phonics instruction over less systematic approaches to teaching phonics has been established by extensive research.[5]

I have spoken of the alphabet method as if it were wholly in the past. In fact, the method has never died. Only a generation ago several countries used the alphabet method, crucially accompanied by writing, so that words were spelled and written at the same time. (I suspect that some still do so.) In Ireland, my mother-in-law, Pauline Monaghan, learned that way, as did, in India, my friend Shaista Rahman. Moreover, the alphabet method is still used in some remedial work with dyslexics and other children having severe difficulties learning to read and write.[6] But in one sense we were once all abcedarians, as those in their A B C's used to be known, at the beginning of our own literacy journeys. When, in turn, we start teaching our own children, we begin instinctively with the first letter of the alphabet, in its capital form ("great A"). In fact, it is my happy duty as a grandmother to warn Conor, Quinn, Jane, and Jake, who have just set out on this not "ordinary Road" but extraordinary road that, to adapt Henry Dixon's old spelling-book poem,

If you cry A, you must cry B,
And then go on to C, and D,
And that won't do, but still there's Jod,
Lurks in the way with X, Y, Zod.
And so no End you'll find there'll be,
If you but once learn A, B, C.

But I very much doubt that you will rue it . . .

APPENDIX I

Signature Literacy in Colonial America, the
United States, and the Atlantic World, 1650 to 1810

GRAPH 1. Rates of Signature Literacy among Men as Reported for the Atlantic World, 1650 to 1810

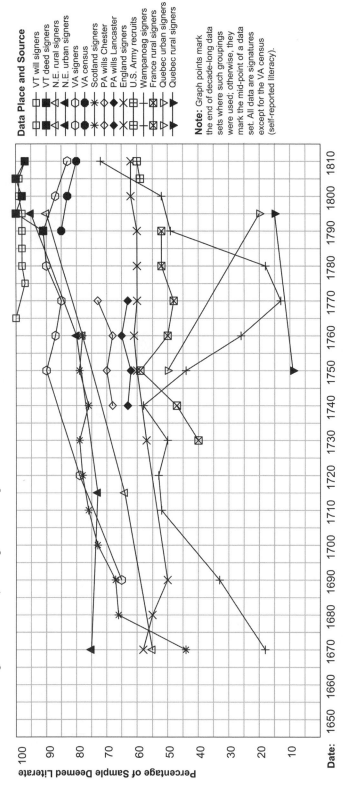

Data Place and Source

■	VT will signers
■	VT deed signers
◁	N.E. rural signers
◀	N.E. urban signers
⬡	VA signers
●	VA census
◇	Scotland signers
◆	PA wills Chester
✳	PA wills Lancaster
✕	England signers
⊞	U.S. Army recruits
⊠	Wampanoag signers
▷	France rural signers
▶	Quebec urban signers
▶	Quebec rural signers

Note: Graph points mark the end of decade-long data sets where such groupings were used; otherwise, they mark the mid-point of a data set. All data are signatures except the VA census (self-reported literacy).

SOURCES: **VT will signers, VT deed signers:** William J. Gilmore, *Reading Becomes a Necessity of Life: Material and Cultural Life in Rural New England, 1780–1835* (Knoxville: University of Tennessee Press, 1989), 122–23, graphs 3-1 and 3-2 (deeds and wills). **N.E. rural signers, N.E. urban signers:** Kenneth A. Lockridge, *Literacy in Colonial New England: An Enquiry into the Social Context of Literacy in the Early Modern West* (New York: Norton, 1974), 24, graph 3 (wills). **VA signers:** For 1650–1720: Darrett B. Rutman and Anita H. Rutman, *A Place in Time: Explicatus* (New York: Norton, 1984), 167, fig. 29 (various legal documents); for 1750–1810: David A. Rawson, "Guardians of Their Own Liberty" (Ph.D. diss., College of William and Mary, 1998), chap. 1, fig. 29 (various legal documents). **VA census:** Rawson, "Guardians of Their Own Liberty," chap. 1, fig. 29 (self-reported literacy). **Scotland signers:** R. A. Houston, "The Literacy Myth? Illiteracy in Scotland 1630–1760," *Past and Present* 96 (1982): 86–90, tables I and II (various legal documents). **England signers:** For 1650–1720: David Cressy, "Levels of Literacy in England, 1530–1730," *Historical Journal* 20 (1977): 11, table 3; for 1750–1810: R. S. Schofield, "Dimensions of Illiteracy, 1750–1850," *Explorations in Economic* **PA wills Chester, PA wills Lancaster:** Alan Tully, "Literacy Levels and Educational Development in Rural Pennsylvania, 1729–1775," *Pennsylvania History* 39 (1972): 304, table I (will-makers). *History* 10 (1973): 445, fig. 2 (various legal documents). **U.S. Army recruits:** Lee Soltow and Edward Stevens, *The Rise of Literacy and the Common School in the United States: A Socioeconomic Analysis to 1870* (Chicago: University of Chicago Press, 1981), 52, tables 2.2 and 2.3 (enlistment papers). **Wampanoag signers:** David J. Silverman, "Conditions for Coexistence, Climates for Collapse: The Challenges of Indian Life on Martha's Vineyard, 1524–1871" (Ph.D. diss., Princeton University, 2000), 367, fig. 2 (various legal documents). **France rural signers:** Thomas F. Sheppard, *Lourmarin in the Eighteenth Century* (Baltimore: Johns Hopkins University Press, 1971), 69–72, tables III-4 and III-5 (marriage act signatures). **Quebec urban signers, Quebec rural signers:** Allan Greer, "The Pattern of Literacy in Quebec," *Histoire Sociale/Social History* 44 (1978): 299, table 1 (marriage contract signatures). Graph adapted and expanded from Rawson, "Guardians," table 29, following p. 69.

GRAPH 2. Rates of Signature Literacy among Women as Reported for the Atlantic World, 1650 to 1810

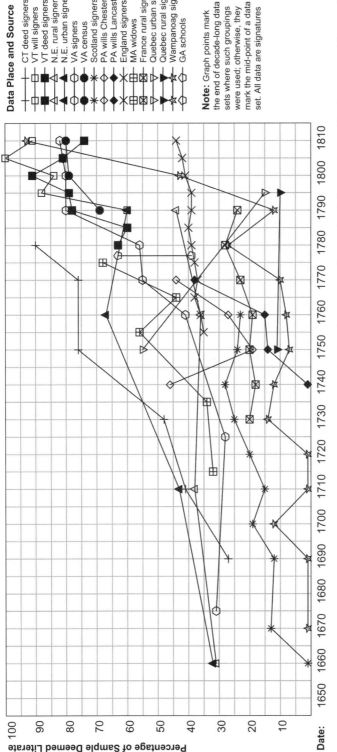

Data Place and Source

- CT deed signers
- VT will signers
- VT deed signers
- N.E. rural signers
- N.E. urban signers
- VA signers
- VA census
- Scotland signers
- PA wills Chester
- PA wills Lancaster
- England signers
- MA widows
- France rural signers
- Quebec urban signers
- Quebec rural signers
- Wampanoag signers
- GA schools

Note: Graph points mark the end of decade-long data sets where such groupings were used; otherwise, they mark the mid-point of a data set. All data are signatures.

SOURCES: CT deed signers: Linda Auwers, "Reading the Marks of the Past: Exploring Female Literacy in Colonial Windsor Connecticut," *Historical Methods* 13 (1980): 205, table 1. (Because Auwers' figures are for the dates of the women's births, I have arbitrarily added 30 years to her data to approximate the date of signing given by other sources.) VT will signers: Gilmore, *Reading Becomes a Necessity*, 122–23, graphs 3-1 and 3-2. VT deed signers: Gilmore, *Reading Becomes a Necessity*, 122–23, graphs 3-1 and 3-2. N.E. rural signers: Lockridge, *Literacy in Colonial New England*, 41, graph 8 (wills). N.E. urban signers: Lockridge, *Literacy in Colonial New England*, 41, graph 8 (wills). VA signers: For 1650–1720: Rutman and Rutman, *Place in Time*, 167, fig. 29; for 1750–1810: Rawson, "Guardians of Their Own Liberty," chap. 1, fig. 29 (various legal documents). VA census: Rawson, "Guardians of Their Own Liberty," chap. 1, fig. 29 (self-reported literacy). Scotland signers: Houston, "The Literacy Myth?" 86–90, tables I and II (various legal documents). PA wills Chester: Tully, "Literacy Levels," 304, table I. PA wills Lancaster: Tully, "Literacy Levels," 304, table I. England signers: Schofield, "Dimensions of Illiteracy," 445, fig. 2 (various legal documents). MA widows: Gloria L. Main, "An Inquiry Into When and Why Women Learned to Write in Colonial New England," *Journal of Social History* 24 (1990–91): 585, table 4 (letters of guardianship, etc.) (Because Main's figures are for the dates of the women's births, I have arbitrarily added 30 years to her data to approximate the date of signing given by other sources.) France rural signers: Sheppard, *Lourmarin in the Eighteenth Century*, 69–72, tables III-4 and III-5 (marriage registers). Quebec urban signers: Greer, "Pattern of Literacy in Quebec," 299, table 1 (marriage registers). Quebec rural signers: Greer, "Pattern of Literacy in Quebec," 299, table 1 (marriage registers). GA schools: Linda L. Arthur, "A New Look at Schooling and Literacy: The Colony of Georgia," *Georgia Historical Quarterly* 84 (2000): 587, table 1 (deeds, St. Matthew's Parish, inside and outside school district). Graph adapted and expanded from Rawson, "Guardians," table 30, following p. 69.

APPENDIX 2

The Alphabet Method of Reading Instruction

The alphabet (or alphabetic) method used in colonial reading, spelling, and writing instruction is often confused with the phonic approach, but the two were very different, and nineteenth-century sources—which are the earliest to discuss different reading instructional methods—always distinguish between them. No such distinction was made in the eighteenth or earlier centuries because the alphabet method of reading instruction was the only method known.

As its name suggests, the alphabet method was dependent on children's learning to match the shapes of the printed alphabetic letters to their names (not to their "sounds," as children would have done in a phonic approach). This matching was done orally, without writing the letters. Children learned to recognize each letter and name it, so that "reading" the letters *a b* of the nonsense syllable *ab* required them to utter "ay, bee" before saying "ab." Children's initial reading experiences, as they tackled syllables, words, and finally sentences, involved this oral spelling and pronouncing in a process that I call "spelling-for-reading." The syllable was the transitional unit at which a child aimed, and the point at which he or she would move from oral spelling of individual letters to the pronunciation of an entire syllabic unit. Most instructors required the students to spell out words in cumulative syllables, repeating each earlier syllable once they had achieved its pronunciation. The schoolmaster William Kempe, in his *Education of Children in Learning*, printed in London in 1588, describes the process. The "scholler" should tackle the word *mercifulness* as follows: "m-e-r [to be read as "em, ee, ar"], mer: c-i, ci, merci: f-u-l, ful, merciful: n-e-s, nes, mercifulnes."[1]

Spelling aloud in this way was the key to word recognition. Here, for instance, is a description of how children would have "read" the first lesson that they found in an American edition of Thomas Dilworth's spelling book of 1747, which Noah Webster later reproduced as the first lesson of his own spelling book, in 1783. (To make sense of this, you will need to read it aloud.) "En-o, No, emm-ai-en, man, emm-ai-wy, may, pee-you-tee, put, o-double-eff, off, tee-aitch-ee, the, ell-ai-double you, law, o-eff, of, gee-o-dee, God." That was children's first rendering of "No man may put off the law of God."[2] The limitations of this approach are self-evident: its critics would later say that "tee-aitch-ee" would lead a child more readily to the word "teacher" than to the word *the*. Nonetheless, it was the only method of "decoding," as reading professionals call it (cracking the code between the written or printed letters and the speech sounds they represent), that was prevalent during the sixteenth, seventeenth, and eighteenth centuries on either side of the Atlantic. Children were considered able to "read" satisfactorily once they were able to drop the crutch of oral spelling and pronounce a word at sight.

If children were not taught phonics in any direct way under this approach, how did they learn the correspondences between letters and speech sounds? The best explanation is probably that they learned them by association, analogy, and much repetition. If "bee ay dee" was "bad," then "ess ay dee" must be "sad." The spelling book, the key innovation of eighteenth-century America, gave children an inordinate amount of practice in pronouncing lists of syllables and words divided into syllables, because the heart of the spelling book lay in these long lists that were to be read out and pronounced aloud, often long before children met up with any connected reading matter. All this recitation was viewed as preparation for teaching children how to divide an unfamiliar word into its constituent syllables as a guide to pronouncing it.

A second use of oral spelling, which I call "spelling-for spelling," proceeded in much the same way, except that it moved from whole to part, from a word pronounced aloud down to the constituent letters of its written form. Once again, these words were presented in groups of syllables. The chief use of this process was in the school spelling competitions that surface early in the sources.

The final use of spelling, spelling-for-writing, is the most familiar to us today. Ironically, because of the pedagogical fixation, during the colonial period, on writing as penmanship rather than composition, this aspect of spelling is the least visible in the colonial record.

APPENDIX 3

Production of American Imprints, 1695 to 1790

GRAPH 3. Extant Editions of Primers Printed in Colonial America and the United States, 1695 to 1790

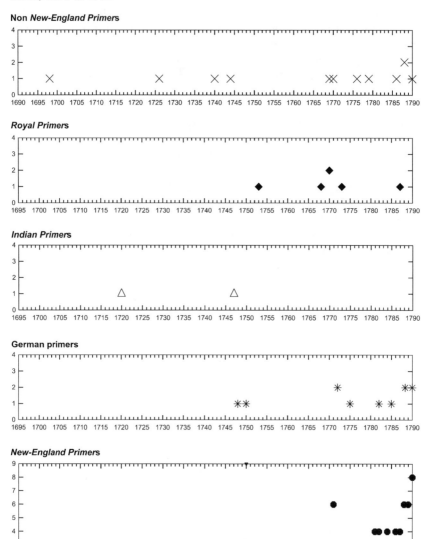

SOURCES: All the books graphed above are extant. Their titles were obtained from the American Antiquarian Society's online catalogue, which lists titles in other libraries as well as its own. The genre searched was *primers*. **Non-New England Primers:** This category includes Francis Daniel Pastorius, *A New Primer* (1698), Benjamin Harris, *The Protestant Tutor for Children* (1685, 1726?), *The American Primer* (ca. 1740), *A Primmer for Children* (1744), Stephen Crisp, *A New Book for Children to Learn in* (1769), David Manson, *A New Primer. Or, Child's Best Guide* (1770?), *A New Primer* (1776), *The Newest American Primer* (1779), *A New Primer, or Little Boy and Girls Spelling Book* (1786?), Anna Letitia Barbauld, *Lessons for Children, from Two to Four Years Old* (1788), Robert Ross, *The New Primer, or Little Boy and Girls Spelling Book* (1788), and Samuel Freeman, *The Columbian Primer, or The School Mistresses Guide to Children* (1790). **Royal Primers:** *The Royal Primer Improved* (1753), *The Royal Primer* (1768, 1770, 1773, 1787), and *A Primer: or, An Easy and Pleasant Guide to the Art of Reading* (1790). **Indian Primers:** *The Indian Primer or The First Book: By Which Children May Know Truely to Read the Indian Language. And Milk for Babes* (1720, 1747). **German primers:** Die *Schule der Weisheit* (1748, 1750), *Hoch-Deutsches Lutherisches A B C* (1772, 1774 or 1775, 1790, 1790), *Verbessertes Hochdeutsch-Reformirtes Namen-Büchlein* (1772), *Hoch-Deutsches Evangelisch-Lutherisches A B C* (1782), and *Hoch-Deutsches Reformirtes A B C* (1785, 1788, 1788). **New-England Primers:** Some 85 primers printed between 1727 and 1789 and titled *The New-England Primer* are extant. (From 1790 on, printers were less likely to include a date.) Editions either added "enlarged" or "improved" to the main title. Publication began in Boston, which remained by far the largest source of imprints, then expanded to Germantown (1754) and Philadelphia, Pa. (including 1760 and 1764 editions by Benjamin Franklin and David Hall). In the early 1770s, editions began to be printed in Salem and Newburyport, Mass., as well as Providence, R.I. The 1780s saw a new expansion to Hartford (including Noah Webster's revision of 1781), New Haven, New London, and Norwich, all in Connecticut; to Plymouth, Salem, and Springfield, Mass.; to Exeter and Portsmouth, N.H.; and finally to New York (1788) and Wilmington, Del. (1788).

GRAPH 4. Extant Editions of Spelling Books Printed in Colonial America and the United States, 1695 to 1790

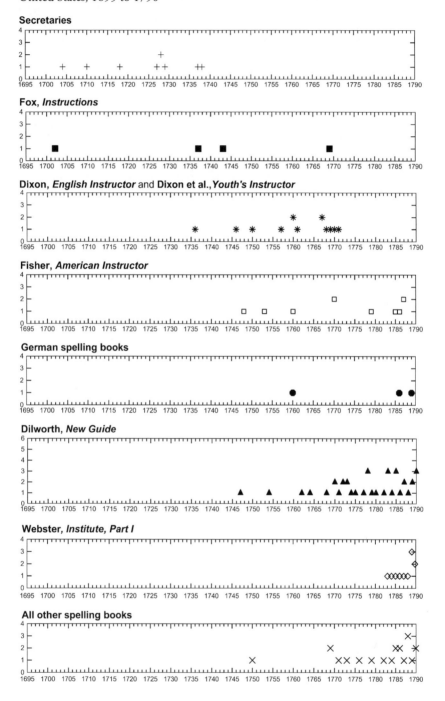

SOURCES: All the books graphed above are extant. Their titles were obtained from the American Antiquarian Society's online catalogue, which lists titles in other libraries as well as its own. The genres searched were *spellers* and *textbooks*. **Secretaries:** The "Secretaries" category comprises works for young men aspiring to be clerks. It includes *England's Perfect School-Master, The Young Man's Companion, and The Secretary's Guide, or, Young Mans Companion.* **Fox, *Instructions:*** George Fox, *Instructions for Right Spelling* (1702 on), was a combination of a primer and a speller for members of the Society of Friends. **Dixon, *English Instructor* and Dixon et al., *Youth's Instructor:*** Henry Dixon, *The English Instructor.* Designed to teach children to read, Dixon's contribution became part of the compilation, *The Youth's Instructor in the English Tongue: or, the Art of Spelling Improved,* Collected from Dixon, Bailey, Owen, Strong and Watts, in 1757 and thereafter. **Fisher, *American Instructor:*** George Fisher's *American Instructor* (1748 and thereafter) was an omnibus self-instructional book for young men. Its title, *The American Instructor; or, Young Man's Best Companion,* was alternatively titled *The Instructor; or, American Young Man's Best Companion.* **German spelling books:** This category includes German spelling books printed in 1760, 1786, and 1789. **Dilworth, *New Guide:*** Thomas Dilworth, *A New Guide to the English Tongue* (1747 on), was, like Dixon's, a speller designed for children. **Webster, *Institute, Part I:*** Noah Webster, *A Grammatical Institute of the English Language,* Part 1 (1783 on), titled *An American Spelling Book* from 1787 on, introduced children to reading. **All other spelling books:** *The Child's New Play-Thing* (1750); anon., *The Spelling-book, and Child's Plaything* (1769); Daniel Fenning, *Universal Spelling-Book* (1769 on); Anthony Benezet, *The Pennsylvania Spelling-Book* (1776 on); William Perry, *The Only Sure Guide* (1785 on); Ross, Robert, *The New American Spelling-Book* (c. 1785); John Barry, *The Philadelphia Spelling Book* (1790). Note that the 1750 edition of *The Child's New Play-Thing* is the only colonial American edition extant. *The Child's New Play-Thing* (Philadelphia: W[illiam] Dunlap, 1763) is spurious: apparently written by its printer, its title page is the only page taken from the genuine speller. Not graphed is David Zeisberger, *Essay of a Delaware-Indian and English Spelling-Book* (1776).

GRAPH 5. Production of Imprints in Colonial America and the United States, 1700 to 1790. Annual totals versus moving average.

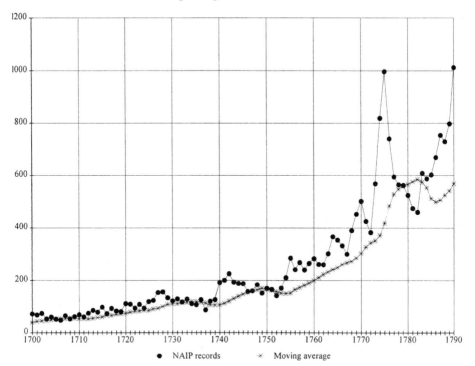

● NAIP records   ⨯ Moving average

SOURCE: *A History of the Book in America,* ed. David D. Hall, vol. 1, *The Colonial Book in the Atlantic World,* ed. Hugh Amory and David D. Hall ([Worcester, Mass.]: American Antiquarian Society; New York: Cambridge University Press, 2000), 506, graph 1b.

APPENDIX 4

American Imprints versus English Exports, 1710 to 1780

GRAPH 6. Records of the North American Imprints Program (NAIP) Compared with English Exports, 1710 to 1780. Rate of change (10 year moving average)

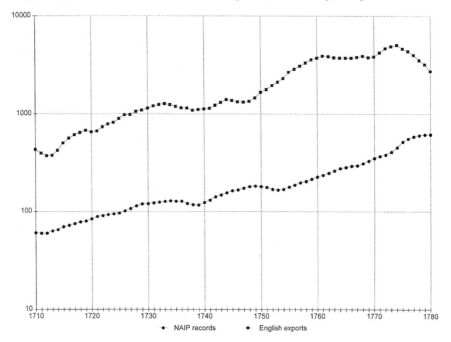

SOURCE: *A History of the Book in America*, ed. David D. Hall, vol. 1, *The Colonial Book in the Atlantic World*, ed. Hugh Amory and David D. Hall ([Worcester, Mass.]: American Antiquarian Society; New York: Cambridge University Press, 2000), 514, graph 7b.

NOTES

Introduction

1. Carl F. Kaestle, "Standardization and Diversity in American Print Culture, 1880 to the Present," in Carl F. Kaestle, Helen Damon-Moore, Lawrence C. Stedman, Katherine Tinsley, and William Vance Trollinger Jr., *Literacy in the United States: Readers and Reading since 1880* (New Haven: Yale University Press, 1991), 291–93. Among those who are less enthusiastic about the fruits of literacy is Harvey Graff. See, in particular, Harvey J. Graff, *The Literacy Myth: Cultural Integration and Social Structure in the Nineteenth Century* (1979; repr., New Brunswick, N.J.: Transaction Publishers, 1991). See also Brian V. Street, *Literacy in Theory and Practice* (Cambridge: Cambridge University Press, 1984).

2. Lawrence A. Cremin, *American Education: The Colonial Experience, 1607–1783* (New York: Harper & Row, 1970), 600; Nila Banton Smith, *American Reading Instruction: Its Development and Its Significance in Gaining a Perspective on Current Practices in Reading* (New York: Silver, Burdett, 1934; rpt. with changes in 1965; updated by others in 1986 and 2002; Newark, Del.: International Reading Association, 1965, 1986, 2002); Mitford M. Mathews, *Teaching to Read, Historically Considered* (Chicago: University of Chicago Press, 1966); Ray Nash, *American Writing Masters and Copybooks: History and Bibliography through Colonial Times* (Boston: Colonial Society of Massachusetts, 1959); Edward E. Gordon and Elaine H. Gordon, *Literacy in America: Historic Journey and Contemporary Solutions* (Westport, Conn.: Praeger, 2003).

3. E.g., Harvey J. Graff, *The Legacies of Literacy: Continuities and Contradictions in Western Culture and Society* (Bloomington: Indiana University Press, 1987).

4. J. T. Hooker, introd., *Reading the Past: Ancient Writing from Cuneiform to the Alphabet* (Berkeley: University of California Press, 1990); William V. Harris, *Ancient Literacy* (Cambridge, Mass.: Harvard University Press, 1989); Jo Ann Hoeppner Moran, *The Growth of English Schooling, 1340–1548: Learning, Literacy, and Laicization in Pre-Reformation York Diocese* (Princeton, N.J.: Princeton University Press, 1984); R. A. Houston, *Scottish Literacy and the Scottish Identity: Illiteracy and Society in Scotland and Northern England, 1600–1800* (1985; repr., New York: Cambridge University Press, 2002); Jeffrey Brooks, *When Russia Learned to Read: Literacy and Popular Culture, 1861–1917* (Princeton, N.J.: Princeton University Press, 1985); Kaestle et al., *Literacy in the United States*; Daniel A. Wagner, ed., *The Future of Literacy in a Changing World*, rev. ed. (1987; repr., Cresskill, N.J.: Hampton Press, 1999).

5. Kenneth A. Lockridge, *Literacy in Colonial New England: An Enquiry into the Social Context of Literacy in the Early Modern West* (New York: Norton, 1974).

6. E. Jennifer Monaghan, "Literacy Instruction and Gender in Colonial New England," *American Quarterly* 40 (1988): 18–41; reprinted in *Reading in America: Literature and Social History*, ed. Cathy N. Davidson (Baltimore: Johns Hopkins University Press, 1989), 53–80, and *The Book History Reader*, ed. David Finkelstein and Alistair McCleery (London: Routledge, 2002), 297–315.

7. Jonathan Edwards, *The Works of Jonathan Edwards*, vol. 16, *Letters and Personal Writings*, ed. George S. Claghorn (New Haven: Yale University Press, 1998), 407. I am indebted to David Hall for this reference.

8. Jack P. Greene, *Pursuits of Happiness: The Social Development of Early Modern British Colonies and the Formation of American Culture* (Chapel Hill: University of North Carolina Press, 1988).

9. T. H. Breen, *The Marketplace of Revolution: How Consumer Politics Shaped American Independence* ([London]: Oxford University Press, 2004), 53.

10. Ross W. Beales and E. Jennifer Monaghan, "Literacy and Schoolbooks," in *A History of the Book in America*, ed. David D. Hall, vol. 1, *The Colonial Book in the Atlantic World*, ed. Hugh Amory and David D. Hall ([Worcester, Mass.:] American Antiquarian Society; New York: Cambridge University Press, 2000), 380–87.

11. Charles Hoole, *A New Discovery of the Old Art of Teaching School*, with an introduction by Thistleton Mark (London, 1660; repr., Syracuse, N.Y.: Bardeen, 1912), 89, 159. Hoole was discussing teaching Latin grammar, but the model was adopted wholesale to teaching English.

Prelude to Part I

1. Laurel Thatcher Ulrich, *Good Wives: Image and Reality in the Lives of Women in Northern New England, 1650–1750* (1980; rpt., New York: Vintage Books, 1991).

2. James K. Hosmer, *Winthrop's Journal, "History of New England, 1630–1649,"* 2 vols. (New York: Charles Scribner's Sons, 1908), 2:225. Ann Hopkins was the aunt of Elihu Yale, for whom Yale College was named. Letter, John Winthrop to Margaret Winthrop, Oct., 3, 1623, quoted in Alice Morse Earle, *Margaret Winthrop* (1895; rpt., Williamstown, Mass.: Corner House Publishers, 1975), 50.

3. Hall, "The Uses of Literacy in New England, 1600–1850," in *Cultures of Print: Essays in the History of the Book* (Amherst: University of Massachusetts Press, 1996), 56–57.

4. Kenneth A. Lockridge, *Literacy in Colonial New England: An Enquiry into the Social Context of Literacy in the Early Modern West* (New York: Norton, 1974).

5. Richard D. Brown, *Knowledge Is Power: The Diffusion of Information in Early America, 1700–1865* (New York: Oxford University Press, 1989), chap. 1. For female scolding, see Jane Kamensky, *Governing the Tongue: The Politics of Speech in Early New England* (New York: Oxford University Press, 1997).

6. John Winthrop, "A Modell of Christian Charity" (1630), available at http://history.hanover.edu/texts/winthmod.html; James Axtell, *The School upon a Hill: Education and Society in Colonial New England* (1974; rpt., New York: Norton, 1976).

7. James L. Axtell, ed., *Educational Writings of John Locke: A Critical Edition with Introduction and Notes* (Cambridge: Cambridge University Press, 1968), 260.

8. Robert R. Roden, *The Cambridge Press, 1638–1692: A History of the First Printing Press Established in English America, Together with a Bibliographical List of the Issues of the Press* (New York: Dodd, Mead, 1905), 36.

9. Coote, *The English Schoole-Maister* (London: Widow Orwin, 1596); for editions of Coote, see William R. Hart, "*The English Schoole-Maister* (1596) by Edmund Coote: An Edition of the Text with Critical Notes and Introductions" (Ph.D. diss., University of Michigan, 1963), 8–21; for the quotation from Coote, *English Schoole-Maister*, 12, see Hart, "*English Schoole-Maister*," 144. Cf. John Brinsley: the "Secretarie hand," he remarks in a 1627 edition of his book, "is almost wholly in vse amongst us." Brinsley, *Ludus Literarius or the Grammar Schoole*, ed. E. T. Campagnac (Liverpool: University Press, 1917), xviii, 27 (this is a reprint of the 1627 edition).

10. Ray Nash, *American Writing Masters and Copybooks: History and Bibliography through Colonial Times* (Boston: Colonial Society of Massachusetts, 1959), 2–3; Joyce I. Whalley, *The Pen's Excellencie: A Pictorial History of Western Calligraphy* (New York: Taplinger, 1980), 145; Coote, *English Schoole-Maister*, [95], in Hart, "*English Schoole-Maister*," 227. The secretary script had evolved from the Italian "running chancery" hand, a product of the Renaissance. A. S. Osley, "Canons of Renaissance Handwriting," *Visible Language* 13 (1979): 70–94.

11. Whalley, *Pen's Excellencie*, 162, 181–83, 216.

12. Kempe, *The Education of Children in Learning* (London: Iohn Porter and Thomas Gubbin, 1588), n.p., in *Four Tudor Books on Education . . .* , facsimile reproduction with an introduction by Robert D. Pepper (Gainesville, Fla.: Scholars' Facsimiles and Reprints, 1966), 226.

13. Nash, *American Writing Masters*, 1–3; for the evolution of Italian-derived scripts, see Tamara Plakins Thornton, *Handwriting in America: A Cultural History* (New Haven: Yale University Press, 1996), 18–22. See Figure 14 below, p. 298, for an illustration of the scripts.

14. Laetitia Yeandle, "The Evolution of Handwriting in the English-Speaking Colonies of America," *American Archivist*, Summer 1980, 298.

15. Nash, *American Writing Masters*, 4. See also Yeandle, "Evolution of Handwriting," 298; Yeandle provides illustrations of Winthrop's and Bradford's handwriting, among others. Town records show how scripts changed over the years. In Watertown, Massachusetts, for example, when Ephraim Child kept the town book in 1656, he wrote a swift secretary. When Richard Norcross, long the schoolmaster of the Watertown town school and a Latinist, signed a new contract with the town in 1693, he wrote his name in italic. *Watertown Records Comprising the First and Second Books of Town Proceedings* (Watertown, Mass.: Historical Society, 1894), 1: facing p. 45; 2: facing p. 62.

Chapter 1. Literacy and the Law in Orthodox New England

1. Franklin Bowditch Dexter, ed., *Ancient Town Records*, vol. 1, *New Haven Town Records, 1649–1662* (New Haven: New Haven Colony Historical Society, 1917), 212; reelected: 241 (1655), 277 (1656), 313 (1657).

2. For lawmaking and record keeping in the Chesapeake context in the seventeenth century, see David D. Hall, "The Chesapeake in the Seventeenth Century," in *A History of the Book in America*, ed. David D. Hall, vol. 1, *The Colonial Book in the Atlantic World*, ed. Hugh Amory and David D. Hall ([Worcester, Mass.:] American Antiquarian Society; New York: Cambridge University Press, 2000), 57–65. For histories of New Haven colony, see Edward E. Atwater, *History of the Colony of New Haven to Its Absorption into Connecticut* (New Haven: printed for the author, 1881); Isabel MacBeath Calder, *The New Haven Colony* (New Haven: Yale University Press, 1934).

3. Calder, *New Haven Colony*, 4–31, 46, 28.

4. Ibid., 116–17. By 1657, the other townships were, in addition to Guilford and Milford, Stamford, Southold, and Branford. Charles J. Hoadly, ed., *Records of the Colony or Jurisdiction of New Haven, from May, 1653, to the Union. Together with the Code of 1656* (Hartford: Case, Lockwood, 1858), 221 (hereafter cited as Hoadly, *New Haven Colony Records, from May 1653*).

5. Charles J. Hoadly, ed., *Records of the Colony and Plantation of New-Haven, from 1638 to 1649* (Hartford: Case, Tiffany, 1857), 1, 5, 7. Mantowese was the son of the Indian sachem of Mattabezeck (ibid., 53).

6. My dating system needs an explanation. Most continental countries had long adopted the calendar reforms made by Pope Gregory in 1582 to the old Roman (Julian) calendar. In 1752, Britain and her colonies also switched to the Gregorian calendar, changing the date on which each year began from Mar. 25 to Jan. 1. Until 1752, some English writers indicated the first three months of the (Gregorian) year by writing dual dates, such as Feb. 1664/65. In this book, I have silently "modernized" the dates as if the Gregorian dating system had been in force throughout the colonial period.

7. Hoadly, *New Haven Colony Records, 1638–1649*, 9–12, 17–18, quot. 12.

8. Ibid., 23–24.

9. Ibid., 25–27, 61, 75, 77.

10. Patricia Cline Cohen, *A Calculating People: The Spread of Numeracy in Early America* (Chicago: University of Chicago Press, 1982), 120–22.

11. Hoadly, *New Haven Colony Records, 1638–1649*, 62, 156.

12. Lawrence A. Cremin, *American Education: The Colonial Experience, 1607–1783* (New York: Harper & Row, 1970), 503.

13. Hoadly, *New Haven Colony Records, 1638–1649*, 191, 210.

14. Quoted in Calder, *New Haven Colony*, 94. Dexter, *New Haven Town Records, 1649–1662*, 68, 74, 91, 93, quot. 68. The "Janes" in the town records is identified as William Jeanes by Dexter, ibid., 68.

15. Dexter, *New Haven Town Records, 1649–1662*, 97, 99–100. Dexter identifies the "Handford" of the records as Thomas Hanford (97).

16. Ibid., 111–12, 130.

17. Ibid., 153.

18. Ibid., 153n, 181, 206–7.

19. Ibid., 228, 448.

20. Dexter, *New Haven Town Records, 1649–1662*, 280.

21. Hoadly, *New Haven Colony Records, from May 1653*, 583–84.

22. Ibid., 219–20, quot. 220.

23. Ibid., 301, 372–76, quot. 372. The estate was that of Edward Hopkins. Franklin Bowditch Dexter, ed., *Ancient Town Records*, vol. 2, *New Haven Town Records, 1662–1684* (New Haven: New Haven Colony Historical Society, 1919), 218.

24. Hoadly, *New Haven Colony Records, from May 1653*, 374, 376.

25. Ibid., 377; Calder, *New Haven Colony*, 136.

26. Hoadly, *New Haven Colony Records, from May 1653*, 407–8.

27. Ibid., 458, 471; Franklin Bowditch Dexter, ed., *Ancient Town Records*, vol. 2, *New Haven Town Records, 1662–1684* (New Haven: New Haven Colony Historical Society, 1919), 5, 15.

28. Dexter, *New Haven Town Records, 1662–1684*, 15.

29. Ibid., 19, 48–49. There were similar objections in April 1664 "against alloweing a Sallary to teach English" (ibid., 86). Israel Chauncy, who graduated from Harvard in 1661, was supposed to replace Pardee at the end of the year but received a call to help out with the ministry at Stratford instead (ibid., 94; Calder, *New Haven Colony*, 142).

30. Calder, *New Haven Colony*, 143. For details of Connecticut's education laws, see below, notes 43 and 71.

31. Dexter, *New Haven Town Records, 1662–1684*, 332, 318–19, 332–33; service as attorney: 147.

32. Ibid., 363–65.

33. Cremin, *American Education*, 187, also emphasizes the range of instruction provided.

34. On the New Haven courts, see Gail Sussman Marcus, "'Due Execution of the Generall Rules of Righteousnesse': Criminal Procedure in New Haven Town and Colony, 1638–1658," in *Saints and Revolutionaries: Essays on Early American History*, ed. David D. Hall, John M. Murrin, and Thad W. Tate (New York: Norton, 1984), 99–137.

35. Hoadly, *New Haven Colony Records, 1638–1649*, 174–76.

36. Paul L. Ford, *The New-England Primer: A History of Its Origin and Development with a Reprint of the Unique Copy of the Earliest Known Edition* (New York: Dodd, Mead, 1899). (See Figures 5–7.)

37. Nathaniel B. Shurtleff, ed., *Records of the Colony of New Plymouth in New England*, vol. 1, *1633–1640* (Boston: William White, 1855), 38 (1636), 82 (1638); George Francis Dow, *Every Day Life in the Massachusetts Bay Colony* (1935; repr., New York: Benjamin Blom, 1967), 242–43.

38. Dexter, *New Haven Town Records, 1649–1662*, 88–89. I am indebted to Claire Monaghan for this interpretation. Puritans regarded the taking of an oath as of the utmost significance, under the assumption that no defendant or witness would jeopardize the fate of his or her soul by lying under oath (Marcus, "'Due Execution,'" 113–14).

39. Dexter, *New Haven Town Records, 1649–1662*, 437–38. While the records say "Bower," this was presumably the schoolmaster John Bowers.

40. Hoadly, *New Haven Colony Records, from May 1653*, 443.

41. "The Commonplace Book of Joseph Green," in *Publications of the Colonial Society of Massachusetts*, vol. 34, *Transactions 1937–1942* (Boston: Colonial Society of Massachusetts, 1943), 236. For examples of dame schools in England in the seventeenth century, see David Cressy, *Literacy and the Social Order: Reading and Writing in Tudor and Stuart England* (New York: Cambridge University Press, 1980), 37–38; Margaret Spufford, *Small Books and Pleasant Histories: Popular Fiction and Its Readership in Seventeenth-Century England* (Cambridge: Cambridge University Press, 1981), 35–36. See also J. H. Higginson, "Dame Schools," *British Journal of Educational Studies* 22 (1974): 166–81; and D. D. P. Leinster-MacKay, "Dame Schools: A Need for Review," *British Journal of Educational Studies* 24 (1976): 38–48, cited in

Joan Burstyn, "Women in the History of Education," paper presented at the annual meeting of the American Educational Research Association, Montreal, April 1983.

42. Shurtleff, *Records of the Colony of New Plymouth*, vol. 4, *1661–1668*, 83–84.

43. Nathaniel B. Shurtleff, ed., *Records of the Governor and Company of the Massachusetts Bay in New England*, vol. 2, *1642–1649* (Boston: William White, 1853), 6–7 (law of 1642), repeated with minimal change, 8–9 (1642); Boston, Registry Department, *Records Relating to the Early History of Boston*, [vol. 7], *A Report of the Record Commissioners of the City of Boston, Containing the Boston Records from 1660 to 1701* (Boston: Rockwell and Churchill, 1881), 26 (law of 1672).

44. [Connecticut Colony], *The Code of 1650, Being a Compilation of the Earliest Laws and Orders of General Court of Connecticut . . .* (Hartford: Silas Andrus, 1822), 40–41.

45. [New Plymouth Colony], *The Generall Laws and Liberties of New Plimouth Colony, Revised and Published by Order of the General Court, in June 1671* (Cambridge, Mass., 1672); Cremin, *American Education*, 125–26. *Laws of New Hampshire; Including Public and Private Acts and Resolves . . .* , vol. 2, ed. A. S. Batchellor (Manchester, N.H.: John B. Clarke, 1904), 115.

46. John Demos, *A Little Commonwealth: Family Life in Plymouth Colony* (New York: Oxford University Press, 1970), 69–75, 107–17, 120–22; Edmund S. Morgan, *Puritan Family: Religion and Domestic Relations in Seventeenth-Century New England*, rev. ed. (1944; New York: Harper and Row, 1966), 109–10, 117–22. For a review of the motivations for "putting out" children, see Judith S. Graham, *Puritan Family Life: The Diary of Samuel Sewall* (Boston: Northeastern University Press, 2000), chap. 9.

47. Cremin, *American Education*, 125. For examples of indentures, see Morgan, *Puritan Family*, 120–21 (from a 1692 Boston almanac); Judith Walter, "Apprenticeship Education and Family Structure in Seventeenth Century Massachusetts Bay" (master's thesis, Bryn Mawr College, 1971), 29–30.

48. David D. Hall, *Worlds of Wonder, Days of Judgment: Popular Religious Belief in Early New England* (New York: Knopf, 1989), 18, 22–23, quot. 23.

49. For the paradoxical status of the Bible as both inviolate text and physical object, as immaterial truth yet a text that invited annotations, see Hall, *Worlds of Wonder*, 23–27.

50. *Watertown Records Comprising the First and Second Books of Town Proceedings* (Watertown: Historical Society, 1894), 71 (hereafter cited as *Watertown Records, First and Second Books*).

51. [Connecticut], *Code of 1650*, 40. Much of the land settled by the newcomers was not wilderness at all but land cleared by the Indians. Nonetheless, the wilderness continued to be a powerful, if evolving, symbol in Puritan thought. Peter N. Carroll, *Puritanism and the Wilderness: The Intellectual Significance of the New England Frontier, 1629–1700* (New York: Columbia University Press, 1969), esp. 62, 127, 196, 213, 222.

52. Wales was one among several who were summoned either for being unemployed or for having children who were not under family government. Dorchester Antiquarian and Historical Society, *History of the Town of Dorchester, Massachusetts* (Boston: Ebenezer Clapp, Jr., 1859), 223–24; *Watertown Records, First and Second Books*, 104.

53. Dexter, *New Haven Town Records, 1649–1662*, 135.

54. Ibid., 280, 426–27.

55. *Watertown Records, First and Second Books*, 1:121.

56. Shurtleff, *Records of the Governor*, 2:9.

57. *The Records of the Town of Cambridge (Formerly Newtowne) Massachusetts, 1630–1703* (Cambridge, 1901), 47.

58. Convers Francis, *An Historical Sketch of Watertown, in Massachusetts, from the First Settlement of the Town to the Close of its Second Century* (Cambridge, Mass.: E. W. Metcalf, 1830), 48–49 (John Sherman). *Watertown Records, First and Second Books*, 1: 71. Inspections are noted in ibid., 71 (1661), 86 (1665), 104 (1671), 113 (1672), 121 (1674), 137 (1679), 145 (1680); *Watertown Records Comprising the Third Book of Town Proceedings . . . to End of 1737 . . .* (Watertown, Mass.: Historical Society, 1900), 13 (1683), 17 (1684), 26 (1686). The inspection of 1683 was a little different: two men were to go "to the Farmes that those that cannot cum downe conueniantly to Be caticysed" by the pastor, to check on their catechizing and reading.

Edmund Morgan was the first to spot the unusual activity of Watertown in relation to the reading law (Morgan, *Puritan Family*, 148 n. 53).

59. *Watertown Records, First and Second Book,* 1:102–3, 114, 122; the three families received yet another inspection in 1677 (ibid., 128).

60. Ibid., 103–4, 105, 107.

61. *New Haven Town Records, 1649–1662,* 129, 200. For another example of monitoring children's reading acquisition, in Salem, Massachusetts, in 1673, see *Town Records of Salem, Massachusetts,* vol. 2, *1659–1680* (Salem, Mass., 1913), 180.

62. Walter, "Apprenticeship Education," 33, 43, 37–38. Of the total 267, Walter found only 31 who were promised an education in their indentures—though, of course, all were covered by the colony's educational legislation (ibid., 42).

63. *Watertown Records, First and Second Books,* 1:104, 107, 109.

64. Ibid., 135–36 ("Goodwife Eiues").

65. Robert A. Arnove and Harvey J. Graff, eds., *National Literacy Campaigns and Comparative Perspectives* (New York: Plenum Press, 1987).

66. Shurtleff, *Records of the Governor,* 2:203.

67. See Perry Miller, *The New England Mind, the Seventeenth Century* (New York: Macmillan, 1939).

68. Quoted in Thomas Jefferson Wertenbaker, *The Puritan Oligarchy: The Founding of American Civilization* (New York: Grosset & Dunlap, 1947), 137.

69. *Oxford English Dictionary,* compact edition (1971), s.v. "Illiterate": "1748. . . . The word, illiterate, in its common acceptation, means a man who is ignorant of those two languages [Greek and Latin]."

70. Geraldine Joanne Murphy takes a similar view of the purpose of the law. "Massachusetts Bay Colony: The Role of Government in Education" (Ph.D. diss., Radcliffe College, 1960), 88–92.

71. Cremin, *American Education,* 182; J. Hammond Trumbull, ed., *The Public Records of the Colony of Connecticut* (Hartford: Lockwood and Brainard, 1850), 1:554–55; Nathaniel B. Shurtleff, ed., *Records of the Colony of New Plymouth in New England, Court Orders,* vol. 5, *1668–1678* (1856; repr., New York: AMS Press, 1968), 107–8; David Pulsifer, ed., *Records of the Colony of New Plymouth in New England,* [vol. 11], *Laws, 1623–1682* (1861; repr., New York: AMS Press, 1968), 142.

72. Between 1630 and 1642, seven towns (Boston, Charlestown, Cambridge, Dorchester, Ipswich, Newbury, and Salem) of the twenty-two towns then in existence had schooling of some kind; by 1647, eight (Dedham and Roxbury, both Latin grammar schools, were added) out of thirty-three did. Murphy, "Massachusetts Bay Colony," 12–13, 30–33, 52–53. Murphy later identifies the total as twenty-four towns and identifies only six as sponsoring schools, omitting Cambridge (ibid., 34).

73. Ibid., 17–18, 25–26. According to Murphy, all but two of the earliest towns offered Latin instruction; Newbury and Salem alone provided just reading and writing instruction. Furthermore, Salem was already paying John Fiske as a Latin teacher before the town began to employ Edward Norris Jr. in 1639 to teach literacy skills.

74. Ibid., 1.

75. The five Massachusetts townships (out of fourteen) that complied with the fifty-family law in some fashion between 1647 and 1657 were Dover, Hampton, Rowley, Salisbury, and Weymouth. (In addition, the hamlet of Medfield voted in 1654 for a writing and reading school, despite having only thirty-nine families.) The two of nine towns complying in the 1660s were Hadley and Northampton (ibid., 138–39, 152, 154, 141). For details of presentations of towns for failing to comply with the one-hundred-family law, see Robert Middlekauff, *Ancients and Axioms: Secondary Education in Eighteenth-Century New England* (New Haven: Yale University Press, 1963), 33–40.

76. Don Gleason Hill, ed., *The Early Records of the Town of Dedham,* Massachusetts, 6 vols. (vol. 6 ed. Julius H. Tuttle) (Dedham, Mass.: Dedham Transcript, 1886–1936), 4:83 (hereafter cited as *Dedham Records*); Carlos Slafter, *A Record of Education: The Schools and Teachers of*

Dedham, Massachusetts, 1644–1904 ([Dedham:] Dedham Transcript Press, 1905), 21. Murphy, "Massachusetts Bay Colony," 99, 131–32; Cremin, *American Education*, 187. A few examples out of dozens of other towns that insisted on writing instruction, no matter what else the master taught, include Cambridge, Mass., in 1690: *Records of the Town of Cambridge*, 293, "Sir Hancock to keep scoole for the Town to teach both Gramer & English with writeing & siphering"; Derby, Conn., in 1703: Samuel Orcutt, *The History of the Old Town of Derby, Conn.* (Springfield, Mass.: Springfield Printing Company, 1880), 107, Mr. James "to teach reading and writing"; Fairfield, Conn., in 1674: Thomas J. Farnham, *Fairfield: The Biography of a Community, 1639–1989* (West Kennebunk, Me.: Fairfield Historical Society, 1988), 46, Josiah Harvey to teach students "the rules of grammar both Lattin & greeke & to read write & cast acctt."; Norwalk, Conn., in 1678: Edwin Hall, comp., *The Ancient Historical Records of Norwalk, Conn.* (Norwalk: Ivison, Phinney, Blakeman, 1865), 69, Mr. Cornish to "teach all the childring in the towne to lerne to Rede and write"; Plymouth, Plymouth Colony, in 1674: [William T. Davis, ed.], *Records of the Town of Plymouth, Published by Order of the Town*, vol. 1, *1636–1705* (Plymouth, Mass.: Avery & Doten, 1889), 141, which proposed that "their Children be perfected in Reading when they are entered [into] the bible: and alsoe that they be taught to wright and Sifor"; Wethersfield, Conn., in 1668, Henry R. Stiles, *The History of Ancient Wethersfield, Connecticut* (New York: Grafton Press, 1904), 1:359, which instructed Samuel Butler "to teach children to read and write."

77. *Watertown Records, First and Second Books*, 26. Cf. the threepence charged for reading instruction and fourpence for writing and ciphering instruction in Lynn in 1703 and the fees in Plymouth in 1705: children living within a mile of the school were to pay "4 pence per weke for latten writing or sifering & 2 pence a weke for reading." *Records of ye Towne Meetings of Lyn, 1691–1701/2, Part I* (Lynn: Lynn Historical Society, 1949), 13; [William T. Davis, ed.], *Records of the Town of Plymouth . . .* , vol. 2, *1705 to 1743* (Plymouth: Avery & Doten, 1892), 1.

78. Newbury and Salisbury, quoted in Murphy, "Massachusetts Bay Colony," 98, 142; New Haven in 1651: Dexter, *New Haven Town Records, 1649–1662*, 97; New Haven in 1684: [Henry Barnard,] "History of Common Schools in Connecticut," *American Journal of Education* 4 (1858): 710n; Farmington, in Murphy, "Massachusetts Bay Colony," 142.

79. *Dedham Records*, 3:202; Stiles, *History of Ancient Wethersfield*, 358. In 1699 boys between six and twelve were to pay (360).

80. Quoted in Slafter, *Record of Education*, 15, 17.

81. Question raised on admission of girls: Hill, *Dedham Records*, 3:202, 5:164, 222. "Male children": ibid., 4:3 (1659), 35 (1661), 5:87 (1679), 164 (1685), 222 (1693); Hopkins Grammar School: [Barnard,] "History of Common Schools," 710n.

82. *Watertown Records, First and Second Books*, 21.

83. Murphy, "Massachusetts Bay Colony," 143.

84. For examples of boys in Boston records as "children," see the proposal to open a free school for the "teachinge of Children to write & Cypher" in *Boston Records from 1660 to 1701*, 158.

85. Quoted in Walter H. Small, "Girls in Colonial Schools," *Education* 22 (1902): 532–33. Small used primary sources such as town records for his study but did not document his sources. Where I have been able to cross-check them, I have found them largely accurate, although he modernized the spelling.

86. Charles B. Kinney Jr., *Church and State: The Struggle for Separation in New Hampshire, 1630–1900* (New York: Teachers College, 1955), 146; Murphy, "Massachusetts Bay Colony," 142.

87. Small, "Girls in Colonial Schools," 532–33; Walter H. Small, *Early New England Schools* (Boston: Ginn, 1914), 275–78, quot. 277.

88. For details, see E. Jennifer Monaghan, "Literacy Instruction and Gender in Colonial New England," in *Reading in America: Literature and Social History*, ed. Cathy N. Davidson (Baltimore: Johns Hopkins University Press, 1989), 64–65; Walter, "Apprenticeship Education," 33–34, 42–43. For girls taught only reading and sewing (and perhaps knitting and spinning) in England, see Spufford, *Small Books and Pleasant Histories*, 34–36.

89. Quoted in Monaghan, "Literacy Instruction and Gender," 65.

90. Charles H. S. Davis, *History of Wallingford, Conn., From Its Settlement in 1670 to the Present Time . . .* (Meriden, Conn.: By the author, 1870), 310, 311.

91. "Autobiography of the Rev. John Barnard," *Collections of the Massachusetts Historical Society,* 3rd ser., 5 (1836): 178.

92. *The General Laws and Liberties of the Massachusetts Colony: Revised and Reprinted* (Cambridge: Samuel Green for John Usher of Boston, 1672), 26; Small, *Early New England Schools,* 167.

93. For examples, see Small, *Early New England Schools,* chap. 6; esp. 168, 165; Monaghan, "Literacy Instruction and Gender," 68–69.

94. John D. Cushing, ed., *Acts and Laws of New Hampshire, 1680–1712* (Wilmington, Del.: Michael Glazier, 1978), 140; cf. a 1714 school law, 52.

95. William W. Hening, ed., *The Statutes at Large: Being a Collection of All the Laws of Virginia, from the First Session of the Legislature, in the Year 1619,* 13 vols. (imprint varies, 1819–1823), 1:157; see also 1:181–82, 311, where the penalty for noncompliance was set at five hundred pounds of tobacco, and 2:47, an act that reinforced the sole use of the catechism in the Book of Common Prayer (catechism); 1:336 (Poor Law); 2:170 (children of Negroes). For the first act related to the Syms free school, see 1:336.

96. R. A. Houston, *Scottish Literacy and the Scottish Identity: Illiteracy and Society in Scotland and Northern England, 1600–1800* (Cambridge: Cambridge University Press, 1985).

Chapter 2. Literacy and the Indians of Massachusetts Bay

1. Neal Salisbury, *Manitou and Providence: Indians, Europeans, and the Making of New England, 1500–1643* (New York: Oxford University Press, 1982), 21; Kathleen J. Bragdon, "Another Tongue Brought In": An Ethnohistorical Study of Native Writings in Massachusett" (Ph.D. diss., Brown University, 1981), 16, 18 (for Massachusett dialect variation, see 17–28).

2. Salisbury, *Manitou and Providence,* 22–30. See also Bert Salwen, "Indians of Southern New England and Long Island: Early Period," in *Handbook of North American Indians,* ed. William C. Sturtevant, vol. 15, *Northeast,* ed. Bruce G. Trigger (Washington, D.C.: Smithsonian Institution, 1978), 160–76. For a reappraisal of the relationship between infectious diseases and native susceptibility, see David S. Jones, "Virgin Soils Revisited," *William and Mary Quarterly,* 3rd ser., 60 (2003): 703–42.

3. James Axtell, *The European and the Indian: Essays in the Ethnohistory of Colonial North America* (New York: Oxford University Press, 1981), 85–86; Dane Morrison, *A Praying People: Massachusett Acculturation and the Failure of the Puritan Mission, 1600–1690* (New York: Peter Lang, 1995), 3–17, 25–35.

4. John Winthrop, *The History of New England from 1630 to 1649,* ed. James Savage (Boston: Phelps and Farnham, 1825), 1:254; William S. Simmons, "Conversion from Indian to Puritan," *New England Quarterly* 52 (1979): 202; Bragdon, "Another Tongue," 42.

5. For record keeping, see Karen Ordahl Kupperman, *Settling with the Indians: The Meeting of English and Indian Cultures in America, 1580–1640* (London: J. M. Dent, 1980), 95.

6. James Axtell, "The Power of Print in the Eastern Woodlands," *William and Mary Quarterly* 44 (1987): 300–309.

7. Quoted in ibid., 302.

8. Amy C. Schutt, "Forging Identities in a Multiethnic World: Indians and Moravians in the Middle Colonies and the Ohio Country" (Ph.D. diss., Colgate University, 1999), 267. See also David D. Hall, Introduction to *A History of the Book in America,* ed. David D. Hall, vol. 1, *The Colonial Book in the Atlantic World,* ed. Hugh Amory and David D. Hall ([Worcester, Mass.:] American Antiquarian Society; New York: Cambridge University Press, 2000), 25.

9. For a full account of missionary efforts to educate native Americans, see Margaret Connell Szasz, *Indian Education in the American Colonies, 1607–1783* (Albuquerque: University of New Mexico Press, 1988).

10. The wording in the Massachusetts seal echoes the appeal of the Macedonian to Paul (Acts 16.9); cf. Kupperman, *Settling with the Indians*, 160–66.

11. Works in this vein are reviewed in James P. Ronda, " 'We are Well as we Are': An Indian Critique of Seventeenth-Century Christian Missions," *William and Mary Quarterly*, 3rd ser., 34 (1977): 66. For the debate in general, see J. Frederick Fausz, "Anglo-Indian Relations in Colonial North America," in *Scholars and the Indian Experience: Critical Reviews of Recent Writing in the Social Sciences*, ed. W. R. Swagerty (Bloomington: Indiana University Press, 1984), 79–105.

12. For example, Q. Stitt Robinson Jr., "Indian Education and Missions in Colonial Virginia," *Journal of Southern History* 18 (1952): 152–68; Norman Earl Tanis, "Education in John Eliot's Indian Utopias, 1646–1675," *History of Education Quarterly* 10 (1970): 308–23. See also Lawrence A. Cremin, *American Education: The Colonial Experience, 1607–1783* (New York: Harper & Row, 1970), 157–63, 194.

13. Ronda, " 'We are Well as we Are,' " 67, summarizes this approach; Francis Jennings, *The Invasion of America: Indians, Colonialism, and the Cant of Conquest* (1975; New York: Norton, 1976); Henry Warner Bowden, *American Indians and Christian Missions: Studies in Cultural Conflict* (Chicago: University of Chicago Press, 1981), chap. 4. "Cultural revolutionary" is in James P. Ronda and James Axtell, *Indian Missions: A Critical Bibliography* (Bloomington: Indiana University Press, 1978), 4; "delimited" is in, for the postcolonial period, Robert F. Berkhofer Jr., *Salvation and the Savage: An Analysis of Protestant Missions and American Indian Response, 1787–1862* (Lexington: University of Kentucky Press, 1965), xi.

14. James Axtell is one of the leading proponents of this view. See his *European and the Indian* and *The Invasion Within: The Contest of Cultures in Colonial North America* (New York: Oxford University Press, 1985).

15. James Axtell, "Some Thoughts on the Ethnohistory of Missions," *Ethnohistory* 29 (1982): 35–41; quotation in Axtell, *Invasion Within*, 332. Szasz evaluates the "success" of educating the Indians by whether or not they became "cultural brokers" (*Indian Education*, chap. 11).

16. Jill Lepore, *The Name of War: King Philip's War and the Origins of American Identity* (New York: Alfred A. Knopf, 1998), 27.

17. For a list of the eleven Eliot Tracts, see Wilberforce Eames, ed., *John Eliot and the Indians, 1652–1657 . . .* (New York: Adams and Grace Press, 1915), 28–31.

18. For the distinction between a pastor and a teacher, see David D. Hall, *The Faithful Shepherd: A History of the New England Ministry in the Seventeenth Century* (Williamsburg, Va., 1972), 11, 95–96. As Hall has noted, the distinction between "teachers" and "pastors" blurred in practice.

19. Assessments of Eliot's life and work have undergone reevaluation since the glowing account of Ola E. Winslow, *John Eliot, "Apostle to the Indians"* (Boston: Houghton Mifflin, 1968). For reassessments, see the authors cited in Szasz, *Indian Education*, 111, 279 n. 37. The definitive account is that by Richard W. Cogley, *John Eliot's Mission to the Indian before King Philip's War* (Cambridge, Mass.: Harvard University Press, 1999).

20. *The Day-Breaking if not the Sun-Rising of the Gospell with the Indians in New England* (London, 1647; repr., New York: Joseph Sabin, 1865). Eames lists this as the second tract, regarding *New Englands First Fruits* as the first.

21. William Kellaway, *The New England Company, 1649–1776: Missionary Society to the American Indians* (New York: Barnes & Noble, 1962).

22. David Pulsifer, ed., *Records of the Colony of New Plymouth in New England. Acts of the Commissioners of the United Colonies of New England*, vol. 2, *1653–1679* [bound as vol. 10 of the *Records of the Colony of New Plymouth*] (Boston, 1859; repr., New York: AMS Press, 1968), 139, 141.

23. Quot., Henry Whitfield, *The Light appearing more and more towards the perfect Day. Or, A farther Discovery of the present state of the Indians in New-England* (London, 1651); reprinted under the title *A Farther Discovery of the Present State of the Indians in New England* (New York: J. Sabin, 1865), 2; Thomas Shepard, *The Clear Sunshine of the Gospel Breaking forth upon the Indians in New-England* (London, 1648; repr., New York: Joseph Sabin, 1865); Henry Whit-

field, *Strength out of Weakness: or a Glorious Manifestation of the Further Progresse of the Gospel amongst the Indians in New England* (London, 1652; repr., New York: Joseph Sabin, 1865).

24. On Eliot as a linguist, see, e.g., Bragdon, "Another Tongue," 34–37; Salisbury, *Manitou and Providence*, 221–24. For the Pequot War, see Alfred A. Cave, *The Pequot War* (Amherst: University of Massachusetts Press, 1996); William Wallace Tooker, *John Eliot's First Indian Teacher and Interpreter, Cockenoe-de-Long Island* (New York: Francis P. Harper, 1896), 9–12; Szasz, *Indian Education*, 111–13.

25. John Eliot, letter, Feb. 2, 1648/9, in "The Glorious Progress[e] of the Gospel, Amongst the Indians in New-England," *Collections of the Massachusetts Historical Society*, 3rd ser., 4 (1834): 90. The identification of Eliot's first Indian interpreter (whom John Eliot never named) as Cockenoe is made by Tooker, *First Indian Teacher*, 11–12.

26. [John Eliot], *A Grammar of the Massachusetts Indian Language by John Eliot*, ed. Peter S. du Ponceau (Boston: Phelps and Pharnum, 1822), 66. This is a reprint of John Eliot, *The Indian Grammar Begun: or, An Essay to Bring the Indian Language into Rules* (Cambridge, Mass.: Marmaduke Johnson, 1666). The "Interpreter" present during John Eliot's sermon in Waaubon's tent, Oct. 1646, was undoubtedly Cockenoe (*Day-Breaking*, 4; Tooker, *First Indian Teacher*, 14).

27. *Day-Breaking*, 1–3.

28. Ibid., 3–9, quot. 4; Cogley, *John Eliot's Mission*, 41.

29. *Day-Breaking*, 9–10, 28; Cogley, *John Eliot's Mission*, 52–54. The laws are reproduced in Morrison, *Praying People*, 189.

30. Eliot maintained that the hair cutting was voluntary (*Day-Breaking*, 31).

31. Axtell, *European and the Indian*, 59–60.

32. Cotton Mather, *The Life and Death of the Reverend Mr. John Eliot, Who was the First Preacher of the Gospel to the Indians in America,* 3rd ed. (London: John Dunton, 1694), 36–37.

33. John Eliot, letter, Nov. 13, 1648 [erroneously dated 1649], in "Glorious Progresse of the Gospel," 88. The school dame mentioned here may or may not be the same as the woman whom Eliot mentions that he paid to teach, who lived near the Indians before their move to Natick. John Eliot, letter, Apr. 18, 1650, in Whitfield, *Farther Discovery*, 42. Another woman who taught Indian children was the wife of "William Daniell of Dorchester," who, the commissioners said in 1653, had been teaching the Indians for the previous three years for the sum of £6. They gave her a back payment of £9 and an advance of £3 for the coming year. She received another £10 from the commissioners in 1668, although she taught four years in all. John W. Ford, *Some Correspondence between the Governors and Treasurers of the New England Company in London . . . Between the Years 1657 and 1712* (1896; repr., New York: Burt Franklin, 1970), 19.

34. Eliot, letter, July 8, 1649, in Whitfield, *Farther Discovery*, 17.

35. *Day-Breaking*, 27–28 (spelled Noonatomen).

36. John Eliot, letter, Nov. 12, 1648, in "Glorious Progresse of the Gospel," 81. For a detailed account of the creation of Natick, see Morrison, *Praying People*, 76–94.

37. John Eliot, letter, Feb. 28, 1651, in Whitfield, *Strength out of Weakness*, 13–14; John Wilson, letter, Oct. 27, 1651, in ibid., 25–26.

38. John Eliot, letter, Oct. 21, 1650, in Whitfield, *Farther Discovery*, 42–43. Szasz, *Indian Education*, 113, identifies the reader-writer as Job Nesutan (or Nesuton).

39. John Eliot, letter, Feb. 28, 1651, in Whitfield, *Strength out of Weakness*, 10, 11.

40. Wilson, in ibid., 25–26, 28.

41. The relations are recorded in "Tears of Repentance: Or, A further Narrative of the Progress of the Gospel Amongst the Indians in New-England" [London, 1653], *Collections of the Massachusetts Historical Society*, 3rd ser., 4 (1834): 227–45. For another discussion of the occasion, see Morrison, *Praying People*, 104–8.

42. "Tears," 227–28, 243, quot. 244. Eliot insisted that he had not knowingly made the confessions any better than they were; if anything, they were weaker, because he missed some words and had to give "short and curt touches of what they more fully spake" (ibid., 245).

43. "Tears of Repentance," 244.

44. Ibid., 237–38. Cf. Monequassun's first relation, ibid., 234–37.

45. Ibid., 238.

46. Ibid., 238–39.

47. Ibid., 240, 243–45.

48. John Eliot, letter, June 13, 1654, in "A Late and Further Manifestation of the Progress of the Gospel Amongst the Indians in Nevv-England" (London, 1655), reprinted in *Collections of the Massachusetts Historical Society,* 3rd ser., 4 (1834), 272–73, 284–85.

49. Charles E. Banks, *The History of Martha's Vineyard, Dukes County, Massachusetts,* vol. 1, *General History* (Edgartown, Mass.: Dukes County Historical Society, 1966), 80–83.

50. For contacts between the Vineyard Indians and Europeans before 1642, see Salisbury, *Manitou and Providence,* 87–89, 95–96, 120, 129. The Indian population of Martha's Vineyard and Nantucket combined has been estimated to be five thousand in 1642. Sherburne F. Cook, *The Indian Population of New England in the Seventeenth Century* (Berkeley: University of California Press, 1976), 40. Some three thousand of these were on the Vineyard. The 1616–19 epidemics struck the offshore islands "relatively lightly." Salwen, "Indians of Southern New England," 171. The Wampanoags are also called the Pokanokets, but their descendants in Gay Head in Martha's Vineyard name themselves the Wampanoags.

51. For "Nope" or "Noepe" as the name of the Martha's Vineyard dialect, see James C. Pilling, *Bibliography of the Algonquian Languages* (Washington, D.C.: Government Printing Office, 1891), 252. Opinions differ on the extent of the differences between the dialect of the mainland (which was also the dialect of Nantucket) and that of the Vineyard Indians. Ives Goddard, "Eastern Algonquian Languages," in Sturtevant, *Handbook of North America,* 15:72, cites (in support of his contention that the dialects "differed enough . . . to make communication difficult") a 1710 letter by Cotton Mather that Samuel Sewall had copied into his letter book. *Proceedings of the Massachusetts Historical Society,* 1st ser., 12 (1873): 373. Mather, however, was using the differences as part of his argument against printing a new edition of the Indian Bible. In contrast, Experience Mayhew considered the dialects very similar and believed that the Indian Bible had helped reduce the differences between them. Mayhew, *Observations on the Indian Language* (Boston: John S. H. Fogg, 1884), 5–6. Since Mayhew spoke the language and Mather did not, Mayhew is the more credible witness. For a full discussion of dialect variation, see Bragdon, "Another Tongue," chap. 1. In Bragdon's view, dialect differences probably did not hinder interaction among speakers of different dialects (ibid., 24).

52. Thomas Mayhew, letter, Sept. 7, 1650, in Whitfield, *Farther Discovery,* 3–4.

53. Experience Mayhew, *Indian Converts: Or, Some Account of the Lives and Dying Speeches of a Considerable Number of the Christianized Indians of Martha's Vineyard, in New-England* (London: Samuel Gerrish, 1727), 1. For Hiacoomes, see David J. Silverman, "Conditions for Coexistence, Climates for Collapse: The Challenges of Indian Life on Martha's Vineyard, 1524–1871," (Ph.D. diss., Princeton University, 2000), 63–72, 87.

54. Matthew Mayhew, *A Brief Narrative of the Success which the Gospel hath had, among the Indians of Martha's Vineyard . . .* (Boston: Bartolomew Green, 1694), 17.

55. Mayhew, in Whitfield, *Farther Discovery,* 4. Silverman interprets the primer as a charm against epidemics ("Conditions for Coexistence," 66–67).

56. Whitfield, *Farther Discovery,* 4, 6.

57. Ibid., 11; quotation in Thomas Mayhew, letter, Nov. 18, 1647, in "Glorious Progresse of the Gospel," 77. For the importance of Hiacoomes's continuing health amid disease as a "turning point" in the conversion effort, see Simmons, "Conversion from Indian to Puritan," 206–10. For the powers of Indian priests, see Kupperman, *Settling with the Indians,* 72.

58. Whitfield, *Farther Discovery,* 1–2 (italics romanized).

59. Ibid., 2 (italics romanized).

60. Thomas Mayhew, letter, Oct. 16, 1651, in Whitfield, *Strength out of Weakness,* 45–46.

61. Mayhew, *Brief Narrative,* 22; Thomas Mayhew, letter, Oct. 22, 1652, in "Tears of Repentance," 208. Foulger's bilingualism is not specified but can be inferred: his student Japheth

Hannit was taught to be literate in both Indian and English (Mayhew, *Indian Converts*, 45). In 1652 Foulger had a grant of land near the schoolhouse in Edgartown, so he presumably taught there. Banks, *History of Martha's Vineyard*, vol. 2, *Annals of Edgartown*, 67–69.

62. Mayhew, *Observations on the Indian Language*, 7.

63. Thomas Mayhew, letter, Oct. 22, 1652, in "Tears of Repentance," 208.

64. Pulsifer, Acts of the Commissioners, 2:167.

65. John Eliot, letter, Aug. 29, 1654, in Eames, *John Eliot and the Indians*, 11; e.g., requests in Pulsifer, *Acts of the Commissioners*, 2:133, 139 (hornbooks and "old Common primers"); accounts paid in ibid., 2:206 (Bibles, spectacles, primers, books, paper, inkhorns—for the Indian scholars).

66. Quoted in Lloyd C. M. Hare, *Thomas Mayhew, Patriarch to the Indians (1593–1682)* (New York: Appleton, 1932), 110.

67. Ibid.; Mayhew, *Indian Converts*, 79.

68. Hare, *Thomas Mayhew*, 110–11.

69. Pulsifer, *Acts of the Commissioners*, 2:202, quot. 203; John Eliot, letter, Dec. 8, 1658, quoted in Banks, *History of Martha's Vineyard*, 1:249; Thomas senior quoted in Hare, *Thomas Mayhew*, 112; [Thomas Prince], *Some Account of Those English Ministers who have successively presided over the Work of Gospelizing the Indians on Martha's Vineyard, and the adjacent Islands* (London, 1727), in Mayhew, *Indian Converts*, 292.

70. Len Travers, "The Missionary Journal of John Cotton, Jr., 1666–1678," *Proceedings of the Massachusetts Historical Society* 109 (1997): 52–101.

71. Mayhew, *Indian Converts*, 10, 14; Daniel Gookin, *Historical Collections of the Indians in New England* (Boston: Belknap and Hall, 1792), 66, reproduced on microfiche from publications documented in *Early American Imprints. Series I, Evans (1639-1800)* [electronic resource], ([New Canaan, Conn.]: Readex; [Worcester, Mass.]: American Antiquarian Society, [2002–]) (hereafter cited as Evans), #24362.

72. Pulsifer, *Acts of the Commissioners*, 2:205, 245, 262, 277, 296, 317, 331; John Eliot, letter, Aug. 25, 1664, in ibid., 384, 356. There are no records for 1665 and 1666, or for missionary-related matters between Sept. 1667 and Sept. 1672.

73. As Szasz points out in *Indian Education*, 106.

74. Pulsifer, *Acts of the Commissioners*, 2:105; Gookin, *Historical Collections*, 58.

75. Gookin, *Historical Collections*, 52–53. Gookin spells Caleb's name "Cheeschaumuck." Experience Mayhew spells it "Cheshechaamog" (*Indian Converts*, 148). Caleb, however, spelled his name "Cheeshahteaumauk" in his signature to an address to the corporation, reproduced in Arthur R. Railton, "The Vineyard's First Harvard Men Were Indians," *Dukes County Intelligencer* 29 (1988): 107.

76. Gookin, *Historical Collections*, 53; Railton, "Vineyard's First Harvard Men," 91–112.

77. Gookin, *Historical Collections*, 52, 53–54.

78. [Eliot], *Grammar of the Massachuset Indian Language*.

79. *The Massachuset Psalter; or, Psalms of David with the Gospel according to John, in columns of Indian and English. Being an introduction for training up the aboriginal natives, in reading and understanding the Holy Scriptures* (Boston: printed by B. Green and J. Printer, for the Honourable Company for the Propagation of the Gospel in New-England, 1709).

80. Scholars have only recently acknowledged the importance of the Indians' contribution to these translations (Salisbury, "Red Puritans," 43). For Printer, see Szasz, *Indian Education*, 115–17; Lepore, *Name of War*, 94, 126, 136–41, 145–49. Not until 1709 would Wowaus's contributions to the Boston press be acknowledged. In that year, his name, as James Printer, appeared beside that of Bartholomew Green as the printer of the *Massachuset Psalter*.

81. [Eliot], *Grammar of the Massachusetts Indian Language*, 3. Eliot said that diphthongs were "many, and of much use" (ibid.). See also Pulsifer, *Acts of the Commissioners*, 2:105, 120 (catechism); Kellaway, *New England Company*, 130.

82. Kellaway, *New England Company*, 131, 133–34.

83. Ibid., 135–36, 139–41. For a convenient list of the publications of the Indian Library up to 1689, see Lepore, *Name of War*, 35.

84. *A Letter of the Reverend John Eliot of Roxbury to the Reverend Thomas Shepard of Charlestown, Aug. 22, 1673* (Portland, Me.: Boston University, 1952).

85. Gookin, *Historical Collections*, 90–92, quot. 93. The villages and their totals are tabulated in Lepore, *Name of War*, 37–38, where percentages are based on the total 497.

86. Gookin, *Historical Collections*, 94, 101–3, 104.

87. Ibid., 95.

88. John Eliot, letter, Aug. 25, 1664, in *Records of Plymouth Colony*, 2:383, 384. For how to name Philip and the war, see Lepore, *Name of War*, xv–xvi, xix–xx. Sassamon is also spelled Sosomon in the sources. Philip's *P*: Nathaniel B. Shurtleff, ed., *Records of the Colony of New Plymouth in New England. Court Orders*, vol. 4, *1661–1668* (Boston, 1855; repr., New York: AMS Press, 1968), 26. For another *P* Philip put on a document in 1671, see Shurtleff, *Records of the Colony of New Plymouth*, vol. 5, *1668–1678*, 79. This time the letter is standing upright, but with a 45-degree slant to the right.

89. Cotton Mather, *Life and Death of the Renown'd Mr. John Eliot*, 2nd ed. (London: For John Dunton, 1691), 95. For a full description of Eliot's attempts to convert Philip, see Lepore, *Name of War*, 39–41.

90. For the murderers and the motive, see Lepore, *Name of War*, 21–26. For the subsequent trial and execution of his alleged Indian killers, see Douglas E. Leach, *Flintlock and Tomahawk: New England in King Philip's War* (New York: Macmillan, 1958), 30–33; Eric B. Scult and Michael Tougias, *King Philip's War: The History and Legacy of America's Forgotten Conflict* (Woodstock, Vt.: Countryman Press, 1999), 25–29.

91. Daniel Gookin, "An Historical Account of the Doings and Sufferings of the Christian Indians in New England, in the Years 1675, 1676, 1677 . . . ," *Transactions and Collections of the American Antiquarian Society* 2 (1836): 423–534. For details of the Indians' suffering, see Morrison, *Praying People*, 166–80.

92. Gookin, "Historical Accoount," 444, quots. 449, 450, 436, 485.

93. Ibid., 449, 509–13.

94. Ibid., 485, 494. Cf. a letter from the Indians who had captured Mary Rowlandson in response to a message by the Massachusetts Council trying to negotiate her release: "Because you know, and we know, you have great sorrowful with crying; for you lost many, many hundred men, and all your house, all your land, and woman, child, and cattle, and all your things that you have lost" (ibid., 508); see also Lepore, *Name of War*, 146.

95. Mayhew, *Brief Narrative*, 35, 34.

96. William S. Simmons, "Cultural Bias in the New England Puritans' Perceptions of Indians," *William and Mary Quarterly*, 3rd. ser., 38 (1981): 69. Similarly, Simmons calls it "an example of deep and rapid voluntary change to colonial ideology," in his "Conversion from Indian to Puritan," *New England Quarterly* 52 (1979): 215.

97. James P. Ronda, "Generations of Faith: The Christian Indians of Martha's Vineyard," *William and Mary Quarterly*, 3rd ser., 38 (1981): 369–94. Ronda's discussion of the literacy of the Vineyard Indians in this article inspired me to explore it further, and his article provided a broader context for my own discussion. For Vineyard naming practices, see ibid., 391.

98. [Prince], *Some Account of Those English Ministers*, 280, 302, 305, 306; Banks, *History of Martha's Vineyard*, 1:127, 213–14.

99. "An Appendix. The Present Condition of the Indians on Martha's Vineyard, Extracted from an Account of Mr. Experience Mayhew," in Cotton Mather, *India Christiana* (Boston: B. Green, 1721), 88–89, quots. 89, 93.

100. Kellaway, *New England Company*, 142–47, quot. 144. For the destruction of Indian Bibles, see Lepore, *Name of War*, 43.

101. Kellaway, *New England Company*, 147–50. The all-Indian nature of the primer is indicated by Rawson's being asked to send a copy of it "in English" to the commissioners for their perusal (ibid., 148).

102. Ibid., 150–57, 160–61, quots. 156, 157. Cotton Mather's letter opposing the reprinting of the Indian Bible was copied by Samuel Sewall into his letter book. The letter is reproduced in *Proceedings of the Massachusetts Historical Society*, 1st ser., 12 (1873): 373. For more on

Mather's unflattering view of the Massachusett tongue, see Mather, *Life and Death of the Renown'd Mr. John Eliot*, 76–77.

103. Kellaway, *New England Company*, 152–53. The date of copyright of the *Massachuset Psalter* is actually 1709, but, as Kellaway demonstrates, the book did not appear until 1710.

104. Ibid., 160–63; *The Indian Primer or The First Book. By which Children may know truely to read the Indian Language. And Milk for Babes* (Boston: B. Green, 1720).

105. Kellaway, *New England Company*, 164.

106. I used the New York Public Library's copy of Mayhew's *Indian Converts*. For an earlier discussion, see E. Jennifer Monaghan "'She loved to read in good Books': Literacy and the Indians of Martha's Vineyard, 1643–1725," *History of Education Quarterly* 30 (1990), 493–521.

107. Mayhew, *Indian* Converts, x. Mayhew records with obvious regret that he mistimed Jabob Sockakonnit's impending death in 1721 and so missed it (ibid., 119); John Eliot, *The Dying Speeches of Several Indians* (Cambridge, Mass.: 1685?), [1].

108. Mayhew, *Indian Converts*, 11-12, x-xi; Ronda, "Generations of Faith," 372. For Experience's bilingualism, see Mayhew, *Observations on the Indian Language*, 8.

109. Ronda, "Generations of Faith," 388–89, points out the stereotyping.

110. Mayhew, *Indian Converts*, ix-x. Mayhew took such pains over the accuracy of his work that at one point in his manuscript he left a space for a place name he intended to ascertain. The gap is faithfully reproduced in the printed text; "and set him on Shore at————" (ibid., 245). C. John Sommerville, "Breaking the Icon: The First Real Children in English Books," *History of Education Quarterly* 21 (1981): 51–75.

111. The figures in Mayhew, *Indian Converts* are as follows. Chapter 1 (church-related men): total 22 (15 readers, 3 writers), supplement total 8 (2 readers, 0 writers); chapter 2 (men not holding a church position): total 20 (8 readers, 2 writers), supplement total 17 (0 readers, 0 writers); chapter 3 (women): total 30 (19 readers, 1 writer), supplement total 9 (0 readers, 0 writers); chapter 4 (children): total 22 (16 readers, 3 writers), no supplement; grand total (chapters and supplements): 128 (60 readers, 9 writers).

112. Ibid., xxiii; David D. Hall, "The Uses of Literacy in New England, 1600–1850," in *Cultures of Print: Essays in the History of the Book* (Amherst: University of Massachusetts Press, 1996), 56–57.

113. Mayhew, *Indian Converts*, 101, 202, 176.

114. Ibid., 68–70, quots. 68, 70; Neesnummin's assistance: Bragdon, "Another Tongue," 26.

115. Mayhew, *Indian Converts*, 57; cf. 119, 163, 188. Mayhew was probably in error about Perkins's *Six Principles*: it is not documented as part of the Indian Library. John Eliot is said to have translated this work: Pilling, *Bibliography of the Algonquian Languages*, 131; but Pilling's source may have been this reference in *Indian Converts*. For the wear and tear of the *Massachuset Psalter*, see Ives Goddard and Kathleen J. Bragdon, *Native Writings in Massachusett*, pt. 1 (Philadelphia: American Philosophical Society, 1988), 20.

116. Mayhew, *Indian Converts*, 10, 14–15, quots. 15, 20. Compare Hiacoomes, who used to drop in on the younger Thomas Mayhew for help. See also Janawannit, who visited Experience's father, John, once a week for help in the preparation of his sermons (ibid., 21). Similarly, four Indians who were "Teachers" (of doctrine) at Indian villages near Eastham, Cape Cod, visited Samuel Treat, the Congregational minister at Eastham, weekly for instruction, as Treat reported in 1693. Jean Fittz Hankins, "Bringing the Good News: Protestant Missionaries to the Indians of New England and New York, 1700–1775" (Ph.D. diss., University of Connecticut, 1993), 106–7. For other examples of men reading the Bible, see Mayhew, *Indian Converts*, 18, 57, 65, 87, 92, 119.

117. Mayhew, *Indian Converts*. The three ministers were Janawannit, Joash Panu, and Japheth Hannit; the laymen were Japheth Skuhwhannan (grandson of Japheth Hannit) and Job Somannan (Hannit's son-in-law); and the woman was Rachel Wompanummoo; quot., ibid., 57. Writers who were not the subject of biographies, 240, 245.

118. Ibid., 212.

119. Ibid., 91, 79.

120. Ibid., 63–64.

121. Ibid., 113–15.

122. Adult converts who learned to read as children: ibid., 37, 45, 106, 110, 148 (Abigail Ammapoo), 151, 154, 156, 158, 175, 188 (Abigail Sekitchahkomun), 197, 203 (Sarah Peag), 207, 212. Of a fourth woman, Margaret Osooit (197), Mayhew does not say whether her parents were "godly," but her grandfather was the praying Indian convert Noquittompany (ibid., 84–85).

123. Ronda, "Generations of Faith." Mayhew, *Indian Converts*, 91; cf. Job Somannon (111).

124. Mayhew, *Indian Converts*, 44–50, quot. 168.

125. Ibid., 223, 232, quot. 222.

126. Ibid., 102–3. For another example of generational literacy (two generations), see the Jonathan Amos family (ibid., 37, 154, 156, 158, 179).

127. Ibid., 18. His name is spelled Wunnannauhkomun in ibid., 255.

128. Ibid., 184, 255–56. Cf. Elizabeth Uhquat, who went to live on the mainland with an English family that taught her neither reading nor religion, "which is the unhappy Case of many of our *Indian* Youth that go to live among the *English*" (ibid., 194). On instruction by neighbors, compare Matthew Mayhew's comment, in 1694, that some Indians "who are too far distant from any School are often taught by some of their Neighbours" (Mayhew, *Brief Narrative*, 39).

129. Mayhew, *Indian Converts*, 135; Ronda, "Generations of Faith," 384–88; Edmund S. Morgan, "New England Puritanism: Another Approach," *William and Mary Quarterly*, 3rd ser., 18 (1961): 236–42. On church membership skewed by gender, see Patricia U. Bonomi, *Under the Cope of Heaven: Religion, Society, and Politics in Colonial America* (New York: Oxford University Press, 1986), 111–13.

130. Mayhew, *Indian Converts*, 198, 199, 199–200.

131. Ibid., 222, 235, 224.

132. Ibid., 269, quot. 234–35. See also Bragdon, "Another Tongue," 29, 54.

133. Grindal Rawson and Samuel Danforth, "Account of an Indian Visitation A.D. 1698," *Collections of the Massachusetts Historical Society*, 1st ser., 10 (1809): 132. Bethia Sissetom, born in 1702 or 1703, had no school nearby; Hannah Soopasun, born in 1712, and Jesse Quannoohuh, born in 1717, both attended schools that failed (Mayhew, *Indian Converts*, 255, 261, 269).

134. Mayhew, *Indian Converts*, 247–48, 232.

135. Ibid., 256, 236–37; cf. 226–27.

136. Ibid., 71 (italics romanized).

137. Goddard and Bragdon, *Native Writings in Massachusett*, 20.

138. Ibid., 14–15, 18–20.

139. Ibid., 270–337 (Natick), 176–81, quot. 179 (Mashpee), 226–29 (marriage bans), 68–73 (marriages by Hossueit). Quotations are taken from the translations provided by Goddard and Bragdon from the Massachusett in ibid.

140. Ibid., 414 (Laben Hossuit), 379 (book of Nahum), 377 (Thomas), 423, cf. 439 (Papenau), 445, 415 (Zachary Hosueit, who signed in Sept. 1738 and again in Feb. 1747). For the much admired Zachary (or Zachariah) Hosueit (or Hossueit), see Silverman, "Conditions for Coexistence," 280–311.

141. Silverman, "Conditions for Coexistence," 366–69, graphs the following figures by decades (367). 1700–1749: signature literacy among men ranged from 47 to 57 percent; among women, never more than about 15 percent. 1750–1769: men dropped to 43 percent, then 10 percent; women to 6 or 7 percent. 1770–1799: men climbed from 19 percent in the 1770s to over 50 percent in the 1780s and 1790s; women averaged just under 20 percent, with a spike of almost 30 percent in the 1780s.

142. Daniel R. Mandell, *Behind the Frontier: Indians in Eighteenth-Century Eastern Massachusetts* (Lincoln: University of Nebraska Press, 1996).

143. For the English approach to pious reading, see Charles E. Hambrick-Stowe, *The Practice of Piety: Puritan Devotional Disciplines in Seventeenth-Century New England* (Chapel Hill, N.C.: Institute of Early American History and Culture, 1982), 157–75; David D. Hall, "The Uses of

Literacy in New England, 1600–1850," in Hall, *Cultures of Print: Essays in the History of the Book* (Amherst: University of Massachusetts Press, 1996), 56–57. See also Hall, *Worlds of Wonder*, 41–42.

144. Bragdon, "Another Tongue," 50.

Chapter 3. Books Read by Children at Home and at School

1. David Pulsifer, ed., *Records of the Colony of New Plymouth in New England. Acts of the Commissioners of the United Colonies of New England*, vol. 2, *1653–1679* [bound as vol. 10 of the *Records of the Colony of New Plymouth*] (Boston, 1859; repr., New York: AMS Press, 1968), 139.

2. For hornbooks in America, see George A. Plimpton, *The Hornbook and Its Use in America* (Worcester, Mass.: American Antiquarian Society, 1916). Plimpton cites an entry in his ledger by a man named Charles Lidgett, who paid "For horning book and papr 8d" in 1678. The ledger also shows an entry for "1 Alphabott." Nila Banton Smith, *American Reading Instruction* (Newark, Del.: International Reading Association, 1965), 17, notes the absence of A B C books in colonial America. (See Figure 3.)

3. Quoted in Andrew W. Tuer, *History of the Horn Book* (1897; repr., New York: Arno Press, 1979), 201–2. Tuer's work remains the definitive treatment of the hornbook.

4. *The B A C bothe in latyn and in Englysshe* (London: Thomas Petyt, n.d.); first page reproduced in Tuer, *History of the Horn Book*, 378.

5. For a full discussion of the relationship between spelling and reading in the seventeenth century, see Ian Michael, *The Teaching of English from the Sixteenth Century to 1870* (Cambridge: Cambridge University Press, 1987), 111–22. Michael correctly states that the prevailing view of learning was that "knowledge was . . . most firmly acquired when it was presented in the form of particles that could be systematically aggregated" (ibid., 117). Letters were aggregated into syllables, syllables into words.

6. On the crucial role of the syllable in reading instruction, see ibid., 72–89; for the terminology of "short" and "long" vowels, see Francis Clement, *The Petie Schole with an English Orthographie* (London, 1587), 23, in *Four Tudor Books on Education . . .* , facsimile reproduction with an introduction by Robert D. Pepper (Gainesville, Fla.: Scholars' Facsimiles & Reprints, 1966), 71. The *Petie Schole* was first published in 1576.

7. Samuel Sewall, *The Diary of Samuel Sewall, 1674–1729*, ed. M. Halsey Thomas, 2 vols. (New York: Farrar, Straus and Giroux, 1973), 1:277; Samuel Sewall, *Letter Book*, 1:248, as cited in Thomas Goddard Wright, *Literary Culture in Early New England, 1620–1730* (New Haven: Yale University Press, 1920), 119. For Hannah Penn Townsend, see Judith S. Graham, *Puritan Family Life: The Diary of Samuel Sewall* (Boston: Northeastern University Press, 2000), 113.

8. David D. Hall, "The Chesapeake in the Seventeenth Century," in *A History of the Book in America*, ed. David D. Hall, vol. 1, *The Colonial Book in the Atlantic World*, ed. Hugh Amory and David D. Hall ([Worcester, Mass.]: American Antiquarian Society; New York: Cambridge University Press, 2000), 69–70; James N. Green, "The Book Trade in the Middle Colonies, 1680–1720," in ibid., 218.

9. J[ohn] B[unyan], *A Book for Boys and Girls; or Country Rhimes for Children* (London, 1686); quoted in Tuer, *History of the Hornbook*, 198.

10. *Oxford English Dictionary*, compact edition (1971), s.v. "Primer." Cf. Chaucer's "The Prioress's Prologue and Tale" ("This litel child, his litel book lernynge / As he sat in the scole at his prymer"), in *The Riverside Chaucer*, 3rd ed., ed. Larry D. Benson (general editor) and F. N. Robinson (Boston: Houghton Mifflin, 1987), 210.

11. The primer was published in 1545 with the title, *The Primer, set foorth by the Kynges maiestie and his Clergie, to be taught, lerned, and read; and non other to be used throughout all his dominion*. For English primers, see Charles C. Butterworth, *The English Primers, 1529–1545: Their Publication and Connection with the English Bible and the Reformation in England* (Philadelphia: University of Pennsylvania Press, 1953).

12. Thomas Shepard, *Eye-Salve, or A Watch-Word From our Lord Iesus Christ unto his Church*

... (Cambridge, Mass.: Samuel Green, 1673), 31, *Early American Imprints. Series I, Evans (1639–1800)* [electronic resource], ([New Canaan, Conn.]: Readex; [Worcester, Mass.]: American Antiquarian Society, [2002–]) (hereafter cited as Evans), #182.

13. Samuel Eliot Morison, *The Intellectual Life of Colonial New England* (New York: New York University Press, 1956), 81.

14. *The VVhole Booke of Psalmes, Faithfully Translated into English Metre* ... ([Cambridge, Mass.: Stephen Daye], 1640) (Evans #4); Robert R. Roden, *The Cambridge Press, 1638–1692: A History of the First Printing Press Established in English America, Together with a Bibliographical List of the Issues of the Press* (New York: Dodd, Mead, 1905), chap. 2.

15. Advertisement, in William Brattle, *Unius Labor* ... *An Ephemeris of Celestial Motions* (Cambridge: Samuel Green, 1682), [10] (#314); Hugh Amory, "Reinventing the Colonial Book," in Hall, *History of the Book*, 1:52.

16. Amory, "Reinventing the Colonial Book," 45. For imports, see Hall, "Chesapeake in the Seventeenth Century," 66. Worthington C. Ford, *The Boston Book Market, 1679–1700* (Boston: Club of Odd Volumes, 1917).

17. Hugh Amory, "Under the Exchange: The Unprofitable Business of Michael Perry, a Seventeenth-Century Boston Bookseller," *Proceedings of the American Antiquarian Society* 103 (1993): 31–60, esp. 43, 55–56. Hornbooks in a store in York County, Maryland, in 1675 were valued at twopence for gilt and a penny for plain; Hall, "Chesapeake in the Seventeenth Century," 70.

18. Quot., Paul Leicester Ford, ed., The *New-England Primer. A History of Its Origin and Development with a Reprint of the Unique Copy of the Earliest Known Edition* ... (New York: Dodd, Mead, 1897), n.p.; for the catechism in England, see Ian Green, *The Christian's ABC: Catechism and Catechizing in England* (New York: Oxford University Press, 1996).

19. Cotton Mather, *Magnalia Christi Americana; or, the Ecclesiastical History of New-England* ... (Hartford: Silas Andrus & Son, 1853), 2:179. For catechisms, see Wilberforce Eames, "Early New England Catechisms," *Proceedings of the American Antiquarian Society*, n.s., 12 (1899): 76–182.

20. William Kempe said that when the scholar "shall haue ended his first booke the Catechisme, he wil be able to passe through the Primer commendably without spelling; some harde words here and there excepted." Kempe, *The Education of Children in Learning* (London: Iohn Porter and Thomas Gubbin, 1588), n.p., in Pepper, *Four Tudor Books*, 225–26. Watertown: see Chapter 1, n. 50. See also Ian Green, *The Christian's ABC: Catechisms and Catechizing in England c. 1530–1740* (New York: Oxford University Press), 1996.

21. Edmund Coote, *The English Schoole-Maister* (London: Widow Orwin, 1596).

22. Roden, *Cambridge Press*, 36.

23. Coote, *English Schoole-Maister*, 4, in William R. Hart, "*The English Schoole-Maister* (1596) by Edmund Coote: An Edition of the Text with Critical Notes and Introductions" (Ph.D. diss., University of Michigan, 1963), 136 (hereafter cited as Coote, in Hart, "*English Schoole-Maister*"). In its modern dress, the conflict takes the form of "systematic sequential instruction" versus "authentic text."

24. For a discussion of two conflicting views on the nature of English orthographic systems, see E. Jennifer Monaghan, *A Common Heritage: Noah Webster's Blue-Back Speller* (Hamden, Conn.: Archon Books, 1983), 110–13.

25. Coote, 94, in Hart, "*English Schoole-Maister*," 228.

26. Coote, 32–33, in Hart, "*English Schoole-Maister*," 164–65. The distinction, in the colonial period, between at least two different stages of childhood—children and youth—has been well established. See Ross W. Beales Jr., "In Search of the Historical Child: Miniature Adulthood and Youth in Colonial New England," *American Quarterly* 27 (1975): 379– 98; Gusti Wiesenfeld Frankel, "Between Parent and Child in Colonial New England: An Analysis of the Religious Child-Oriented Literature and Selected Children's Works" (Ph.D. diss., University of Minnesota, 1977), chap.1. Boundaries between child and youth, and youth and adult, were distinguished by levels of maturity rather than a specific age.

27. [John Eliot], *A Grammar of the Massachusetts Indian Language by John Eliot*, ed. Peter S.

du Ponceau (Boston: Phelps and Pharnum, 1822), 66. The request came from the English scientist Robert Boyle, secretary of the New England Corporation.

28. Ibid., 3–5.

29. Ibid., 6–18; verbs declined, 28–63; quots. 6, 11, 36, 28.

30. Ibid., 4–5.

31. J[ohn] E[liot], *The Indian Primer; Or, the way of training up of our Indian Youth in the good Knowledge of God* (Cambridge, 1669); reprinted as John Small, introd., *The Indian Primer; or, the way of training up of our Indian Youth in the good Knowledge of God, 1669, by John Eliot,* with an introduction by John Small (Edinburgh: Andrew Elliot, 1880).

32. E[liot], *Indian Primer,* n.p. Note that in the only surviving copy of the *Indian Primer,* it is clear from the wrapover word for the next page that the introductory pages have been mispaginated. I have referred to the pages in the order that Eliot intended rather than to the order in which they actually appear in print.

33. See, for example, the syllables *peemb poomd peamn poamp* in a 1654 work published in London by John Brooksbank, quoted in Michael, *Teaching of English,* 96–97.

34. The translation is not in the text but is provided in James C. Pilling, *Bibliography of the Algonquian Languages* (Washington, D.C.: Government Printing Office, 1891), 129.

35. E[liot], *Indian Primer,* n.p.

36. See Michael, *Teaching of English,* 103–8.

37. Compare Coote's "Da dad dass da dam daw day" (Coote, 3, in Hart, "*English Schoole-Maister,*" 135), with Eliot's "da de di do du bad dad" (*Indian Primer,* n.p.). As the vowels are short in CVC words, a more logical approach would have been to treat them as an extension of VC syllables rather than CV syllables.

38. Coote, 13, 17, in Hart, "*English Schoole-Maister,*" 145, 149.

39. Coote, 35, in Hart, "*English Schoole-Maister,*" 167. For discussion of "the power and sound of c," see Francis Clement, *The Petie Schole . . .* (London: Thomas Vautrollier, 1587), 13, in Pepper, *Four Tudor Books,* 61. For Coote's debt to Mulcaster, see Miriam Balmuth, *The Roots of Phonics: A Historical Introduction* (New York: McGraw-Hill, 1982), 126. For examples of discussions by spelling book authors of such topics as the status of *J* and *V,* the names of the letters, the "sound" and "power" of the letters, see Michael, *Teaching of English,* 25–58, and the discussion in Chapter 8, notes 13–15.

40. These figures are calculated from the texts listed in Michael, *Teaching of English,* when reordered by date. See also his charts (ibid., 9). The figure for the 1670s omits Richard Hodges's *Most plain directions for true-writing* (1653), because it was written in Hodges's innovative orthography.

41. F[rancis] D[aniel] P[astorius], *A New Primmer Or Methodical Directions To Attain the True Spelling, Reading and Writing of English. Whereunto are added, some Things Necessary and Useful both for the Youth of this Province, and likewise for those, who from foreign Countries and Nations come to settle amongst us . . .* (New York: William Bradford, 1698); "sold by the Author in Pennsilvania" (Evans #851). See M[arion] D. Learned, *The Life of Francis Daniel Pastorius, the Founder of Germantown* (Philadelphia: William J. Campbell, 1908).

42. George Fox's *A Primer and Catechism for Children* was coauthored by Ellis Hookes, whose name never appears in American editions (Michael, *Teaching of English,* 459). After the 1702 Jansen edition (Evans #1049), Fox's work was reprinted at least three more times in the colonies: *Instructions for Right Spelling* (Philadelphia: B[enjamin] Franklin, 1737) (#4138) and *Instructions for Right Spelling* (Newport: S. Southwick, 1769) (#11258). For Jansen, see Green, "Book Trade," 215–16. (See Appendix 3.)

43. Strong's *England's Perfect Schoolmaster* was in its second London edition in 1676 and its third in 1681 (under "Nathanael"). Konstantin Dierks, "American Writing Skills Imprints, 1698–1800: A Bibliography," unpublished manuscript, 20. Michael Perry of Boston had twelve copies in his inventory in 1700, priced at a shilling each (Amory, "Under the Exchange," 52).

44. Pastorius, *New Primmer,* 50; Fox, *Instructions for Right-Spelling* (1702), 72; Nathanael Strong, *England's Perfect School-Master: or, Directions for exact Spelling, Reading and Writing,* 3rd ed. (London: Benjamin Billingsley, 1681), 65.

45. Pastorius, *New Primmer*, 58, 67; Fox, *Instructions for Right-Spelling* (1702), 22, 83; Fox, *Instructions for Right Spelling* (1769), 44.

46. Fox, *Instructions for Right-Spelling* (1702), 4–9; Pastorius, *A New Primmer*, 4–7, 8.

47. Strong, *England's Perfect School-Master*, 14.

48. Ibid., 16–19; Michael, *Teaching of English*, 106.

49. Pastorius, *New Primmer*, 18–20; Strong, *England's Perfect School-Master*, 124–28.

50. Pastorius, *New Primmer*, 18–20 (punctuation), 72–77 (arithmetic); Strong, *England's Perfect School-Master*, 124–28 (punctuation), 91–112 (pieces), 126–62 (arithmetic and accounting).

51. E[ward] Young, *The Compleat English-Scholar. in Spelling, Reading and Writing* (London, 1682).

52. Advt., *Pennsylvania Gazette*, July 14, 1748, for a copy printed by Franklin and Hall (Evans #6176).

53. Anon., *The Church Catechism Broke into Short Questions, with an Explanation of some Words, for the Easier Understanding of it: To which are added, Prayers for the Charity-Schools* (London: J. Downing, 1709), [1]. Compare a similar work, *An Easy Method of Instructing Youth in the Principles and Practice of the Christian Religion: For the better understanding of the Church-Catechism . . .* (Oxford, for Anth[ony] Peisley, 1715).

54. John Lewis, *The Church Catechism Explained, By Way of Question and Answer; And Confirmed by Scripture Proofs* (London: B. Dod, 1759), v–vi, vii, ix–x.

55. Ibid., 17–19.

56. Ibid., 69, 103.

57. The advertisement is reproduced in Ford, *New-England Primer*, facing p. 16; and in Nila Banton Smith, *American Reading Instruction* (Newark, Del.: International Reading Association, 1965), 19. For the murky origins of the *New-England Primer* and a discussion of its authorship, see Gillian Avery, "Origins and English Predecessors of the *New-England Primer*," *Proceedings of the American Antiquarian Society* 108, pt. 2 (1998): 33–61.

58. *A Primer for the Colony of Connecticut, or an Introduction to the true Reading* of English. *To Which is Added, Milk for Babes* [New London: T. Green, 1715]. Known only from an advertisement in Joseph Moss, *An Election Sermon . . .* (New-London, [Conn.]: Timothy Green, 1715), [41] (Evans #1769).

59. An analysis by David Watters of the ten *New-England Primers* that survive before 1761 shows the features that were replicated in most later editions. (Features missing from what was, until recently, the only extant 1727 edition and conjectured by Ford from later imprints in Ford, *New-England Primer*, may now be substantiated from a newly discovered primer, also believed to be a 1727 imprint, that has been acquired by the American Antiquarian Society.) David H. Watters, "'I Spake as a Child': Authority, Metaphor, and the New-England Primer," *Early American Literature* 20 (1985–86): 193–213, presents the key features up to 1761, the date of their first appearance, and the number of texts in which they are found. Those in the 1727 edition that are not reproduced in all of the first ten editions are: Choice Sentences (in 6 of 10, reflecting its filler status); The Ten Commandments (8); Duty of Children Towards Their Parents (9); I in the Burying Place may see (9); Good Children must (9), Awake, arise (8); Have Communion with few (8); The Names and Order of the Books of the Old and New Testament (7); the numeral Letters and Figures (5); The short Catechism (8).

60. Ford, *New-England Primer*, 19.

61. Patricia Crain, *The Story of A: The Alphabetization of America from the "New England Primer" to "The Scarlet Letter"* (Stanford: Stanford University Press, 2000), 43–48.

62. Ibid., 43, 44–45.

63. Watters, "'I Spake as a Child,'" esp. 194.

64. Ford, *New-England Primer*, n.p.; Watters, "'I Spake as a Child,'" 201. For a somewhat different interpretation, see Crain, *Story of A*, 45, 49–51.

65. Watters, "'I Spake as a Child,'" 203–4. Watters presents evidence that Cotton Mather may have written this verse. However, Mather might also have borrowed it from an early edition of the *New-England Primer*.

66. Compare Henry Scudder's warning in 1627 that "sleepe and the bed doe aptly resemble death and the grave." Quoted in David D. Hall, *Worlds of Wonder, Days of Judgment; Popular Religious Belief in Early New England* (New York: Alfred A. Knopf, 1989), 134.

67. In fact, it was not John Rogers but Robert Smith who wrote this poem as he awaited execution at the stake in 1555, but Rogers had died similarly a year earlier as "the first Martyr in Q Mary's Reign," as the primer identifies him (Ford, *New-England Primer*, 32–37). John Foxe, *Actes and Monuments . . .* (London: John Day, [1563]), 1263: "The extortacion of Robert Smith, unto his children, commenly set out in the name of maister Rogers." The work, extolling Protestants martyred for their faith, was popularly known as the *Book of Martyrs*.

68. Watters, "'I Spake as a Child,'" 206–8.

69. *The Protestant Tutor for Children . . . To which is Added Verses made by Mr. John Rogers, a Martyr in Queen Mareis Reign* (Boston: Samuel Green, 1685), 3 (Evans, #387); cf. [Benjamin Harris], *The Protestant Tutor for Children* (London: B. Harris, 1680). R. C. Alston cautions against confusing this with [Benjamin Harris], *The Protestant Tutor, Instructing Youth and Others, in the Compleat Method of Spelling, Reading, and Writing, True English: also Discovering to Them the Notorious Errors, Damnable Doctrines, and Cruel Massacres of the Bloody Papists, which England May expect from a Popish Successor* (1685; London: T. Norris, 1720); R. C. Alston, *Spelling Books* (Bradford [Yorkshire]: Printed for the author by Earnest Cummings, 1967), 24.

70. Keach, *Instructions for Children, or the Child's and Youth's Delight, Teaching An easie way to Spell and Read True English . . .* (New York: William Bradford, 1695), [3], 134, 41. Pastorius owned a copy (Learned, *Life of Francis Daniel Pastorius*, 283).

71. Cotton Mather, *A Faithful Man, Described and Rewarded. Some Observable and Serviceable Passages in the Life and Death of Mr. Michael Wigglesworth, Late Pastor of Maldon . . . With a Funeral Sermon Preached (for him) at Maldon, June 24, 1705 . . .* (Boston: Printed by B. Green, for Benjamin Eliot, 1705) (Evans #1212), 24; quoted in Robert Daly, *God's Altar: The World and the Flesh in Puritan Poetry* (Berkeley: University of California Press, 1978), 132. For Wigglesworth's life, see Richard Crowder, *No Featherbed to Heaven: A Biography of Michael Wigglesworth, 1631–1705* ([East Lansing]: Michigan State University Press, 1962). For sales of the *Day of Doom* (the title of the collection in which the poem appeared), see Hugh Amory, "Printing and Bookselling in New England, 1683–1713," in Hall, *History of the Book*, 1:107–8.

72. Michael Wigglesworth, *The Day of Doom* [Cambridge, 1666], 1, 3 (stanzas 1, 7) (Evans #112). The beginning and closing stanzas are designed to stir the emotions and are drawn, as John Adams has suggested, from Wigglesworth's own longstanding experience with physical pain. Alan Pope demonstrates that Christ's arguments were modeled on Petrus Ramos's exposition of logic, in which Wigglesworth was well versed. Richard Crowder shows how Wigglesworth used tenses to intensify the drama. John C. Adams, "Alexander Richardson and the Ramist Poetics of Michael Wigglesworth," *Early American Literature* 25 (1990): 271–88; Alan H. Pope, "Petrus Ramus and Michael Wigglesworth: The Logic of Poetic Structure," in *Puritan Poets and Poetics: Seventeenth-Century American Poetry in Theory and Practice*, ed. Peter White (University Park: Pennsylvania State University Press, 1985), 210–26; Richard Crowder, "The Day of Doom as Chronomorph," *Journal of Popular Culture* 9 (1975–76): 948–59.

73. Wigglesworth, *Day of Doom*, 41 (stanzas 121–22).

74. The records of John Usher, a Boston bookseller, show that he imported forty-two copies of *War with the Devil* in the 1680s (Ford, *Boston Book Market*, 128, 142; Avery, "Origins and English Predecessors," 47–49). The intended audience is suggested by the frontispiece of the first English edition of 1673, which features a converted and an unconverted youth, both identified as aged sixteen.

75. B[enjamin] K[each], *War with the Devil, or, the Young Man's Conflict with the Powers of Darkness . . .*, 12th ed. ([New York: William Bradford, 1705] (Evans #1207), 119, 120, 177.

76. Keach's *War with the Devil* was already in its twelfth English edition when William Bradford reprinted it in New York in 1705 (Evans #1207). For steady sellers, see Hall, *Worlds of Wonder*, 48–49.

77. See, e.g., Janeway, *A Token for Children: Being An Exact Account of the Conversion, Holy and Exemplary Lives, and Joyful Deaths of several young Children* (London: Dorman Newman,

1672); Janeway, *A Token for Children. The Second Part. Being a further Account of the Converson, Holy and Exemplary Lives, and Joyful Deaths of several other young Children, not published in the First Part* (London: D. Newman, 1672). Increase Mather quoted in Hall, *Worlds of Wonder*, 50. Evidence of *A Token*'s popularity is that sixty copies were imported between Mar. 1684 and Apr. 1685 by just one Boston publisher, John Usher (Foster, "Godly in Transit," 222, n. 5). In 1741, an advertisement appeared for the fourth edition of a separate printing of *Early Piety, exemplified in Elizabeth Butcher of Boston*; *Boston Weekly News-Letter*, Feb. 19, 1741. The 1771 edition is Evans #12085. Sarah Osborn to Rev. Joseph Fish, June 17, 1766, Sarah Osborn, letters, Miscellaneous MSS. O, American Antiquarian Society.

78. Gusti Wiesenfeld Frankel, "Between Parent and Child in Colonial New England: An Analysis of the Religious Child-Oriented Literature and Selected Children's Works" (Ph.D. diss., University of Minnesota, 1977), 173. Frankel's work has been very helpful to my discussion.

79. James Janeway, *A Token for Children, Being an Exact Account of the Conversion, Holy and Exemplary Lives and Joyful Deaths of several Young Children* (Boston: T. Hancock, 1728) (Evans #3042), viii, vi.

80. Ibid., 46.

81. Ibid., 74, 77. Cf. John Langham, added to a 1771 edition of James Janeway, *A Token for Children . . .* (Boston: Z. Fowle, 1771) (Evans #12085), 104.

82. Mary A. in Janeway, *Token for Children* (1771), 22; Janeway, *Token for Children* (1728), 39.

83. [Thomas White], *A Little Book for Little Children . . .* (Boston: T. Green, for Nicholas Buttolph, 1702), 19 (#1056).

84. Jos[eph] Porter, *The Holy Seed: Or, The Life of Mr. Tho. Beard, Wrote by Himself: With Some Account of his Death, September 15. 1710. Soon after he had compleated the 17th Year of his Age*, 2nd ed. (London: N. Cliff & D. Jackson, 1711), 16, 18, 30. Cotton Mather's personal copy is in the New York Public Library.

85. Thomas Reynolds, *Practical Religion Exemplify'd in the Lives of Mrs. Mary Terry . . . and Mrs. Clissould* (Boston: Samuel Gerrish, 1713), 4, 37. 46.

86. Amory, "Under the Exchange," 54.

87. Margaret Spufford, *Small Books and Pleasant Histories: Popular Fiction and Its Readership in Seventeenth-Century England* (New York: Cambridge University Press, 1981), chap. 5.

88. Ibid., 132, 262–67. For definitions of chapbooks and a discussion of the problem of when chapbooks price themselves out of the chapbook market, see ibid., 130–31. For Spufford's discussion of Samuel Pepys's collection of "Godliness, Merriments and Vulgaria," housed in the Samuel Pepys Library, Magdalene College, Cambridge, England, see ibid., 130–35; for "godly" books, chap. 8, and for "merry" books, chap. 7. For "merry books," see also Roger Thompson, "Popular Reading and Humour in Restoration England," *Journal of Popular Culture* 9 (1975–76): 653–71.

89. For chapbooks in America, see Victor Neuburg, "Chapbooks in America: Reconstructing the Popular Reading of Early America," in *Reading in America: Literature and Social History*, ed. Cathy N. Davidson (Baltimore: Johns Hopkins University Press), 81–113. Hall, *Worlds of Wonder*, 132–35, tells the tale of Spira and documents references to it in many times and places in New England. Learned, *Life of Francis Daniel Pastorius*, 282.

90. Benjamin Franklin, *The Autobiography and Other Writings*, edited and with an introduction by Kenneth Silverman (New York: Penguin Books, 1986), 13; Gillian Avery, *Behold the Child: American Children and Their Books 1621–1922* (Baltimore: Johns Hopkins University Press, 1994), 30.

91. In the 1680s, the Boston bookseller John Usher was sent "without ordre" from London multiple copies of several romances, including two of *Parismus* and six each of *Guy of Warwick, Reynard the Fox*, and *Fortunatus*. Ford, *Boston Book Market*, 88, 89 (Parismus) (cf. 85), 104 (*Guy* and *Reynard the Fox*), 105 (Fortunatus); Sarah Kemble Knight, *The Journal of Madam Knight*, with an introductory note by George Parker Winship (New York: Peter Smith, 1935), 4; Mather quot. in Avery, *Behold the Child*, 30.

92. [Cotton Mather], *Bethiah. The Glory Which Adorns the Daughters of God* (Boston: J.

Franklin, for S. Gerrish, 1722), 58; quoted in Hall, *World of Wonders*, 55. For the "ungodly" books available, see Hall, *World of Wonders*, 52–55. There was a large gap between English and colonial tastes. For example, in 1682 the London book dealer Robert Boulter sent off a consignment of books to John Usher, a Boston importer, without specific instructions: some 20 percent of the order were titles of the romantic genre. In contrast, over the next few years Usher's own orders included only 5 percent of "romance" literature. Stephen Botein, "The Anglo-American Book Trade before 1776: Personnel and Strategies," in *Printing and Society in Early America*, ed. William L. Joyce, David D. Hall, Richard D. Brown, and John B. Hench (Worcester, Mass.: American Antiquarian Society, 1983), 52.

Chapter 4. Death and Literacy in Two Devout Boston Families

1. Samuel Sewall, *The Diary of Samuel Sewall, 1674–1729*, ed. M. Halsey Thomas, 2 vols. (New York: Farrar, Straus and Giroux), 1:249.

2. Ibid, 1:345–46.

3. Ibid., 1:348. For Spira, who suffered mental agonies from being convinced he was damned after renouncing Protestantism, see Chapter 3, note 89; David D. Hall, *Worlds of Wonder: Days of Judgment; Popular Religious Belief in Early New England* (New York: Alfred A. Knopf, 1989), 132–35. For the spiritual conflict within adults between fear and hope, see ibid., 119–37. The tale of Spira was still being imported in the 1750s (advt., *Pennsylvania Gazette*, Feb. 6, 1750).

4. Sewall, *Diary*, 1:355, 359. The dates of Betty's outbursts of a month apart are probably not a coincidence: she showed the symptoms of menstrual stress.

5. For Elijah Corlett's reminiscence, see *Publications of the Colonial Society of Massachusetts*, vol. 34, *Transactions 1937–1942* (Boston: Colonial Society of Massachusetts, 1943), 236.

6. The best-known proponent of the view that Puritan parents frightened their children unconscionably is Sandford Fleming, *Children and Puritanism: The Place of Children in the Life and Thought of the New England Churches, 1620–1847* (New Haven: Yale University Press, 1933). See also M. Halsy Thomas's views in Sewall, *Diary*, 1:345, n. 3; Lloyd deMause, "The Evolution of Childhood," in *The History of Childhood*, ed. Lloyd deMause (New York: Psychohistory Press, 1974), 1. Those who find the Puritans' warnings of death and the corresponding fears of their children rational are best represented by David E. Stannard, "Death and the Puritan Child," *American Quarterly* 26 (1974): 456–76, esp. 475; David E. Stannard, *The Puritan Way of Death: A Study in Religion, Culture, and Social Change* (New York: Oxford University Press, 1977), 68–71. See also Peter Gregg Slater, *Children in the New England Mind: In Death and in Life* (Hamden, Conn.: Archon Books, 1977), 15–16, 166. Scholars do not agree on the fear that death inspired; for a view that contrasts directly with that of Stannard, see Gordon E. Geddes, *Welcome Joy: Death in Puritan New England* (Riverside, Calif.: UMI Research Press, 1981). For a review of scholars' approaches to the family, see Judith S. Graham, *Puritan Family Life: The Diary of Samuel Sewall* (Boston: Northeastern University Press, 2000), 4–12.

7. Stannard, "Death and the Puritan Child," 463, 465. For discussions of children's mortality rates, see works cited in Slater, *Children in the New England Mind*, 166–67; and Maris A. Vinovskis, "Angels' Heads and Weeping Willows: Death in Early America," *Proceedings of the American Antiquarian Society* 86 (1976): 286; David T. Courtwright, "New England Families in Historical Perspective," in *Families and Children: The Dublin Seminar for New England Folklife: Annual Proceedings 1985*, ed. Peter Benes (Boston: Boston University, 1987), 14, 17.

8. For Samuel Sewall's mental world, see Hall, *Worlds of Wonder*, chap. 5.

9. On typology, see Mason I. Lowance Jr., *The Language of Canaan: Metaphor and Symbol in New England from the Puritans to the Transcendentalists* (Cambridge: Harvard University Press, 1980), esp. 150–59, chap. 7; defined 4–6.

10. The exact date of birth and year of death of the children of each man to live much past the age of two are as follows. For the Sewall family: Samuel, June 11, 1678–1750/1; Hannah, Feb. 3, 1679/80–1724; Elizabeth ("Betty"), December 29, 1681–1716; Joseph, Aug. 15, 1688–1769; Mary, October 28, 1691–1710; Judith, Jan. 2, 1702–40 (Sewall, *Diary*, 2:1076–77, 1086–89). For the Mather family, four of the nine children born to Abigail and survived their

infancy: Katharin (Katy), Sept. 1, 1689–1716; Abigail ("Nibby"), June 14, 1694–1721; Hannah ("Nancy"), Feb. 7, 1697– ?; Increase ("Creasy"), July 9, 1699–1724. Three of the six children born to Elizabeth lived past their second year: Elizabeth ("Liza"), July 13, 1704–26; Samuel ("Sammy"), October 30, 1706–85; and Jerusha, Apr. 1, 1711–13. (Dates of birth provided courtesy of Thomas G. Knoles, American Antiquarian Society.)

11. For Mather's publications, see below, note 38. For his political involvements, see Kenneth Silverman, *The Life and Times of Cotton Mather* (New York: Harper & Row, 1984), 65–76, 209–21, 373–78. For Sewall's publications, see Sewall, *Diary*, 2:1097–102. Samuel Sewall's sixty-page ruminations on New England as the New Jerusalem, *Phaenomena Quaedam Apocalyptica*, appeared in 1697; his *The Selling of Joseph: A Memorial*, America's first antislavery attack, appeared in 1700. Other publications related to his immediate circle, especially his family: a broadside rejoicing that his minister, Samuel Willard, was restored to his congregation after a long illness; an elegy for his mother-in-law, Judith; or a remembrance of his son-in-law Grove Hirst. See also Hall, *Worlds of Wonder*, 236.

12. Sewall, *Diary*, 1:463; Mather, *Diary*, 1:421. Mather mentions Sewall by name in Mather, *Diary*, 2:368, 481, 701.

13. Hall, *Worlds of Wonder*, 234–38, quot. 237. For Sewall's relationship with his family, see Graham, *Puritan Family Life*.

14. Ibid., 1:114. For discussions of family prayer, see Charles E. Hambrick-Stowe, *The Practice of Piety: Puritan Devotional Disciplines in Seventeenth-Century New England* (Williamsburg, Va.: Institute of Early American History and Culture, 1982), 143–50.

15. Sewall, *Diary*, 1:249.

16. Ibid. 1:384.

17. Stannard, *Puritan Way of Death*, 98–105, 108–10; Geddes, *Welcome Joy*, 104–15.

18. For the need for ritual at death, see Stannard, *Puritan Way of Death*, 110–18; Geddes, *Welcome Joy*, 115–25, 133–35; for the role of ritual in general, see Hall, *Worlds of Wonder*, chap. 4.

19. Sewall gave gloves at the funeral of his son Hull, just under two years old; for the funeral of two-year-old Sarah, he gave five rings but gave gloves only to the bearers (*Diary*, 1:117, 364–65).

20. Hambricke-Stowe, *Practice of Piety*, 143; on manuals that guided family prayers, see ibid., 144–48. On ritual, see Hall, *Worlds of Wonder*, chap. 4. See also Graham, *Puritan Family Life*, ch. 5.

21. Sewall, *Diary*, 1:89–90.

22. Ibid., 1:117, 145.

23. Ibid., 1:267, 313. Samuel does not note his children's readings at Jane's funeral. She died at the age of five weeks.

24. Ibid., 1:364.

25. Ibid.

26. Ibid., 1:403–4.

27. *Collections of the Dorchester Antiquarian and Historical Society*, 3; [Richard Mather], *Journal of Richard Mather. 1635. His Life and Death. 1670* (Boston: David Clapp, 1850), [iii]; Increase Mather, *The Autobiography of Increase Mather*, ed. M. G. Hall (Worcester, Mass.: American Antiquarian Society, 1962); "Diary of Increase Mather," *Proceedings of the Massachusetts Historical Society*, 2nd ser., 13 (1899–1900): 337–74.

28. Mather, *Autobiography*, 302–3; Silverman, *Life and Times*, 7.

29. David Levin, *Cotton Mather: The Young Life of the Lord's Remembrancer, 1663–1703* (Cambridge, Mass.: Harvard University Press, 1978), 13; Ronald A. Bosco, ed., *Paterna: The Autobiography of Cotton Mather* (Delmar, N.Y., 1976), 6–7. Mather took notes on sermons until his thirties: Cotton Mather, *Diary of Cotton Mather*, 2 vols., ed. Worthington Chauncey Ford (New York: Frederick Ungar, 1957), 1:265. For a more extensive discussion of Mather and family literacy, see E. Jennifer Monaghan, "Family Literacy in Early 18th-Century Boston: Cotton Mather and His Children," *Reading Research Quarterly* 26 (1991): 342–70.

30. Bosco, *Paterna*, 7; Levin, *Cotton Mather*, 10–13; Silverman, *Life and Times*, 13–14.

31. Silverman, *Life and Times*, 15, 23, 42–45, 50; Carol Gay, "The Fettered Tongue: A Study of the Speech Defect of Cotton Mather," *American Literature* 46 (1975): 451–64; Sewall, *Diary*, 1:63.

32. Mather, *Diary*, 1:127–28.

33. Thomas Prince, "The Preface," in Samuel Mather, *The Life of the Very Reverend and Learned Cotton Mather, D.D. & F.R.S.* (Boston: S. Gerrish, 1729), 3 (italics reversed). For the "Biblia Americana," see Mather, *Diary*, 1:169–71, 231, 563; Silverman, *Life and Times*, 166–68.

34. Mather, *Diary*, 1:323; Cotton Mather, *The Religious Mariner . . .* (Boston: S. Phillips, 1700). For an example of Mather's summarizing and paraphrasing, see Jeffrey Jeske, "Cotton Mather: Physico-theologian." *Journal of the History of Ideas*, 47 (1986): 587. On his manuscripts, see Mather, *Diary*, 1:532 n. 2.

35. Mather, *Dairy*, 1:101.

36. Ibid., 1:368, 548.

37. Ibid., 2:40–41, 162.

38. Ibid., 1:547–48; Silverman, *Life and Times*, 197–98; Thomas J. Holmes, *Cotton Mather: A Bibliography of His Works*, 3 vols. Newton, Mass.: Crofton Publishing, 1974), 1:ix.

39. Mather, Diary, 1:369, 555–56, quots. 1:572, 2:216; James Janeway, *A Token for Children . . . To Which is Added, A Token for the Children of New-England* (1700; repr., Boston, Z. Fowle, 1771); Cotton Mather, *The A, B, C, of Religion. Lessons Relating the Fear of God, Fitted Unto the Youngest and Lowest Capacities, and Children Suitably Instructed in the Maxims of Religion* (Boston: Timothy Green, 1713); reprinted in *Early American Imprints. Series I, Evans (1639–1800)* [electronic resource], ([New Canaan, Conn.]: Readex; [Worcester, Mass.]: American Antiquarian Society, [2002–]) (hereafter cited as Evans), #1614.

40. Silverman, *Life and Times*, 199. Silverman located 569 letters after a search in fifteen states and twenty-one countries (Silverman, *Selected Letters of Cotton Mather*, ix).

41. "contrivance," Mather, *Diary*, 2–41. On writing as a spiritual exercise, see Hambrick-Stowe, *Practice of Piety*, 186–93; Daniel B. Shea Jr., *Spiritual Autobiography in Early America* (Princeton: Princeton University Press, 1968).

42. For the criticism, see Virginia Bernhard, "Cotton Mather's 'most unhappy wife': Reflections on the Uses of Historical Evidence," *New England Quarterly* 60 (1987): 341–62.

43. Mather, *Diary*, 1:240; cf. Cotton Mather, *The Diary of Cotton Mather, D.D., F.R.S., for the Year 1712*, edited and with an introduction and notes by William R. Manierre II (Charlottesville: University Press of Virginia, 1964), 66 (hereafter cited as Mather, *Diary for 1712*). See also Mather, *Diary*, 1:580 ("my Sons, to whom I leave these poor Memorials"); Cotton Mather, *Paterna: The Autobiography of Cotton Mather*, ed. Ronald A. Bosco (Delmar, N.Y.: Scholars' Facsimiles and Reprints, 1976).

44. Mather, *Diary*, 1:239–40. The book Mather referred to was probably Cotton Mather, *Help for Distressed Parents Or, Counsels and Comforts for Godly Parents Afflicted with Ungodly Children: And Warnings Unto Children, to Beware of All Those Evil Courses, Which Would Be Afflictive Unto Their Parents* (Boston: John Allen, 1695) (Evans #723).

45. Mather, *Diary*, 1:135–36, 1:423.

46. Ibid., 1:423–24. (For other examples of Mather's altering the evening prayers, see ibid., 1:372.) According to the National Union Catalogue, *An Exposition of the Book of Job* by George Hucheson (1615–74) was published in London in 1669.

47. Mather, *Diary*, 1:435, 445–47, quot. 447.

48. Ibid., 1:447–49. Mather first mentions Abigail's ill health in ibid., 1:368–69. For the deaths of the five, see ibid., 1:163 (Joseph in 1693), 1:174 (Mary in 1693, aged just under two), 1:185 (Mehetabel in 1696—identified by Mather as the fourth death, and as overlain by her nurse), and 1:382 (Samuel in 1701). Their firstborn, Abigail, died in 1688 at five months (Silverman, *Life and Times*, 76; see also 274; Mather, *Diary*, 2:290).

49. Mather, *Diary*, 1:450.

50. Ibid., 1:545, 548.

51. Ibid, 1:545-46.

52. Ibid., 1:546.

53. Ibid., 1:534–36, quots. 536; Mather, *Journal of Richard Mather. 1635*, 44.

54. Mather, *Diary*, 1:534–35.

55. Ibid., 1:555–56; 2:68. Despite a second edition, no copy of *Good Lessons*, printed by T. Green in 1706, seems to have survived.

56. Mather, *Diary*, 1:583.

57. Ibid., 2:9, 25. Mather made successive efforts to devote Saturday evenings to his family, at one point resolving to get home by nine o'clock in order to instruct and converse with his children, rather than sitting with his neighbors (ibid., 2:227).

58. Ibid., 2:41. Mather details his daily questions in ibid., 2:24–28, quot. 25. He numbered the days of the week successively 1 through 7, no matter what the actual day of the month was; his "Good Devised" for his family can therefore be found under each number 2, until 1716, when he began numbering the days of the month as every one else did and moved the family G.D.'s to Tuesdays. At this point, entries on his children may be found in every second entry after the asterisk that denotes Sundays in each week (ibid., 2:334 n. 1).

59. Mather, *Diary for 1712*, 122, 91, 97.

60. Mather, *Diary*, 2:41, 193.

61. Ibid., 2:65 (cf. 59–60), 81.

62. Ibid., 2:94, 84, 106–7; cf. ibid., 2:136, 161, 207, 219.

63. Ibid., 2:149, 153 (cf. ibid., 199).

64. Ibid., 2:97, 132.

65. Mather, *Diary for 1712*, 3.

66. Mather, *Diary*, 2:49; *Diary for 1712*, 9, 77–78, 85.

67. Mather, *Diary for 1712*, 25, 71, 111–12.

68. Ibid., 71, 102.

69. Ibid., 94–95, 112. The book was reprinted in Boston as Thomas Reynolds, *Practical Religion Exemplify'd in the Lives of Mrs. Clissold, and Mrs. Mary Terry . . .* (Boston: Timothy Green, 1713) (Evans #1645).

70. Mather, *Diary for 1712*, 40; *Diary*, 2:353.

71. Mather, *Diary for 1712*, 18; *Diary*, 2:70, 205.

72. Mather, *Diary*, 2:182, 202.

73. Ibid., 2:248–61.

74. Ibid., 2:261, 236, 26.

75. Ibid., 2:262; Cotton Mather, *The Religion of the Cross . . . Occasioned by What Was Encountered in the Death of That Vertuous Gentlewoman, Mrs. Elizabeth Mather . . .* (Boston: John Allen, 1714) (Evans #1697); Cotton Mather, *A Christian Funeral. A Brief Essay, on That Case, What Should Be the Behaviour of a Christian at a Funeral?* (Boston, B. Green, 1713) (#1618).

76. Mather, *Diary*, 2:266, 268, 497, 204.

77. Ibid., 2:224, 249 (cf. Mather, *Diary for 1712*, 23); see also Joseph Porter, *The Holy Seed: Or, the Life of Mr. Thomas Beard, Wrote by Himself: With Some Account of His Death, September 15, 1710 . . .* 2nd ed. (London: N. Cliff & D. Jackson, 1711). The copy Mather owned is housed in the New York Public Library. Similarly, Mather used the accidental death of a fourteen-year-old, crushed by a cart, as an occasion to warn his children (particularly Increase), to "become serious, and prayerful and afraid of Sin" (Mather, *Diary*, 2:64).

78. Mather, *Diary*, 2:273–74.

79. Ibid., 2: 271–72. Onesimus married and had two sons who died in infancy. A few months after the second baby died, Mather accused Onesimus of growing "wicked" and "Froward" and gave him his freedom in exchange for Onesimus's purchase of a replacement servant (Mather, *Diary*, 2:271–72, 282, 342, 363, 363 n 1).

80. Ibid., 2:322, 338. Lydia's daughter married Samuel Sewall, a nephew of the diarist Samuel Sewall, after the death of her first husband, Nathan Howell. For Mather's courtship, see Silverman, *Life and Times*, 281–90.

81. Ibid., 2:334, 335–36, 438 (cf. 2:376). Cotton Mather, *Utilia: Real and Vital Religion . . .* (Boston: for Daniel Henchman, 1716) (Evans #1834); Johann Arndt, *De Vero Christianismo*

Libri Quatuor . . . Tomus I (London: J. Downing, 1708); for Arndt, see Silverman, *Life and Times*, 231.

82. Mather, *Diary*, 2:373, 388, 391; Cotton Mather, *Victorina. A Sermon Preach'd on the Decease and at the Desire of Mrs. Katharin Mather, by Her Father. Wherunto there is added, a Further Account of That Young Gentlewoman, by Another Hand* (Boston: D. Henchman, 1717). Mather first mentions her illness in Mather, *Diary*, 2:350 (May 8, 1716). The claim in the title that this "*Further Account of that Young Gentlewoman*" was "*by Another Hand*" was deliberately misleading: Mather appears to have employed the hand, literally, of his nephew Thomas Walter by getting him to copy out Mather's own reminiscences.

83. Mather, *Victorina*, 50, 59, 67, 68; Samuel Mather, *Life of the Very Reverend and Learned Cotton Mather* (Boston, Mass.: Samuel Gerrish, 1729), 14.

84. Mather, Diary, 2:469 (cf. 523) (grammar school), quot. 459 (play), 379, 525 (translations), 463 (French), 523 (writing school), 473 (geography), 498-99 (prayer), 476 (books), quot. 557 (manliness and Latin), 782 (theology).

85. Ibid., 2:352, 489, 484.

86. Ibid., 2:487, 526 (cf. 2:665).

87. Ibid., 2:762, 628, 782, 465, 373; Richard Baxter, *Poor Man's Family Book*, in William Orme, *Practical Works, with a Life of the Author, and a Critical Examination of His Writings* (London: J. Duncan, 1830), vol. 20.

88. Mather, *Diary*, 2:534, 548 (cf. 537, 549), 583 (outbursts), 712 (Nancy), 338. For the deterioration of Lydia's relationship with Nancy, see ibid., 2:553, 579, 582.

89. Ibid., 2:583 nn. 1, 2, 584–85.

90. Mather, *Diary*, 2:630 (poverty), 606 (Harvard) (cf. 629), quots. 620.

91. Ibid., 2:712, 715, 749–50. Lydia took her niece and the niece's maid with her. For Cotton's distress at this time, see ibid., 2:705–708; Silverman, *Life and Times*, chap. 13.

92. Mather, *Diary*, 2:611, 612, 664, 647 (sloth), 753.

93. Ibid., 753, 777 (papers), 776, 753 (sincere); Cotton Mather, *The Words of Understanding . . .* (Boston: J. Edwards, 1724).

94. Mather, *Diary*, 2:701, 772, 721.

95. Ibid., 2:647–49 (Nibby); 745 n. 1 (Liza); Silverman, *Life and Times*, 427. As Silverman suggests, Nancy was probably disfigured as the result of a childhood accident, which burned her right arm and face; see also Silverman, *Life and Times*, 348; Mather, *Diary*, 1:282–83.

96. Mather, *Diary*, 2:786.

97. Sewall, *Diary*, 1:474–75, 2:705–6n, 726; Bruce Tucker, "Joseph Sewall's Diary and the Rhythm of Puritan Spirituality," *Early American Literature* 22 (1987): 3–18. Tucker notes that between April 27 and November 16, 1707, Joseph wrote 180 pages of self-examination.

Chapter 5. The Literacy Mission of the S.P.G.

1. John Calam, *Parsons and Pedagogues: The S.P.G. Adventure in American Education* (New York: Columbia University Press, 1971), 8–9, 177, 198–99; Patricia U. Bonomi, *Under the Cope of Heaven* (New York: Oxford University Press, 1986), 46; the S.P.G. even funded some ministers for a brief time in early Maryland (Bonomi, *Under the Cope of Heaven*, 232 n. 17). See also David Humphreys, *An Historical Account of the Incorporated Society for the Propagation of the Gospel in Foreign Parts* (London, 1730; repr., New York: Arno Press, 1969).

2. Calam, *Parsons and Pedagogues*, 108.

3. Ibid., 65–73, quot. 33.

4. John Thomas to Sec., Feb. 20, 1712, Society for the Propagation of the Gospel Papers (hereafter cited as S.P.G. Papers), 7:8, Library of Congress Records, Washington, D.C. (LC). Cf. James Honyman to Sec., May 7, 1714, S.P.G. Papers, ser. B, 1:176, Rhodes House, Oxford, U.K. (RH).

The LC records I consulted are handwritten transcripts of the originals of the S.P.G. papers; those in RH are the originals. Series A, however, at RH consists of copies of letters transcribed by S.P.G. clerks into their letter books; series B consists of the original letters sent by overseas correspondents to the S.P.G. Unfortunately, the two sets of numbers (the last entry in the documentation) at the two depositories do not correspond for series A. The numbers of series A at LC refer to the numbered letters, no matter how many pages a letter has; but the numbers at RH refer to the page numbers of the letter books. For example, William Huddlestone to Sec., Feb. 23, 1711/12, S.P.G. Papers, ser. A, 7:10 (LC) (cited in note 5) is the same as 7:146 (RH). The numbers in series B, at both depositories, in contrast, usually refer to the numbered letters, not to page numbers. Therefore each entry identifies which source I consulted.

5. The following discussion is drawn from "Instructions for Schoolmasters, 1706," reproduced in William Webb Kemp, *The Support of Schools in Colonial New York by the Society for the Propagation of the Gospel in Foreign Parts* (New York: Teachers College, Columbia University, 1913), 58–59. For an example of receiving the printed regulations, see William Huddlestone to Sec., Feb. 23, 1711/12, S.P.G. Papers, ser. A, 7:10 (LC).

6. John Lewis, *The Church Catechism Explained, By Way of Question and Answer; And Confirmed by Scripture Proofs: Divided into Five Parts, and Twelve Sections*, 27th ed. (London, for B. Dod, 1759).

7. For a refusal by a clergyman to sign the "Notitia," see Samuel Seabury to Sec., Oct. 8, 1771, S.P.G. Papers, ser. B, 2:182 (RH).

8. Thomas Fishwicke to Mr. Shute, June 14, 1711, S.P.G. Papers, ser. A, 6:84 (LC).

9. Kemp, *Support of Schools*, 54. For additional problems that affected S.P.G. missionaries in particular (missionary quarrels and the lack of a colonial bishop), see Calam, *Parsons and Pedagogues*, 57–59.

10. Calam, *Parsons and Pedagogues*, 31, n. 2.

11. Rev. Leonard Cutting to Sec., Jan. 5, 1771, S.P.G. Papers, ser. B, 2:147 (RH); William Leahy to Sec., Dec. 29, 1770, ser. B, 3:214 (RH). By this time Leahy had seven children and a salary totaling only £17-5-0. See also George Taylor to Sec., Oct. 25, 1743, S.P.G. Papers, ser. B, 13:151 (RH). Taylor then had six small children.

12. Petition, received Jan. 1733, S.P.G. Papers, ser. B, 1:43 (RH). Similarly, "Humble Address" to Henry Lord Bishop of London, [1704], S.P.G. Papers, ser. A, 2:45, signed by twenty-one persons requesting that Joseph Cleator be made schoolmaster of Rye and Mamaroneck (LC).

13. Thomas Standard to Sec., Nov. 4, 1733, S.P.G. Papers, ser. B, 1:11 (RH); William Forster to Sec., Nov. 2, 1717, S.P.G. Papers, ser. A, 12:364 (RH). For another charge of drunkenness, see Samuel Seabury to Sec., Oct. 8, 1771, S.P.G. Papers, ser. B, 2:182 (RH).

14. Robert Jenney to Sec., Dec. 22, 1729, S.P.G. Papers, ser. B, 1:45 (RH).

15. Thomas Gildensleave to Sec., Dec. 1, 1729, S.P.G. Papers, ser. B, 1:47 (RH); Gildensleave to Sec., Nov. 22, 1729, S.P.G. Papers, ser. B, 1:48 (RH); Robert Jenney to Sec., Dec. 22, 1729, S.P.G. Papers, ser. B, 1:45 (RH).

16. E.g., Samuel Purdy to Sec., Dec. 6, 1744, S.P.G. Papers, ser. B, 13:268 (RH); Lewis, *Church Catechism Explained*.

17. For objections voiced in New York, see Elias Neau to Sec., July 4, 1704, S.P.G. Papers, ser. A, 1:177 (LC); Neau to [John] Chamberlayne [Sec.], Oct. 3, 1705, S.P.G. Papers, ser. A, 2:124 (LC); in South Carolina, Francis Le Jau to Sec., Feb. 19, 1709/10, S.P.G. Papers, ser. A, 5:82 (LC). The argument that baptism might confer freedom was spurious, because between 1664 and 1706 Maryland, Virginia, North and South Carolina, New Jersey, and New York had passed laws affirming that baptism did not confer emancipation. Marcus W. Jernegan, "Slavery and Conversion in the American Colonies," in Paul Finkelman, ed., *Articles on American Slavery*, vol. 16, *Religion and Slavery* (New York: Garland, 1989), 504–27.

18. Robert Jenney to Sec., Nov. 19, 1725, S.P.G. Papers, ser. B, 1:78 (RH). Jenney speaks of "sureties."

19. Samuel Purdy to Sec., June 28, 1739, S.P.G. Papers, ser. B, 7:147 (RH); Rev. Samuel Johnson to Sec., Sept 20, 1727, S.P.G. Papers, ser. B, 1:224, mentions that there were two schools run by dissenters at Stratford, Conn.

20. Rev. Leonard Cutting to Sec., Jan. 1, 1770, S.P.G. Papers, ser. B, 2:146 (RH).

21. Joseph Cleator to Sec., May 16, 1710, S.P.G. Papers, ser. A, 5:150 (LC); Basil Bartow to

Sec., Oct. 28, 1745, S.P.G. Papers, ser. B, 13:337 (RH); Rev. Samuel Seabury to Sec., Dec. 28, 1767, S.P.G. Papers, ser. B, 2:172 (RH).

22. William Huddlestone to Sec., Jan. 16, 1710/11, S.P.G. Papers, ser. A, 6:51 (LC); Thomas Huddlestone to Sec., July 10, 1729, S.P.G. Papers, ser. B, 1:61 (RH); [Thomas Noxon] to Sec., Oct. 6, 1740, S.P.G. Papers, ser. B, 7, pt. 2, no. 109 (thanks for books received) (RH); Joseph Hildreth to Sec., Apr. 27, 1763, S.P.G. Papers, ser. B, 3:156 (RH).

23. Requests from missionaries: Aeneas MacKenzie to Sec., June 13, 1709, S.P.G. Papers, ser. A, 5:18 (LC); Rev. Charlton to Sec., Oct. 12, 1768, S.P.G. Papers, ser. B, 3:85 (RH). Requests for books for schools (or letters from the S.P.G. secretary on books dispatched): Joseph Cleator to Sec., June 24, 1709, S.P.G. Papers, ser. A, 5:10 (LC); Alexander Adams to Sec., July 2, 1711, S.P.G. Papers, ser. A, 6:128 (LC); Benjamin Dennis to Sec., Sept. 3, 1711, S.P.G. Papers, ser. A, 6:143 (LC); Philip Bearcroft [Sec.], to Commissary [Alexander] Garden, July 4, 1748, S.P.G. Papers, ser. B, 15:247 (RH) (books dispatched); Joseph Hildreth to Sec., Apr. 27, 1763, S.P.G. Papers, ser. B, 3:156 (RH).

24. Examples of the many requests for church catechisms with Lewis's *Church Catechism Explained*, or a response to such requests: Elias Neau to Sec., July 22, 1707, S.P.G. Papers, ser. A, 3:80 (LC) (requests catechisms in general); William Huddlestone to Sec., Nov. 27, 1714, S.P.G. Papers, ser. A, 10:166 (RH) (requests Lewis's); Philip Bearcroft [Sec.] to Thomas Keeble [*sic*], June 14, 1743, S.P.G. Papers, ser. B, 10:195 (RH) (sends 25 Wall's *Abridgment of Infant Baptism* and 25 Lewis's *Exposition)*; John Ogilvie (at Fort Hunter) to Sec., Apr. 14, 1751, S.P.G. Papers, ser. B, 19:71 (RH); Joseph Hildreth to Sec., Apr. 27, 1763, S.P.G. Papers, ser. B, 3:156 (RH).

25. Examples of lost or delayed books: William Huddlestone to Sec., Jan. 16, 1710/11, S.P.G. Papers, ser. A, vol. 6 (LC); William Forster to Sec., May 10, 1723, S.P.G. Papers, ser. A, 17: 228. P. Bearcroft [Sec.] to Mr. Miller, bookseller, Aug. 27, 1761, S.P.G. Papers, ser. B, 1:245 (RH). Books for S.P.G. missionaries were sometimes ordered through New England booksellers: in the instance above, Philip Bearcroft, the S.P.G. secretary, placed an order with Mr. Miller, a bookseller in New England, for Bibles, Common Prayer Books, John Lewis's *Expositions,* and above all, catechisms. Miller was to forward them along with various other books to six different missionaries. The ratio of catechisms to any other title was 2 to 1: Bearcroft ordered 100 church catechisms or 100 Lewis's *Expositions,* or both, for four of the six recipients. Each man received either a half or a quarter of that number of small Common Prayer Books. Besides catechisms, Lewis's *Expositions,* Common Prayer Books, and a few folio Bibles, the list of books included, for Mr. Fayerweather only, "Bishop Beveridge on the Common Prayer, The Sin and Danger of neglecting the publick Service of the Church, Reasonable Communicant, Husbandman's Man-ual, Pastoral letter from a minister to his Parishioners," and "Plain Directions for Reading the Holy Scriptures" (50 copies of each). Mr. Graves, a New London missionary, was to receive, in addition to his 25 Common Prayer Books with the 29 articles of religion, 50 copies of "Wall's abridgment of infant Baptism." For a similar list, see Philip Bearcroft, Feb. 19, 1761, S.P.G. Papers, ser. B, 1:284 (RH).

26. Joseph Cleator to Sec., Sept. 24, 1710, S.P.G. Papers, ser. A, 5:182 (LC); Joseph Hildreth to Sec., Oct. 16, 1770, S.P.G. Papers, ser. B, 3:165 (RH).

27. Joseph Cleator to Sec., June 24, 1709, S.P.G. Papers, ser. A, 5:10 (LC).

28. Joseph Cleator to Sec., Sept. 24, 1710, S.P.G. Papers, ser. A, 5:182 (LC); Cleator to Sec., May 21, 1712, S.P.G. Papers, ser. A, 7:27 (LC). Similarly, Alexander Adams to Sec., July 2, 1711, S.P.G. Papers, ser. A, 6:107 (LC): he asks for primers, catechisms, Lewis's *Explanations,* psalters, Common Prayer Books with Tate and Brady Psalms, and Bibles. See also Thomas Huddlestone to Sec., July 10, 1729, S.P.G. Papers, ser. B, 1:61 (RH).

29. "Common Prayer books with the new Version of Psalms are greatly wanted," Rev. Richard Charlton to Sec., Sept. 30, 1745, S.P.G. Papers, ser. B, 14:103 (RH); N[icholas] Brady and N. Tate, *A New Version of the Psalms of David Fitted to the Tunes Used in Churches* (London, 1704; repr., Boston: J. Allen for Nicolas Boone, 1713), reprinted *in Early American Imprints. Series I, Evans (1639–1800)* [electronic resource], ([New Canaan, Conn.]: Readex; [Worcester, Mass.]: American Antiquarian Society, [2002–]), #1594.

30. The praise for Joseph Cleator's teaching occurred in the context of a petition of twenty-one persons whose children he was already teaching, requesting financial support, "Humble Address" to Henry Lord Bishop of London, n.d. [1704], S.P.G. Papers, ser. A, 2:45 (LC). The number of children in Cleator's school or schools in any one year ranged from thirty-five to eighty, depending on how many schools he taught at any one time. He reported eighty students (in three schools): Joseph Cleator to Sec., June 24, 1709, S.P.G. Papers, ser. A, 5:10 (LC); fifty students in three schools: Cleator to Sec., Feb. 23, 1708/9, S.P.G. Papers, ser. A, 4:133 (LC). References to two schools: Cleator to Sec., Sept, 6, 1711, S.P.G. Papers, ser. A, 6:135 (LC); 35 in one school: Cleator to Sec., Dec. 10, 1711, S.P.G. Papers, ser. A, 7:4 (LC); forty children under the age of thirteen in one school: Cleator to Sec., Jan. 9, 1716, S.P.G. Papers, ser. A, 12: 271 (RH); to a school in his own house near the church: Cleator to Sec., Oct. 14, 1717, S.P.G. Papers, ser. A, 12:356 (RH).

31. Joseph Cleator to Sec., Oct. 14, 1717, S.P.G. Papers, ser. A, 12:354 (RH).

32. Christopher Bridge to Sec., Nov. 14, 1717, S.P.G. Papers, ser. A, 12:345–46, cited in Calam, *Parsons and Pedagogues*, 145; cf. Sec. to Cleator, Apr. 5, 1717, S.P.G. Papers, ser. A, 12: 424 (RH); blind: Daniell Chubb to Sec., n.d. (received June 15, 1733), S.P.G. Papers, ser. B, 1: 26 (RH).

33. [William] Forster to Sec., Nov 2, 1717, S.P.G. Papers ser. A, 12:364–65 (RH).

34. Compare the English workhouse schools, such as the Great Yarmouth Children's Hospital, which registered the admission of 132 boys and 85 girls between 1698 and 1715. David Cressy, *Literacy and the Social Order: Reading and Writing in Tudor and Stuart England* (Cambridge: Cambridge University Press, 1980), 30–34. None of the girls learned to write, a fact that I interpret as a function of their sex rather than, with Cressy, their lack of preparation.

35. Ed[ward] Davies to Sec., Nov. 6, 1733, S.P.G. Papers, ser. B, 1:9 (RH); Alexander Garden to Sec., Oct. 10, 1743, S.P.G. Papers, ser. B, 11:204 (RH) (requests one hundred spelling books); Dr. Philip Bearcroft [Sec.] to Commissary [Alexander] Garden, July 7, 1744, S.P.G. Papers, ser. B, 13:52 (RH) (has sent one hundred); Garden to Sec., Oct. 18, 1744, S.P.G. Papers, ser. B, 12:119 (RH) (books in use); Bearcroft [Sec.] to Commissary [Alexander] Garden, July 4, 1748, S.P.G. Papers, ser. B, 15:247 (RH) (sends fifty); Kemp, *Support of Schools*, 104, n. 174. Advertisements for imported copies of Dyche's spelling book: *The South Carolina Gazette*, June 23, 1735; in Hennig Cohen, *The South Carolina Gazette, 1732–75* (Columbia: University of South Carolina Press, 1953), 128; *Pennsylvania Gazette*, Dec. 22, 1730.

36. Samuel Purdy to Sec., Aug. 29, 1733, S.P.G. Papers, ser. B, 1:20 (RH).

37. Rowland Ellis to Sec., Sept. 21, 1725, S.P.G. Papers, ser. B, 1:90 (RH).

38. For Jones, see also Calam, *Parsons and Pedagogues*, 124–26.

39. Rowland Jones to Sec., June 17, 1730, S.P.G. Papers, ser. A, 23:162–63 (RH).

40. Frank J. Klingberg, ed., *The Carolina Chronicle of Dr. Francis le Jau, 1706–1717* (Berkeley: University of California Press, 1956), 70, n. 84. Klingberg's book provides a valuable and accessible transcript of Le Jau's letters. Goose Creek was actually still in Carolina at this time: Carolina would be split into North and South in 1713.

41. Francis Le Jau to Sec., Dec. 2, 1706, S.P.G. Papers, ser. A, 3:68 (LC).

42. Francis Le Jau to Sec., Feb. 18, 1708/9, S.P.G. Papers, ser. A, 4:101 (LC); Le Jau to Sec., Sept. 15, 1708, S.P.G. Papers, ser. A, 4:125 (LC).

43. Gideon Johnston to Sec., July 5, 1710, S.P.G. Papers, ser. A, 5:158 (LC).

44. Francis Le Jau to Sec., Sept. 5, 1711, S.P.G. Papers, ser. A, 6:141 (LC); Benjamin Dennis to Sec., Sept. 3, 1711, S.P.G. Papers, ser. A, 6:143 (LC).

45. Benjamin Dennis to Sec., Feb. 26, 1711/12, S.P.G. Papers, ser. A, 7:12 (LC); Le Jau to Sec., May 26, 1712, S.P.G. Papers, ser. A, 7:13 (LC).

46. Benjamin Dennis to Sec., Feb. 26, 1711/12, S.P.G. Papers, ser. A, 7:12 (LC).

47. Benjamin Dennis to Sec., Dec. 18, 1712, S.P.G. Papers, ser. A, 8:335 (RH); Dennis to Sec., Mar. 20, 1712/13, S.P.G. Papers, ser. A, 8:349 (RH).

48. Benjamin Dennis to Sec., May 30, 1713, S.P.G. Papers, ser. A, 8:351 (RH); Sec. to Dennis, Nov. 30, 1713, S.P.G. Papers, ser. A, 8:455–56 (RH).

49. Benjamin Dennis to Sec., Feb. 9, 1713/14, S.P.G. Papers, ser. A, 9:260–61 (RH).

50. Benjamin Dennis to Sec., Aug. 12, 1714, S.P.G. Papers, ser. A, 9:283 (RH); Klingberg, *Carolina Chronicle*, 118.

51. Benjamin Dennis to Sec., Feb. 9, 1714, S.P.G. Papers, ser. A, 9:261 (RH).

52. Sec. to Benjamin Dennis, July 16, 1714, S.P.G. Papers, ser. A, 9:304 (RH).

53. Benjamin Dennis to Sec., Apr. 22, 1714, S.P.G. Papers, ser. A, 9:267 (RH).

54. Benjamin Dennis to Sec., Aug. 12, 1714, S.P.G. Papers, ser. A, 9:284 (RH); Francis Le Jau to Sec., July 4, 1714, S.P.G. Papers, ser. A, 9:269 (RH); Klingberg, *Carolina Chronicle*, 143.

55. Benjamin Dennis to Sec., Sept. 2, 1715, S.P.G. Papers, ser. A, 11:62–63 (RH); Francis Le Jau to Sec., Nov. 28, 1715, S.P.G. Papers, as quoted in Klingberg, *Carolina Chronicle*, 170. For the Yamasee War of 1715, see Robert M. Weir, *Colonial South Carolina, A History* (Millwood, N.Y.: kto press, 1983), 28–30.

56. Benjamin Dennis to Sec., Nov. 14, 1716, S.P.G. Papers, ser. B, 4:79 (RH).

57. Huddlestone said in 1712 that he had been teaching for over twenty years: William Huddlestone to Sec., Feb. 23, 1711/12, S.P.G. Papers, ser. A, 7:146 (RH); Kemp, *Support of Schools*, 77, 80; Rev. William Vesey to Sec., Nov. 21, 1705, S.P.G. Papers, ser. A, 2:130 (LC); similarly, Vesey to Sec., Nov. 28, 1705, S.P.G. Papers, ser. A, 2:132 (LC). For Trinity Church, then and now, see Dena Merriam, *Trinity: A Church, a Parish, a People*, with photography by David Finn (New York: Cross River Press, 1996).

58. William Huddlestone to Sec., Oct. 9, 1706, S.P.G. Papers, ser. A, 3:8 (LC); William Huddlestone to Sec., July 24, 1710, S.P.G. Papers, ser. A, 5:163 (LC); quot., Merriam, *Trinity*, 17.

59. William Huddlestone to Sec., July 24, 1710, S.P.G. Papers, ser. A, 5:163 (LC).

60. Ibid.; inadequate clothing, William Huddlestone to Sec., Feb. 23, 1711/12, S.P.G. Papers, ser. A, 7:146 (RH).

61. William Huddlestone to Sec., Jan. 16, 1710/11, S.P.G. Papers, ser. A, 6:51 (LC); William Huddlestone to Sec., Feb. 23, 1711/12, S.P.G. Papers, ser. A, 7:146 (RH).

62. Certificate of Col. Hunter, Col. Heathcote, and Col. Morris, Feb. 19, 1711/12, S.P.G. Papers, 7:2 (LC); mentioned in William Huddlestone to Sec., Feb. 23, 1771/12, S.P.G. Papers, ser. A, 7:146 (RH).

63. Sec. to William Huddlestone, Dec. 18, 1713, S.P.G. Papers, ser. A, 8:326–67 (RH); William Huddlestone, petition to Gen. Francis Nicholson, May 11, 1714, S.P.G. Papers, ser. A, 9:212–13 (RH).

64. William Huddlestone to Sec., Feb. 23, 1711/12, S.P.G. Papers, ser. A, 7:146 (RH).

65. Caleb Heathcote, certificate, Sept. 26, 1713, S.P.G. Papers, ser. A, 9:179–80 (RH); Mayor John Johnston to Sec., July 21, 1715, S.P.G. Papers, ser. A, 10:265 (RH).

66. Kemp, *Support of Schools*, 88 n. 58.

67. William Huddlestone to Sec., Sept. 14, 1716, S.P.G. Papers, ser. A, 12:244–45 (RH).

68. William Huddlestone to Sec., Sept. 14, 1716, S.P.G. Papers, ser. A, 12:245–46 (RH).

69. Kemp (*Support of Schools*, 92, n. 84) notes that there is an uncertainty over the date of William Huddlestone's death. The rector of Trinity Church set it at Aug. 1724, in a letter to the society that year. Rev. William Vesey to Sec., Nov. 8, 1725, S.P.G. Papers, ser. B, 1:85 (RH). However, in a letter a year earlier, Vesey had notified the society that he had appointed Thomas Huddlestone to the school after William Huddlestone's death, and the S.P.G. certified Thomas's appointment in Mar. 1724. Vesey to Sec., Nov. 20, 1723, S.P.G. Papers, ser. A, 17:247 (RH); Sec. to Thomas Huddlestone, Mar. 2, 1723/24, S.P.G. Papers, ser. A, 17:328 (RH). Huddlestone therefore died in Aug. 1723.

70. Thomas Huddlestone to Sec., n.d., rec'd. Mar. 18, 1725, S.P.G. Papers, ser. B, 1:106 (RH).

71. Thomas Huddlestone to Sec., May 23, 1730, S.P.G. papers, ser. A, 23:57–58 (RH). For details on the numbers enrolled from 1726 to 1731, see Kemp, *Support of Schools*, 95 n. 101.

72. "Petition of Mrs. Huddlestone," Oct. 21, 1731, S.P.G. Papers, ser. A, 23:375 (RH).

73. Ibid., 375–76.

74. "A list of the Gent. who subscribed to the Pettition of Mrs. Sarah Huddleston [*sic*]," S.P.G. Papers, ser. A, 23:377–80 (RH).

75. Kemp, *Support of Schools*, 96.

76. Quoted in ibid., 89.

77. *Supplement to the Vindication of Mr. Alex. Campbell . . .* , Aug. 15, 1732, quoted in Kemp, *Support of Schools*, 96, n.116 (Evans #3514).

78. Kemp, *Support of Schools*, 97, n.123.

79. Thomas Noxon to Sec., June 5, 1733, S.P.G. Papers, ser. B, 1:35 (RH); Kemp, *Support of Schools*, 98–99.

80. Thomas Noxon to Sec., May 22, 1742, S.P.G. Papers, ser. B, 10:69 (RH); Philip Bearcroft to Thomas Noxon, June 14, 1743, S.P.G. Papers, ser. B, 10:141 (RH); Kemp, *Support of Schools*, 97.

81. Kemp, *Support of Schools*, 101.

82. Rev. William Vesey to Sec., Dec. 9, 1743, S.P.G. Papers, ser. B, 11:118–19 (RH).

83. Dr. Philip Bearcroft to Commissary [William] Vesey, May 21, 1744, S.P.G. Papers, ser. B, 13:38 (RH); Bearcroft to Joseph Hildreth, May 21, 1744, S.P.G. Papers, ser. B, 13:38 (RH). The society's support was increased to £15 in 1748: Joseph Hildreth to Sec., Jan. 8, 1747/8, S.P.G. Papers, ser. B, 15:120 (RH). Quots., Vesey's death: Churchwardens and Vestry to Sec., Dec 5, 1746, S.P.G. Papers, ser. B., 14:95; Henry Barclay to Sec., Dec. 2, 1746, S.P.G. Papers, ser. B., 14:95 (RH).

84. Kemp, *Support of Schools*, 101–4, 114, 103; spelling books (in 1747) (ibid., 104, n. 174).

85. Kemp, *Support of Schools*, 109–10, quots. 109; Samuel Auchmuty to Sec., Dec. 30, 1749, S.P.G. Papers, ser. B, 17:116 (RH). For the role of the vestry in the affairs of the church, see Mary Sudman Donovan, "Shaping a Vision of Urban Ministry: The Role of the Colonial Vestry of Trinity Church," unpublished paper in the possession of the author.

86. Joseph Hildreth to Sec., Dec. 22, 1761, S.P.G. Papers, ser. B, 3:153 (RH); Hildreth to Sec., May 11, 1762, S.P.G. Papers, ser. B, 3:155 (RH); Hildreth to Sec., Apr. 27, 1763, S.P.G. Papers, ser. B, 3:156 (RH); Hildreth to Sec., May 29, 1764, S.P.G. Papers, ser. B, 3:157 (RH). The reading taught to the girls by the schoolmistress is implied in Hildreth to Sec., Dec. 22, 1761, S.P.G. Papers, ser. B, 3:153 (RH), but not mentioned directly until Hildreth to Sec., May 29, 1764, S.P.G. Papers, ser. B, 3:157 (RH). It was undoubtedly taught by her from the first, however, as was the fact that she taught spelling, mentioned only in Hildreth to Sec., Sept. 29, 1766, S.P.G. Papers, ser. B, 3:159 (RH).

87. Rev. Richard Charlton to Sec., July 14, 1745, S.P.G. Papers, ser. B, 14:115 (RH); Samuel Auchmuty to Sec., Mar. 30, 1748, S.P.G. Papers, ser. B, 15:80 (RH).

88. Joseph Hildreth to Sec., Apr. 27, 1765, S.P.G. Papers, ser. B, 3:158 (RH).

89. Trinity Vestry Minutes, 1:245, Aug. 10, 1747, quoted in Kemp, *Support of Schools*, 104 n. 174.

90. Joseph Hildreth to Sec., Oct. 18, 1769, S.P.G. Papers, ser. B, 3:164 (RH).

91. Joseph Hildreth to Sec., Oct. 16, 1770, S.P.G. Papers, ser. B, 3:165 (RH); Hildreth to Sec., Nov. 7, 1773, S.P.G. Papers, ser. B, 3:169 (RH).

92. Joseph Hildreth to Sec., Oct. 18, 1768, S.P.G. Papers, ser. B, 3:163 (RH).

93. Kemp's chart shows that no nonconformist children were listed by Hildreth from 1764 on (*Support of Schools*, 106); three children were dismissed for poor attendance. Joseph Hildreth to Sec., Oct. 18, 1768, S.P.G. Papers, ser. B, 3:163 (RH).

94. Kemp, *Support of Schools*, 106; see also Joseph Hildreth to Sec., in S.P.G. Papers, ser. B (RH), for the following dates: May 29, 1764, 3:157; Oct. 20, 1767, 3:162; Oct. 18, 1768, 3:163; Oct. 18, 1769, 3:164; Oct. 16, 1770, 3:165; Oct. 16, 1771, 3:167; Nov. 7, 1773, 3:169; Dec. 30, 1775, 3:170; quot., n.d. [1772], 3:168.

95. John Johnston, certificate, July 21, 1715, S.P.G. Papers, ser. A, 10:265 (RH); John Johnston, Mayor of New York, to Sec., Sept. 14, 1716, S.P.G. Papers, ser. A, 12:403 (RH), and Aug. 15, 1717, S.P.G. Papers, ser. A, 12:408–10 (RH). Ratio in 1719: nine girls to forty-two boys; in 1721: fifteen girls to thirty-three boys; in 1722: fourteen girls to thirty-two boys. Kemp, *Support of Schools*, 88 n. 58.

96. Lists, S.P.G. Papers, ser. A, 12:403, 409–10 (RH).

97. The figures are tabulated in Kemp, *Support of Schools*, 106; Joseph Hildreth to Sec., May 27, 1764, S.P.G. Papers, ser. B, 3:157 (RH).

Chapter 6. Literacy and the Mohawks

1. *The Book of Common Prayer, and Administration of the Sacraments . . . Formerly Collected, and Translated into the Mohawk Language under the direction of the Missionaries of the Society for the Propagation of the Gospel in Foreign Parts, to the Mohawk Indians. A New Edition: to which is added the Gospel according to St. Mark, Translated into the Mohawk Language, by Captn. Joseph Brant, An Indian of the Mohawk Nation* (London: C. Buckton, 1787), frontispiece. The Mohawk name of Brant is spelled T'hayendanegea on the frontispiece, but Tayendanegea on p. 177. I presume that the former is more correct. For the life of Joseph Brant, see Isabel Thompson Kelsay, *Joseph Brant, 1743–1807, Man of Two Worlds* (Syracuse, N.Y.: Syracuse University Press, 1984).

2. Jean Fittz Hankins, "Bringing the Good News: Protestant Missionaries to the Indians of New England and New York, 1700–1775" (Ph.D. diss., University of Connecticut, 1993), 171, n.17, 543–55.

3. Another Indian imprint not in the Massachusett language was the product of the Moravians, who carried out missions to the Mahican and Delaware Indians beginning in 1765, first on the banks of the upper Susquehanna and soon, as the Indians were pushed west by white encroachment, along the Allegheny and Muskingum rivers of Ohio. See Amy C. Schutt, " 'What will become of our young people?': Goals for Indian Children in Moravian Missions," *History of Education Quarterly* 38 (1998): 268–86. The German-speaking Moravian David Zeisberger (1721–1808) prepared a spelling book in 1776, bilingual in the Delaware language and English, and later translated some hymns into Delaware. Zeisberger, *Essay of a Delaware-Indian and English Spelling-Book, for the Use of the Schools of the Christian Indians on Muskingum river* (Philadelphia: Henry Miller, 1776); *Early American Imprints. Series I, Evans (1639–1800)* [electronic resource], ([New Canaan, Conn.]: Readex; [Worcester, Mass.]: American Antiquarian Society, [2002–]) (hereafter cited as Evans), #15228; Zeisberger, *A Collection of Hymns, for the Use of the Christian Indians, of the Missions of the United Brethren, in North America* (Philadelphia: Henry Sweitzer, 1803). See Earl P. Olmstead, *David Zeisberger: A Life among the Indians* (Kent, Ohio: Kent State University Press, 1997).

4. For cultural brokers, see Szasz, *Indian Education in the American Colonies, 1607–1783* (Albuquerque: University of New Mexico Press, 1988), 171, 263.

5. William Bryan Hart, "For the Good of Our Souls: Mohawk Authority, Accommodation, and Resistance to Protestant Evangelism, 1700–1780" (Ph.D. diss., Brown University, 1998), 94–99.

6. Daniel K. Richter, *The Ordeal of the Longhouse: The Peoples of the Iroquois League in the Era of European Colonization* (Chapel Hill, N.C.: Institute of Early American History and Culture, 1992), 134–38.

7. Hart, "For the Good of Our Souls," 32.

8. Richter, *Ordeal of the Longhouse*, 211–12; John Wolfe Lydekker, *The Faithful Mohawks* (1938; repr., Port Washington, N.Y.: Ira J. Friedman, 1968), 11. Lydekker quotes extensively from the manuscripts in the archives of the S.P.G., all of which are now housed at Rhodes House, Oxford, U.K. (RH). (All quotations by Lydekker are therefore RH but not indicated as such.) My quotations are either from the handwritten transcripts housed at the Library of Congress (LC) or from the original manuscripts at Rhodes House (RH). (See Chapter 5, note 4, for an explanation of the depositories for S.P.G. Papers.) H. P. Thompson, *Into All Lands: The History of the Society for the Propagation of the Gospel in Foreign Parts, 1701–1950* (London: S.P.C.K., 1951), 76.

9. Lydekker, *Faithful Mohawks*, 16–17.

10. Thorogood Moor to Sec., Nov. 13, 1705, S.P.G. Papers, ser. A, 2:122, quoted in Lydekker, *Faithful Mohawks*, 21–23, quot. 22; Richter, *Ordeal of the Longhouse*, 222. See Hart,

"For the Good of Our Souls," 136–49 (a fuller description of Moor's mission and the mistakes he made), 49–68 (details of Catholic conversion efforts among the Mohawks), 68–75 (Protestant efforts).

11. Lydekker, *Faithful Mohawks*, 24.

12. Richter, *Ordeal of the Longhouse*, 222–23. For Freeman, see Hart, "For the Good of Our Souls," 125–28. The entry in Charles Evans, *American Bibliography*, 14 vols. (1903; repr., New York: Peter Smith, 1941–59), #1740, states, "The translation by Lawrence Claesse[n], was based on the translation in manuscript of Rev. Bernardus Freeman, which had been placed freely in the hands of the Rev. William Andrews by the Propagation Society for this use." For pronunciation, see *Book of Common Prayer, and Administration of the Sacraments*, [506], "They pronounce a broad, like the Scots and Germans; e as we pronounce a, and i like our ee."

13. Richter, *Ordeal of the Longhouse*, 226–27. Although Cornbury's successor, John, Lord Lovelace, died not long after he arrived in New York, Cornbury's designs for the "Glorious Enterprise" were carried out (ibid., 225).

14. Lydekker, *Faithful Mohawks*, 25–28, 30; Richter, *Ordeal of the Longhouse*, 227, 367–68 n. 29. See Richmond Pugh Bond, *Queen Anne's American Kings* (Oxford: Clarendon Press, 1952). For the relationships between the two Brants, see the family tree in Lydekker, *Faithful Mohawks*, 196–97.

15. Lydekker, *Faithful Mohawks*, 30–32; Thompson, *Into All Lands*, 78–79; Indian Sachems to S.P.G., enclosed with Archbishop's of Apr. 20, 1710, S.P.G. Papers, ser. A, 5:88 (LC). The letter is reproduced as plate III in Lydekker, *Faithful Mohawks*, facing p. 30.

16. Lydekker, *Faithful Mohawks*, 28–33; Thompson, *Into All Lands*, 79–80. A photograph of Queen Anne's communion plate is reproduced as plate IV in Lydekker, *Faithful Mohawks*, facing p. 31.

17. Lydekker, *Faithful Mohawks*, 34, 40. Conajoharie is spelled differently nearly every time it occurs in the manuscripts. For thirty-eight miles, see John Ogilvie to Sec., July 27, 1750, S.P.G. Papers, ser. B, 18:102 (RH), quoted in Lydekker, *Faithful Mohawks*, 67.

18. William Andrews to Sec., Sept. 7, 1713, S.P.G. Papers, ser. A, 8:184, quoted in Lydekker, *Faithful Mohawks*, 39, and Thompson, *Into All Lands*, 80.

19. Lydekker, *Faithful Mohawks*, 34, 41, 42; Thompson, *Into All Lands*, 80; William Andrews to Sec., Oct. 17, 1714, S.P.G. Papers, ser. A, 10:158–60, quots. 159 (RH); Lydekker, *Faithful Mohawks*, 45. Lawrence Claessen is also spelled Laurence Claesse or Cláese.

20. William Andrews to Sec., Nov. 23, 1713, S.P.G. Papers, ser. B, 1:153 (RH).

21. William Andrews to Sec., Sept. 7, 1713, S.P.G. Papers, ser. A, 8:184, quoted in Lydekker, *Faithful Mohawks*, 39–40.

22. Lydekker, *Faithful Mohawks*, 40; cf. William Andrews to Sec., Nov. 23, 1713, S.P.G. Papers, ser. B, 1:153 (RH). The "Liturgy" in Lydekker, *Faithful Mohawks*, 40, is presumably Andrews's error for "Litany."

23. *The Morning and Evening Prayer, the Litany, Church Catechism, Family Prayers, and Several Chapters of the Old and New-Testament, Translated into the Mahaque Indian Language, by Lawrence Claesse, interpreter to William Andrews, Missionary to the Indians, from the Honourable and Reverend the Society for the Propogation* [sic] *of the Gospel in Foreign Parts . . .* (New York: Printed by William Bradford, 1715) (Evans #1740).

24. Ibid. The Old and New Testament chapters take up pp. 41–58 (16 percent) and the scriptural sentences pp. 59–88 (another 24 percent) of the total 115 pages; quot. on "procured," *Book of Common Prayer . . . Translated into the Mohawk Language* (1787), [i], which cites this version as one of the two earlier editions.

25. William Andrews to Sec., July 12, 1715, S.P.G. Papers, ser. A, 10:185–86 (RH); "Invoyce of Goods sent Mr Andrews," London June 20, 1714, S.P.G. Papers, ser. A, 9:72 (RH).

26. William Andrews to Sec., July 12, 1715, S.P.G., ser. A, 10:185–86 (RH); Lydekker, *Faithful Mohawks*, 46, 51 (dismissal of Oliver). For Andrews's teaching of Christian doctrine, see Hankins, "Bringing the Good News," 256–57.

27. William Andrews to Sec., July 12, 1715, S.P.G. Papers, ser. A, 10:186 (RH).

28. William Andrews to Sec., Oct. 17, 1714, S.P.G. Papers, ser. A, 10:155–56, quoted in Lydekker, *Faithful Mohawks*, 43–44. For the "feminization" of the Anglican mission, see Hart, "For the Good of Our Souls," 188-95.

29. Lydekker, *Faithful Mohawks*, 50.

30. William Andrews to Sec., July 12, 1715, S.P.G. Papers, ser. A, 10:186, and Apr. 20, 1716, S.P.G. Papers, ser. A, 11:322, quoted in Lydekker, *Faithful Mohawks*, 46–47, 50. For the Tuscarora and Yamasee uprisings, see J. Leitch Wright Jr., *The Only Land They Knew: The Tragic Story of the American Indians in the Old South* (New York: Free Press, 1981), 117–25.

31. William Andrews to Sec., Oct 17, 1715, S.P.G. Papers, ser. A, 11:270–71 (RH); Lydekker, *Faithful Mohawks*, 48–49.

32. William Andrews to Sec., Apr. 20, 1716, S.P.G. Papers, ser. A, 11:317–19, 323 (RH).

33. William Andrews to Sec., Apr. 23, 1717, S.P.G. Papers, ser. A, 12:310 (RH); Lydekker, *Faithful Mohawks*, 51. For a fuller account of Andrews' mission, see Hart, "For the Good of Our Souls," 176–88.

34. Lydekker, *Faithful Mohawks*, 51.

35. For evaluations by historians on the apparent failure of the mission, see Hart, "For the Good of Our Souls," 155–58, 179–80.

36. Lydekker, *Faithful Mohawks*, 52–53.

37. Henry Barclay to John Sergeant, June 11, 1736, quoted in Samuel Hopkins, *Historical Memoirs, Relating to the Hoosatannuk Indians . . .* (Boston: S. Kneeland, 1753), 67–68. Sergeant was employed by the New England Company as their Congregationalist minister to the Housatonick Indians (Hankins, "Bringing the Good News," 66). For Sergeant, see Hilary E. Wyss, *Writing Indians: Literacy, Christianity, and Native Community in Early America* (Amherst: University of Massachusetts Press, 2000), 81–105.

38. Henry Barclay to Sec., Aug. 31, 1736, S.P.G. Papers, ser. A, 26:283 (RH); Lydekker, *Faithful Mohawks*, 54.

39. Henry Barclay to Sec., Oct. 15, 1740, S.P.G. Papers, ser. B, 7:141 (RH); Lydekker, *Faithful Mohawks*, 54–55; John Barclay to John Sergeant, Aug. 21, 1740, as quoted in Hopkins, *Historical Memoirs*, 67.

40. Henry Barclay to Sec., Nov. 9, 1741, S.P.G. Papers, ser. B, 9:81; names of schoolmasters: Barclay to Sec., Nov. 17, 1742, S.P.G. Papers, ser. B, 10:112, and Dec. 7, 1741, S.P.G. Papers, ser. B, 9:83 (all RH).

41. Henry Barclay to Sec., Nov. 9, 1741, S.P.G. Papers, ser. B, 9:81 (RH); Lydekker, *Faithful Mohawks*, 55. Barclay consistently calls the Lower and Upper Castles Lower and Upper Towns.

42. Henry Barclay to Sec., Nov. 17, 1742, ser. B, 10:112 (RH).

43. Philip Bearcroft to Henry Barclay, June 14, 1743, S.P.G. Papers, ser. B, 10:196 (RH).

44. Henry Barclay to Sec., May 31, 1743, S.P.G. Papers, ser. B, 11:153 (RH).

45. Henry Barclay to Sec., Nov. 4, 1743, S.P.G. Papers, ser. B, 11:155; June 20, 1743, S.P.G. Papers, ser. B, 11:154; Nov. 4, 1743, S.P.G. Papers, ser. B, 11:155; June 4, 1744, S.P.G. Papers, ser. B, 13:313 (all RH).

46. Henry Barclay to Sec., Mar. 12, 1744/45, S.P.G. Papers, ser. B, 13:314 (RH); Lydekker, *Faithful Mohawks*, 56–57.

47. Henry Barclay to Sec., Oct 21, 1745, S.P.G. Papers, ser. B, 13:316 (RH), and Dec. 2, 1746, S.P.G. Papers, ser. B, 14:95 (RH); Lydekker, *Faithful Mohawks*, 59–60. Barclay continued to hold onto Indian property even after he left the Mohawks: for the dispute over land given by the Mohawks for his use only as long as he was their missionary, see Hankins, "Bringing the Good News," 404–5.

48. Henry Barclay to Sec., Dec. 2, 1746, S.P.G. Papers, ser. B, 14:95 (RH); Lydekker, *Faithful Mohawks*, 58–59.

49. Henry Barclay to Sec., Dec. 2, 1746, S.P.G. Papers, ser. B, 14:95 (RH).

50. John Ogilvie to Sec., July 27, 1750, S.P.G. Papers, ser. B, 18:102 (RH); Lydekker, *Faithful Mohawks*, 64–68, quot. 66.

51. John Ogilvie to Sec., July 27, 1750, S.P.G. Papers, ser. B, 18:102 (RH); Lydekker, *Faithful Mohawks*, 67.

52. John Ogilvie to Sec., July 27, 1750, S.P.G. Papers, ser. B, 18:102 (RH).

53. Ibid., 104, quoted in Lydekker, *Faithful Mohawks*, 67.

54. Ibid.; Henry Barclay to Sec., Apr. 29, 1751. S.P.G. Papers, ser. B, 19:65 (RH). The S.P.G. gave Abraham a "present."

55. William Johnson to George Clinton, Sept. 20, 1749, in *The Papers of Sir William Johnson*, 14 vols. (Albany: University of the State of New York, 1921–62), 9:53 (hereafter *Johnson Papers*). In this source, Clinton's extract of Johnson's letter, Paulus is identified as Abraham's son. However, both Barclay and Ogilvie denied that Abraham had a living son, and Hendrick did indeed have a son named Paulus (although not, it seems, Petrus Paulus). I am arbitrarily assuming that they are one and the same person, and that the error crept in through Clinton's extract. For the confusion over whose son Paulus was, see Lydekker, *Faithful Mohawks*, 69 n. 4.

56. John Ogilvie to Sec., Aug. 7, 1751, S.P.G. Papers, ser. B, 19:72 (RH); Lydekker, *Faithful Mohawks*, 69, 74. For Oel and the name of the Lower Castle, see ibid., 63–64, 68.

57. John Ogilvie to Sec., June 29, 1752, S.P.G. Papers, ser. B, 20:55; Lydekker, *Faithful Mohawks*, 72–73 (Ogilvie's marriage). See also Hart, "For the Good of Our Souls," 188–95.

58. Lydekker, *Faithful Mohawks*, 76–81.

59. John Ogilvie to Sec., Dec. 25, 1755, summarized in S.P.G. *Journal*, 13:182–85, quoted in Lydekker, *Faithful Mohawks*, 83.

60. Lydekker, *Faithful Mohawks*, 86–91.

61. Ibid., 98–106.

62. Lyddeker, *Faithful Mohawks*, 117. Another view is that work among the Indians *was* part of his job description, and he was appointed as such in 1764, but neither the Indians nor the local Presbyterians accepted him as an appropriate Indian missionary. Hankins, "Bringing the Good News," 355; Frank J. Klingberg, *Anglican Humanitarianism in Colonial New York* (Philadelphia: Church Historical Society, 1940), 83.

63. Daniel Claus to Sir William Johnson, Mar. 19, 1761, May 1, 1761, Feb. 16, 1762, in *Johnson Papers*, 3:363, 10:264, 3:369, respectively; Sir William Johnson to Daniel Claus, Nov. 22, 1761, Feb. 9, 1762, in *Johnson Papers*, 10:333, 3:630. For a chronology of Daniel Claus's life, see *Johnson Papers*, 10:ix–xiv.

64. Henry Barclay to Sir William Johnson, Oct. 5, 1763, in *Johnson Papers*, 13:300; Sir William Johnson to Henry Barclay, Nov. 24, 1763, in *Johnson Papers*, 10:935–36; *The Morning and Evening Prayer, the Litany, and Church Catechism . . .* (Boston: Richard and Samuel Draper, 1763). Despite a request that his name be included, Johnson is not acknowledged, nor is anyone else (Sir William Johnson to Henry Barclay, Nov. 24, 1763, in *Johnson Papers*, 10:935–36).

65. Sir William Johnson to Daniel Burton, Sec., S.P.G., Dec. 6, 1769, in *Johnson Papers*, 7:290; cf. Sec. to Sir William Johnson, Dec. 2, 1767, and May 8, 1769, in *Johnson Papers*, 5:847 and 6:747, respectively. See Colin McLelland's receipt for £25 "in full for a years Service as Indian Schoolmaster to the Mohawks" from Apr. 17, 1769 to Apr. 17, 1770, in *Johnson Papers*, 7:574. The expense of £127-16-0 is noted for Sept 2 [1769], in Johnson's expenses in *Johnson Papers*, 12:762: "near 500 Indian Prayer Books, a Bible &c." For gilt lettering, see James T. Flexner, *Lord of the Mohawks: A Biography of Sir William Johnson* (1959; repr., Boston: Little Brown, 1979), 291.

66. *The Order For Morning and Evening Prayer, and Administration of the Sacraments, and Some Other Offices of the Church, Together with A Collection of Prayers, and some Sentences of the Holy Scriptures necessary for Knowledge Practice . . . Collected, and Translated into the Mohawk Language under the Direction of the Late Rev. Mr. William Andrews, the Late Rev. Dr. Henry Barclay, and the Rev. Mr. John Ogilvie* ([New York]: printed [by William Wyman and Hugh Gaine], 1769. The new material is on pp. 157–96: 157 (communion); 177 (baptism); 186 (matrimony); 191 (burial). Gaine took over as printer when Wyman died (Lydekker, *Faithful Mohawks*, 182).

67. For details, see Szasz, *Indian Education*, chap. 10, esp. 236; quots., 249.

68. Hart, "For the Good of Our Souls," 254–67.

69. Lydekker, *Faithful Mohawks*, 111, 121; Harry Munro to Sec., Sept. 25, 1770, S.P.G. Papers, ser. B, 3:271, quoted in Lydekker, *Faithful Mohawks*, 128.

70. Lydekker, *Faithful Mohawks*, 121–29, 196–97 (Little Abraham's sister married Nickus Brant, son the Brant who went to England in 1710). For Inglis, see Hart, "For the Good of Our Souls," 292–95. Rev. Charles Ingliss's remarks on Stuart are quoted in Thompson, *Into All Lands*, 83, and Lydekker, *Faithful Mohawks*, 121, n. 3. See John W. Lydekker, "The Rev. John Stuart, D.D., (1740–1811). Missionary to the Mohawks," *Historical Magazine of the Protestant Episcopal Church* 11 (1942): 18–64.

71. John Stuart to Sec., Jan. 30, 1771, S.P.G. Papers, ser. B, 2:196; Jan. 8, 1772, S.P.G. Papers, ser. B, 2:198; June 22, 1772, S.P.G. Papers, ser. B, 2:197 (all RH).

72. John Stuart to Sec., Jan. 8, 1772, S.P.G. Papers, ser. B, 2:198 (RH). The figure of 200 is in John Stuart to Sec., Aug. 9, 1774, S.P.G. Papers, ser. B, 2:201 (RH); Lydekker, *Faithful Mohawks*, 135.

73. John Stuart to Sec., July 20, 1772, S.P.G. Papers, ser. B, 2:199 (RH); Lydekker, *Faithful Mohawks*, 130–31.

74. Lydekker, *Faithful Mohawks*, 129–30; John Stuart to Sec., Jan. 30, 1771, S.P.G. Papers, ser. B, 2:196, and Jan. 8, 1772, S.P.G. Papers, ser. B, 2:198. Stuart says he provided "windows," but the chapel must have had windows earlier, so presumably he means glass. Sir William Johnson to Sec., Oct. 16, 1772, S.P.G. Papers, ser. B, 2:93 (RH).

75. John Stuart to Sec., Feb 13, 1774, S.P.G. Papers, ser. B, 2:200, and Aug. 9, 1774, S.P.G. Papers, ser. B, 2:201 (both in RH); Lydekker, *Faithful Mohawks*, 135–36.

76. John Stuart to Sec., Oct. 27, 1775, S.P.G. Papers, ser. B, 2:203 (RH).

77. Hart, "For the Good of Our Souls," 244.

78. Hart calls Old Abraham the "perhaps most pious" of the Mohawk catechists (ibid., 245).

79. Ibid., 246.

80. Szasz, *Indian Education*, 171, 263.

Prelude to Part II

1. Hugh Amory, "A Note on Statistics," in *A History of the Book in America*, ed. David D. Hall, vol.1, *The Colonial Book in the Atlantic World*, ed. Hugh Amory and David D. Hall ([Worcester, Mass.]: American Antiquarian Society; New York: Cambridge University Press, 2000), 506, 514; Jack P. Greene, *Pursuits of Happiness: The Social Development of Early Modern British Colonies and the Formation of American Culture* (Chapel Hill: University of North Carolina Press, 1988), 178–79. Greene's figures for the Atlantic Islands and the Caribbean have been deducted from his totals. For 1740 as a turning point in trans-Atlantic communication, see Charles E. Clark, *The Public Prints: The Newspaper in Anglo-American Culture, 1665–1740* (New York: Oxford University Press, 1994), and Ian K. Steele, *The English Atlantic, 1675–1740: An Exploration of Communication and Community* (New York: Oxford University Press, 1986).

2. Advts., *Boston Weekly News-Letter*, Aug. 13, 1741, May 12, 1747; Isaiah Thomas, *The History of Printing in America*, ed. Marcus A. McCorison from 2d ed. (New York, Weathervane Books, 1970), 568n; Timothy Cutler, letter, Dec. 30, 1752, in *The Great Awakening and American Education: A Documentary History*, ed. Douglas Sloan, 237–38 (New York: Teachers College Press, 1973).

3. Robert F. Seybolt, *The Private Schools of Colonial Boston* (Cambridge: Harvard University Press, 1935).

4. Ibid., 27, 32–33, 16.

5. Harlan Updegraff, *The Origin of the Moving School in Massachusetts* (New York: Columbia University, Teachers College, 1907). For an example of a moving school in the 1740s, see *Copy of the Old Records of the Town of Duxbury, Mass. from 1642 to 1770* (Plymouth, Mass.: Avery and Doten, 1893), 245–47, 269–70.

6. Thomas Bullock, "Schools and Schooling in Eighteenth Century Virginia" (Ed.D. diss., Duke University, 1961), quot. 128 (by Emanuel Jones, of Petsworth Parish, Gloucester County).

7. George Staughton, Benjamin M. Nead, and Thomas McCamant, eds., *Charter to William Penn, and Laws of the Province of Pennsylvania, Passed Between the Years 1682 and 1700* (Harris-

burg: Lane S. Hart, 1879), 142; quot. in Lawrence A. Cremin, *American Education: The Colonial Experience, 1607–1783* (New York: Harper & Row, 1970), 125.

8. Marion Dexter Learned, *The Life of Francis Daniel Pastorius* (Philadelphia: William J. Campbell, 1908), 175.

9. Carl Bridenbaugh, *Cities in the Wilderness: The First Century of Urban Life in America, 1625–1742* (1938; repr., London: Oxford University Press, 1971), 283–84. The Anglicans established Christ Church School in 1695. German Lutherans opened the German Reformed Church in the 1730s, and Roman Catholics and Presbyterians soon opened their own schools. For details, see Julia Nash Murphy, "Schools and Schooling in Eighteenth-Century Philadelphia" (Ph.D. diss., Bryn Mawr College, 1977).

10. Joan R. Soderlund, "Women's Authority in Pennsylvania and New Jersey Quaker Meetings, 1680–1760," *William and Mary Quarterly*, 3rd. ser., 44 (1987): 722–49.

Chapter 7. Schools, Schoolteachers, and Schoolchildren

1. Benjamin Franklin, *The Autobiography and Other Writings*, ed. and with an introduction by Kenneth Silverman (New York: Penguin Books, 1986), 9. For Samuel Mather's and Benjamin Franklin's attendance at Sarah Kemble Knight's school, see Alice Morse Earle, *Colonial Dames and Good Wives* (Boston: Houghton Mifflin, 1895), 139–42. Franklin's mother, Abiah, was the daughter of Peter Folger, schoolmaster to the Wampanoags on Martha's Vineyard.

2. Franklin, *Autobiography*, 8–9. Boston's second grammar school was opened in 1712.

3. Ibid., 13; Cotton Mather, *Bonifacius: An Essay upon the Good . . .* (Boston: Samuel Gerrish, 1710), *Early American Imprints. Series I, Evans (1639–1800)* [electronic resource], ([New Canaan, Conn.]: Readex; [Worcester, Mass.]: American Antiquarian Society, [2002–]) (hereafter cited as Evans), #1460. Franklin identifies this as "Essays to do Good" (*Autobiography*, 13).

4. Franklin, *Autobiography*, 13.

5. Ibid., 14–15.

6. Ibid., 14.

7. Ibid., 14–15; see below, Chapter 10, for writing instruction as penmanship.

8. Ibid., 15–16.

9. Ibid., 16–17. Michael Warner, *Letters of the Republic: Publication and the Public Sphere in Eighteenth-Century America* (Cambridge, Mass.: Harvard University Press, 1990), 78–80.

10. Franklin, *Autobiography*, 20–21.

11. [Benjamin Franklin], *Proposals Relating to the Education of Youth in Pensylvania* (Philadelphia: n.p., 1740) (Evans #6321), 11, 13–14, 16–18.

12. George Whitefield, *An Extract of the Preface to the Reverend Mr. Whitefield's Account of the Orphan-House in Georgia. Together with An Extract of some Letters sent him from the Superintendents of the Orphan-House, and from some of the Children* (Edinburgh, 1741), 13–16, quots. 13, 14. Barber's name, printed here as B * * * * r, is given in full in George Whitefield, *A Continuation of the Account of the Orphan-House in Georgia, from January 1740/1 to January 1742/3* (London, 1743) (see p. 23 for later accounts of weeping children); James Habersham, *A Letter from Mr. Habersham . . . to the Reverend Mr. Whitefield* (London: J. Lewis, 1744), 6.

13. Whitefield, *Extract of the Preface*, 21, 26; cf. Ezekiel 37.1–6.

14. Whitefield, *Extract of the Preface*, 22, 19–20, 18–19.

15. Ibid., 27.

16. Misspellings: ibid., 18 (tris), 22, 20 (tris), 21.

17. Warren M. Billings, John E. Selby, and Thad W. Tate, *Colonial Virginia: A History* (New York: KTO Press, 1986), 211–12.

18. Devereux Jarratt, *The Life of the Reverend Devereux Jarratt . . .* (Baltimore, 1806; repr., New York: Arno Press and New York Times, 1969), 12–14.

19. Ibid., 14. For a full interpretation of clothing in relation to social status, see Rhys Isaac, *The Transformation of Virginia, 1740–1790* (Chapel Hill, N.C.: Institute of Early American History and Culture, 1982), 43–44.

20. Jarratt, *Life*, 15–16.

21. Ibid., 18. For Jarratt and Chevy Chase, see Rhys Isaac, "Stories and Constructions of Self: Folk Tellings and Diary Inscriptions in Revolutionary Virginia," in *Through a Glass Darkly: Reflections on Personal Identity in Early America*, ed. Ronald Hoffman, Mechal Sobel, and Fredrika J. Teute (Chapel Hill: Omohundro Institute of Early American History and Culture, 1997), 212–13.

22. Jarratt, *Life*, 18–19.

23. Ibid., 16–20, quot. 19–20.

24. Ibid., 20, 24–25.

25. Ibid., 25.

26. Ibid., 26–27, 28. For "New Lights" and "old Lights," see above, p. 192.

27. Ibid., 29–31.

28. Ibid., 31, 33.

29. Ibid., 33–34. John Flavel (1628?–1691), an Englishman, was ordained as a Presbyterian minister in 1650. He was the author of numerous printed works, many of them his sermons.

30. Jarratt, *Life*, 34–36, quots. 34.

31. Ibid., 38–39.

32. Ibid. 39–40. The sermons of Robert Russel, of Wadhurst, Sussex, England, were first published in London in the early 1690s. Russel's *Seven Sermons on Different Important Subjects* was soon reprinted in the colonies and became a steady seller. The earliest documented American edition is a fourth in Boston in 1701 (Evans #1021). By 1766, William Dunlap was selling a fifty-second edition in Philadelphia (#10485). In Virginia, imported copies were advertised in the *Virginia Gazette* from the late 1760s; e.g., *Virginia Gazette*, Purdie & Dixon, Feb. 25, 1768, in John E. Molnar, "Publication and Retail Book Advertisements in the *Virginia Gazette*, 1736–1780" (Ph.D. diss., University of Michigan, 1978), 734. Imported copies were occasionally advertised elsewhere (e.g., in *New-York Mercury*, Nov. 13, 1752, May 13, 1754).

33. Jarratt read an imported copy of William Burkitt's [spelled Burkett by Jarratt], *Expository Notes, With Practical Observations, on the New Testament of Our Lord and Saviour Jesus Christ* . . . , which was first published in London in 1724; Isaac, *Transformation of Virginia*, 378, n. 19. The first American edition was Burkitt, *Expository Notes* . . . (New York: T. Dunning and W. W. Hyer, 1796) (Evans #30085).

34. Jarratt, *Life*, 40–41.

35. Ibid., 42–45, 53, 59, quot. 25.

36. Martin G. Brumbaugh, *The Life and Works of Christopher Dock: America's Pioneer Writer on Education* (Philadelphia: Lippincott, 1908), 12–14, 20, 102. For the Mennonites, see J. C. Wenger, *The Mennonite Church in America, Sometimes Called the Old Mennonites* (Scottsdale, Pa.: Herald Press, 1966).

37. Brumbaugh, *Life and Works*, 14–16, 94–95; Christoph Dock, *Schul-Ordnung* (Germantown: Christoph Saur, 1770), translated and reprinted in English in Brumbaugh, *Life and Works*, 87–156 (hereafter all cites to Dock, *School-Management* are to the translation in Brumbaugh, *Life and Works*). In *Life and Works* Brumbaugh has provided translations of all Dock's known publications. For the elder Christopher Saur, see Anna Kathryn Oller, "Christopher Saur: Colonial Printer: A Study of the Publications of Press, 1738–1758" (Ph.D. diss, University of Michigan, 1963). Saur's output included an ABC (p. 302) but no spelling books.

38. I am indebted to Joachim, Renate, and Anya Henke for this explanation of "0," which is not the letter but the numeral. This marker of zero mistakes is still used by teachers in Germany today.

39. Dock, *School-Management*, 111 ("piecemeal"), 110 (blackboard), 106 (crayon), 105 (slate), 109 (wooden tag), 105 (coeducation), 105 (scriptures), 108 (speller). Children apparently also took slates to church (Dock, *Spiritual Magazine* no. 40, translated and reprinted in Brumbaugh, *Life and Works*, 211).

40. Brumbaugh, *Life and Works*, 19; Dock, *School-Management*, 124.

41. Dock, *School-Management*, 104, 105, 107.

42. Ibid., 105.

43. Ibid., 107.

44. Ibid., 108.

45. Ibid., 110–11.

46. Ibid., 132–33, quots. 137, 133.

47. Brumbaugh, *Life and Works*, 21–22. Some *Schriften* are reproduced and translated in ibid., 239–53, but scholars debate whether they are indeed by Dock.

48. Dock, *School-Management*, 111.

49. Brumbaugh, *Life and Works*, 191–237 (Evans #9676).

50. Christopher Dock, "A Hundred Necessary Rules of Conduct for Children," *Spiritual Magazine* no. 40, in Brumbaugh, *Life and Works*, 208–9.

51. The spelling books were presumably imported copies, since the elder Christopher Saur did not print any spellers.

Chapter 8. The Rise of the Spelling Book

1. These figures have been reordered by date and calculated from the texts listed in Ian Michael, *The Teaching of English from the Sixteenth Century to 1870* (New York: Cambridge University Press, 1987). See also Michael's graph of spelling and elementary reading texts, tabulated at five-year intervals (10). For editions of Edmund Coote, see William R. Hart, "*The English Schoole-Maister* (1596) by Coote: An Edition of the Text with Critical Notes and Introductions" (Ph.D. diss., University of Michigan, 1963), 8.

2. Isaac Watts, *The Art of Reading and Writing English, 1721* (1721; repr., Menston. Eng.: Scolar Press, 1972), 26. This book seems never to have been reprinted in America, but imported copies were occasionally advertised (e.g., *South Carolina Gazette*, Aug. 10, 1752).

3. *The Youth's Instructor in the English Tongue: Or, The Art of Spelling Improved . . . In Three Parts . . . Collected from Dixon, Bailey, Owen, Strong and Watts* (Boston: J. Green & J. Russell, for D. Henchman, 1757) (hereafter cited as Dixon et al., *Youth's Instructor*), 97, Early American Imprints. Series I, Evans (1639–1800) [electronic resource], ([New Canaan, Conn.]: Readex; [Worcester, Mass.]: American Antiquarian Society, [2002–]) (hereafter cited as Evans), #7884. Earlier authors did not always use cumulative spelling: "In this order then let him spell it, saying: m,a,ma:n,i,ni:f,o,l,d,fold,manifold." Francis Clement, *The Petie Schole with an English Orthographie* (London: Thomas Vautrollier, 1587), 14, in *Four Tudor Books on Education, Facsimile Reproduction* by Robert D. Pepper (Gainesville, Fla.: Scholars' Facsimiles and Reprints, 1966), 62 (spacing as printed). For a fuller discussion of kinds of spelling, see Michael, *Teaching of English*, 90–96.

4. T. Goodman, *The Experienc'd Secretary: or, Citizen and Countryman's Companion* (Boston, 1708), 3–33, 45–48, 49–56. Evans #1354 misidentifies the work as *The Young Secretary's Guide* by John Hill.

5. Thomas [*sic*] Hill, *The Young Secretary's Guide: Or, A speedy help to Learning. In Two Parts* (Boston: Printed by B. Green for Nicolas Butteph, 1707) (Evans #39448). John Hill wrote the first edition in London in 1687. Konstantin Dierks, "Letter Writing, Gender, and Class in America, 1750–1800" (Ph.D. diss., Brown University, 1999), 45–46.

6. *The Young Man's Companion* (New York: William and Andrew Bradford, 1710) (Evans #39517), contents, 5, 45, 12–31; *The Young Man's Companion* (Philadelphia: Andrew Bradford, 1718) (#39697), 5, 11, 6; Dierks, "Letter Writing," 46.

7. *The Secretary's Guide, Or Young Man's Companion. In Four Parts . . . To which is added, The Family Companion* (Philadelphia: Andrew Bradford, 1737) (Evans #4127), title page, 14 (italics reversed).

8. George Fisher, *The American Instructor: Or, Young Man's Best Companion . . . To which is added, The Poor Planters Physician*, 9th ed., revised and corrected (Philadelphia: B. Franklin & D. Hall, 1748) (Evans #6238), title page, v (italics reversed).

9. Ibid., 12.

10. Gaine included the *Poor Planter's Physician* and another book: George Fisher, *The American Instructor; or, Young Man's Best Companion . . . To which is added, The Poor Planter's Physician . . . and also Prudent Advice to young Tradesmen and Dealers*, 12th ed., revised and corrected

(New York: H. Gaine, 1760) (Evans #8736). Gaine also issued later editions, including one in 1766 (Evans #10495) (no copy extant). For other editions of Fisher, *American Instructor*, see Evans #7120 (1753), #11859 (1770), #14458 (1775).

11. Watts, *Art of Reading*, 48–49. For a useful discussion of Watts's works on reading, see Norman A. Stahl's review of *Isaac Watts, Improvement of the Mind*, edited and abridged by Stephen B. Halfant and J. David Coecoli, in *Reading Research and Instruction* 29 (1990): 99–102.

12. Thomas Dilworth, *A New Guide to the English Tongue* (Philadelphia: B. Franklin, 1747), v. The preface is dated 1740. Cf. Joseph Aickin, 1693, "Letters compose Syllables: Syllables, words: words, Sentences: and Sentences make Orations or Books. Wherefore you must first learn the Letters" (quoted in Michael, *Teaching of English*, 72). For theories of pronunciation and orthography in spelling books, see E. Jennifer Monaghan, *A Common Heritage: Noah Webster's Blue-Back Speller* (Hamden, Conn.: Archon Books, 1983), chap. 6. The phoneme is the smallest phonetic difference in speech that also signals a difference in meaning.

13. Michael, *Teaching of English*, 50, 25–27, 53 (after 1800 the proportion of spellers discussing "sounds" dropped still further), 54, 77–89. For a discussion of the naming of letters with a consonant-vowel (CV) pattern as in *b* ("bee"), or a vowel-consonant (VC) pattern as in *f* ("eff"), see ibid., 41–48.

14. For the importance of the syllable as the "central feature" in both reading and writing, the link between letters and words/words and letters, see ibid., 72–75.

15. The terms *short* and *long*: Clement, *Petie Schole*, 25, in Pepper, *Four Tudor Books*, 71; Coote, *English Schoole-Maister*, 15, in Hart, "*English Schoole-Maister*," 147; Watts, *Art of Reading*, 12–13. See also Richard Mulcaster, *Mulcaster's Elementarie*, edited and with an introduction by E. T. Campagnac (Oxford: Clarendon Press, 1925), who distinguishes between a "loud and sharp" vowel and a "flat and short" one; and Nathaniel Strong, "True / *E* at the end must written be, from whence / Words are made long, and so preserve their sense." Nathaniel Strong, *England's Perfect School-Master: or, Directions for exact Spelling, Reading and Writing*, 3rd ed. (London: Benjamin Billingsley, 1681), 13–14. For rules in Coote, see *English Schoole-Maister*, 13–32, in Hart, "*English Schoole-Maister*," 145–64. For an introduction to the evolution of the so-called short and long vowels and their written representation, see Miriam Balmuth, *The Roots of Phonics: A Historical Introduction* (New York: McGraw-Hill, 1982), 83–84, 101–6, and, for Coote's indebtedness to Mulcaster, 126. For a caution, see Richard L. Venezky, *The Structure of English Orthography* (The Hague: Mouton, 1970), 14n: "The terms LONG and SHORT as applied . . . to English vowel sounds are neither historically accurate nor mnemonically useful."

16. Examples are taken from Dixon et al., *Youth's Instructor*, 23, 32, 21, 27.

17. Thomas Dyche, *A Guide to the English Tongue, 1707*, ed. R. C. Alston (Menston, Eng.: The Scolar Press, 1968), editor's note, n.p. Dyche authored a Latin vocabulary (1709), *The Youth's Guide to the Latin Tongue* (1716), a *Spelling Dictionary* (1723), and *A New General English Dictionary* (1735). For the pronunciation of Dyche's name, see Michael, *Teaching of English*, 441. Charles Ackers: John Feather, *The Provincial Book Trade in Eighteenth-Century England* (Cambridge: Cambridge University Press, 1985), 34.

18. Dyche, *Guide*, 1–12; Michael, *Teaching of English*, 101.

19. Dyche, *Guide*, preface; quots. in Michael, *Teaching of Reading*, 101.

20. Michael, *Teaching of English*, 104; Dyche, *Guide*, preface, 88. Dyche does not use the terms *long* and *short vowels* but claims instead that, as Michael puts it, "the stressed vowel attracted to itself the following consonant" (*Teaching of English*, 83; see also 82–84, for a discussion of various resolutions of the rule conflicts).

21. Dyche, *Guide*, 48.

22. Gaine's edition (1753) is known only from an advertisement (Evans #6995); the other edition was advertised as "In press" in the *North Carolina Gazette*, Nov. 7, 1778 (#15783). Ed. Davies to Sec., Nov. 6, 1733, Society for the Propagation of the Gospel Papers, ser. B, 1:9 (Rhodes House, Oxford, U.K.). Dyche's *Guide to the English Tongue* is advertised alongside Cocker's *Arithmetick*, psalters, and history books in the *South Carolina Gazette*, June 23, 1735. Hennig Cohen, *The South Carolina Gazette, 1732–1775* (Columbia: University of South Car-

olina Press, 1953), 128. Fifteen later advertisements specifying Dyche's speller appeared in the *South Carolina Gazette* on Dec. 15, 1739, Oct. 18, 1746, May 11, 1747, Feb 19, 1750, Aug. 20, 1750, Nov. 5, 1753, July 1, 1756, Aug. 25, 1757, Dec. 8, 1759, Dec. 29, 1759, May 16, 1761, Oct. 1, 1764 (bis), June 22, 1765, June 22, 1767, July 20, 1767, in Cohen, *South Carolina Gazette*, 131, 133 (bis), 135 (bis), 138, 141, 143, 144 (tris), 149 (bis), 150 (tris). Two advertisements for Dyche's speller appear in the *Virginia Gazette* (Purdie & Dixon), Feb. 25, 1764, June 10, 1773, in John E. Molnar, "Publication and Retail Book Advertisements in the *Virginia Gazette*, 1736–1780" (Ph.D. diss., University of Michigan, 1978), 477. (Molnar incorrectly identifies the advertisement for "Dyche. Spelling book" as "Dyche's Spelling Dictionary.") It was advertised in the *Pennsylvania Gazette* on Dec. 22, 1730, Oct. 6, 1737, Jan. 18, 1739, Mar. 22 1739, May 21, 1741, June 4, 1741, Dec. 2, 1742, July 12, 1744, Aug. 15, 1745, Jan. 28, 1746, July 2 and 9, 1747, May 28, 1752, July 18, 1754, Dec. 25, 1755, May 26, 1757, Aug. 10, 1758, Nov. 19, 1761, and in the *Georgia Gazette*, Apr. 7, 1763. Francis Jerdone, "Account Book, 1750–1772," 147, Jerdone Family Papers, Swem Library, College of William and Mary.

23. Henry Dixon, *The English Instructor*, 1728 (Menston, Eng.: Scolar Press, 1967), title page; Henry Dixon, *The English Instructor; or, the Art of Spelling Improved. Being a more Plain, Easy, and Regular Method of Teaching Young Children, than any extant. In Two Parts*, 23rd ed. (London, 1760). Michael, *Teaching of English*, 437. Advt., *Pennsylvania Gazette*, Jan. 18, 1739.

24. For these as well as bibliographical references to other spelling books, such as that of Thomas Dilworth (see Appendix 3), I am much indebted to Konstantin Dierks's unpublished manuscript, "American Writing Skills Imprints, 1698–1800: A Bibliography," which greatly eased my tracing of these imprints. Extant books are documented in and available from the American Antiquarian Society's online catalogs (www.americanantiquarian.org/library.htm). For editions of Henry Dixon's *English Instructor*, see Evans #4011 (Boston: J. Draper, 1736), #5762 (Boston: D. Henchman, 1746), and a Boston: D. Henchman imprint from 1750 that has no Evans # but appears on R. C. Alston, *A Bibliography of the English Language from the Invention of Printing to the Year 1800*, vol. 4, *Spelling Books* (Bradford, Eng.: for the author, 1967), 329.

25. Dixon et al., *Youth's Instructor* (Evans #7884).

26. Isaiah Thomas, *The History of Printing in America*, ed. Marcus A. McCorison from 2nd ed. (New York: Weathervane Books, 1970), 133, 146, 155; the Fowle and Draper edition must have been in the late 1750s or early 1760s (Dierks, "Bibliography"). The postrevolutionary copies are Evans #24726 (1792) and #27599 (1794).

27. Michael, *Teaching of English*, 437, 396, 536, 579, 593–94.

28. Dixon, *English Instructor* (1746), 19; cf. Dixon et al., *Youth's Instructor*, 18.

29. Dixon et al., *Youth's Instructor*, 20–21; cf. Dixon, *English Instructor* (1728), 17–18, and *English Instructor* (1746), 22–23.

30. Dixon, *English Instructor* (1728), 18.

31. Dixon et al., *Youth's Instructor*, 27 (italics reversed).

32. Dixon, *English Instructor* (1746), 43, 46; Dixon et al., *Youth's Instructor*, 32, 34.

33. Dixon et al., *Youth's Instructor*, 39, 42; Dixon, *English Instructor* (1746), 53, 56–57.

34. Dixon et al., *Youth's Instructor*, 59–68. (One of the poems on writing appears above, in Chapter 10, p. 274.)

35. Ibid., 81.

36. E.g., ibid., 74–79, quot. 77.

37. Dixon et al., *Youth's Instructor*, 89; Dixon, *English Instructor* (1746), 108.

38. Dixon et al., *Youth's Instructor*, 103–4; Dixon, *English Instructor*, 124–26.

39. Dixon et al., *Youth's Instructor*, 104–7; Dixon, *English Instructor*, 126–29.

40. Dixon et al., *Youth's Instructor*, 108–31; Strong, *England's Perfect School-Master*, 126–49.

41. Dixon et al., *Youth's Instructor*, 132–39, 158–59; quots., 134, 138, 158, 159; Watts, *Art of Reading*, 71–82, quots., 74, 80–81, 153, 154; *The New-England Psalter Improved* (Philadelphia: W. Dunlap, 1760), A2–A3.

42. Michael, *Teaching of English*, 437.

43. Dyche's speller was advertised for the last time in the *Pennsylvania Gazette* on Nov. 19, 1761, but advertisements in the *Georgia Gazette* began in its first issue on Apr. 7, 1763, and continued. Jeremiah Condy was still selling copies in New England in 1762. Jeremiah Condy, "Account Book, 1759–1770," American Antiquarian Society, Worcester, Mass., 14, 68, 96.

44. Advts. for Dilworth's speller, *South Carolina Gazette*, Jan. 8, 1741, June 22, 1765, June 22, 1767, July 20, 1767, in Cohen, *South Carolina Gazette*, 131, 150 (tris). Imported copies were advertised in the *Virginia Gazette* (Purdie & Dixon), Feb. 25, 1768, June 10, 1773; *Virginia Gazette* (Dixon & Hunter), Aug. 24, 1776 (Molnar, "Publication and Retail Book Advertisements in the *Virginia Gazette*," 463). Dilworth's speller was advertised in the *Pennsylvania Gazette* on Jan. 28, 1746, Feb. 3, 1747, July 2, 1747, and beyond. The three years when it was not advertised are 1759, 1766, and 1777 (s.v. "Dilworth's spelling" in the computerized index to the *Pennsylvania Gazette* [Malvern, Pa.: Accessible Archives, 1991]). A storekeeper's memorandum book for the year 1768 records a half dozen each of Bibles, testaments, and psalters, but two dozen primers and Dilworth spelling books (Memorandum, Apr. 1768, Dwight-Howard Papers, 1672–1803, box 2, Massachusetts Historical Society, Boston). A Boston bookseller sold, in Apr. 1759, 24 testaments, 24 psalters, and 12 Dilworth spellers to a New Haven merchant, but by 1761 he was selling a ratio of 24 testaments and 24 Dilworth's spellers to 12 psalters (Condy, "Account Book," 1, 14).

45. No copy is extant of Franklin's own *A New and Complete Guide to the English Tongue. Collected from the best Authors. In Two Books* (Evans #4566), but it was advertised in the *Pennsylvania Gazette* July 31, 1740; there may have been another edition in 1745 (#5648, no copy, cites "Title from Hildeburn"). Its authorship was designated as "By an ingenious hand": whose hand was more ingenious than Franklin's? Thomas Dilworth, *A New Guide to the English Tongue: In Five Parts*, 8th ed. (Philadelphia: B. Franklin, 1747) (#40424).

46. Dilworth, *New Guide* (1747), vi, vii (italics reversed).

47. Ibid., vii, ix.

48. Ibid., vii, [xii–xiv], quot. [xii]. Dilworth explains (vii) that he put the mark immediately after any vowel, "which according to the Sound, ought to be joined with the following Consonant, which is nevertheless contrary to the Rules of Grammar." See above, note 20, and Figure 11.

49. Ibid., 3, 15. A digraph such as *sh* represents a new speech sound not derived from its constituent letters; but in a consonant blend such as *scr*, each of the speech sounds represented by the individual letters is pronounced.

50. Ibid., 5, 28, 62, 67.

51. Ibid., 121. For English grammars see Michael, *Teaching of English*, chap. 7; see also Grace W. Landrum, "The First Colonial Grammar in English," *William and Mary Quarterly*, ser. 2, 19 (1939): 272–85.

52. For selected illustrations in Dilworth's New Guide, see Elizabeth Carroll Reilly, *A Dictionary of Colonial American Printers' Ornaments and Illustrations: A Tribute to Alden Porter Johnson* (Worcester, Mass.: American Antiquarian Society, 1975), 313–30. Reilly believes that Franklin carved the woodcuts himself, partly on the grounds that one of the illustrations includes a picture of a Franklin stove (313–14, 326; illustration of the stove, Evans #1344). Michael documents earlier English spelling books with illustrations, such as Tobias Ellis's *The Poors English Spelling-Book* (1684) (Michael, *Teaching of English*, 445).

53. Advts., *Pennsylvania Gazette*, July 2, 1747 (Franklin for Owen's speller), June 20, 1754 (Philip Benezet for Markham's), Nov. 19, 1761. See Michael, *Teaching of English*, for the spelling books of William Markham (512), Edward Young (603), Philip Sproson (577), Isaac Watts (593), Henry Boad (405), John Deane (435), John Palairet (536), and Daniel Fenning (455).

54. In the *Pennsylvania Gazette*, for example, Dilworth appears as one of several spelling books appearing in seven advertisements from Feb. 1747 to May 1752 but as the only speller in forty-two of forty-eight advertisements (two of which advertised Dilworth and Dyche together) between November 1752 and the close of 1765. Quot., June 25, 1761.

Prelude to Part III

1. Jack Greene, *Pursuits of Happiness: The Social Development of Early Modern British Colonies and the Formation of American Culture* (Chapel Hill: University of North Carolina Press, 1988).

2. Mark M. Smith, "Culture, Commerce, and Calendar Reform in Colonial America," *William and Mary Quarterly*, 3rd ser., 55 (1998): 569. The switch from the Julian calendar to the Gregorian also changed the beginning of the new year from Mar. 25 to Jan. 1.

3. John Feather, *The Provincial Book Trade in Eighteenth-Century England* (Cambridge: Cambridge University Press, 1985), 19, 33–35.

4. Hugh Amory, "A Note on Statistics," in *A History of the Book in America*, ed. David D. Hall, vol. 1, *The Colonial Book in the Atlantic World*, ed. Hugh Amory and David D. Hall ([Worcester, Mass.]: American Antiquarian Society; New York: Cambridge University Press, 2000), 514, graph 7b.

5. Ibid., 506, graph 1b. Amory voices caution on the use of the North American Imprints Program (NAIP) records for measuring book production (514–15), but the unit of measurement is constant across the period and can certainly be used to confirm increasing production. Note that in this reckoning, weekly newspapers count as 52 units a year.

6. David D. Hall, "The Atlantic Economy in the Eighteenth Century," in *History of the Book in America*, 1:158–59 (fig. 5.1); Charles E. Clark, "Early American Journalism: News and Opinion in the Popular Press," in ibid., 361; Richard D. Brown, *Knowledge Is Power: The Diffusion of Information in Early America, 1700–1865* (New York: Oxford University Press, 1989), 111 (see chap. 5 for communication networks from the 1760s).

7. Amory, "Note on Statistics," 513, graph 6.

8. Jeremiah Condy, "Account Book, 1759–1770," American Antiquarian Society, Worcester, Mass. For the Dyche copies, see pp. 14 (1762), 68 (1762), 96 (1760).

9. Robert F. Seybolt, *Source Studies in American Colonial Education: The Private School* (1925; repr., New York: Arno Press and New York Times, 1971), chap. 2, 66–67; quot., Robert F. Seybolt, *The Private Schools of Colonial Boston* (Cambridge, Mass.: Harvard University Press, 1935), 75; see also chap. 9.

10. Inscription by David Chapin dated Oct. 3, 1775, to *The New-England Primer Improved* (Boston: Seth Adams, 1773) (copy at American Antiquarian Society).

11. Adams talks of a child he thinks of as a future minister, "wrangling in his mind about Adam's fall in which we sinned all as his primmer has it." John Adams, *Diary and Autobiography of John Adams*, vol. 1, *Diary, 1755–1770*, ed. L. H. Butterfield (Cambridge, Mass.: Harvard University Press, Belknap Press, 1961), 13.

12. Charles S. Grant, *Democracy in the Connecticut Frontier Town of Kent* (New York: Columbia University Press, 1961), 157.

13. Kathryn Kish Sklar, "The Schooling of Girls and Changing Community Values in Massachusetts Towns, 1750–1820," *History of Education Quarterly* 33 (1993): 512–42.

14. Robert Middlekauff, *Ancients and Axioms: Secondary Education in Eighteenth-Century New England* (New Haven: Yale University Press, 1963), 40–42.

15. See, for example, a 1748 Boston advertisement placed by Mrs. Hiller for "Wax-work, Transparent and Filligree, Painting upon Glass, Japanning, Quill-work, Feather-Work, and Embroidering with Gold and Silver" at her boarding school (Seybolt, *Private Schools*, 89).

16. Middlekauff, *Ancients and Axioms*, 49–51; "Schools: North School house, Providence, North School Proprietors, Minutes of meetings held by the Proprietors for the North School house, Providence, RI, 1768–1794," Rhode Island Historical Society, Providence. Whipple Hall was transferred to the town in 1785 and renamed the North School House.

17. Schoolteacher advertisements appeared in the *Pennsylvania Gazette*, first issued in 1728, as follows: 3 in the 1720s, 12 in the 1730s, 19 in the 1740s, 36 in the 1750s, 61 in the 1760s, and 45 in the 1770s. Julia Nash Murphy, "Schools and Schooling in Eighteenth-Century Philadelphia" (Ph.D. diss., Bryn Mawr College, 1977), 156–96. Since Murphy identified schoolteachers by the street location of their schools, any man who moved appears more than once. In the *South Carolina Gazette*: 33 first-time advertisements were published in the 1730s, 55 in the

1740s, 35 in the 1750s, 69 in the 1760s, and 42 up to 1775. Hennig Cohen, *The "South Carolina Gazette," 1732–1775* (Columbia: University of South Carolina Press, 1953). Cohen used the first advertisement only for each schoolmaster or schoolmistress, so his data underestimate the number of schools still in existence in a following decade but advertised earlier.

18. Gloria Main, "The Standard of Living in Southern New England, 1640–1773," *William and Mary Quarterly*, 3rd ser., 45 (1988): 124–34; Lois Green Carr and Lorena S. Walsh, "The Standard of Living in the Colonial Chesapeake," *William and Mary Quarterly*, 3rd ser., 45 (1988): 135–59.

19. T. H. Breen, *The Marketplace of Revolution: How Consumer Politics Shaped American Independence* ([London]: Oxford University Press, 2004), chap. 2; advt., *Boston Weekly News-Letter*, May 24, 1739 (china).

20. Breen, *Marketplace of Revolution*, 56–57; ibid., 57 (carpets); *Boston Gazette and Country Journal*, Aug. 10. 1767 (fans, lawns, damask, silks), Dec. 16, 1771 (decanter items); *Boston News-Letter*, Oct. 19, 1758 (broadcloth); *Massachusetts Gazette and Boston News-Letter*, Sept. 22 postscript, 1768 (lace); *Boston News-Letter*, June 10, 1756 (children's knives); *Massachusetts Gazette and Boston News-Letter*, June 13, 1765 (children's ivory knives).

Chapter 9. Literacy Instruction and the Enslaved

1. Joseph Hildreth to Sec., n.d., and Jan. 1747/8, Society for the Propagation of the Gospel Papers (hereafter cited as S.P.G. Papers; see Chapter 5, note 4 for a discussion of the depositories of the papers), ser. B, 15:88, 120, Rhodes House, Oxford, U.K. (RH).

2. David Brion Davis, *The Problem of Slavery in Western Culture* (Ithaca, N.Y.: Cornell University Press, 1966), 248–51; William M. Wiecek, "The Statutory Law of Slavery and Race in the Thirteen Mainland Colonies of British America," *William and Mary Quarterly*, 3rd ser., 34 (1977): 258–80. For the slave codes of New England, see Lorenzo Johnston Greene, *The Negro in Colonial New England, 1620–1776* (1942; repr., Port Washington, N.Y.: Kennikat Press, 1966), chap. 5.

3. Samuel Sewall, *The Selling of Joseph: A Memorial* (Boston: Bartholomew Green and John Allen, 1700), 3; Edmund Gibson, *Two Letters of the Lord Bishop of London: The First, to the Masters and Mistresses of Families in the English Plantations Abroad . . . The Second, to the Missionaries there . . .* , 2nd ed. [London, 1728?], 3 (italics reversed).

4. The "margins" of literacy, Jack Goody, ed., *Literacy in Traditional Societies* (Cambridge: Cambridge University Press, 1968), 4–5, quoted in Janet Duitsman Cornelius, *"When I Can Read My Title Clear": Literacy, Slavery, and Religion in the Antebellum South* (Columbia: University of South Carolina Press, 1991), 12.

5. Olaudah Equiano, *The Interesting Narrative of the Life of Olaudah Equiano*, in *The Classic Slave Narratives*, ed. Henry Louis Gates Jr. (New York: Penguin, 1987), 43–44. Cornelius, *"When I Can Read,"* 16–17, notes that the authors of four out of five of the first African narratives published in the eighteenth century made similar comments about their first encounters with books.

6. Cornelius, *"When I Can Read"*; see also E. Jennifer Monaghan, "Reading for the Enslaved, Writing for the Free: Reflections on Liberty and Literacy," *Proceedings of the American Antiquarian Society* 108 (1998): 323–24; Gates, *Classic Slave Narratives*, xii.

7. For Whitefield and the Great Awakening, see Frank Lambert, *Pedlar in Divinity: George Whitefield and the Transatlantic Revivals, 1737–1770* (Princeton, N.J.: Princeton University Press, 1994); John C. Pollock, *George Whitefield and the Great Awakening* (Garden City, N.Y.: Doubleday, 1972); Harry S. Stout, *The Divine Dramatist: George Whitefield and the Rise of Modern Evangelicalism* (Grand Rapids, Mich.: W. B. Eerdmans, 1991). See also Edwin S. Gaustad, *The Great Awakening in New England* (New York: Harper, 1957).

8. Cornelius, *"When I Can Read,"* 19–23; Edward E. Gordon and Elaine H. Gordon, *Literacy in America: Historic Journey and Contemporary Solutions* (Westport. Conn.: Praeger, 2003), 227–31.

9. For advertisements for runaways in the colonial period, see Farley Grubb, *Runaway*

Servants, Convicts, and Apprentices Advertised in the Pennsylvania Gazette, 1728–1796 (Baltimore: Genealogical Publishing, 1992); Graham Russell Hodges and Alan Edward Brown, eds., *"Pretends to Be Free": Runaway Slave Advertisements from Colonial and Revolutionary New York and New Jersey* (New York: Garland, 1994); Lathan A. Windley, *A Profile of Runaway Slaves in Virginia and South Carolina from 1730 through 1787* (New York: Garland, 1995); Maureen A. Taylor, *Runaways, Deserters, and Notorious Villains from Rhode Island Newspapers*, vol. 1, *The Providence Gazette, 1762–1800* (Camden, Me.: Picton Press, 1995); Robert L. Hall, "Slave Resistance in Baltimore City and County, 1747–1790," *Maryland Historical Magazine* 84 (1989): 305–18; literate slaves: 310, 312, 313. See also David Waldstreicher, "Reading the Runaways: Self-Fashioning, Print Culture, and Confidence in Slavery in the Eighteenth-Century Mid-Atlantic," *William and Mary Quarterly*, 3rd ser., 56 (1999): 263–64.

10. For the slave's 1723 letter, see Thomas N. Ingersoll, "'Releese us out of this Cruell Bondegg': An Appeal from Virginia in 1723," *William and Mary Quarterly*, 3rd ser., 51 (1994): 777-82; Monaghan, "Reading for the Enslaved," 323–24; Edmund Gibson, *Two Letters of the Lord Bishop of London.* Cf. Gibson's first letter, *A Letter of the Lord Bishop of London to the Masters and Mistresses of Families in the English Plantations Abroad; Exhorting Them to Encourage and Promote the Instruction of Their Negroes in the Christian Faith* (London: Joseph Downing, 1727).

11. Frank J. Klingberg, ed., *The Carolina Chronicle of Dr. Francis le Jau, 1706–1717* (Berkeley: University of California Press, 1956), 3; Eliza Lucas Pinckney, *The Letterbook of Eliza Lucas Pinckney, 1739–1762*, ed. Elise Pinckney (Chapel Hill: University of North Carolina Press, 1972), xvi, 34; cf. 12. For Fithian, see below, Chapter 12. For Osborn, see Mary Beth Norton, *Liberty's Daughters: The Revolutionary Experience of American Women, 1750–1800* (Boston: Little, Brown, 1980), 129–32; Mary Beth Norton, "'My Resting Reaping Times': Sarah Osborn's Defense of Her "Unfeminine" Activities, 1767," *Signs: Journal of Women in Culture and Society* (1976): 515–29.

12. George S. Brookes, *Friend Anthony Benezet* (Philadelphia: University of Pennsylvania Press, 1937), 29–30, 38, 40, 42–44. The years missed at the girls' school were 1755 to 1757.

13. Letter of Marquis François de Barbé-Marbois, 1779–1780, quoted in ibid., 452; Anthony Benezet to John Pemberton, May 29, 1783, quoted in ibid., 388; for 1754, see ibid., 80–81. Benezet's antislavery publications, published first anonymously but later under his own name, included two editions of his *Observations on the Inslaving, Importing, and Purchasing of Negroes* (Germantown, Pa.: Christopher Sower, 1759), *Early American Imprints. Series I, Evans (1639–1800)* [electronic resource], ([New Canaan, Conn.]: Readex; [Worcester, Mass.]: American Antiquarian Society, [2002–]) (hereafter cited as Evans), #8298, and 2nd ed. (Germantown: Christopher Sower, 1760) (Evans #8542); also, *A Short Account of that Part of Africa, Inhabited by the Negroes* (Philadelphia, 1762) (#9066); *A Short Account of that Part of Africa Inhabited by the Negroes*, 2nd ed. (Philadelphia: W. Dunlap, 1762) (#9067); *A Short Account of that Part of Africa Inhabited by the Negroes* (London: W. Baker and J. W. Galabin, 1768) (which identified itself as a copy of a third Philadelphia edition); *A Caution and Warning to Great Britain and her Colonies* (Philadelphia: Henry Miller, 1766) (#41702); *A Caution and Warning to Great Britain and her Colonies* (Philadelphia: D. Hall and N. Sellers, 1767) (#10555)—which aroused international interest—and the eight-page anonymous *Notes on the Slave Trade* ([Philadelphia, 1781]) (#17095).

14. Brookes, *Friend Anthony Benezet*, 46–47, quot. 47, from Roberts Vaux, *Memoirs of the Life of A. Benezet* (Philadelphia: James P. Parke, 1817), 30. See also Nancy Slocum Hornick, "Anthony Benezet and the Africans' School: Toward a Theory of Full Equality," *Pennsylvania Magazine of History and Biography* 99 (1975): 399–421.

15. Cotton Mather, *Diary of Cotton Mather*, ed. Worthington C. Ford, 2 vols. (New York: Frederick Ungar, 1957), 2:500, 663, 271–72 (Onesimus), 721 (Ezer); cf. Cotton Mather, *Rules for the Society of Negroes. 1693*, ([Boston], 1714) (Evans #653), which requires the enslaved to learn only a catechism.

16. Pompey Fleet was "an ingenious man . . . [who] cut, on wooden blocks, all the pictures which decorated the ballads and small books of his master." Isaiah Thomas, *The History of*

Printing in America, ed. Marcus A. McCorison from the 2nd ed. (New York: Weathervane Books, 1970), 94. The initials P.F. appear in a surviving copy of the *Prodigal Daughter*. Elizabeth Carroll Reilly, *A Dictionary of Colonial American Printers' Ornaments and Illustrations* (Worcester, Mass.: American Antiquarian Society, 1975), 332; see also 334, 335, 337 (Evans #41867, #41996). Fleet died in 1758, and his sons Thomas and John Fleet continued the newspaper. Thomas implies that they did not continue the chapbook side of their father's business. If so, the undated copies of the *Prodigal Daughter* must precede 1758, currently the conjectured date of an extant copy of the *Prodigal Daughter* (#41867). "Newport Gardner": William D. Piersen, *Black Yankees: The Development of an Afro-American Subculture in Eighteenth-Century New England* (Amherst: University of Massachusetts Press, 1988), 45–46.

17. Phillis Wheatley, *The Poems of Phillis Wheatley*, revised and enlarged, ed. Julian D. Mason Jr. (1966; repr., Chapel Hill: University of North Carolina Press, 1989) (hereafter cited as Mason, *Phillis Wheatley*), 2–3.

18. Ibid., 3; quots., John Wheatley, letter to the publisher, Nov. 14, 1772, in Phillis Wheatley, *Poems on Various Subjects, Religious and Moral* (London: A. Bell, 1773), reprinted in Mason, *Phillis Wheatley*, 47 (hereafter citations to Wheatley, *Poems on Various Subjects*, are to this reprinted version).

19. John Wheatley, letter to the publisher, Nov. 14, 1772. John Wheatley gives the year 1765 as the date of Phillis's first letter; because of the timing of Occum's departure for England, Mason corrects this to 1766 (Mason, *Phyllis Wheatley*, 183).

20. For Wheatley's classical references and sophisticated adoption of Roman verse forms, see John C. Shields, "Phillis Wheatley's Use of Classicism," *American Literature* 52 (1980): 97–111; for her biblical ones, used to make oblique antislavery statements, see Sondra O'Neale, "A Slave's Subtle War: Phillis Wheatley's Use of Biblical Myth and Symbol," *Early American Literature* 21 (1986): 144–65; for the relevance of the poetry of Homer, Milton, and Pope to Wheatley's aspirations as a poet, see Charles Scruggs, "Phillis Wheatley and the Poetical Legacy of Eighteenth-Century England," *Studies in Eighteenth-Century Culture* 10 (1981): 279–95. See also M[erle] A. Richmond, *Bid the Vassal Soar: Interpretive Essays on the Life and Poetry of Phillis Wheatley . . . and George Moses Horton . . .* (Washington, D.C.: Howard University Press, 1974); William H. Robinson, *Phillis Wheatley and Her Writings* (New York: Garland, 1981). See Mason, *Phillis Wheatley*, 3 (Wheatley's membership in Old South Church), 120, 133 (her age); see also 217–21 for a useful bibliography.

21. Mason, *Phillis Wheatley*, 117, 131. Revised versions of both poems were published in Wheatley, *Poems on Various Subjects*.

22. Mason, *Phillis Wheatley*, 115 n.1, 132 n. 18; for publishing details of Wheatley's elegy for Whitefield, see ibid., 133n.

23. "An Elegiac Poem, On the Death of that celebrated Divine, and eminent Servant of Jesus Christ, the late Reverend, and pious George Whitefield" ([Boston]: sold by Ezekiel Russell . . . and John Boyles, [1770]) (Evans #11812); reprinted in Mason, *Phillis Wheatley*, 132–35, quot. 134; Wheatley's later revision of the poem appears in Wheatley, *Poems on Various Subjects*, 55–57. See also William D. Piersen, *Black Yankees: The Development of an Afro-American Subculture in Eighteenth-Century New England* (Amherst: University of Massachusetts Press, 1988), 68–69.

24. Mason, *Phillis Wheatley*, 48.

25. Ibid., 164 (italics reversed).

26. Davis, *Problem of Slavery*, 219–21; J. Harry Bennett Jr., *Bondsmen and Bishops: Slavery and Apprenticeship on the Codrington Plantation of Barbados, 1710–1838* (Berkeley: University of California Press, 1958). According to Bennett, the S.P.G. did not distinguish itself for its philanthropic Christianity in Barbados. The only school that eventually opened was restricted to white children. As late as 1793 only three of the enslaved Africans at Codrington could read, none of them well (98–99).

27. William Webb Kemp, *The Support of Schools in Colonial New York by the Society for the Propagation of the Gospel in Foreign Parts* (New York: Teachers College, Columbia University, 1913), 236; Elias Neau to Hodges, July 10, 1703, S.P.G. Papers, ser. A, 1:106, Library of

Congress Records, Washington, D.C. (LC); Elias Neau to Chamberlayne, Nov. 15, 1705, S.P.G. Papers, ser. A, 2:125 (LC). Neau's letters are written in French. The translations were provided by the S.P.G., but I have on occasion corrected them.

28. Edgar J. McManus, *A History of Negro Slavery in New York* (Syracuse, N.Y.: Syracuse University Press, 1966), 7–25. For slavery in its early Dutch context, see Russell Shorto, *The Island at the Center of the World: The Epic Story of Dutch Manhattan and the Forgotten Colony that Shaped America* (New York: Doubleday, 2004), 273–74.

29. Elias Neau to Chamberlayne, Oct. 3, 1705, S.P.G. Papers, ser. A, 2:124 (LC); Elias Neau to Sec., Mar. 1, 1705/6, S.P.G. Papers, ser. A, 2:159 (LC).

30. W. Jernegan, "Slavery and Conversion in the American Colonies," in *Articles on American Slavery*, ed. Paul Finkelman, vol. 16, *Religion and Slavery* (New York: Garland, 1989), 504–27.

31. Rev. John Sharpe, Mar. 11, 1712/13, in Lambeth Archives, 841, fol. 18, quoted in Kemp, *Support of Schools*, 237.

32. For a full account, see John C. Van Horne, ed., with an introduction, *Religious Philanthropy and Colonial Slavery: The American Correspondence of the Associates of Dr. Bray, 1717–1777* (Urbana: University of Illinois Press), 2–16.

33. For details, see ibid., 16–17.

34. Ibid., 72, n. 1, 91.

35. Rev. Alexander Garden to Rev. Samuel Smith, [Sept. 24, 1742], in ibid., 93.

36. For a somewhat different viewpoint about native Americans, suggesting that English opinions were more influenced by the Indians' social status, see Karen Ordahl Kupperman, *Settling with the Indians: The Meeting of English and Indian Cultures in America, 1580–1640* (London: J M Dent, 1980), esp. chaps. 5–6.

37. Betty Wood, *Slavery in Colonial Georgia, 1730–1775* (Athens: University of Georgia Press, 1984), 1–11, quot. 5.

38. In 1738, 117 male settlers signed a petition asking for the repeal of the prohibition against slavery. Counter representations came from the Salzburgers, Highland Scots, and Oglethorpe (ibid., 15–17, 20–23, 24–26, 29–31).

39. Ibid., 77–85.

40. Van Horne, *Religious Philanthropy*, 344; Petition, J[oseph] Ottolenghe to S.P.G., n. d. [1750 on back], S.P.G. Letters, ser. B, 18:80 (RH); Julia Floyd Smith, *Slavery and Rice Culture in Low Country Georgia, 1750–1860* (Knoxville: University of Tennessee Press, 1985), 19, 22. By 1776, there would be 17,000 whites and 16,000 enslaved (Smith, *Slavery and Rice Culture*, 22).

41. Joseph Ottolenghe to S.P.G. Sec., Sept. 9, 1751, S.P.G. Letters, ser. B, 19:149 (RH). Church notice of the school: Joseph Ottolenghe to [Sec.], Dec. 4, 1751, in Van Horne, *Religious Philanthropy*, 104.

42. Joseph Ottolenghe to [Rev. Samuel Smith], Dec. 4, 1751, in Van Horne, *Religious Philanthropy*, 104.

43. Joseph Ottolenghe to [Rev. Samuel Smith], June 8, 1752, in ibid., 109.

44. Joseph Ottolenghe to [Rev. Rev. John Waring], Nov. 19, 1753, in ibid., 112.

45. See Davis, *Problem of Slavery*, 203–5; Wood, *Slavery in Colonial Georgia*, 161–62.

46. Joseph Ottolenghe to [Rev. Rev. John Waring], Nov. 19, 1753, in Van Horne, *Religious Philanthropy*, 112, 113; U.S.P.G. Thomas Bray Papers, "Catalogues of Books for Home and Foreign Libraries, A.D. 1753 to A.D. 1817," [1] (RH).

47. Joseph Ottolenghe to [Rev. John Waring], Nov. 18, 1754, in Van Horne, *Religious Philanthropy*, 116, 117.

48. Joseph Ottolenghe to Rev. John Waring, July 12, 1758, in ibid., 127–32, quot. 128.

49. Ibid., 129.

50. Ibid., 130–31, quots. 130.

51. Elizabeth Donnan, "The Slave Trade into South Carolina before the Revolution," *American Historical Review* 33 (1928): 807.

52. John D. Cushing, comp., *The First Laws of the State of South Carolina*, 2 pts. (Wilmington, Del.: Michael Glazier, 1981), pt. 1, 174. Most scholars who have discussed this law have

incorrectly interpreted it as a prohibition against reading as well as writing. See Monaghan, "Reading for the Enslaved," 317 n. 17, 319, n. 20.

53. Samuel Thomas to [Sec.], Mar. 10, 1703/4, S.P.G. Papers, ser. A, 1:180.

54. Frank J. Klingberg, *An Appraisal of the Negro in Colonial South Carolina: A Study in Americanization* (Washington, D.C.: Associated Publishers, 1941), 103; Van Horne, *Religious Philanthropy*, 338.

55. Klingberg, *Negro in Colonial South Carolina*, 104.

56. Rev. Alexander Garden to Sec., May 6, 1740, S.P.G. Papers, ser. B, 7:235 (RH).

57. Rev. Alexander Garden to Sec., Apr. 9, 1742, S.P.G. Papers, ser. B, 9:124 (RH).

58. Rev. Alexander Garden to Sec., Sept. 24, 1742, S.P.G. Papers, ser. B, 10:140 (RH). The identification of which, Harry or Andrew, was the "excellent Genius" is made in Rev. Alexander Garden to Sec., Oct. 18. 1744, S.P.G. Papers, ser. B, 12:119 (RH).

59. Rev. Alexander Garden to Sec., Oct. 10, 1743, S.P.G. Papers, ser. B, 11:204 (RH).

60. Philip Bearcroft, the S.P.G. secretary, informs Garden that the books are on their way in Dr. Philip Bearcroft to Commissary [Alexander] Garden, July 7, 1744, in S.P.G. Papers, ser. B, 13:52. Garden acknowledges receipt of the books in Rev. Alexander Garden to Sec., Apr. 24, 1745, S.P.G. Papers, ser. B, 12:80 (RH).

61. Rev. Alexander Garden to Sec., Oct. 18, 1744, S.P.G. Papers, ser. B, 12:119 (RH).

62. Klingberg, *Negro in Colonial South Carolina*, 115–17; quoted from *An Abstract of the Proceedings of the S.P.G. Printed with Thomas Sermon* (London, 1746), 55–56.

63. Rev. Alexander Garden to Sec., Oct. 22, 1748, S.P.G. Papers, ser. B, 16:146 (RH).

64. Dr. Philip Bearcroft to Commissary [Alexander] Garden, July 4, 1748, S.P.G. Papers, ser. B, 15:247 (RH).

65. Rev. Alexander Garden to Sec., Feb. 14, 1750/51, S.P.G. Papers, ser. B, 18:183, quoted in Klingberg, *Negro in Colonial South Carolina*, 118.

66. Klingberg, *Negro in Colonial South Carolina*, 118–21; Robert Olwell, *Masters, Slaves, and Subjects: The Culture of Power in the South Carolina Low Country, 1740–1790* (Ithaca, N.Y.: Cornell University Press, 1998), 121.

67. See the acrimonious discussion between Rev. John Waring and Robert Carter Nicholas about the latter's spending over the limit that Waring thought he had set for the financial support of the Williamsburg school, in Van Horne, *Religious Philanthropy*, 266–67, 275–77.

68. Rev. John Waring to Benjamin Franklin, Jan. 24, 1757, in Van Horne, *Religious Philanthropy*, 122–23.

69. Gary B. Nash, "Slaves and Slaveowners in Colonial Philadelphia," *William and Mary Quarterly*, 3rd ser., 30 (1973): 226–27, 229–31.

70. Benjamin Franklin to Rev. John Waring, [London], Jan. 3, 1758, in Van Horne, *Religious Philanthropy*, 124. For Sturgeon, see ibid., 349.

71. Frederick Douglass, *Narrative of the Life of Frederick Douglass, an American Slave*, ed. David W. Blight (Boston: Bedford Books, 1993), 57.

72. Benjamin Franklin to Rev. John Waring, in Van Horne, *Religious Philanthropy*, 125–26. Enrollment: in Nov. 1759, there were 35 students, 24 girls and 11 boys (ibid., 142); by June 1759 the school had grown to 36 students, 22 girls and 14 boys (ibid., 162–63); and in Nov. 1762 it had 32 students, 20 girls and 12 boys (ibid., 199–200).

73. U.S.P.G. Thomas Bray Papers, "Catalogues of Books for Home and Foreign Libraries, A.D. 1753 to A.D. 1817," 60 (RH).

74. Rev. William Sturgeon to Rev. John Waring, Nov. 9, 1758, June 12, 1759, in Van Horne, *Religious Philanthropy*, 135–36, quots. 136. The school was first called the Negro or Negroe School (ibid., 286, 290) or the Charity Negro(e) School (ibid., 288), but from fall 1770 on, the "Negroe Charity School" (ibid., 302, 304, 308, 313, 318). When Sturgeon retired in 1768 from his post as assistant minister, he was replaced in his supervisory capacity by two of his church wardens, Francis Hopkinson and Anthony Duffield.

75. [Deborah Franklin to Benjamin Franklin], Aug. 9, 1759, in Van Horne, *Religious Philanthropy*, 137; Benjamin Franklin to Rev. John Waring, Dec. 17, 1763, in ibid., 203–4.

76. The following statistics, indicated by page number, are from Van Horne, *Religious Philan-*

thropy. Salary of £20: in 1758 (136), 1761 (170), 1770 (290). Enrollment: 36 children admitted between Nov. 1758 and June 1759 (136, 162–63); 35 children in Nov. 1759 (142); 32 children in Nov. 1762 (199–200); drop in numbers to 15 in 1764 (214); 59 children admitted between Nov. 1764 and Mar. 1768, of whom 27 were attending in 1768 (266); school "full," in 1769 (286), in 1770 (290), in Feb. 1775 (326) (Feb. 1775); 30 children in 1774 (318), in May 1775 (326). Applications for vacancies in 1770 (290).

77. Ibid., 135, 142, 160–61, 162 n. 2, 200 (Elizabeth Harrison).

78. Ibid., 222 n. 3, 232, 266. For the spelling Ayres rather than Ayers, see ibid., 270.

79. Ibid., 270, 318.

80. Ibid., 143–44, 355.

81. Biographical sketch in ibid., 330; Samuel Auchmuty to Sec., July 1, 1747, in S.P.G. Papers, ser. B, 15:80 (RH), and Mar. 30, 1748, in S.P.G. Papers, ser. B, 3:153 (RH); advt., *New-York Mercury*, Sept. 15, 1760, quoted in Van Horne, *Religious Philanthropy*, 156.

82. Samuel Auchmuty to Sec., Sept. 19, 1761, in S.P.G. Papers, ser. B, 2:2 (RH); Van Horne, *Religious Philanthropy*, 155, 160, 167–68.

83. Van Horne, *Religious Philanthropy*, 168–69. The average age of the first fifteen children admitted was 8.7 years; that of the second fifteen, 6.3.

84. Ibid., 167. For the 1741 "Great Negro Plot," see Thomas J. Davis, *A Rumor of Revolt: The "Great Negro Plot" in Colonial New York* (1985; repr., Amherst: University of Massachusetts Press, 1990).

85. Samuel Auchmuty to Sec., June 29, 1762, in S.P.G. Papers, ser. B, 2:4; Jan. 2, 1767, in S.P.G. Papers, ser. B, 2:3; Mar. 29, 1764, in S.P.G. Papers, ser. B, 2:7 (RH). Without an Anglican bishop in America, confirmation in America was impossible.

86. Samuel Auchmuty to John Waring, Oct. 18, 1762, Apr. 19, 1763, in Van Horne, *Religious Philanthropy*, 192, 197.

87. Samuel Auchmuty to John Waring, Oct. 20, 1763, May 2, 1764, [May 31, 1765], May 1, 1767, May 9, 1768, [May 31, 1765], in ibid., 202 (cf. 257), 213, 231, 257, 268, 231.

88. Samuel Auchmuty to John Waring, Oct. 26, 1765, Sept. 28, 1774, Oct. 20, 1774, in ibid., 238, 320, 322. Auchmuty became rector in Trinity Church in 1764, succeeding the Rev. Henry Barclay.

89. Davis, *Problem of Slavery*, 144.

90. Van Horne, *Religious Philanthropy*, 333.

91. Rev. Marmaduke Brown to John Waring, Nov. 6, 1764, and [July 1, 1766], in Van Horne, *Religious Philanthropy*, 220, 248.

92. Rev. Marmaduke Brown to John Waring, Nov. 6, 1764, in ibid., 221.

93. Rev. Marmaduke Brown to John Waring, [July 1, 1766], and [June 4, 1767], in ibid., 247, 259.

94. Ibid., 332 (the grammar school was Mr. Kay's); Rev. George Bisset to John Waring, Oct. 17, 1772, [Nov 13, 1773], and Oct 17, 1772, in ibid., 309, 315, 309–10.

95. Rev. George Bisset to John Waring, Apr. 8, 1773, Rev. Marmaduke Browne to John Waring, [June 4, 1767], and summary of Bisset to Waring, [Apr. 12, 1775], in ibid., 312–13, 259, 326.

96. Thad W. Tate Jr., *The Negro in Eighteenth-Century Williamsburg* (Williamsburg, Va.: Colonial Williamsburg, 1965), 1–24, 47–49.

97. Van Horne, *Religious Philanthropy*, 144; Rev. John Waring to Rev. Thomas Dawson, Feb. 29, 1760, in ibid., 144–46, 336. See also Tate, *Negro in Eighteenth-Century Williamsburg*, 134–52, for a concise summary of the associates' dealings with the Williamsburg school. Some of the relevant minutes of the associates have been reproduced in Edgar W. Knight, ed., *A Documentary History of Education in the South before 1860*, 5 vols. (Chapel Hill: University of North Carolina Press, 1949–53), vol. 1, chap. 4.

98. William Hunter to John Waring, Feb. 16, 1761, and John Waring to William Hunter, June 1, 1761, in Van Horne, *Religious Philanthropy*, 152–53, 157–58.

99. John Waring to Thomas Dawson, Feb. 29, 1760, and John Waring to William Hunter, June 1, 1761, in ibid., 146, 158. For *The Church Catechism Broke,* see above, p. 96.

100. William Hunter to Rev. John Waring, Feb. 16, 1761, in ibid., 153. For Nicholas, see ibid., 344. For Nicholas as a slaveholder, see Tate, *Negro in Eighteenth-Century Williamsburg*, 132.

101. Robert Carter Nicholas to John Waring, Sept. 17, 1761, and John Waring to Robert Carter Nicholas, [Apr. 4, 1762], in Van Horne, *Religious Philanthropy*, 164, 171.

102. Robert Carter Nicholas to John Waring, June 23, 1762, in ibid., 174.

103. Enclosure in William Yates and Robert Carter Nicholas to [John Waring], Sept. 30, 1762, in ibid., 188.

104. All quotations from "Regulations" appear in ibid., 189–91.

105. Robert Carter Nicholas to [John Waring], Sept. 13, 1765, in ibid., 236.

106. For a review of arguments based on the Bible for and against slavery, see Carolina L. Shanks, "The Biblical Anti-Slavery Argument of the Decade, 1830–1840," in Finkelman, *Articles on American Slavery*, 16:616–41.

107. Van Horne, *Religious Philanthropy*, 352.

108. John Waring to Robert Carter Nicholas, [Mar. 1764], in ibid., 205.

109. Robert Carter Nicholas to Rev. John Waring, Dec. 21, 1764, in ibid., 223.

110. Robert Carter Nicholas to Rev. John Waring, Dec. 27, 1765, in ibid., 240–41.

111. Enclosure, Robert Carter Nicholas to John Waring, Feb. 16, 1769, in ibid., 277–78. The four continuing children were Mary Ashby (sent by Mrs. Campbell), Jerry (sent by Mr. Hay), and Catherine and Johanna (sent by Blair); Blair also sent new children, Nancy and Clara Bee. The craftsmen included Anthony Hay, Hugh Orr, and Jane Vobe. The professions of the slaveholders are identified in Tate, *Negro in Eighteenth-Century Williamsburg*, 145.

112. Rev. John Waring to Robert Carter Nicholas, April 20, 1768, in Van Horne, *Religious Philanthropy*, 267. For Waring's contributions of two to three guineas annually, see ibid., 267. For Nicholas's accounts, see ibid., 253. For the correspondence between the two men on the issue of the school's financial support see ibid., 266–68, 275–77, 283–85, 288–89. Waring was sufficiently disturbed about slavery to print his own pamphlet on the topic that falls just short of attacking the institution itself: [John Waring], *A Letter to an American Planter from his Friend in London* [1770], reprinted in Van Horne, *Religious Philanthropy*, 293–301. The identification of Waring as the author of this anonymous pamphlet is made by Van Horne in *Religious Philanthropy*, 301.

113. Robert Carter Nicholas to Rev. John Waring, Jan. 1, 1770, Dec. 1, 1772, in Van Horne, *Religious Philanthropy*, 288, 310.

114. Frederick Dalcho, *An Historical Account of the Protestant Episcopal Church in South Carolina . . .* (Charles Town: E. Thayer, 1820), 149n; Klingberg, *Negro in Colonial South Carolina*, 121, 56n.

115. Douglass, *Narrative of the Life*, 61.

116. Tate, *Negro in Eighteenth-Century Williamsburg*, 76.

117. Francis Le Jau to Secretary, Mar. 19 1715/16, S.P.G. Papers, ser. B, 4, no. 58 (RH).

118. Francis Le Jau to Secretary, Feb. 1 1709/10, in S.P.G. Papers, ser. A, 5, 98 (LC).

119. Ibid.

120. Francis Le Jau to Secretary, Feb. 19 1709/10, in S.P.G. Papers, ser. A, 5, 82 (LC).

121. Francis Le Jau to Secretary, June 13, 1710, in S.P.G. Papers, ser. A, 5, 120 (LC).

122. Monaghan, "Reading for the Enslaved."

Chapter 10. Writing Instruction

1. *The Youth's Instructor in the English Tongue: Or, The Art of Spelling Improved . . . Collected from Dixon, Bailey, Owen, Strong and Watts* (Boston: J. Green and J. Russell, for D. Henchman, 1757), 59; *Early American Imprints. Series I, Evans (1639–1800)* [electronic resource] ([New Canaan, Conn.]: Readex; [Worcester, Mass.]: American Antiquarian Society, [2002–]) (hereafter cited as Evans), #7884.

2. Dixon et al., *Youth's Instructor*, 60. Pounce, referred to in the line "Use Pounce to Paper, if

the ink go thro'," was a fine powder, made from pulverized cuttlefish shell, and used to prevent ink from spreading on unsized paper or paper damaged by ink erasures.

3. George Bickham's *A Poem on Writing* (n.p., n.d.). The poem is mentioned in an "Advertisement" in Charles Snell, *The Art of Writing; In it's* [sic] *Theory and Practice* (London: [Overton & Hoole], 1712). Cf. Thomas Weston, *Ancilla Calligraphiae or The Handmaid to Fair Writing* ([London, n.d.]), 208, who ends his copybook with the sentiments, "Tis Writing doth Facilitate / Commerce, and all Societie / Is jointed, and made strong thereby. / Friends absent hereby do Communicate / Each secret thought and Sentiment." See also Tamara Plakins Thornton, *Handwriting in America: A Cultural History* (New Haven: Yale University Press, 1996), 15–16.

4. Charles J. Hoadly, ed., *Records of the Colony and Plantation of New-Haven, from 1638 to 1649* . . . (Hartford: Case, Tiffany, 1857), 156 (Pearce); Robert F. Seybolt, *The Private Schools of Colonial Boston* (Cambridge, Mass.: Harvard University Press, 1935), 3 (Howard); Thornton, *Handwriting in America*, 6–12.

5. Konstantin Dierks, "Letter Writing, Gender, and Class in America, 1750–1800" (Ph.D. diss., Brown University, 1999).

6. Jon Teaford, "The Transformation of Massachusetts Education, 1670–1780," in *History of Education Quarterly* 10 (1970): 287–307; Robert Middlekauff, *Ancients and Axioms: Secondary Education in Eighteenth-Century New England* (New Haven: Yale University Press, 1963), 31–45.

7. In 1666, Daniel Hinchman was employed to assist the master of the Boston grammar school and "teach Childere to wright." Hinchman left in 1671 and subsequently demanded that the town give him a year's unpaid salary. Boston, *Early History,* [vol. 7,] *A Report of the Record Commissioners of the City of Boston, Containing the Boston Records from 1660 to 1701* (Boston: Rockwell and Churchill, 1881), 30, 63; Robert F. Seybolt, "Schoolmasters of Colonial Boston," *Publications of the Colonial Society of Massachusetts* 27 (1928): 136.

8. Connecticut: Middlekauff, *Ancients and Axioms,* 44; Samuel Pepys: Ambrose Heal, *The English Writing-Masters and Their Copy-Books, 1570–1800: A Biographical Dictionary and a Bibliography* (Cambridge: Cambridge University Press, 1931), xi; *Boston Records,* 7:158; Seybolt, "Schoolmasters of Colonial Boston," 137.

9. Boston, *A Report of the Record Commissioners of the City of Boston, Containing the Records of Boston Selectmen, 1736 to 1742* [vol. 15 of the Town Records] (Boston: Rockwell and Churchill, 1886), 246, 349, 369 (populations). There were 160 boys at the North in 1743; Boston, *A Report of the Record Commissioners of the City of Boston, Containing the Selectmen's Minutes from 1742–3 to 1753* [vol. 17] (Boston: Rockwell and Churchill, 1887), 20; Nash, *American Writing Masters,* 15–16 (numbers for 1755).

10. Robert F. Seybolt, *Public Schoolmasters of Colonial Boston* ([Cambridge, Mass.:] privately printed at the Harvard University Press, 1939), 17, 28–30.

11. Nash, *American Writing Masters,* 14; Seybolt, *Public Schoolmasters,* 14–16, 18–19; Seybolt, *Private Schools,* 41; see also Samuel Holbrook, manuscript petition for a raise, Apr. 1774, "Miscellaneous Specimens of American Calligraphy," pfMS Typ 473.2, Houghton Library, Harvard University, Cambridge, Mass.

12. Quot., *Records of Boston Selectmen, 1736 to 1742,* 292; Seybolt, "Schoolmasters of Colonial Boston," 147, 155; Seybolt, *Public Schoolmasters,* 15, 16, 18.

13. Nash, *American Writing Masters,* 13; Seybolt, *Public Schoolmasters,* esp. 21–23 for salary figures.

14. Anthony Benezet to John Smith, Mar. 2, 1765, in George S. Brookes, *Friend Anthony Benezet* (Philadelphia: University of Pennsylvania Press, 1937), 208–9, quot. 257; advt., *Pennsylvania Gazette,* Nov. 3, 1763, for William Thorne, *A New Sett of Copies* (Evans #9522); advts., *Newport Mercury,* Sept. 17, 24, 1764, and *New-York Mercury,* Apr. 1765, for Thomas Powell, *The Writing Master's Assistant* . . . (Evans #9801), both quoted in Robert F. Seybolt, *Source Studies in American Colonial Education: The Private School* (1925; repr., New York: Arno Press, 1971), 46–47.

15. George Fisher, *The American Instructor: Or, Young Man's Best Companion* . . . *To which is*

added, The Poor Planters Physician . . . , 9th ed., revised and corrected (Philadelphia: B. Franklin & D. Hall, 1748) (Evans #6238), 27–32; Nash, *American Writing Masters*, 23–25.

16. Ray Nash, "A Colonial Writing Master's Collection of English Copybooks," *Harvard Library Bulletin* 14 (1960): 12–19; see p. 13 for the authors and titles in Holbrook's collection; *Copy-Books to Write By, Sold by H. Overton, at the White-House without Newgate* (London, 1750).

17. George Bickham, *The Universal Penman, Engraved by George Bickham London 1743*, with an introductory essay by Philip Hofer (1954; rpt., New York: Dover, 1968).

18. Advts., *Pennsylvania Gazette*, May 30, 1751, Dec. 10, 1751 (for Bickman's penmanship); Thomas Woody, *Early Quaker Education in Pennsylvania* (1920; repr., New York: Arno Press and New York Times, 1969), 195 (Seaton); advt., *Pennsylvania* Gazette, Oct. 17, 1755 (Milne); advt., *South Carolina Gazette*, July 20, 1767; J. Champion in Bickham, *Universal Penman*, 11; advt., *South Carolina Gazette*, Nov. 7, 1768, in Hennig Cohen, *The "South Carolina Gazette," 1732–1775* (Columbia: University of South Carolina Press, 1953), 152.

19. Richard L. Bushman, *The Refinement of America: Persons, Houses, Cities* (New York: Vintage Books, 1993); for desks, see 95–96.

20. Billingsley is quoted in Joyce I. Whalley, *The Pen's Excellencie: A Pictorial History of Western Calligraphy* (New York: Taplinger, 1980), 255.

21. William Brooks, *A Delightful Recreation for the Industrious* (London: n.p., [1717], 14, reproduced in Whalley, *Pen's Excellencie*, 255.

22. Bickham, *Universal Penman*, 29. The poem, along with its companion poem "To Young Gentlemen," was reproduced in James Carver, *A New and Easy Introduction to the Art of Analytical Penmanship, on an improved plan . . .* (Philadelphia: W. Hall, Jun. & G. W. Pierie, 1808), 27.

23. Jack P. Greene, *Pursuits of Happiness: The Social Development of Early Modern British Colonies and the Formation of American Culture* (Chapel Hill: University of North Carolina Press, 1988). See above, p. 5.

24. Advt., *Maryland Gazette*, quoted in Calhoun Winton, "The Southern Book Trade in the Eighteenth Century," in *A History of the Book in America*, ed. David D. Hall, vol. 1, *The Colonial Book in the Atlantic World*, ed. Hugh Amory and David D. Hall ([Worcester, Mass.]: American Antiquarian Society; New York: Cambridge University Press, 2000), 228; advt., *Boston Weekly News-Letter*, Dec. 29, 1743.

25. For advertisements for slates and slate pencils, see *Pennsylvania Gazette*, Nov. 2, 1749; *Boston Weekly News-Letter*, Apr. 26, 1750; *New-York Mercury*, May 27, 1754; *South Carolina Gazette*, Oct. 23–30, 1755; *Virginia Gazette*, July 25, 1766. Advt. for sealing wax, *Providence (Rhode Island) Gazette; and Country Journal*, Nov. 6, 1762. See also Jeremiah Condy, "Account Book, 1759–1770," American Antiquarian Society, Worcester, Mass. (hereafter cited as AAS), recording the sale in 1760 of "16 small slates framed @ 1/2 [one shilling two pence]," 100.

26. For writing paper, see "Appendix E, Manufactures and other products listed in the rates on imports established by the House of Parliament June 24 1660," in George F. Dow, *Every Day Life in the Massachusetts Bay Colony* (Boston: Society for the Preservation of New England Antiquities, 1935), 252; John Bidwell, "Printer' Supplies and Capitalization," in Hall, *History of the Book*, 1:176–77; advts., *New-York Mercury*, Oct. 2, 1752, Aug. 27, 1753, May 27, 1754. Cf. "Imperial, Super-royal, Royal, Medium, Demy, Double-post [paper]," *Pennsylvania Gazette*, May 30, 1751.

27. Philip Vickers Fithian, *Journal and Letters of Philip Vickers Fithian, 1773–1774: A Plantation Tutor of the Old Dominion*, ed. Hunter Dickinson Farish (Williamsburg, Va.: Colonial Williamsburg, 1943), 269. An American reprint of *A Universal Spelling Book* by the British author Daniel Fenning offered recipes for making "good red Ink": most of the ingredients, such as vinegar or stale beer, were ready-to-hand; Daniel Fenning, *The Universal Spelling-Book or, A New and Easy Guide to the English Language*, 15th ed. (Providence: John Carter, 1773), 136 (Evans #42437); cf. Daniel Fenning, *The Universal Spelling-Book . . . Revised, Corrected, and Improved By the Rev. J. Malham* (London: S. Crowder and B. C. Collins, 1794), 136. The Boston writing master John Tileston recorded a recipe for black ink ("4 ounces of Galls of Aleppo, 2 ounces of Copperas, 2 ounces of Gum Arabic") in his diary in 1764. D[aniel]

C[lement] Colesworthy, *John Tileston's School. Boston, 1778–1789: 1761–1766. Also, his Diary from 1761 to 1766* (Boston: Antiquarian Book Store, 1887), 72–86. Ink would not be manufactured and bottled in America until the Thaddeus Davids Ink Company (established in 1825) did so. Harry B. Weiss, "The Writing Masters and Ink Manufacturers of New York City, 1737–1820," *Bulletin of The New York Public Library* 56 (1952): 387; see 386–87 for other recipes for ink making. Experiments on old manuscripts show that "Iron gall inks were used almost exclusively in this country during the seventeenth and eighteenth centuries." William J. Barrow, "Black Writing Ink of the Colonial Period," *American Archivist* 9 (1948): 306.

28. Advts. by Joshua Blanchard for "Ink-Powder," *Boston Weekly Newsletter*, Dec. 29, 1743, Apr. 26, 1750; by Joshua Blanchard for Holman's ink powder, ibid., June 10, 1756; see also Condy, "Account Book," 100. Cf. advertisements for ink powder in the *Pennsylvania Gazette*, Nov. 2, 1749, May 30, 1751; *New-York Mercury*, Mar. 12, 1753; *South Carolina Gazette*, July 1, 1756; *Providence Gazette; and Country Journal*, Dec. 4, 1762; *Georgia Gazette*, June 2, 1763; for "black and red ink-powder," *Georgia Gazette*, Nov. 10, 1763; *Virginia Gazette*, July 25, 1766; for "Holman's best London ink powder," *New-York Mercury*, Feb. 27, 1764; "Holman's ink-powder," *Providence Gazette; and Country Journal*, Mar. 10, 1764.

29. Price of ink powder packets: Condy, "Account Book," 100 (10 pence each); Francis Jerdone, "Account Book, 1750–1772," 128 (1/- per packet), Jerdone Papers, Swem Library, College of William and Mary, Williamsburg, Va.; James Poyas, "Day Book, 1764–1766," May 2, 1764, South Carolina Historical Society, Charleston. See also the wholesale purchase of a two dozen packets (4/- a dozen), Nov. 21, 1769, by Johnston & Bennehan, Cameron Family Papers, box I, Southern Historical Collection #133, Library of the University of North Carolina at Chapel Hill.

30. Advts. for inkpots: *Pennsylvania Gazette*, Nov. 2, 1749 (horn, "double screw" leather); *Boston Weekly News-Letter*, Mar. 6, 1746 (brass, horn, and leather), May 29, 1755 (brass), Sept. 8, 1757 (brass and horn); *New-York Mercury*, Aug. 27, 1753, May 27, 1754 (leather, pewter, flint glass), Feb. 27, 1764 (Clark's best leather); *Providence Gazette; and Country Journal*, Dec. 25, 1762 (brass); *Georgia Gazette*, Nov. 10, 1763 (pewter); cf. Condy, "Account Book," 100 (brass). Inkstands ("standishes"): *Pennsylvania Gazette*, Nov. 2, 1749 (wood), May 30, 1751 (wood); *South Carolina Gazette*, July 1, 1756; *Virginia Gazette*, Apr. 27, 1757 (no material specified). "Pewter-Standishes and Ink-Pots": *New-York Mercury*, Oct 14, 1754; similarly, *Georgia Gazette*, Nov. 10, 1763; *South Carolina Gazette*, July 20, 1767; *Virginia Gazette*, Nov. 29, 1770 (all pewter).

31. Advts, *Pennsylvania Gazette*, Nov. 2, 1749 (fountain pen); *Georgia Gazette*, Nov. 10, 1763 (tin pen and brass fountain pens). Maygene Daniels, "The Ingenious Pen: American Writing Implements from the Eighteenth Century to the Twentieth," *American Archivist* (Summer 1980): 312–24; William H. Harris and Judith S. Levey, eds., *New Columbia Encyclopedia* (New York: Columbia University Press, 1975), s.v. "pen"; Ray Nash, *American Penmanship, 1800–1850: A History of Writing and a Bibliography of Copybooks from Jenkins to Spencer* (Worcester, Mass.: American Antiquarian Society, 1969), 57–59. Steel slip-on nibs were first manufactured in England at Birmingham in 1828, and American manufacturers soon followed suit. Metal nibs would not eliminate quills, however, until perhaps the 1860s, after their price had plummeted.

32. Colesworthy, *John Tileston's School*, 72–86.

33. Advts. for "Quills": South Carolina Gazette, Oct. 22, 1753; *Virginia Gazette*, Apr. 22, 1757; *Georgia Gazette*, Nov. 10, 1763. Advts. for Dutch quills: *Pennsylvania Gazette*, Nov. 2, 1749; *New-York Mercury*, Aug. 27, 1753; *Boston Weekly News-Letter*, May 29, 1755; *South Carolina Gazette*, July 20, 1767. For writing materials advertised in the *Virginia Gazette*, see John E. Molnar, "Publication and Retail Advertisements in the *Virginia Gazette*, 1736–1780" (Ph.D. diss., University of Michigan, 1978), pt. 1, 185

34. Advts. for "black-lead pencils" or "lead-pencils": *Boston Weekly Newsletter*, Dec. 29, 1743, Mar. 6, 1746, Apr. 26, 1750, Oct. 19, 1758; "cedar pencils": *New-York Mercury*, Nov. 13, 1752; *Boston [Weekly] News-Letter*, Oct. 19, 1758; "Pencils and Steel Cases": *Providence Gazette; and Country Journal*, Nov. 6, 1762.

35. Advts. for "Penknives": *Pennsylvania Gazette*, Dec. 19, 1749; *South Carolina Gazette*, Oct.

22, 1753; *Boston Weekly News-Letter*, Nov. 1, 1739, May 29, 1755, Jan 17, 1760, May 15, 1760; *Georgia Gazette*, Nov. 10, 1763; *Virginia Gazette* (Purdie & Dixon), Aug 29, 1771 (Dixon & Hunter), July 6, Aug. 24, 1776, in Molnar, "Publication and Retail," pt. 1, 185; see also Jerdone, "Account Book," 126, 146.

36. Advts. for pounce and pounce boxes: *New-York Mercury*, Oct. 14, 1754, June 23, 1755. Condy, "Account Book," 106. A recipe for making pounce is given in Dwight Foster to Algernon Foster, Foster Family Papers, Nov. 18, 1796, AAS.

37. Advts. for sealing wax: *Boston Weekly News-Letter*, Dec. 29, 1743; *New-York Mercury*, Dec. 11, 1752; *Virginia Gazette*, Apr. 22, 1757. Advts. for wafers, in "large and small Boxes": *New-York Mercury*, Aug. 27, 1753; *Providence Gazette; and Country Journal*, Nov. 6, 1762; "sealing wax and wafers: *Georgia Gazette*, Nov. 10, 1763; red and black wafers: *South Carolina Gazette*, July 1, 1756.

38. Advts. for both Dutch quills and Holman's ink powder: *Boston Weekly News-Letter*, May 29, 1755, June 10, 1756 (by Joshua Blanchard); *Providence Gazette; and Country Journal*, Mar. 10, 1764 (by Peleg Thurston at his Newport store); cf. advts. for ink powder: *Providence Gazette; and Country Journal*, Dec. 4, 1762; for Dutch quills: *Boston Weekly News-Letter*, June 5, 1760; advt. for "Holman's best London ink powder": *New-York Mercury*, Feb. 27, 1764. Advt. for Dutch sealing-wax: *Virginia Gazette*, Nov. 29, 1770.

39. Advts., *Providence Gazette; and Country Journal*, Nov. 6, 1762; *Georgia Gazette*, Nov. 10, 1763; Douglas C. McMurtrie, "Pioneer Printing in Georgia," *Georgia Historical Quarterly* 16 (1932): 77–93; advt. for "steel-blade pen-knives": *South Carolina Gazette*, Dec. 29, 1759.

40. Advts. for "Clark's best leather ink pots": *New-York Mercury*, Feb. 27, 1764; "Clark's leather ink holders": *Virginia Gazette*, July 25, 1766; "Jones's best Pen Knives": *New-York Mercury*, Aug. 23, 1756; "supersuperfine" sealing-wax: *New-York Mercury*, July 18, 1757.

41. Advt., *Boston Weekly News-Letter*, Sept. 19 [error for 16], 1742; Seybolt, *Private Schools*, 64.

42. Walter H. Small, *Early New England Schools* (Boston: Ginn, 1914), 317; Robert F. Seybolt, *The Evening School in Colonial America* (Urbana: University of Illinois Press, 1925), 23.

43. Advts., *Maryland Gazette*, quoted in Winton, "Southern Book Trade," 228; "Copy-books for Children": *Pennsylvania Gazette*, May 30, 1751; "Copy Books for School Boys": *New-York Mercury*, Oct 2, 1752; "cyphering and copy books for Children": *New-York Mercury*, Feb. 27, 1764; Condy, "Account Book," 26; cf. 100.

44. Molnar, "Publication and Retail," pt. 1, 66–67.

45. Dierks, "Letter Writing," 390-92; Robert F. Seybolt, *Apprenticeship and Apprenticeship Education in Colonial New England and New York* (New York: Teachers College, Columbia University, 1917), 47; E. Jennifer Monaghan, "Literacy Instruction and Gender in Colonial New England," in *Reading in America: Literature and Social History*, ed. Cathy N. Davidson (Baltimore: Johns Hopkins University Press, 1989), 63.

46. Advt., *Boston News-Letter and New-England Chronicle*, Dec. 16, 1762.

47. MSS, "Miscellaneous Specimens of American Calligraphy," Houghton Library. For a full discussion of the collection and the procedure by which the curriculum was inferred, see E. Jennifer Monaghan, "Readers Writing: The Curriculum of the Writing Schools of Eighteenth-Century Boston," *Visible Language* 21 (1987): 167–213. The spread of the collection by date is not uniform, but between 1751 and 1774, every year except 1758 and 1761 is represented by at least one piece. In the 1740s: 3 (all dated 1748); 1750s: 38 (14 in 1751 and 12 in 1757); 1760s: 70 (10 in 1763, 13 in 1767, and 15 in 1769); 1770s: 32 (up to 1774); 1780s: 1 (in 1782). Where dates and schools are both known, the manuscripts from the Queen School are dated 1767–74 (under the successive masterships of Samuel Holyoke, John Proctor Jr., and James Carter); the North Writing School, 1764–73 (John Tileston); and the South Writing School, 1760–74 (Abiah Holbrook, Joseph Ward, and Samuel Holbrook). For other manuscripts from the three Boston writing schools, see Tristram Plummer, "On the Pen," July 29, 1788 (North Writing School), MS (Newberry Library, Chicago). For the inspection, see Boston, *Records of Boston Selectmen, 1736–1742*, 20.

48. Tamara Plakins Thornton, *Handwriting in America: A Cultural History* (New Haven: Yale

University Press), 41. The nomenclature for the scripts has been borrowed from George Bickham's *Universal Penman*, 210–11, which provides the upper- and lowercase alphabets of twelve different scripts and identifies them by name. The scripts, issued separately by Henry Overton of London, are reproduced in Thornton, *Handwriting in America*, 20–21.

49. James Brown Mason, Writing Book, 1771, Rhode Island Historical Society, Providence (hereafter cited as RIHS).

50. Ray Nash, *An American Colonial Calligraphic Sheet of King Charles's Twelve Good Rules at Dartmouth College Library* (London: Bibliographical Society, 1952); the town of Worcester agreed that Richard Rogers should keep the school longer in 1738 (MSS, Worcester, Mass., Collection, School Records, 1738, AAS).

51. Abiah Holbrook, "The Writing Master's Amusement, 1767," MS, Houghton Library; Will of Abiah Holbrook, MS, Houghton Library; Ray Nash, "Abiah Holbrook and His 'Writing Master's Amusement,'" *Harvard Library Bulletin* 7 (1953): 88–104. For an identification of the scripts, see Bickham, *Universal Penman*, 210–11.

52. Lindley Murray, *Memoirs of the Life and Writings of Lindley Murray . . .* (York, England: Longman, Rees, Orme, Brown, and Green, 1826), 10–11; quoted in Charles Monaghan, *The Murrays of Murray Hill* (Brooklyn: Urban History Press, 1988), 25. I am indebted to Charles Monaghan for this reference.

53. Whalley, *Pen's Excellencie*, 243; Bickham, *Universal Penman*, 9, 113; George Bickham, *The United Pen-Men for Forming the Man of Business: Or, the Young Man's Copy-Book* (London: n.p., 1743).

54. John Bland to George Bickham, Nov. 21, 1738, in Bickham, *Universal Penman*, 143. See also "Specimens of the Running Hand, from the Performances of the best Masters" (dated Sept. 4, 1739), in ibid., 163.

55. B. F. Foster, *Foster's System of Penmanship: or, the Art of Rapid Writing* (Boston: Perkins, Marvin, 1835), 39–42.

56. John Jenkins, *The Art of Writing, Reduced to a Plain and Easy System . . . Book I . . .* (Boston: Isaiah Thomas and Ebenezer T. Andrews, 1791) (Evans #23469); John Jenkins, *The Art of Writing: Reduced to a Plain and Easy System . . . revised, enlarged and improved*, 3rd ed. (Elizabeth Town, N.J.: J. E. Sanderson, 1816), 75; *Early American Imprints*, 2nd ser., *1801–1819*, a Readex microprint [of the works listed in Shaw's *American Bibliography*] Shaw-Shoemaker numbers 1–50192 (Worcester, Mass.: American Antiquarian Society, 1964–), #37951. Nash, *American Writing Masters*, 26–34.

57. Boston, *Records of Boston Selectmen, 1736–1742*, 288; Boston, *Early History* [vol. 13], *A Report of the Record Commissioners of the City of Boston, Containing the Records of Boston Selectmen, 1716–1736* (Boston: Rockwell and Churchill, 1885), 53.

58. For manuscript schoolbooks in general, see James Mulhern, "Manuscript School-Books," *Papers of the Bibliographical Society of America* 32 (1938), 17–37. See, for example, William Collis's MS, "Compleat System of Practical Arithmetic," 1763, AM 824, Historical Society of Pennsylvania, Philadelphia (hereafter cited as HSP).

59. Photocopy, MS, "Arithmetic book, 1751–1766," 252, Virginia Historical Society, Richmond. See Figure 15.

60. Mary Clough, arithmetic book, 1762, Penmanship Collection, 1762–1848, AAS.

61. John C. Fitzpatrick, ed., *The Writings of George Washington from the Original Manuscript Sources, 1745–1799*, vol. 1, *1745–1756* (Washington, D.C.: U.S. Government Printing Office, 1931), 1–2.

62. Alice Gould, copybook 1755 (the front page gives the name Alice Chase), RIHS; Samuel Coates, "Cyphring Book," 1724, Am 3665, HSP. For other examples of the rule of three see Clough, arithmetic book, 1762; Grace Hoope's "Ciphering Book," Am 823, HSP, internally dated to 1719 or thereafter. For calligraphic arithmetic books by girls and women, see Rebeccah Salisbury, Aug. 1788, Penmanship Collection, 1762–1848, AAS.

63. John Brown, "Cyphering Book 1749/50," RIHS.

64. Collis, "Compleat System of Practical Arithmetic"; Lamb, "Andrew Lamb's new Rules for finding Longitude," 1754, Am 860, HSP. See also Patricia Cline Cohen, "Numeracy in

Nineteenth-Century America," in *A School History of Mathematics*, ed. George M. A. Stanic and Jeremy Kilpatrick, 2 vols. (Reston, Va.: National Council of Teachers of Mathematics, 2003), 1: 47–53.

65. James Hodder, *Hodder's Arithmetick: Or, That necessary Art made most easie . . .* 4th ed., much enlarged (London: Tho. Rooks, 1667) (http://wwwlib.umi.com/eebo/fullcite?id= 16963617, accessed July 30, 2004); *Hodder's Arithmetick: Or, That Necessary Art made most easie . . . 15th ed., revised, augmented, and above a Thousand Faults amended, by Henry Mose* (London: Ric. Chiswel, 1685) (http://wwwlib.umi.com/eebo/fullcite?id=19335788, accessed July 30, 2004); Edward Cocker, *Cockers Arithmetick: Being a plain and familiar Method suitable to the meanest capacity . . . perused and published by John Hawkins* (London: T. Passinger and T. Lacy, 1678) (http://wwwlib.umi.com/eebo/fullcite?id=11982220, accessed July 30, 2004).

66. George Fisher, *Arithmetic in the Plainest and Most Concise Methods Hitherto Extant. With new Improvements for Dispatch of Business in all the Several Rules*, was first published in London in 1730; Edward Cocker's *Arithmetick* was reprinted as "Carefully Corrected and Amended by George Fisher" and had reached a 56th edition in London by 1767; John Hill, *Arithmetick, Both in the Theory and Practice, Made Plain and Easie . . .* was in print by 1713 (Molnar, "Publication and Retail," pt. 2, 502, 432, 565). Advts. for Fisher's arithmetic: *Pennsylvania Gazette*, Dec. 10, 1751; *South Carolina Gazette*, June 2, 1759, July 20, 1767 (in Hennig Cohen, *The "South Carolina Gazette," 1732–1775* [Columbia: University of South Carolina, 1953], 143, 151); *Virginia Gazette*, July 18, 1771 (in Molnar, "Publication and Retail," pt. 2, 502); Cocker's *Arithmetick*: *South Carolina Gazette*, Jan. 25, 1735, July 20, 1767, Nov. 7, 1768 (in Cohen, *"South Carolina Gazette,"* 128, 151, 152); Cocker's and Fisher's *Arithmetick*: *New-York Mercury*, Dec, 11, 1752; "Hodder's, Cocker's and Hill's Arithmetick": *New-York Mercury*, Oct. 14, 1754; Hill's arithmetic: Nov. 7, 1768 (in Cohen, *"South Carolina Gazette,"* 152). Other arithmetics advertised in the *South Carolina Gazette*: unidentified, Mar. 9, 1752; Marsh's arithmetic, Aug. 10, 1752; Wingate's, Wise's, July 20, 1767, Nov. 7, 1768; Webster's, Nov. 7, 1768 (in Cohen, *"South Carolina Gazette,"* 135, 136, 151, 152).

67. David D. Hall, "Learned Culture in the Eighteenth Century," in Hall, *History of the Book*, 1:411–33; David S. Shields, "Eighteenth-Century Literary Culture," in ibid., 434–76. For Turell, see E. Jennifer Monaghan, "The Uses of Literacy by Girls in Colonial America," in *Girls and Literacy in America: Historical Perspectives to the Present*, ed. Jane Greer (Santa Barbara, Calif.: ABC-CLIO, 2003), 7–10. Some of Turell's writings are reproduced in ibid., 249–56.

68. R. T. Paine, letter of June 17, 1757, Massachusetts Historical Society, Boston; James Brown Mason, "Writing Book, 1771," RIHS.

69. John Gorton, in book of Sarah Gorton, 1778, [1] RIHS; Gorton gives his date of birth as Aug. 13, 1753, [1, 13]. "Practice" is defined as "a short Method of casting or finding the value of any quantity of Merchandize" in Francis Gardiner, copybook, [?1769], RIHS.

70. Collis, "Compleat System of Practical Arithmetic"; Benjamin Carr, "Account Books, 1772–95," internally dated to 1768, RIHS.

71. Advt., 1772, in Seybolt, *Private Schools*, 67, for teaching "Writing, Arithmetic, English Grammar, Logic, and Composition"; advt., *Gazette of the State of Georgia*, Jan. 22, 1784, for teaching "Young Ladies . . . Writing, Arithmetick, English Grammar, Composition, Geography, &c."

72. Dierks, "Letter Writing"; see esp., chap. 1, and on Richardson, 60–63.

73. See above, Chapter 8, p. 214.

74. Dierks, "Letter Writing," 372; J[ohn] Hill, *The Young Secretary's Guide: Or, A Speedy Help to Learning*, 24th ed. (Boston: Thomas Fleet, 1750) (Evans # 6517), [3], 20–67; letters to girls or women appear in 11 of the 48 pages devoted to letters.

75. Dierks, "Letter Writing," 373–76; quot., Seybolt, *Private Schools*, 72.

76. Dierks, "Letter Writing," 395–442. Of the 31 sets of family letters that Dierks cites in his chap. 6, only 2 are dated before 1770 (1750s: 1; 1760s: 1; 1770s: 6; 1780s: 9; 1790s: 11; 1800s: 3). Most of these are from parent to child. See also Bushman, *Refinement of America*, 90–92.

77. Paine, letter, June 17, 1757.

78. "Diary of Sally Fairfax, 1771–1772," dated Jan. 3, 1772, and letter, Sally Fairfax to Bryan Fairfax (1737–1802), Oct. 18, 1777, Virginia Historical Society, Richmond.

79. Fred Anderson, *A People's Army: Massachusetts Soldiers and Society in the Seven Years' War* (Chapel Hill, N.C.: Institute of Early American History and Culture, 1984), ix–x.

80. "Diary of John Thomas," *Nova Scotia Historical Society Collections* 1 (1878): 123.

81. Quoted in Richard E. Hodges, "American Spelling Instruction: Retrospect and Prospect," *Visible Language* 21 (1987): 216; Philip Dormer Stanhope, Earl of Chesterfield, *Letters Written to His Son, Philip Stanhope . . .* , 4 vols., 3rd ed. (London: 1774; rpt., New York: J. Rivington and H. Gaine, 1775) (Evans # 14471). Philip Fithian (see Chapter 12) saw the book, was "charm'd" by it and decided to buy a copy (Fithian, *Journal and Letters*, 255).

82. For the varying commitment of Massachusetts towns to educating girls, see Kathryn Kish Sklar, "The Schooling of Girls and Changing Community Values in Massachusetts Towns, 1750–1820," *History of Education Quarterly* 33 (1993): 511–42.

83. E. Jennifer Monaghan, "Reading for the Enslaved, Writing for the Free: Reflections on Liberty and Literacy," *Proceedings of the American Antiquarian Society* 108 (1999): 335–36. The states were Alabama, Georgia, Louisiana, North Carolina, and South Carolina (of which Alabama, Georgia, and South Carolina also prohibited literacy instruction for free blacks); Virginia defined all schools for blacks, free or enslaved, as illegal assembly and prohibited whites from teaching at any such school for pay.

Chapter 11. The New World of Children's Books

1. *The History of the Holy Jesus*, 4th ed. (Boston: D[aniel] Gookin, 1747), frontispiece, *Early American Imprints. Series I, Evans (1639–1800)* [electronic resource] ([New Canaan, Conn.]: Readex; [Worcester, Mass.]: American Antiquarian Society, [2002–]) (hereafter cited as Evans), #5967; Gillian Avery, *Behold the Child: American Children and Their Books, 1621–1922* (Baltimore: Johns Hopkins University Press, 1994), 42–44.

2. I have used the categorization of Ruth K. MacDonald, *Literature for Children in England and America from 1646 to 1774* (Troy, N.Y.: Whitston, 1982). See also William Sloane, *Children's Books in England and America in the Seventeenth Century: A History and Checklist, Together with the Young Christian's Library, the First Printed Catalogue of Books for Children* (New York: Kimg's Crown Press, Columbia University, 1955); Jane Bingham and Grayce Scholt, *Fifteen Centuries of Children's Literature: An Annotated Chronology of British and American Works in Historical Context* (Westport, Conn.: Greenwood Press, 1980).

3. James Raven, "The Importation of Books in the Eighteenth Century," in *A History of the Book in America*, ed. David D. Hall, vol. 1, *The Colonial Book in the Atlantic World*, ed. Hugh Amory and David D. Hall ([Worcester, Mass.]: American Antiquarian Society; New York: Cambridge University Press, 2000), 183–85; Hugh Amory, "A Note on Statistics," ibid., 514.

4. Lorraine Smith Pangle and Thomas L. Pangle, *The Learning of Liberty: The Educational Ideas of the American Founders* (Lawrence: University Press of Kansas, 1993), 61–66. For Locke's views on original sin, see Peter A. Schouls, *Reasoned Freedom: John Locke and Enlightenment* (Ithaca, N.Y.: Cornell University Press, 1992), 190–203.

5. James L. Axtell, *The Educational Writings of John Locke: A Critical Edition with Introduction and Notes* (Cambridge: Cambridge University Press, 1968), 257, 260, 255, 256.

6. Samuel Pickering, *John Locke and Children's Books in Eighteenth-Century England* (Knoxville: University of Tennessee Press, 1981), 11–12; cf. Pangle and Pangle, *Learning of Liberty*, 75. Imported copies of Locke's *Some Thoughts* were advertised in, e.g., *Pennsylvania Gazette*, May 30, 1751; *New-York Mercury*, June 16, 1755, Oct. 27, 1755; *South Carolina Gazette*, June 2, 1759, in Hennig Cohen, *The South Carolina Gazette, 1732–1775* (Columbia: University of South Carolina Press, 1953), 144.

7. Margaret Spufford's evidence that chapbooks were used as toilet paper is relevant here. Spufford, *Small Books and Pleasant Histories: Popular Fiction and Its Readership in Seventeenth-Century England* (New York: Cambridge University Press, 1981), 48–49.

8. *A Catalogue of Books, Sold by Noel and Hazard at their Book and Stationary* [sic] *Store* (New York: Inslee and Car., 1771) (Evans #12168), 29.

9. *Faults on All Sides. The Case of Religion Consider'd* . . . (Newport, R.I.: printed for the author, and sold by E. Nearegreas and J. Franklin, 1728), [154]; Victor Neuburg, "Chapbooks in America: Reconstructing the Popular Reading of Early America," in *Reading in America: Literature and Social History*, ed. Cathy N. Davidson (Baltimore: Johns Hopkins University Press, 1989), 85.

10. Advts., *New York-Mercury*, Oct. 14, 1754, June 23, 1755; see also Aug. 23, 1756, July 18, 1757. For histories, see Worthington C. Ford, *The Boston Book Market, 1679–1700* (Boston: Club of Odd Volumes, 1917), 85, 89, 90, 134. London editions of the *History of Parismus* were in print from at least 1615 on. *Valentine and Orson* began as a French prose romance printed in Lyons, France, in 1489, and all versions derive from this source. The first English translation was published in London in about 1510 and was the source for later English versions. Arthur Dickson, *Valentine and Orson: A Study in Late Medieval Romance* (New York: Columbia University Press, 1929), 3.

11. Neuburg, "Chapbooks in America," 85–90. Cf. *The History of Valentine and Orson, Two Sons of the Emperor of Greece* (Dublin: for Luke Dillon, 1734). The bookseller Jeremiah Condy sold one copy of the *Seven Champions* between 1759 and 1768. "Jeremiah Condy, "Account Book, 1759–1770," American Antiquarian Society, Worcester, Mass., 67.

12. Elizabeth Carroll Reilly and David D. Hall, "Customers and the Market for Books," in Hall, *History of the Book in America*, 1:391.

13. Advt., *Boston Evening-Post*, May 31, 1736; *The Prodigal Daughter* (Boston: n.p., [1767?]) (Evans #41754).

14. *A New Gift for Children. Delightful and Entertaining Stories For little Masters and Misses* (Boston: D[aniel] Fowle, n.d.) (Evans # 40555); see also *A New Gift for Children* (Boston: G[amaliel] Rogers, 1750) (#6511). D'Alte A. Welch, *A Bibliography of American Children's Books Printed prior to 1821* (Worcester, Mass.: American Antiquarian Society, 1972), 48. For Daniel Fowle, who printed at Boston from 1742 to 1755, see Isaiah Thomas, *The History of Printing in America*, ed. Marcus A. McCorison from the 2nd edition (New York: Weathervane Books, 1970), 120–21, 127–30.

15. Avery, *Behold the Child*, 48.

16. *New Gift*, 26, 8, 30. For the verse in Watts, see above, p. 309.

17. Elizabeth Carroll Reilly, *A Dictionary of Colonial American Printers' Ornaments and Illustrations* (Worcester, Mass.: American Antiquarian Society, 1975), 338, 332–37. For Thomas Fleet's children's books, see Benjamin Franklin V, ed., *Boston Printers, Publishers, and Booksellers: 1640–1800* (Boston, Mass.: G. K. Hall, 1980), 163–64.

18. *Aesops Fables, with their Moralls, in Prose and Verse Grammatically translated* (London: n.p., 1655); Lawrence A. Cremin, *American Education: The Colonial Experience, 1607–1783* (New York: Harper & Row, 1970), 175, 185, 505; Axtell, *Educational Writings of John Locke*, 259; Pickering, *John Locke*, 22; Thomas Noel, *Theories of the Fable in the Eighteenth Century* (New York: Columbia University Press, 1975), 6–8.

19. Michael, *Teaching of* English, 161. On fables for children, see MacDonald, *Literature for Children*, chap. 5. For the relationship between cultural inclination and fable choice, see Eugene F. Provenzo Jr., "Education and the Aesopic Tradition" (Ph.D. diss., Washington University, 1976). For the status of the fable in England, see Noel, *Theories of the Fable*, chaps. 3, 9.

20. A characteristic work in the courtesy vein was Francis Hawkins, *Youths Behavior or Decency in Conversation Among Men, Translated out of French* (1640); see Michael V. Belok, "The Courtesy Tradition and Early Schoolbooks," *History of Education Quarterly* 8 (1968): 307–18; Michael V. Belok, *Forming the American Minds: Early School-Books and Their Compilers, 1783–1837* (Moti Katra, Agra-U.P., India: Satish Book Enterprise, 1973), 46. For the courtesy tradition, see Richard L. Bushman, *The Refinement of America: Persons, Houses, Cities* (1992; repr., New York: Vintage Books, 1993), chap. 2.

21. *The School of Good Manners*, documented in 1715 (Evans #1778), 1725 (#2699), and 1732 (#3603) (advertised as "Just republished," *Boston Weekly News-Letter*, Aug 17, 1732)—

none extant; the 1772 Fleet edition (Boston: T. & J. Fleet, 1772) appears in Evans #12553. George Washington, *George Washington's Rules of Civility: Complete with the Original French Text and New French-to-English Translations*, 2nd ed. (Leesburg, Va.: Goose Creek Productions, 2000), ed. John T. Phillips II. An early version was written by John Garretson, *The School of Manners. Or Rules for Childrens Behaviour*, 4th ed. (London, 1701; repr., London: Victoria and Albert Museum, 1983). I am indebted to David Mikosz for this reference.

22. *School of Good Manners* (1772), 6, 15, 16, 30.

23. Advts., *Boston Weekly News-Letter*, Aug. 17, 1732. The work was in a fourth edition and the publisher was Benjamin Eliot of Boston.

24. Michael Wigglesworth, *Day of Doom*, was reprinted in 1701, its 5th edition (Evans #1030), 1715, 6th ed. (#1794), and 1751 (#6796). Advt. for 4th edition of *Early Piety: Boston Weekly News-Letter*, Feb 19, 1741. For examples of advertisements for *Pilgrim's Progress*, see *New-York Mercury*, May 13, 1754; "bunyan's pilgrims progress in 3 parts": *South Carolina Gazette*, May 11, 1747 (in Cohen, *South Carolina Gazette*, 133); advertised extensively from 1770 to 1773 in the *Virginia Gazette* (in John E. Molnar, "Publication and Retail Book Advertisements in the *Virginia Gazette*, 1736–1780" [Ph.D. diss., University of Michigan, 1978], 402–3).

25. Only four of many editions of the *Holy Bible in Verse* are extant. Its woodcuts are said to have been borrowed from a now vanished *New-England Primer*. Avery, *Behold the Child*, 42.

26. Geoffrey Summerfield, *Fantasy and Reason: Children's Literature in the Eighteenth Century* ([London]: Methuen, 1984), 73.

27. I[saac] Watts, *Divine Songs for Children*, 7th ed. (Boston: W. Kneeland and T. Green for D. Henchman, 1730) (Evans #39960). For additional American editions of Watts's *Divine Songs*, see Evans #2085 (1719), #4206 (1737), #5508 (1744), #6080 (1747), #6438 (1749), #7134 (1753), #8059 (1757), #13065 (1773).

28. Watts, *Divine Songs for Children* (1730), 2, 12.

29. Ibid., 8, 9.

30. Ibid., 9, 17.

31. Ibid., 17, 18.

32. John Lewis, *The Church Catechism Explained, By Way of Question and Answer; And Confirmed by Scripture Proofs* (London: B. Dod, 1759), v–vi, vii, ix–x.

33. For example, Elias Neau used *The Church Catechism Explained* for catechizing some white apprentices in 1710; Thomas Huddleston requested it for his New York scholars at the Trinity Charity School in 1729; and Thomas Keeble, schoolmaster of a charity school at Oyster Bay, Long Island, was sent twenty-five copies from London in 1743. Elias Neau to Sec., July 5, 1710, S.P.G. Papers, ser. A, 5:134, Library of Congress Records, Washington, D.C.; Thomas Huddleston to Sec., July 10, 1729, S.P.G. Papers, ser. B, 1:61, Rhodes House, Oxford, U.K.; Philip Bearcroft to Thomas Keeble, June 14, 1743, S.P.G. Papers, ser. B, 10:140, Rhodes House.

34. John Lewis's *Church Catechism Explained* was published in 1748 (Evans #6178), 1753 (#7039), and 1765 (#10039). The *South Carolina Gazette* never advertised it; however, the *Virginia Gazette* advertised it once in 1752, and seventeen times between 1771 and 1777 (Molnar, "Publication and Retail Book Advertisements," 618–19).

35. The publisher of the 1746 edition of *The History of Holy Jesus* is listed as "for B. C——[illegible]" (Evans #40398); others include the 4th ed. (see above, note 1); 6th ed. (Boston: J[ohn] Bushnell and J[ohn] Green, 1749) (#6331); 7th ed. (New-London: John Green, 1754) (#7211); 8th ed. (New-London: T[imothy] Green, 1762) (#9138); 24th ed. (Boston: Ez[ekiel] Russell, 1771) (#12073) (most of the presumed intermediary editions are no longer extant).

36. *The History of the Holy Jesus* (Boston: Zechariah Fowle, 1766) (Evans #41626); see the illustrations in Reilly, *Dictionary*, 383. The initials I.T. appear in the woodcut of this last edition. Because Thomas copied the earlier woodcut from an earlier book, his illustrations appear as mirror images of the earlier ones.

37. *History of the Holy Jesus* (1746) (Evans # 40398), n.p.

38. For the ordinary person's hopefulness about death, see David D. Hall, *Worlds of Wonder, Days of Judgment: Popular Religious Belief in Early New England* (New York: Alfred A. Knopf, 1989), 207–9.

39. *The Friendly Instructor: Or, A companion for Young Ladies and Young Gentlemen* (London; repr., Philadelphia: Joseph Crukshank, 1782) (Evans #44200). Doddridge became coeditor of the collected works of Isaac Watts after the latter's death.

40. Advts. for *Friendly Instructor: Pennsylvania Gazette*, Dec. 10, 1745 (for sixpence), Feb. 13, 1749/50 (for sixpence single or fourpence by the dozen, 6th ed.); Feb. 20, 1749/50 (for eight pence single or sixpence by the dozen); *Boston Weekly News-Letter*, Jan. 9, 1746; Aug. 10, 1749; *South Carolina Gazette*, May 11, 1747 (in Cohen, *South Carolina Gazette*, 133); *New York Gazette*, Dec. 22, 1760; Evans #5600, 5774, 5775, 6503, 6323, 11660; *The Friendly Instructor: Or, A companion for Young Ladies and Young Gentlemen* (London; repr., Philadelphia: Joseph Crukshank, 1782) (#44200).

41. *Friendly Instructor* (1782) (Evans #44200), table of contents, [xii], 5, 6.

42. Ibid., 9–12, quot. 11; 2 Kings 2.23.

43. *Friendly Instructor* (1782), 20, 73.

44. Ibid., 32–48.

45. Advt., *Boston Weekly News-Letter*, May 28, 1747; *Present for an Apprentice* (London; repr., Boston: Rogers & Fowle, 1747), 81 (Evans #5904).

46. Advt., *Boston Weekly News-Letter*, Aug. 20, 1747; for Locke and "Esteem," see Schouls, *Reasoned Freedom*, 212.

47. Advts., *Philadelphia Gazette*, Dec. 19, 1749; Jan. 22, 1750/51.

48. Advt., *Boston Weekly News-Letter*, Jan. 26, 1744. No copy is extant.

49. *The Child's New Play-Thing*, American editions after 1744: 1750 (Evans #6477), 1757 (#7871), 1761 (#8813), 1765 (#9927); advts., *Virginia Gazette*, June 10, 1773 (in Molnar, "Publication and Retail Book Advertisements," 423). (It is not advertised by title in the *South Carolina Gazette*.) Advts., *Pennsylvania Gazette*, July 2, 1747; *New-York Mercury*, Dec. 11, 1752, Mar. 12, 1753, Oct. 14, 1754, June 7, 1756. Condy, "Account Book" shows sales of 499 Dilworth's spellers to 22 of the *New Play-Thing* between 1759 and 1768.

50. *The Child's New Play-Thing* (Boston: J. Draper & J. Edwards, 1750) (Evans #6477), 4.

51. Patricia Crain, *The Story of A: The Alphabetization of America from the "New England Primer" to "The Scarlet Letter"* (Stanford: Stanford University Press, 2000), 64–73, quot. 64. Cf. "alphabets of different sizes," advt. *Georgia Gazette*, Nov. 10, 1763.

52. *Child's New Play-Thing*, 17.

53. Ibid., 48–49 (italics reversed).

54. Ibid., 65–67.

55. Ibid., 73.

56. For romances in their medieval form, see Roberta L. Krueger, ed., *The Cambridge Companion to Medieval Romance* (Cambridge: Cambridge University Press, 2000).

57. The many London versions of Guy of Warwick include Humphrey Crouch, *The Heroick History of Guy Earl of Warwick* (London: Edward Brewster, 1671); an undated twenty-four-page twopenny chapbook, *Renowned Guy, Earl of Warwick* (London: for the booksellers, n.d.); cf. *The History of Guy, Earl of Warwick* (London: printed and sold in Aldermary Church Yard, n.d.), and the lavishly illustrated *The Noble and Renowned History of Guy Earl of Warwick*, 6th. ed. (London: A. Bettesworth, 1729). For the continuing popularity of Guy, see Ronald Crane, "The Vogue of Guy of Warwick from the Close of the Middle Ages to the Romantic Revival," *Publications of the Modern Language Association of America* 30 (1915): 125–94; for a modern reproduction, see John Simons, ed., *Guy of Warwick and Other Chapbook Romances: Six Tales from the Popular Literature of Pre-Industrial England* (Exeter: University of Exeter Press, 1998).

58. *Child's New Play-Thing* (1750), 96, 98, 99.

59. Ibid., title page.

60. This edition of *The Friar and the Boy* is cited in Avery, *Behold the Child*, 38. For fairy tales, see MacDonald, *Literature for Children*, chap. 6; for Isaac Watts's warnings against them, see Summerfield, *Fantasy and Reason*, 79–81.

61. Neuburg, "Chapbooks in America," 89–90. *Arabian Nights* was on sale from 1752 on in New York, from 1768 in Charles Town, South Carolina, and from 1770 in Williamsburg, Virginia, advertised in *New-York Mercury* (as "Arabian Nights Entertainments"), Dec. 11, 1752

(as "Arabian Tales"), Aug. 27, 1753, May 13, 1754; *Massachusetts Gazette and Boston News-Letter*, Oct. 31, 1765; *South Carolina Gazette*, Nov. 7, 1768 (in Cohen, *South Carolina Gazette*, 152); see also advts. from 1770 on in *Virginia Gazette* in Molnar, "Publication and Retail Book Advertisements," 351. Nicholas Rigby owned a copy; May 6, 1756, Georgia (Colony) Estate Records, Inventories and Appraisements, Book F, 1754–1770, Georgia State Archives, 34.

62. Avery, *Behold the Child*, 38.

63. For a full discussion, from which some of the wording has been taken, as well as the quotations from the boys' pieces (and so, indirectly, copybooks), see E. Jennifer Monaghan, "Readers Writing: The Curriculum of the Writing Schools of Eighteenth Century Boston," *Visible Language* 21 (1987): 194–208.

64. Ibid., 198.

65. Ibid., 199–200 (moral), 200–202 (commerce), 202–3 (political).

66. Ibid., 206–7.

67. Charles Welsh, *A Bookseller of the Last Century* (London: Griffith, Farran, Okedan, and Walsh, 1885), 6–8, 19–23; John Newbery, *A Little Pretty Pocket-Book, facsimile, with introductory essay and bibliography* by M. F. Thwaite (London: Oxford University Press, 1966), 28–34. The Thwaite facsimile is of the 1767 London edition.

68. For a description of the appearance of Newbery books, see MacDonald, *Literature for Children*, 141.

69. Newbery, *Little Pretty Pocket-Book*, 6, 7–8, 10.

70. The Maryland subscribers are detailed in Avery, *Behold the Child*, 41. For publications by Newbery and his successors from 1740 to 1800, see Welsh, *Bookseller of the Last Century*, 168–336; Sydney Roscoe, *Newbery-Carnan-Power: A Provisional Check-List of Books for the Entertainment, Instruction and Education of Children and Young People, Issued under the Imprints of John Newbery and his Family in the Period 1742–1802* ([London: Dawsons], 1966). See also MacDonald, *Literature for Children*, 135–51; John Rowe Townsend, ed., *John Newbery and His Books: Trade and Plum-Cake for Ever, Huzza!* (Metuchen, N.J.: Scarecrow Press, 1996).

71. This does not attempt to do justice to the complexity of Locke's views: for a good discussion, see Schouls, *Reasoned Freedom*, chaps. 7–8, esp. 211–17.

72. Newbery, *Little Pretty Pocket-Book*, 71–72.

73. Advt., *Virginia Gazette* (Purdie & Dixon), Feb 25, 1768; in Molnar, "Publication and Retail Book Advertisements," 800; John Newbery, *The Valentine's Gift, or, A Plan to enable Children of all Sizes and Denominations To behave with Honour, Integrity, and Humanity* (London: T. Carnan & F. Newbery, Jr., 1777), 19–23. The work had no American imprint until after the Revolution.

74. Newbery, *Valentine's Gift*, 24–25.

75. *The Renowned History of Giles Gingerbread: A Little Boy who lived upon Learning* (Boston: Mein & Fleeming, 1768) (Evans #41870), 14–22, quots. 20, 22.

76. Ibid., 23–[35], quots. 23, 26, [34]. (Pages missing from the torn 1768 edition have been supplied from a later edition.) For the illustration of the lion, see Reilly, *Dictionary*, 348.

77. *The History of Goody Two Shoes; Otherwise called Mrs. Margery Two Shoes* (London: H. Abel, n.d.), 14–15. The wording in this London edition is virtually identical in the first extant colonial edition, although the latter uses many more capitalizations. *The History of Little Goody Two-Shoes: Otherwise called, Mrs. Margery Two-Shoes* (New-York: H[ugh] Gaine, 1775) (Evans #14117), quots. 23, 25.

78. *History of Little Goody Two-Shoes* (1775), 27–37, quots. 27, 29, 32, 34, 36; *History of Goody Two Shoes* (London edition), 16–21.

79. *History of Little Goody Two-Shoes* (1775), 66; *History of Goody Two Shoes* (London edition), 39.

80. J[ohn] H. Plumb, "The New World of Children in Eighteenth-Century England," *Past and Present* 67 (1975): 64–95, esp. 71, 85–91, quot. 90.

81. Cary Carson, Ronald Hoffman, and Peter J. Albert, eds., *Of Consuming Interests: The Style of Life in the Eighteenth Century* (Charlottesville: University Press of Virginia, published for the United States Capitol Historical Society, 1994).

82. Avery, *Behold the Child*, 40; advts., *Pennsylvania Gazette*, July 2, 1747, Nov. 15, 1750; *Boston Weekly News-Letter*, June 24, 1756. Cohen, *South Carolina Gazette*, 125. The following phrases appeared in advertisements in the *South Carolina Gazette*: "new invented Books for Children": Sept. 11, 1749; "sundry sorts of useful and entertaining books for children": Oct. 22, 1753; "with many entertaining novels, books for children, &c.": Oct. 23, 1755; "all sorts of Primmers and other small Books for Children" July 1, 1756; "sundry little books for the amusement and instruction of children": Dec. 29, 1759; "little history books for children, with sundry other books in small octavo both instructive and entertaining": May 30, 1761; "a great variety of small picture books for children, entertaining and instructive": July 20, 1767 (in Cohen, *South Carolina Gazette*, 134, 138, 140, 142, 144 [bis], 151).

83. Catalogue, circa 1772, published by Cox & Berry of Boston, quoted in Neuburg, "Chapbooks in America," 86–87; advt., *Boston Gazette and Country Journal*, Jan. 13, 1772. See also Thomas, *History of Printing*, 210–11.

84. Advt., *Pennsylvania Gazette*, Nov. 15, 1750; Avery, *Behold the Child*, 40. For other primers, see Charles F. Heartman, *American Primers, Indian Primers, Royal Primers, and Thirty-Seven Other Types of Non-New England Primers Issued Prior to 1830* (Highland Park, N.J.: for H. B. Weiss, 1935).

85. Advts., *New-York Mercury*, July 18, 1757, Aug. 30, 1762.

86. *The Royal Primer; Or, an easy and pleasant Guide to the Art of Reading. Authoriz'd by His Majesty King George II* (London: J. Newbery, n.d.). (George II died in 1760.) *The Royal Primer Improved* (Philadelphia: James Chattin, 1753); *The Royal Primer. Or, an Easy and Pleasant Guide To the Art of Reading. Authorized by His Majesty King George II . . .* (Boston: William McAlpine, 1773) (Evans #12989). William McAlpine advertised Boston copies of *The Royal Primer* in 1768; advt., *Boston Gazette and Country Journal*, Nov. 21, 1768. At least two Philadelphia booksellers stocked imported copies of it in 1761; advts., *Pennsylvania Gazette*, Feb. 19, 1761 (Solomon Fussell), May 7, 1761 (William Wilson). It was not advertised by title in the *South Carolina Gazette* or the *Virginia Gazette*. It was occasionally reprinted even after the American Revolution, in 1784 (#8768), 1795 (#29443), and 1796 (#31131). *The Famous Tommy Thumb's Little Story-Book* (Boston: William McAlpine, 1768 [#41890]). For its illustrations, see Reilly, *Dictionary*, 351–52. Isaiah Thomas is the presumed printer of another Boston edition circa 1765 (#10189).

87. One London edition actually begins with an advertisement—for Newbery's *Royal Psalter; Royal Primer* (London), opposite title page. According to Welsh, *Bookseller of the Last Century*, 302, Benjamin Collins was the author of the *Royal Primer*.

88. *Royal Primer* (1773), [1].

89. Crain, *Story of A*, 91–93, quot. 91.

90. *Royal Primer* (1773), 14, 19.

91. Ibid., 22.

92. In the nineteenth century, several British reading instructional texts were printed with hyphenated syllables, even in the more advanced readers. See, for example, [Mrs. Mortimer], *Reading Without Tears; Or, a Pleasant Mode of Learning to Read, Part Second* (New York: Harper & Brothers, 1866) (originally an English imprint), where the entire text indicates syllabic division by hyphens: "Fox-es are sly and clev-er" (5).

93. *Royal Primer* (1773), 27.

94. Ibid., 54, 51–52.

95. Ibid., 49–50.

96. Electronic search of the genre "primers," courtesy American Antiquarian Society.

Chapter 12. Literacy in Three Families of the 1770s

1. Anna Green Winslow, *Diary of Anna Green Winslow: A Boston School Girl of 1771*, ed. Alice Morse Earle (1894; repr., Williamstown, Mass.: Corner House Publishers, 1974), 64.

2. Ibid., x, xi.

3. Ibid., 23 (warmth), 75 n.1 (Sarah and John Deming), 83 n. 12 (Sally Winslow; see also

22, 25, 47, 72). Family members in Boston included Anna's father's brother, John Winslow, his wife, and their daughters, Sally (mentioned above) and Bessy, who was Anna's age (80 n. 5), as well as Anna's mother's sister, Elizabeth Storer, and her husband, Ebenezer (96 n. 28), who lived next door to Elizabeth's younger sister, Susanna, who had married her cousin Frank Green (91 n. 21).

4. Ibid., 86 n.14; for another slave, see "Mr. Soley's Charlstown," 8.

5. Ibid., 76 n. 3 (Bacon), 80 n. 4 (Hunt), 23–24 (lectures on the catechism), quot. 25. For Hunt, see also 50, 56, 63.

6. Ibid., 1, 73, 62, 63, vi, quot. 18.

7. Ibid., manuscript page reproduced on xxiii, 72, 49. See Figure 19.

8. Ibid., 29–31 (Uncle Ned); 36–37, 62, 65 (Bet Smith); quots. 4, 29, 65. For Uncle Ned (Edward Green), see 104 n. 43.

9. Ibid., 46, quots. 22, 44. The "Dim eyes" poem is attributed to Governor Thomas Dudley, who is said to have written it for his epitaph. He died in 1653 (ibid., 106 n. 46).

10. Ibid., 34, 55 (text journal), 56 (loose paper); quots. 15, 1–2, 56. For other examples of Anna's verbal recall or summaries of sermons or lectures, see 24–25, 50–51, 53–54.

11. Ibid., 42–43 (see Prov. 27.1), 21 (Judges 15.8), 15 (I Peter 5.2, 3).

12. Winslow, *Diary*, 21, 41; see also 51, 72.

13. Ibid., 34, 13, 15, 60, 70. Advts, *Providence (Rhode Island) Gazette; and Country Journal*, Nov. 6, 1762 ("The Histories of Tom Jones, Joseph Andrews . . ."), and Aug. 27, 1763 ("The Histories of Pamela, Clarissa, Tom Jones, Joseph Andrews, &c"); *Boston Gazette and Country Journal*, Jan. 20, 1772 (quoted in Winslow, *Diary*, 116 n. 65). The 1772 advertisement includes the *Puzzling Cap*, the "History of Joseph Andrews," the "History of Clarissa," and the "History of Grandison." *Early American Imprints. Series I, Evans (1639-1800)* [electronic resource] ([New Canaan, Conn.]: Readex; [Worcester, Mass.]: American Antiquarian Society, [2002–]), (hereafter cited as Evans), #27623, records Samuel Hall's first Boston edition of *The History of Sir Charles Grandison* in 1794 as having some fifty-four pages.

14. Winslow, *Diary*, 22 (health), 35 (weather); for specific schools, see 18, 72, 103 n. 42 (William Turner's dancing school); 12, 22, 35, 36, 64, 70, 72 (Mrs. Smith's sewing school); 12, 35, 36, 45, 46, 52, 57, 59, 70, 72, 92 n.23 (Samuel Holbrook's writing school).

15. Ibid., vi (italics romanized). For Anna's handiwork, see 10, 12, 47 (sewing), 34 (spinning), 28, 34, 63 (knitting), 62 (patchwork).

16. Ibid., 29, 46, 47–48.

17. Ibid., 5, 48, 39.

18. Ibid., 41–42, 16; 18 (Caty's age).

19. Ibid., 9, 70, 8.

20. Ibid., 52, 9.

21. Ibid., 12.

22. Ibid., 27–28 (newspaper article); 36–37, 62, 65 (Betty Smith), quot. 40 (cf. 34).

23. Ibid., 7, 13, 17, 42, 62–67 (clothing); 13, 17, 20 (jewelry); 31, 63, 71 (headgear); 17 (shoes), quots. 52 ("frolicks"), 17, 31.

24. Philip Vickers Fithian, *Journal and Letters of Philip Vickers Fithian, 1773–1774: A Plantation Tutor of the Old Dominion*, edited and with an introduction by Hunter Dickinson Farish (Williamsburg, Va.: Colonial Williamsburg, 1943), 3 nn. 1–2, 22.

25. Fithian, *Journal*, 8. For Robert Carter, see Louis Morton, *Robert Carter of Nomini Hall: A Virginia Tobacco Planter of the Eighteenth Century* (Williamsburg, Va.: Colonial Williamsburg, 1941). He was the grandson of "King" Robert Carter, a well-known plantation owner.

26. Fithian, *Journal*, 62. Cf. Elizabeth Brown Pryor, "An Anomalous Person: The Northern Tutor in Plantation Society, 1773–1860," *Journal of Southern History* 47 (1981): 363–92.

27. Fithian, *Journal*, 109, 106 (acres), 184 (Gmby); Morton, *Robert Carter*, 205 (see 63–67 for Carter's landholdings).

28. Fithian, *Journal*, 107–8, 175 (Harry's last name); Morton, *Robert Carter*, 205–9.

29. Fithian, *Journal*, 40.

30. Ibid., 41. The routine was tightened up the following June: school hours were from

Fithian's entry until eight (the children arrived at about seven); breakfast 8:00–9:00; school 9: 00–12:00; school play hours, 12:00–2:00; dinner, 2:00–3:00; school, 3:00–5:30 (ibid., 157).

31. Ibid., 37, 48 (three times a week), 57 (twice a week), 105 (Nancy was later instructed by Stadley, 159), 187, 123.

32. Ibid., 25–26. The dates of birth of the Carter children surviving in 1773 are: Benjamin, Nov. 9, 1756; Robert Bladen, Mar. 18, 1759; Priscilla, June 15, 1760; Anne Tasker (Nancy), Jan. 17, 1762; Frances (Fanny), May 25, 1764; Betty Landon (Betsy), Oct. 25, 1765; Harriot Lucy, July 8, 1768; John Tasker, Mar. 2, 1772; Sarah Fairfax Apr. 10, 1773. A daughter born between Nancy and Fanny had died at birth; Mary, born between Betty and Harriot had died at the age of four; and two daughters born since Harriot had died within the year. Four more children would be born after Fithian departed, three of whom, George, Sophia, and Julia, would survive; Morton, *Robert Carter*, 220n.

33. Fithian, *Journal*, 39; Morton, *Robert Carter*, 49. A "harmonica" was not the modern instrument but one made of glass tubes.

34. Fithian, *Journal*, 26, 66.

35. Ibid., 46, 34; Morton, *Robert Carter*, 32; [James Buchanan], *The British Grammar: Or, an Essay in Four Parts, Towards Speaking and Writing the English Language Grammatically and Inditing Elegantly . . .* (Boston: Nathaniel Coverly for John Norman, 1784) (Buchanan first published this book in London anonymously in 1762); Ian Michael, *The Teaching of English from the Sixteenth Century to 1870* (New York: Cambridge University Press, 1987), 410. An imported copy of Buchanan's grammar was first advertised in the *Virginia Gazette*, July 18, 1771. Advt. reprinted in John E. Molnar, "Publication and Retail Book Advertisements in the *Virginia Gazette*, 1736–1780" (Ph.D. diss., University of Michigan, 1978), 399.

36. Fithian, *Journal*, 26, 46. For Dilworth's recommendation, see above, p. 227. For examples of imported *Spectator*s, see advts., *South Carolina Gazette*, July 1, 1756, June 18, 1763, July 20, 1767, in Hennig Cohen, *The "South Carolina Gazette," 1732–1775* (Columbia: University of South Carolina, 1953), 142, 148, 151. For editions and of *The Complete Letter-Writer*, see Ian Michael, *The Teaching of English from the Sixteenth Century to 1870* (Cambridge: Cambridge University Press, 1987), 427. *The Complete Letter-Writer: Containing Familiar Letters on the Most Common Occasions in Life . . .* was published in Boston by John West Folsom in 1785. Konstantin Dierks, "American Writing Skills Imprints, 1698–1800: A Bibliography," unpublished MS, 10. (Not in Evans, *American Bibliography*.)

37. Fithian, *Journal*, 64, 57, 50.

38. Ibid., 50.

39. Ibid., 54.

40. Ibid., 149.

41. Ibid., 186. Wingate's arithmetic (probably the 1760 edition) was advertised in the *South Carolina Gazette*, July 20, 1767, Nov. 7, 1768, in Cohen, *South Carolina Gazette*, 151, 152.

42. Fithian, *Journal*, 178, 254.

43. Ibid., 66, 26, 58, 66, 110, 157.

44. Ibid., 57, 160 (see also 154).

45. Ibid., 88 (flute), quots. 65, 96, 113.

46. Ibid., 178–80. An advertisement for the Newbery publication, advertised as "Fables," appeared in the *Virginia Gazette*, Feb. 25, 1768; in Molnar, "Publication and Retail Book Advertisements," 343.

47. Fithian, *Journal*, 88, 111.

48. Kevin Hayes, *A Colonial Woman's Bookshelf* (Knoxville: University of Tennessee Press, 1996); see ibid., 1, for his discussion of the women and soul episode; Fithian, *Journal*, 138–39.

49. Fithian, *Journal*, 157, 285–94 (catalogue of Carter's library), 286 (Wingate's arithmetic), 122 (Junius), 148–49 (probably Henry Hammond, *A Paraphrase and Annotations upon All the Books of the New Testament . . .* [London: for Margaret Royston . . . , 1689]—inferred from Fithian's designation of it as "Mr Hammond's Exposition of the New Testament"), 159 (German Spa), 224 (Swift), 170 (*Tristram Shandy*), 177 (cf. 248 [reading outdoors]), 160 (censured), 93 (*Gentleman's Magazine*), 54 (*Pennsylvania Gazette*), 246 (history).

50. Ibid., 223–24; for Fithian's letters from Nomini Hall, see 275–84.

51. Ibid., 133, 146.

52. Ibid., 148, 168.

53. Ibid., 175.

54. Ibid., 176–77.

55. Ibid., 264.

56. Ibid., 8, 53, 243, 245 (Nelson); 53, 68 (finger); 272 (Dennis); quot. 240.

57. Ibid., 184–85.

58. Ibid., 188 (cf. Fithian's long letter of advice, 208–22), 267 (Bob), quots. 188, 268, 270.

59. Ibid., 79–80; John Harrower, *The Journal of John Harrower: An Indentured Servant in the Colony of Virginia, 1773–1776*, edited and with an introduction by Edward Miles Riley (Williamsburg, Va.: Colonial Williamsburg, 1963), xiii–xv, 3, quot., 17.

60. Harrower, *Journal*, xv, 20, 32, 35, 166–68.

61. Ibid., xv–xvi, 37, 40.

62. Ibid., xvi–xvii, 41, 56.

63. Ibid., 56, 48.

64. Ibid., 41, 18, 56.

65. Ibid., 42. Harrower taught from 6 to 8 a.m., from 9 a.m. to 12 noon., and from 3 to 6 p.m.

66. Ibid., 42, 49. For the spelling "Bathurst," see ibid., 180 n. 54. Harrower spelled the name "Bathurest." Edwin was born in 1766, Bathurst on May 29,1767, and William on October 13, 1769; ibid., 180 n. 54.

67. Ibid., 54, 73, 108, 134.

68. Ibid., 42, 54, 73, 140.

69. Ibid., 42, 54, 150.

70. Ibid., 72.

71. Ibid., 83, 109; quots. 91, 104, 148.

72. Ibid., 46, 100 (Evans), 46, 51, 52, 100, 105 (the Patties); 47, 52, 63, 119 (the Edges); 47, 72 (John Edge); 88, 96–97, 121 (Samuel Edge); quots. 47, 72. Philip Fithian once met a "deaf, & dumb" youth of about twenty who could write his name, Coley Reed, "in a good legible Hand, better indeed, than the Bulk of planters are able to do! But he can write nothing more—" (Fithian, *Journal*, 247–48).

73. Harrower, *Journal*, 59, 81, quots. 72–73, 120.

74. Ibid., 153, 154, 155. Harrower mentions "a page each" later, 157.

75. Ibid., 118, 92.

76. Ibid., 144; cf. "the Lucy friggat," 143.

77. Ibid., 162–63.

78. Ibid., 158.

Epilogue

1. Isaiah Thomas, *The History of Printing in America*, ed. Marcus A. McCorison from the 2nd edition (New York: Weathervane Books, 1970), 150, 152; Alfred Lawrence Lorenz, *Hugh Gaine: A Colonial Printer-Editor's Odyssey to Loyalism* (Carbondale: Southern Illinois University Press, 1972), 133–34.

2. Anthony Benezet, *A First Book for Children* (Philadelphia: Crukshank, 1778), 3, 22–25, 29–30, 31.

3. The following paragraphs draw from E. Jennifer Monaghan, *A Common Heritage: Noah Webster's Blue-Back Speller* (Hamden, Conn.: Archon Books, 1983).

4. Ibid., 36, 44.

5. For sales of Webster's *Elementary Spelling Book*, see ibid., 218–20, 228.

6. William Holmes McGuffey, *Eclectic First Reader, for Young Children* (Cincinnati: Truman and Smith, 1836). McGuffey's innovations were not entirely his own: he plagiarized so much from the *Worcester Readers* of Samuel Worcester that his publishers were brought to court.

Richard L. Venezky, "A History of the American Reading Textbook," *Elementary School Journal* 87 (1987): 251–52.

7. For the Webster spellers in slave communities, see Janet Duitsman Cornelius, "*When I Can Read My Title Clear*": *Literacy, Slavery and Religion in the Antebellum South* (Columbia: University of South Carolina Press, 1991), 68–71, 89–90, 93, 108, 109, 112–13; for the spurt of 1866, see Monaghan, *Common Heritage*, 192, 194–95.

Conclusion

1. For Robert Carter's teaching, see Mary Beth Norton, *Liberty's Daughters: The Revolutionary Experience of American Women, 1750–1800* (Boston: Little, Brown, 1980), 258. Ray Nash, *American Writing Masters and Copybooks: History and Bibliography Through Colonial Times* (Boston: Colonial Society of Massachusetts, 1959), 10. In general, see Gloria Main, "An Inquiry into When and Why Women Learned to Write in Colonial New England," *Journal of Social History* 24 (1991): 579–89.

2. Carl F. Kaestle, *Pillars of the Republic: Common Schools and American Society, 1780–1860* (New York: Hill and Wang, 1983), 60.

3. Noah Webster, "Modes of Teaching the English Language," in *A Collection of Papers on Political, Literary and Moral Subjects* (1843; repr., New York: Burt Franklin, 1968), 307, 309.

4. For advertisements for hornbooks over the decades, see, e.g., *South Carolina Gazette*, July 12, 1735 (in Hennig Cohen, *The "South Carolina Gazette," 1732–1775* [Columbia: University of South Carolina, 1953], 128); *Pennsylvania Gazette*, Jan. 28, 1746; *New-York Mercury*, May 27, 1754; *South Carolina Gazette*, May 30, 1761, Apr. 30, 1772 (in Cohen, *South Carolina Gazette*, 144, 154); *Georgia Gazette*, Nov. 10, 1763.

5. E. Jennifer Monaghan, "Literacy Instruction and Gender in Colonial New England," *American Quarterly* 40 (1988): 18–41. (For later reprints, see Introduction, n. 6.)

6. Carl Bridenbaugh, *Cities in the Wilderness: The First Century of Urban Life in America, 1625–1742* (1938; rpt., London: Oxford University Press, 1971), 283–84.

7. For "learned" and literary women, see David S. Shields, "Eighteenth-Century Literary Culture," in *A History of the Book in America*, ed. David D. Hall, vol. 1, *The Colonial Book in the Atlantic World*, ed. Hugh Amory and David D. Hall ([Worcester, Mass.]: American Antiquarian Society; New York: Cambridge University Press, 2000), 460–64; quot., *The Book of Abigail and John: Selected Letters of the Adams Family, 1762–1784*, ed. L. H. Butterfield, Marc Friedlaender, and Mary-Jo Kline (Cambridge, Mass.: Harvard University Press, 1975), 153; Norton, *Liberty's Daughters*; Linda K. Kerber, *Women of the Republic: Intellect and Ideology in Revolutionary America* (1980; rpt., New York: Norton, 1986). Abigail Adams, in an 1817 letter, said that she never attended any district school because she was constantly ill. John Adams, *Diary and Autobiography of John Adams*, vol. 1, *Diary, 1755–1770*, ed. L. H. Butterfield (Cambridge, Mass.: Harvard University Press, Belknap Press, 1961), x.

8. Jack Greene, *Pursuits of Happiness: The Social Development of Early Modern British Colonies and the Formation of American Culture* (Chapel Hill: University of North Carolina Press, 1988); quot. T. H. Breen, *The Marketplace of Revolution: How Consumer Politics Shaped American Independence* ([London]: Oxford University Press, 2004), 58. See above, p. 5.

9. Stereotyping was invented in England in the early eighteenth century. This revolutionary process allowed plates to be cast from every page of type, freeing up the type for other imprints. But it would not be used widely in the United States until 1813, when a copy of Lindley Murray's *English Reader* was stereotyped. It would then prove to be so valuable for textbook production that it would soon be used extensively. Charles Monaghan, *The Murrays of Murray Hill* (Brooklyn, N.Y.: Urban History Press, 1998), 132.

10. David D. Hall, "The Atlantic Economy in the Eighteenth Century," in Hall, *History of the Book in America*, 1:153–57. For details on the changes in book printing and publishing (in English), see, for the middle colonies after 1720, James N. Green, "English Books and Printing in the Age of Franklin," in ibid., 248–98; for New England, Hugh Amory, "The New England

Book Trade, 1713–1790," in ibid., chap. 9; for the south, Calhoun Winton, "The Southern Book Trade in the Eighteenth Century," in ibid., chap. 7.

11. Lawrence A. Cremin, *American Education: The Colonial Experience, 1607–1783* (New York: Harper & Row, 1970), 400–404, 499–500, 503–5, 544–46.

12. David Zeisberger, *Essay of a Delaware-Indian and English Spelling-Book, for the Use of the Schools of the Christian Indians on Muskingum River* (1776; reprint, n.p.: Arthur M. McGraw, 1991).

13. Konstantin Dierks, "Letter Writing, Gender, and Class in America, 1750–1800" (Ph.D. diss., Brown University, 1999).

14. Joel Perlmann, Silvana R. Siddali, and Keith Whitescarver, "Literacy, Schooling, and Teaching among New England Women, 1730–1820," *History of Education Quarterly* 37 (1997): 117–39.

15. Mary Beth Norton, "Communications," *William and Mary Quarterly*, 3rd ser., 48 (1991): 639–45.

16. Norton, *Liberty's Daughters*.

17. [James Burgh], *The Art of Speak ing . . .* , 4th ed. (Philadelphia: Aitken, 1775), 10; John Newbery, *A Little Pretty Pocket-Book* [facsimile], ed. M. F. Thwaite (London: Oxford University Press, 1966), 47–48; Adams, *Diary and Autobiography*, 219.

18. Dierks, "Letter Writing"; Lucille M. Schultz, *The Young Composers: Composition's Beginnings in Nineteenth-Century Schools* (Carbondale: Southern Illinois University Press, 1999), chap. 2. Schultz identifies Richard Green Parker's 1832 *Progressive Exercises* as "the first full-fledged exercise/activity composition book [for primary-school children] in our history" (35).

19. Tamara Plakins Thornton, *Handwriting in America: A Cultural History* (New Haven: Yale University Press, 1996), 37–40, quot. 40.

20. Victor E. Neuburg [Neuberg], *Popular Education in Eighteenth Century England* (London: Woburn Press, 1971), 3, quot. 4. For nineteenth-century views, see Gretchen R. Galbraith, *Reading Lives: Reconstructing Childhood, Books, and Schools in Britain, 1870–1920* (New York: St. Martin's Press. 1997).

21. For "'Appropriate' Literacy" versus "Appropriating Literacy" for girls, see Jane Greer, "Introduction," in *Girls and Literacy in America: Historical Perspectives to the Present*, ed. Jane Greer (Santa Barbara, Calif.: ABC-CLIO, 2003), xvi–xxiv. For adult self-definition, see Ronald Hoffman, Mechal Sobel, and Fredrika J. Teute, eds., *Through a Glass Darkly: Reflections on Personal Identity in Early America* (Chapel Hill, N.C.: Omohundro Institute of Early American History and Culture, 1997).

22. Richard L. Venezky, "The Development of Literacy in the Industrialized Nations of the West," in *Handbook of Reading Research*, vol. 2, ed. Rebecca Barr, Michael L. Kamil, and Peter M. Rosenthal (New York: Longman, 1991), 48.

23. Kevin J. Hayes, *A Colonial Woman's Bookshelf* (Knoxville: University of Tennessee Press, 1996); Cathy N. Davidson, *Revolution and the Word: The Rise of the Novel in America* (New York: Oxford University Press, 1986).

24. E. Jennifer Monaghan, *Reading for the Enslaved, Writing for the Free: Reflections on Liberty and Literacy* (Worcester, Mass.: American Antiquarian Society, 2000).

Afterword

1. E. Jennifer Monaghan and E. Wendy Saul, "The Reader, the Scribe, the Thinker: A Critical Look at the History of American Reading and Writing Instruction," in *The Formation of School Subjects: The Struggle for Creating an American Institution*, ed. Thomas S. Popkewitz (Philadelphia: Falmer, 1987), 86–87.

2. For a charming account of composing experiences in the early 1900s, see Alvina Treut Burrows, "Learning to Write: Early 1900s," *History of Reading News* 10, no. 2 (Spring 1987): 3, available at www.historyliteracy.org, "newsletters, back issues."

3. E. Jennifer Monaghan, 'Phonics and Whole Word/Whole Language Controversies, 1948–

1998: An Introductory History," in *Finding Our Literacy Roots: Eighteenth Yearbook of the American Reading Forum*, ed. Richard J. Telfer (Whitewater, Wisc.: American Reading Forum, 1998), 9–11.

4. For the role of Webster's spellers in the reading acquisition of slaves, see Janet Duitsman Cornelius, *"When I Can Read My Title Clear": Literacy, Slavery, and Religion in the Antebellum South* (Columbia: University of South Carolina Press, 1991), 68–71, 89–90, 108–9, illustration between 112 and 113.

5. Systematic phonics teaches children letter-sound correspondences explicitly along with blending. Less systematic approaches (known as intrinsic, analytic, or embedded phonics) presuppose that words have been learned as sight words and that sounds are inferred from known words as the need arises. For the research, see Jeanne S. Chall, *Learning to Read: The Great Debate*, 3rd ed. (1967; Fort Worth, Tex.: Harcourt Brace College Publishers, 1996); Marilyn Jager Adams, *Beginning to Read: Thinking and Learning about Print* (1990; Cambridge, Mass.: MIT Press, 1994), 7, 38, 42, 49; Michael Pressley, *Reading Instruction That Works: The Case for Balanced Reading*, 2nd ed. (New York: Guilford Press, 2002), 144–55.

6. E.g. the "Alphabetic Phonics" approach and the Slingerland approach: Aylett Royall Cox, Alphabetic Phonics series (Cambridge, Mass.: Educators Publishing Service, 1994–2003); Beth H. Slingerland, *A Multi-Sensory Approach to Language Arts for Specific Language Disability Children: A Guide for Primary Teachers* (1971; Cambridge, Mass.: Educators Publishing Service, 1975).

INDEX

E. Jennifer Monaghan (née Walker) is internationally known as a reading educator and as a historian of literacy education.

A native of Cambridge, England, she attended the Perse School for Girls in Cambridge after returning from Ottawa, Canada, where she was evacuated during World War II. She holds bachelor's and master's degrees in Literae Humaniores (classics) from Oxford University, another master's in classical Greek from the University of Illinois, and a doctorate in reading education from Yeshiva University, New York. She taught reading at the elementary level and, when she became a faculty member of Brooklyn College of The City University of New York in 1978, taught reading and composition there. In 2001, she retired from the English Department as professor emerita. She is the founder of the History of Reading Special Interest Group of the International Reading Association.

As a historian, she is the author of *A Common Heritage: Noah Webster's Blue-Back Speller* and *Reading for the Enslaved, Writing for the Free: Reflections on Liberty and Literacy*. She has written numerous articles on topics that range from literacy instruction and gender in colonial New England to twentieth-century reading methodology. She has also won "best article" awards from the American Studies Association and the History of Education Society and has been invited to be the keynote speaker at many conferences. In 1990, she gave the inaugural Esther Clarke Wright Lecture at Acadia University, Wolfville, Nova Scotia. In 1997, she was the first plenary speaker at the International Reading Association's reading research conference. In 1998, she was chosen to deliver the annual James Russell Wiggins Lecture at the American Antiquarian Society.

Her scholarly activities have been recognized by her election as a Member of the American Antiquarian Society and an Associate Member of Darwin College, Cambridge.

She lives with her husband Charles in Charlottesville, Virginia, where she pursues her interest in choral music by singing with The Oratorio Society of Charlottesville and Albemarle. She continues to write, but her greatest joys revolve around her extended family, which now includes seven grandchildren.